GUIDE TO USING PLAYFAIR

The basic layout of *Playfair* has remained the same for this edition. The Annual is divided into five sections, as follows: Test match cricket, county cricket, international limited-overs cricket (including Twenty20), other cricket (universities, IPL and Champions League and women's international cricket), and fixtures for the coming season. Each section, where applicable, begins with a preview of forthcoming events, followed by events during the previous year, then come the player records, and finally the records sections.

Within the players' register, I have added one new feature to the biographies. Where players have scored 1000 or more Test or LOI runs in a calendar year, or taken 50 wickets, these achievements are noted, as for first-class cricket. Players' Second XI Championship debuts and their England Under-19 Test appearances are given for those under the age of 25.

In the county limited-overs records in the Register, those records denoted by '50ov' cover any limited-overs game of 50 or more overs – in the early days, each team could have as many as 65 overs per innings. The '40ov' section refers to games of 40 or 45 overs per innings.

Records are provided for two formats of the women's game – limited-overs and T20 – and there is an England women's register. Fixtures for the new season's Super League are provided. The women's game continues to go from strength to strength, with participation numbers increasing at club level, in contrast to the men's game.

ACKNOWLEDGEMENTS AND THANKS

As ever, this book could not have been compiled without the help of many people giving freely of their time and expertise, so I must thank the following for all they have done to help ensure this edition of *Playfair Cricket Annual* could be written:

At the counties, I would like to thank the following for their help over the last year: Derbyshire – Neil Bates and John Brown; Durham – Brian Hunt (this year, he will be sharing his scoring duties with William Dobson, but he has been a stalwart of the county over many years); Essex – Tony Choat; Glamorgan – Andrew Hignell; Gloucestershire – Lizzie Allen and Adrian Bull; Hampshire – Tim Tremlett and Kevin Baker; Kent – Thomas Brown and Lorne Hart; Lancashire – Diana Lloyd, James Price and Darrin White; Leicestershire – Jen Wilks and Paul Rogers; Middlesex – Steven Fletcher, Rebecca Hart and Don Shelley; Northamptonshire – Tony Kingston; Nottinghamshire – Helen Palmer and Roger Marshall; Somerset – Spencer Bishop and Gerald Stickley; Surrey – Steve Howes and Keith Booth; Sussex – Colin Bowley and Mike Charman; Warwickshire – Tom Rawlings and Mel Smith; Worcestershire – Christine Cameron and Dawn Pugh; Yorkshire – Janet Bairstow and John Potter.

Thanks as ever to Alan Fordham for the Principal and Second XI Fixtures, and Philip August for the Minor Counties. Philip Bailey once again provided the first-class and List A career records, for which I am hugely grateful.

At Headline, many thanks go to [...] encouragement; Louise Rothwell nud[...] sure I didn't miss it, before ensuring [...] administers the *Playfair* website with [...] it a visit. John Skermer did his usual [...] turnarounds demanded. At Letterpart [...] Leggett did a brilliant job to ensure [...] edition.

I have to thank my daughters, Kir[...] and how I am NOT to be disturbed [...] memorable performance in the scho[...] my biggest thanks go to my wife, Sugra. She does a brilliant job [...] sane in the final days of the process.

ENGLAND v SRI LANKA

1981-82 to 2014

HIGHEST INNINGS TOTALS

England	in England	575-9d	Lord's	2014
	in Sri Lanka	460	Colombo (PSS)	2011-12
Sri Lanka	in England	591	The Oval	1998
	in Sri Lanka	628-8d	Colombo (SSC)	2003-04

LOWEST INNINGS TOTALS

England	in England	181	The Oval	1998
	in Sri Lanka	81	Galle	2007-08
Sri Lanka	in England	82	Cardiff	2011
	in Sri Lanka	81	Colombo (SSC)	2000-01

HIGHEST MATCH AGGREGATE 1496 for 36 wickets Lord's 2014
LOWEST MATCH AGGREGATE 645 for 36 wickets Colombo (SSC) 2000-01

HIGHEST INDIVIDUAL INNINGS

England	in England	203	I.J.L.Trott	Cardiff	2011
	in Sri Lanka	151	K.P.Pietersen	Colombo (PSS)	2011-12
Sri Lanka	in England	213	S.T.Jayasuriya	The Oval	1998
	in Sri Lanka	213*	D.P.M.D.Jayawardena	Galle	2007-08

HIGHEST AGGREGATE OF RUNS IN A SERIES

England	in England	390	(av 97.50)	A.N.Cook	2011
	in Sri Lanka	278	(av 46.33)	A.N.Cook	2007-08
Sri Lanka	in England	342	(av 85.50)	K.C.Sangakkara	2014
	in Sri Lanka	474	(av 158.00)	D.P.M.D.Jayawardena	2007-08

RECORD WICKET PARTNERSHIPS – ENGLAND

1st	168	M.E.Trescothick (76)/M.P.Vaughan (115)	Lord's	2002
2nd	202	M.E.Trescothick (161)/M.A.Butcher (94)	Birmingham	2002
3rd	251	A.N.Cook (133)/I.J.L.Trott (203)	Cardiff	2011
4th	128	G.A.Hick (107)/M.R.Ramprakash (53)	The Oval	1998
5th	173	K.P.Pietersen (158)/P.D.Collingwood (57)	Lord's	2006
6th	171	J.E.Root (200*)/M.J.Prior (86)	Lord's	2014
7th	109	I.R.Bell (74)/M.J.Prior (63)	Kandy	2007-08
8th	102	A.J.Stewart (123)/A.F.Giles (45)	Manchester	2002
9th	81	J.E.Root (200*)/L.E.Plunkett (39)	Lord's	2014
10th	91	G.P.Thorpe (123)/M.J.Hoggard (17*)	Birmingham	2002

RECORD WICKET PARTNERSHIPS – SRI LANKA

1st	207	N.T.Paranavitana (65)/T.M.Dilshan (193)	Lord's	2011
2nd	109	W.U.Tharanga (52)/K.C.Sangakkara (65)	Lord's	2006
3rd	262	T.T.Samaraweera (142)/D.P.M.D.Jayawardena (134)	Colombo (SSC)	2003-04
4th	153	D.P.M.D.Jayawardena (52)/T.M.Dilshan (100)	Kandy	2003-04
5th	150	S.Wettimuny (190)/L.R.D.Mendis (111)	Lord's	1984
6th	138	S.A.R.Silva (102*)/L.R.D.Mendis (94)	Lord's	1984
7th	183	D.P.M.D.Jayawardena (213*)/W.P.J.U.C.Vaas (90)	Galle	2007-08
8th	149	A.D.Mathews (160)/H.M.R.K.B.Herath (48)	Leeds	2014
9th	105	W.P.J.U.C.Vaas (50*)/M.D.N.Kulasekara (64)	Lord's	2006
10th	64	J.R.Ratnayeke (59*)/G.F.Labrooy (42)	Lord's	1988

BEST INNINGS BOWLING ANALYSIS

England	in England	7-70	P.A.J.DeFreitas	Lord's	1991
	in Sri Lanka	6-33	J.E.Emburey	Colombo (PSS)	1981-82
Sri Lanka	in England	9-65	M.Muralitharan	The Oval	1998
	in Sri Lanka	7-46	M.Muralitharan	Galle	2003-04

BEST MATCH BOWLING ANALYSIS

England	in England	8-115	P.A.J.DeFreitas	Lord's	1991
	in Sri Lanka	10-181	G.P.Swann	Colombo (PSS)	2011-12
Sri Lanka	in England	16-220	M.Muralitharan	The Oval	1998
	in Sri Lanka	12-171	H.M.R.K.B.Herath	Galle	2011-12

HIGHEST WICKET AGGREGATE IN A SERIES

England	in England	15	(av 24.60)	M.J.Hoggard	2006
		15	(av 23.40)	C.T.Tremlett	2011
	in Sri Lanka	18	(av 29.94)	A.F.Giles	2003-04
Sri Lanka	in England	24	(av 16.87)	M.Muralitharan	2006
	in Sri Lanka	26	(av 12.30)	M.Muralitharan	2003-04

RESULTS SUMMARY

ENGLAND v SRI LANKA – IN ENGLAND

		Series			Lord's			The Oval			Birmingham			Manchester			Nottingham			Cardiff			Southampton			Leeds		
	Tests	E	SL	D	E	SL	D	E	SL	D	E	SL	D	E	SL	D	E	SL	D	E	SL	D	E	SL	D	E	SL	D
1984	1	–	–	1	–	–	1																					
1988	1	1	–	–	1	–	–																					
1991	1	1	–	–	1	–	–																					
1998	1	–	1	–				–	1	–																		
2002	3	2	–	1	–	–	1				1	–	–	1	–	–												
2006	3	1	1	1	–	–	1				1	–	–				–	1	–									
2011	3	1	–	2	–	–	1													1	–	–	–	–	1			
2014	2	–	1	1	–	–	1																			–	1	–
15		6	3	6	2	–	5	–	1	–	2	–	–	1	–	–	–	1	–	1	–	–	–	–	1	–	1	–

ENGLAND v SRI LANKA – IN SRI LANKA

		Series			Colombo (PSS)			Colombo (SSC)			Galle			Kandy		
	Tests	E	SL	D	E	SL	D	E	SL	D	E	SL	D	E	SL	D
1981-82	1	1	–	–	1	–	–									
1992-93	1	–	1	–				–	1	–						
2000-01	3	2	1	–				1	–	–	–	1	–	1	–	–
2003-04	3	–	1	2				–	1	–	–	–	1	–	–	1
2007-08	3	–	1	2				–	–	1	–	–	1	–	1	–
2011-12	2	1	1	–	1	–	–				–	1	–			
13		4	5	4	2	–	–	1	2	1	–	2	2	1	1	1
Totals	**28**	10	8	10												

ENGLAND v PAKISTAN

HIGHEST INNINGS TOTALS

England	in England	558-6d		Nottingham	1954
	in Pakistan	546-8d		Faisalabad	1983-84
	in UAE	598-9d		Abu Dhabi	2015-16
Pakistan	in England	708		The Oval	1987
	in Pakistan	636-8d		Lahore	2005-06
	in UAE	523-8d		Abu Dhabi	2015-16

LOWEST INNINGS TOTALS

England	in England	130		The Oval	1954
	in Pakistan	130		Lahore	1987-88
	in UAE	72		Abu Dhabi	2011-12
Pakistan	in England	72		Birmingham	2010
	in Pakistan	158		Karachi	2000-01
	in UAE	99		Dubai	2011-12

HIGHEST INDIVIDUAL INNINGS

England	in England	278	D.C.S.Compton	Nottingham	1954
	in Pakistan	205	E.R.Dexter	Karachi	1961-62
	in UAE	263	A.N.Cook	Abu Dhabi	2015-16
Pakistan	in England	274	Zaheer Abbas	Birmingham	1971
	in Pakistan	223	Mohammad Yousuf	Lahore	2005-06
	in UAE	245	Shoaib Malik	Abu Dhabi	2015-16

HIGHEST AGGREGATE OF RUNS IN A SERIES

England	in England	453	(av 90.60)	D.C.S.Compton	1954
	in Pakistan	449	(av 112.25)	D.I.Gower	1983-84
	in UAE	450	(av 90.00)	A.N.Cook	2015-16
Pakistan	in England	631	(av 90.14)	Mohammad Yousuf	2006
	in Pakistan	431	(av 107.75)	Inzamam-ul-Haq	2005-06
	in UAE	380	(av 63.33)	Mohammad Hafeez	2015-16

RECORD WICKET PARTNERSHIPS – ENGLAND

1st	198	G.Pullar (165)/R.W.Barber (86)	Dacca	1961-62
2nd	248	M.C.Cowdrey (182)/E.R.Dexter (172)	The Oval	1962
3rd	267	M.P.Vaughan (120)/G.P.Thorpe (138)	Manchester	2001
4th	233	A.N.Cook (105)/P.D.Collingwood (186)	Lord's	2006
5th	219	P.D.Collingwood (82)/E.J.G.Morgan (130)	Nottingham	2010
6th	166	G.P.Thorpe (118)/C.White (93)	Lahore	2000-01
7th	167	D.I.Gower (152)/V.J.Marks (83)	Faisalabad	1983-84
8th	332	I.J.L.Trott (184)/S.C.J.Broad (169)	Lord's	2010
9th	76	T.W.Graveney (153)/F.S.Trueman (29)	Lord's	1962
10th	79	R.W.Taylor (54)/R.G.D.Willis (28*)	Birmingham	1982

RECORD WICKET PARTNERSHIPS – PAKISTAN

1st	173	Mohsin Khan (104)/Shoaib Mohammad (80)	Lahore	1983-84
2nd	291	Zaheer Abbas (274)/Mushtaq Mohammad (100)	Birmingham	1971
3rd	363	Younus Khan (173)/Mohammad Yousuf (192)	Leeds	2006
4th	322	Javed Miandad (153*)/Salim Malik (165)	Birmingham	1992
5th	248	Shoaib Malik (245)/Asad Shafiq (107)	Abu Dhabi	2015-16
6th	269	Mohammad Yousuf (223)/Kamran Akmal (154)	Lahore	2005-06
7th	112	Asif Mujtaba (51)/Moin Khan (105)	Leeds	1996
8th	130	Hanif Mohammad (187*)/Asif Iqbal (76)	Lord's	1967
9th	190	Asif Iqbal (146)/Intikhab Alam (51)	The Oval	1967
10th	62	Sarfraz Nawaz (53)/Asif Mahmood (4*)	Leeds	1974

BEST INNINGS BOWLING ANALYSIS

Team	Location	Figures	Player	Ground	Year
England	in England	8-34	I.T.Botham	Lord's	1978
	in Pakistan	7-66	P.H.Edmonds	Karachi	1977-78
	in UAE	6-62	M.S.Panesar	Abu Dhabi	2011-12
Pakistan	in England	7-40	Imran Khan	Leeds	1987
	in Pakistan	9-56	Abdul Qadir	Lahore	1987-88
	in UAE	7-55	Saeed Ajmal	Dubai	2011-12

BEST MATCH BOWLING ANALYSIS

Team	Location	Figures	Player	Ground	Year
England	in England	13- 71	D.L.Underwood	Lord's	1974
	in Pakistan	11- 83	N.G.B.Cook	Karachi	1983-84
	in UAE	7-149	M.S.Panesar	Dubai	2011-12
Pakistan	in England	12- 99	Fazal Mahmood	The Oval	1954
	in Pakistan	13-101	Abdul Qadir	Lahore	1987-88
	in UAE	10- 97	Saeed Ajmal	Dubai	2011-12

HIGHEST AGGREGATE OF WICKETS IN A SERIES

Team	Location	Wkts	Average	Player	Year
England	in England	23	(av 13.73)	J.M.Anderson	2010
	in Pakistan	17	(av 24.11)	A.F.Giles	2000-01
	in UAE	14	(av 21.57)	M.S.Panesar	2011-12
Pakistan	in England	22	(av 25.31)	Waqar Younis	1992
	in Pakistan	30	(av 14.56)	Abdul Qadir	1987-88
	in UAE	24	(av 14.70)	Saeed Ajmal	2011-12

RESULTS SUMMARY – ENGLAND v PAKISTAN – IN ENGLAND

	Tests	Series			Lord's			Nottingham			Manchester			The Oval			Birmingham			Leeds		
		E	P	D	E	P	D	E	P	D	E	P	D	E	P	D	E	P	D	E	P	D
1954	4	1	1	2	–	–	1	1	–	–	–	–	1	–	1	–						
1962	5	4	–	1	1	–	–	–	–	1				1	–	–	1	–	–	1	–	–
1967	3	2	–	1	–	–	1	1	–	–				1	–	–						
1971	3	1	–	2	–	–	1										–	–	1	1	–	–
1974	3	–	–	3	–	–	1							–	–	1				–	–	1
1978	3	2	–	1	1	–	–										1	–	–	–	–	1
1982	3	2	1	–	–	1	–										1	–	–	1	–	–
1987	5	–	1	4	–	–	1				–	–	1	–	–	1	–	–	1	–	1	–
1992	5	1	2	2	–	1	–				–	–	1	–	1	–	–	–	1	1	–	–
1996	3	–	2	1	–	1	–							–	1	–				–	–	1
2001	2	1	1	–	1	–	–				–	1	–									
2006	4	3	–	1	–	–	1				1	–	–	1	–	–				1	–	–
2010	4	3	1	–	1	–	–	1	–	–				–	1	–	1	–	–			
	47	20	9	18	4	3	6	3	–	1	1	1	3	3	4	2	4	–	3	5	1	3

ENGLAND v PAKISTAN – IN PAKISTAN

	Tests	Series			Lahore			Dacca			Karachi			Hyderabad			Faisalabad			Multan		
		E	P	D	E	P	D	E	P	D	E	P	D	E	P	D	E	P	D	E	P	D
1961-62	3	1	–	2	1	–	–	–	–	1	–	–	1									
1968-69	3	–	–	3	–	–	1	–	–	1	–	–	1									
1972-73	3	–	–	3	–	–	1				–	–	1	–	–	1						
1977-78	3	–	–	3	–	–	1				–	–	1	–	–	1						
1983-84	3	–	1	2	–	–	1				–	1	–				–	–	1			
1987-88	3	–	1	2	–	1	–				–	–	1				–	–	1			
2000-01	3	1	–	2	–	–	1				1	–	–				–	–	1			
2005-06	3	–	2	1	–	1	–										–	–	1	–	1	–
	24	2	4	18	1	2	5	–	–	2	1	1	5	–	–	2	–	–	4	–	1	–

ENGLAND v PAKISTAN – IN UNITED ARAB EMIRATES

	Tests	Series			Dubai			Abu Dhabi (SZ)			Sharjah		
		E	P	D	E	P	D	E	P	D	E	P	D
2011-12	3	–	3	–	–	2	–	–	1	–			
2015-16	3	–	2	1	–	1	–	–	–	1	–	1	–
	6	–	5	1	–	3	–	–	1	1	–	1	–

	Tests	Series		
		E	P	D
Totals	77	22	18	37

TOURING TEAMS REGISTER 2016

Neither Sri Lanka nor Pakistan had selected their 2016 touring teams at the time of going to press. The following players, who had represented those teams in Test matches since 1 December 2014, were still available for selection:

SRI LANKA

Full Names	Birthdate	Birthplace	Team	Type	F-C Debut
CHAMEERA, P.V.Dushmantha	11.01.92	Ragama	Nondescripts	RHB/RF	2011-12
CHANDIMAL, Lokuge Dinesh	18.11.89	Balapitiya	Nondescripts	RHB/WK	2009
DICKWELLA, D.P.D.Niroshan	23.06.93	Kandy	Nondescripts	LHB/WK	2012-13
ERANGA, R.M.Shaminda	23.06.86	Chilaw	Tamil Union	RHB/RFM	2006-07
FERNANDO, A.Nuwan Pradeep R.	19.10.86	Negombo	Sinhalese	RHB/RFM	2007-08
HERATH, H.M.Rangana K.B.	19.03.78	Kurunegala	Tamil Union	LHB/SLA	1996-97
JAYASUNDERA, M.D.Udara S.	03.01.91	Minuwangoda	Ragama	LHB/LB	2009-10
KARUNARATNE, F.Dimuth M.	21.04.88	Colombo	Sinhalese	LHB/RM	2008-09
KAUSHAL, P.H.Tharindu	05.03.93	Galle	Nondescripts	RHB/OB	2012-13
LAKMAL, R.A.Suranga	10.03.87	Matara	Tamil Union	RHB/RFM	2007-08
MATHEWS, Angelo Davis	02.06.87	Colombo	Colts	RHB/RMF	2006-07
MENDIS, B.Kusal G.	02.02.95		Colombo	RHB/WK	2014-15
MUBARAK, Jehan	10.01.81	Washington, US	Nondescripts	LHB/OB	1999-00
PERERA, M.Dilruwan K.	22.07.89	Panadura	Colts	RHB/OB	2000-01
PRASAD, K.T.G.Dhammika	30.05.83	Ragama	Sinhalese	RHB/RFM	2001-02
SILVA, Jayan Kaushal	27.05.86	Colombo	Sinhalese	RHB/WK	2002-03
SIRIWARDANA, T.A.Milinda	04.12.85	Nagoda	Badureliya	LHB/SLA	2005-06
THARANGA, W.Upul	02.02.85	Balapitiya	Nondescripts	LHB/WK	2000-01
THIRIMANNE, H.D.R.Lahiru	08.09.89	Moratuwa	Ragama	LHB/RMF	2008-09
VITHANAGE, K.D.Kithuruwan	26.02.91	Colombo	Tamil Union	LHB/LB	2010-11

NB: A.N.P.R.Fernando is also known as Nuwan Pradeep.

PAKISTAN

Full Names	Birthdate	Birthplace	Team	Type	F-C Debut
AHMED SHEHZAD	23.11.91	Lahore	Habib Bank	RHB/LB	2006-07
ASAD SHAFIQ	28.01.86	Karachi	Habib Bank	RHB/LB	2007-08
AZHAR ALI	19.02.85	Lahore	Sui Northern	RHB/LB	2001-02
EHSAN ADIL	15.03.93	Sheikhupura	United Bank	RHB/RFM	2012-13
IMRAN KHAN, Mohammad	15.07.87	Lower Dir	Peshawar	RHB/RMF	2007-08
JUNAID KHAN	24.12.89	Matra	WAPDA	RHB/LFM	2006-07
MISBAH-UL-HAQ Khan Niazi	28.05.74	Mianwali	Sui Northern	RHB/LB	1998-99
MOHAMMAD HAFEEZ	17.10.80	Sargodha	Sui Northern	RHB/OB	1998-99
RAHAT ALI	12.09.88	Multan	Khan Research	RHB/LFM	2007-08
SAMI ASLAM	12.12.95	Lahore	Lahore Whites	LHB/RM	2012-13
SARFRAZ AHMED	22.05.87	Karachi	PIA	RHB/WK	2005-06
SHAN MASOOD	14.10.89	Kuwait	United Bank	LHB/RMF	2007-08
WAHAB RIAZ	28.06.85	Lahore	National Bank	RHB/LF	2001-02
YASIR SHAH	02.05.86	Swabi	Sui Northern	RHB/LB	2001-02
YOUNUS KHAN	29.11.77	Mardan	United Bank	RHB/LB	1998-99
ZULFIQAR BABAR	10.12.78	Okara	WAPDA	RHB/SLA	2001-02

STATISTICAL HIGHLIGHTS IN 2015 TESTS

Including Tests from No. 2150 (Australia v India, 4th Test), No. 2153 (South Africa v West Indies, 3rd Test) and No. 2155 (New Zealand v Sri Lanka, 2nd Test) to No. 2194 (Australia v West Indies, 2nd Test) and No. 2196 (South Africa v England, 1st Test). † = National record

TEAM HIGHLIGHTS

HIGHEST INNINGS TOTALS

628	Pakistan v Bangladesh	Khulna
624	New Zealand v Australia	Perth

HIGHEST FOURTH INNINGS TOTAL

382-3	Pakistan (set 377) v Sri Lanka	Pallekele

LOWEST INNINGS TOTALS

60	Australia v England	Nottingham
79	South Africa v India	Nagpur

HIGHEST MATCH AGGREGATES

1672-28	Australia (559-9d & 385-7d) v New Zealand (624 & 104-2)	Perth
1610-40	England (389 & 478) v New Zealand (523 & 220)	Lord's
1550-30	Australia (572-7d & 251-6d) v India (475 & 252-7)	Sydney
1515-26	Bangladesh (332 & 555-6) v Pakistan (628)	Khulna

LARGE MARGINS OF VICTORY

Inns & 212 runs	Australia (583-4d) beat West Indies (223 & 148)	Hobart
405 runs	Australia (566-8d & 254-2d) beat England (312 & 103)	Lord's

FOUR HUNDREDS IN AN INNINGS

Australia (551-3d) v West Indies	Melbourne

SIX FIFTIES IN AN INNINGS

Australia (572-7d) v India	Sydney

The first time all of the first six batsmen for Australia had scored 50+ in an innings.

MOST EXTRAS IN AN INNINGS

	B	LB	W	NB		
67	26	34	6	1	New Zealand (523) v England	Lord's

BATTING HIGHLIGHTS

DOUBLE HUNDREDS

Azhar Ali	226	Pakistan v Bangladesh	Mirpur
A.N.Cook	263	England v Pakistan	Abu Dhabi
Mohammad Hafeez	224	Pakistan v Bangladesh	Khulna
K.C.Sangakkara	203	Sri Lanka v New Zealand	Wellington
Shoaib Malik	245	Pakistan v England	Abu Dhabi
S.P.D.Smith	215	Australia v England	Lord's
Tamim Iqbal	206	Bangladesh v Pakistan	Khulna
L.R.P.L.Taylor	290	New Zealand v Australia	Perth
A.C.Voges	269*	Australia v West Indies	Hobart
D.A.Warner	253	Australia v New Zealand	Perth
K.S.Williamson	242*	New Zealand v Sri Lanka	Wellington

HUNDREDS IN THREE CONSECUTIVE INNINGS

D.A.Warner	163	116	Australia v New Zealand	Brisbane
	253		Australia v New Zealand	Perth

HUNDRED IN EACH INNINGS OF A MATCH

A.M.Rahane	127	100*	India v South Africa	Delhi
D.A.Warner	163	116	Australia v New Zealand	Brisbane

FASTEST HUNDRED

B.A.Stokes	(101) 85 balls	England v New Zealand	Lord's

200 RUNS IN A DAY

L.R.P.L.Taylor (26-235*)	New Zealand v Australia	Perth
D.A.Warner (0-244*)	Australia v New Zealand	Perth

150 RUNS OR MORE IN BOUNDARIES IN AN INNINGS

Runs	*6s*	*4s*			
172	0	43	L.R.P.L.Taylor	New Zealand v Australia	Perth

HUNDRED ON TEST DEBUT

A.C.Voges (130*)	Australia v West Indies	Roseau

CARRYING BAT THROUGH COMPLETED INNINGS

D.Elgar (118*)	South Africa (214) v England	Durban
C.A.Pujara (145*)	India (312) v Sri Lanka	Colombo (SSC)

60% OF A COMPLETED INNINGS TOTAL

%			
63.51	K.C.Brathwaite (94/148)	West Indies v Australia	Hobart

LONG INNINGS (Qualification: 600 mins and/or 400 balls)

Mins	*Balls*			
562	428	Azhar Ali (226)	Pakistan v Bangladesh	Mirpur
836	528	A.N.Cook (263)	England v Pakistan	Abu Dhabi

The third longest innings in Test match history.

639	420	Shoaib Malik (245)	Pakistan v England	Abu Dhabi
623	438	K.S.Williamson (242*)	New Zealand v Sri Lanka	Wellington

FIRST-WICKET PARTNERSHIP OF 100 IN EACH INNINGS

Mins	*Balls*			
161/237		J.A.Burns/D.A.Warner	Australia v New Zealand	Brisbane

OTHER NOTABLE PARTNERSHIPS

Qualifications: 1st-4th wkts: 250 runs; 5th-6th: 225; 7th: 200; 8th: 175; 9th: 150; 10th: 100.

First Wicket

312†	Tamim Iqbal/Imrul Kayes	Bangladesh v Pakistan	Khulna

Highest partnership for any wicket for Bangladesh.

283	M.Vijay/S.Dhawan	India v Bangladesh	Fatullah

Second Wicket

302	D.A.Warner/U.T.Khawaja	Australia v New Zealand	Perth
284	C.J.L.Rogers/S.P.D.Smith	Australia v England	Lord's
258	J.A.Burns/U.T.Khawaja	Australia v West Indies	Melbourne

Third Wicket

265	K.S.Williamson/L.R.P.L.Taylor	New Zealand v Australia	Perth
250	Azhar Ali/Younus Khan	Pakistan v Bangladesh	Mirpur

Fourth Wicket
449†   A.C.Voges/S.E.Marsh   Australia v West Indies   Hobart
  A world record fourth-wicket partnership in Tests.

Fifth Wicket
248   Shoaib Malik/Asad Shafiq   Pakistan v England   Abu Dhabi

Sixth Wicket
365†   K.S.Williamson/B.J.Watling   New Zealand v Sri Lanka   Wellington
  A then world record sixth-wicket partnership in Tests.

BOWLING HIGHLIGHTS
EIGHT WICKETS IN AN INNINGS
S.C.J.Broad   8-15   England v Australia   Nottingham

TEN WICKETS IN A MATCH
R.Ashwin (2)   10-160   India v Sri Lanka   Galle
                     12- 98   India v South Africa   Nagpur
H.M.R.K.B.Herath   10-147   Sri Lanka v West Indies   Galle

FIVE WICKETS IN AN INNINGS ON DEBUT
A.U.Rashid   5-64   England v Pakistan   Abu Dhabi
  Having conceded the worst analysis on debut (0-163) in first innings.

MOST OVERS IN AN INNINGS
Zulfiqar Babar   72-17-183-1   Pakistan v England   Abu Dhabi

MOST RUNS CONCEDED IN AN INNINGS
Zulfiqar Babar   72-17-183-1   Pakistan v England   Abu Dhabi
Taijul Islam   51-3-179-3   Bangladesh v Pakistan   Mirpur
D.Bishoo   51-10-177-4   West Indies v England   St George's

MOST CONSECUTIVE DELIVERIES WITHOUT CONCEDING A RUN
R.A.Jadeja   109   India v South Africa   Delhi

WICKET-KEEPING HIGHLIGHTS
SIX WICKET-KEEPING DISMISSALS IN AN INNINGS
L.D.Chandimal   5ct, 1st   Sri Lanka v Pakistan   Colombo (PSS)
B.J.Watling   6ct   New Zealand v Sri Lanka   Dunedin

NINE OR MORE WICKET-KEEPING DISMISSALS IN A MATCH
B.J.Watling   9ct   New Zealand v Sri Lanka   Dunedin

NO BYES CONCEDED IN AN INNINGS OF 550
572-7d   W.P.Saha   India v Australia   Sydney
557-8d   Mushfiqur Rahim   Bangladesh v Pakistan   Mirpur
556-4d   B.J.Watling   New Zealand v Australia   Brisbane
555-6   Sarfraz Ahmed   Pakistan v Bangladesh   Khulna
551-3d   D.Ramdin   West Indies v Australia   Melbourne

FIELDING HIGHLIGHTS
FIVE CATCHES IN AN INNINGS IN THE FIELD
J.Blackwood   5ct   West Indies v Sri Lanka   Colombo (PSS)
A.M.Rahane   5ct   India v Sri Lanka   Galle

SIX CATCHES IN A MATCH IN THE FIELD

A.M.Rahane   8ct   India v Sri Lanka   Galle

A world record number of catches in a Test match.

LEADING TEST AGGREGATES IN 2015
1000 RUNS IN 2015

	M	I	NO	HS	Runs	Avge	100	50
S.P.D.Smith (A)	13	24	4	215	**1474**	73.70	6	5
J.E.Root (E)	14	26	3	182*	**1385**	60.21	3	10
A.N.Cook (E)	14	26	1	263	**1364**	54.56	3	8
D.A.Warner (A)	13	24	–	253	**1317**	54.87	4	7
K.S.Williamson (NZ)	8	16	3	242*	**1172**	90.15	5	4
A.C.Voges (A)	12	18	6	269*	**1028**	85.66	4	3

RECORD CALENDAR YEAR RUNS AGGREGATE

	M	I	NO	HS	Runs	Avge	100	50
M.Yousuf (P) (2006)	11	19	1	202	**1788**	99.33	9	3

RECORD CALENDAR YEAR RUNS AVERAGE

	M	I	NO	HS	Runs	Avge	100	50
G.St A.Sobers (WI) (1958)	7	12	3	365*	**1193**	132.55	5	3

1000 RUNS IN DEBUT CALENDAR YEAR

	M	I	NO	HS	Runs	Avge	100	50
M.A.Taylor (A) (1989)	11	20	1	219	**1219**	64.15	4	5
A.C.Voges (A) (2015)	12	18	6	269*	**1028**	85.66	4	3
A.N.Cook (E) (2006)	13	24	2	127	**1013**	46.04	4	3

50 WICKETS IN 2015

	M	O	R	W	Avge	Best	5wI	10wM
R.Ashwin (I)	9	376.4	1067	62	**17.20**	7-66	7	2
S.C.J.Broad (E)	14	450.3	1334	56	**23.82**	8-15	2	–
J.R.Hazlewood (A)	12	403.3	1191	51	**23.35**	6-70	2	–

RECORD CALENDAR YEAR WICKETS AGGREGATE

	M	O	R	W	Avge	Best	5wI	10wM
M.Muralitharan (SL) (2006)	11	588.4	1521	90	**16.90**	8-70	9	5
S.K.Warne (A) (2005)	14	691.4	2043	90	**22.70**	6-46	6	2

MOST WICKET-KEEPING DISMISSALS IN 2015

	M	Dis	Ct	St
J.C.Buttler (E)	12	38	38	–

RECORD CALENDAR YEAR DISMISSALS AGGREGATE

	M	Dis	Ct	St
I.A.Healy (A) (1993)	16	67	58	9
M.V.Boucher (SA) (1998)	13	67	65	2

20 CATCHES BY FIELDERS IN 2015

	M	Ct
J.E.Root (E)	14	24
A.M.Rahane (I)	9	20

RECORD CALENDAR YEAR FIELDER'S AGGREGATE

	M	Ct
G.C.Smith (SA) (2008)	15	30

TEST MATCH SCORES
WEST INDIES v ENGLAND (1st Test)

At Sir Vivian Richards Stadium, North Sound, Antigua, on 13, 14, 15, 16, 17 April 2015.
Toss: West Indies. Result: **MATCH DRAWN**.
Debuts: None.

ENGLAND

*A.N.Cook	b Roach	11		c Benn b Taylor	13
I.J.L.Trott	c Bravo b Taylor	0		c Ramdin b Taylor	4
G.S.Ballance	c Bravo b Holder	10		c Blackwood b Benn	122
I.R.Bell	c Ramdin b Roach	143		run out	11
J.E.Root	b Taylor	83		b Holder	59
B.A.Stokes	c Holder b Taylor	79		st Ramdin b Benn	35
J.C.Tredwell	c Bravo b Holder	8			
†J.C.Buttler	c Ramdin b Roach	0	(7)	not out	59
C.J.Jordan	not out	21	(8)	c Bravo b Roach	13
S.C.J.Broad	c Blackwood b Roach	0			
J.M.Anderson	c Holder b Samuels	20			
Extras	(B 7, LB 3, W 8, NB 6)	24		(B 1, LB 6, W 5, NB 5)	17
Total	**(110.4 overs)**	**399**		**(7 wkts dec; 86 overs)**	**333**

WEST INDIES

K.C.Brathwaite	c Jordan b Tredwell	39		c Root b Broad	5
D.S.Smith	c Buttler b Anderson	11		c Ballance b Tredwell	65
D.M.Bravo	c Buttler b Jordan	10		c Jordan b Root	32
M.N.Samuels	c Buttler b Broad	33		c Tredwell b Anderson	23
S.Chanderpaul	c Stokes b Tredwell	46		lbw b Root	13
J.Blackwood	not out	112		c Buttler b Jordan	31
*†D.Ramdin	c Buttler b Broad	9		c Cook b Anderson	57
J.O.Holder	c Ballance b Tredwell	16		not out	103
K.A.J.Roach	c Buttler b Tredwell	5		not out	15
J.E.Taylor	run out				
S.J.Benn	c Root b Anderson	2			
Extras	(LB 4, W 6, NB 2)	12		(B 2, LB 2, NB 2)	6
Total	**(113 overs)**	**295**		**(7 wkts; 129.4 overs)**	**350**

WEST INDIES	O	M	R	W		O	M	R	W	FALL OF WICKETS			
											E	WI	E	WI
Taylor	20	4	90	3		14	5	42	2					
Roach	29	6	94	4		14	1	53	1	Wkt	1st	1st	2nd	2nd
Holder	25	11	69	2		17	5	63	1	1st	1	19	15	7
Benn	26	3	85	0		26	3	115	2	2nd	22	42	20	90
Samuels	10.4	0	51	1		15	0	53	0	3rd	34	89	52	119
										4th	211	99	166	127
ENGLAND										5th	341	192	226	155
Anderson	23	9	67	2		24.4	3	72	2	6th	357	227	281	189
Broad	22	2	67	2		21	5	61	1	7th	357	276	333	294
Jordan	23	8	46	1	(4)	18	6	48	1	8th	361	292	–	–
Stokes	19	3	64	0	(5)	13	0	50	0	9th	361	292	–	–
Tredwell	26	12	47	4	(3)	40	14	93	1	10th	399	295	–	–
Root						13	6	22	2					

Umpires: B.F.Bowden (*New Zealand*) (83) and S.J.Davis (*Australia*) (56).
Referee: A.J.Pycroft (*Zimbabwe*) (34).   **Test No. 2156/149 (WI504/E953)**

13

WEST INDIES v ENGLAND (2nd Test)

At National Cricket Stadium, St George's, Grenada, on 21, 22, 23, 24, 25 April 2015.
Toss: England. Result: **ENGLAND** won by nine wickets.
Debuts: None.

WEST INDIES

K.C.Brathwaite	b Anderson	1	c Root b Anderson		116
D.S.Smith	c Buttler b Jordan	15	b Anderson		2
D.M.Bravo	c Cook b Broad	35	c Buttler b Broad		69
M.N.Samuels	c Bell b Anderson	103	c Buttler b Anderson		37
S.Chanderpaul	c Ali b Stokes	1	c Cook b Anderson		7
J.Blackwood	lbw b Jordan	26	c Anderson b Jordan		10
*†D.Ramdin	c Buttler b Broad	31	lbw b Ali		28
J.O.Holder	c Buttler b Broad	22	run out		2
K.A.J.Roach	c Root b Broad	1	c Anderson b Ali		10
D.Bishoo	lbw b Ali	30	not out		15
S.T.Gabriel	not out	20	lbw b Ali		0
Extras	(B 5, LB 6, W 1, NB 2)	14	(B 8, LB 2, NB 1)		11
Total	**(104.4 overs)**	**299**	**(112 overs)**		**307**

ENGLAND

*A.N.Cook	b Gabriel	76	not out	59
I.J.L.Trott	c Blackwood b Bishoo	59	b Gabriel	0
G.S.Ballance	b Samuels	77	not out	81
I.R.Bell	b Gabriel	1		
J.E.Root	not out	182		
M.M.Ali	run out	0		
B.A.Stokes	c Blackwood b Bishoo	8		
†J.C.Buttler	st Ramdin b Bishoo	13		
C.J.Jordan	run out	16		
S.C.J.Broad	c Smith b Bishoo	0		
J.M.Anderson	run out	2		
Extras	(B 9, LB 2, W 1, NB 18)	30	(W 1, NB 3)	4
Total	**(144.1 overs)**	**464**	**(1 wkt; 41.1 overs; 157 mins)**	**144**

ENGLAND	O	M	R	W	O	M	R	W	FALL OF WICKETS
Anderson	24	10	47	2	22	7	43	4	
Broad	24	9	61	4	21	2	71	1	WI E WI E
Jordan	25	4	65	2	(4) 21	6	69	1	*Wkt 1st 1st 2nd 2nd*
Ali	13.4	1	47	1	(3) 24	9	51	3	1st 2 125 3 2
Stokes	17	7	66	1	8	0	34	0	2nd 28 159 145 –
Trott	1	0	2	0					3rd 65 164 224 –
Root					(6) 16	7	29	0	4th 74 329 238 –
									5th 129 335 239 –
WEST INDIES									6th 223 364 257 –
Roach	28	4	100	0	7	1	18	0	7th 233 387 260 –
Gabriel	22	3	67	2	7	3	20	1	8th 246 426 282 –
Holder	21.1	6	57	0	1.4	0	11	0	9th 247 431 307 –
Bishoo	51	10	177	4	(5) 8	0	32	0	10th 299 464 307 –
Samuels	21	4	38	1	(4) 12.3	1	54	0	
Blackwood	1	0	14	0					
Brathwaite					(6) 5	1	9	0	

Umpires: S.J.Davis (*Australia*) (57) and B.N.J.Oxenford (*Australia*) (22).
Referee: A.J.Pycroft (*Zimbabwe*) (35).   Test No. 2157/150 (WI505/E954)

WEST INDIES v ENGLAND (3rd Test)

At Kensington Oval, Bridgetown, Barbados, on 1, 2, 3 May 2015.
Toss: England. Result: **WEST INDIES** won by five wickets.
Debut: West Indies – S.D.Hope.

ENGLAND

*A.N.Cook	c Ramdin b Samuels	105	c Brathwaite b Gabriel		4
I.J.L.Trott	c Permaul b Gabriel	0	lbw b Taylor		9
G.S.Ballance	b Holder	18	c Bravo b Permaul		23
I.R.Bell	c and b Holder	0	lbw b Taylor		0
J.E.Root	c Ramdin b Permaul	33	c Bravo b Holder		1
M.M.Ali	run out	58	b Permaul		8
B.A.Stokes	c Hope b Gabriel	22	c Chanderpaul b Permaul		32
†J.C.Buttler	not out	3	not out		35
C.J.Jordan	c Ramdin b Taylor	3	lbw b Holder		2
S.C.J.Broad	b Taylor	10	b Holder		0
J.M.Anderson	b Taylor	0	lbw b Taylor		2
Extras	(LB 1, W 1, NB 3)	5	(B 4, LB 2, NB 1)		7
Total	**(96.3 overs)**	**257**	**(42.1 overs)**		**123**

WEST INDIES

K.C.Brathwaite	c Jordan b Anderson	0	c Jordan b Ali		25
S.D.Hope	c Cook b Anderson	5	lbw b Jordan		9
D.M.Bravo	c Jordan b Ali	9	c Broad b Stokes		82
M.N.Samuels	lbw b Anderson	0	b Broad		20
S.Chanderpaul	c Jordan b Root	25	b Anderson		0
J.Blackwood	c Ali b Anderson	85	not out		47
*†D.Ramdin	c Buttler b Broad	13	not out		0
J.O.Holder	c Buttler b Stokes	4			
V.Permaul	c sub (A.Lyth) b Anderson	18			
J.E.Taylor	b Anderson	15			
S.T.Gabriel	not out	0			
Extras	(B 4, LB 1)	5	(B 5, LB 6)		11
Total	**(49.4 overs)**	**189**	**(5 wkts; 62.4 overs)**		**194**

WEST INDIES	O	M	R	W		O	M	R	W
Taylor	18.3	8	36	3		11.1	1	33	3
Gabriel	15	3	47	2		7	4	16	1
Holder	16	4	34	2		9	3	15	3
Samuels	27	5	53	1	(5)	4	1	10	0
Permaul	20	1	86	1	(4)	11	3	43	3

ENGLAND	O	M	R	W		O	M	R	W
Anderson	12.4	5	42	6		13	4	35	1
Broad	10	3	31	1		13	5	29	1
Ali	10	2	56	1	(4)	12.4	1	54	1
Root	9	1	34	1	(5)	8	4	16	0
Jordan	6	3	4	0	(3)	11	5	24	1
Stokes	2	0	17	1		5	0	25	1

FALL OF WICKETS				
	E	W	E	W
	I	I	I	I
Wkt	1st	1st	2nd	2nd
1st	0	0	11	35
2nd	38	5	13	35
3rd	38	21	18	70
4th	91	37	28	80
5th	189	82	39	188
6th	233	107	62	–
7th	240	124	95	–
8th	247	162	98	–
9th	257	178	98	–
10th	257	189	123	–

Umpires: B.F.Bowden (*New Zealand*) (84) and B.N.J.Oxenford (*Australia*) (23).
Referee: A.J.Pycroft (*Zimbabwe*) (36).   Test No. 2158/151 (WI506/E955)

BANGLADESH v PAKISTAN (1st Test)

At Sheikh Abu Naser Stadium, Khulna, on 28, 29, 30 April, 1, 2 May 2015.
Toss: Bangladesh. Result: **MATCH DRAWN**.
Debuts: Bangladesh – Mohammad Shahid, Soumya Sarkar; Pakistan – Sami Aslam.

BANGLADESH

Tamim Iqbal	c Azhar b Shah	25	st Ahmed b Hafeez		206
Imrul Kayes	c and b Hafeez	51	c sub (Babar Azam) b Babar		150
Mominul Haque	lbw b Babar	80	b Junaid		21
Mahmudullah	c Ahmed b Riaz	49	lbw b Junaid		40
Shakib Al Hasan	c Shafiq b Babar	25	not out		76
*†Mushfiqur Rahim	c Misbah b Shah	32	lbw b Hafeez		0
Soumya Sarkar	c Shafiq b Hafeez	33	c Hafeez b Shafiq		33
Shuvagata Hom	not out	12	not out		20
Taijul Islam	b Shah	1			
Mohammad Shahid	c Misbah b Riaz	10			
Rubel Hossain	c Ahmed b Riaz	2			
Extras	(LB 5, NB 7)	12	(LB 4, W 2, NB 3)		9
Total	**(120 overs)**	**332**	**(6 wkts; 136 overs)**		**555**

PAKISTAN

Mohammad Hafeez	c Mahmudullah b Shuvagata	224
Sami Aslam	c Mushfiqur b Taijul	20
Azhar Ali	b Shuvagata	83
Younus Khan	b Taijul	33
*Misbah-ul-Haq	c Rubel b Taijul	59
Asad Shafiq	c and b Shakib	83
†Sarfraz Ahmed	c sub (Liton Das) b Shahid	82
Wahab Riaz	b Taijul	0
Yasir Shah	lbw b Taijul	13
Zulfiqar Babar	st Mahmudullah b Taijul	11
Junaid Khan	not out	0
Extras	(B 5, LB 8, W 3, NB 4)	20
Total	**(168.4 overs)**	**628**

PAKISTAN	O	M	R	W		O	M	R	W
Junaid Khan	16	2	40	0		21	5	88	2
Wahab Riaz	26	7	55	3	(4)	20	3	75	0
Mohammad Hafeez	18	5	47	2		20	0	82	2
Zulfiqar Babar	32	3	99	2	(2)	32	1	125	1
Yasir Shah	28	4	86	3		30	2	123	0
Azhar Ali						6	1	26	0
Asad Shafiq						7	0	32	1

BANGLADESH	O	M	R	W
Rubel Hossain	22	3	82	0
Mohammad Shahid	19	4	59	1
Taijul Islam	46.4	14	163	6
Shuvagata Hom	34	1	120	2
Shakib Al Hasan	37	4	146	1
Mahmudullah	4	0	30	0
Soumya Sarkar	1	0	2	0
Mominul Haque	5	0	13	0

FALL OF WICKETS

		B	P	B
Wkt	1st	1st	2nd	
1st	52	50	312	
2nd	92	277	345	
3rd	187	339	399	
4th	236	402	463	
5th	243	468	464	
6th	305	594	524	
7th	310	595	–	
8th	312	617	–	
9th	329	617	–	
10th	332	628	–	

Umpires: N.J.Llong (*England*) (27) and R.E.J.Martinesz (*Sri Lanka*) (7).
Referee: J.J.Crowe (*New Zealand*) (70).

Test No. 2159/9 (B89/P388)

BANGLADESH v PAKISTAN (2nd Test)

At Shere Bangla National Stadium, Mirpur, on 6, 7, 8, 9 May 2015.
Toss: Bangladesh. Result: **PAKISTAN** won by 328 runs.
Debuts: None.

‡ (Abul Hasan)

PAKISTAN

Mohammad Hafeez	c Mushfiqur b Shahid	8	c Mushfiqur b Shahid		0
Sami Aslam	c Shahadat b Taijul	19	c Mahmudullah b Shahid		8
Azhar Ali	c Mahmudullah b Shuvagata	226	c Shuvagata b Soumya		25
Younus Khan	c Shuvagata b Shahid	148	c and b Taijul		39
*Misbah-ul-Haq	b Shakib	9	c sub ‡ b Mahmudullah		82
Asad Shafiq	c Mahmudullah b Shuvagata	107	b Shuvagata		15
†Sarfraz Ahmed	not out	21	not out		18
Wahab Riaz	c Imrul b Taijul	4			
Yasir Shah	lbw b Taijul	0			
Junaid Khan					
Imran Khan					
Extras	(LB 8, W 2, NB 5)	15	(LB 2, W 6)		8
Total	**(8 wkts dec; 152 overs)**	**557**	**(6 wkts dec; 41.1 overs)**		**195**

BANGLADESH

Tamim Iqbal	lbw b Junaid	4	c Sarfraz b Imran		42
Imrul Kayes	b Shah	32	b Shah		16
Mominul Haque	c Sarfraz b Junaid	13	c Shafiq b Shah		68
Mahmudullah	c Ali b Riaz	28	c Younus b Imran		2
Shakib Al Hasan	not out	89	c Riaz b Hafeez		13
*†Mushfiqur Rahim	b Shah	8	b Shah		0
Soumya Sarkar	c Ali b Riaz	3	c Sarfraz b Riaz		1
Shuvagata Hom	c Shafiq b Riaz	0	b Junaid		39
Taijul Islam	b Hafeez	15	c Aslam b Shah		10
Mohammad Shahid	c Ali b Shah	-1	not out		14
Shahadat Hossain	absent hurt	–	absent hurt		–
Extras	(LB 2, W 2, NB 2)	6	(B 4, LB 4, NB 8)		16
Total	**(47.3 overs)**	**203**	**(56.5 overs)**		**221**

BANGLADESH	O	M	R	W		O	M	R	W	FALL OF WICKETS			
											P	B	P	B
Shahadat Hossain	0.2	0	4	0									
Soumya Sarkar	17.4	1	57	0	(3)	9	0	45	1	*Wkt*	*1st*	*1st*	*2nd*	*2nd*
Mohammad Shahid	31	10	72	2	(1)	10	4	23	2	1st	9	4	0	48
Taijul Islam	51	3	179	3	(2)	10	0	56	1	2nd	58	38	25	86
Shuvagata Hom	16	0	76	2		2	0	18	1	3rd	308	69	49	95
Shakib Al Hasan	30	3	136	1	(4)	8	0	45	0	4th	323	85	107	121
Mominul Haque	3	0	12	0						5th	530	107	140	126
Mahmudullah	2	0	12	0	(6)	2.1	0	8	1	6th	545	113	195	139
Imrul Kayes	1	0	1	0						7th	552	119	–	143
										8th	557	140	–	177
PAKISTAN										9th	–	203	–	221
Junaid Khan	6	2	26	2		10.5	1	45	1	10th	–	–	–	–
Imran Khan	7	0	31	0		11	1	56	2					
Wahab Riaz	15	2	73	3	(4)	11	1	36	1					
Yasir Shah	15.3	4	58	3	(3)	21	3	73	4					
Mohammad Hafeez	4	1	13	1		3	0	3	1					

Umpires: N.J.Llong (*England*) (28) and P.R.Reiffel (*Australia*) (16).
Referee: J.J.Crowe (*New Zealand*) (71).   Test No. 2160/10 (B90/P389)

ENGLAND v NEW ZEALAND (1st Test)

At Lord's, London, on 21, 22, 23, 24, 25 May 2015.
Toss: New Zealand. Result: **ENGLAND** won by 124 runs.
Debuts: England – A.Lyth, M.A.Wood; New Zealand – M.J.Henry.

ENGLAND

A.Lyth	c Watling b Southee	7	c Southee b Boult		12
*A.N.Cook	c Watling b Henry	16	c Latham b Boult		162
G.S.Ballance	c Southee b Boult	1	b Southee		0
I.R.Bell	b Henry	1	c Latham b Southee		29
J.E.Root	c Latham b Henry	98	c Boult b Henry		84
B.A.Stokes	b Craig	92	c Taylor b Craig		101
†J.C.Buttler	lbw b Boult	67	c Latham b Henry		14
M.M.Ali	c Latham b Boult	58	lbw b Boult		43
S.C.J.Broad	c Latham b Boult	3	b Boult		10
M.A.Wood	not out	8	not out		4
J.M.Anderson	c and b Henry	11	b Boult		0
Extras	(B 16, LB 6, W 2, NB 3)	27	(B 2, LB 12, W 5)		19
Total	**(100.5 overs)**	**389**	**(129 overs)**		**478**

NEW ZEALAND

M.J.Guptill	c Ballance b Broad	70	c Ballance b Anderson		0
T.W.M.Latham	lbw b Ali	59	lbw b Broad		0
K.S.Williamson	c Ballance b Ali	132	c Root b Stokes		27
L.R.P.L.Taylor	c Buttler b Broad	62	lbw b Broad		8
*B.B.McCullum	c Root b Wood	42	(6) c Stokes		0
C.J.Anderson	c Buttler b Wood	9	(7) lbw b Root		67
†B.J.Watling	not out	61	(5) c Buttler b Wood		59
M.D.Craig	lbw b Ali	0	b Stokes		4
T.G.Southee	c Wood b Anderson	11	c and b Ali		20
M.J.Henry	c Root b Wood	10	not out		10
T.A.Boult	c Anderson b Broad	0	c Ali b Broad		10
Extras	(B 26, LB 34, W 6, NB 1)	67	(B 5, LB 7, W 2, NB 1)		15
Total	**(131.2 overs)**	**523**	**(67.3 overs)**		**220**

NEW ZEALAND	O	M	R	W	O	M	R	W
Boult	29	6	79	4	34	8	85	5
Southee	24	1	104	1	34	4	162	2
Henry	24.5	3	93	4	29	3	106	2
Craig	18	2	77	1	28	3	96	1
Anderson	5	1	14	0	3	0	13	0
Williamson					1	0	2	0

ENGLAND	O	M	R	W	O	M	R	W
Anderson	29	7	88	1	14	5	31	1
Broad	26.2	4	77	3	16.3	3	50	3
Wood	27	2	93	3	13	3	47	1
Stokes	21	2	105	0	11	3	38	3
Ali	26	4	94	3	8	3	35	1
Root	2	0	6	0	5	3	7	1

FALL OF WICKETS

	E	NZ	E	NZ
Wkt	1st	1st	2nd	2nd
1st	17	148	14	0
2nd	25	148	25	0
3rd	25	337	74	12
4th	30	403	232	61
5th	191	420	364	61
6th	251	470	389	168
7th	354	470	455	174
8th	363	493	467	198
9th	368	515	478	198
10th	389	523	478	220

Umpires: M.Erasmus (*South Africa*) (30) and S.Ravi (*India*) (5).
Referee: D.C.Boon (*Australia*) (25).   Test No. 2161/100 (E956/NZ400)

ENGLAND v NEW ZEALAND (2nd Test)

At Headingley, Leeds, on 29, 30, 31 May, 1, 2 June 2015.
Toss: England. Result: **NEW ZEALAND** won by 199 runs.
Debut: New Zealand – L.Ronchi.

NEW ZEALAND

M.J.Guptill	c Bell b Anderson	0	(2) c Root b Wood		70
T.W.M.Latham	c Root b Broad	84	(1) c Buttler b Broad		3
K.S.Williamson	c Buttler b Anderson	0	c Buttler b Broad		6
L.R.P.L.Taylor	lbw b Broad	20	c Stokes b Wood		48
*B.B.McCullum	c Wood b Stokes	41	lbw b Wood		55
B.J.Watling	b Wood	14	c Root b Anderson		120
†L.Ronchi	c Anderson b Broad	88	c Buttler b Anderson		31
M.D.Craig	not out	41	not out		58
T.G.Southee	c Lyth b Wood	1	c Anderson b Ali		40
M.J.Henry	c Buttler b Broad	27	not out		12
T.A.Boult	c Lyth b Broad	15			
Extras	(B 4, LB 14, NB 1)	19	(B 4, LB 6, W 1)		11
Total	**(72.1 overs)**	**350**	**(8 wkts dec; 91 overs)**		**454**

ENGLAND

A.Lyth	run out	107	c Ronchi b Boult		24
*A.N.Cook	lbw b Craig	75	lbw b Williamson		56
G.S.Ballance	b Boult	29	b Boult		6
I.R.Bell	c Craig b Southee	12	c Williamson b Craig		1
J.E.Root	c Ronchi b Southee	1	c Latham b Craig		0
B.A.Stokes	c Craig b Boult	6	c Ronchi b Williamson		29
†J.C.Buttler	c Taylor b Southee	10	lbw b Craig		73
M.M.Ali	c Guptill b Southee	1	b Henry		2
S.C.J.Broad	b Henry	46	b Williamson		23
M.A.Wood	c Ronchi b Craig	19	c Craig b Southee		17
J.M.Anderson	not out	10	not out		8
Extras	(B 19, LB 5, W 5, NB 5)	34	(B 12, LB 2, W 2)		16
Total	**(108.2 overs)**	**350**	**(91.5 overs)**		**255**

ENGLAND	O	M	R	W	O	M	R	W		FALL OF WICKETS			
											NZ	E	NZ	E
Anderson	13	3	43	2	23	4	96	2	Wkt	1st	1st	2nd	2nd
Broad	17.1	0	109	5	16	1	94	2	1st	2	177	15	47
Wood	14	4	62	2	19	2	97	3	2nd	2	215	23	61
Stokes	17	4	70	1	12	1	61	0	3rd	68	238	122	62
Ali	11	3	48	0	16	0	73	1	4th	123	239	141	62
Root					5	0	23	0	5th	144	247	262	102
									6th	264	257	315	141
NEW ZEALAND									7th	265	266	368	153
Boult	30	7	98	2	23	4	61	2	8th	281	267	435	188
Southee	30	5	83	4	18	7	43	1	9th	310	318	–	230
Henry	20.2	4	92	1	(4) 12	2	49	1	10th	350	350	–	255
Craig	26	12	48	2	(3) 31.5	12	73	3					
Williamson	3	1	5	0	7	1	15	3					

Umpires: S.Ravi (*India*) (6) and R.J.Tucker (*Australia*) (36).
Referee: D.C.Boon (*Australia*) (26). **Test No. 2162/101 (E957/NZ401)**

19

WEST INDIES v AUSTRALIA (1st Test)

At Windsor Park, Roseau, Dominica, on 3, 4, 5 June 2015.
Toss: West Indies. Result: **AUSTRALIA** won by nine wickets.
Debuts: West Indies – S.O.Dowrich; Australia – A.C.Voges.

WEST INDIES

K.C.Brathwaite	c Haddin b Hazlewood	10	b Starc		15
S.D.Hope	c Marsh b Johnson	36	c Clarke b Johnson		2
D.M.Bravo	c Clarke b Lyon	19	c Warner b Hazlewood		5
S.O.Dowrich	b Hazlewood	15	c Watson b Hazlewood		70
M.N.Samuels	c Hazlewood b Starc	7	c Starc b Johnson		74
J.Blackwood	c Clarke b Hazlewood	2	st Haddin b Lyon		12
*†D.Ramdin	b Johnson	19	b Lyon		3
J.O.Holder	c Marsh b Starc	21	not out		12
J.E.Taylor	c Voges b Smith	6	lbw b Starc		0
D.Bishoo	not out	9	b Starc		1
S.T.Gabriel	c Clarke b Johnson	2	b Starc		0
Extras	(W 1, NB 1)	2	(B 11, LB 10, W 1)		22
Total	**(53.5 overs)**	**148**	**(86 overs)**		**216**

AUSTRALIA

D.A.Warner	c Blackwood b Taylor	8	(2) c Bravo b Taylor		28
S.E.Marsh	c Bravo b Holder	19	(1) not out		13
S.P.D.Smith	st Ramdin b Bishoo	25	not out		5
*M.J.Clarke	c Ramdin b Bishoo	18			
A.C.Voges	not out	130			
S.R.Watson	c Holder b Bishoo	11			
†B.J.Haddin	b Bishoo	8			
M.G.Johnson	c Samuels b Bishoo	20			
M.A.Starc	b Bishoo	0			
N.M.Lyon	lbw b Gabriel	22			
J.R.Hazlewood	b Samuels	39			
Extras	(B 9, LB 3, W 1, NB 5)	18	(NB 1)		1
Total	**(107 overs)**	**318**	**(1 wkt; 5 overs; 27 mins)**		**47**

AUSTRALIA	O	M	R	W		O	M	R	W	FALL OF WICKETS				
Johnson	13.5	2	34	3		15	3	38	2		WI	A	WI	A
Hazlewood	15	7	33	3	(3)	16	7	17	2	Wkt	1st	1st	2nd	2nd
Starc	15	5	48	2	(2)	18	7	28	4	1st	23	13	21	42
Lyon	6	1	20	1		24	7	67	2	2nd	63	38	21	–
Watson	3	1	11	0	(6)	7	3	6	0	3rd	75	61	37	–
Smith	1	0	2	1	(5)	2	0	16	0	4th	85	97	181	–
Voges						2	0	15	0	5th	87	112	198	–
Clarke						2	0	8	0	6th	91	126	198	–
										7th	121	178	206	–
WEST INDIES										8th	133	178	206	–
Taylor	20	0	72	1		3	0	22	1	9th	144	221	216	–
Gabriel	15	3	38	1		2	0	25	0	10th	148	318	216	–
Holder	14	3	30	1										
Bishoo	33	10	80	6										
Samuels	22	2	71	1										
Blackwood	3	0	15	0										

Umpires: Alim Dar (*Pakistan*) (95) and R.A.Kettleborough (*England*) (27).
Referee: R.S.Mahanama (*Sri Lanka*) (57).　　　　Test No. 2163/112 (WI507/A773)

20

WEST INDIES v AUSTRALIA (2nd Test)

At Sabina Park, Kingston, Jamaica, on 11, 12, 13, 14 June 2015.
Toss: West Indies. Result: **AUSTRALIA** won by 277 runs.
Debut: West Indies – R.Chandrika.

AUSTRALIA

D.A.Warner	c Hope b Taylor	0	(2) c Ramdin b Roach		62
S.E.Marsh	lbw b Taylor	11	(1) c Holder b Permaul		69
S.P.D.Smith	lbw b Taylor	199	not out		54
*M.J.Clarke	c Ramdin b Holder	47	not out		14
A.C.Voges	c Ramdin b Taylor	37			
S.R.Watson	b Taylor	25			
†B.J.Haddin	c Taylor	22			
M.G.Johnson	c Bravo b Roach	5			
M.A.Starc	b Holder	6			
J.R.Hazlewood	c Blackwood b Permaul	24			
N.M.Lyon	not out	5			
Extras	(B 5, LB 7, NB 6)	18	(B 9, LB 4)		13
Total	**(126.5 overs)**	**399**	**(2 wkts dec; 65 overs)**		**212**

WEST INDIES

K.C.Brathwaite	b Lyon	4	b Starc		0
R.Chandrika	c Haddin b Starc	0	c Marsh b Starc		0
D.M.Bravo	lbw b Lyon	14	c Marsh b Hazlewood		11
S.O.Dowrich	c Haddin b Hazlewood	13	b Starc		4
S.D.Hope	c Haddin b Lyon	26	b Johnson		16
J.Blackwood	c Warner b Hazlewood	51	b Hazlewood		0
*†D.Ramdin	lbw b Hazlewood	8	c Clarke b Johnson		29
J.O.Holder	not out	82	c Starc b Watson		1
V.Permaul	c Haddin b Johnson	0	not out		23
K.A.J.Roach	c Haddin b Hazlewood	7	c Smith b Lyon		3
J.E.Taylor	lbw b Hazlewood	0	b Lyon		0
Extras	(B 6, LB 2, W 1, NB 1, Pen 5)	15	(B 13, LB 11, W 2, NB 1)		27
Total	**(59.5 overs)**	**220**	**(42 overs)**		**114**

WEST INDIES	O	M	R	W		O	M	R	W
Taylor	25	10	47	6		10	2	24	0
Roach	25	2	113	1		9	2	26	1
Holder	22	3	64	2	(4)	10	2	24	0
Permaul	34.5	7	124	1	(3)	21	3	83	1
Brathwaite	19	2	39	0		11	3	23	0
Blackwood	20	2	10	0		4	1	19	0

AUSTRALIA	O	M	R	W	O	M	R	W
Starc	14	2	50	1	13	5	34	3
Hazlewood	15.5	8	38	5	10	5	18	2
Lyon	14	4	55	3	7	3	12	2
Johnson	14	2	54	1	8	1	23	2
Watson	2	0	10	0	4	2	3	1

FALL OF WICKETS

	A	WI	A	WI
Wkt	1st	1st	2nd	2nd
1st	0	1	117	0
2nd	16	9	163	1
3rd	134	25	–	20
4th	210	44	–	27
5th	264	77	–	33
6th	296	119	–	55
7th	306	142	–	62
8th	330	143	–	111
9th	393	220	–	114
10th	399	220	–	114

Umpires: I.J.Gould (*England*) (44) and R.A.Kettleborough (*England*) (28).
Referee: R.S.Mahanama (*Sri Lanka*) (58). **Test No. 2164/113 (WI508/A774)**

BANGLADESH v INDIA (Only Test)

At Khan Shaheb Osman Ali Stadium, Fatullah, on 10, 11 (*no play*), 12, 13, 14 June 2015.
Toss: India. Result: **MATCH DRAWN**.
Debut: Bangladesh – Liton Das.

INDIA

M.Vijay	lbw b Shakib	150
S.Dhawan	c and b Shakib	173
R.G.Sharma	b Shakib	6
*V.Kohli	b Jubair	14
A.M.Rahane	b Shakib	98
†W.P.Saha	b Jubair	6
R.Ashwin	not out	2
Harbhajan Singh	not out	7
U.T.Yadav		
I.Sharma		
V.R.Aaron		
Extras	(B 4, LB 1, NB 1)	6
Total	**(6 wkts dec; 103.3 overs)**	**462**

BANGLADESH

Tamim Iqbal	st Saha b Ashwin	19	not out	16
Imrul Kayes	st Saha b Harbhajan	72	not out	7
Mominul Haque	c Yadav b Harbhajan	30		
*Mushfiqur Rahim	c R.G.Sharma b Ashwin	2		
Shakib Al Hasan	c Saha b Ashwin	9		
Soumya Sarkar	b Aaron	37		
†Liton Das	c R.G.Sharma b Ashwin	44		
Shuvagata Hom	c R.G.Sharma b Ashwin	9		
Taijul Islam	not out	16		
Mohammad Shahid	c Dhawan b Harbhajan	6		
Jubair Hossain	run out	0		
Extras	(LB 9, NB 3)	12		–
Total	**(65.5 overs)**	**256**	**(0 wkts; 15 overs; 46 mins)**	**23**

BANGLADESH	O	M	R	W	O	M	R	W	FALL OF WICKETS
Mohammad Shahid	22	2	88	0					I B B
Soumya Sarkar	3	0	11	0					Wkt 1st 1st 2nd
Shuvagata Hom	14	0	52	0					1st 283 27 –
Shakib Al Hasan	24.3	1	105	4					2nd 291 108 –
Taijul Islam	20	0	85	0					3rd 310 110 –
Jubair Hossain	19	1	113	2					4th 424 121 –
Imrul Kayes	1	0	3	0					5th 445 172 –
									6th 453 176 –
INDIA									7th – 219 –
I.Sharma	7	0	24	0					8th – 232 –
Ashwin	25	6	87	5	6	2	8	0	9th – 246 –
Yadav	7	0	45	0	(1) 2	1	4	0	10th – 256 –
Aaron	9	0	27	1					
Harbhajan Singh	17.5	2	64	3	(3) 5	2	11	0	
Vijay					(4) 1	1	0	0	
Dhawan					(5) 1	1	0	0	

Umpires: H.D.P.K.Dharmasena (*Sri Lanka*) (30) and N.J.Llong (*England*) (29).
Referee: A.J.Pycroft (*Zimbabwe*) (37). **Test No. 2165/8 (B91/1488)**

SRI LANKA v PAKISTAN (1st Test)

At Galle International Stadium, on 17 (*no play*), 18, 19, 20, 21 June 2015.
Toss: Pakistan. Result: **PAKISTAN** won by ten wickets.
Debuts: None.

SRI LANKA

Batsman	Dismissal	Runs		2nd innings	Runs
F.D.M.Karunaratne	c Sarfraz b Riaz	21	(2)	st Sarfraz b Shah	79
J.K.Silva	c Sarfraz b Babar	125	(1)	c Ali b Riaz	5
K.C.Sangakkara	c Younus b Riaz	50		c Ali b Shah	18
H.D.R.L.Thirimanne	c Babar b Hafeez	8	(5)	c Younus b Riaz	44
*A.D.Mathews	b Riaz	19	(6)	c Ali b Shah	38
†L.D.Chandimal	b Babar	23	(7)	st Sarfraz b Shah	38
K.D.K.Vithanage	c and b Hafeez	18	(8)	c Babar b Shah	1
M.D.K.Perera	c Sarfraz b Shah	15	(4)	b Shah	0
K.T.G.D.Prasad	lbw b Babar	0		st Sarfraz b Babar	2
H.M.R.K.B.Herath	not out	6		c Hafeez b Shah	1
A.N.P.R.Fernando	c and b Shah	4		not out	0
Extras	(LB 5, W 2, NB 4)	11		(B 5, LB 1, W 6, NB 1)	13
Total	**(109.3 overs; 466 mins)**	**300**		**(77.1 overs; 341 mins)**	**206**

PAKISTAN

Batsman	Dismissal	Runs		2nd innings	Runs
Mohammad Hafeez	c Karunaratne b Prasad	2		not out	46
Ahmed Shehzad	lbw b Prasad	9		not out	43
Azhar Ali	lbw b Herath	8			
Younus Khan	b Perera	47			
*Misbah-ul-Haq	c Sangakkara b Fernando	20			
Asad Shafiq	st Chandimal b Perera	131			
†Sarfraz Ahmed	b Prasad	96			
Wahab Riaz	b Perera	14			
Yasir Shah	c Chandimal b Fernando	23			
Zulfiqar Babar	c Vithanage b Perera	56			
Junaid Khan	not out	6			
Extras	(LB 1, W 1, NB 3)	5		(B 3)	3
Total	**(113.1 overs; 493 mins)**	**417**		**(0 wkts; 11.2 overs; 47 mins)**	**92**

PAKISTAN	O	M	R	W		O	M	R	W
Junaid Khan	16	5	38	0	(2)	7	1	23	0
Wahab Riaz	26	3	74	3	(1)	16	4	46	2
Zulfiqar Babar	27	8	64	3	(5)	14	4	31	1
Yasir Shah	30.3	6	79	2	(3)	30.1	6	76	7
Mohammad Hafeez	10	0	40	2	(4)	10	3	24	0

SRI LANKA	O	M	R	W		O	M	R	W
Prasad	24	4	91	3	(2)	2	1	10	0
Fernando	19	1	71	2	(3)	2	0	18	0
Herath	30	4	99	1	(1)	4.2	0	30	0
Perera	31.1	3	122	4		3	0	31	0
Mathews	6	1	12	0					
Vithanage	3	0	21	0					

FALL OF WICKETS

Wkt	SL 1st	P 1st	SL 2nd	P 2nd
1st	30	2	18	–
2nd	142	11	63	–
3rd	154	35	63	–
4th	189	86	132	–
5th	226	96	144	–
6th	261	235	167	–
7th	277	273	175	–
8th	288	302	200	–
9th	291	403	203	–
10th	300	417	206	–

Umpires: R.K.Illingworth (*England*) (15) and P.R.Reiffel (*Australia*) (17).
Referee: B.C.Broad (*England*) (68). **Test No. 2166/49 (SL236/P390)**

SRI LANKA v PAKISTAN (2nd Test)

At P.Sara Oval, Colombo, on 25, 26, 27, 28, 29 June 2015.
Toss: Pakistan. Result: **SRI LANKA** won by seven wickets.
Debut: Sri Lanka – P.V.D.Chameera.

PAKISTAN

Batsman	1st innings		2nd innings	
Mohammad Hafeez	b Kaushal	42	c Sangakkara b Mathews	8
Ahmed Shehzad	c Sangakkara b Prasad	1	c Chandimal b Prasad	69
Azhar Ali	c Chandimal b Prasad	26	st Chandimal b Herath	117
Younus Khan	c Chandimal b Prasad	6	c Chandimal b Mathews	40
*Misbah-ul-Haq	run out	7	lbw b Prasad	22
Asad Shafiq	lbw b Kaushal	2	c Chandimal b Chameera	27
†Sarfraz Ahmed	c Mathews b Kaushal	14	c Chandimal b Prasad	16
Wahab Riaz	lbw b Kaushal	4	(11) lbw b Chameera	6
Yasir Shah	c Sangakkara b Kaushal	15	(8) b Prasad	0
Zulfiqar Babar	b Chameera	5	(9) not out	7
Junaid Khan	not out	2	(10) c Chandimal b Chameera	3
Extras	(LB 4, W 3, NB 7)	14	(B 2, LB 2, W 5, NB5)	14
Total	**(42.5 overs; 223 mins)**	**138**	**(118.2 overs; 553 mins)**	**329**

SRI LANKA

Batsman	1st innings		2nd innings	
F.D.M.Karunaratne	c Sarfraz b Junaid	28	lbw b Shah	50
J.K.Silva	run out	80		
K.C.Sangakkara	c Shafiq b Babar	34	c Ali b Shah	0
H.D.R.L.Thirimanne	c Ali b Shah	7	(5) not out	20
*A.D.Mathews	lbw b Shah	77	(4) not out	43
†L.D.Chandimal	b Shah	1		
K.D.K.Vithanage	b Shah	3	(2) c Hafeez b Babar	34
K.T.G.D.Prasad	lbw b Hafeez	35		
H.M.R.K.Herath	not out	18		
P.H.T.Kaushal	c Misbah b Shah	18		
P.V.D.Chameera	c Younus b Shah	5		
Extras	(B 6, LB 4, W 1, NB 1)	12	(LB 6)	6
Total	**(121.3 overs; 524 mins)**	**315**	**(3 wkts; 26.3 overs; 117 mins)**	**153**

SRI LANKA	O	M	R	W		O	M	R	W
Prasad	13	6	43	3		29.3	3	92	4
Mathews	9	4	16	0		11	5	15	2
Chameera	10	0	33	1	(4)	18.5	1	53	3
Kaushal	10.5	0	42	5	(5)	25	3	76	0
Herath					(3)	34	7	89	1

PAKISTAN	O	M	R	W		O	M	R	W
Wahab Riaz	9	2	19	0					
Junaid Khan	29	5	89	1	(1)	4	0	30	0
Zulfiqar Babar	32	8	82	1		8	0	42	1
Yasir Shah	41.3	5	96	6		10.3	0	55	2
Mohammad Hafeez	10	2	19	1	(2)	4	0	20	0

FALL OF WICKETS

	P	SL	P	SL
Wkt	1st	1st	2nd	2nd
1st	30	47	9	49
2nd	51	98	129	49
3rd	74	119	202	121
4th	89	191	234	–
5th	95	194	274	–
6th	96	202	301	–
7th	113	275	303	–
8th	117	275	313	–
9th	124	303	323	–
10th	138	315	329	–

Umpires: R.K.Illingworth (*England*) (16) and S.Ravi (*India*) (7).
Referee: B.C.Broad (*England*) (69). **Test No. 2167/50 (SL237/P391)**

SRI LANKA v PAKISTAN (3rd Test)

At Pallekele International Cricket Stadium, on 3, 4, 5, 6, 7 July 2015.
Toss: Pakistan. Result: **PAKISTAN** won by seven wickets.
Debuts: None.

SRI LANKA

F.D.M.Karunaratne	st Sarfraz b Azhar	130	b Rahat	10
J.K.Silva	c Sarfraz b Rahat	9	c Misbah b Adil	3
W.U.Tharanga	c Younus b Shah	46	c Azhar b Shah	48
H.D.R.L.Thirimanne	c sub (Babar Azam) b Shah	11	b Rahat	0
*A.D.Mathews	c sub (Babar Azam) b Shah	3	c Sarfraz b Imran	122
J.Mubarak	st Sarfraz b Shah	25	c Azhar b Shah	35
†L.D.Chandimal	lbw b Rahat	24	lbw b Imran	67
K.T.G.D.Prasad	c Shah b Azhar	0	c Sarfraz b Imran	0
P.H.T.Kaushal	lbw b Rahat	18	c Sarfraz b Imran	8
R.A.S.Lakmal	not out	6	c Sarfraz b Imran	0
A.N.P.R.Fernando	lbw b Shah	0	not out	4
Extras	(LB 3, W 3)	6	(B 4, LB 9, W 3)	16
Total	**(89.5 overs; 410 mins)**	**278**	**(95.4 overs; 463 mins)**	**313**

PAKISTAN

Shan Masood	lbw b Prasad	13	st Chandimal b Kaushal	125
Ahmed Shehzad	c Chandimal b Fernando	21	b Lakmal	0
Azhar Ali	c Karunaratne b Fernando	52	c Chandimal b Prasad	5
Younus Khan	run out	3	not out	171
Asad Shafiq	lbw b Prasad	15		
†Sarfraz Ahmed	not out	78		
*Misbah-ul-Haq	lbw b Fernando	6	(5) not out	59
Ehsan Adil	lbw b Kaushal	0		
Yasir Shah	c Chandimal b Prasad	18		
Rahat Ali	lbw b Kaushal	2		
Imran Khan	b Kaushal	0		
Extras	(LB 4, W 1, NB 2)	7	(B 5, LB 10, W 2, NB 5)	22
Total	**(66 overs; 308 mins)**	**215**	**(3 wkts; 103.1 overs; 462 mins)**	**382**

PAKISTAN	O	M	R	W	O	M	R	W
Rahat Ali	21	4	74	0	21	3	82	2
Ehsan Adil	14	3	37	0	17	4	66	1
Imran Khan	16	3	51	0	20.4	3	58	5
Yasir Shah	31.5	4	78	5	32	7	80	2
Azhar Ali	0	0	35	2	5	1	14	0

SRI LANKA	O	M	R	W	O	M	R	W
Prasad	19	1	78	3	20	2	65	1
Lakmal	14	1	64	0	19	5	48	1
Fernando	15	5	29	3	17	3	51	0
Mathews	4	1	3	0	13	2	34	0
Kaushal	14	1	37	3	31	1	153	1
Mubarak					3.1	0	16	0

FALL OF WICKETS

	SL	P	SL	P
Wkt	1st	1st	2nd	2nd
1st	15	32	12	0
2nd	106	40	22	13
3rd	133	45	35	255
4th	137	91	80	–
5th	204	135	161	–
6th	248	151	278	–
7th	248	152	278	–
8th	264	197	290	–
9th	277	202	306	–
10th	278	215	313	–

Umpires: I.J.Gould (*England*) (45) and P.R.Reiffel (*Australia*) (18).
Referee: B.C.Broad (*England*) (70).   **Test No. 2168/51 (SL238/P392)**

ENGLAND v AUSTRALIA (1st Test)

At Sophia Gardens, Cardiff, on 8, 9, 10, 11 July 2015.
Toss: England. Result: **ENGLAND** won by 169 runs.
Debuts: None.

ENGLAND

A.Lyth	c Warner b Hazlewood	6	c Clarke b Lyon	37
*A.N.Cook	c Haddin b Lyon	20	c Lyon b Starc	12
G.S.Ballance	lbw b Hazlewood	61	c Haddin b Hazlewood	0
I.R.Bell	lbw b Starc	1	b Johnson	60
J.E.Root	c Watson b Starc	134	b Hazlewood	60
B.A.Stokes	b Starc	52	b Starc	42
†J.C.Buttler	c Johnson b Hazlewood	27	c Haddin b Lyon	7
M.M.Ali	c Watson b Starc	77	c Haddin b Johnson	15
S.C.J.Broad	c Haddin b Lyon	18	c Hazlewood b Lyon	4
M.A.Wood	not out	7	not out	32
J.M.Anderson	b Starc	1	b Lyon	1
Extras	(B 17, LB 3, W 5, NB 1)	26	(B 7, LB 6, W 6)	19
Total	(102.1 overs; 456 mins)	430	(70.1 overs; 306 mins)	289

AUSTRALIA

C.J.L.Rogers	c Buttler b Wood	95	c Bell b Broad	10
D.A.Warner	c Cook b Anderson	17	lbw b Ali	52
S.P.D.Smith	c Cook b Ali	33	c Bell b Broad	33
*M.J.Clarke	c and b Ali	38	c Stokes b Broad	4
A.C.Voges	c Anderson b Stokes	31	c Buttler b Wood	1
S.R.Watson	lbw b Broad	30	lbw b Wood	19
N.M.Lyon	lbw b Wood	6	(11) not out	0
†B.J.Haddin	c Buttler b Anderson	22	(7) c Cook b Ali	7
M.G.Johnson	c Ballance b Broad	14	(8) c Lyth b Root	77
M.A.Starc	c Root b Anderson	0	(9) c Lyth b Root	17
J.R.Hazlewood	not out	2	(10) c Root b Ali	14
Extras	(B 6, LB 11, W 3)	20	(B 4, LB 3, NB 1)	8
Total	(84.5 overs; 368 mins)	308	(70.3 overs; 305 mins)	242

AUSTRALIA	O	M	R	W		O	M	R	W
Starc	24.1	4	114	5	(3)	16	4	60	2
Hazlewood	23	8	83	3		13	2	49	2
Johnson	25	3	111	0	(1)	16	2	69	2
Lyon	20	4	69	2		20.1	4	75	4
Watson	8	0	24	0		5	0	23	0
Warner	2	0	9	0					

ENGLAND	O	M	R	W		O	M	R	W
Anderson	18.5	6	43	3		12	3	33	0
Broad	17	4	60	2		14	3	39	3
Wood	20	5	66	2	(5)	14	4	53	2
Ali	15	1	71	2	(3)	16.3	4	59	3
Stokes	14	5	51	1	(4)	8	2	23	0
Root						6	1	28	2

FALL OF WICKETS

	E	A	E	A
Wkt	1st	1st	2nd	2nd
1st	7	52	17	19
2nd	42	129	22	97
3rd	43	180	73	101
4th	196	207	170	106
5th	280	258	207	106
6th	293	265	236	122
7th	343	265	240	151
8th	395	304	245	223
9th	419	306	288	242
10th	430	308	289	242

Umpires: H.D.P.K.Dharmasena (*Sri Lanka*) (31) and M.Erasmus (*South Africa*) (31).
Referee: R.S.Madugalle (*Sri Lanka*) (156). **Test No. 2169/337 (E958/A775)**

ENGLAND v AUSTRALIA (2nd Test)

At Lord's, London, on 16, 17, 18, 19 July 2015.
Toss: Australia. Result: **AUSTRALIA** won by 405 runs.
Debut: Australia – P.M.Nevill.

AUSTRALIA

Batsman	1st innings		2nd innings	
C.J.L.Rogers	b Broad	173	retired hurt	49
D.A.Warner	c Anderson b Ali	38	c Cook b Ali	83
S.P.D.Smith	lbw b Root	215	b Ali	58
*M.J.Clarke	c Ballance b Wood	7	not out	32
A.C.Voges	c Buttler b Broad	25		
M.R.Marsh	b Broad	12	(5) not out	27
†P.M.Nevill	c Ali b Root	45		
M.G.Johnson	c Anderson b Broad	15		
M.A.Starc	not out	12		
J.R.Hazlewood				
N.M.Lyon				
Extras	(B 8, LB 14, W 1, NB 1)	24	(LB 5)	5
Total	**(8 wkts dec; 149 overs)**	**566**	**(2 wkts dec; 49 overs)**	**254**

ENGLAND

Batsman	1st innings		2nd innings	
A.Lyth	c Nevill b Starc	0	c Nevill b Starc	7
*A.N.Cook	b Marsh	96	c Nevill b Johnson	11
G.S.Ballance	b Johnson	23	c Nevill b Marsh	14
I.R.Bell	b Hazlewood	1	c sub (S.E.Marsh) b Lyon	11
J.E.Root	c Nevill b Johnson	1	b Hazlewood	17
B.A.Stokes	b Marsh	87	run out	0
†J.C.Buttler	c Nevill b Lyon	13	c Nevill b Johnson	11
M.M.Ali	lbw b Hazlewood	39	c sub (S.E.Marsh) b Johnson	0
S.C.J.Broad	c sub (S.E.Marsh) b Johnson	21	c Voges b Lyon	25
M.A.Wood	b Hazlewood	4	not out	2
J.M.Anderson	not out	6	b Hazlewood	0
Extras	(B 12, LB 8, NB 1)	21	(B 4, LB 1)	5
Total	**(90.1 overs)**	**312**	**(37 overs)**	**103**

ENGLAND	O	M	R	W		O	M	R	W
Anderson	26	4	99	0		7	0	38	0
Broad	27	5	83	4		8	2	42	0
Wood	28	7	92	1	(4)	10	3	39	0
Ali	36	4	138	1	(3)	16	0	78	2
Stokes	19	2	77	0		3	0	20	0
Root	12	0	55	2		5	0	32	0
Lyth	1	1	0	0					

AUSTRALIA	O	M	R	W		O	M	R	W
Starc	22	1	86	1		7	3	16	1
Hazlewood	22	2	68	3		8	2	20	2
Johnson	20.1	8	53	3		10	3	27	3
Lyon	16	1	53	1	(5)	9	3	27	2
Marsh	8	3	23	2	(4)	3	2	8	1
Smith	2	0	9	0					

FALL OF WICKETS

	A	E	A	E
Wkt	1st	1st	2nd	2nd
1st	78	0	165	12
2nd	362	28	210	23
3rd	383	29	–	42
4th	426	30	–	48
5th	442	175	–	52
6th	533	210	–	64
7th	536	266	–	64
8th	566	294	–	101
9th	–	306	–	101
10th	–	312	–	103

Umpires: H.D.P.K.Dharmasena (*Sri Lanka*) (32) and M.Erasmus (*South Africa*) (32).
Referee: R.S.Madugalle (*Sri Lanka*) (157).   **Test No. 2170/338 (E959/A776)**
C.J.L.Rogers retired hurt at 114-0.

ENGLAND v AUSTRALIA (3rd Test)

At Edgbaston, Birmingham, on 29, 30, 31 July 2015.
Toss: Australia. Result: **ENGLAND** won by eight wickets.
Debuts: None.

AUSTRALIA

C.J.L.Rogers	lbw b Broad	52	lbw b Broad		6
D.A.Warner	lbw b Anderson	2	c Lyth b Anderson		77
S.P.D.Smith	c Cook b Finn	7	c Buttler b Finn		8
*M.J.Clarke	b Finn	10	c Lyth b Finn		3
A.C.Voges	c Buttler b Anderson	16	c Bell b Finn		0
M.R.Marsh	c Buttler b Anderson	0	b Finn		6
†P.M.Nevill	b Anderson	2	c Buttler b Finn		59
M.G.Johnson	c Stokes b Anderson	3	c Stokes b Finn		14
M.A.Starc	c Buttler b Broad	11	c sub (J.E.Poysden) b Ali		58
J.R.Hazlewood	not out	14	c Root b Stokes		11
N.M.Lyon	b Anderson	11	not out		12
Extras	(LB 7, NB 1)	8	(B 2, LB 9)		11
Total	(36.4 overs; 173 mins)	136	(79.1 overs; 348 mins)		265

ENGLAND

A.Lyth	c Voges b Hazlewood	10	lbw b Hazlewood		12
*A.N.Cook	c Voges b Lyon	34	b Starc		7
I.R.Bell	c Warner b Lyon	53	not out		65
J.E.Root	c Voges b Starc	63	not out		38
J.M.Bairstow	c Nevill b Johnson	5			
B.A.Stokes	c Nevill b Johnson	0			
†J.C.Buttler	lbw b Lyon	9			
M.M.Ali	c Warner b Hazlewood	59			
S.C.J.Broad	c Marsh b Hazlewood	31			
S.T.Finn	not out	0			
J.M.Anderson	c Nevill b Starc	3			
Extras	(B 6, LB 4, W 4)	14	(W 2)		2
Total	(67.1 overs; 297 mins)	281	(2 wkts; 32.1 overs; 138 mins)		124

ENGLAND	O	M	R	W	O	M	R	W		FALL OF WICKETS			
Anderson	14.4	2	47	6	8.3	5	15	1			A	E	A	E
Broad	12	2	44	2	20	4	61	1		Wkt	1st	1st	2nd	2nd
Finn	10	1	38	2	21	3	79	6		1st	7	19	17	11
Ali					16.1	3	64	1		2nd	18	76	62	51
Stokes					11	3	28	1		3rd	34	132	76	–
Root					2.3	0	7	0		4th	77	142	76	–
										5th	82	142	92	–
AUSTRALIA										6th	86	182	111	–
Starc	16.1	1	71	2	6	1	33	1		7th	94	190	153	–
Hazlewood	15	0	74	3	7	0	21	1		8th	110	277	217	–
Johnson	16	2	66	2	(4) 7	3	10	0		9th	119	278	245	–
Marsh	7	2	24	0	(5) 1.1	0	8	0		10th	136	281	265	–
Lyon	13	2	36	3	(3) 11	1	52	0						

Umpires: Alim Dar (*Pakistan*) (96) and C.B.Gaffaney (*New Zealand*) (3).
Referee: R.S.Madugalle (*Sri Lanka*) (158).   **Test No. 2171/339 (E960/A777)**

ENGLAND v AUSTRALIA (4th Test)

At Trent Bridge, Nottingham, on 6, 7, 8 August 2015.
Toss: England. Result: **ENGLAND** won by an innings and 78 runs.
Debuts: None.

AUSTRALIA

C.J.L.Rogers	c Cook b Broad	0	c Root b Stokes		52
D.A.Warner	c Buttler b Wood	0	c Broad b Stokes		64
S.P.D.Smith	c Root b Broad	6	c Stokes b Broad		5
S.E.Marsh	c Bell b Broad	0	c Root b Stokes		2
*M.J.Clarke	c Cook b Broad	10	c Bell b Wood		13
A.C.Voges	c Stokes b Broad	1	not out		51
†P.M.Nevill	b Finn	2	lbw b Stokes		17
M.G.Johnson	c Root b Broad	13	c Cook b Stokes		5
M.A.Starc	c Root b Broad	1	c Bell b Stokes		0
J.R.Hazlewood	not out	4	b Wood		0
N.M.Lyon	c Stokes b Broad	9	b Wood		4
Extras	(LB 11, NB 3)	14	(B 20, LB 16, W 1, NB 3)		40
Total	**(18.3 overs; 94 mins)**	**60**	**(72.4 overs; 311 mins)**		**253**

ENGLAND

A.Lyth	c Nevill b Starc	14
*A.N.Cook	lbw b Starc	43
I.R.Bell	lbw b Starc	1
J.E.Root	c Nevill b Starc	130
J.M.Bairstow	c Rogers b Hazlewood	74
M.A.Wood	b Starc	28
B.A.Stokes	c Nevill b Hazlewood	5
†J.C.Buttler	b Starc	12
M.M.Ali	c Smith b Johnson	38
S.C.J.Broad	not out	24
S.T.Finn	not out	0
Extras	(B 14, LB 2, W 2, NB 4)	22
Total	**(9 wkts dec; 85.2 overs; 376 mins)**	**391**

ENGLAND	O	M	R	W	O	M	R	W		FALL OF WICKETS			
Broad	9.3	5	15	8	16	5	36	1			A	E	A
Wood	3	0	13	1	17.4	3	69	3		Wkt	1st	1st	2nd
Finn	6	0	21	1	12	4	42	0		1st	4	32	113
Stokes					21	8	36	6		2nd	10	34	130
Ali					6	0	34	0		3rd	10	96	136
										4th	15	269	136
AUSTRALIA										5th	21	297	174
Starc	27	2	111	6						6th	29	306	224
Hazlewood	24	4	97	2						7th	33	320	236
Johnson	21.2	2	102	1						8th	46	332	242
Lyon	10	1	47	0						9th	47	390	243
Warner	3	0	18	0						10th	60	–	253

Umpires: Alim Dar (*Pakistan*) (97) and S.Ravi (*India*) (8).
Referee: R.S.Madugalle (*Sri Lanka*) (159).   **Test No. 2172/340 (E961/A778)**

ENGLAND v AUSTRALIA (5th Test)

At The Oval, London, on 20, 21, 22, 23 August 2015.
Toss: England. Result: **AUSTRALIA** won by an innings and 46 runs.
Debuts: None.

AUSTRALIA

C.J.L.Rogers	c Cook b Wood	43
D.A.Warner	c Lyth b Ali	85
S.P.D.Smith	b Finn	143
*M.J.Clarke	c Buttler b Stokes	15
A.C.Voges	lbw b Stokes	76
M.R.Marsh	c Bell b Finn	3
†P.M.Nevill	c Buttler b Ali	18
M.G.Johnson	b Ali	0
M.A.Starc	lbw b Stokes	58
P.M.Siddle	c Lyth b Finn	1
N.M.Lyon	not out	5
Extras	(B 1, LB 24, W 6, NB 3)	34
Total	**(125.1 overs)**	**481**

ENGLAND

A.Lyth	c Starc b Siddle	19	c Clarke b Siddle	10
*A.N.Cook	b Lyon	22	c Voges b Smith	85
I.R.Bell	b Siddle	10	c Clarke b Marsh	13
J.E.Root	c Nevill b Marsh	6	c Starc b Johnson	11
J.M.Bairstow	c Lyon b Johnson	13	c Voges b Lyon	26
B.A.Stokes	c Nevill b Marsh	15	c Clarke b Lyon	0
†J.C.Buttler	b Lyon	1	c Starc b Marsh	42
M.M.Ali	c Nevill b Johnson	30	(9) c Nevill b Siddle	35
S.C.J.Broad	c Voges b Marsh	0	(10) b Siddle	11
M.A.Wood	c Starc b Johnson	24	(8) lbw b Siddle	6
S.T.Finn	not out	0	not out	9
Extras	(B 1, LB 7, NB 1)	9	(B12, LB 18, W 7, NB 1)	38
Total	**(48.4 overs)**	**149**	**(101.4 overs)**	**286**

ENGLAND	O	M	R	W	O	M	R	W
Broad	20	4	59	0				
Wood	26	9	59	1				
Stokes	29	6	133	3				
Finn	29.1	7	90	3				
Ali	18	1	102	3				
Root	3	0	13	0				

AUSTRALIA	O	M	R	W	O	M	R	W
Starc	8	3	18	0	(2) 16	4	40	0
Johnson	8.4	4	21	3	(1) 16	2	65	1
Lyon	10	2	40	2	28	7	53	2
Siddle	13	5	32	2	24.4	12	35	4
Marsh	9	2	30	3	16	4	56	2
Smith					1	0	7	1

FALL OF WICKETS

	A	E	E
Wkt	1st	1st	2nd
1st	110	30	19
2nd	161	46	62
3rd	186	60	99
4th	332	64	140
5th	343	83	140
6th	376	84	199
7th	376	92	221
8th	467	92	223
9th	475	149	263
10th	481	149	286

Umpires: Alim Dar (*Pakistan*) (98) and H.D.P.K.Dharmasena (*Sri Lanka*) (33).
Referee: J.J.Crowe (*New Zealand*) (72). **Test No. 2173/341 (E962/A779)**

ENGLAND v AUSTRALIA 2015

ENGLAND – BATTING AND FIELDING

	M	I	NO	HS	Runs	Avge	100	50	Ct/St
J.E.Root	5	9	1	134	460	57.50	2	2	8
A.N.Cook	5	9	–	96	330	36.66	–	2	9
M.M.Ali	5	8	–	77	293	36.62	–	2	2
J.M.Bairstow	3	4	–	74	118	29.50	–	1	–
I.R.Bell	5	9	1	65*	215	26.87	–	3	7
M.A.Wood	4	7	3	32*	103	25.75	–	–	–
B.A.Stokes	5	8	–	87	201	25.12	–	2	6
G.S.Ballance	2	4	–	61	98	24.50	–	1	2
S.C.J.Broad	5	8	1	31	134	19.14	–	–	1
J.C.Buttler	5	8	–	42	122	15.25	–	–	12
A.Lyth	5	9	–	37	115	12.77	–	–	6
J.M.Anderson	3	5	1	6*	11	2.75	–	–	3
S.T.Finn	3	4	4	9*	9	–	–	–	–

ENGLAND – BOWLING

	O	M	R	W	Avge	Best	5wI	10wM
S.C.J.Broad	143.3	34	439	21	20.90	8-15	1	–
S.T.Finn	78.1	15	270	12	22.50	6-79	1	–
J.M.Anderson	87	20	275	10	27.50	6-47	1	–
B.A.Stokes	105	26	368	11	33.45	6-36	1	–
M.A.Wood	118.4	31	391	10	39.10	3-69	–	–
M.M.Ali	123.4	13	546	12	45.50	3-59	–	–

Also bowled: A.Lyth 1-1-0-0; J.E.Root 28.3-1-135-4.

AUSTRALIA – BATTING AND FIELDING

	M	I	NO	HS	Runs	Avge	100	50	Ct/St
C.J.L.Rogers	5	9	1	173	480	60.00	1	3	1
S.P.D.Smith	5	9	–	215	508	56.44	2	1	1
D.A.Warner	5	9	–	85	418	46.44	–	5	3
A.C.Voges	5	8	1	76	201	28.71	–	2	7
P.M.Nevill	4	6	–	59	143	23.83	–	1	17
M.A.Starc	5	8	1	58	157	22.42	–	2	4
M.G.Johnson	5	8	–	77	141	17.62	–	1	1
M.J.Clarke	5	9	1	38	132	16.50	–	–	4
J.R.Hazlewood	4	6	3	14*	45	15.00	–	–	1
M.R.Marsh	3	5	1	27*	48	12.00	–	–	1
N.M.Lyon	5	7	3	12*	47	11.75	–	–	2

Also batted (one Test each): B.J.Haddin 22, 7 (5 ct); S.E.Marsh 0, 2; P.M.Siddle 1; S.R.Watson 30, 19 (2 ct).

AUSTRALIA – BOWLING

	O	M	R	W	Avge	Best	5wI	10wM
P.M.Siddle	37.4	17	67	6	11.16	4- 35	–	–
M.R.Marsh	44.1	13	149	8	18.62	3- 30	–	–
J.R.Hazlewood	112	28	412	16	25.75	3- 68	–	–
N.M.Lyon	137.1	25	452	16	28.25	4- 75	–	–
M.A.Starc	142.2	23	549	18	30.50	6-111	2	–
M.G.Johnson	140.1	29	524	15	34.93	3- 21	–	–

Also bowled: S.P.D.Smith 3-0-16-1; D.A.Warner 5-0-27-0; S.R.Watson 13-0-47-0.

BANGLADESH v SOUTH AFRICA (1st Test)

At Zohur Ahmed Chowdhury Stadium, Chittagong, on 21, 22, 23, 24‡, 25‡ July 2015.
Toss: South Africa. Result: **MATCH DRAWN**.
Debut: Bangladesh – Mustafizur Rahman.   ‡ *(no play)*

SOUTH AFRICA

D.Elgar	c Liton b Taijul	47	(2) not out		28
S.van Zyl	c Liton b Mahmudullah	34	(1) not out		33
F.du Plessis	lbw b Shakib	48			
*H.M.Amla	c Liton b Mustafizur	13			
T.Bavuma	c Jubair b Mustafizur	54			
J.P.Duminy	lbw b Mustafizur	0			
†Q.de Kock	b Mustafizur	0			
V.D.Philander	c Shakib b Jubair	24			
S.R.Harmer	c Mominul b Jubair	9			
D.W.Steyn	c Tamim b Jubair	2			
M.Morkel	not out	3			
Extras	(B 8, LB 5, NB 1)	14			–
Total	**(83.4 overs)**	**248**	**(0 wkts; 21.1 overs)**		**61**

BANGLADESH

Tamim Iqbal	b Elgar	57
Imrul Kayes	st de Kock b van Zyl	26
Mominul Haque	b Harmer	6
Mahmudullah	lbw b Philander	67
*Mushfiqur Rahim	lbw b Steyn	28
Shakib Al Hasan	c Duminy b Harmer	47
†Liton Das	c de Kock b Harmer	50
Mohammad Shahid	c van Zyl b Philander	25
Taijul Islam	c Elgar b Steyn	9
Mustafizur Rahman	c Duminy b Steyn	3
Jubair Hossain	not out	0
Extras	(LB 7, NB 1)	8
Total	**(116.1 overs)**	**326**

BANGLADESH	O	M	R	W		O	M	R	W	FALL OF WICKETS			
											SA	B	SA
Mohammad Shahid	17	9	34	0	(5)	6	1	12	0	Wkt	*1st*	*1st*	*2nd*
Mustafizur Rahman	17.4	6	37	4	(1)	5	0	21	0	1st	58	46	–
Shakib Al Hasan	14	2	45	1	(4)	5	0	19	0	2nd	136	55	–
Mahmudullah	3	0	9	1	(3)	1	1	0	0	3rd	136	144	–
Taijul Islam	18	3	57	1	(2)	2	0	4	0	4th	173	178	–
Jubair Hossain	14	1	53	3		2.1	1	5	0	5th	173	195	–
										6th	173	277	–
SOUTH AFRICA										7th	208	311	–
Steyn	22.1	5	78	3						8th	237	319	–
Philander	20	2	40	2						9th	239	325	–
Morkel	19	2	52	0						10th	248	326	–
Harmer	35	8	105	3									
Van Zyl	13	4	23	1									
Elgar	3	0	6	1									
Duminy	4	0	15	0									

Umpires: R.A.Kettleborough (*England*) (29) and J.S.Wilson (*West Indies*) (1).
Referee: B.C.Broad (*England*) (71).   **Test No. 2174/9 (B92/SA391)**

BANGLADESH v SOUTH AFRICA (2nd Test)

At Shere Bangla National Stadium, Mirpur, on 30, 31 July‡, 1‡, 2‡, 3‡ August 2015.
Toss: Bangladesh. Result: **MATCH DRAWN**.
Debut: South Africa – D.J.Vilas.   ‡ *(no play)*

BANGLADESH

Tamim Iqbal	c Amla b Steyn	6
Imrul Kayes	lbw b Duminy	30
Mominul Haque	c Vilas b Duminy	40
Mahmudullah	c Bavuma b Steyn	35
*Mushfiqur Rahim	c Vilas b Elgar	65
Shakib Al Hasan	c Elgar b Morkel	35
†Liton Das	c Elgar b Duminy	3
Nasir Hossain	not out	13
Mohammad Shahid	b Steyn	1
Mustafizur Rahman		
Jubair Hossain		
Extras	(B 5, LB 11, NB 2)	18
Total	**(8 wkts; 88.1 overs)**	**246**

SOUTH AFRICA

D.Elgar
S.van Zyl
F.du Plessis
*H.M.Amla
T.Bavuma
J.P.Duminy
†D.J.Vilas
V.D.Philander
D.W.Steyn
S.R.Harmer
M.Morkel
Extras
Total

SOUTH AFRICA	O	M	R	W		FALL OF WICKETS	
Steyn	16.1	4	30	3			B
Philander	11	2	25	0		*Wkt*	*1st*
Morkel	14	2	45	1		1st	12
Harmer	23	3	76	0		2nd	81
Van Zyl	2	1	5	0		3rd	86
Elgar	7	0	22	1		4th	180
Duminy	15	4	27	3		5th	215
						6th	220
						7th	245
						8th	246
						9th	–
						10th	–

Umpires: R.A.Kettleborough (*England*) (30) and P.R.Reiffel (*Australia*) (19).
Referee: B.C.Broad (*England*) (72).   **Test No. 2175/10 (B93/SA392)**

SRI LANKA v INDIA (1st Test)

At Galle International Stadium, on 12, 13, 14, 15 August 2015.
Toss: Sri Lanka. Result: **SRI LANKA** won by 63 runs.
Debuts: None.

SRI LANKA

F.D.M.Karunaratne	c Rahane b I.Sharma	9	b Ashwin	0
J.K.Silva	c Dhawan b Aaron	5	b Mishra	0
H.D.R.L.Thirimanne	c Rahane b Ashwin	13	(7) c Rahane b Ashwin	44
K.C.Sangakkara	c Rahul b Ashwin	5	c Rahane b Ashwin	40
*A.D.Mathews	c R.G.Sharma b Ashwin	64	c Rahul b Mishra	39
J.Mubarak	c Rahul b Ashwin	0	(8) c Rahane b Harbhajan	49
†L.D.Chandimal	c Rahane b Mishra	59	(6) not out	162
K.T.G.D.Prasad	lbw b Ashwin	0	(3) c Rahane b Aaron	3
H.M.R.K.B.Herath	b Ashwin	23	c Rahane b Mishra	1
P.H.T.Kaushal	c R.G.Sharma b Mishra	0	c Saha b I.Sharma	7
A.N.P.R.Fernando	not out	0	b Ashwin	3
Extras	(B 1, LB 1, NB 3)	5	(B 3, W 8, NB 8)	19
Total	**(49.4 overs; 234 mins)**	**183**	**(82.2 overs; 360 mins)**	**367**

INDIA

K.L.Rahul	lbw b Prasad	7	lbw b Herath	5
S.Dhawan	b Fernando	134	c and b Kaushal	28
R.G.Sharma	lbw b Mathews	9	(4) b Herath	4
*V.Kohli	lbw b Kaushal	103	(5) c Silva b Kaushal	3
A.M.Rahane	lbw b Kaushal	0	(6) c Mathews b Herath	36
†W.P.Saha	c Chandimal b Fernando	60	(7) st Chandimal b Herath	2
R.Ashwin	b Fernando	14	c Prasad b Herath	3
Harbhajan Singh	b Kaushal	14	c Silva b Herath	1
A.Mishra	b Kaushal	10	(10) c Karunaratne b Kaushal	15
I.Sharma	not out	3	(3) lbw b Herath	10
V.R.Aaron	c Mathews b Kaushal	4	not out	1
Extras	(LB 10, W 3, NB 11)	24	(LB 2, W 1, NB 1)	4
Total	**(117.4 overs; 506 mins)**	**375**	**(49.5 overs; 210 mins)**	**112**

INDIA	O	M	R	W		O	M	R	W
I.Sharma	11	3	30	1	(5)	13	0	77	1
Aaron	11	0	68	1	(4)	7	0	39	1
Ashwin	13.4	2	46	6	(1)	28.2	6	114	4
Mishra	6	1	20	2	(2)	17	2	61	3
Harbhajan Singh	8	1	17	0	(3)	17	0	73	1

SRI LANKA	O	M	R	W		O	M	R	W
Prasad	22	4	54	1		4	2	4	0
Fernando	26	2	98	3	(4)	6	3	8	0
Mathews	4	1	12	1	(5)	1	0	3	0
Kaushal	32.4	2	134	5	(3)	17.5	1	47	3
Herath	33	4	67	0	(2)	21	6	48	7

FALL OF WICKETS				
	SL	I	SL	I
Wkt	1st	1st	2nd	2nd
1st	15	14	0	12
2nd	15	28	1	30
3rd	27	255	5	34
4th	54	257	92	45
5th	60	294	95	60
6th	139	302	220	65
7th	155	330	302	67
8th	179	344	319	81
9th	179	366	360	102
10th	183	375	367	112

Umpires: N.J.Llong (*England*) (30) and B.N.J.Oxenford (*Australia*) (24).
Referee: A.J.Pycroft (*Zimbabwe*) (38). **Test No. 2176/36 (SL239/I489)**

SRI LANKA v INDIA (2nd Test)

At P.Sara Oval, Colombo, on 20, 21, 22, 23, 24 August 2015.
Toss: India. Result: **INDIA** won by 278 runs.
Debuts: None.

INDIA

M.Vijay	lbw b Prasad	0	lbw b Kaushal		82
K.L.Rahul	c Chandimal b Chameera	108	b Prasad		2
A.M.Rahane	c Karunaratne b Prasad	4	c Chandimal b Kaushal		126
*V.Kohli	c Mathews b Herath	78	lbw b Kaushal		10
R.G.Sharma	lbw b Mathews	79	c Mubarak b Kaushal		34
S.T.R.Binny	c Chameera b Herath	10	c Thirimanne b Prasad		17
†W.P.Saha	lbw b Herath	56	not out		13
R.Ashwin	c Silva b Mathews	2	c Chandimal b Prasad		19
A.Mishra	c Chandimal b Chameera	24	c Mubarak b Prasad		10
I.Sharma	lbw b Herath	2			
U.T.Yadav	not out	2	(10) not out		4
Extras	(B 8, LB 13, W 4, NB 3)	28	(LB 4, W 3, NB 1)		8
Total	**(114 overs; 517 mins)**	**393**	**(8 wkts dec; 91 overs; 414 mins)**		**325**

SRI LANKA

F.D.M.Karunaratne	lbw b Yadav	1	(2) b Ashwin		46
J.K.Silva	c Ashwin b Mishra	51	(1) c Binny b Ashwin		1
K.C.Sangakkara	c Rahane b Ashwin	32	c Vijay b Ashwin		18
H.D.R.L.Thirimanne	c Saha b I.Sharma	62	(6) c sub (C.A.Pujara) b Ashwin		11
*A.D.Mathews	c Vijay b Binny	102	(4) c Rahul b Yadav		23
†L.D.Chandimal	c Rahul b I.Sharma	11	(5) b Mishra		15
J.Mubarak	b Mishra	22	c Kohli b I.Sharma		0
K.T.G.D.Prasad	c Rahane b Mishra	5	c Mishra b Ashwin		0
H.M.R.K.B.Herath	lbw b Ashwin	1	not out		4
P.H.T.Kaushal	st Saha b Mishra	6	lbw b Mishra		5
P.V.D.Chameera	not out	0	lbw b Mishra		4
Extras	(B 2, LB 6, NB 5)	13	(B 4, W 1, NB 2)		7
Total	**(108 overs; 503 mins)**	**306**	**(43.4 overs; 199 mins)**		**134**

SRI LANKA	O	M	R	W		O	M	R	W
Prasad	24	7	84	2		15	0	43	4
Mathews	15	7	24	2	(4)	2	1	1	0
Chameera	20	2	72	2		14	0	63	0
Herath	25	3	81	4	(2)	29	4	96	0
Kaushal	30	2	111	0		31	1	118	4
INDIA									
I.Sharma	21	3	68	2	(3)	11	2	41	1
Yadav	19	5	67	1		7	1	18	1
Binny	18	4	44	1					
Ashwin	29	3	76	2	(1)	16	6	42	5
Mishra	21	3	43	4	(4)	9.4	3	29	3

FALL OF WICKETS				
	I	SL	I	SL
Wkt	1st	1st	2nd	2nd
1st	4	1	3	8
2nd	12	75	143	33
3rd	176	114	171	72
4th	231	241	256	91
5th	267	259	262	106
6th	319	284	283	111
7th	321	289	311	114
8th	367	300	318	123
9th	386	306	–	128
10th	393	306	–	134

Umpires: B.N.J.Oxenford (*Australia*) (25) and R.J.Tucker (Australia) (37).
Referee: A.J.Pycroft (*Zimbabwe*) (39). **Test No. 2177/37 (SL240/I1490)**
W.P.Saha retired hurt at 267-5 and resumed at 318-8.

SRI LANKA v INDIA (3rd Test)

At Sinhalese Sports Club, Colombo, on 28, 29, 30, 31 August, 1 September 2015.
Toss: Sri Lanka. Result: **INDIA** won by 117 runs.
Debuts: Sri Lanka – M.D.K.J.Perera; India – N.V.Ojha.

INDIA

K.L.Rahul	b Prasad	2	(2)	b Fernando	2
C.A.Pujara	not out	145	(1)	b Prasad	0
A.M.Rahane	lbw b Fernando	8		lbw b Fernando	4
*V.Kohli	c Perera b Mathews	18		c Tharanga b Fernando	21
R.G.Sharma	c Tharanga b Prasad	26		c Fernando b Prasad	50
S.T.R.Binny	lbw b Prasad	0		c Tharanga b Prasad	49
†N.V.Ojha	c Tharanga b Kaushal	21		c Karunaratne b Herath	35
R.Ashwin	c Perera b Prasad	5	(9)	c Perera b Prasad	58
A.Mishra	st Perera b Herath	59	(8)	run out	39
I.Sharma	b Herath	6	(11)	not out	2
U.T.Yadav	b Herath	4	(10)	c Herath b Fernando	4
Extras	(LB 2, W 4, NB 7, Pen 5)	18		(B 1, LB 1, W 3, NB 5)	10
Total	**(100.1 overs; 456 mins)**	**312**		**(76 overs; 353 mins)**	**274**

SRI LANKA

W.U.Tharanga	c Rahul b I.Sharma	4		c Ojha b I.Sharma	0
J.K.Silva	b Yadav	3		c Pujara b Yadav	27
F.D.M.Karunaratne	c Rahul b Binny	11		c Ojha b Yadav	0
L.D.Chandimal	lbw b Binny	23		c Kohli b I.Sharma	18
*A.D.Mathews	c Ojha b I.Sharma	1		lbw b I.Sharma	110
H.D.R.L.Thirimanne	c Rahul b I.Sharma	0		c Rahul b Ashwin	12
†M.D.K.J.Perera	c Kohli b I.Sharma	55		c R.G.Sharma b Ashwin	70
K.T.G.D.Prasad	st Ojha b Mishra	27	(10)	c Binny b Ashwin	6
H.M.R.K.B.Herath	c Ojha b I.Sharma	49	(8)	lbw b Ashwin	11
P.H.T.Kaushal	lbw b Mishra	16	(9)	not out	1
A.N.P.R.Fernando	not out	2		lbw b Mishra	0
Extras	(LB 1, W 2, NB 7)	10		(B 4, LB 2, NB 7)	13
Total	**(52.2 overs; 258 mins)**	**201**		**(85 overs; 388 mins)**	**268**

SRI LANKA	O	M	R	W		O	M	R	W		FALL OF WICKETS			
Prasad	26	4	100	4		19	3	69	4			I	SL	I	SL
Fernando	22	6	52	1		17	2	62	4		*Wkt*	*1st*	*1st*	*2nd*	*2nd*
Mathews	13	6	24	1	(4)	6	3	11	0		1st	4	11	0	1
Herath	27.1	3	84	3	(3)	22	0	89	1		2nd	14	11	2	2
Kaushal	12	2	45	1		12	2	41	0		3rd	64	40	7	21
											4th	119	45	64	74
INDIA											5th	119	47	118	107
I.Sharma	15	2	54	5		19	5	32	3		6th	173	47	160	242
Yadav	13	2	64	1		15	3	65	2		7th	180	127	179	249
Binny	9	3	24	2		13	3	49	0		8th	284	156	234	257
Ashwin	8	1	33	0	(5)	20	2	69	4		9th	298	183	269	263
Mishra	7.2	1	25	2	(4)	18	1	47	1		10th	312	201	274	268

Umpires: N.J.Llong (*England*) (31) and R.J.Tucker (Australia) (38).
Referee: A.J.Pycroft (*Zimbabwe*) (40).   **Test No. 2178/38 (SL241/I491)**
K.T.G.D.Prasad retired hurt at 48-6 and resumed at 156-8.

PAKISTAN v ENGLAND (1st Test)

At Sheikh Zayed Stadium, Abu Dhabi, on 13, 14, 15, 16, 17 October 2015.
Toss: Pakistan. Result: **MATCH DRAWN**.
Debut: England – A.U.Rashid.

PAKISTAN

Mohammad Hafeez	lbw b Stokes	98	run out		34
Shan Masood	b Anderson	2	b Anderson		1
Shoaib Malik	c Bell b Stokes	245	c Bairstow b Anderson		0
Younus Khan	c Cook b Broad	38	c Stokes b Rashid		45
*Misbah-ul-Haq	c Buttler b Anderson	3	b Ali		51
Asad Shafiq	lbw b Wood	107	c Buttler b Rashid		6
†Sarfraz Ahmed	c Bell b Stokes	2	c Anderson b Rashid		27
Wahab Riaz	not out	2	c Bairstow b Ali		1
Zulfiqar Babar	c Anderson b Stokes	0	c Anderson b Rashid		1
Rahat Ali			not out		0
Imran Khan			c Anderson b Rashid		0
Extras	(B 4, LB 21, NB 1)	26	(B 3, LB 2, NB 2)		7
Total	(8 wkts dec; 151.1 overs)	523	(57.5 overs)		173

ENGLAND

*A.N.Cook	c Masood b Malik	263			
M.M.Ali	c Sarfraz b Imran	35	(1) c Malik b Babar		11
I.R.Bell	c Hafeez b Riaz	63	(6) not out		5
M.A.Wood	b Riaz	4			
J.E.Root	c Sarfraz b Rahat	85	(3) not out		33
J.M.Bairstow	lbw b Riaz	8	(5) st Sarfraz b Babar		15
B.A.Stokes	b Malik	57	(4) c Hafeez b Malik		2
†J.C.Buttler	c Shafiq b Babar	23	(2) lbw b Malik		4
A.U.Rashid	b Imran	12			
S.C.J.Broad	not out	17			
J.M.Anderson	not out	3			
Extras	(B 7, LB 7, W 3, NB 11)	28	(LB 2, W 2)		4
Total	(9 wkts dec; 206 overs)	598	(4 wkts; 11 overs)		74

ENGLAND	O	M	R	W		O	M	R	W
Anderson	22	7	42	2		10	3	30	2
Broad	21	8	44	1		8	5	8	0
Stokes	17.1	3	57	4	(5)	7	4	9	0
Wood	22	5	58	1	(3)	7	2	29	0
Rashid	34	0	163	0	(4)	18.5	3	64	5
Ali	30	2	121	0		7	0	28	2
Root	5	1	13	0					
PAKISTAN									
Rahat Ali	28	1	86	1					
Imran Khan	27	7	74	2					
Zulfiqar Babar	72	17	183	1	(1)	5	0	27	2
Wahab Riaz	37	3	125	3	(3)	2	0	20	0
Asad Shafiq	7	0	19	0					
Shoaib Malik	35	4	97	2	(2)	4	0	25	2

FALL OF WICKETS

	P	E	P	E
Wkt	1st	1st	2nd	2nd
1st	5	116	3	13
2nd	173	281	3	29
3rd	247	285	47	35
4th	251	426	113	66
5th	499	443	139	
6th	514	534	159	
7th	521	549	165	
8th	523	563	168	
9th	–	590	173	
10th	–	–	173	–

Umpires: B.N.J.Oxenford (*Australia*) (26) and P.R.Reiffel (*Australia*) (20).
Referee: A.J.Pycroft (*Zimbabwe*) (41). **Test No. 2179/75 (P393/E963)**

PAKISTAN v ENGLAND (2nd Test)

At Dubai Sports City Stadium, on 22, 23, 24, 25, 26 October 2015.
Toss: Pakistan. Result: **PAKISTAN** won by 178 runs.
Debuts: None.

PAKISTAN

Batsman	1st innings		2nd innings	
Mohammad Hafeez	c Bairstow b Ali	19	c Root b Wood	51
Shan Masood	c Buttler b Anderson	54	c Buttler b Anderson	1
Shoaib Malik	c Bairstow b Stokes	2	b Wood	7
Younus Khan	c Buttler b Wood	56	c Ali b Rashid	118
*Misbah-ul-Haq	lbw b Broad	102	c Cook b Anderson	87
Asad Shafiq	c Root b Wood	83	lbw b Ali	79
†Sarfraz Ahmed	c Anderson b Ali	32	not out	3
Wahab Riaz	c Anderson b Ali	6		
Yasir Shah	c Stokes b Rashid	16		
Zulfiqar Babar	lbw b Wood	3		
Imran Khan	not out	0		
Extras	(LB 4, W 1)	5	(B 6, LB 1, NB 1)	8
Total	**(118.5 overs)**	**378**	**(6 wkts dec; 95 overs)**	**354**

ENGLAND

Batsman	1st innings		2nd innings	
*A.N.Cook	c sub (Ahmed Shehzad) b Shah	65	c Riaz b Shah	10
M.M.Ali	c Masood b Riaz	1	c Younus b Imran	1
I.R.Bell	c Sarfraz b Imran	4	c Younus b Babar	46
J.E.Root	c Sarfraz b Riaz	88	c Younus b Babar	71
J.M.Bairstow	lbw b Shah	46	b Shah	22
B.A.Stokes	c Sarfraz b Riaz	4	c Misbah b Imran	13
†J.C.Buttler	c Sarfraz b Riaz	0	c Younus b Shah	7
A.U.Rashid	c Hafeez b Shah	0	c Babar b Shah	61
S.C.J.Broad	not out	15	b Riaz	30
M.A.Wood	c Younus b Shah	1	c Hafeez b Babar	29
J.M.Anderson	c Sarfraz b Imran	4	not out	0
Extras	(B 4, LB 1, W 5, NB 4)	14	(B 12, LB 4, W 1, NB 5)	22
Total	**(75.2 overs)**	**242**	**(137.3 overs)**	**312**

ENGLAND	O	M	R	W		O	M	R	W
Anderson	20	5	40	1		15	7	22	2
Broad	17	4	48	1		10	1	34	0
Ali	25	3	108	3	(4) 11	0	60	1	
Wood	19.5	7	39	3	(3) 14	3	44	2	
Stokes	17	3	55	1		17	3	54	0
Rashid	20	1	84	1		25	1	107	1
Root						3	0	26	0

PAKISTAN	O	M	R	W		O	M	R	W
Imran Khan	13.2	4	33	2		14	4	41	2
Wahab Riaz	19	5	66	4		25	4	78	1
Zulfiqar Babar	10	2	35	0	(5) 47	23	53	3	
Yasir Shah	29	4	93	4	(3) 41.3	15	87	4	
Shoaib Malik	4	1	10	0	(4) 10	2	37	0	

FALL OF WICKETS

	P	E	P	E
Wkt	1st	1st	2nd	2nd
1st	51	5	1	9
2nd	58	14	16	19
3rd	85	127	83	121
4th	178	206	224	157
5th	282	212	337	163
6th	334	216	354	178
7th	342	218	–	193
8th	370	223	–	253
9th	377	233	–	308
10th	378	242	–	312

Umpires: B.N.J.Oxenford (*Australia*) (27) and P.R.Reiffel (*Australia*) (21).
Referee: A.J.Pycroft (*Zimbabwe*) (42).   Test No. 2180/76 (P394/E964)

PAKISTAN v ENGLAND (3rd Test)

At Sharjah Cricket Stadium, on 1, 2, 3, 4, 5 November 2015.
Toss: Pakistan. Result: **PAKISTAN** won by 127 runs.
Debuts: None.

PAKISTAN

Mohammad Hafeez	c Broad b Ali	27		c Bell b Ali	151
Azhar Ali	c Bairstow b Anderson	0		run out	34
Shoaib Malik	c Bairstow b Broad	38		lbw Anderson	0
Younus Khan	lbw b Anderson	31		lbw b Broad	14
*Misbah-ul-Haq	c Root b Anderson	71	(6)	lbw b Broad	38
Asad Shafiq	c Bairstow b Patel	5	(7)	b Broad	46
†Sarfraz Ahmed	c Root b Ali	39	(8)	b Patel	36
Wahab Riaz	b Patel	0	(10)	run out	21
Yasir Shah	c Patel b Broad	7		c Broad b Rashid	4
Zulfiqar Babar	not out	6	(11)	not out	0
Rahat Ali	c Ali b Anderson	4	(5)	b Anderson	0
Extras	(B 1, LB 5)	6		(B 6, LB 5)	11
Total	**(85.1 overs)**	**234**		**(118.2 overs)**	**355**

ENGLAND

*A.N.Cook	c Azhar b Shah	49	(2)	st Sarfraz b Malik	63
M.M.Ali	c Younus b Malik	14	(1)	lbw b Malik	22
I.R.Bell	st Sarfraz b Shah	40		b Malik	0
J.E.Root	c Sarfraz b Rahat	4		lbw b Shah	6
J.W.A.Taylor	c Sarfraz b Rahat	76		c Younus b Babar	2
†J.M.Bairstow	b Babar	43		lbw b Shah	0
S.R.Patel	b Shah	42		lbw b Babar	0
A.U.Rashid	c Azhar b Malik	8		b Rahat	22
S.C.J.Broad	not out	13		c Malik b Shah	20
J.M.Anderson	b Malik	7		st Sarfraz b Shah	12
B.A.Stokes	b Malik	0		not out	0
Extras	(LB 6, NB 4)	10		(B 7, W 1, NB 1)	9
Total	**(126.5 overs)**	**306**		**(60.3 overs)**	**156**

ENGLAND	O	M	R	W		O	M	R	W		FALL OF WICKETS			
Anderson	15.1	7	17	4		26	8	52	2			P	E	P	E
Broad	13	8	13	2		23	6	44	3		Wkt	1st	1st	2nd	2nd
Stokes	11	4	23	0							1st	5	19	101	34
Patel	23	3	85	2	(3)	19	1	79	1		2nd	49	90	105	34
Ali	13	3	49	2	(4)	21.2	1	72	1		3rd	88	97	146	48
Rashid	10	1	41	0	(5)	29	3	97	1		4th	103	139	152	57
											5th	116	228	245	58
PAKISTAN											6th	196	245	257	59
Rahat Ali	22	12	48	2		5	1	23	1		7th	196	285	312	108
Yasir Shah	36	3	99	2	(5)	17.3	2	44	4		8th	224	287	319	138
Wahab Riaz	20	5	33	0	(2)	5	0	25	0		9th	224	296	354	150
Zulfiqar Babar	37	6	80	1	(3)	18	5	31	2		10th	234	306	355	156
Shoaib Malik	9.5	3	33	4	(4)	15	4	26	3						
Azhar Ali	2	0	7	0											

Umpires: C.B.Gaffaney (*New Zealand*) (4) and B.N.J.Oxenford (*Australia*) (28).
Referee: A.J.Pycroft (*Zimbabwe*) (43). **Test No. 2181/77 (P395/E965)**

SRI LANKA v WEST INDIES (1st Test)

At Galle International Stadium, on 14, 15, 16, 17 October 2015.
Toss: Sri Lanka. Result: **SRI LANKA** won by an innings and 6 runs.
Debut: Sri Lanka – T.A.M.Siriwardana.

SRI LANKA

F.D.M.Karunaratne	c and b Samuels	186
J.K.Silva	c Ramdin b Roach	17
H.D.R.L.Thirimanne	c sub (R.Chandrika) b Bishoo	16
L.D.Chandimal	c Blackwood b Taylor	151
*A.D.Mathews	c and b Holder	48
T.A.M.Siriwardana	c Ramdin b Taylor	1
†M.D.K.J.Perera	b Gabriel	23
K.T.G.D.Prasad	c Holder b Bishoo	13
H.M.R.K.B.Herath	lbw b Bishoo	0
P.H.T.Kaushal	not out	9
A.N.P.R.Fernando	c Gabriel b Bishoo	0
Extras	(B 4, LB 5, W 5, NB 6)	20
Total	**(152.3 overs)**	**484**

WEST INDIES

K.C.Brathwaite	lbw b Herath	19		lbw b Herath	34
S.D.Hope	b Herath	23		b Siriwardana	6
D.M.Bravo	c Chandimal b Herath	50		c Perera b Fernando	31
M.N.Samuels	b Herath	11	(5)	lbw b Herath	0
J.Blackwood	c Siriwardana b Prasad	11	(6)	c Silva b Prasad	92
†D.Ramdin	c Perera b Fernando	23	(7)	c Silva b Siriwardana	11
*J.O.Holder	c Perera b Prasad	19	(8)	run out	18
K.A.J.Roach	st Perera b Herath	22	(9)	st Perera b Herath	5
J.E.Taylor	c Mathews b Kaushal	31	(10)	lbw b Prasad	5
D.Bishoo	not out	23	(4)	c Mathews b Herath	10
S.T.Gabriel	b Herath	0		not out	7
Extras	(B 5, LB 6, W 1, NB 7)	19		(LB 3, W 2, NB 3)	8
Total	**(82 overs)**	**251**		**(68.3 overs)**	**227**

WEST INDIES	O	M	R	W	O	M	R	W
Taylor	20	4	65	2				
Roach	19	3	57	1				
Holder	21	4	36	1				
Gabriel	20	2	76	1				
Samuels	27	4	84	1				
Bishoo	40.3	2	143	4				
Brathwaite	5	0	14	0				

SRI LANKA	O	M	R	W	O	M	R	W
Prasad	15	6	38	2	9.3	3	28	2
Fernando	15	4	56	1	(3) 14	1	28	1
Herath	33	9	68	6	(2) 22	5	79	4
Kaushal	14	4	65	1	(5) 11	3	29	0
Siriwardana	5	2	13	0	(4) 12	1	60	2

FALL OF WICKETS			
	SL	WI	WI
Wkt	1st	1st	2nd
1st	56	33	18
2nd	101	49	60
3rd	339	70	74
4th	425	111	74
5th	427	132	88
6th	448	165	136
7th	467	171	172
8th	467	217	178
9th	475	251	189
10th	484	251	227

Umpires: M.Erasmus (*South Africa*) (33) and R.K.Illingworth (*England*) (17).
Referee: D.C.Boon (*Australia*) (27).　　　　　**Test No. 2182/16 (SL242/WI509)**

SRI LANKA v WEST INDIES (2nd Test)

At P.Sara Oval, Colombo, on 22, 23, 24, 25 (*no play*), 26 October 2015.
Toss: Sri Lanka. Result: **SRI LANKA** won by 72 runs.
Debuts: Sri Lanka – B.K.G.Mendis; West Indies – J.A.Warrican.

SRI LANKA

F.D.M.Karunaratne	lbw b Holder	13		c Bishoo b Taylor	0
J.K.Silva	c Ramdin b Taylor	0		c Blackwood b Warrican	32
B.K.G.Mendis	c Ramdin b Roach	13		c Ramdin b Warrican	39
L.D.Chandimal	b Taylor	25		c Ramdin b Taylor	12
*A.D.Mathews	c Brathwaite b Holder	14		c Blackwood b Brathwaite	46
T.A.M.Siriwardana	c Taylor b Warrican	68		c Blackwood b Brathwaite	42
†M.D.K.J.Perera	c and b Warrican	16		c Ramdin b Brathwaite	5
M.D.K.Perera	st Ramdin b Bishoo	5	(9)	c Roach b Brathwaite	7
H.M.R.K.B.Herath	not out	26	(8)	c Blackwood b Brathwaite	18
K.T.G.D.Prasad	c Ramdin b Warrican	7		not out	1
A.N.P.R.Fernando	lbw b Warrican	0		c Blackwood b Brathwaite	0
Extras	(B 10, LB 3)	13		(B 2, LB 2)	4
Total	**(66 overs; 333 mins)**	**200**		**(75.3 overs; 304 mins)**	**206**

WEST INDIES

K.C.Brathwaite	c M.D.K.J.Perera b Siriwardana	47		lbw b Prasad	3
S.D.Hope	lbw b Prasad	4		st M.D.K.J.Perera b Siriwardana	35
D.Bishoo	c M.D.K.J.Perera b Prasad	13	(10)	run out	0
D.M.Bravo	b Prasad	2	(3)	c Mathews b Herath	61
M.N.Samuels	c Mathews b Siriwardana	13	(4)	c Mathews b M.D.K.Perera	16
J.Blackwood	c M.D.K.J.Perera b Prasad	16	(5)	lbw b Siriwardana	5
†D.Ramdin	b Herath	14	(6)	c Mathews b Herath	10
*J.O.Holder	c Mathews b M.D.K.Perera	21	(7)	lbw b Siriwardana	7
K.A.J.Roach	not out	17	(8)	lbw b Herath	13
J.E.Taylor	lbw b M.D.K.Perera	1	(9)	c Siriwardana b Herath	1
J.A.Warrican	c and b M.D.K.Perera	1		not out	2
Extras	(B 9, LB 3, W 1, NB 1)	14		(B 3, LB 1, W 1, NB 6)	11
Total	**(64.2 overs; 269 mins)**	**163**		**(65.5 overs; 251 mins)**	**171**

WEST INDIES	O	M	R	W	O	M	R	W
Taylor	15	2	50	2	8	3	26	2
Roach	12	4	30	1	6	1	15	0
Holder	11	1	22	2	5	1	9	0
Warrican	20	2	67	4	25	2	62	2
Bishoo	8	0	18	1	20	3	61	0
Brathwaite					11.3	4	29	6

SRI LANKA	O	M	R	W	O	M	R	W
Prasad	12	3	34	4	10	2	38	1
Fernando	11	3	24	0	3	0	11	0
Herath	20	5	39	1	19.5	3	56	4
M.D.K.Perera	11.2	3	28	3	20	4	37	1
Siriwardana	19	2	26	2	13	1	25	3

FALL OF WICKETS				
	SL	WI	SL	WI
Wkt	*1st*	*1st*	*2nd*	*2nd*
1st	1	7	0	20
2nd	34	33	55	80
3rd	34	37	84	97
4th	59	76	84	102
5th	90	89	151	124
6th	127	105	165	125
7th	149	137	195	133
8th	173	149	203	136
9th	200	151	206	138
10th	200	161	206	171

Umpires: S.D.Fry (*Australia*) (1) and R.J.Tucker (*Australia*) (39).
Referee: D.C.Boon (*Australia*) (28). Test No. 2183/17 (SL243/WI510)

AUSTRALIA v NEW ZEALAND (1st Test)

At Woolloongabba, Brisbane, on 5, 6, 7, 8, 9 November 2015.
Toss: Australia. Result: **AUSTRALIA** won by 208 runs.
Debuts: None.

AUSTRALIA

J.A.Burns	c Watling b Southee	71		c Taylor b Craig	129
D.A.Warner	c Taylor b Neesham	163		c Boult b Craig	116
U.T.Khawaja	c Guptill b Williamson	174		not out	9
*S.P.D.Smith	b Boult	48		c Williamson b Boult	1
A.C.Voges	not out	83	(6)	not out	1
M.R.Marsh			(5)	c McCullum b Craig	2
†P.M.Nevill					
M.G.Johnson					
M.A.Starc					
J.R.Hazlewood					
N.M.Lyon					
Extras	(LB 7, W 4, NB 6)	17		(LB 1, W 1, NB 4)	6
Total	**(4 wkts dec; 130.2 overs; 559 mins)**	**556**		**(4 wkts dec; 42 overs)**	**264**

NEW ZEALAND

M.J.Guptill	c Warner b Hazlewood	23	(2)	c Smith b Lyon	23
T.W.M.Latham	c Lyon b Starc	47	(1)	lbw b Starc	29
K.S.Williamson	c Nevill b Starc	140		lbw b Lyon	59
L.R.P.L.Taylor	c Smith b Johnson	0		c Smith b Hazlewood	26
*B.B.McCullum	c Voges b Johnson	6		c Smith b Marsh	80
J.D.S.Neesham	b Starc	0		c Burns b Johnson	3
†B.J.Watling	c Nevill b Johnson	32		lbw b Lyon	14
M.D.Craig	c Marsh b Lyon	24		not out	26
D.A.J.Bracewell	b Marsh	16		lbw b Marsh	0
T.G.Southee	b Starc	14		c Nevill b Hazlewood	5
T.A.Boult	not out	0		c Nevill b Starc	15
Extras	(LB 4, W 1, NB 7)	12		(B 7, LB 5, W 2, NB 1)	15
Total	**(82.2 overs)**	**317**		**(88.3 overs)**	**295**

NEW ZEALAND	O	M	R	W		O	M	R	W		FALL OF WICKETS				
												A	NZ	A	NZ
Southee	24	8	70	1						*Wkt*	*1st*	*1st*	*2nd*	*2nd*
Boult	29	3	127	1	(1)	8	0	61	1	1st	161	56	237	44
Bracewell	27	3	107	0	(2)	11	1	63	0	2nd	311	102	254	98
Craig	31	3	156	0		14	0	78	3	3rd	399	105	258	136
Neesham	11	1	50	1	(3)	9	0	61	0	4th	556	114	263	165
Williamson	8.2	0	39	1						5th	–	118	–	205
										6th	–	185	–	242
AUSTRALIA										7th	–	231	–	243
Starc	17.2	4	57	4		20.3	5	69	2	8th	–	273	–	243
Johnson	21	3	105	3		19	6	58	1	9th	–	310	–	249
Hazlewood	21	5	70	1		18	3	68	2	10th	–	317	–	295
Lyon	17	3	46	1	(5)	21	3	63	3					
Marsh	5	0	32	1	(4)	10	3	25	2					
Voges	1	0	3	0										

Umpires: R.K.Illingworth (*England*) (18) and N.J.Llong (*England*) (32).
Referee: R.S.Mahanama (*Sri Lanka*) (59).   Test No. 2184/53 (A780/NZ402)

AUSTRALIA v NEW ZEALAND (2nd Test)

At W.A.C.A. Ground, Perth, on 13, 14, 15, 16, 17 November 2015.
Toss: Australia. Result: **MATCH DRAWN**.
Debuts: None.

AUSTRALIA

J.A.Burns	b Henry	40	c Taylor b Southee		0
D.A.Warner	c Craig b Boult	253	c Latham b Boult		24
U.T.Khawaja	c Latham b Bracewell	121			
*S.P.D.Smith	c Watling b Henry	27	(3) c Watling b Boult		138
A.C.Voges	c Watling b Boult	41	(4) lbw b Southee		119
M.R.Marsh	c and b Bracewell	34	(5) lbw b Bracewell		1
†P.M.Nevill	st Watling b Craig	19	(6) c Watling b Southee		35
M.G.Johnson	st Watling b Craig	2	(7) c Watling b Southee		29
M.A.Starc	c Latham b Craig	0	(8) not out		28
J.R.Hazlewood	not out	8	(9) not out		2
N.M.Lyon	not out	4			
Extras	(B 4, LB 2, W 1, NB 4)	10	(B 4, LB 3, W 1, NB 1)		9
Total	**(9 wkts dec; 133 overs; 562 mins)**	**559**	**(7 wkts dec; 103 overs; 427 mins)**		**385**

NEW ZEALAND

M.J.Guptill	lbw b Starc	1	(2) c Burns b Johnson		17
T.W.M.Latham	c Smith b Lyon	36	(1) c Hazlewood b Johnson		15
K.S.Williamson	c Johnson b Hazlewood	166	not out		32
L.R.P.L.Taylor	c sub (J.W.Wells) b Lyon	290	not out		36
*B.B.McCullum	b Marsh	27			
†B.J.Watling	c Lyon b Starc	1			
D.A.J.Bracewell	c Nevill b Johnson	12			
M.D.Craig	c Johnson b Lyon	15			
M.J.Henry	b Starc	6			
T.G.Southee	c and b Starc	21			
T.A.Boult	not out	23			
Extras	(B 7, LB 11, W 5, NB 3)	26	(B 4)		4
Total	**(153.5 overs; 691 mins)**	**624**	**(2 wkts; 28 overs; 115 mins)**		**104**

NEW ZEALAND	O	M	R	W	O	M	R	W		FALL OF WICKETS			
											A	NZ	A	NZ
Southee	29	6	88	0	25	4	97	4		Wkt	1st	1st	2nd	2nd
Boult	26	2	123	2	19	2	77	2		1st	101	6	8	34
Henry	22	2	105	2	(4) 20	7	53	0		2nd	403	87	46	44
Bracewell	25	1	81	2	(3) 20	5	62	1		3rd	427	352	270	–
Craig	23	0	123	3	18	1	81	0		4th	462	432	277	–
Williamson	3	0	11	0	1	0	8	0		5th	512	447	294	–
Guptill	3	0	7	0						6th	539	485	355	–
McCullum	2	0	16	0						7th	547	525	366	–
										8th	547	554	–	–
AUSTRALIA										9th	547	587	–	–
Starc	37	7	119	4	6	1	33	0		10th	–	624	–	–
Hazlewood	32	2	134	1	6	3	3	0						
Johnson	28	2	157	1	6	2	20	2						
Lyon	37.5	6	107	3	7	0	35	0						
Marsh	15	1	73	1	3	0	9	0						
Smith	4	0	16	0										

Umpires: N.J.Llong (*England*) (33) and S.Ravi (*India*) (9).
Referee: R.S.Mahanama (*Sri Lanka*) (60).   Test No. 2185/54 (A781/NZ403)

AUSTRALIA v NEW ZEALAND (3rd Test)

At Adelaide Oval, on 27, 28, 29 November 2015.
Toss: New Zealand. Result: **AUSTRALIA** won by three wickets.
Debut: New Zealand – M.J.Santner.

NEW ZEALAND

M.J.Guptill	lbw b Hazlewood	1	(2) c M.R.Marsh b Hazlewood		17
T.W.M.Latham	c Nevill b Lyon	50	(1) c Nevill b Hazlewood		10
K.S.Williamson	lbw b Starc	22	c Nevill b M.R.Marsh		9
L.R.P.L.Taylor	c Nevill b Siddle	21	lbw b Hazlewood		32
*B.B.McCullum	c Nevill b Starc	4	lbw b M.R.Marsh		20
M.J.Santner	b Starc	31	st Nevill b Lyon		45
†B.J.Watling	c Smith b Hazlewood	29	c Smith b Hazlewood		7
M.D.Craig	b Lyon	11	c Nevill b Hazlewood		15
D.A.J.Bracewell	c Burns b Siddle	11	not out		27
T.G.Southee	c Warner b Hazlewood	16	c Lyon b M.R.Marsh		13
T.A.Boult	not out	2	b Hazlewood		5
Extras	(LB 1, W 2, NB 1)	4	(B 6, LB 2)		8
Total	**(65.2 overs; 278 mins)**	**202**	**(62.5 overs; 284 mins)**		**208**

AUSTRALIA

J.A.Burns	b Bracewell	14	(2) lbw b Boult		11
D.A.Warner	c Southee b Boult	1	(1) c Southee b Bracewell		35
*S.P.D.Smith	c Watling b Craig	53	lbw b Boult		14
A.C.Voges	c Guptill b Southee	13	c Southee b Boult		28
S.E.Marsh	run out	2	c Taylor b Boult		49
M.R.Marsh	c Watling b Bracewell	4	c Williamson b Santner		28
†P.M.Nevill	c Santner b Bracewell	66	c Watling b Boult		10
P.M.Siddle	c Latham b Craig	0	not out		9
J.R.Hazlewood	b Santner	4			
N.M.Lyon	c Williamson b Boult	34			
M.A.Starc	not out	24	(9) not out		0
Extras	(B 5, LB 3, W 1)	9	(LB 2, W 1)		3
Total	**(72.1 overs; 245 mins)**	**224**	**(7 wkts; 51 overs; 235 mins)**		**187**

AUSTRALIA	O	M	R	W		O	M	R	W	FALL OF WICKETS				
											NZ	A	NZ	A
Starc	9	3	24	3						*Wkt*	*1st*	*1st*	*2nd*	*2nd*
Hazlewood	17.2	3	66	3	(1)	24.5	5	70	6	1st	7	6	29	34
Siddle	17	5	54	2	(2)	14	6	35	0	2nd	59	34	32	62
Lyon	15	1	42	2		10	1	36	1	3rd	94	63	52	66
M.R.Marsh	5	1	12	0	(3)	14	2	59	3	4th	98	67	84	115
Smith	2	0	3	0						5th	98	80	98	161
										6th	142	109	116	176
NEW ZEALAND										7th	164	109	140	185
Southee	17	1	50	1		16	1	58	0	8th	184	116	175	–
Boult	17	5	41	2		16	3	60	5	9th	194	190	192	–
Bracewell	12.1	3	18	3		11	2	37	1	10th	202	224	208	–
Santner	16	1	54	1	(5)	2	0	8	1					
Craig	10	1	53	2	(4)	6	0	22	0					

Umpires: R.K.Illingworth (*England*) (19) and S.Ravi (*India*) (10).
Referee: R.S.Mahanama (*Sri Lanka*) (61).   **Test No. 2186/55 (A782/NZ404)**

INDIA v SOUTH AFRICA (1st Test)

At Punjab CA Stadium, Mohali, Chandigarh, on 5, 6, 7 November 2015.
Toss: India. Result: **INDIA** won by 108 runs.
Debut: South Africa – K.Rabada.

INDIA

M.Vijay	lbw b Harmer	75	c sub (T.Bavuma) b Tahir	47
S.Dhawan	c Amla b Philander	0	c de Villiers b Philander	0
C.A.Pujara	lbw b Elgar	31	c Amla b Tahir	77
*V.Kohli	c Elgar b Rabada	1	c Vilas b van Zyl	29
A.M.Rahane	c Amla b Elgar	15	c sub (T.Bavuma) b Harmer	2
†W.P.Saha	c Amla b Elgar	0	c Vilas b Tahir	20
R.A.Jadeja	lbw b Philander	38	lbw b Harmer	8
A.Mishra	c Steyn b Elgar	6	c du Plessis b Harmer	2
R.Ashwin	not out	20	c Amla b Tahir	3
U.T.Yadav	b Tahir	5	b Harmer	1
V.R.Aaron	b Tahir	0	not out	1
Extras	(B 6, LB 1, NB 3)	10	(B 9, LB 1)	10
Total	**(68 overs; 298 mins)**	**201**	**(75.3 overs; 303 mins)**	**200**

SOUTH AFRICA

D.Elgar	c Jadeja b Ashwin	37	c Kohli b Aaron	6
S.van Zyl	lbw b Ashwin	5	(6) c Rahane b Ashwin	36
F.du Plessis	b Jadeja	0	c Rahane b Ashwin	0
*H.M.Amla	st Saha b Ashwin	43	b Jadeja	0
A.B.de Villiers	b Mishra	63	b Mishra	16
†D.J.Vilas	c Jadeja b Ashwin	1	b Jadeja	7
V.D.Philander	c Rahane b Jadeja	3	(2) lbw b Jadeja	1
S.R.Harmer	lbw b Mishra	7	c Rahane b Jadeja	11
D.W.Steyn	st Saha b Jadeja	6	c Vijay b Ashwin	2
K.Rabada	not out	1	not out	1
Imran Tahir	c Pujara b Ashwin	4	lbw b Jadeja	0
Extras	(B 6, LB 7, NB 1)	14	(B 8, LB 5, W 1)	14
Total	**(68 overs; 274 mins)**	**184**	**(39.5 overs; 159 mins)**	**109**

SOUTH AFRICA	O	M	R	W		O	M	R	W	FALL OF WICKETS				
											I	SA	I	SA
Steyn	11	3	30	0							*1st*	*1st*	*2nd*	*2nd*
Philander	15	5	38	2	(1)	12	3	23	1	Wkt	1st	1st	2nd	2nd
Harmer	14	1	51	1	(2)	24	5	61	4	1st	0	9	9	8
Rabada	10	0	30	1	(5)	12	7	19	0	2nd	63	9	95	9
Elgar	8	1	22	4	(3)	7	1	34	0	3rd	65	85	161	9
Imran Tahir	10	3	23	2	(4)	16.3	1	48	4	4th	102	105	164	32
Van Zyl					(6)	4	1	5	1	5th	102	107	164	45
										6th	140	136	178	60
INDIA										7th	154	170	182	102
Ashwin	24	5	51	5		14	5	39	3	8th	196	179	185	102
Yadav	6	1	12	0	(5)	3	0	7	0	9th	201	184	188	105
Aaron	8	1	18	0	(4)	3	0	3	1	10th	201	184	200	109
Jadeja	18	0	55	3	(2)	11.5	4	21	5					
Mishra	12	3	35	2	(3)	8	0	26	1					

Umpires: H.D.P.K.Dharmasena (*Sri Lanka*) (34) and R.A.Kettleborough (*England*) (31).
Referee: J.J.Crowe (*New Zealand*) (73).   **Test No. 2187/30 (1492/SA393)**

INDIA v SOUTH AFRICA (2nd Test)

At M.Chinnaswamy Stadium, Bangalore, on 14, 15‡, 16‡, 17‡, 18‡ November 2015.
Toss: India. Result: **MATCH DRAWN**.
Debuts: None.   ‡ *(no play)*

SOUTH AFRICA

S.van Zyl	lbw b Ashwin	10
D.Elgar	b Jadeja	38
F.du Plessis	c Pujara b Ashwin	0
*H.M.Amla	b Aaron	7
A.B.de Villiers	c Saha b Jadeja	85
J.P.Duminy	c Rahane b Ashwin	15
†D.J.Vilas	c and b Jadeja	15
K.J.Abbott	run out	14
K.Rabada	c Pujara b Jadeja	0
M.Morkel	c Binny b Ashwin	22
Imran Tahir	not out	0
Extras	(LB 2, NB 6)	8
Total	**(59 overs; 267 mins)**	**214**

INDIA

M.Vijay	not out	28
S.Dhawan	not out	45
C.A.Pujara		
*V.Kohli		
A.M.Rahane		
†W.P.Saha		
R.A.Jadeja		
S.T.R.Binny		
R.Ashwin		
I.Sharma		
V.R.Aaron		
Extras	(B 4, NB 3)	7
Total	**(0 wkts; 22 overs; 107 mins)**	**80**

INDIA	O	M	R	W
Sharma	13	3	40	0
Binny	3	2	1	0
Ashwin	18	2	70	4
Aaron	9	0	51	1
Jadeja	16	2	50	4

SOUTH AFRICA	O	M	R	W
Morkel	7	1	23	0
Abbott	6	1	18	0
Rabada	5	1	17	0
Duminy	2	0	9	0
Imran Tahir	2	0	9	0

FALL OF WICKETS

	SA	I
Wkt	1st	1st
1st	15	—
2nd	15	—
3rd	45	—
4th	78	—
5th	120	—
6th	159	—
7th	177	—
8th	177	—
9th	214	—
10th	214	—

Umpires: I.J.Gould (*England*) (46) and R.A.Kettleborough (*England*) (32).
Referee: J.J.Crowe (*New Zealand*) (74).   **Test No. 2188/31 (I493/SA394)**

INDIA v SOUTH AFRICA (3rd Test)

At Vidarbha CA Stadium, Nagpur, on 25, 26, 27 November 2015.
Toss: India. Result: **INDIA** won by 124 runs.
Debuts: None.

INDIA

M.Vijay	lbw b Morkel	40	c Amla b Morkel		5
S.Dhawan	c and b Elgar	12	c Vilas b Tahir		39
C.A.Pujara	lbw b Harmer	21	b Duminy		31
*V.Kohli	c Vilas b Morkel	22	c du Plessis b Tahir		16
A.M.Rahane	b Morkel	13	c Duminy b Tahir		9
R.G.Sharma	c de Villiers b Harmer	2	c Elgar b Morkel		23
†W.P.Saha	c Duminy b Harmer	32	c Amla b Tahir		7
R.A.Jadeja	b Rabada	34	b Harmer		5
R.Ashwin	b Tahir	15	lbw b Morkel		7
A.Mishra	lbw b Harmer	3	b Tahir		14
I.Sharma	not out	0	not out		1
Extras	(B 15, LB 3, W 2, NB 1)	21	(B 8, LB 5, NB 3)		16
Total	**(78.2 overs; 340 mins)**	**215**	**(46.3 overs; 210 mins)**		**173**

SOUTH AFRICA

D.Elgar	b Ashwin	7	lbw b Ashwin		18
S.van Zyl	c Rahane b Ashwin	0	c R.G.Sharma b Ashwin		5
Imran Tahir	b Jadeja	4	lbw b Mishra		8
*H.M.Amla	c Rahane b Ashwin	1	c Kohli b Mishra		39
A.B.de Villiers	c and b Jadeja	0	lbw b Ashwin		9
F.du Plessis	b Jadeja	10	b Mishra		39
J.P.Duminy	lbw b Mishra	35	lbw b Ashwin		19
†D.J.Vilas	b Jadeja	1	c Saha b Ashwin		12
S.R.Harmer	b Ashwin	13	not out		0
K.Rabada	not out	6	c Kohli b Ashwin		6
M.Morkel	c and b Ashwin	1	b Ashwin		4
Extras	(LB 1)	1	(B 9, LB 5, NB 4)		18
Total	**(33.1 overs; 127 mins)**	**79**	**(89.5 overs; 344 mins)**		**185**

SOUTH AFRICA	O	M	R	W		O	M	R	W
Morkel	16.1	7	35	3		10	5	19	3
Rabada	17	8	30	1	(3)	5	1	15	0
Harmer	27.2	2	78	4	(2)	18	3	64	1
Elgar	4	0	7	1					
Imran Tahir	12.5	1	41	1		11.3	2	38	5
Duminy	1	0	6	0	(4)	2	0	24	1
INDIA									
I.Sharma	2	1	4	0		15	6	20	0
Ashwin	16.1	6	32	5		29.5	7	66	7
Jadeja	12	3	33	4		25	12	34	0
Mishra	3	0	9	1		20	2	51	3

FALL OF WICKETS

	I	SA	I	SA
Wkt	1st	1st	2nd	2nd
1st	50	4	8	17
2nd	69	9	52	29
3rd	94	11	97	40
4th	115	12	102	58
5th	116	12	108	130
6th	125	35	122	135
7th	173	47	128	164
8th	201	66	150	167
9th	215	76	171	177
10th	215	79	173	185

Umpires: I.J.Gould (*England*) (47) and B.N.J.Oxenford (*Australia*) (29).
Referee: J.J.Crowe (*New Zealand*) (75).　　　**Test No. 2189/32 (I494/SA395)**

INDIA v SOUTH AFRICA (4th Test)

At Feroz Shah Kotla, Delhi, on 3, 4, 5, 6, 7 December 2015.
Toss: India. Result: **INDIA** won by 337 runs.
Debuts: None.

INDIA

M.Vijay	c Amla b Piedt	12		c Vilas b Morkel	3
S.Dhawan	lbw b Piedt	33		b Morkel	21
C.A.Pujara	b Abbott	14	(4)	b Tahir	28
*V.Kohli	c Vilas b Piedt	44	(5)	lbw b Abbott	88
A.M.Rahane	c de Villiers b Tahir	127	(6)	not out	100
R.G.Sharma	c Tahir b Piedt	1	(3)	b Morkel	0
†W.P.Saha	b Abbott	1		not out	23
R.A.Jadeja	c Elgar b Abbott	24			
R.Ashwin	c de Villiers b Abbott	56			
U.T.Yadav	not out	10			
I.Sharma	lbw b Abbott	0			
Extras	(B 8, W 1, NB 3)	12		(LB 2, NB 2)	4
Total	**(117.5 overs; 501 mins)**	**334**		**(5 wkts dec; 100.1 overs; 459 mins)**	**267**

SOUTH AFRICA

D.Elgar	c Saha b Yadav	17		c Rahane b Ashwin	4
T.Bavuma	b Jadeja	22		b Ashwin	34
*H.M.Amla	c Saha b Jadeja	3		b Jadeja	25
A.B.de Villiers	c I.Sharma b Jadeja	42		c Jadeja b Ashwin	43
F.du Plessis	c Rahane b Jadeja	0		lbw b Jadeja	10
J.P.Duminy	b Yadav	1		lbw b Ashwin	0
†D.J.Vilas	b I.Sharma	11		b Yadav	13
K.J.Abbott	lbw b Ashwin	4		b Yadav	0
D.L.Piedt	c Rahane b Jadeja	5		c Saha b Yadav	1
M.Morkel	not out	9		b Ashwin	2
Imran Tahir	c sub (K.L.Rahul) b Ashwin	6		not out	0
Extras	(B 5, NB 1)	6		(B 8, LB 3)	11
Total	**(49.3 overs; 221 mins)**	**121**		**(143.1 overs; 525 mins)**	**143**

SOUTH AFRICA	O	M	R	W		O	M	R	W
Morkel	24	5	58	0		21	6	51	3
Abbott	24.5	7	40	5		22	9	47	1
Piedt	38	6	117	4		18	1	53	0
Imran Tahir	16	2	66	1		26.1	4	74	1
Elgar	11	0	33	0		13	1	40	0
Duminy	4	0	12	0					

INDIA	O	M	R	W		O	M	R	W
I.Sharma	12	5	28	1		20	12	23	0
Yadav	12	3	32	2	(4)	21	16	9	3
Ashwin	13.3	5	26	2	(2)	49.1	26	61	5
Jadeja	12	2	30	5	(3)	46	33	26	2
Dhawan						3	1	9	0
Vijay						2	0	2	0
Kohli						1	1	0	0
Pujara						1	0	2	0

FALL OF WICKETS

	I	SA	I	SA
Wkt	1st	1st	2nd	2nd
1st	30	36	4	5
2nd	62	40	8	49
3rd	66	56	53	76
4th	136	62	57	111
5th	138	65	211	112
6th	139	79	–	136
7th	198	84	–	136
8th	296	103	–	140
9th	334	118	–	143
10th	334	121	–	143

Umpires: H.D.P.K.Dharmasena (*Sri Lanka*) (35) and B.N.J.Oxenford (*Australia*) (30).
Referee: J.J.Crowe (*New Zealand*) (76).　　　　**Test No. 2190/33 (I495/SA396)**

NEW ZEALAND v SRI LANKA (1st Test)

At University Oval, Dunedin, on 10, 11, 12, 13, 14 December 2015.
Toss: Sri Lanka. Result: **NEW ZEALAND** won by 72 runs.
Debut: Sri Lanka – M.D.U.S.Jayasundera.

NEW ZEALAND

Batsman	Dismissal	Runs		Dismissal	Runs
M.J.Guptill	c Chandimal b Mathews	156	(2)	b Herath	46
T.W.M.Latham	c and b Lakmal	22	(1)	not out	109
K.S.Williamson	c Karunaratne b Fernando	88		b Chameera	71
L.R.P.L.Taylor	lbw b Fernando	8		b Herath	15
*B.B.McCullum	c Vithanage b Siriwardana	75		not out	17
M.J.Santner	c Chandimal b Chameera	12			
†B.J.Watling	c Vithanage b Chameera	5			
D.A.J.Bracewell	lbw b Fernando	47			
T.G.Southee	c Siriwardana b Lakmal	2			
N.Wagner	c Jayasundera b Fernando	7			
T.A.Boult	not out	0			
Extras	(B 4, LB 3, W 1, NB 1)	9		(B 4, NB 5)	9
Total	**(96.1 overs; 421 mins)**	**431**		**(3 wkts dec; 65.4 overs; 304 mins)**	**267**

SRI LANKA

Batsman	Dismissal	Runs	Dismissal	Runs
F.D.M.Karunaratne	c Watling b Santner	84	c Watling b Southee	29
B.K.G.Mendis	c Watling b Boult	8	c Watling b Southee	46
M.D.U.S.Jayasundera	c Watling b Wagner	1	c Watling b Wagner	3
†L.D.Chandimal	c Guptill b Southee	83	lbw b Santner	58
*A.D.Mathews	c Watling b Southee	2	b Wagner	25
K.D.K.Vithanage	c Watling b Southee	22	lbw b Southee	38
T.A.M.Siriwardana	c Taylor b Wagner	35	c McCullum b Boult	29
H.M.R.K.B.Herath	c Boult b Wagner	15	c Guptill b Boult	6
P.V.D.Chameera	c Taylor b Boult	14	b Santner	14
R.A.S.Lakmal	not out	18	c and b Bracewell	23
A.N.P.R.Fernando	c Watling b Santner	3	not out	4
Extras	(B 1, LB 4, NB 4)	9	(B 2, LB 4, W 1)	7
Total	**(117.1 overs; 505 mins)**	**294**	**(95.2 overs; 412 mins)**	**282**

SRI LANKA	O	M	R	W		O	M	R	W
Lakmal	16	1	69	2		13	0	40	0
Fernando	23.1	2	112	4	(4)	13	1	52	0
Mathews	9	2	28	1	(2)	4	1	4	0
Chameera	20	2	112	2	(3)	14	0	61	1
Herath	19	1	46	0		11.4	1	62	2
Jayasundera	5	0	33	0	(7)	2	0	12	0
Siriwardana	4	0	24	1	(6)	8	0	32	0

NEW ZEALAND	O	M	R	W		O	M	R	W
Boult	22	7	52	2		15	2	58	2
Southee	27	4	71	3		21	6	52	3
Bracewell	21	6	42	0		19.2	5	46	1
Wagner	25	5	87	3	(5)	17	1	56	2
Santner	21.1	8	37	2	(4)	22	6	53	2
Williamson						1	0	1	0

FALL OF WICKETS

	NZ	SL	NZ	SL
Wkt	1st	1st	2nd	2nd
1st	56	19	79	54
2nd	229	29	220	64
3rd	245	151	247	109
4th	334	156	–	165
5th	359	198	–	165
6th	365	209	–	213
7th	394	252	–	236
8th	399	273	–	249
9th	426	287	–	268
10th	431	294	–	282

Umpires: R.A.Kettleborough (*England*) (33) and N.J.Llong (*England*) (34).
Referee: D.C.Boon (*Australia*) (29). **Test No. 2191/31 (NZ405/SL244)**

NEW ZEALAND v SRI LANKA (2nd Test)

At Seddon Park, Hamilton, on 18, 19, 20, 21 December 2015.
Toss: New Zealand. Result: **NEW ZEALAND** won by five wickets.
Debuts: None.

‡ (J.D.F.Vandersay)

SRI LANKA

Batsman	Dismissal 1	R	Dismissal 2	R
F.D.M.Karunaratne	c Watling b Southee	12	c Southee b Bracewell	27
B.K.G.Mendis	c Watling b Southee	31	c Santner b Southee	46
M.D.U.S.Jayasundera	run out	26	c Watling b Bracewell	0
†L.D.Chandimal	c Watling b Bracewell	47	c Guptill b Wagner	4
*A.D.Mathews	c Latham b Southee	77	c Watling b Southee	2
T.A.M.Siriwardana	c Taylor b Boult	62	c Boult b Wagner	26
K.D.K.Vithanage	c McCullum b Boult	0	c Bracewell b Wagner	9
H.M.R.K.B.Herath	run out	4	b Southee	0
P.V.D.Chameera	c McCullum b Bracewell	4	run out	2
R.A.S.Lakmal	c Williamson b Wagner	4	not out	1
A.N.P.R.Fernando	not out	2	c Watling b Southee	0
Extras	(LB 11, W 12)	23	(B 4, LB 2, W 7, NB 3)	16
Total	(80.1 overs; 353 mins)	292	(36.3 overs; 191 mins)	133

NEW ZEALAND

Batsman	Dismissal 1	R	Dismissal 2	R
M.J.Guptill	c Mathews b Herath	50	(2) c Karunaratne b Chameera	1
T.W.M.Latham	c Karunaratne b Chameera	28	(1) c Fernando b Chameera	4
K.S.Williamson	c Lakmal b Chameera	1	not out	108
L.R.P.L.Taylor	c Chandimal b Chameera	0	c sub‡ b Chameera	35
*B.B.McCullum	c Mendis b Herath	18	c Mathews b Chameera	18
M.J.Santner	c Chandimal b Fernando	38	c Chandimal b Lakmal	4
†B.J.Watling	c Vithanage b Lakmal	28	not out	13
D.A.J.Bracewell	not out	35		
T.G.Southee	c Jayasundera b Chameera	4		
N.Wagner	c Vithanage b Chameera	17		
T.A.Boult	c Herath b Fernando	0		
Extras	(LB 3, W 8, NB 7)	18	(B 1, NB 5)	6
Total	(79.4 overs; 360 mins)	237	(5 wkts; 54.3 overs; 260 mins)	189

NEW ZEALAND	O	M	R	W	O	M	R	W
Boult	20	2	51	2	7	1	30	0
Southee	21	5	63	3	12.3	2	26	4
Bracewell	22.1	4	81	2	8	1	31	2
Wagner	9	1	51	1	9	2	40	3
Santner	7	0	34	0				
Williamson	1	0	1	0				

SRI LANKA	O	M	R	W		O	M	R	W
Lakmal	16	4	48	1	(2)	12	4	20	1
Mathews	11	7	25	0	(5)	1	0	4	0
Fernando	17.4	4	39	2	(4)	12	1	43	0
Herath	22	1	75	2	(3)	11	0	48	0
Chameera	13	3	47	5	(1)	17	1	68	4
Siriwardana						1.3	0	5	0

FALL OF WICKETS

	SL	NZ	SL	NZ
Wkt	1st	1st	2nd	2nd
1st	39	81	71	4
2nd	44	83	71	11
3rd	115	86	77	78
4th	121	89	87	130
5th	259	128	110	142
6th	259	168	123	–
7th	264	196	123	–
8th	284	201	131	–
9th	288	232	133	–
10th	292	237	133	–

Umpires: N.J.Llong (*England*) (35) and P.R.Reiffel (*Australia*) (22).
Referee: D.C.Boon (*Australia*) (30).　　　Test No. 2192/32 (NZ406/SL245)

AUSTRALIA v WEST INDIES (1st Test)

At Bellerive Oval, Hobart, on 10, 11, 12 December 2015.
Toss: Australia. Result: **AUSTRALIA** won by an innings and 212 runs.
Debuts: None.

AUSTRALIA

J.A.Burns	b Gabriel	33
D.A.Warner	c Ramdin b Warrican	64
*S.P.D.Smith	c Blackwood b Warrican	10
A.C.Voges	not out	269
S.E.Marsh	c Bravo b Warrican	182
M.R.Marsh	not out	1
†P.M.Nevill		
P.M.Siddle		
J.L.Pattinson		
J.R.Hazlewood		
N.M.Lyon		
Extras	(B 4, LB 3, W 3, NB 14)	24
Total	**(4 wkts dec; 114 overs; 510 mins)**	**583**

WEST INDIES

K.C.Brathwaite	lbw b Hazlewood	2	b Hazlewood		94
R.Chandrika	c Smith b Lyon	25	c Smith b Pattinson		0
D.M.Bravo	c Lyon b Siddle	108	b Pattinson		4
M.N.Samuels	c and b Lyon	9	c Warner b Pattinson		3
J.Blackwood	c Burns b Lyon	0	b Pattinson		0
†D.Ramdin	b Hazlewood	8	c Warner b M.R.Marsh		4
*J.O.Holder	lbw b Siddle	15	c Nevill b Pattinson		17
K.A.J.Roach	c Nevill b Hazlewood	31	c Nevill b Hazlewood		3
J.E.Taylor	b Hazlewood	0	c Pattinson b Hazlewood		12
J.A.Warrican	not out	2	not out		6
S.T.Gabriel	absent hurt	–	absent hurt		–
Extras	(B 7, LB 10, W 1, NB 5)	23	(LB 1, W 1, NB 3)		5
Total	**(70 overs; 292 mins)**	**223**	**(36.3 overs; 166 mins)**		**148**

WEST INDIES	O	M	R	W	O	M	R	W
Taylor	17	0	108	0				
Roach	16	1	99	0				
Gabriel	10	1	59	1				
Holder	24	3	75	0				
Warrican	28	1	158	3				
Brathwaite	13	0	52	0				
Blackwood	6	0	25	0				
AUSTRALIA								
Hazlewood	18	5	45	4	10.3	3	33	3
Pattinson	15	0	68	0	8	2	27	5
Siddle	15	5	36	2	7	1	34	0
Lyon	19	6	43	3	(5) 4	0	17	0
M.R.Marsh	3	1	14	0	(4) 7	0	36	1

FALL OF WICKETS

	A	WI	WI
Wkt	1st	1st	2nd
1st	75	17	2
2nd	104	58	20
3rd	121	78	24
4th	570	78	24
5th	–	89	30
6th	–	116	60
7th	–	215	91
8th	–	215	117
9th	–	223	148
10th	–	–	–

Umpires: M.Erasmus (*South Africa*) (34) and I.J.Gould (*England*) (48).
Referee: B.C.Broad (*England*) (73).　　　　Test No. 2193/114 (A783/WI511)

51

AUSTRALIA v WEST INDIES (2nd Test)

At Melbourne Cricket Ground, on 26, 27, 28, 29 December 2015.
Toss: West Indies. Result: **AUSTRALIA** won by 177 runs.
Debut: West Indies – C.R.Brathwaite.

AUSTRALIA

J.A.Burns	st Ramdin b K.C.Brathwaite	128	c K.C.Brathwaite b Holder		5
D.A.Warner	c Samuels b Taylor	23	c Holder b C.R.Brathwaite		17
U.T.Khawaja	c Ramdin b Taylor	144	c Ramdin b Holder		56
*S.P.D.Smith	not out	134	not out		70
A.C.Voges	not out	106			
M.R.Marsh			(5) not out		18
†P.M.Nevill					
P.M.Siddle					
J.L.Pattinson					
J.R.Hazlewood					
N.M.Lyon					
Extras	(LB 10, W 4, NB 2)	16	(LB 6, W 2, NB 5)		13
Total	(3 wkts dec; 135 overs; 554 mins)	551	(3 wkts dec; 32 overs; 144 mins)		179

WEST INDIES

K.C.Brathwaite	c Burns b Lyon	17	c Smith b Lyon		31
R.Chandrika	lbw b Pattinson	25	lbw b Pattinson		37
D.M.Bravo	c Smith b Pattinson	81	c Nevill b Siddle		21
M.N.Samuels	lbw b Pattinson	0	c Nevill b Marsh		19
J.Blackwood	c and b Lyon	28	lbw b Lyon		20
†D.Ramdin	c Burns b Siddle	0	c Nevill b Marsh		59
*J.O.Holder	b Siddle	0	c Hazlewood b Marsh		68
C.R.Brathwaite	c and b Lyon	59	b Lyon		2
K.A.J.Roach	lbw b Pattinson	22	c Warner b Pattinson		11
J.E.Taylor	c Nevill b Lyon	15	c Pattinson b Marsh		0
J.A.Warrican	not out	11	not out		4
Extras	(B 5, LB 3, NB 5)	13	(LB 7, W 1, NB 2)		10
Total	(100.3 overs; 422 mins)	271	(88.3 overs; 391 mins)		282

WEST INDIES	O	M	R	W		O	M	R	W		FALL OF WICKETS			
												A	WI	A	WI
Taylor	22	2	97	2		3	0	25	0		*Wkt*	*1st*	*1st*	*2nd*	*2nd*
Roach	17	1	97	0	(4)	4	0	22	0		1st	29	35	7	35
Holder	22	7	47	0	(2)	11	1	49	2		2nd	287	50	46	83
C.R.Brathwaite	30	3	109	0	(3)	6	1	30	1		3rd	328	50	123	91
Warrican	26	2	113	0		8	0	47	0		4th	–	82	–	118
K.C.Brathwaite	18	1	78	1							5th	–	83	–	150
											6th	–	83	–	250
AUSTRALIA											7th	–	173	–	253
Hazlewood	21	6	49	0		20	6	40	0		8th	–	215	–	274
Pattinson	22.3	1	72	4		17	4	49	2		9th	–	239	–	278
Lyon	29	8	66	4		23	7	85	3		10th	–	271	–	282
Siddle	18	3	40	2		9	2	35	1						
Marsh	7	4	15	0		17.3	2	61	4						
Smith	3	0	21	0		2	1	5	0						

Umpires: M.Erasmus (*South Africa*) (35) and C.B.Gaffaney (*New Zealand*) (5).
Referee: B.C.Broad (*England*) (74).   Test No. 2194/115 (A784/WI512)

AUSTRALIA v WEST INDIES (3rd Test)

At Sydney Cricket Ground, on 3, 4, 5 (*no play*), 6 (*no play*), 7 January 2016.
Toss: West Indies. Result: **MATCH DRAWN**.
Debuts: None.

WEST INDIES

K.C.Brathwaite	c Smith b Lyon	85
S.D.Hope	c Nevill b Hazlewood	9
D.M.Bravo	c Khawaja b Pattinson	33
M.N.Samuels	run out	4
J.Blackwood	b Lyon	10
†D.Ramdin	c Smith b O'Keefe	62
*J.O.Holder	c Burns b O'Keefe	1
C.R.Brathwaite	b Pattinson	69
K.A.J.Roach	c Burns b Lyon	15
J.E.Taylor	c Lyon b O'Keefe	13
J.A.Warrican	not out	21
Extras	(B 5, LB 2, NB 1)	8
Total	**(112.1 overs)**	**330**

AUSTRALIA

D.A.Warner	not out	122
J.A.Burns	c Roach b Warrican	26
M.R.Marsh	c Blackwood b Warrican	21
†P.M.Nevill	not out	7
U.T.Khawaja		
*S.P.D.Smith		
A.C.Voges		
S.N.J.O'Keefe		
J.L.Pattinson		
J.R.Hazlewood		
N.M.Lyon		
Extras		–
Total	**(2 wkts; 38 overs; 150 mins)**	**176**

AUSTRALIA	O	M	R	W
Hazlewood	18	5	49	1
Pattinson	18	3	76	2
Lyon	46	12	120	3
Marsh	4	1	15	0
O'Keefe	26.1	7	63	3

WEST INDIES	O	M	R	W
Taylor	4	0	27	0
Holder	4	1	15	0
Roach	4	0	29	0
Warrican	15	1	62	2
C.R.Brathwaite	7	0	23	0
K.C.Brathwaite	4	0	20	0

FALL OF WICKETS

	WI	A
Wkt	*1st*	*1st*
1st	13	100
2nd	104	154
3rd	115	–
4th	131	–
5th	158	–
6th	159	–
7th	246	–
8th	296	–
9th	300	–
10th	330	–

Umpires: C.B.Gaffaney (*New Zealand*) (6) and I.J.Gould (*England*) (49).
Referee: B.C.Broad (*England*) (75).   Test No. 2195/116 (A785/WI513)

SOUTH AFRICA v ENGLAND (1st Test)

At Kingsmead, Durban, on 26, 27, 28, 29, 30 December 2015.
Toss: South Africa. Result: **ENGLAND** won by 241 runs.
Debut: England – A.D.Hales.

ENGLAND

*A.N.Cook	c Elgar b Steyn	0	lbw b Piedt		7
A.D.Hales	c de Villiers b Steyn	10	c Abbott b Piedt		26
N.R.D.Compton	c de Villiers b Morkel	85	c de Villiers b Morkel		49
J.E.Root	lbw b Piedt	24	c van Zyl b Abbott		73
J.W.A.Taylor	c de Villiers b Steyn	70	st de Villiers b Piedt		42
B.A.Stokes	c Duminy b Morkel	21	c Elgar b Piedt		5
†J.M.Bairstow	c Elgar b Abbott	41	c Duminy b van Zyl		79
M.M.Ali	c de Villiers b Morkel	0	lbw b Piedt		16
C.R.Woakes	lbw b Morkel	0	c Duminy b van Zyl		23
S.C.J.Broad	not out	32	c de Villiers b van Zyl		0
S.T.Finn	lbw b Steyn	12	not out		0
Extras	(B 1, LB 3, W 1, NB 3)	8	(B 3, LB 3)		6
Total	**(100.1 overs; 475 mins)**	**303**	**(102.1 overs; 444 mins)**		**326**

SOUTH AFRICA

S.van Zyl	b Broad	0	(2) b Stokes		33
D.Elgar	not out	118	(1) c Root b Finn		40
*H.M.Amla	c Bairstow b Broad	7	c Bairstow b Finn		12
†A.B.de Villiers	c Bairstow b Broad	49	lbw b Ali		37
F.du Plessis	b Ali	2	c Cook b Finn		9
T.Bavuma	b Broad	10	(7) st Bairstow b Ali		0
J.P.Duminy	c Stokes b Ali	2	(8) not out		26
K.J.Abbott	c Taylor b Ali	0	(9) lbw b Ali		2
D.W.Steyn	c Woakes b Ali	17	(6) b Finn		2
D.L.Piedt	c Bairstow b Finn	1	c Taylor b Woakes		0
M.Morkel	c Root b Finn	0	lbw b Broad		8
Extras	(B 4, LB 3, W 1)	8	(B 2, LB 3)		5
Total	**(81.4 overs; 386 mins)**	**214**	**(71 overs; 311 mins)**		**174**

SOUTH AFRICA	O	M	R	W		O	M	R	W	FALL OF WICKETS				
											E	SA	E	SA
Steyn	25.1	5	70	4		3.5	0	10	0	Wkt	1st	1st	2nd	2nd
Abbott	24	4	66	1	(3)	21.4	3	62	1	1st	3	0	13	53
Morkel	26	5	76	4	(2)	20.3	5	38	1	2nd	12	14	48	85
Piedt	16	2	63	1		36	4	153	5	3rd	49	100	119	88
Van Zyl	2	1	2	0	(6)	10.1	3	20	3	4th	174	113	192	136
Elgar	7	2	22	0	(5)	9	0	32	0	5th	196	137	197	136
Duminy						1	0	5	0	6th	247	150	224	136
										7th	253	156	272	138
ENGLAND										8th	253	210	315	143
Broad	15	6	25	4		13	5	29	1	9th	267	214	315	155
Woakes	14	1	28	0		10	5	25	1	10th	303	214	326	174
Ali	25	3	69	4	(5)	26	9	47	3					
Finn	15.4	1	49	2	(3)	15	6	42	4					
Stokes	9	1	25	0	(4)	7	1	26	1					
Root	3	1	11	0										

Umpires: Alim Dar (*Pakistan*) (99) and R.J.Tucker (*Australia*) (40).
Referee: R.S.Madugalle (*Sri Lanka*) (160). **Test No. 2196/142 (SA397/E966)**

SOUTH AFRICA v ENGLAND (2nd Test)

At Newlands, Cape Town, on 2, 3, 4, 5, 6 January 2016.
Toss: England. Result: **MATCH DRAWN**.
Debut: South Africa – C.H.Morris.

ENGLAND

Batsman	1st innings			2nd innings	
*A.N.Cook	c Morris b Rabada	27		c de Kock b Rabada	8
A.D.Hales	c de Villiers b Morkel	60		c Morris b Morkel	5
N.R.D.Compton	c Bavuma b Rabada	45		c du Plessis b Piedt	15
J.E.Root	c de Kock b Morris	50		b Morris	29
J.W.A.Taylor	c de Kock b Rabada	0		c Bavuma b Piedt	27
B.A.Stokes	run out	258		c Morkel b Piedt	26
†J.M.Bairstow	not out	150		not out	30
M.M.Ali	not out	0		not out	10
S.C.J.Broad					
J.M.Anderson					
S.T.Finn					
Extras	(B 12, LB 6, W 13, NB 8)	39		(LB 4, NB 5)	9
Total	(6 wkts dec; 125.5 overs; 582 mins)	629		(6 wkts; 65 overs; 281 mins)	159

SOUTH AFRICA

D.Elgar	c Compton b Stokes	44
S.van Zyl	run out	4
*H.M.Amla	b Broad	201
A.B.de Villiers	c Anderson b Finn	88
F.du Plessis	c Stokes b Anderson	86
T.Bavuma	not out	102
†Q.de Kock	c Anderson b Broad	5
C.H.Morris	c Root b Finn	69
K.Rabada	not out	2
D.L.Piedt		
M.Morkel		
Extras	(B 4, LB 9, W 13)	26
Total	(7 wkts dec; 211 overs; 929 mins)	627

SOUTH AFRICA	O	M	R	W		O	M	R	W
Morkel	29	5	114	1		16	7	26	1
Morris	28	3	150	1	(3)	12	4	24	1
Rabada	29.5	2	175	3	(2)	13	2	57	1
Piedt	25	5	112	0		18	8	38	3
Van Zyl	10	0	43	0					
Elgar	4	0	17	0	(5)	6	2	10	0

ENGLAND	O	M	R	W
Anderson	35	12	77	1
Broad	34	8	94	2
Ali	52	14	155	0
Finn	39	5	132	2
Root	20	4	54	0
Stokes	28	4	100	1
Hales	3	1	2	0

FALL OF WICKETS

	E	SA	E
Wkt	1st	1st	2nd
1st	55	7	17
2nd	129	85	19
3rd	167	268	55
4th	167	439	85
5th	223	439	115
6th	622	449	116
7th	–	616	–
8th	–	–	–
9th	–	–	–
10th	–	–	–

Umpires: Alim Dar (*Pakistan*) (100) and B.N.J.Oxenford (*Australia*) (31).
Referee: R.S.Madugalle (*Sri Lanka*) (161).　　　Test No. 2197/143 (SA398/E967)

SOUTH AFRICA v ENGLAND (3rd Test)

At New Wanderers, Johannesburg, on 14, 15, 16 January 2016.
Toss: South Africa. Result: **ENGLAND** won by seven wickets.
Debut: South Africa – G.C.Viljoen.

SOUTH AFRICA

D.Elgar	c Bairstow b Ali	46	c Bairstow b Broad	15
S.van Zyl	c Bairstow b Stokes	21	c Stokes b Broad	11
H.M.Amla	c Bairstow b Finn	40	c Taylor b Broad	5
*A.B.de Villiers	c Bairstow b Stokes	36	c Bairstow b Broad	0
F.du Plessis	c Hales b Finn	16	c and b Broad	14
T.Bavuma	run out	23	b Broad	0
†D.J.Vilas	c Ali b Broad	26	c Taylor b Finn	8
C.H.Morris	c Bairstow b Broad	28	b Stokes	1
K.Rabada	c Bairstow b Anderson	24	c Bairstow b Stokes	16
G.C.Viljoen	not out	20	lbw b Anderson	6
M.Morkel	c Cook b Stokes	12	not out	4
Extras	(B 9, LB 9, W 1, NB 2)	21	(LB 2, NB 1)	3
Total	**(99.3 overs; 443 mins)**	**313**	**(33.1 overs; 167 mins)**	**83**

ENGLAND

*A.N.Cook	c Vilas b Viljoen	18	c Vilas b Morris	43
A.D.Hales	c de Villiers b Rabada	1	lbw b Elgar	18
N.R.D.Compton	c Elgar b Rabada	26	c Morkel b Elgar	0
J.E.Root	c Vilas b Rabada	110	not out	4
J.W.A.Taylor	c Bavuma b Morkel	7	not out	2
B.A.Stokes	c and b Morkel	58		
†J.M.Bairstow	c van Zyl b Rabada	45		
M.M.Ali	c Vilas b Morris	19		
S.C.J.Broad	b Rabada	12		
S.T.Finn	c Vilas b Morkel	0		
J.M.Anderson	not out	0		
Extras	(B 1, LB 14, W 9, NB 3)	27	(B 4, LB 2, W 1)	7
Total	**(76.1 overs; 368 mins)**	**323**	**(3 wkts; 22.4 overs; 92 mins)**	**74**

ENGLAND	O	M	R	W		O	M	R	W
Anderson	25.2	5	60	1		10	1	26	1
Broad	22	5	82	2		12.1	6	17	6
Finn	18	4	50	2	(4)	3	0	14	1
Ali	16	4	50	1					
Stokes	18.1	1	53	3	(3)	8	1	24	2

SOUTH AFRICA	O	M	R	W		O	M	R	W
Morris	15	1	71	1	(4)	6	2	8	1
Rabada	23.1	5	78	5		4	0	28	0
Morkel	20	1	76	4	(1)	5	2	7	0
Viljoen	15	0	79	1	(3)	4	2	15	0
Van Zyl	3	0	4	0					
Elgar					(5)	3.4	1	10	2

FALL OF WICKETS				
	SA	E	SA	E
Wkt	1st	1st	2nd	2nd
1st	44	10	23	64
2nd	117	22	28	68
3rd	127	74	30	71
4th	161	91	31	–
5th	185	202	35	–
6th	212	242	45	–
7th	225	279	47	–
8th	281	309	67	–
9th	281	311	77	–
10th	313	323	83	–

Umpires: Alim Dar (*Pakistan*) (101) and R.J.Tucker (*Australia*) (41).
Referee: R.S.Madugalle (*Sri Lanka*) (162).   **Test No. 2198/144 (SA399/E968)**

SOUTH AFRICA v ENGLAND (4th Test)

At Centurion Park, on 22, 23, 24, 25, 26 January 2016.
Toss: South Africa. Result: **SOUTH AFRICA** won by 280 runs.
Debut: South Africa – S.C.Cook.

SOUTH AFRICA

Batsman	First innings		Second innings	
S.C.Cook	b Woakes	115	c Bairstow b Anderson	25
D.Elgar	c Taylor b Ali	20	c Bairstow b Anderson	1
H.M.Amla	b Stokes	109	c Bairstow b Broad	96
*A.B.de Villiers	c Root b Broad	0	lbw b Anderson	0
J.P.Duminy	lbw b Ali	16	c Bairstow b Stokes	29
T.Bavuma	c Bairstow b Broad	35	not out	78
†Q.de Kock	not out	129	not out	9
K.Rabada	lbw b Anderson	0		
K.J.Abbott	lbw b Stokes	16		
D.L.Piedt	c Bairstow b Stokes	19		
M.Morkel	lbw b Stokes	0		
Extras	(LB 12, W 4)	16	(B 2, LB 5, W 3)	10
Total	**(132 overs; 580 mins)**	**475**	**(5 wkts dec; 83.2 overs; 367 mins)**	**248**

ENGLAND

Batsman	First innings		Second innings	
*A.N.Cook	c de Kock b Morkel	76	c and b Morkel	5
A.D.Hales	c Piedt b Rabada	15	lbw b Rabada	1
N.R.D.Compton	lbw b Rabada	19	c de Kock b Rabada	6
J.E.Root	c de Kock b Rabada	76	c Elgar b Piedt	20
J.W.A.Taylor	c de Kock b Rabada	14	c de Kock b Morkel	24
B.A.Stokes	c Amla b Rabada	33	c Cook b Morkel	10
†J.M.Bairstow	c de Kock b Rabada	0	c de Kock b Rabada	14
M.M.Ali	c Piedt b Morkel	61	not out	10
C.R.Woakes	c Elgar b Duminy	26	c de Kock b Rabada	5
S.C.J.Broad	c Cook b Rabada	5	c de Villiers b Rabada	2
J.M.Anderson	not out	5	lbw b Rabada	4
Extras	(B 2, LB 7, W 3)	12	(LB 2, W 1, NB 1)	4
Total	**(104.2 overs; 432 mins)**	**342**	**(34.4 overs; 151 mins)**	**101**

ENGLAND	O	M	R	W		O	M	R	W
Anderson	30	6	91	1		18	5	47	3
Broad	28	4	91	2		15	4	33	1
Ali	25	5	104	2	(5)	17	3	60	0
Woakes	22	3	91	1		13.2	0	53	0
Stokes	27	3	86	4	(3)	16	4	36	1
Root						4	0	12	0

SOUTH AFRICA	O	M	R	W		O	M	R	W
Abbott	19	9	36	0	(3)	2	0	10	0
Rabada	29	6	112	7		10.4	2	32	6
Piedt	24	4	78	0	(4)	7	2	11	1
Morkel	23.2	4	73	2	(1)	12	5	36	3
Elgar	4	0	13	0		2	1	8	0
Duminy	5	0	21	1		1	0	2	0

FALL OF WICKETS

	SA	E	SA	E
Wkt	1st	1st	2nd	2nd
1st	35	22	5	2
2nd	237	78	49	8
3rd	238	177	49	18
4th	271	208	106	58
5th	273	211	223	58
6th	335	211	–	83
7th	336	252	–	83
8th	386	295	–	91
9th	468	320	–	101
10th	475	342	–	101

Umpires: H.D.P.K.Dharmasena (*Sri Lanka*) (36) and C.B.Gaffaney (*New Zealand*) (7).
Referee: R.S.Madugalle (*Sri Lanka*) (163). **Test No. 2199/145 (SA400/E969)**

NEW ZEALAND v AUSTRALIA (1st Test)

At Basin Reserve, Wellington, on 12, 13, 14, 15 February 2016.
Toss: Australia. Result: **AUSTRALIA** won by an innings and 52 runs.
Debut: New Zealand – H.M.Nicholls.

NEW ZEALAND

M.J.Guptill	c Smith b Hazlewood	18	(2) c Marsh b Lyon		45
T.W.M.Latham	c Nevill b Hazlewood	6	(1) c Khawaja b Lyon		63
K.S.Williamson	c Nevill b Siddle	16	c Nevill b Hazlewood		22
H.M.Nicholls	c Nevill b Siddle	8	b Bird		59
*B.B.McCullum	c Warner b Hazlewood	0	lbw b Marsh		10
C.J.Anderson	c Khawaja b Lyon	38	lbw b Marsh		0
†B.J.Watling	c Nevill b Hazlewood	17	b Lyon		10
D.A.J.Bracewell	c Voges b Siddle	5	lbw b Hazlewood		14
M.D.Craig	not out	41	not out		33
T.G.Southee	c Hazlewood b Lyon	0	c Khawaja b Lyon		48
T.A.Boult	c Khawaja b Lyon	24	b Marsh		12
Extras	(B 4, LB 1, NB 5)	10	(B 2, LB 5, NB 4)		11
Total	**(48 overs; 223 mins)**	**183**	**(104.3 overs; 436 mins)**		**327**

AUSTRALIA

J.A.Burns	c Watling b Southee	0
D.A.Warner	c Watling b Southee	5
U.T.Khawaja	lbw b Boult	140
*S.P.D.Smith	c and b Craig	71
A.C.Voges	c and b Craig	239
M.R.Marsh	c and b Boult	0
†P.M.Nevill	c Watling b Anderson	32
P.M.Siddle	c Anderson b Bracewell	49
J.R.Hazlewood	c Southee b Bracewell	8
N.M.Lyon	c and b Anderson	3
J.M.Bird	not out	3
Extras	(B 4, LB 3, W 2, NB 3)	12
Total	**(154.2 overs; 651 mins)**	**562**

AUSTRALIA	O	M	R	W	O	M	R	W		FALL OF WICKETS		
Hazlewood	14	2	42	4	29	7	75	2		NZ	A	NZ
Bird	10	1	52	0	19	4	51	1	Wkt	1st	1st	2nd
Siddle	12	5	37	3	8	0	30	0	1st	17	0	81
Marsh	6	1	15	0	17.3	2	73	3	2nd	38	5	121
Lyon	6	0	32	3	31	10	91	4	3rd	44	131	157
									4th	47	299	178
NEW ZEALAND									5th	51	299	185
Southee	31	5	87	2					6th	88	395	214
Boult	33	6	101	2					7th	97	494	218
Bracewell	33	4	127	2					8th	137	508	242
Anderson	18	0	79	2					9th	137	532	301
Craig	35.2	2	153	2					10th	183	562	327
Williamson	4	0	8	0								

Umpires: R.K.Illingworth (*England*) (20) and R.A.Kettleborough (*England*) (34).
Referee: B.C.Broad (*England*) (76).   **Test No. 2200/56 (NZ407/A786)**

NEW ZEALAND v AUSTRALIA (2nd Test)

At Hagley Oval, Christchurch, on 20, 21, 22, 23, 24 February 2016.
Toss: Australia. Result: **AUSTRALIA** won by seven wickets.
Debuts: None.

NEW ZEALAND

M.J.Guptill	c Burns b Pattinson	18	(2) c Nevill b Pattinson		0
T.W.M.Latham	c Smith b Bird	4	(1) c Nevill b Pattinson		39
K.S.Williamson	c Smith b Marsh	7	b Bird		97
H.M.Nicholls	lbw b Hazlewood	7	c Smith b Pattinson		2
*B.B.McCullum	c Lyon b Pattinson	145	c Warner b Hazlewood		25
C.J.Anderson	c Voges b Lyon	72	b Bird		40
†B.J.Watling	c Burns b Bird	58	c Burns b Pattinson		46
T.G.Southee	c Hazlewood b Lyon	5	c Smith b Bird		0
M.J.Henry	c Khawaja b Lyon	21	b Bird		66
N.Wagner	c Nevill b Hazlewood	10	not out		3
T.A.Boult	not out	14	c Pattinson b Bird		0
Extras	(LB 2, W 5, NB 2)	9	(B 2, LB 14, NB 1)		17
Total	**(65.4 overs; 301 mins)**	**370**	**(111.1 overs; 489 mins)**		**335**

AUSTRALIA

D.A.Warner	c Guptill b Boult	12	(2) c Watling b Wagner		22
J.A.Burns	c Guptill b Wagner	170	(1) b Boult		65
U.T.Khawaja	c McCullum b Boult	24	c McCullum b Southee		45
*S.P.D.Smith	c Guptill b Wagner	138	not out		53
A.C.Voges	c Latham b Wagner	60	not out		10
N.M.Lyon	c McCullum b Williamson	33			
M.R.Marsh	c Nicholls b Wagner	18			
†P.M.Nevill	c Watling b Wagner	13			
J.L.Pattinson	c Boult b Anderson	1			
J.R.Hazlewood	c McCullum b Wagner	13			
J.M.Bird	not out	4			
Extras	(B 9, LB 10)	19	(LB 4, NB 2)		6
Total	**(153.1 overs; 642 mins)**	**505**	**(3 wkts; 54 overs; 241 mins)**		**201**

AUSTRALIA	O	M	R	W	O	M	R	W		FALL OF WICKETS			
Hazlewood	18	5	98	2	34	11	92	1			NZ	A	NZ	A
Pattinson	15	2	81	2	26	8	77	4		*Wkt*	*1st*	*1st*	*2nd*	*2nd*
Bird	14.4	4	66	2	17.1	5	59	5		1st	21	25	8	49
Marsh	8	1	62	1	(5) 17	4	49	0		2nd	23	67	66	113
Lyon	10	0	61	3	(4) 17	3	42	0		3rd	32	356	72	179
										4th	74	357	105	
NEW ZEALAND										5th	253	438	207	
Southee	25	4	85	0	(2) 7	2	30	1		6th	266	464	210	
Boult	31	5	108	2	(1) 17	1	60	1		7th	273	483	210	
Henry	32	8	101	0	9	1	33	0		8th	297	484	328	
Anderson	22	2	66	1	(5) 3	0	14	0		9th	333	496	335	
Wagner	32.1	6	106	6	(4) 18	4	60	1		10th	370	505	335	
Williamson	7	0	17	1										
McCullum	4	2	3	0										

Umpires: R.A.Kettleborough (*England*) (35) and R.E.J.Martinesz (*Sri Lanka*) (8).
Referee: B.C.Broad (*England*) (77). **Test No. 2201/57 (NZ408/A787)**

INTERNATIONAL UMPIRES AND REFEREES 2016

ELITE PANEL OF UMPIRES 2016

The Elite Panel of ICC Umpires and Referees was introduced in April 2002 to raise standards and guarantee impartial adjudication. Two umpires from this panel stand in Test matches while one officiates with a home umpire from the Supplementary International Panel in limited-overs internationals.

Full Names	Birthdate	Birthplace	Tests	Debut	LOI	Debut
ALIM Sarwar DAR	06.06.68	Jhang, Pakistan	101	2003-04	178	1999-00
DHARMASENA, H.D.P.Kumar	24.04.71	Colombo, Sri Lanka	36	2010-11	70	2008-09
ERASMUS, Marais	27.02.64	George, South Africa	35	2009-10	62	2007-08
GAFFANEY, Christopher Blair	30.11.75	Dunedin, New Zealand	7	2014	46	2010
GOULD, Ian James	19.08.57	Taplow, England	49	2008-09	111	2006
ILLINGWORTH, Richard Keith	23.08.63	Bradford, England	20	2012-13	44	2010
KETTLEBOROUGH, Richard Allan	15.03.73	Sheffield, England	35	2010-11	62	2009
LLONG, Nigel James	11.02.69	Ashford, England	35	2007-08	100	2006
OXENFORD, Bruce Nicholas James	05.03.60	Southport, Australia	31	2010-11	72	2007-08
RAVI, Sundaram	22.04.66	Bangalore, India	10	2013-14	26	2011-12
REIFFEL, Paul Ronald	19.04.66	Box Hill, Australia	22	2012	41	2008-09
TUCKER, Rodney James	28.08.64	Sydney, Australia	41	2009-10	64	2008-09

ELITE PANEL OF REFEREES 2016

Full Names	Birthdate	Birthplace	Tests	Debut	LOI	Debut
BOON, David Clarence	29.12.60	Launceston, Australia	30	2011	81	2011
BROAD, Brian Christopher	29.09.57	Bristol, England	77	2003-04	271	2003-04
CROWE, Jeffrey John	14.09.58	Auckland, New Zealand	76	2004-05	229	2003-04
MADUGALLE, Ranjan Senerath	22.04.59	Kandy, Sri Lanka	163	1993-94	302	1993-94
PYCROFT, Andrew John	06.06.56	Harare, Zimbabwe	43	2009	120	2009
SRINATH, Javagal	31.08.69	Mysore, India	33	2006	177	2006-07

INTERNATIONAL UMPIRES PANEL 2016

Nominated by their respective cricket boards, members from this panel officiate in home LOIs and supplement the Elite panel for Test matches. Specialist third umpires have been selected to undertake adjudication involving television replays. The number of Test matches/LOI in which they have stood is shown in brackets.

			Third Umpire
Australia	J.D.Ward (-/7)	S.D.Fry (1/25)	M.D.Martell (-/4)
			P.Wilson (-/4)
Bangladesh	Enamul Haque (1/54)	Sharfuddoula (-/23)	Anisur Rahman (-/3)
England	R.J.Bailey (-/12)	M.A.Gough (-/25)	R.T.Robinson (-/7)
India	C.Shamshuddin (-/7)	V.A.Kulkarni (-/25)	C.K.Nandan (-/-)
			A.K.Chaudhary (-/5)
New Zealand	D.J.Walker (-/9)	B.F.Bowden (84/200)	P.D.Jones (-/3)
Pakistan	Shozab Raza (-/13)	Ahsan Raza (-/20)	Ahmed Shahab (-/4)
South Africa	J.D.Cloete (-/60)	S.George (-/14)	A.T.Holdstock (-/4)
Sri Lanka	R.E.J.Martinesz (8/37)	R.S.A.Palliyaguruge (-/32)	R.R.Wimalasiri (-/6)
West Indies	P.J.Nero (-/22)	J.S.Wilson (1/25)	G.O.Brathwaite (-/13)
			N.Duguid (-/-)
Zimbabwe	R.B.Tiffin (44/146)	T.J.Matibiri (-/16)	L.Rusere (-/1)

Test Match and LOI statistics to 23 February 2016.

TEST MATCH CAREER RECORDS

These records, complete to 7 April 2016, contain all players registered for county cricket in 2016 at the time of going to press, plus those who have played Test cricket since 1 December 2014 (Test No. 2147). Records are for performances for the country shown, and do not include figures for multi-national teams.

ENGLAND – BATTING AND FIELDING

	M	I	NO	HS	Runs	Avge	100	50	Ct/St
M.M.Ali	23	38	4	108*	949	27.91	1	5	13
T.R.Ambrose	11	16	1	102	447	29.80	1	3	31
J.M.Anderson	113	156	56	81	1032	10.32	–	1	73
J.M.Bairstow	24	41	4	150*	1204	32.54	1	6	42/1
G.S.Ballance	15	27	2	156	1194	47.76	4	6	14
G.J.Batty	7	8	1	38	144	20.57	–	–	3
I.R.Bell	118	205	24	235	7727	42.69	22	46	100
R.S.Bopara	13	19	1	143	575	31.94	3	–	6
S.G.Borthwick	1	2	–	4	5	2.50	–	–	2
T.T.Bresnan	23	26	4	91	575	26.13	–	3	8
S.C.J.Broad	91	130	18	169	2565	22.90	1	10	26
J.C.Buttler	15	24	3	85	630	30.00	–	5	49
M.A.Carberry	6	12	–	60	345	28.75	–	1	7
R.Clarke	2	3	–	55	96	32.00	–	1	1
P.D.Collingwood	68	115	10	206	4259	40.56	10	20	96
N.R.D.Compton	13	25	2	117	724	31.47	2	2	5
A.N.Cook	126	226	12	294	9964	46.56	28	47	125
S.T.Finn	29	36	19	56	190	11.17	–	1	6
J.S.Foster	7	12	3	48	226	25.11	–	–	17/1
A.D.Hales	4	8	–	60	136	17.00	–	1	1
C.J.Jordan	8	11	1	35	180	18.00	–	–	14
S.C.Kerrigan	1	1	1	1*	1	–	–	–	–
R.W.T.Key	15	26	1	221	775	31.00	1	3	11
A.Lyth	7	13	–	107	265	20.38	1	–	8
E.J.G.Morgan	16	24	1	130	700	30.43	2	3	11
G.Onions	9	10	7	17*	30	10.00	–	–	–
S.R.Patel	6	9	–	42	151	16.77	–	–	3
L.E.Plunkett	13	20	5	55*	238	15.86	–	1	3
W.B.Rankin	1	2	–	13	13	6.50	–	–	–
A.U.Rashid	3	5	–	61	103	20.60	–	1	–
C.M.W.Read	15	23	4	55	360	18.94	–	1	48/6
S.D.Robson	7	11	–	127	336	30.54	1	1	5
J.E.Root	39	72	10	200*	3406	54.93	9	19	41
A.Shahzad	1	1	–	5	5	5.00	–	–	2
R.J.Sidebottom	22	31	11	31	313	15.65	–	–	5
B.A.Stokes	23	41	–	258	1383	33.73	3	6	15
J.W.A.Taylor	7	13	1	76	312	26.00	–	2	7
J.C.Tredwell	2	2	–	37	45	22.50	–	–	2
M.E.Trescothick	76	143	10	219	5825	43.79	14	29	95
I.J.L.Trott	49	87	6	226	3763	46.45	9	18	29
C.R.Woakes	6	9	3	26*	129	21.50	–	–	3
M.A.Wood	8	14	5	32*	185	20.55	–	–	2

ENGLAND – BOWLING

	O	M	R	W	Avge	Best	5wI	10wM
M.M.Ali	689	103	2545	64	39.76	6-67	1	–
J.M.Anderson	4197.3	1023	12638	433	29.18	7-43	18	2
G.S.Ballance	2	1	5	0	–	–	–	–
G.J.Batty	232.2	34	733	11	66.63	3-55	–	–
I.R.Bell	18	3	76	1	76.00	1-33	–	–
R.S.Bopara	72.2	10	290	1	290.00	1-39	–	–
S.G.Borthwick	13	0	82	4	20.50	3-33	–	–
T.T.Bresnan	779	185	2357	72	32.73	5-48	1	–
S.C.J.Broad	3147.3	697	9545	333	28.66	8-15	15	2
R.Clarke	29	11	60	4	15.00	2- 7	–	–
P.D.Collingwood	317.3	51	1018	17	59.88	3-23	–	–
A.N.Cook	3	0	7	1	7.00	1- 6	–	–
S.T.Finn	893.3	166	3203	113	28.34	6-79	5	–
A.D.Hales	3	1	2	0	–	–	–	–
C.J.Jordan	255	74	752	21	35.80	4-18	–	–
S.C.Kerrigan	8	0	53	0	–	–	–	–
A.Lyth	1	1	0	0	–	–	–	–
G.Onions	267.4	50	957	32	29.90	5-38	1	–
S.R.Patel	143	23	421	7	60.14	2-27	–	–
L.E.Plunkett	443.1	71	1536	41	37.46	5-64	1	–
W.B.Rankin	20.5	0	81	1	81.00	1-47	–	–
A.U.Rashid	136.5	9	556	8	69.50	5-64	1	–
J.E.Root	206.3	50	613	12	51.08	2- 9	–	–
A.Shahzad	17	4	63	4	15.75	3-45	–	–
R.J.Sidebottom	802	188	2231	79	28.24	7-47	5	1
B.A.Stokes	617	108	2170	57	38.07	6-36	2	–
J.C.Tredwell	131	39	321	11	29.18	4-47	–	–
M.E.Trescothick	50	6	155	1	155.00	1-34	–	–
I.J.L.Trott	117	11	398	5	79.60	1- 5	–	–
C.R.Woakes	154.2	37	510	8	63.75	3-30	–	–
M.A.Wood	254.3	59	860	25	34.40	3-39	–	–

TESTS

AUSTRALIA – BATTING AND FIELDING

	M	I	NO	HS	Runs	Avge	100	50	Ct/St
J.M.Bird	5	6	5	6*	14	14.00	–	–	1
J.A.Burns	10	17	–	170	838	49.29	3	4	12
M.J.Clarke	115	198	22	329*	8643	49.10	28	27	134
B.J.Haddin	66	112	13	169	3266	32.98	4	18	262/8
R.J.Harris	27	39	11	74	603	21.53	–	3	13
J.W.Hastings	1	2	–	32	52	26.00	–	–	1
J.R.Hazlewood	17	16	8	39	175	21.87	–	–	8
M.G.Johnson	73	109	16	123*	2065	22.20	1	11	27
U.T.Khawaja	15	25	3	174	1090	49.54	4	3	11
N.M.Lyon	54	62	28	40*	528	15.52	–	–	28
C.J.McKay	1	1	–	10	10	10.00	–	1	–
M.R.Marsh	15	23	4	87	437	23.00	–	1	6
S.E.Marsh	17	30	1	182	1094	37.72	3	4	12
P.M.Nevill	12	13	1	66	325	27.08	–	2	44/1
S.N.J.O'Keefe	2	2	1	6	6	6.00	–	–	–
J.L.Pattinson	17	19	7	42	332	27.66	–	–	4
C.J.L.Rogers	25	48	1	173	2015	42.87	5	14	15
P.M.Siddle	61	84	13	51	1032	14.53	–	2	16
S.P.D.Smith	41	75	11	215	3852	60.18	14	16	43
M.A.Starc	25	37	11	99	700	26.92	–	6	13
A.C.Voges	15	21	7	269*	1337	95.50	5	4	11
D.A.Warner	51	94	4	253	4506	50.06	16	20	39
S.R.Watson	59	109	3	176	3731	35.19	4	24	45

AUSTRALIA – BOWLING

	O	M	R	W	Avge	Best	5wI	10wM
J.M.Bird	166.2	50	531	21	25.28	5- 59	1	–
M.J.Clarke	405.5	62	1184	31	38.19	6- 9	2	–
R.J.Harris	956	258	2658	113	23.52	7-117	5	–
J.W.Hastings	39	3	153	1	153.00	1- 51	–	–
J.R.Hazlewood	595.5	145	1804	70	25.77	6- 70	3	–
M.G.Johnson	2666.5	514	8891	313	28.40	8- 61	12	3
N.M.Lyon	2039.5	399	6410	195	32.87	7- 94	7	1
C.J.McKay	28	5	101	1	101.00	1- 56	–	–
M.R.Marsh	244.1	50	863	25	34.52	4- 61	–	–
S.N.J.O'Keefe	83.1	13	282	7	40.28	3- 63	–	–
J.L.Pattinson	546.3	116	1831	70	26.15	5- 27	4	–
P.M.Siddle	2118.5	563	6216	208	29.88	6- 54	8	–
S.P.D.Smith	193	19	837	16	52.31	3- 18	–	–
M.A.Starc	815.1	157	2783	91	30.58	6-111	4	–
A.C.Voges	3	0	18	0	–	–	–	–
D.A.Warner	55	1	254	4	63.50	2- 45	–	–
S.R.Watson	915.5	240	2526	75	33.68	6- 33	3	–

SOUTH AFRICA – BATTING AND FIELDING

	M	I	NO	HS	Runs	Avge	100	50	Ct/St
K.J.Abbott	7	9	–	16	59	6.55	–	–	3
H.M.Amla	92	156	13	311*	7358	51.45	25	29	78
T.Bavuma	9	12	2	102*	383	38.30	1	2	5
S.C.Cook	1	2	–	115	140	70.00	1	–	2
Q.de Kock	8	12	3	129*	407	45.22	1	2	31/2
A.B.de Villiers	106	176	16	278*	8074	50.46	21	39	197/5
F.du Plessis	29	45	4	137	1682	41.02	4	8	15
J.P.Duminy	34	53	9	166	1423	32.34	4	6	26
D.Elgar	25	39	5	121	1249	36.73	4	3	27
S.R.Harmer	5	6	1	13	58	11.60	–	–	1
Imran Tahir	20	23	9	29*	130	9.28	–	–	8
R.K.Kleinveldt	4	5	2	17*	27	9.00	–	–	2
R.McLaren	2	3	1	33*	47	23.50	–	–	–
M.Morkel	71	82	15	40	775	11.56	–	–	19
C.H.Morris	2	3	–	69	98	32.66	–	1	2
A.N.Petersen	36	64	4	182	2093	34.88	5	8	31
V.D.Philander	32	39	10	74	725	25.00	–	4	8
D.L.Piedt	5	6	–	19	39	6.50	–	–	4
K.Rabada	6	9	4	24	56	11.20	–	–	–
J.A.Rudolph	48	83	9	222*	2622	35.43	6	11	29
D.W.Steyn	82	102	21	76	1143	14.11	–	2	22
S.van Zyl	11	15	2	101*	355	27.30	1	–	5
D.J.Vilas	6	9	–	26	94	10.44	–	–	13
G.C.Viljoen	1	2	1	20*	26	26.00	–	–	–

SOUTH AFRICA – BOWLING

	O	M	R	W	Avge	Best	5wI	10wM
K.J.Abbott	207.1	60	537	21	25.57	7- 29	2	–
H.M.Amla	9	0	37	0	–	–	–	–
A.B.de Villiers	34	6	104	2	52.00	2- 49	–	–
F.du Plessis	13	0	69	0	–	–	–	–
J.P.Duminy	388	42	1380	37	37.29	4- 73	–	–
D.Elgar	147.5	10	530	13	40.76	4- 22	–	–
S.R.Harmer	191.2	34	588	20	29.40	4- 61	–	–
Imran Tahir	654.1	86	2294	57	40.24	5- 32	2	–
R.K.Kleinveldt	111.1	21	422	10	42.20	3- 65	–	–
R.McLaren	44	8	162	3	54.00	2- 72	–	–
M.Morkel	2273.2	490	7098	242	29.33	6- 23	6	–
C.H.Morris	61	10	253	4	63.25	1- 8	–	–
A.N.Petersen	19	1	62	1	62.00	1- 2	–	–
V.D.Philander	1010.5	245	2783	126	22.08	6- 44	9	2
D.L.Piedt	231	36	777	22	35.31	5-153	1	–
K.Rabada	158.4	34	593	24	24.70	7-112	3	1
J.A.Rudolph	110.4	13	432	4	108.00	1- 1	–	–
D.W.Steyn	2826	608	9150	406	22.53	7- 51	25	5
S.van Zyl	64.1	14	143	6	23.83	3- 20	–	–
G.C.Viljoen	19	2	94	1	94.00	1- 79	–	–

WEST INDIES – BATTING AND FIELDING

	M	I	NO	HS	Runs	Avge	100	50	Ct/St
S.J.Benn	26	39	5	42	486	14.29	–	–	14
D.Bishoo	15	27	11	30	244	15.25	–	–	9
J.Blackwood	15	27	3	112*	800	33.33	1	6	17
C.R.Brathwaite	2	3	–	69	130	43.33	–	2	–
K.C.Brathwaite	27	51	2	212	1686	34.40	4	8	10
D.J.Bravo	40	71	1	113	2200	31.42	3	13	41
D.M.Bravo	42	76	4	218	2988	41.50	7	14	41
S.Chanderpaul	164	280	49	203*	11867	51.37	30	66	66
R.Chandrika	3	6	–	37	87	14.50	–	–	–
S.S.Cottrell	2	4	–	5	11	2.75	–	–	–
S.O.Dowrich	2	4	–	70	102	25.50	–	1	–
F.H.Edwards	55	88	28	30	394	6.56	–	–	10
S.T.Gabriel	16	20	8	20*	53	4.41	–	–	9
C.H.Gayle	103	182	11	333	7214	42.18	15	37	96
J.O.Holder	13	23	3	103*	546	27.30	1	3	10
S.D.Hope	6	11	–	36	171	15.54	–	–	2
L.R.Johnson	4	7	–	66	275	39.28	–	2	1
V.Permaul	6	9	1	23*	98	12.25	–	–	2
K.K.Peters	1	1	–	0	0	0.00	–	–	–
D.Ramdin	74	126	14	166	2898	25.87	4	15	205/12.
K.A.J.Roach	37	59	10	41	509	10.38	–	–	10
M.N.Samuels	64	114	6	260	3622	33.53	7	22	27
D.S.Smith	38	67	2	108	1593	24.50	1	6	30
J.E.Taylor	46	73	7	106	856	12.96	1	1	8
J.A.Warrican	4	7	6	21*	65	65.00	–	–	1

WEST INDIES – BOWLING

	O	M	R	W	Avge	Best	5wI	10wM
S.J.Benn	1220.1	229	3402	87	39.10	6-81	6	–
D.Bishoo	668.1	100	2093	55	38.05	6-80	2	–
J.Blackwood	38.3	4	157	2	78.50	2-14	–	–
C.R.Brathwaite	43	4	162	1	162.00	1-30	–	–
K.C.Brathwaite	95.1	11	316	8	39.50	6-29	1	–
D.J.Bravo	1077.4	213	3426	86	39.83	6-55	2	–
D.M.Bravo	1	0	2	0	–	–	–	–
S.Chanderpaul	290	50	883	9	98.11	1- 2	–	–
S.S.Cottrell	46	4	196	2	98.00	1-72	–	–
F.H.Edwards	1600.2	183	6249	165	37.87	7-87	12	–
S.T.Gabriel	365.3	68	1281	34	37.67	3-10	–	–
C.H.Gayle	1184.5	230	3120	73	42.73	5-34	2	–
J.O.Holder	304.5	72	819	21	39.00	3-15	–	–
L.R.Johnson	4	0	9	0	–	–	–	–
V.Permaul	228.3	34	788	18	43.77	3-32	–	–
K.K.Peters	20	7	69	2	34.50	2-69	–	–
K.A.J.Roach	1129.5	214	3689	122	30.23	6-48	6	1
M.N.Samuels	732	79	2445	41	59.63	4-13	–	–
D.S.Smith	1	0	3	0	–	–	–	–
J.E.Taylor	1292.5	258	4480	130	34.46	6-47	4	–
J.A.Warrican	122	8	509	11	46.27	4-67	–	–

TESTS

NEW ZEALAND – BATTING AND FIELDING

	M	I	NO	HS	Runs	Avge	100	50	Ct/St
C.J.Anderson	13	22	1	116	683	32.52	1	4	7
T.A.Boult	39	54	26	52*	442	15.78	–	1	17
D.A.J.Bracewell	25	43	4	47	520	13.33	–	–	8
M.D.Craig	14	23	9	67	586	41.85	–	3	14
J.E.C.Franklin	31	46	7	122*	808	20.71	1	2	12
M.J.Guptill	40	77	1	189	2274	29.92	3	15	42
M.J.Henry	4	7	2	66	152	30.40	–	1	1
T.W.M.Latham	18	35	1	137	1292	38.00	3	7	18
B.B.McCullum	101	176	9	302	6453	38.64	12	31	198/11
H.J.H.Marshall	13	19	2	160	652	38.35	2	2	1
J.D.S.Neesham	9	17	1	137*	612	38.25	2	3	7
H.M.Nicholls	2	4	–	59	76	19.00	–	1	1
J.S.Patel	19	30	7	27*	276	12.00	–	–	12
L.Ronchi	1	2	–	88	119	59.50	–	1	4
H.D.Rutherford	16	29	1	171	755	26.96	1	1	11
J.D.Ryder	18	33	2	201	1269	40.93	3	6	12
M.J.Santner	3	5	–	45	130	26.00	–	–	2
T.G.Southee	48	78	6	77*	1209	16.79	–	3	30
L.R.P.L.Taylor	69	127	12	290	5232	45.49	13	24	112
N.Wagner	19	27	7	37	237	11.85	–	–	4
B.J.Watling	38	65	9	142*	2092	37.35	5	11	124/5
K.S.Williamson	48	89	7	242*	4037	49.23	13	19	39

NEW ZEALAND – BOWLING

	O	M	R	W	Avge	Best	5wI	10wM
C.J.Anderson	217	34	659	16	41.18	3- 47	–	–
T.A.Boult	1425.4	306	4285	147	29.14	6- 40	5	1
D.A.J.Bracewell	777.2	130	2626	69	38.05	6- 40	2	–
M.D.Craig	564.3	91	2187	48	45.56	7- 94	1	1
J.E.C.Franklin	794.3	143	2786	82	33.97	6-119	3	–
M.J.Guptill	58.2	3	265	5	53.00	3- 37	–	–
M.J.Henry	169.1	30	632	10	63.20	4- 93	–	–
B.B.McCullum	29.1	5	88	1	88.00	1- 1	–	–
H.J.H.Marshall	1	0	4	0	–	–	–	–
J.D.S.Neesham	129.5	13	472	12	39.33	3- 42	–	–
J.S.Patel	787.1	164	2520	52	48.46	5-110	1	–
H.D.Rutherford	1	0	2	0	–	–	–	–
J.D.Ryder	82	23	280	5	56.00	2- 7	–	–
M.J.Santner	68.1	15	186	6	31.00	2- 37	–	–
T.G.Southee	1746.2	360	5332	166	32.12	7- 64	4	1
L.R.P.L.Taylor	16	3	48	2	24.00	2- 4	–	–
N.Wagner	696.5	137	2400	74	32.43	6-106	2	–
K.S.Williamson	329.3	45	1100	29	37.93	4- 44	–	–

TESTS

INDIA – BATTING AND FIELDING

	M	I	NO	HS	Runs	Avge	100	50	Ct/St
V.R.Aaron	9	14	5	9	35	3.88	–	–	1
R.Ashwin	32	48	10	124	1204	31.68	2	6	13
S.T.R.Binny	6	10	1	78	194	21.55	–	1	4
S.Dhawan	19	33	–	187	1308	40.87	4	2	15
M.S.Dhoni	90	144	16	224	4876	38.09	6	33	256/38
Harbhajan Singh	103	145	23	115	2224	18.22	2	9	42
R.A.Jadeja	16	24	2	68	473	21.50	–	1	16
V.Kohli	41	72	4	169	2994	44.02	11	12	36
B.Kumar	12	18	3	63*	393	26.20	–	3	4
A.Mishra	18	29	2	84	574	21.25	–	3	7
Mohammed Shami	12	19	6	51*	166	12.76	–	1	1
N.V.Ojha	1	2	–	35	56	28.00	–	–	4/1
C.A.Pujara	32	56	5	206*	2420	47.45	7	7	24
A.M.Rahane	22	40	4	147	1619	44.97	6	7	27
K.L.Rahul	5	10	–	110	256	25.60	2	–	10
S.K.Raina	18	31	2	120	768	26.48	1	7	23
W.P.Saha	11	19	2	60	367	21.58	–	2	14/5
I.Sharma	68	100	38	31*	550	8.87	–	–	14
K.V.Sharma	1	2	1	4*	8	8.00	–	–	–
R.G.Sharma	16	29	2	177	896	33.18	2	4	17
M.Vijay	37	65	1	167	2630	41.09	6	12	31
U.T.Yadav	17	22	8	30	109	7.78	–	–	4

INDIA – BOWLING

	O	M	R	W	Avge	Best	5wI	10wM
V.R.Aaron	198.1	12	947	18	52.61	3- 97	–	–
R.Ashwin	1537.2	320	4470	176	25.39	7- 66	16	4
S.T.R.Binny	75	12	258	3	86.00	2- 24	–	–
S.Dhawan	9	2	18	0	–	–	–	–
M.S.Dhoni	16	1	67	0	–	–	–	–
Harbhajan Singh	4763.2	871	13537	417	32.46	8- 84	25	5
R.A.Jadeja	711.3	200	1616	68	23.76	6-138	4	–
V.Kohli	25	2	70	0	–	–	–	–
B.Kumar	318.5	68	1015	29	35.00	6- 82	2	–
A.Mishra	704.5	95	2208	65	33.96	5- 71	1	–
Mohammed Shami	446.3	62	1699	47	36.14	5- 47	2	–
C.A.Pujara	1	0	2	0	–	–	–	–
S.K.Raina	173.3	22	603	13	46.38	2- 1	–	–
I.Sharma	2236.3	429	7417	201	36.90	7- 74	7	1
K.V.Sharma	49	3	238	4	59.50	2- 95	–	–
R.G.Sharma	54.4	3	197	2	98.50	1- 26	–	–
M.Vijay	38	5	107	1	107.00	1- 12	–	–
U.T.Yadav	471	74	1911	53	36.05	5- 93	1	–

TESTS

PAKISTAN – BATTING AND FIELDING

	M	I	NO	HS	Runs	Avge	100	50	Ct/St
Ahmed Shehzad	11	21	1	176	861	43.05	3	3	3
Asad Shafiq	41	65	5	137	2597	43.28	8	13	36
Azhar Ali	45	84	5	226	3427	43.37	9	20	48
Azhar Mahmood	21	34	4	136	900	30.00	3	1	14
Ehsan Adil	3	4	–	12	21	5.25	–	–	–
Imran Khan	7	4	2	0*	0	0.00	–	–	–
Junaid Khan	22	28	11	17	122	7.17	–	–	4
Misbah-ul-Haq	61	106	17	161*	4352	48.89	9	32	44
Mohammad Hafeez	47	90	8	224	3350	40.85	9	12	38
Rahat Ali	14	19	7	35*	98	8.16	–	–	7
Sami Aslam	2	3	–	20	47	15.66	–	–	1
Sarfraz Ahmed	21	37	9	112	1296	46.28	3	7	46/17
Shahid Afridi	27	48	1	156	1716	36.51	5	8	10
Shan Masood	7	14	–	125	361	25.78	1	2	6
Shoaib Malik	35	60	6	245	1898	35.14	3	8	18
Umar Akmal	16	30	2	129	1003	35.82	1	6	12
Wahab Riaz	15	21	4	27	149	8.76	–	–	3
Yasir Arafat	3	3	1	50*	94	47.00	–	1	–
Yasir Shah	12	14	1	25	136	10.46	–	–	7
Younus Khan	104	186	17	313	9116	53.94	31	30	117
Zulfiqar Babar	13	15	7	56	128	16.00	–	1	3

PAKISTAN – BOWLING

	O	M	R	W	Avge	Best	5wI	10wM
Ahmed Shehzad	8	0	28	0	–	–	–	–
Asad Shafiq	14	0	51	1	51.00	1- 32	–	–
Azhar Ali	57	5	214	4	53.50	2- 35	–	–
Azhar Mahmood	502.3	111	1402	39	35.94	4- 50	–	–
Ehsan Adil	80.1	19	263	5	52.60	2- 54	–	–
Imran Khan	174.3	32	562	20	28.10	5- 58	1	–
Junaid Khan	767.3	157	2253	71	31.73	5- 38	5	–
Mohammad Hafeez	658.5	113	1763	52	33.90	4- 16	–	–
Rahat Ali	470.4	89	1450	40	36.25	6-127	2	–
Shahid Afridi	532.2	69	1709	48	35.60	5- 52	1	–
Shoaib Malik	452	61	1519	32	47.46	4- 33	–	–
Wahab Riaz	440.2	72	1469	43	34.16	5- 63	1	–
Yasir Arafat	104.3	12	438	9	48.66	5-161	1	–
Yasir Shah	613.4	92	1837	76	24.17	7- 76	4	–
Younus Khan	134	18	491	9	54.55	2- 23	–	–
Zulfiqar Babar	679.2	128	1980	51	38.82	5- 74	2	–

SRI LANKA – BATTING AND FIELDING

	M	I	NO	HS	Runs	Avge	100	50	Ct/St
P.V.D.Chameera	4	7	1	14	40	6.66	–	–	1
L.D.Chandimal	25	44	4	162*	1835	45.87	5	10	46/8
D.P.D.N.Dickwella	4	7	–	72	144	20.57	–	1	15/2
R.M.S.Eranga	16	21	10	45*	186	16.90	–	–	5
A.N.P.R.Fernando	17	29	10	17*	75	3.94	–	–	3
H.M.R.K.B.Herath	67	99	22	80*	1049	13.62	–	1	17
M.D.U.S.Jayasundera	2	4	–	26	30	7.50	–	–	2
H.A.P.W.Jayawardena	58	83	11	154*	2124	29.50	4	5	124/32
F.D.M.Karunaratne	25	48	2	186	1622	35.26	3	7	19
P.H.T.Kaushal	7	12	2	18	106	10.60	–	–	3
R.A.S.Lakmal	26	38	14	23	196	8.16	–	–	6
A.D.Mathews	56	97	17	160	4015	50.18	7	23	37
B.K.G.Mendis	3	6	–	46	183	30.50	–	–	1
J.Mubarak	13	23	1	49	385	17.50	–	–	15
M.D.K.Perera	9	14	–	95	155	11.07	–	1	6
M.D.K.J.Perera	3	5	–	70	169	33.80	–	2	9/4
K.T.G.D.Prasad	25	39	2	47	476	12.86	–	–	6
K.C.Sangakkara	134	233	17	319	12400	57.40	38	52	182/20
J.K.Silva	24	44	–	139	1404	31.90	2	9	25/1
T.A.M.Siriwardana	4	7	–	68	263	37.57	–	2	3
W.U.Tharanga	21	38	1	165	1117	30.18	1	5	17
H.D.R.L.Thirimanne	23	45	6	155*	969	24.84	1	4	9
K.D.K.Vithanage	10	16	2	103*	370	26.42	1	1	10

SRI LANKA – BOWLING

	O	M	R	W	Avge	Best	5wI	10wM
P.V.D.Chameera	126.5	9	509	18	28.27	5- 47	1	–
R.M.S.Eranga	561.5	115	1814	52	34.88	4- 49	–	–
A.N.P.R.Fernando	530.3	71	1953	42	46.50	4- 62	–	–
H.M.R.K.B.Herath	3187.2	604	8873	297	29.87	9-127	23	5
M.D.U.S.Jayasundera	7	0	45	0	–	–	–	–
F.D.M.Karunaratne	2	0	5	0	–	–	–	–
P.H.T.Kaushal	276.2	22	1105	25	44.20	5- 42	2	–
R.A.S.Lakmal	795.2	147	2655	54	49.16	4- 78	–	–
A.D.Mathews	535	125	1487	30	49.56	4- 44	–	–
J.Mubarak	17.1	2	66	0	–	–	–	–
M.D.K.Perera	428.4	77	1301	44	29.56	5- 69	3	–
K.T.G.D.Prasad	721.1	96	2698	75	35.97	5- 50	1	–
K.C.Sangakkara	14	0	49	0	–	–	–	–
T.A.M.Siriwardana	53.3	6	185	8	23.12	3- 25	–	–
H.D.R.L.Thirimanne	14	1	51	0	–	–	–	–
K.D.K.Vithanage	29	1	133	1	133.00	1- 73	–	–

A.N.P.R.Fernando is also known as N.Pradeep.

TESTS

ZIMBABWE – BATTING AND FIELDING *

	M	I	NO	HS	Runs	Avge	100	50	Ct/St
R.W.Chakabva	8	16	1	101	495	33.00	1	3	9
B.B.Chari	2	4	–	25	29	7.25	–	–	1
T.L.Chatara	7	14	2	22	82	6.83	–	–	–
E.Chigumbura	14	27	–	88	569	21.07	–	4	6
C.R.Ervine	7	14	2	49	286	23.83	–	–	8
S.M.Ervine	5	8	–	86	261	32.62	–	3	7
K.M.Jarvis	8	14	6	25*	58	7.25	–	–	3
T.Kamungozi	1	2	–	5	5	2.50	–	–	–
H.Masakadza	29	58	2	158	1712	30.57	4	6	18
S.W.Masakadza	5	9	1	24	88	11.00	–	–	2
N.M'shangwe	2	4	–	8	8	2.00	–	–	2
R.Mutumbami	6	12	1	43	217	19.72	–	–	17/2
J.C.Nyumbu	2	4	–	14	30	7.50	–	–	1
T.Panyangara	9	18	6	40*	201	16.75	–	–	3
V.Sibanda	14	28	–	93	591	21.10	–	2	16
Sikandar Raza	4	8	–	82	327	40.87	–	4	–
B.R.M.Taylor	23	46	3	171	1493	34.72	4	7	23
M.N.Waller	9	18	1	72*	396	23.29	–	3	6

ZIMBABWE – BOWLING

	O	M	R	W	Avge	Best	5wI	10wM
B.B.Chari	2	0	9	0	–	–	–	–
T.L.Chatara	241.1	70	585	20	29.25	5- 61	1	–
E.Chigumbura	301	61	966	21	46.00	5- 54	1	–
S.M.Ervine	95	18	388	9	43.11	4-116	–	–
K.M.Jarvis	261.3	47	952	30	31.73	5- 54	2	–
T.Kamungozi	26	6	58	1	58.00	1- 51	–	–
H.Masakadza	149	38	360	13	27.69	3- 24	–	–
S.W.Masakadza	176.1	34	515	16	32.18	4- 32	–	–
N.M'shangwe	131.4	16	435	7	62.14	4- 82	–	–
J.C.Nyumbu	69.3	8	250	5	50.00	5-157	1	–
T.Panyangara	314.5	87	813	31	26.22	5- 59	1	–
Sikandar Raza	82	4	303	5	60.60	3-123	–	–
B.R.M.Taylor	7	0	38	0	–	–	–	–
M.N.Waller	53	8	132	6	22.00	4- 59	–	–

* Zimbabwe have played no Tests since their series with Bangladesh in Oct-Nov 2014, and this list includes all who played in that series, plus those registered to play county cricket in 2016.

TESTS

BANGLADESH – BATTING AND FIELDING

	M	I	NO	HS	Runs	Avge	100	50	Ct/St
Imrul Kayes	24	46	1	150	1252	27.82	3	3	20
Jubair Hossain	6	5	2	7*	13	4.33	–	–	2
Liton Das	3	3	–	50	97	32.33	–	1	3
Mahmudullah	27	50	2	115	1506	31.37	1	12	28/1
Mohammad Shahid	5	6	1	25	57	11.40	–	–	–
Mominul Haque	17	30	4	181	1456	56.00	4	9	13
Mushfiqur Rahim	48	88	6	200	2650	32.31	3	15	76/11
Mustafizur Rahman	2	1	–	3	3	3.00	–	–	–
Nasir Hossain	17	28	2	100	971	37.34	1	6	10
Rubel Hossain	23	39	.17	45*	197	8.95	–	–	11
Shahadat Hossain	38	69	17	40	521	10.01	–	–	9
Shakib Al Hasan	42	78	7	144	2823	39.76	3	19	19
Shuvagata Hom	7	13	3	50	213	21.30	–	1	5
Soumya Sarkar	3	5	–	37	107	21.40	–	–	–
Taijul Islam	9	14	2	32	137	11.41	–	–	6
Tamim Iqbal	42	80	1	206	3118	39.46	7	18	11

BANGLADESH – BOWLING

	O	M	R	W	Avge	Best	5wI	10wM
Imrul Kayes	4	0	12	0	–	–	–	–
Jubair Hossain	119.1	10	493	16	30.81	5- 96	1	–
Mahmudullah	491.3	50	1680	37	45.40	5- 51	1.	–
Mohammad Shahid	105	30	288	5	57.60	2- 23	–	–
Mominul Haque	53.1	1	192	1	192.00	1- 10	–	–
Mustafizur Rahman	22.4	6	58	4	14.50	4- 37	–	–
Nasir Hossain	143.3	22	413	8	51.62	3- 52	–	–
Rubel Hossain	622	64	2429	32	75.90	5-166	1	–
Shahadat Hossain	896.4	92	3731	72	51.81	6- 27	4	–
Shakib Al Hasan	1630.2	307	4897	147	33.31	7- 36	14	1
Shuvagata Hom	131	10	473	8	59.12	2- 66	–	–
Soumya Sarkar	30.4	1	115	1	115.00	1- 45	–	–
Taijul Islam	374.5	53	1222	36	33.94	8- 39	3	–
Tamim Iqbal	5	0	20	0	–	–	–	–

INTERNATIONAL TEST MATCH RESULTS

Complete to 7 April 2016.

	Opponents	Tests	\<--- Won by ---\>										Tied	Drawn
			E	A	SA	WI	NZ	I	P	SL	Z	B		
England	Australia	341	108	140	–	–	–	–	–	–	–	–	–	93
	South Africa	145	58	–	32	–	–	–	–	–	–	–	–	55
	West Indies	151	46	–	–	54	–	–	–	–	–	–	–	51
	New Zealand	101	48	–	–	–	9	–	–	–	–	–	–	44
	India	112	43	–	–	–	–	21	–	–	–	–	–	48
	Pakistan	77	22	–	–	–	–	–	18	–	–	–	–	37
	Sri Lanka	28	10	–	–	–	–	–	–	8	–	–	–	10
	Zimbabwe	6	3	–	–	–	–	–	–	–	0	–	–	3
	Bangladesh	8	8	–	–	–	–	–	–	–	–	0	–	0
Australia	South Africa	91	–	50	21	–	–	–	–	–	–	–	–	20
	West Indies	116	–	58	–	32	–	–	–	–	–	–	1	25
	New Zealand	57	–	31	–	–	8	–	–	–	–	–	–	18
	India	90	–	40	–	–	–	24	–	–	–	–	1	25
	Pakistan	59	–	28	–	–	–	–	14	–	–	–	–	17
	Sri Lanka	26	–	17	–	–	–	–	–	1	–	–	–	8
	Zimbabwe	3	–	3	–	–	–	–	–	–	0	–	–	0
	Bangladesh	4	–	4	–	–	–	–	–	–	–	0	–	0
South Africa	West Indies	28	–	–	18	3	–	–	–	–	–	–	–	7
	New Zealand	40	–	–	23	–	4	–	–	–	–	–	–	13
	India	33	–	–	13	–	–	10	–	–	–	–	–	10
	Pakistan	23	–	–	12	–	–	–	4	–	–	–	–	7
	Sri Lanka	22	–	–	11	–	–	–	–	5	–	–	–	6
	Zimbabwe	8	–	–	7	–	–	–	–	–	0	–	–	1
	Bangladesh	10	–	–	8	–	–	–	–	–	–	0	–	2
West Indies	New Zealand	45	–	–	–	13	13	–	–	–	–	–	–	19
	India	90	–	–	–	30	–	16	–	–	–	–	–	44
	Pakistan	46	–	–	–	15	–	–	16	–	–	–	–	15
	Sri Lanka	17	–	–	–	3	–	–	–	8	–	–	–	6
	Zimbabwe	8	–	–	–	6	–	–	–	–	0	–	–	2
	Bangladesh	12	–	–	–	8	–	–	–	–	–	2	–	2
New Zealand	India	54	–	–	–	–	10	18	–	–	–	–	–	26
	Pakistan	53	–	–	–	–	8	–	24	–	–	–	–	21
	Sri Lanka	32	–	–	–	–	14	–	–	8	–	–	–	10
	Zimbabwe	15	–	–	–	–	9	–	–	–	0	–	–	6
	Bangladesh	11	–	–	–	–	8	–	–	–	–	0	–	3
India	Pakistan	59	–	–	–	–	–	9	12	–	–	–	–	38
	Sri Lanka	38	–	–	–	–	–	16	–	7	–	–	–	15
	Zimbabwe	11	–	–	–	–	–	7	–	–	2	–	–	2
	Bangladesh	8	–	–	–	–	–	6	–	–	–	0	–	2
Pakistan	Sri Lanka	51	–	–	–	–	–	–	19	14	–	–	–	18
	Zimbabwe	17	–	–	–	–	–	–	10	–	3	–	–	4
	Bangladesh	10	–	–	–	–	–	–	9	–	–	0	–	1
Sri Lanka	Zimbabwe	15	–	–	–	–	–	–	–	10	0	–	–	5
	Bangladesh	16	–	–	–	–	–	–	–	14	–	0	–	2
Zimbabwe	Bangladesh	14	–	–	–	–	–	–	–	–	6	5	–	3
		2201	346	371	145	164	83	127	126	75	11	7	2	744

	Tests	Won	Lost	Drawn	Tied	Toss Won
England	969	346	282	341	–	465
Australia	788†	372†	208	206	2	398†
South Africa	400	145	134	121	–	191
West Indies	513	164	177	171	1	267
New Zealand	408	83	164	160	–	204
India	495	127	157	210	1	252
Pakistan	394	126	111	158	–	187
Sri Lanka	245	75	90	80	–	134
Zimbabwe	97	11	60	26	–	55
Bangladesh	93	7	71	15	–	49

† total includes Australia's victory against the ICC World XI.

INTERNATIONAL TEST CRICKET RECORDS

(To 7 April 2016)

TEAM RECORDS

HIGHEST INNINGS TOTALS

952-6d	Sri Lanka v India	Colombo (RPS)	1997-98
903-7d	England v Australia	The Oval	1938
849	England v West Indies	Kingston	1929-30
790-3d	West Indies v Pakistan	Kingston	1957-58
765-6d	Pakistan v Sri Lanka	Karachi	2008-09
760-7d	Sri Lanka v India	Ahmedabad	2009-10
758-8d	Australia v West Indies	Kingston	1954-55
756-5d	Sri Lanka v South Africa	Colombo (SSC)	2006
751-5d	West Indies v England	St John's	2003-04
749-9d	West Indies v England	Bridgetown	2008-09
747	West Indies v South Africa	St John's	2004-05
735-6d	Australia v Zimbabwe	Perth	2003-04
730-6d	Sri Lanka v Bangladesh	Dhaka	2013-14
729-6d	Australia v England	Lord's	1930
726-9d	India v Sri Lanka	Mumbai	2009-10
713-3d	Sri Lanka v Zimbabwe	Bulawayo	2003-04
710-7d	England v India	Birmingham	2011
708	Pakistan v England	The Oval	1987
707	India v Sri Lanka	Colombo (SSC)	2010
705-7d	India v Australia	Sydney	2003-04
701	Australia v England	The Oval	1934
699-5	Pakistan v India	Lahore	1989-90
695	Australia v England	The Oval	1930
692-8d	West Indies v England	The Oval	1995
690	New Zealand v Pakistan	Sharjah	2014-15
687-8d	West Indies v England	The Oval	1976
682-6d	South Africa v England	Lord's	2003
681-8d	West Indies v England	Port-of-Spain	1953-54
680-8d	New Zealand v India	Wellington	2013-14
679-7d	Pakistan v India	Lahore	2005-06
676-7	India v Sri Lanka	Kanpur	1986-87
675-5d	India v Pakistan	Multan	2003-04
674	Australia v India	Adelaide	1947-48
674-6	Pakistan v India	Faisalabad	1984-85

674-6d	Australia v England	Cardiff	2009
671-4	New Zealand v Sri Lanka	Wellington	1990-91
668	Australia v West Indies	Bridgetown	1954-55
664	India v England	The Oval	2007
660-5d	West Indies v New Zealand	Wellington	1994-95
659-8d	Australia v England	Sydney	1946-47
659-4d	Australia v India	Sydney	2011-12
658-8d	England v Australia	Nottingham	1938
658-9d	South Africa v West Indies	Durban	2003-04
657-8d	Pakistan v West Indies	Bridgetown	1957-58
657-7d	India v Australia	Calcutta	2000-01
656-8d	Australia v England	Manchester	1964
654-5	England v South Africa	Durban	1938-39
653-4d	England v India	Lord's	1990
653-4d	Australia v England	Leeds	1993
652-8d	West Indies v England	Lord's	1973
652	Pakistan v India	Faisalabad	1982-83
652-7d	England v India	Madras	1984-85
652-7d	Australia v South Africa	Johannesburg	2001-02
651	South Africa v Australia	Cape Town	2008-09
650-6d	Australia v West Indies	Bridgetown	1964-65

The highest for Zimbabwe is 563-9d (v WI, Harare, 2001), and for Bangladesh 638 (v SL, Galle, 2012-13).

LOWEST INNINGS TOTALS

† One batsman absent

26	New Zealand v England	Auckland	1954-55
30	South Africa v England	Port Elizabeth	1895-96
30	South Africa v England	Birmingham	1924
35	South Africa v England	Cape Town	1898-99
36	Australia v England	Birmingham	1902
36	South Africa v Australia	Melbourne	1931-32
42	Australia v England	Sydney	1887-88
42	New Zealand v Australia	Wellington	1945-46
42†	India v England	Lord's	1974
43	South Africa v England	Cape Town	1888-89
44	Australia v England	The Oval	1896
45	England v Australia	Sydney	1886-87
45	South Africa v Australia	Melbourne	1931-32
45	New Zealand v South Africa	Cape Town	2012-13
46	England v West Indies	Port-of-Spain	1993-94
47	South Africa v England	Cape Town	1888-89
47	New Zealand v England	Lord's	1958
47	West Indies v England	Kingston	2003-04
47	Australia v South Africa	Cape Town	2011-12
49	Pakistan v South Africa	Johannesburg	2012-13

The lowest for Sri Lanka is 71 (v P, Kandy, 1994-95), for Zimbabwe 51 (v NZ, Napier, 2011-12), and for Bangladesh 62 (v SL, Colombo PPS, 2006-07).

BATTING RECORDS
5000 RUNS IN TESTS

Runs			M	I	NO	HS	Avge	100	50
15921	S.R.Tendulkar	I	200	329	33	248*	53.78	51	68
13378	R.T.Ponting	A	168	287	29	257	51.85	41	62
13289	J.H.Kallis	SA/ICC	166	280	40	224	55.37	45	58

Runs			M	I	NO	HS	Avge	100	50
13288	R.S.Dravid	I/ICC	164	286	32	270	52.31	36	63
12400	K.C.Sangakkara	SL	134	233	17	319	57.40	38	52
11953	B.C.Lara	WI/ICC	131	232	6	400*	52.88	34	48
11867	S.Chanderpaul	WI	164	280	49	203*	51.37	30	66
11814	D.P.M.D.Jayawardena	SL	149	252	15	374	49.84	34	50
11174	A.R.Border	A	156	265	44	205	50.56	27	63
10927	S.R.Waugh	A	168	260	46	200	51.06	32	50
10122	S.M.Gavaskar	I	125	214	16	236*	51.12	34	45
9964	A.N.Cook	E	126	226	12	294	46.56	28	47
9265	G.C.Smith	SA/ICC	117	205	13	277	48.25	27	38
9116	Younus Khan	P	104	186	17	313	53.94	31	30
8900	G.A.Gooch	E	118	215	6	333	42.58	20	46
8832	Javed Miandad	P	124	189	21	280*	52.57	23	43
8830	Inzamam-ul-Haq	P/ICC	120	200	22	329	49.60	25	46
8781	V.V.S.Laxman	I	134	225	34	281	45.97	17	56
8643	M.J.Clarke	A	115	198	22	329*	49.10	28	27
8625	M.L.Hayden	A	103	184	14	380	50.73	30	29
8586	V.Sehwag	I/ICC	104	180	6	319	49.34	23	32
8540	I.V.A.Richards	WI	121	182	12	291	50.23	24	45
8463	A.J.Stewart	E	133	235	21	190	39.54	15	45
8231	D.I.Gower	E	117	204	18	215	44.25	18	39
8181	K.P.Pietersen	E	104	181	8	227	47.28	23	35
8114	G.Boycott	E	108	193	23	246*	47.72	22	42
8074	A.B.de Villiers	SA	106	176	16	278*	50.46	21	39
8032	G.St A.Sobers	WI	93	160	21	365*	57.78	26	30
8029	M.E.Waugh	A	128	209	17	153*	41.81	20	47
7728	M.A.Atherton	E	115	212	7	185*	37.70	16	46
7727	I.R.Bell	E	118	205	24	235	42.69	22	46
7696	J.L.Langer	A	105	182	12	250	45.27	23	30
7624	M.C.Cowdrey	E	114	188	15	182	44.06	22	38
7558	C.G.Greenidge	WI	108	185	16	226	44.72	19	34
7530	Mohammad Yousuf	P	90	156	12	223	52.29	24	33
7525	M.A.Taylor	A	104	186	13	334*	43.49	19	40
7515	C.H.Lloyd	WI	110	175	14	242*	46.67	19	39
7487	D.L.Haynes	WI	116	202	25	184	42.29	18	39
7422	D.C.Boon	A	107	190	20	200	43.65	21	32
7358	H.M.Amla	SA	92	156	13	311*	51.45	25	29
7289	G.Kirsten	SA	101	176	15	275	45.27	21	34
7249	W.R.Hammond	E	85	140	16	336*	58.45	22	24
7214	C.H.Gayle	WI	103	182	11	333	42.18	15	37
7212	S.C.Ganguly	I	113	188	17	239	42.17	16	35
7172	S.P.Fleming	NZ	111	189	10	274*	40.06	9	46
7110	G.S.Chappell	A	87	151	19	247*	53.86	24	31
7037	A.J.Strauss	E	100	178	6	177	40.91	21	27
6996	D.G.Bradman	A	52	80	10	334	99.94	29	13
6973	S.T.Jayasuriya	SL	110	188	14	340	40.07	14	31
6971	L.Hutton	E	79	138	15	364	56.67	19	33
6868	D.B.Vengsarkar	I	116	185	22	166	42.13	17	35
6806	K.F.Barrington	E	82	131	15	256	58.67	20	35
6744	G.P.Thorpe	E	100	179	28	200*	44.66	16	39
6453	B.B.McCullum	NZ	101	176	9	302	38.64	12	31
6361	P.A.de Silva	SL	93	159	11	267	42.97	20	22
6235	M.E.K.Hussey	A	79	137	16	195	51.52	19	29
6227	R.B.Kanhai	WI	79	137	6	256	47.53	15	28
6215	M.Azharuddin	I	99	147	9	199	45.03	22	21
6167	H.H.Gibbs	SA	90	154	7	228	41.95	14	26

75

Runs			M	I	NO	HS	Avge	100	50
6149	R.N.Harvey	A	79	137	10	205	48.41	21	24
6080	G.R.Viswanath	I	91	155	10	222	41.93	14	35
5949	R.B.Richardson	WI	86	146	12	194	44.39	16	27
5842	R.R.Sarwan	WI	87	154	8	291	40.01	15	31
5825	M.E.Trescothick	E	76	143	10	219	43.79	14	29
5807	D.C.S.Compton	E	78	131	15	278	50.06	17	28
5768	Salim Malik	P	103	154	22	237	43.69	15	29
5764	N.Hussain	E	96	171	16	207	37.19	14	33
5762	C.L.Hooper	WI	102	173	15	233	36.46	13	27
5719	M.P.Vaughan	E	82	147	9	197	41.44	18	18
5570	A.C.Gilchrist	A	96	137	20	204*	47.60	17	26
5515	M.V.Boucher	SA/ICC	147	206	24	125	30.30	5	35
5502	M.S.Atapattu	SL	90	156	15	249	39.02	16	17
5492	T.M.Dilshan	SL	87	145	11	193	40.98	16	23
5462	T.T.Samaraweera	SL	81	132	20	231	48.76	14	30
5444	M.D.Crowe	NZ	77	131	11	299	45.36	17	18
5410	J.B.Hobbs	E	61	102	7	211	56.94	15	28
5357	K.D.Walters	A	74	125	14	250	48.26	15	33
5345	I.M.Chappell	A	75	136	10	196	42.42	14	26
5334	J.G.Wright	NZ	82	148	7	185	37.82	12	23
5312	M.J.Slater	A	74	131	7	219	42.84	14	21
5248	Kapil Dev	I	131	184	15	163	31.05	8	27
5234	W.M.Lawry	A	67	123	12	210	47.15	13	27
5232	L.R.P.L.Taylor	NZ	69	127	12	290	45.49	19	24
5200	I.T.Botham	E	102	161	6	208	33.54	14	22
5138	J.H.Edrich	E	77	127	9	310*	43.54	12	24
5105	A.Ranatunga	SL	93	155	12	135*	35.69	4	38
5062	Zaheer Abbas	P	78	124	11	274	44.79	12	20

The most for Zimbabwe is 4794 (112 innings) by A.Flower, and for Bangladesh 3026 by Habibul Bashar (99 innings).

750 RUNS IN A SERIES

Runs			Series	M	I	NO	HS	Avge	100	50
974	D.G.Bradman	A v E	1930	5	7	–	334	139.14	4	–
905	W.R.Hammond	E v A	1928-29	5	9	1	251	113.12	4	–
839	M.A.Taylor	A v E	1989	6	11	1	219	83.90	2	5
834	R.N.Harvey	A v SA	1952-53	5	9	–	205	92.66	4	3
829	I.V.A.Richards	WI v E	1976	4	7	–	291	118.42	3	2
827	C.L.Walcott	WI v A	1954-55	5	10	–	155	82.70	5	2
824	G.St A.Sobers	WI v P	1957-58	5	8	2	365*	137.33	3	3
810	D.G.Bradman	A v E	1936-37	5	9	–	270	90.00	3	1
806	D.G.Bradman	A v SA	1931-32	5	5	1	299*	201.50	4	–
798	B.C.Lara	WI v E	1993-94	5	8	–	375	99.75	2	2
779	E.de C.Weekes	WI v I	1948-49	5	7	–	194	111.28	4	2
774	S.M.Gavaskar	I v WI	1970-71	4	8	3	220	154.80	4	3
769	S.P.D.Smith	A v I	2014-15	4	8	2	192	128.16	4	2
766	A.N.Cook	E v A	2010-11	5	7	1	235*	127.66	3	2
765	B.C.Lara	WI v E	1995	6	10	1	179	85.00	3	3
761	Mudassar Nazar	P v I	1982-83	6	8	2	231	126.83	4	1
758	D.G.Bradman	A v E	1934	5	8	–	304	94.75	2	1
753	D.C.S.Compton	E v SA	1947	5	8	–	208	94.12	4	2
752	G.A.Gooch	E v I	1990	3	6	–	333	125.33	3	2

HIGHEST INDIVIDUAL INNINGS

400*	B.C.Lara	WI v E	St John's	2003-04
380	M.L.Hayden	A v Z	Perth	2003-04

375	B.C.Lara	WI v E	St John's	1993-94
374	D.P.M.D.Jayawardena	SL v SA	Colombo (SSC)	2006
365*	G.St A.Sobers	WI v P	Kingston	1957-58
364	L.Hutton	E v A	The Oval	1938
340	S.T.Jayasuriya	SL v I	Colombo (RPS)	1997-98
337	Hanif Mohammed	P v WI	Bridgetown	1957-58
336*	W.R.Hammond	E v NZ	Auckland	1932-33
334*	M.A.Taylor	A v P	Peshawar	1998-99
334	D.G.Bradman	A v E	Leeds	1930
333	G.A.Gooch	E v I	Lord's	1990
333	C.H.Gayle	WI v SL	Galle	2010-11
329*	M.J.Clarke	A v I	Sydney	2011-12
329	Inzamam-ul-Haq	P v NZ	Lahore	2001-02
325	A.Sandham	E v WI	Kingston	1929-30
319	V.Sehwag	I v SA	Chennai	2007-08
319	K.C.Sangakkara	SL v B	Chittagong	2013-14
317	C.H.Gayle	WI v SA	St John's	2004-05
313	Younus Khan	P v SL	Karachi	2008-09
311*	H.M.Amla	SA v E	The Oval	2012
311	R.B.Simpson	A v E	Manchester	1964
310*	J.H.Edrich	E v NZ	Leeds	1965
309	V.Sehwag	I v P	Multan	2003-04
307	R.M.Cowper	A v E	Melbourne	1965-66
304	D.G.Bradman	A v E	Leeds	1934
302	L.G.Rowe	WI v E	Bridgetown	1973-74
302	B.B.McCullum	NZ v I	Wellington	2013-14
299*	D.G.Bradman	A v SA	Adelaide	1931-32
299	M.D.Crowe	NZ v SL	Wellington	1990-91
294	A.N.Cook	E v I	Birmingham	2011
293	V.Sehwag	I v SL	Mumbai	2009-10
291	I.V.A.Richards	WI v E	The Oval	1976
291	R.R.Sarwan	WI v E	Bridgetown	2008-09
290	L.R.P.L.Taylor	NZ v A	Perth	2015-16
287	R.E.Foster	E v A	Sydney	1903-04
287	K.C.Sangakkara	SL v SA	Colombo (SSC)	2006
285*	P.B.H.May	E v WI	Birmingham	1957
281	V.V.S.Laxman	I v A	Calcutta	2000-01
280*	Javed Miandad	P v I	Hyderabad	1982-83
278*	A.B.de Villiers	SA v P	Abu Dhabi	2010-11
278	D.C.S.Compton	E v P	Nottingham	1954
277	B.C.Lara	WI v A	Sydney	1992-93
277	G.C.Smith	SA v E	Birmingham	2003
275*	D.J.Cullinan	SA v NZ	Auckland	1998-99
275	G.Kirsten	SA v E	Durban	1999-00
275	D.P.M.D.Jayawardena	SL v I	Ahmedabad	2009-10
274*	S.P.Fleming	NZ v SL	Colombo (SSC)	2002-03
274	R.G.Pollock	SA v A	Durban	1969-70
274	Zaheer Abbas	P v E	Birmingham	1971
271	Javed Miandad	P v NZ	Auckland	1988-89
270*	G.A.Headley	WI v E	Kingston	1934-35
270	D.G.Bradman	A v E	Melbourne	1936-37
270	R.S.Dravid	I v P	Rawalpindi	2003-04
270	K.C.Sangakkara	SL v Z	Bulawayo	2004
269*	A.C.Voges	A v WI	Hobart	2015-16
268	G.N.Yallop	A v P	Melbourne	1983-84
267*	B.A.Young	NZ v SL	Dunedin	1996-97
267	P.A.de Silva	SL v NZ	Wellington	1990-91

267	Younus Khan	P v I	Bangalore	2004-05
266	W.H.Ponsford	A v E	The Oval	1934
266	D.L.Houghton	Z v SL	Bulawayo	1994-95
263	A.N.Cook	E v P	Abu Dhabi	2015-16
262*	D.L.Amiss	E v WI	Kingston	1973-74
262	S.P.Fleming	NZ v SA	Cape Town	2005-06
261*	R.R.Sarwan	WI v B	Kingston	2004
261	F.M.M.Worrell	WI v E	Nottingham	1950
260	C.C.Hunte	WI v P	Kingston	1957-58
260	Javed Miandad	P v E	The Oval	1987
260	M.N.Samuels	WI v B	Khulna	2012-13
259*	M.J.Clarke	A v SA	Brisbane	2012-13
259	G.M.Turner	NZ v WI	Georgetown	1971-72
259	G.C.Smith	SA v E	Lord's	2003
258	T.W.Graveney	E v WI	Nottingham	1957
258	S.M.Nurse	WI v NZ	Christchurch	1968-69
258	B.A.Stokes	E v SA	Cape Town	2015-16
257*	Wasim Akram	P v Z	Sheikhupura	1996-97
257	R.T.Ponting	A v I	Melbourne	2003-04
256	R.B.Kanhai	WI v I	Calcutta	1958-59
256	K.F.Barrington	E v A	Manchester	1964
255*	D.J.McGlew	SA v NZ	Wellington	1952-53
254	D.G.Bradman	A v E	Lord's	1930
254	V.Sehwag	I v P	Lahore	2005-06
253*	H.M.Amla	SA v I	Nagpur	2009-10
253	S.T.Jayasuriya	SL v P	Faisalabad	2004-05
253	D.A.Warner	A v NZ	Perth	2015-16
251	W.R.Hammond	E v A	Sydney	1928-29
250	K.D.Walters	A v NZ	Christchurch	1976-77
250	S.F.A.F.Bacchus	WI v I	Kanpur	1978-79
250	J.L.Langer	A v E	Melbourne	2002-03

The highest for Bangladesh is 206 by Tamim Iqbal (v P, Khulna, 2015).

20 HUNDREDS

			200	Inn	E	A	SA	WI	NZ	I	P	SL	Z	B
51	S.R.Tendulkar	I	6	329	7	11	7	3	4	–	2	9	3	3
45	J.H.Kallis	SA	2	280	8	5	–	8	6	7	6	1	3	1
41	R.T.Ponting	A	6	287	8	–	8	7	2	8	5	1	1	1
38	K.C.Sangakkara	SL	11	233	3	1	3	3	4	5	10	–	2	7
36	R.S.Dravid	I	5	286	7	2	2	5	6	–	5	3	3	3
34	S.M.Gavaskar	I	4	214	4	8	–	13	2	–	5	2	–	–
34	B.C.Lara	WI	9	232	7	9	4	–	1	2	4	5	1	1
34	D.P.M.D.Jayawardena	SL	7	252	8	2	6	1	3	6	2	–	1	5
32	S.R.Waugh	A	1	260	10	–	2	7	2	2	3	3	1	2
31	Younus Khan	P	5	186	3	3	4	2	2	5	–	8	1	3
30	M.L.Hayden †	A	2	184	5	–	6	5	1	6	1	3	2	–
30	S.Chanderpaul	WI	2	280	5	5	5	–	2	7	1	–	1	4
29	D.G.Bradman	A	12	80	19	–	4	2	–	4	–	–	–	–
28	M.J.Clarke	A	4	198	7	–	5	1	4	7	1	3	–	–
28	A.N.Cook	E	3	226	–	4	2	5	3	5	4	3	–	2
27	G.C.Smith	SA	5	205	7	3	–	7	2	–	4	–	1	3
27	A.R.Border	A	2	265	8	–	–	3	5	4	6	1	–	–
26	G.St A.Sobers	WI	2	160	10	4	–	–	1	8	3	–	–	–
25	H.M.Amla	SA	4	156	6	5	–	1	4	5	2	1	–	1
25	Inzamam-ul-Haq	P	2	200	5	1	–	4	3	3	–	5	2	2

			200	Inn	E	A	SA	WI	NZ	I	P	SL	Z	B
24	G.S.Chappell	A	4	151	9	–	–	5	3	1	6	–	–	
24	Mohammad Yousuf	P	4	156	6	1	–	7	1	4	–	1	2	2
24	I.V.A.Richards	WI	3	182	8	5	–	–	1	8	2	–	2	2
23	V.Sehwag	I	6	180	2	3	5	2	2	–	4	5	–	–
23	K.P.Pietersen	E	3	181	–	4	3	3	2	2	6	2	3	–
23	J.L.Langer	A	3	182	5	–	2	3	4	3	4	2	–	–
22	Javed Miandad	P	6	189	2	6	–	2	7	5	–	1	–	–
22	W.R.Hammond	E	7	140	–	9	6	1	4	2	–	–	–	–
22	M.Azharuddin	I	–	147	6	2	2	4	–	2	–	3	5	–
22	M.C.Cowdrey	E	–	188	–	5	3	6	2	3	3	–	–	–
22	G.Boycott	E	1	193	–	7	1	5	2	4	3	–	–	–
22	I.R.Bell	E	1	205	–	4	2	2	1	4	4	2	–	3
21	R.N.Harvey	A	2	137	6	–	8	3	–	4	–	–	–	–
21	A.B.de Villiers	SA	2	176	2	5	–	6	–	3	4	5	–	–
21	G.Kirsten	SA	3	176	5	2	–	3	2	3	2	1	1	2
21	A.J.Strauss	E	–	178	–	4	3	6	3	3	2	–	–	–
21	D.C.Boon	A	1	190	7	–	3	3	6	1	1	–	–	–
20	K.F.Barrington	E	1	131	–	5	2	3	3	3	4	–	–	–
20	P.A.de Silva	SL	2	159	2	1	–	–	2	5	8	–	1	3
20	M.E.Waugh	A	–	209	6	–	4	4	1	1	3	1	–	–
20	G.A.Gooch	E	2	215	–	4	–	5	4	5	1	1	–	–

† Includes century scored for Australia v ICC in 2005-06.

The most for New Zealand is 17 by M.D.Crowe (131 innings), for Zimbabwe 12 by A.Flower (112), and for Bangladesh 7 by Tamim Iqbal (80 innings).

The most double hundreds by batsmen not included above are 6 by M.S.Atapattu (16 hundreds for Sri Lanka), 4 by L.Hutton (19 for England), 4 by C.G.Greenidge (19 for West Indies), 4 by Zaheer Abbas (12 for Pakistan), and 4 by B.B.McCullum (12 for New Zealand).

HIGHEST PARTNERSHIP FOR EACH WICKET

1st	415	N.D.McKenzie/G.C.Smith	SA v B	Chittagong	2007-08
2nd	576	S.T.Jayasuriya/R.S.Mahanama	SL v I	Colombo (RPS)	1997-98
3rd	624	K.C.Sangakkara/D.P.M.D.Jayawardena	SL v SA	Colombo (SSC)	2006
4th	449	A.C.Voges/S.E.Marsh	A v WI	Hobart	2015-16
5th	405	S.G.Barnes/D.G.Bradman	A v E	Sydney	1946-47
6th	399	B.A.Stokes/J.M.Bairstow	E v SA	Cape Town	2015-16
7th	347	D.St E.Atkinson/C.C.Depeiza	WI v A	Bridgetown	1954-55
8th	332	I.J.L.Trott/S.C.J.Broad	E v P	Lord's	2010
9th	195	M.V.Boucher/P.L.Symcox	SA v P	Johannesburg	1997-98
10th	198	J.E.Root/J.M.Anderson	E v I	Nottingham	2014

BOWLING RECORDS

200 WICKETS IN TESTS

Wkts			M	Balls	Runs	Avge	5 wI	10 wM
800	M.Muralitharan	SL/ICC	133	44039	18180	22.72	67	22
708	S.K.Warne	A	145	40705	17995	25.41	37	10
619	A.Kumble	I	132	40850	18355	29.65	35	8
563	G.D.McGrath	A	124	29248	12186	21.64	29	3
519	C.A.Walsh	WI	132	30019	12688	24.44	22	3
434	Kapil Dev	I	131	27740	12867	29.64	23	2
433	J.M.Anderson	E	113	25185	12638	29.18	18	2
431	R.J.Hadlee	NZ	86	21918	9612	22.30	36	9
421	S.M.Pollock	SA	108	24453	9733	23.11	16	1

Wkts			M	Balls	Runs	Avge	5 wI	10 wM
417	Harbhajan Singh	I	103	28580	13537	32.46	25	5
414	Wasim Akram	P	104	22627	9779	23.62	25	5
406	D.W.Steyn	SA	82	16956	9150	22.53	25	5
405	C.E.L.Ambrose	WI	98	22104	8500	20.98	22	3
390	M.Ntini	SA	101	20834	11242	28.82	18	4
383	I.T.Botham	E	102	21815	10878	28.40	27	4
376	M.D.Marshall	WI	81	17584	7876	20.94	22	4
373	Waqar Younis	P	87	16224	8788	23.56	22	5
362	Imran Khan	P	88	19458	8258	22.81	23	6
362	D.L.Vettori	NZ/ICC	113	28814	12441	34.36	20	3
355	D.K.Lillee	A	70	18467	8493	23.92	23	7
355	W.P.J.U.C.Vaas	SL	111	23438	10501	29.58	12	2
333	S.C.J.Broad	E	91	18885	9545	28.66	15	2
330	A.A.Donald	SA	72	15519	7344	22.25	20	3
325	R.G.D.Willis	E	90	17357	8190	25.20	16	–
313	M.G.Johnson	A	73	16001	8891	28.40	12	3
311	Z.Khan	I	92	18785	10247	32.94	11	1
310	B.Lee	A	76	16531	9554	30.81	10	–
309	L.R.Gibbs	WI	79	27115	8989	29.09	18	2
307	F.S.Trueman	E	67	15178	6625	21.57	17	3
297	D.L.Underwood	E	86	21862	7674	25.83	17	6
297	H.M.R.K.B.Herath	SL	67	19124	8873	29.87	23	5
292	J.H.Kallis	SA/ICC	166	20232	9535	32.65	5	–
291	C.J.McDermott	A	71	16586	8332	28.63	14	2
266	B.S.Bedi	I	67	21364	7637	28.71	14	1
261	Danish Kaneria	P	61	17697	9082	34.79	15	2
259	J.Garner	WI	58	13169	5433	20.97	7	–
259	J.N.Gillespie	A	71	14234	6770	26.13	8	–
255	G.P.Swann	E	60	15349	7642	29.96	17	3
252	J.B.Statham	E	70	16056	6261	24.84	9	1
249	M.A.Holding	WI	60	12680	5898	23.68	13	2
248	R.Benaud	A	63	19108	6704	27.03	16	1
248	M.J.Hoggard	E	67	13909	7564	30.50	7	1
246	G.D.McKenzie	A	60	17681	7328	29.78	16	3
242	M.Morkel	SA	71	13640	7099	29.33	6	–
242	B.S.Chandrasekhar	I	58	15963	7199	29.74	16	2
236	A.V.Bedser	E	51	15918	5876	24.89	15	5
236	J.Srinath	I	67	15104	7196	30.49	10	1
236	Abdul Qadir	P	67	17126	7742	32.80	15	5
235	G.St A.Sobers	WI	93	21599	7999	34.03	6	–
234	A.R.Caddick	E	62	13558	6999	29.91	13	1
233	C.S.Martin	NZ	71	14026	7878	33.81	10	1
229	D.Gough	E	58	11821	6503	28.39	9	–
228	R.R.Lindwall	A	61	13650	5251	23.03	12	–
226	S.J.Harmison	E/ICC	63	13375	7192	31.82	8	1
226	A.Flintoff	E/ICC	79	14951	7410	32.78	3	–
218	C.L.Cairns	NZ	62	11698	6410	29.40	13	1
216	C.V.Grimmett	A	37	14513	5231	24.21	21	7
216	H.H.Streak	Z	65	13559	6079	28.14	7	–
212	M.G.Hughes	A	53	12285	6017	28.38	7	1
208	S.C.G.MacGill	A	44	11237	6038	29.02	12	2
208	Saqlain Mushtaq	P	49	14070	6206	29.83	13	3
208	P.M.Siddle	A	61	12713	6216	29.88	8	–
202	A.M.E.Roberts	WI	47	11136	5174	25.61	11	2
202	J.A.Snow	E	49	12021	5387	26.66	8	1
201	I.Sharma	I	68	13779	7417	36.90	7	1
200	J.R.Thomson	A	51	10535	5601	28.00	8	–

The most for Bangladesh is 147 in 42 Tests by Shakib Al Hasan.

35 OR MORE WICKETS IN A SERIES

Wkts			Series	M	Balls	Runs	Avge	5 wI	10 wM
49	S.F.Barnes	E v SA	1913-14	4	1356	536	10.93	7	3
46	J.C.Laker	E v A	1956	5	1703	442	9.60	4	2
44	C.V.Grimmett	A v SA	1935-36	5	2077	642	14.59	5	3
42	T.M.Alderman	A v E	1981	6	1950	893	21.26	4	–
41	R.M.Hogg	A v E	1978-79	6	1740	527	12.85	5	2
41	T.M.Alderman	A v E	1989	6	1616	712	17.36	6	1
40	Imran Khan	P v I	1982-83	6	1339	558	13.95	4	2
40	S.K.Warne	A v E	2005	5	1517	797	19.92	3	2
39	A.V.Bedser	E v A	1953	5	1591	682	17.48	5	1
39	D.K.Lillee	A v E	1981	6	1870	870	22.30	2	1
38	M.W.Tate	E v A	1924-25	5	2528	881	23.18	5	1
37	W.J.Whitty	A v SA	1910-11	5	1395	632	17.08	2	–
37	H.J.Tayfield	SA v E	1956-57	5	2280	636	17.18	4	1
37	M.G.Johnson	A v E	2013-14	5	1132	517	13.97	3	–
36	A.E.E.Vogler	SA v E	1909-10	5	1349	783	21.75	4	1
36	A.A.Mailey	A v E	1920-21	5	1465	946	26.27	4	2
36	G.D.McGrath	A v E	1997	6	1499	701	19.47	2	–
35	G.A.Lohmann	E v SA	1895-96	3	520	203	5.80	4	2
35	B.S.Chandrasekhar	I v E	1972-73	5	1747	662	18.91	4	–
35	M.D.Marshall	WI v E	1988	5	1219	443	12.65	3	1

The most for New Zealand is 33 by R.J.Hadlee (3 Tests v A, 1985-86), for Sri Lanka 30 by M.Muralitharan (3 Tests v Z, 2001-02), for Zimbabwe 22 by H.H.Streak (3 Tests v P, 1994-95), and for Bangladesh 18 by Enamul Haque II (2 Tests v Z, 2004-05) and 18 by Shakib Al Hasan (3 Tests v Z, 2014-15).

15 OR MORE WICKETS IN A TEST († On debut)

19- 90	J.C.Laker	E v A	Manchester	1956
17-159	S.F.Barnes	E v SA	Johannesburg	1913-14
16-136†	N.D.Hirwani	I v WI	Madras	1987-88
16-137†	R.A.L.Massie	A v E	Lord's	1972
16-220	M.Muralitharan	SL v E	The Oval	1998
15- 28	J.Briggs	E v SA	Cape Town	1888-89
15- 45	G.A.Lohmann	E v SA	Port Elizabeth	1895-96
15- 99	C.Blythe	E v SA	Leeds	1907
15-104	H.Verity	E v A	Lord's	1934
15-123	R.J.Hadlee	NZ v A	Brisbane	1985-86
15-124	W.Rhodes	E v A	Melbourne	1903-04
15-217	Harbhajan Singh	I v A	Madras	2000-01

The best analysis for South Africa is 13-132 by M.Ntini (v WI, Port-of-Spain, 2004-05), for West Indies 14-149 by M.A.Holding (v E, The Oval, 1976), for Pakistan 14-116 by Imran Khan (v SL, Lahore, 1981-82), for Zimbabwe 11-257 by A.G.Huckle (v NZ, Bulawayo, 1997-98), and for Bangladesh 12-200 by Enamul Haque II (v Z, Dhaka, 2004-05).

NINE OR MORE WICKETS IN AN INNINGS

10-53	J.C.Laker	E v A	Manchester	1956
10-74	A.Kumble	I v P	Delhi	1998-99
9-28	G.A.Lohmann	E v SA	Johannesburg	1895-96
9-37	J.C.Laker	E v A	Manchester	1956
9-51	M.Muralitharan	SL v Z	Kandy	2001-02
9-52	R.J.Hadlee	NZ v A	Brisbane	1985-86
9-56	Abdul Qadir	P v E	Lahore	1987-88
9-57	D.E.Malcolm	E v SA	The Oval	1994

9- 65	M.Muralitharan	SL v E	The Oval	1998
9- 69	J.M.Patel	I v A	Kanpur	1959-60
9- 83	Kapil Dev	I v WI	Ahmedabad	1983-84
9- 86	Sarfraz Nawaz	P v A	Melbourne	1978-79
9- 95	J.M.Noreiga	WI v I	Port-of-Spain	1970-71
9-102	S.P.Gupte	I v WI	Kanpur	1958-59
9-103	S.F.Barnes	E v SA	Johannesburg	1913-14
9-113	H.J.Tayfield	SA v E	Johannesburg	1956-57
9-121	A.A.Mailey	A v E	Melbourne	1920-21
9-127	H.M.R.K.B.Herath	SL v P	Colombo (SSC)	2014

The best analysis for Zimbabwe is 8-109 by P.A.Strang (v NZ, Bulawayo, 2000-01), and for Bangladesh 8-39 by Taijul Islam (v Z, Dhaka, 2014-15).

HAT-TRICKS

F.R.Spofforth	Australia v England	Melbourne	1878-79
W.Bates	England v Australia	Melbourne	1882-83
J.Briggs[7]	England v Australia	Sydney	1891-92
G.A.Lohmann	England v South Africa	Port Elizabeth	1895-96
J.T.Hearne	England v Australia	Leeds	1899
H.Trumble	Australia v England	Melbourne	1901-02
H.Trumble	Australia v England	Melbourne	1903-04
T.J.Matthews (2)[2]	Australia v South Africa	Manchester	1912
M.J.C.Allom[1]	England v New Zealand	Christchurch	1929-30
T.W.J.Goddard	England v South Africa	Johannesburg	1938-39
P.J.Loader	England v West Indies	Leeds	1957
L.F.Kline	Australia v South Africa	Cape Town	1957-58
W.W.Hall	West Indies v Pakistan	Lahore	1958-59
G.M.Griffin[7]	South Africa v England	Lord's	1960
L.R.Gibbs	West Indies v Australia	Adelaide	1960-61
P.J.Petherick[1/7]	New Zealand v Pakistan	Lahore	1976-77
C.A.Walsh[3]	West Indies v Australia	Brisbane	1988-89
M.G.Hughes[3/7]	Australia v West Indies	Perth	1988-89
D.W.Fleming[1]	Australia v Pakistan	Rawalpindi	1994-95
S.K.Warne	Australia v England	Melbourne	1994-95
D.G.Cork	England v West Indies	Manchester	1995
D.Gough[7]	England v Australia	Sydney	1998-99
Wasim Akram[4]	Pakistan v Sri Lanka	Lahore	1998-99
Wasim Akram[4]	Pakistan v Sri Lanka	Dhaka	1998-99
D.N.T.Zoysa[7]	Sri Lanka v Zimbabwe	Harare	1999-00
Abdul Razzaq	Pakistan v Sri Lanka	Galle	2000-01
G.D.McGrath	Australia v West Indies	Perth	2000-01
Harbhajan Singh	India v Australia	Calcutta	2000-01
Mohammad Sami[7]	Pakistan v Sri Lanka	Lahore	2001-02
J.J.C.Lawson[7]	West Indies v Australia	Bridgetown	2002-03
Alok Kapali[7]	Bangladesh v Pakistan	Peshawar	2003
A.M.Blignaut	Zimbabwe v Bangladesh	Harare	2003-04
M.J.Hoggard	England v West Indies	Bridgetown	2003-04
J.E.C.Franklin	New Zealand v Bangladesh	Dhaka	2004-05
I.K.Pathan[6/7]	India v Pakistan	Karachi	2005-06
R.J.Sidebottom[7]	England v New Zealand	Hamilton	2007-08
P.M.Siddle	Australia v England	Brisbane	2010-11
S.C.J.Broad	England v India	Nottingham	2011
Sohag Gazi	Bangladesh v New Zealand	Chittagong	2013-14
S.C.J.Broad[7]	England v Sri Lanka	Leeds	2014

[1] On debut. [2] Hat-trick in each innings. [3] Involving both innings. [4] In successive Tests. [5] His first 3 balls (second over of the match). [6] The fourth, fifth and sixth balls of the match. [7] On losing side.

WICKET-KEEPING RECORDS
150 DISMISSALS IN TESTS†

Total			Tests	Ct	St
555	M.V.Boucher	South Africa/ICC	147	532	23
416	A.C.Gilchrist	Australia	96	379	37
395	I.A.Healy	Australia	119	366	29
355	R.W.Marsh	Australia	96	343	12
294	M.S.Dhoni	India	90	256	38
270	B.J.Haddin	Australia	66	262	8
270†	P.J.L.Dujon	West Indies	79	265	5
269	A.P.E.Knott	England	95	250	19
256	M.J.Prior	England	79	243	13
241†	A.J.Stewart	England	82	227	14
228	Wasim Bari	Pakistan	81	201	27
219	R.D.Jacobs	West Indies	65	207	12
219	T.G.Evans	England	91	173	46
217	D.Ramdin	West Indies	74	205	12
206	Kamran Akmal	Pakistan	53	184	22
201†	A.C.Parore	New Zealand	67	194	7
198	S.M.H.Kirmani	India	88	160	38
189	D.L.Murray	West Indies	62	181	8
187	A.T.W.Grout	Australia	51	163	24
178†	B.B.McCullum	New Zealand	52	168	11
176	I.D.S.Smith	New Zealand	63	168	8
174	R.W.Taylor	England	57	167	7
165	R.C.Russell	England	54	153	12
156	H.A.P.W.Jayawardena	Sri Lanka	58	124	32
152	D.J.Richardson	South Africa	42	150	2
151†	K.C.Sangakkara	Sri Lanka	48	131	20
151†	A.Flower	Zimbabwe	55	142	9

The most for Bangladesh is 87 (78 ct, 9 st) by Khaled Masud in 44 Tests.

† *Excluding catches taken in the field*

25 OR MORE DISMISSALS IN A SERIES

29	B.J.Haddin	Australia v England	2013
28	R.W.Marsh	Australia v England	1982-83
27 (inc 2st)	R.C.Russell	England v South Africa	1995-96
27 (inc 2st)	I.A.Healy	Australia v England (6 Tests)	1997
26 (inc 3st)	J.H.B.Waite	South Africa v New Zealand	1961-62
26	R.W.Marsh	Australia v West Indies (6 Tests)	1975-76
26 (inc 5st)	I.A.Healy	Australia v England (6 Tests)	1993
26 (inc 1st)	M.V.Boucher	South Africa v England	1998
26 (inc 2st)	A.C.Gilchrist	Australia v England	2001
26 (inc 2st)	A.C.Gilchrist	Australia v England	2006-07
25 (inc 2st)	I.A.Healy	Australia v England	1994-95
25 (inc 2st)	A.C.Gilchrist	Australia v England	2002-03
25	A.C.Gilchrist	Australia v India	2007-08

TEN OR MORE DISMISSALS IN A TEST

11	R.C.Russell	England v South Africa	Johannesburg	1995-96
11	A.B.de Villiers	South Africa v Pakistan	Johannesburg	2012-13
10	R.W.Taylor	England v India	Bombay	1979-80
10	A.C.Gilchrist	Australia v New Zealand	Hamilton	1999-00

SEVEN DISMISSALS IN AN INNINGS

7	Wasim Bari	Pakistan v New Zealand	Auckland	1978-79
7	R.W.Taylor	England v India	Bombay	1979-80

| 7 | I.D.S.Smith | New Zealand v Sri Lanka | Hamilton | 1990-91 |
| 7 | R.D.Jacobs | West Indies v Australia | Melbourne | 2000-01 |

FIVE STUMPINGS IN AN INNINGS

| 5 | K.S.More | India v West Indies | Madras | 1987-88 |

FIELDING RECORDS
100 CATCHES IN TESTS

Total			Tests	Total			Tests
210	R.S.Dravid	India/ICC	164	120	I.T.Botham	England	102
205	D.P.M.D.Jayawardena	Sri Lanka	149	120	M.C.Cowdrey	England	114
200	J.H.Kallis	South Africa/ICC	166	117	Younus Khan	Pakistan	104
196	R.T.Ponting	Australia	168	115	C.L.Hooper	West Indies	102
181	M.E.Waugh	Australia	128	115	S.R.Tendulkar	India	200
171	S.P.Fleming	New Zealand	111	112	L.R.P.L.Taylor	New Zealand	69
169	G.C.Smith	South Africa/ICC	117	112	S.R.Waugh	Australia	168
164	B.C.Lara	West Indies/ICC	131	110	R.B.Simpson	Australia	62
157	M.A.Taylor	Australia	104	110	W.R.Hammond	England	85
156	A.R.Border	Australia	156	109	G.St A.Sobers	West Indies	93
135	V.V.S.Laxman	India	134	108	S.M.Gavaskar	India	125
134	M.J.Clarke	Australia	115	105	I.M.Chappell	Australia	75
128	M.L.Hayden	Australia	103	105	M.Azharuddin	India	99
125	A.N.Cook	England	126	105	G.P.Thorpe	England	100
125	S.K.Warne	Australia	145	104†	A.B.de Villiers	South Africa	82
122	G.S.Chappell	Australia	87	103	G.A.Gooch	England	118
122	I.V.A.Richards	West Indies	121	100	I.R.Bell	England	118
121	A.J.Strauss	England	100				

The most for Zimbabwe is 60 by A.D.R.Campbell (60) and for Bangladesh 25 by Mohammad Ashraful (61).

† *Excluding catches taken when wicket-keeping.*

15 CATCHES IN A SERIES

| 15 | J.M.Gregory | Australia v England | | 1920-21 |

SEVEN OR MORE CATCHES IN A TEST

8	A.M.Rahane	India v Sri Lanka	Galle	2015
7	G.S.Chappell	Australia v England	Perth	1974-75
7	Yajurvindra Singh	India v England	Bangalore	1976-77
7	H.P.Tillekeratne	Sri Lanka v New Zealand	Colombo (SSC)	1992-93
7	S.P.Fleming	New Zealand v Zimbabwe	Harare	1997-98
7	M.L.Hayden	Australia v Sri Lanka	Galle	2003-04

FIVE CATCHES IN AN INNINGS

5	V.Y.Richardson	Australia v South Africa	Durban	1935-36
5	Yajurvindra Singh	India v England	Bangalore	1976-77
5	M.Azharuddin	India v Pakistan	Karachi	1989-90
5	K.Srikkanth	India v Australia	Perth	1991-92
5	S.P.Fleming	New Zealand v Zimbabwe	Harare	1997-98
5	G.C.Smith	South Africa v Australia	Perth	2012-13
5	D.J.G.Sammy	West Indies v India	Mumbai	2013-14
5	D.M.Bravo	West Indies v Bangladesh	Kingstown	2014
5	A.M.Rahane	India v Sri Lanka	Galle	2015
5	J.Blackwood	West Indies v Sri Lanka	Colombo (PSS)	2015-16

100 TEST MATCH APPEARANCES

Opponents

			E	A	SA	WI	NZ	I	P	SL	Z	B
200	S.R.Tendulkar	India	32	39	25	21	24	–	18	25	9	7
168†	R.T.Ponting	Australia	35	–	26	24	17	29	15	14	3	4
168	S.R.Waugh	Australia	46	–	16	32	23	18	20	8	3	2
166†	J.H.Kallis	South Africa/ICC	31	28	–	24	18	18	19	15	6	6
164	S.Chanderpaul	West Indies	35	20	24	–	21	25	14	7	8	10
164†	R.S.Dravid	India/ICC	21	32	21	23	15	–	15	20	9	7
156	A.R.Border	Australia	47	–	6	31	23	20	22	7	–	–
149	D.P.M.D.Jayawardena	Sri Lanka	23	16	18	11	13	18	29	–	8	13
147†	M.V.Boucher	South Africa/ICC	25	20	–	24	17	14	15	17	6	8
145†	S.K.Warne	Australia	36	–	24	19	20	14	15	13	1	2
134	V.V.S.Laxman	India	17	29	19	22	10	–	15	13	6	3
134	K.C.Sangakkara	Sri Lanka	22	11	17	12	12	17	23	–	5	15
133†	M.Muralitharan	Sri Lanka/ICC	16	12	15	12	14	22	16	–	14	11
133	A.J.Stewart	England	–	33	23	24	16	9	13	9	6	–
132	A.Kumble	India	19	20	21	17	11	–	15	18	7	4
132	C.A.Walsh	West Indies	36	38	10	–	10	15	18	3	2	–
131	Kapil Dev	India	27	20	4	25	10	–	29	14	2	–
131†	B.C.Lara	West Indies/ICC	30	30	18	–	11	17	12	8	2	2
128	M.E.Waugh	Australia	29	–	18	28	14	14	15	9	1	–
126	A.N.Cook	England	–	30	15	17	13	20	14	13	–	4
125	S.M.Gavaskar	India	38	20	–	27	9	–	24	7	–	–
124	Javed Miandad	Pakistan	22	24	–	18	18	28	–	12	3	–
124†	G.D.McGrath	Australia	30	–	17	23	14	11	17	8	1	2
121	I.V.A.Richards	West Indies	36	34	–	–	7	28	16	–	–	–
120†	Inzamam-ul-Haq	Pakistan/ICC	19	13	13	15	12	10	–	20	11	6
119	I.A.Healy	Australia	33	–	12	28	11	9	14	11	1	–
118	I.R.Bell	England	–	33	11	12	13	20	13	10	–	6
118	G.A.Gooch	England	–	42	3	26	15	19	10	3	–	–
117	D.I.Gower	England	–	42	–	19	13	24	17	2	–	–
117†	G.C.Smith	South Africa/ICC	21	21	–	14	13	15	16	7	2	8
116	D.L.Haynes	West Indies	36	33	1	–	10	19	16	1	–	–
116	D.B.Vengsarkar	India	26	24	–	25	11	–	22	8	–	–
115	M.A.Atherton	England	–	33	18	27	11	7	11	4	4	–
115†	M.J.Clarke	Australia	35	–	14	12	11	22	10	8	–	2
114	M.C.Cowdrey	England	–	43	14	21	18	8	10	–	–	–
113	J.M.Anderson	England	–	26	20	14	12	19	10	8	2	2
113	S.C.Ganguly	India	12	24	17	12	8	–	12	14	9	5
113†	D.L.Vettori	New Zealand/ICC	17	18	14	10	–	15	9	11	9	9
111	S.P.Fleming	New Zealand	19	14	15	11	–	13	9	13	11	6
111	W.P.J.U.C.Vaas	Sri Lanka	15	12	11	9	10	14	18	–	15	7
110	S.T.Jayasuriya	Sri Lanka	14	13	15	10	13	10	17	–	13	5
110	C.H.Lloyd	West Indies	34	29	–	–	8	28	11	–	–	–
108	G.Boycott	England	–	38	7	29	15	13	6	–	–	–
108	C.G.Greenidge	West Indies	29	32	–	–	10	23	14	–	–	–
108	S.M.Pollock	South Africa	23	13	–	16	11	12	12	13	5	3
107	D.C.Boon	Australia	31	–	6	22	17	11	11	9	–	–
106	A.B.de Villiers	South Africa	20	20	–	13	10	17	12	7	3	4
105†	J.L.Langer	Australia	21	–	11	18	14	14	13	8	2	4
104	K.P.Pietersen	England	–	27	10	14	8	16	14	11	–	4
104†	V.Sehwag	India/ICC	17	23	15	10	12	–	9	11	3	4
104	M.A.Taylor	Australia	33	–	11	20	11	9	12	8	–	–
104	Wasim Akram	Pakistan	18	13	4	17	9	12	–	19	10	2

			E	A	SA	WI	NZ	I	P	SL	Z	B
104	Younus Khan	Pakistan	13	8	14	10	9	9	–	29	5	7
103	C.H.Gayle	West Indies	20	8	16	–	12	14	8	10	8	7
103	Harbhajan Singh	India	14	18	11	11	13	–	9	16	7	4
103†	M.L.Hayden	Australia	20	–	19	15	11	18	6	7	2	4
103	Salim Malik	Pakistan	19	15	1	7	18	22	–	15	6	–
102	I.T.Botham	England	–	36	–	20	15	14	14	3	–	–
102	C.L.Hooper	West Indies	24	25	10	–	2	19	14	6	2	–
101	G.Kirsten	South Africa	22	18	–	13	13	10	11	9	3	2
101	B.B.McCullum	New Zealand	16	16	13	13	–	10	8	12	4	9
101	M.Ntini	South Africa	18	15	–	15	11	10	9	12	3	8
100	G.P.Thorpe	England	–	16	16	27	13	5	8	9	2	4
100	A.J.Strauss	England	–	20	16	18	9	12	13	8	–	4

† Includes appearance in the Australia v ICC 'Test' in 2005-06. The most for Zimbabwe is 67 by G.W.Flower, and for Bangladesh 61 by Mohammad Ashraful.

100 CONSECUTIVE TEST APPEARANCES

153	A.R.Border	Australia	March 1979 to March 1994
124	A.N.Cook	England	May 2006 to January 2016
107	M.E.Waugh	Australia	June 1993 to October 2002
106	S.M.Gavaskar	India	January 1975 to February 1987
101†	B.B.McCullum	New Zealand	March 2004 to February 2016

† The entire duration of his Test career.

50 TESTS AS CAPTAIN

			Won	Lost	Drawn	Tied
109	G.C.Smith	South Africa	53	29	27	–
93	A.R.Border	Australia	32	22	38	1
80	S.P.Fleming	New Zealand	28	27	25	–
77	R.T.Ponting	Australia	48	16	13	–
74	C.H.Lloyd	West Indies	36	12	26	–
60	M.S.Dhoni	India	27	18	15	–
57	S.R.Waugh	Australia	41	9	7	–
56	A.Ranatunga	Sri Lanka	12	19	25	–
54	M.A.Atherton	England	13	21	20	–
53	W.J.Cronje	South Africa	27	11	15	–
51	M.P.Vaughan	England	26	11	14	–
50	I.V.A.Richards	West Indies	27	8	15	–
50	M.A.Taylor	Australia	26	13	11	–
50	A.J.Strauss	England	24	11	15	–

The most for Pakistan is 48 by Imran Khan, for Zimbabwe 21 by A.D.R.Campbell and H.H.Streak, and for Bangladesh 24 by Mushfiqur Rahim.

50 TEST UMPIRING APPEARANCES

128	S.A.Bucknor	(West Indies)	28.04.1989 to 22.03.2009
108	R.E.Koertzen	(South Africa)	26.12.1992 to 24.07.2010
101	Alim Dar	(Pakistan)	21.10.2003 to 16.01.2016
95	D.J.Harper	(Australia)	28.11.1998 to 23.06.2011
92	D.R.Shepherd	(England)	01.08.1985 to 07.06.2005
84	B.F.Bowden	(New Zealand)	11.03.2000 to 03.05.2015
78	D.B.Hair	(Australia)	25.01.1992 to 08.06.2008
74	S.J.A.Taufel	(Australia)	26.12.2000 to 20.08.2012
73	S.Venkataraghavan	(India)	29.01.1993 to 20.01.2004
66	H.D.Bird	(England)	05.07.1973 to 24.06.1996
57	S.J.Davis	(Australia)	27.11.1997 to 25.04.2015

THE FIRST-CLASS COUNTIES REGISTER, RECORDS AND 2015 AVERAGES

All statistics are to 14 March 2016.

ABBREVIATIONS – General

*	not out/unbroken partnership	IT20	International Twenty20
b	born	l-o	limited-overs
BB	Best innings bowling analysis	LOI	Limited-Overs Internationals
Cap	Awarded 1st XI County Cap	Tests	International Test Matches
f-c	first-class	F-c Tours	Overseas tours involving first-class
HS	Highest Score		appearances

Awards

PCA 2015   Professional Cricketers' Association Player of 2015
Wisden 2014   One of *Wisden Cricketers' Almanack*'s Five Cricketers of 2014
YC 2015   Cricket Writers' Club Young Cricketer of 2015

ECB Competitions

BHC	Benson & Hedges Cup (1972-2002)	CSK	Chennai Super Kings
CB40	Clydesdale Bank 40 (2010-12)	DC	Deccan Chargers
CC	LV= County Championship	DD	Delhi Daredevils
CGT	Cheltenham & Gloucester Trophy (2001-06)	EL	England Lions
FPT	Friends Provident Trophy (2007-09)	EP	Eastern Province
NL	National League (1999-2005)	GW	Griqualand West
NWT	NatWest Trophy (1981-2000)	HB	Habib Bank Limited
P40	NatWest PRO 40 League (2006-09)	HH	Hobart Hurricanes
RLC	Royal London One-Day Cup (2014-15)	KKR	Kolkata Knight Riders
SL	Sunday League (1969-98)	KRL	Khan Research Laboratories
T20	Twenty20 Competition	KXIP	Kings XI Punjab
Y40	Yorkshire Bank 40 (2013)	KZN	KwaZulu-Natal Inland
Education		ME	Mashonaland Eagles
Ac	Academy	MI	Mumbai Indians
BHS	Boys' High School	MR	Melbourne Renegades
C	College	MS	Melbourne Stars
CS	Comprehensive School	MT	Matabeleland Tuskers
GS	Grammar School	MWR	Mid West Rhinos
HS	High School	NBP	National Bank of Pakistan
I	Institute	ND	Northern Districts
S	School	NSW	New South Wales
SFC	Sixth Form College	NT	Northern Transvaal
SS	Secondary School	NW	North West
TC	Technical College	(O)FS	(Orange) Free State
U	University	PDSC	Prime Doleshwar Sporting Club
UWIC	University of Wales Institute, Cardiff	PIA	Pakistan International Airlines
Playing Categories		PS	Perth Scorchers
LBG	Bowls right-arm leg-breaks and googlies	PT	Pakistan Television
LF	Bowls left-arm fast	PTC	Pakistan Telecommunication Co
LFM	Bowls left-arm fast-medium	PW	Pune Warriors
LHB	Bats left-handed	Q	Queensland
LM	Bowls left-arm medium pace	RCB	Royal Challengers Bangalore
LMF	Bowls left-arm medium fast	RR	Rajasthan Royals
OB	Bowls right-arm off-breaks	SH	Sunrisers Hyderabad
RF	Bowls right-arm fast	SJD	Sheikh Jamal Dhanmondi
RFM	Bowls right-arm fast-medium	SNGPL	Sui Northern Gas Pipelines Limited
RHB	Bats right-handed	SR	Southern Rocks
RM	Bowls right-arm medium pace	SS	Sydney Sixers
RMF	Bowls right-arm medium-fast	SSGC	Sui Southern Gas Corporation
SLA	Bowls left-arm 'Chinamen'	ST	Sydney Thunder
SLC	Bowls left-arm leg-breaks	Tas	Tasmania
WK	Wicket-keeper	T&T	Trinidad & Tobago
Teams (see also p 227)		Vic	Victoria
AS	Adelaide Strikers	WA	Western Australia
BH	Brisbane Heat	WAPDA	Water & Power Development Authority.
CC&C	Combined Campuses & Colleges	WP	Western Province
CD	Central Districts	ZTB	Zarai Taraqiati Bank Limited

DERBYSHIRE

Formation of Present Club: 4 November 1870
Inaugural First-Class Match: 1871
Colours: Chocolate, Amber and Pale Blue
Badge: Rose and Crown
County Champions: (1) 1936
NatWest Trophy Winners: (1) 1981
Benson and Hedges Cup Winners: (1) 1993
Sunday League Winners: (1) 1990
Twenty20 Cup Winners: (0) best – Quarter-Finalist 2005

Chief Executive: Simon Storey, Derbyshire County Cricket Club, The 3aaa County Ground, Nottingham Road, Derby, DE21 6DA • Tel: 01332 388101 • Fax: 0844 500 8322 • Email: info@derbyshireccc.com • Web: www. derbyshireccc.com • Twitter: @DerbyshireCCC (20,236 followers)

Elite Performance Director: Graeme Welch. **Elite Performance Coaches**: Ant Botha and John Sadler. **Captain**: W.L.Madsen (f-c) and W.J.Durston (l-o). **Vice-Captain**: B.A.Godleman (f-c) and T.Poynton (l-o). **Overseas Players**: J.D.S.Neesham (T20 only) and H.D.Rutherford. **2016 Beneficiary**: None. **Head Groundsman**: Neil Godrich. **Scorer**: John Brown. ‡ New registration. NQ Not qualified for England.

‡NQ**BROOM, Neil** Trevor, b Christchurch, New Zealand 20 Nov 1983. Older brother of D.J.Broom (Otago 2009-10 to 2012-13). RHB, RM. Squad No 4. Canterbury 2002-03 to 2014-15. Otago 2005-06 to date. LOI (NZ): 22 (2008-09 to 2009-10); HS 71 v B (Napier) 2009-10. IT20 (NZ): 10 (2008-09 to 2013-14); HS 36 v A (Sydney) 2008-09. F-c Tours (NZ A): I 2008-09, 2013-14. HS 203* Otago v ND (Queenstown) 2010-11. BB 1-8 Canterbury v Otago (Christchurch) 2002-03. LO HS 164 Otago v Canterbury (Timaru) 2009-10. LO BB 2-59 NZ A v India A (Chennai) 2008-09. T20 HS 117*. T20 BB 2-19.

‡**CARTER, Andrew** (Lincoln C), b Lincoln 27 Aug 1988. 6'4". RHB, RM. Squad No 7. Nottinghamshire 2009-15. Essex 2010 (on loan). Lincolnshire 2007-10. HS 24* Nt v Worcs (Nottingham) 2015. BB 5-40 Ex v Kent (Canterbury) 2010. LO HS 12 v Sussex (Hove) 2009 (P40). LO BB 4-45 v Durham (Nottingham) 2012 (CB40). T20 HS 5*. T20 BB 4-20.

CORK, Gregory Teodor Gerald (Denstone C), b Derby 29 Sep 1994. Son of D.G.Cork (Derbyshire, Lancashire, Hampshire and England 1990-2011). 6'2". RHB, LMF. Squad No 14. Derbyshire 2nd XI debut 2011. Awaiting f-c debut. LO HS – . LO BB 2-17 v Somerset (Taunton) 2015 (RLC). T20 HS 13*. T20 BB 2-36.

COTTON, Benjamin David (Clayton Hall C; Stoke-on-Trent SFC), b Stoke-on-Trent, Staffs 13 Sep 1993. 6'4". RHB, RMF. Squad No 36. Debut (Derbyshire) 2014. Derbyshire 2nd XI debut 2011. HS 43 v Leics (Derby) 2015. BB 4-20 v Leics (Derby) 2014. LO HS 18* v Yorks (Scarborough) 2014 (RLC). LO BB 3-11 v Somerset (Taunton) 2015 (RLC). T20 HS 8. T20 BB 2-19.

CRITCHLEY, Matthew James John (St Michael's HS, Chorley), b Preston, Lancs 13 Aug 1996. 6'2". RHB, LB. Squad No 20. Debut (Derbyshire) 2015. Derbyshire 2nd XI debut 2014. HS 137* v Northants (Derby) 2015. BB 3-50 v Lancs (Southport) 2015. LO HS 22* v Worcs (Derby) 2015 (RLC). LO BB 4-48 v Northants (Derby) 2015 (RLC).

DAVIS, William Samuel (Stafford GS), b 6 Mar 1996. 6'1". RHB, RFM. Squad No 44. Debut (Derbyshire) 2015. Derbyshire 2nd XI debut 2013. HS 8* and BB 3-63 v Australians (Derby) 2015 – only 1st XI appearance.

DURSTON, Wesley John (Millfield S; University C, Worcester), b Taunton, Somerset 6 Oct 1980. 5'10". RHB, OB. Squad No 3. Somerset 2002-09. Derbyshire debut 2010; cap 2012. Unicorns 2010 (l-o only). 1000 runs (1): 1138 (2011). HS 151 v Glos (Derby) 2011. BB 6-109 v Leics (Derby) 2015. LO HS 134 v Hants (Derby) 2014 (RLC). LO BB 3-7 v Worcs (Derby) 2011 (CB40). T20 HS 111 v Notts (Nottingham) 2010 – De record. T20 BB 3-14.

ELSTONE, Scott Liam (Friary Grange C), b Burton-on-Trent, Staffs 10 Jun 1990. 5'8". RHB, OB. Squad No 10. Debut (Derbyshire) 2014. Nottinghamshire 2nd XI debut 2006, aged 16y 81d. Unicorns (l-o only) 2013. HS 103* v Glamorgan (Cardiff) 2015. BB 3-68 v Northants (Derby) 2015. LO HS 75* Uni v Somerset (Taunton) 2013 (Y40). LO BB 1-22 Nt v Scotland (Nottingham) 2010 (CB40). T20 HS 37. T20 BB – .

GODLEMAN, Billy Ashley (Islington Green S), b Islington, London 11 Feb 1989. 6'3". LHB, LB. Squad No 1. Middlesex 2005-09. Essex 2010-12. Derbyshire debut 2013; cap 2015. 1000 runs (1): 1069 (2015). HS 130 Ex v Leics (Leicester) 2011 and 130 Ex v Glos (Cheltenham) 2012. De HS 108 (and 105*) v Kent (Derby) 2015. BB – . LO HS 109* v Northants (Derby) 2015 (RLC). T20 HS 69.

HEMMINGS, Robert Philip (Sir Thomas Boughey S, Stoke-on-Trent; Denstone C), b Newcastle-under-Lyme, Staffs 28 Feb 1996. RHB, RM. Squad No 24. Derbyshire 2nd XI debut 2015. Awaiting 1st XI debut.

HOSEIN, Harvey Richard (Denstone C), b Chesterfield 12 Aug 1996. 5'10". RHB, WK. Squad No 16. Debut (Derbyshire) 2014, taking seven catches in an innings and UK record-equalling 11 in match v Surrey (The Oval). Derbyshire 2nd XI debut 2010, aged 13y 287d. HS 61 v Glos (Bristol) 2015.

HUGHES, Alex Lloyd (Ounsdale HS, Wolverhampton), b Wordsley, Staffs 29 Sep 1991. 5'10". RHB, RM. Squad No 18. Debut (Derbyshire) 2013. Derbyshire 2nd XI debut 2009. HS 111* v Northants (Northampton) 2015. BB 4-46 v Glamorgan (Derby) 2014. LO HS 59* and LO BB 3-56 v Essex (Leek) 2013 (Y40). And LO BB 3-31 v Leics (Derby) 2015 (RLC). T20 HS 43*. T20 BB 3-32.

HUGHES, Chesney Francis (Albena Lake Hodge CS, Anguilla), b Anguilla 20 January 1991. 6'2". LHB, SLA. Squad No 22. British passport. Debut (Derbyshire) 2010. Derbyshire 2nd XI debut 2009. Leeward Is 2015-16. HS 270* v Yorks (Leeds) 2013. BB 2-9 v Middx (Derby) 2011. LO HS 81 Leeward Is v Windward Is (Kingston) 2010-11. LO BB 5-29 v Unicorns (Wormsley) 2012 (CB40). T20 HS 65. T20 BB 4-23.

KNIGHT, Thomas Craig ('**Tom**') (Eckington C), b Sheffield, Yorks 28 Jun 1993. 6'0½". RHB, SLA. Squad No 27. Debut (Derbyshire) 2011. No f-c appearances 2012-14. HS 25 v Leics (Derby) 2015. BB 2-32 v Glamorgan (Cardiff) 2011. LO HS 10 v Hants (Derby) 2013 (Y40). LO BB 3-36 v Durham (Derby) 2013 (Y40). T20 HS 44*. T20 BB 3-16.

MADSEN, Wayne Lee (Kearsney C, Durban; U of South Africa), b Durban, South Africa 2 Jan 1984. Nephew of M.B.Madsen (Natal 1967-68 to 1978-79), T.R.Madsen (Natal 1976-77 to 1989-90) and H.R.Fotheringham (Natal, Transvaal 1971-72 to 1989-90), cousin of G.S.Fotheringham (KwaZulu-Natal 2008-09 to 2009-10). 5'11". RHB, OB. Squad No 77. KwaZulu-Natal 2003-04 to 2007-08. Dolphins 2006-07 to 2007-08. Derbyshire debut 2009, scoring 170 v Glos (Cheltenham); cap 2011; captain 2012 to date. Qualified for England by residence in February 2015. 1000 runs (3); most – 1239 (2015). HS 231* v Northants (Northampton) 2012. BB 3-45 KZN v EP (Pt Elizabeth) 2007-08. De BB 2-9 v Sussex (Hove) 2013. LO HS 138 v Hants (Derby) 2014 (RLC). LO BB 3-27 v Durham (Derby) 2013 (Y40). T20 HS 65.

MILNES, Thomas Patrick (Heart of England S, Coventry), b Stourbridge, Worcs 6 Oct 1992. RHB, RMF. Squad No 8. Warwickshire 2011-15. Derbyshire debut 2015. England U19 2010-11. HS 52* and BB 7-39 Wa v Oxford MCCU (Oxford) 2013. CC HS 48 Wa v Sussex (Birmingham) 2013. De HS 23 and De BB 1-70 v Leics (Derby) 2015. CC BB 3-96 Wa v Durham (Chester-le-St) 2015. LO HS 16 Wa v Worcs (Birmingham) 2013 (Y40). LO BB 2-73 Wa v Northants (Birmingham) 2013 (Y40).

‡NQ**NEESHAM, James** Douglas Sheahan, b Auckland, New Zealand 17 Sep 1990. LHB, RMF. Squad No 5. Auckland 2009-10 to 2010-11. Otago 2011-12 to date. Joins Derbyshire in 2016 for T20 only. IPL: DD 2014. **Tests** (NZ): 9 (2013-14 to 2015-16); HS 137* v I (Wellington) 2013-14, on debut; BB 3-42 v SL (Wellington) 2014-15. **LOI** (NZ): 19 (2012-13 to 2015); HS 42* v SL (Dambulla) 2013-14; BB 4-42 v B (Dhaka) 2013-14. **IT20** (NZ): 13 (2012-13 to 2015); HS 28 v SA (Centurion) 2015; BB 3-16 v WI (Auckland) 2013-14. F-c Tours (NZ): A 2015-16; WI 2014; I 2013-14 (NZ A); UAE 2014-15 (v P). HS 147 Otago v CD (Nelson) 2013-14. BB 5-65 Otago v ND (Whangarei) 2013-14. LO HS 69 Otago v Wellington (Invercargill) 2011-12. LO BB 5-44 Otago v Wellington (Wellington) 2011-12. T20 HS 59*. T20 BB 3-16.

PALLADINO, Antonio Paul (Cardinal Pole SS; Anglia Polytechnic U), b Tower Hamlets, London 29 Jun 1983. 6'0". RHB, RMF. Squad No 28. Cambridge UCCE 2003-05. Essex 2003-10. Namibia 2009-10. Derbyshire debut 2011; cap 2012. HS 106 v Australia A (Derby) 2012. CC HS 68 v Warwks (Birmingham) 2013. 50 wkts (2); most – 56 (2012). BB 7-53 v Kent (Derby) 2012. Hat-trick v Leics (Leicester) 2012. LO HS 31 Namibia v Boland (Windhoek) 2009-10. LO BB 5-49 v Lancs (Derby) 2014 (RLC). T20 HS 14*. T20 BB 4-21.

POYNTON, Thomas (John Taylor HS, Barton-under-Needwood; Repton S), b Burton upon Trent, Staffs 25 Nov 1989. 5'10". RHB, WK. Squad No 23. Debut (Derbyshire) 2007. No f-c appearances in 2009 and 2011. Missed entire 2014 season after suffering serious injury in a car crash. HS 106 v Northants (Northampton) 2012. BB 2-96 v Glamorgan (Cardiff) 2010. LO HS 40 v Middx (Chesterfield) 2011 (CB40). T20 HS 27*.

NQ**RUTHERFORD, Hamish** Duncan, b Dunedin, New Zealand 27 Apr 1989. Son of K.R.Rutherford (Gauteng, Otago, Transvaal & New Zealand 1982-83 to 1999-00). Nephew of I.A.Rutherford (C Districts, Otago & Worcestershire 1974-75 to 1983-84). LHB, SLA. Squad No 72. Otago 2008-09 to date. Essex 2013. Derbyshire debut 2015. **Tests** (NZ): 16 (2012-13 to 2014-15); HS 171 v E (Dunedin) 2012-13 – on debut. **LOI** (NZ): 4 (2012-13 to 2013-14); HS 11 v E (Napier) 2012-13. **IT20** (NZ): 7 (2012-13 to 2013-14); HS 62 v E (Oval) 2013. F-c Tours (NZ): E 2013, 2014 (NZ A); WI 2014; B 2013-14. 1000 runs (0+1): 1077 (2012-13). HS 239 Otago v Wellington (Dunedin) 2011-12. De HS 108 v Kent (Chesterfield) 2015. BB – . LO HS 126 Otago v Wellington (Invercargill) 2015-16. LO BB – . T20 HS 91*.

SLATER, Benjamin Thomas (Netherthorpe S; Leeds Met U), b Chesterfield 26 Aug 1991. 5'10". LHB, OB. Squad No 26. Debut (Leeds/Bradford MCCU) 2012. Southern Rocks 2012-13. Derbyshire debut 2013. Derbyshire 2nd XI debut 2009. HS 119 v Leics (Derby) 2014, also scored 104 in same match. BB – . LO HS 46 SR v MWR (Masvingo) 2012-13. T20 HS 57.

TAYLOR, Thomas Alex Ian (Trentham HS, Stoke-on-Trent), b Stoke-on-Trent, Staffs 21 Dec 1994. 6'2". RHB, RMF. Squad No 15. Debut (Derbyshire) 2014. Derbyshire 2nd XI debut 2011. HS 49 v Northants (Derby) 2015. BB 6-61 v Lancs (Derby) 2015. LO HS – . LO BB 3-48 v Worcs (Worcester) 2014 (RLC).

THAKOR, Shivsinh Jaysinh (Loughborough GS; Uppingham S), b Leicester 22 Oct 1993. 6'1". RHB, RM. Squad No 57. Leicestershire 2011-13. No f-c appearances in 2014. Derbyshire debut 2015. Leicestershire 2nd XI debut 2008, aged 14y 218d. England U19 2010-11. HS 134 Le v Loughborough MCCU (Leicester) 2011 – on debut. CC HS 114 Le v Kent (Leicester) 2013. De HS 83 v Glos (Bristol) 2015. BB 3-57 Le v Surrey (Leicester) 2011. De BB 2-11 v Glamorgan (Cardiff) 2015. LO HS 83* Le v Lancs (Leicester) 2012 (CB40). LO BB Le 4-49 v Worcs (Leicester) 2014 (RLC). T20 HS 42. T20 BB 3-35.

WHITE, Harry John (John Port S, Etwall; Repton S), b Derby 19 Feb 1995. 6'4". RHB, LM. Squad No 19. Debut (Derbyshire) 2015. Derbyshire 2nd XI debut 2012. HS 3 and BB 2-85 v Australians (Derby) 2015 – only 1st XI game.

RELEASED/RETIRED

(Having made a County 1st XI appearance in 2015)

NQ**AMLA, Hashim** Mahomed, b Durban, South Africa 31 Mar 1983. Younger brother of A.M.Amla (Natal B, KZN, Dolphins 1997-98 to 2012-13). RHB, RM/OB. KZN 1999-00 to 2003-04. Dolphins 2004-05 to 2011-12. Essex 2009. Nottinghamshire 2010; cap 2010. Surrey 2013-14. Derbyshire 2015. Cape Cobras 2015-16. *Wisden* 2012. **Tests** (SA): 92 (2004-05 to 2015-16, 14 as captain); 1000 runs (3); most – 1249 (2010); HS 311* v E (Oval) 2012; BB – . **LOI** (SA): 131 (2007-08 to 2015-16, 9 as captain); 1000 runs (2); most – 1062 (2015); HS 159 v Ireland (Canberra) 2014-15. **IT20** (SA): 33 (2008-09 to 2015-16, 2 as captain); HS 97* v A (Cape Town) 2015-16. F-c Tours (SA) (C=Captain): E 2008, 2012; A 2008-09, 2012-13; WI 2010; NZ 2011-12; I 2004-05, 2007-08 (SA A), 2007-08, 2009-10, 2015-16C; P 2007-08; SL 2005-06 (SA A), 2006, 2014C; Z 2004 (SA A), 2007 (SA A), 2014C; B 2007-08, 2015C; UAE 2010-11, 2013-14 (v P). 1000 runs (0+2); most – 1126 (2005-06). HS 311* (*see Tests*). CC HS 181 Ex v Glamorgan (Chelmsford) 2009 – on debut. De HS 69 v Lancs (Southport) 2015. BB 1-10 SA A v India A (Kimberley) 2001-02. LO HS 159 (*see LOI*). T20 HS 97*.

CLARE, Jonathan Luke (St Theodore's HS), b Burnley, Lancs 14 Jun 1986. 6'4". RHB, RMF. Derbyshire 2007-15, taking 5-90 v Notts (Chesterfield) on debut; cap 2012. HS 130 v Glamorgan (Derby) 2011. BB 7-74 v Northants (Northampton) 2008. LO HS 57 v Warwks (Derby) 2012 (CB40). LO BB 3-39 v Scotland (Derby) 2008 (FPT). T20 HS 35*. T20 BB 2-20.

^{NQ}**DILSHAN, Tillakaratne** Mudiyanselage, b Kalutara, Sri Lanka 14 Oct 1975. RHB, OB. Kulatara 1996-97. Singha SC 1997-98. Sebastianites 1998-99 to 1999-00. Bloomfield 2000-01 to 2008-09. Tamil Union 2012-13 to 2013-14. Surrey 2014. Derbyshire 2015. IPL: DD 2007-08 to 2009-10. RCB 2011-13. Big Bash: ST 2013-14. **Tests** (SL): 87 (1999-00 to 2012-13, 11 as captain); 1000 runs (1): 1097 (2009); HS 193 v E (Lord's) 2011; BB 4-10 v B (Chittagong) 2008-09. **LOI** (SL): 327 (1999-00 to 2015-16, 26 as captain); 1000 runs (4); most – 1207 (2015); HS 161* v B (Melbourne) 2015; BB 4-4 v Z (Pallekele) 2010-11. **IT20** (SL): 74 (2006 to 2015-16, 5 as captain); HS 104* v A (Pallekele) 2011; BB 2-4 v Kenya (Johannesburg) 2007. F-c Tours (SL)(C=Captain): E 1999 (SL A), 2006, 2011C; A 2004, 2012-13; SA 1999-00 (SL A), 2000-01, 2011-12C; WI 2003, 2007-08; NZ 2004-05; I 2001-02 (Bloomfield), 2005-06, 2009-10; P 1999-00, 2008-09; Z 1999-00 (SL A), 2004, 2007-08 (SL A); B 2005-06, 2008-09; UAE (v P) 2011-12C. 1000 runs (0+2); most – 1284. HS 200* NC Prov v Central Prov (Colombo) 2004-05. De HS 27* v Kent (Canterbury) 2015. BB 5-49 Bloomfield v Sinhalese SC (Colombo) 2002-03. BB 1-9 v Leics (Leicester) 2015. LO HS 188 Bloomfield v Colts (Colombo) 2007-08. LO BB 4-4 (*see LOI*). T20 HS 104*. T20 BB 3-16.

FOOTITT, M.H.A. – *see SURREY*.

^{NQ}**GUPTILL, Martin** James (Avondale C), b Auckland, New Zealand 30 Sep 1986. 6'3". RHB, OB. Auckland 2005-06 to date. Derbyshire 2011-15; cap 2012. Big Bash: ST 2012-13. **Tests** (NZ): 40 (2008-09 to 2015-16); HS 189 v B (Hamilton) 2009-10; BB 3-37 v P (Napier) 2009-10. **LOI** (NZ): 129 (2008-09 to 2015-16); 1000 runs (1): 1489 (2015); HS 237* v WI (Wellington) 2014-15; BB 2-7 v B (Napier) 2009-10. **IT20** (NZ): 57 (2008-09 to 2015-16); HS 101* v SA (East London) 2012-13; BB – . F-c Tours (NZ): E 2013, 2015; A 2011-12, 2015-16; SA 2012-13; WI 2012; I 2008-09 (NZ A), 2010-11, 2012; SL 2009, 2012-13; Z 2010-11 (NZ A), 2011-12. HS 227 v Glos (Bristol) 2015. BB 3-37 (*see Tests*). De BB – . LO HS 237* (*see LOI*). LO BB 2-7 (*see LOI*). T20 HS 120*. T20 BB – .

^{NQ}**RIMMINGTON, Nathan** John (Wellington C), b Redcliffe, Queensland, Australia 11 Nov 1982. 5'10". RHB, RFM. Queensland 2005-06 to 2010-11. W Australia 2011-12 to date. Hampshire 2014. Derbyshire T20 only in 2015. IPL: KXIP 2011. Big Bash: PS 2011-12 to 2012-13. MR 2012-13 to date. HS 102* WA v NSW (Sydney) 2011-12. CC HS 65* and BB 2-51 H v Essex (Colchester) 2014. BB 5-27 WA v Q (Perth) 2014-15. LO HS 55 WA v Tas (Sydney) 2014-15. LO BB 4-40 Q v Vic (Melbourne) 2008-09. T20 HS 26. T20 BB 5-27.

WAINWRIGHT, David John (Hemsworth HS and SFC; Loughborough U); b Pontefract, Yorks 21 Mar 1985. 5'9". LHB, SLA. Yorkshire 2004-11; cap 2010. Derbyshire 2012-15; cap 2012. Loughborough UCCE 2005-06. British U 2006. Police Sports Club 2011-12. HS 109 v Leics (Leicester) 2014. 50 wkts (1): 50 (2012). BB 6-33 v Northants (Derby) 2012. LO HS 41 v Notts (Nottingham) 2014 (RLC). LO BB 4-11 v Durham (Derby) 2013 (Y40). T20 HS 20*. T20 BB 3-6.

WHITE, W.A. – *see LEICESTERSHIRE*.

DERBYSHIRE 2015

RESULTS SUMMARY

	Place	Won	Lost	Tied	Drew	NR
LV= County Championship (2nd Division)	8th	3	7		6	
All First-Class Matches		3	7		7	
Royal London One-Day Cup (Group A)	7th	4	4			
NatWest t20 Blast (North Group)	9th	4	10			

LV= COUNTY CHAMPIONSHIP AVERAGES

BATTING AND FIELDING

Cap		M	I	NO	HS	Runs	Avge	100	50	Ct/St
	M.J.Guptill	2	4	1	227	290	96.66	1	–	5
2011	W.L.Madsen	13	26	5	172*	1015	48.33	2	6	13
	H.D.Rutherford	3	6	–	108	273	45.50	1	2	1
2015	B.A.Godleman	14	28	4	108	1069	44.54	3	7	12
	M.J.J.Critchley	6	8	2	137*	246	41.00	1	–	2
	A.L.Hughes	7	11	3	111*	279	34.87	1	–	2
	C.F.Hughes	13	26	1	104	816	32.64	2	4	6
2012	W.J.Durston	11	21	5	85	451	28.18	–	2	12
	B.T.Slater	14	28	–	94	779	27.82	–	7	4
	H.M.Amla	2	4	–	69	101	25.25	–	1	2
	S.J.Thakor	12	17	1	83	349	21.81	–	1	4
	S.L.Elstone	7	12	1	103*	234	21.27	1	–	2
	W.A.White	3	5	1	38*	71	17.75	–	–	–
	T.M.Dilshan	3	6	2	27*	69	17.25	–	–	1
	H.R.Hosein	11	17	2	61	256	17.06	–	1	30/1
	B.D.Cotton	8	12	3	43	126	14.00	–	–	1
2012	A.P.Palladino	12	16	3	35*	173	13.307	–	–	4
	T.A.I.Taylor	9	13	3	49	133	13.300	–	–	2
	T.P.Milnes	2	4	–	23	37	9.25	–	–	–
2014	M.H.A.Footitt	16	21	6	34	110	7.33	–	–	3
	T.Poynton	5	9	–	19	47	5.22	–	–	11/3

Also batted: T.C.Knight (1 match) 25, 14* (1 ct); D.J.Wainwright (2 – cap 2012) 8*, 5, 10.

BOWLING

	O	M	R	W	Avge	Best	5wI	10wM
W.A.White	79.3	18	279	17	16.41	6- 25	2	–
M.H.A.Footitt	537.4	113	1796	76	23.63	7- 71	5	1
A.P.Palladino	356.4	105	890	31	28.70	3- 19	–	–
W.J.Durston	203	23	753	24	31.37	6-109	2	–
T.A.I.Taylor	241.2	34	946	28	33.78	6- 61	1	–
B.D.Cotton	223.1	49	745	15	49.66	3- 26	–	–
S.J.Thakor	188.4	33	667	13	51.30	2- 11	–	–

Also bowled:

A.L.Hughes 81.5 12 281 5 56.20 2- 34 – –

M.J.J.Critchley 76.1-6-363-4; T.M.Dilshan 17-1-76-1; S.L.Elstone 50-7-187-4;
C.F.Hughes 41.2-4-200-3; W.L.Madsen 17.4-2-51-1; T.P.Milnes 41-3-182-1;
D.J.Wainwright 31-0-131-1.

The First-Class Averages (pp 227–243) give the records of Derbyshire players in all
first-class county matches (Derbyshire's other opponents being the Australians), with the
exception of M.J.Guptill, T.P.Milnes and W.A.White, whose first-class figures for Derbyshire are as above, and:
H.J.Rutherford 4-7-0-108-287-41.00-1-2-1ct.

DERBYSHIRE RECORDS

FIRST-CLASS CRICKET

Highest Total	For	801-8d		v	Somerset	Taunton	2007
	V	677-7d		by	Yorkshire	Leeds	2013
Lowest Total	For	16		v	Notts	Nottingham	1879
	V	23		by	Hampshire	Burton upon T	1958
Highest Innings	For	274	G.A.Davidson	v	Lancashire	Manchester	1896
	V	343*	P.A.Perrin	for	Essex	Chesterfield	1904

Highest Partnership for each Wicket

1st	322	H.Storer/J.Bowden	v	Essex	Derby	1929
2nd	417	K.J.Barnett/T.A.Tweats	v	Yorkshire	Derby	1997
3rd	316*	A.S.Rollins/K.J.Barnett	v	Leics	Leicester	1997
4th	328	P.Vaulkhard/D.Smith	v	Notts	Nottingham	1946
5th	302*†	J.E.Morris/D.G.Cork	v	Glos	Cheltenham	1993
6th	212	G.M.Lee/T.S.Worthington	v	Essex	Chesterfield	1932
7th	258	M.P.Dowman/D.G.Cork	v	Durham	Derby	2000
8th	198	K.M.Krikken/D.G.Cork	v	Lancashire	Manchester	1996
9th	283	A.Warren/J.Chapman	v	Warwicks	Blackwell	1910
10th	132	A.Hill/M.Jean-Jacques	v	Yorkshire	Sheffield	1986

† 346 runs were added for this wicket in two separate partnerships

Best Bowling	For	10- 40	W.Bestwick	v	Glamorgan	Cardiff	1921
(Innings)	V	10- 45	R.L.Johnson	for	Middlesex	Derby	1994
Best Bowling	For	17-103	W.Mycroft	v	Hampshire	Southampton	1876
(Match)	V	16-101	G.Giffen	for	Australians	Derby	1886

Most Runs – Season	2165	D.B.Carr	(av 48.11)	1959
Most Runs – Career	23854	K.J.Barnett	(av 41.12)	1979-98
Most 100s – Season	8	P.N.Kirsten		1982
Most 100s – Career	53	K.J.Barnett		1979-98
Most Wkts – Season	168	T.B.Mitchell	(av 19.55)	1935
Most Wkts – Career	1670	H.L.Jackson	(av 17.11)	1947-63
Most Career W-K Dismissals	1304	R.W.Taylor	(1157 ct; 147 st)	1961-84
Most Career Catches in the Field	563	D.C.Morgan		1950-69

LIMITED-OVERS CRICKET

Highest Total	50ov	366-4		v	Comb Univs	Oxford	1991
	40ov	321-5		v	Essex	Leek	2013
	T20	222-5		v	Yorkshire	Leeds	2010
Lowest Total	50ov	73		v	Lancashire	Derby	1993
	40ov	60		v	Kent	Canterbury	2008
	T20	72		v	Leics	Derby	2013
Highest Innings	50ov	173*	M.J.Di Venuto	v	Derbys CB	Derby	2000
	40ov	141*	C.J.Adams	v	Kent	Chesterfield	1992
	T20	111	W.J.Durston	v	Notts	Nottingham	2010
Best Bowling	50ov	8-21	M.A.Holding	v	Sussex	Hove	1988
	40ov	6- 7	M.Hendrick	v	Notts	Nottingham	1972
	T20	5-27	T.Lungley	v	Leics	Leicester	2009

DURHAM

Formation of Present Club: 23 May 1882
Inaugural First-Class Match: 1992
Colours: Navy Blue, Yellow and Maroon
Badge: Coat of Arms of the County of Durham
County Champions: (3) 2008, 2009, 2013
Friends Provident Trophy Winners: (1) 2007
Royal London One-Day Cup Winners: (1) 2014
Twenty20 Cup Winners: (0); best – Semi-Finalist 2008

Chief Executive: David Harker, Emirates Durham International Cricket Ground, Chester-le-Street, Co Durham DH3 3QR • Tel: 0191 387 1717 • Fax: 0191 387 1616 • Email: marketing@durhamccc.co.uk • Web: www.durhamccc.co.uk • Twitter: @DurhamCricket (29,766 followers)

Head Coach: Jon Lewis. **Bowling Coach**: Alan Walker. **Captain**: P.D.Collingwood (f-c) and M.D.Stoneman (l-o). **Vice-Captain**: None. **Overseas Players**: J.W.Hastings and Shoaib Malik. **2016 Beneficiary**: None. **Head Groundsman**: tbc. **Scorer**: Brian Hunt (home) and William Dobson (away). ‡ New registration. NQ Not qualified for England.

Durham initially awarded caps immediately after their players joined the staff but revised this policy in 1998, again capping players on merit, past 'awards' having been nullified. Durham abolished both their capping and 'awards' systems after the 2005 season.

ARSHAD, Usman (Beckfoot GS, Bingley), b Bradford, Yorks 9 Jan 1993. 5'11". RHB, RMF. Squad No 78. Debut (Durham) 2013. Northumberland 2011. HS 83 v Sussex (Hove) 2013. BB 4-78 v Northants (Northampton) 2014. LO HS 25 v Surrey (Chester-le-St) 2015 (RLC). LO BB 3-80 v Somerset (Taunton) 2015 (RLC). T20 HS 28*. T20 BB 3-18.

BORTHWICK, Scott George (Farringdon Community Sports C, Sunderland), b Sunderland 19 Apr 1990. 5'9". LHB, LBG. Squad No 16. Debut (Durham) 2009. Wellington 2015-16. **Tests**: 1 (2013-14); HS 4 and BB 3-33 v A (Sydney) 2013-14. **LOI**: 2 (2011 to 2011-12); HS 15 v Ireland (Dublin) 2011; BB – . **IT20**: 1 (2011); HS 14 and BB 1-15 v WI (Oval) 2011. F-c Tours: A 2013-14; SL 2013-14 (EL). 1000 runs (4); most – 1390 (2015). HS 216 v Middx (Chester-le-St) 2014, sharing Du record 2nd wkt partnership of 274 with M.D.Stoneman. BB 6-70 v Surrey (Oval) 2013. LO HS 87 and LO BB 5-38 v Leics (Leicester) 2015 (RLC). T20 HS 62. T20 BB 3-19.

BUCKLEY, Ryan Sean (Hummersknott Ac, Darlington; Darlington Queen Elizabeth SFC), b Darlington 2 Apr 1994. 5'10". RHB, OB. Squad No 4. Debut (Durham) 2013, taking 5-86 v Surrey (Oval). Durham 2nd XI debut 2011. No 1st XI appearances in 2015. HS 9 v Lancs (Manchester) 2014. BB 5-86 *(see above)*.

BURNHAM, Jack Tony Arthur (Deerness Valley CS, Durham), b Durham 18 Jan 1997. RHB, RM. Debut (Durham) 2015. Durham 2nd XI debut 2014. Northumberland 2015. HS 50 v Yorks (Scarborough) 2015.

CHASE, Peter Karl David (Malahide Community S), b Dublin, Ireland 9 Oct 1993. 6'4". RHB, RMF. Debut (Durham) 2014, taking 5-64 v Notts (Chester-le-St). Durham 2nd XI debut 2011. No 1st XI appearances in 2015. **LOI** (Ire): 1 (2014-15); HS – . HS 4* v Middx (Lord's) 2014. BB 5-64 *(see above)*. LO HS 22* and LO BB 1-60 Ire v Sri Lanka A (Belfast) 2014.

CLARK, Graham (St Benedict's Catholic HS, Whitehaven), b Whitehaven, Cumbria 16 Mar 1993. Younger brother of J.Clark (*see LANCASHIRE*). 6'1". RHB, LB. Squad No 7. Debut (Durham) 2015. Durham 2nd XI debut 2011. MCC YC 2013. HS 36 v Yorks (Scarborough) 2015. LO HS 42 v Yorks (Chester-le-St) 2015 (RLC). T20 HS 91* v Yorks (Leeds) 2015 – Du record. T20 BB – .

COLLINGWOOD, Paul David (Blackfyne CS; Derwentside C), b Shotley Bridge 26 May 1976. 5'11". RHB, RM. Squad No 5. Debut (Durham) 1996 v Northants (Chester-le-St) taking wicket of D.J.Capel with his first ball before scoring 91 and 16; cap 1998; benefit 2007; captain 2012 (*part*) to date. IPL: DD 2009-10. MBE 2005. *Wisden* 2007. **Tests**: 68 (2003-04 to 2010-11); 1000 runs (1): 1121 (2006); HS 206 v A (Adelaide) 2006-07; BB 3-23 v NZ (Wellington) 2007-08. **LOI**: 197 (2001 to 2010-11, 25 as captain); 1000 runs (1): 1064 (2007); HS 120* v A (Melbourne) 2006-07; BB 6-31 v B (Nottingham) 2005 – record analysis for E, and first to score a hundred (112*) and take six wickets in same LOI. **IT20**: 35 (2005 to 2010-11, 30 as captain); HS 79 v WI (Oval) 2007; BB 4-22 v SL (Southampton) 2006. F-c Tours: A 2006-07, 2010-11; SA 2009-10; WI 2003-04, 2008-09; NZ 2007-08; I 2005-06, 2008-09; P 2005-06; SL 2003-04, 2007-08; B 2009-10. 1000 runs (2); most – 1120 (2005), inc six hundreds (Du record). HS 206 (*see Tests*). Du HS 190 v SL (Chester-le-St) 2002 and 190 v Derbys (Derby) 2005, sharing Du record 4th wkt partnership of 250 with D.M.Benkenstein. BB 5-52 v Somerset (Stockton) 2005. LO HS 132 v Northants (Northampton) 2015 (RLC). LO BB 6-31 (*see LOI*). T20 HS 79. T20 BB 5-6 v Northants (Chester-le-St) 2011 – Du record.

COUGHLIN, Paul (St Robert of Newminster Catholic CS, Washington), b Sunderland 23 Oct 1992. 6'3". RHB, RM. Squad No 29. Debut (Durham) 2012. Northumberland 2011. No 1st XI appearances in 2013. HS 85 v Lancs (Chester-le-St) 2014, sharing Du record 9th wkt partnership of 150 with P.Mustard. BB 4-10 v Somerset (Chester-le-St) 2015. LO HS 2* v Yorks (Leeds) 2014 (RLC). LO BB 1-34 v Surrey (Chester-le-St) 2014 (RLC). T20 HS – . T20 BB 2-43.

HARRISON, Jamie (Sedbergh S), b Whiston, Lancs 19 Nov 1990. 6'0". RHB, LMF. Squad No 13. Debut (Durham) 2012. HS 65 v Northants (Northampton) 2014. BB 5-31 v Surrey (Chester-le-St) 2013. LO HS 7* and LO BB 2-51 v Somerset (Chester-le-St) 2012 (CB40).

NQ**HASTINGS, John** Wayne (St Dominic's Catholic C, Sydney; Australian C of PE), b Penrith, NSW, Australia 4 Nov 1985. 6'6". RHB, RFM. Squad No 2. Victoria 2007-08 to date. Durham debut 2014. IPL: CSK 2014. Big Bash: MS 2012-13 to date. **Tests** (A): 1 (2012-13); HS 32 and BB 1-51 v SA (Perth) 2012-13. **LOI** (A): 20 (2010-11 to 2015-16); HS 48* v NZ (Wellington) 2015-16; BB 4-58 v I (Melbourne) 2015-16. **IT20** (A): 7 (2010-11 to 2015-16); HS 15 v SL (Perth) 2010-11; BB 3-14 v SL (Pallekele) 2011. HS 93 Vic v Tas (Hobart) 2009-10. Du HS 91 v Sussex (Arundel) 2015. BB 7-60 v Worcs (Worcester) 2015. LO HS 69* Vic v S Australia (Adelaide) 2012-13. LO BB 5-41 v Somerset (Taunton) 2015 (RLC). T20 HS 80*. T20 BB 4-26.

JENNINGS, Keaton Kent (King Edward VII S, Johannesburg), b Johannesburg, South Africa 19 Jun 1992. Son of R.V.Jennings (Transvaal 1973-74 to 1992-93), brother of D.Jennings (Gauteng and Easterns 1999 to 2003-04), nephew of K.E.Jennings (Northern Transvaal 1981-82 to 1982-83). 6'4". LHB, RMF. Squad No 1. Durham debut 2012. HS 177* v Durham MCCU (Chester-le-St) 2015. CC HS 127 v Sussex (Hove) 2013. BB 2-8 Gauteng v WP (Cape Town) 2011-12. Du BB 1-4 v Northants (Northampton) 2014. LO HS 71* Gauteng v KZN (Johannesburg) 2011-12. LO BB 1-9 v Surrey (Chester-le-St) 2014 (RLC). T20 HS 1*. T20 BB 4-37.

McCARTHY, Barry John (St Michael's C, Dublin; Dublin U), b Dublin, Ireland 13 Sep 1992. 5'11". RHB, RMF. Debut (Durham) 2015. Durham 2nd XI debut 2014. HS 38* and BB 2-51 v Notts (Nottingham) 2015.

NQMacLEOD, Calum Scott (Hillpark S, Glasgow), b Glasgow, Scotland 15 Nov 1988. 6'0''. RHB, RMF. Squad No 14. Scotland 2007 to date. Warwickshire 2008-09. Durham debut 2014. **LOI** (Scot): 34 (2008 to 2015-16); HS 175 v Canada (Christchurch) 2013-14; BB 2-26 v Kenya (Aberdeen) 2013. **IT20** (Scot): 24 (2009 to 2015-16); HS 57 v Netherlands (Dubai) 2011-12; BB 2-17 v Kenya (Aberdeen) 2013. F-c Tours (Scot): UAE 2011-12, 2012-13; Namibia 2011-12. HS 84 v Lancs (Manchester) 2014. BB 4-66 Sc v Canada (Aberdeen) 2009. LO HS 175 (*see LOI*). LO BB 3-37 Sc v UAE (Queenstown) 2013-14. T20 HS 104*. T20 BB 2-17.

MAIN, Gavin Thomas, b Lanark, Scotland 28 Feb 1995. 6'2''. RHB, RMF. Squad No 20. Debut (Durham) 2014. Durham 2nd XI debut 2013. **IT20** (Scot): 3 (2015); HS – ; BB 1-21 v Ireland (Bready) 2015. HS 0*. BB 3-72 v Notts (Nottingham) 2014 – only 1st XI appearance.

MUCHALL, Gordon James (Durham S), b Newcastle upon Tyne, Northumb 2 Nov 1982. 6'0''. RHB, RM. Squad No 24. Northumberland 1999. Older brother of P.B.Muchall (Gloucestershire 2012). Debut (Durham) 2002; cap 2005; benefit 2014. No f-c appearances in 2013. F-c Tour: SL 2002-03 (ECB Acad). HS 219 v Kent (Canterbury) 2006, sharing Du record 6th wkt partnership of 249 with P.Mustard (*see below*). BB 3-26 v Yorks (Leeds) 2003. LO HS 101* v Yorks (Leeds) 2005 (NL). LO BB 1-15 v Sussex (Hove) 2003 (NL). T20 HS 66*. T20 BB 1-8.

MUSTARD, Philip (Usworth CS), b Sunderland 8 Oct 1982. Cousin of C.Rushworth (*see below*). 5'11''. LHB, WK. Squad No 19. Debut (Durham) 2002; captain 2010 (*part*) to 2012 (*part*). Mountaineers 2011-12. Auckland 2012-13. Lancashire 2015 (on loan). **LOI**: 10 (2007-08); HS 83 v NZ (Napier) 2007-08. **IT20**: 2 (2007-08); HS 40 v NZ (Christchurch) 2007-08. HS 130 v Kent (Canterbury) 2006. LO HS 143 v Surrey (Chester-le-St) 2012 (CB40). T20 HS 97*.

ONIONS, Graham (St Thomas More RC S, Blaydon), b Gateshead 9 Sep 1982. 6'1''. RHB, RFM. Squad No 9. Debut (Durham) 2004; benefit 2015. Dolphins 2013-14. MCC 2007-08, 2015. *Wisden* 2009. Missed entire 2010 season through back injury. **Tests**: 9 (2009 to 2012); HS 17* v A (Lord's) 2009; BB 5-38 v WI (Lord's) 2009 – on debut. **LOI**: 4 (2009 to 2009-10); HS 1 v A (Centurion) 2009-10; BB 2-58 v SL (Johannesburg) 2009-10. F-c Tours: SA 2009-10; NZ 2012-13; I 2007-08 (EL), 2012-13; SL 2013-14; B 2006-07 (Eng A); UAE 2011-12 (*part*). HS 41 v Yorks (Leeds) 2007. 50 wkts (6); most – 73 (2013). BB 9-67 v Notts (Nottingham) 2012. LO HS 19 v Derbys (Derby) 2008 (FPT). LO BB 4-45 v Lancs (Chester-le-St) 2013 (Y40). T20 HS 31. T20 BB 3-15.

NQPOYNTER, Stuart William (Teddington S), b Hammersmith, London 18 Oct 1990. Younger brother of A.D.Poynter (Middlesex and Ireland 2005 to date). 5'9''. RHB, WK. Squad No 90. Middlesex 2010. Ireland 2011 to date. Warwickshire 2013. No1st XI appearances for Durham in 2015. **LOI** (Ire): 3 (2014); HS 8 v Scotland (Dublin) 2014. **IT20** (Ire): 10 (2015 to 2015-16); HS 35 v PNG (Townsville) 2015-16. F-c Tour (Ire): Z 2015-16. HS 125 Ire v Zimbabwe A (Harare) 2015-16. CC HS 0. LO HS 109 Ire v Sri Lanka A (Belfast) 2014.

PRINGLE, Ryan David (Durham SFC), b Sunderland 17 Apr 1992. RHB, OB. Squad No 17. Debut (Durham) 2014. Durham 2nd XI debut 2009. Northumberland 2011-12. HS 99 v Hants (Chester-le-St) 2015. BB 5-63 v Hants (Southampton) 2015. LO HS 35 v Surrey (Chester-le-St) 2015 (RLC). LO BB 1-12 v Derbys (Derby) 2013 (Y40). T20 HS 25. T20 BB 2-13.

RICHARDSON, Michael John (Rondebosch HS; Stonyhurst C, Nottingham U), b Pt Elizabeth, South Africa 4 Oct 1986. Son of D.J.Richardson (South Africa, EP and NT 1977-78 to 1997-98), grandson of J.H.Richardson (NE Transvaal and Transvaal B 1952-53 to 1960-61), nephew of R.P.Richardson (WP 1984-85 to 1988-89). 5'10''. RHB, WK. Squad No 18. Debut (Durham) 2010. Colombo CC 2014-15. MCC YC 2008-09. 1000 runs (1): 1007 (2015). HS 148 v Yorks (Chester-le-St) 2014. LO HS 56 v Derbys (Chester-le-St) 2015 (RLC). T20 HS 19.

RUSHWORTH, Christopher (Castle View CS, Sunderland), b Sunderland 11 Jul 1986. Cousin of P.Mustard (*see above*). 6'2". RHB, RMF. Squad No 22. Debut (Durham) 2010. MCC 2013, 2015. Northumberland 2004-05. PCA 2015. HS 46 v Somerset (Taunton) 2014. 50 wkts (2); most – 88 (2015). BB 9-52 (15-95 match) v Northants (Chester-le-St) 2014. LO HS 38* v Derbys (Chester-le-St) 2015 (RLC). LO BB 5-31 v Notts (Chester-le-St) 2010 (CB40). T20 HS 5. T20 BB 3-19.

‡^NQ**SHOAIB MALIK** (Government Arabic SS, Sialkot), b Sialkot, Pakistan 1 Feb 1982. Elder brother of Adeel Malik (*see ESSEX*). 5'6". RHB, OB. Pakistan A 1997. Gujranwala 1997-98 to 1998-99. PIA 1998-99 to 2013-14. Pakistan Reserves 1999-00. Sialkot 2001-02 to 2012-13. Gloucestershire 2003-04. ZTB 2014-15. Joins Durham in 2016 for T20 only. IPL: DD 2007-08. Big Bash: HH 2013-14 to 2014-15. **Tests** (P): 35 (2001 to 2015-16); HS 245 v E (Abu Dhabi) 2015-16; BB 4-33 v E (Sharjah) 2015-16. **LOI** (P): 232 (1999-00 to 2015-16); HS 143 v I (Colombo, RPS) 2004; BB 4-19 v Hong Kong (Colombo, SSC) 2004. **IT20** (P): 74 (2006 to 2015-16); HS 75 v E (Sharjah) 2015-16; BB 2-7 v B (Dhaka) 2011-12. F-c Tours (P): E 1997 (Pak A), 2006, 2010; A 2004-05, 2009-10; WI 2005; NZ 2009-10; I 2007-08; SL 2005-06, 2009. HS 245 (*see Tests*). UK HS 110* P v Leics (Leicester) 2006. LOI HS 63 Gs v Northants (Bristol) 2004. BB 7-81 PIA v WAPDA (Faisalabad) 2000-01. CC BB 3-76 Gs v Worcs (Cheltenham) 2003. LO HS 143 (*see LOI*). LO BB 5-35 PIA v Lahore Blues (Karachi) 2002-03. T20 HS 95*. T20 BB 5-13.

STOKES, Benjamin Andrew (Cockermouth S), b Christchurch, Canterbury, New Zealand 4 Jun 1991. 6'1". LHB, RFM. Squad No 38. Debut (Durham) 2010. Big Bash: MR 2014-15. YC 2013. **ECB Central Contract 2015-16. Tests**: 23 (2013-14 to 2015-16); HS 258 v SA (Cape Town) 2015-16, setting E record fastest double century in 163 balls; BB 6-36 v A (Nottingham) 2015. **LOI**: 39 (2011 to 2015-16); HS 70 v A (Perth) 2014-15; BB 5-61 v A (Southampton) 2013. **IT20**: 11 (2011 to 2015-16); HS 31 v WI (Oval) 2011; BB 2-24 v NZ (Manchester) 2015. F-c Tours: A 2013-14; SA 2015-16; WI 2010-11 (EL), 2014-15; UAE 2015-16 (v P). HS 258 (*see Tests*). Du HS 185 v Lancs (Chester-le-St) 2011, sharing Du record 4th wkt partnership of 331 with D.M.Benkenstein. BB 7-67 (10-121 match) v Sussex (Chester-le-St) 2014. LO HS 164 v Notts (Chester-le-St) 2014 (RLC) – Du record. LO BB 5-61 (*see LOI*). T20 HS 77. T20 BB 2-14.

STONEMAN, Mark Daniel (Whickham CS), b Newcastle upon Tyne, Northumb 26 Jun 1987. 5'11". LHB, RM. Squad No 23. Debut (Durham) 2007; captain (l-o only) 2015 to date. 1000 runs (3); most – 1131 (2015). HS 187 v Middx (Chester-le-St) 2014, sharing Du record 2nd wkt partnership of 274 with S.G.Borthwick. BB – . LO HS 136* v Scotland (Chester-le-St) 2012 (CB40). T20 HS 89*.

WEIGHELL, William James (Stokesley S), b Middlesbrough, Yorks 28 Jan 1994. RHB, RM. Debut (Durham) 2015. Durham 2nd XI debut 2012. Northumberland 2012 to date. HS 25 v Middx (Chester-le-St) 2015. BB 1-72 v Hants (Chester-le-St) 2015.

WOOD, Mark Andrew (Ashington HS; Newcastle C), b Ashington 11 Jan 1990. 5'11". RHB, RF. Squad No 33. Debut (Durham) 2011. Northumberland 2008-10. **ECB Central Contract 2015-16. Tests**: 8 (2015 to 2015-16); HS 32* v A (Cardiff) 2015; BB 3-39 v P (Dubai, DSC) 2015-16. **LOI**: 7 (2015); HS 13 v A (Manchester) 2015; BB 1-25 v Ire (Dublin) 2015. IT20: 1 (2015); HS – ; BB 3-26 v NZ (Manchester) 2015. F-c Tours (EL): SA 2014-15; SL 2013-14; UAE 2015-16 (v P). HS 66 v Notts (Chester-le-St) 2015. BB 5-32 EL v Sri Lanka A (Colombo, RPS) 2013-14. Du BB 5-37 v Somerset (Taunton) 2014. LO HS 15* v Lancs (Chester-le-St) 2013 (Y40). LO BB 3-23 v Scotland (Chester-le-St) 2013 (Y40). T20 HS 12. T20 BB 3-26.

DURHAM 2015

	Place	Won	Lost	Tied	Drew	NR
LV= County Championship (1st Division)	4th	7	8		1	
All First-Class Matches		8	8		1	
Royal London One-Day Cup (Group A)	QF	4	4			1
NatWest t20 Blast (North Group)	6th	5	8			1

LV= COUNTY CHAMPIONSHIP AVERAGES

BATTING AND FIELDING

Cap		M	I	NO	HS	Runs	Avge	100	50	Ct/St
	S.G.Borthwick	16	32	2	103	1286	42.86	1	11	18
2005	G.J.Muchall	11	21	2	145	693	36.47	2	2	10
	M.J.Richardson	16	32	5	96*	964	35.70	–	6	45/3
	M.D.Stoneman	16	32	–	131	1090	34.06	3	5	7
1998	P.D.Collingwood	15	28	4	127	752	31.33	2	2	24
	U.Arshad	3	4	–	60	111	27.75	–	1	3
	B.J.McCarthy	2	4	2	38*	55	27.50	–	–	2
	R.D.Pringle	9	17	1	99	427	26.68	–	3	3
	P.Coughlin	6	10	1	64	213	23.66	–	2	1
	K.K.Jennings	10	20	–	98	473	23.65	–	3	4
	J.W.Hastings	14	24	–	91	449	18.70	–	3	5
	W.J.Weighell	2	4	–	25	69	17.25	–	–	1
	C.Rushworth	16	26	4	43	376	17.09	–	–	6
	C.S.MacLeod	7	13	2	44	161	14.63	–	–	6
	G.Onions	15	24	15	36*	131	14.55	–	–	3
	J.T.A.Burnham	4	8	–	50	115	14.37	–	1	2
	G.Clark	3	6	–	36	65	10.83	–	–	2
	J.Harrison	5	10	–	53	99	9.90	–	1	–
	P.Mustard	5	7	–	22	51	7.28	–	–	19

Also batted: M.A.Wood (1 match) 1, 66.

BOWLING

	O	M	R	W	Avge	Best	5wI	10wM
C.Rushworth	585.4	134	1711	83	20.61	6-39	7	–
P.Coughlin	116	27	412	16	25.75	4-10	–	–
G.Onions	467.5	83	1744	65	26.83	7-68	3	–
R.D.Pringle	160.4	37	566	20	28.30	5-63	1	–
P.D.Collingwood	93.5	20	320	11	29.09	5-57	1	–
J.W.Hastings	401	81	1397	45	31.04	7-60	2	–
S.G.Borthwick	149.1	21	641	15	42.73	4-46	–	–
J.Harrison	115.4	15	436	10	43.60	2-42	–	–

Also bowled:

M.A.Wood	28	6	74	6	12.33	4-39	–	–
U.Arshad	46.2	4	196	5	39.20	3-41	–	–

K.K.Jennings 12-0-51-0; B.J.McCarthy 39-4-154-4; C.S.MacLeod 5-1-16-0; G.J.Muchall 2-0-7-0; M.D.Stoneman 3-0-24-0; W.J.Weighell 36.3-5-179-1.

The First-Class Averages (pp 227–243) give the records of Durham players in all first-class county matches (Durham's other opponents being Durham MCCU), with the exception of M.A.Wood, whose first-class figures for Durham are as above, and:
P.Mustard 6-8-0-39-90-11.25-0-0-21ct.

DURHAM RECORDS

FIRST-CLASS CRICKET

Highest Total	For 648-5d		v	Notts	Chester-le-St[2]	2009
	V 810-4d		by	Warwicks	Birmingham	1994
Lowest Total	For 67		v	Middlesex	Lord's	1996
	V 18		by	Durham MCCU	Chester-le-St[2]	2012
Highest Innings	For 273	M.L.Love	v	Hampshire	Chester-le-St[2]	2003
	V 501*	B.C.Lara	for	Warwicks	Birmingham	1994

Highest Partnership for each Wicket

1st	334*	S.Hutton/M.A.Roseberry	v	Oxford U	Oxford	1996
2nd	274	M.D.Stoneman/S.G.Borthwick	v	Middlesex	Chester-le-St[2]	2014
3rd	212	M.J.Di Venuto/D.M.Benkenstein	v	Essex	Chester-le-St[2]	2010
4th	331	B.A.Stokes/D.M.Benkenstein	v	Lancashire	Chester-le-St[2]	2011
5th	247	G.J.Muchall/I.D.Blackwell	v	Worcs	Worcester	2011
6th	249	G.J.Muchall/P.Mustard	v	Kent	Canterbury	2006
7th	315	D.M.Benkenstein/O.D.Gibson	v	Yorkshire	Leeds	2006
8th	147	P.Mustard/L.E.Plunkett	v	Yorkshire	Leeds	2009
9th	150	P.Mustard/P.Coughlin	v	Lancashire	Chester-le-St[2]	2014
10th	103	M.M.Betts/D.M.Cox	v	Sussex	Hove	1996

Best Bowling (Innings)	For 10- 47	O.D.Gibson	v	Hampshire	Chester-le-St[2]	2007
	V 9- 34	J.A.R.Harris	for	Middlesex	Lord's	2015
Best Bowling (Match)	For 14-177	A.Walker	v	Essex	Chelmsford	1995
	V 13-103	J.A.R.Harris	for	Middlesex	Lord's	2015

Most Runs – Season	1654	M.J.Di Venuto	(av 78.76)		2009
Most Runs – Career	10049	P.D.Collingwood	(av 34.18)		1996-2015
Most 100s – Season	6	P.D.Collingwood			2005
	6	M.J.Di Venuto			2009
Most 100s – Career	21	D.M.Benkenstein			2005-11
	21	P.D.Collingwood			1996-2015
Most Wkts – Season	80	O.D.Gibson	(av 20.75)		2007
Most Wkts – Career	518	S.J.E.Brown	(av 28.30)		1992-2002
Most Career W-K Dismissals	638	P.Mustard	(619 ct; 19 st)		2002-15
Most Career Catches in the Field	200	P.D.Collingwood			1996-2015

LIMITED-OVERS CRICKET

Highest Total	50ov	353-8		v	Notts	Chester-le-St[2]	2014
	40ov	325-9		v	Surrey	The Oval	2011
	T20	225-2		v	Leics	Chester-le-St[2]	2010
Lowest Total	50ov	82		v	Worcs	Chester-le-St[1]	1968
	40ov	72		v	Warwicks	Birmingham	2002
	T20	93		v	Kent	Canterbury	2009
Highest Innings	50ov	164	B.A.Stokes	v	Notts	Chester-le-St[2]	2014
	40ov	150*	B.A.Stokes	v	Warwicks	Birmingham	2011
	T20	91*	G.Clark	v	Yorkshire	Leeds	2015
Best Bowling	50ov	7-32	S.P.Davis	v	Lancashire	Chester-le-St[1]	1983
	40ov	6-31	N.Killeen	v	Derbyshire	Derby	2000
	T20	5- 6	P.D.Collingwood	v	Northants	Chester-le-St[2]	2011

[1] Chester-le-Street CC (Ropery Lane) [2] Emirates Durham International Cricket Ground

ESSEX

Formation of Present Club: 14 January 1876
Inaugural First-Class Match: 1894
Colours: Blue, Gold and Red
Badge: Three Seaxes above Scroll bearing 'Essex'
County Champions: (6) 1979, 1983, 1984, 1986, 1991, 1992
NatWest/Friends Prov Trophy Winners: (3) 1985, 1997, 2008
Benson and Hedges Cup Winners: (2) 1979, 1998
Pro 40/National League (Div 1) Winners: (2) 2005, 2006
Sunday League Winners: (3) 1981, 1984, 1985
Twenty20 Cup Winners: (0); best – Semi-Finalist 2006, 2008, 2010

Chief Executive: Derek Bowden, The Ford County Ground, New Writtle Street, Chelmsford CM2 0PG • Tel: 01245 252420 • Fax: 01245 254030 • Email: administration@essexcricket.org.uk • Web: www.essexcricket.org.uk • Twitter: @EssexCricket (36,666 followers)

Head Coach: Chris Silverwood. **Assistant Head Coach:** Anthony McGrath. **Captain:** R.N.ten Doeschate (f-c) and R.S.Bopara (l-o). **Vice-Captain:** None. **Overseas Players:** A.F.Milne (T20 only), J.D.Ryder and Wahab Riaz (T20 only). **2016 Beneficiary:** None. **Head Groundsman:** Stuart Kerrison. **Scorer:** Tony Choat. ‡ New registration. NQ Not qualified for England.

Syed ASHAR Ahmed ZAIDI, b Karachi, Pakistan 13 Jul 1981. LHB, SLA. Squad No 99. UK citizen. Islamabad 1999-00 to 2009-10. PTC 2003-04 to 2005-06. Rawalpindi 2003-04 to 2004-05. KRL 2006-07. Federal Areas 2007-08. Sussex 2013-15. HS 202 Islamabad v Sialkot (Sialkot) 2009-10. CC HS 106 Sx v Warwks (Birmingham) 2015. BB 4-50 Islamabad v Hyderabad (Islamabad) 2009-10. CC BB 4-57 Sx v Yorks (Hove) 2013. LO HS 141 Rupganj v Old DOHS (Mirpur) 2014-15. LO BB 4-39 Gazi Tank v PDSC (Mirpur) 2013-14. T20 HS 53*. T20 BB 4-11.

BEARD, Aaron Paul (Boswells S, Chelmsford), b Chelmsford 15 Oct 1997. LHB, RFM. Squad No 14. Awaiting 1st XI debut.

BOPARA, Ravinder Singh (Brampton Manor S; Barking Abbey Sports C), b Newham, London 4 May 1985. 5'8". RHB, RM. Squad No 25. Debut (Essex) 2002; cap 2005; benefit 2015; captain (l-o only) 2016. Auckland 2009-10. Dolphins 2010-11. IPL: KXIP 2009-10. MCC 2006, 2008. YC 2008. **Tests:** 13 (2007-08 to 2012); HS 143 v WI (Lord's) 2009; BB 1-39 v SL (Galle) 2007-08. **LOI:** 120 (2006-07 to 2014-15); HS 101* v Ireland (Dublin) 2013; BB 4-38 v B (Birmingham) 2010. **IT20:** 38 (2008 to 2014); HS 65* v A (Hobart) 2013-14; BB 4-10 v WI (Oval) 2011 – England record. F-c Tours: WI 2008-09, 2010-11 (EL); SL 2007-08, 2011-12. 1000 runs (1): 1256 (2008). HS 229 v Northants (Chelmsford) 2007. RHB 5-75 v Surrey (Chelmsford) 2006. LO HS 201* v Leics (Leicester) 2008 (FPT) – Ex record. LO BB 5-63 Dolphins v Warriors (Pietermaritzburg) 2010-11. T20 HS 105*. T20 BB 6-16.

BROWNE, Nicholas Lawrence Joseph (Trinity Catholic HS, Woodford Green), b Leytonstone 24 Mar 1991. 6'3½". LHB, LB. Squad No 10. Debut (Essex) 2013; cap 2015. 1000 runs (1): 1157 (2015). HS 151* v Leics (Leicester) 2015. BB – . LO HS 69 v Hants (Southampton) 2015 (RLC). T20 HS 38.

COOK, Alastair Nathan (Bedford S), b Gloucester 25 Dec 1984. 6'3". LHB, OB. Squad No 26. Debut (Essex) 2003; cap 2005; benefit 2014. MCC 2004-07, 2015. YC 2005. *Wisden* 2011. **ECB central contract 2015-16. Tests**: 126 (2005-06 to 2015-16, 45 as captain); 1000 runs (4) – most – 1364 (2015); HS 294 v I (Birmingham) 2011. Scored 60 and 104* v I (Nagpur) 2005-06 on debut. Third, after D.G.Bradman and S.R.Tendulkar, to score seven Test hundreds before his 23rd birthday. Second, after M.A.Taylor, to score 1000 runs in the calendar year of his debut. BB 1-6 v I (Nottingham) 2014. **LOI**: 92 (2006 to 2014-15, 69 as captain); HS 137 v P (Abu Dhabi) 2011-12. **IT20**: 4 (2007 to 2009-10); HS 26 v SA (Centurion) 2009-10. F-c Tours (C=Captain): A 2006-07, 2010-11, 2013-14C; SA 2009-10, 2015-16C; WI 2005-06 (Eng A), 2008-09, 2014-15C; NZ 2007-08, 2012-13C; I 2005-06, 2008-09, 2012-13C; SL 2004-05 (Eng A), 2007-08, 2011-12; B 2009-10; UAE 2011-12 (v P), 2015-16C (v P). 1000 runs (5+1); most – 1466 (2015). HS 294 (*see Tests*). CC HS 195 v Northants (Northampton) 2005. BB 3-13 v Northants (Chelmsford) 2005. LO HS 137 (*see LOI*). BB – . T20 HS 100*.

‡[NO]**DIXON, Matthew** William, b Subiaco, W Australia 12 Jun 1992. RHB, RF. Squad No 30. W Australia 2010-11 to date. Joins Essex in 2016. UK passport. HS 22 WA v Q (Perth) 2011-12. BB 3-74 WA v Tas (Perth) 2011-12. LO HS 12 Cricket Australia XI v WA (Sydney) 2015-16. LO BB 3-40 CA v Tas (Sydney) 2015-16. T20 HS 4. T20 BB 3-32.

FOSTER, James Savin (Forest S, Snaresbrook; Collingwood C, Durham U), b Whipps Cross 15 Apr 1980. 6'0". RHB, WK. Squad No 7. British U 2000-01. Essex debut 2000; cap 2001; captain 2010 (*part*) to 2015; benefit 2011. Durham UCCE 2001. MCC 2004, 2008-10. **Tests**: 7 (2001-02 to 2002-03); HS 48 v I (Bangalore) 2001-02. **LOI**: 11 (2001-02); HS 13 v I (Bombay) 2001-02. **IT20**: 5 (2009); HS 14* v P (Oval) 2009. F-c Tours: A 2002-03; WI 2000-01 (Eng A); NZ 2001-02; I 2001-02, 2007-08 (Eng A). 1000 runs (1): 1037 (2004). HS 212 v Leics (Chelmsford) 2004. BB 1-122 v Northants (Northampton) 2008 – in contrived circumstances. LO HS 83* v Durham, inc 5 sixes in 5 balls off S.G.Borthwick (Chester-le-St) 2009 (P40). T20 HS 65*.

LAWRENCE, Daniel William (Trinity Catholic HS, Woodford Green), b Whipps Cross 12 Jul 1997. 6'2". RHB, LB. Squad No 28. Debut (Essex) 2015. Essex 2nd XI debut 2013, aged 15y 321d. England U19 2015. HS 161 v Surrey (Oval) 2015. T20 HS 3.

MASTERS, David Daniel (Fort Luton HS; Mid Kent CHE), b Chatham, Kent 22 Apr 1978. Son of K.D.Masters (Kent 1983-84), elder brother of D.Masters (Leicestershire 2009-10). 6'4". RHB, RMF. Squad No 9. Kent 2000-02. Leicestershire 2003-07; cap 2007. Essex debut/cap 2008; benefit 2013. HS 119 Le v Sussex (Hove) 2003. Ex HS 67 v Leics (Chelmsford) 2009. 50 wkts (4); most – 93 (2011). BB 8-10 v Leics (Southend) 2011. LO HS 39 Le v Glos (Cheltenham) 2006 (P40). LO BB 5-17 v Surrey (Oval) 2008 (FPT). T20 HS 14. T20 BB 3-7.

MICKLEBURGH, Jaik Charles (Bungay HS), b Norwich, Norfolk 30 Mar 1990. 5'10". RHB, RM. Squad No 32. Debut (Essex) 2008; cap 2013. Mid West Rhinos 2012-13. Norfolk 2007. England U19 2009. HS 243 v Leics (Chelmsford) 2013. BB – . LO HS 73 MWR v ME (Kwekwe) 2012-13. T20 HS 47*.

‡[NO]**MILNE, Adam** Fraser, b Palmerston North, New Zealand 13 Apr 1992. RHB, RF. Squad No 20. C Districts 2009-10 to date. Joins Essex in 2016 for T20 only. **LOI** (NZ): 33 (2012-13 to 2015-16); HS 36 v A (Wellington) 2015-16; BB 3-49 v P (Auckland) 2015-16. **IT20** (NZ): 14 (2010-11 to 2015-16); HS 10* v SA (Centurion) 2015; BB 4-37 v P (Auckland) 2015-16. F-c Tour (NZ A): SL 2013-14. HS 97 and BB 5-47 CD v Otago (Napier) 2012-13. LO HS 45 NZ A v Sri Lanka A (Lincoln) 2015-16. LO BB 5-61 NZ A v Sri Lanka A (Pallekele) 2013-14. T20 HS 18*. T20 BB 4-37.

MOORE, Thomas Cambridge (St Martin's S, Brentwood; Brentwood S), b Basildon 29 Mar 1992. 6'5". RHB, RMF. Squad No 33. Debut (Essex) 2014. Essex 2nd XI debut 2011. HS 17 and BB 4-78 v Glamorgan (Chelmsford) 2014. T20 HS – .

NAPIER, Graham Richard (The Gilberd S, Colchester), b Colchester 6 Jan 1980. 5'9½". RHB, RM. Squad No 17. Debut (Essex) 1997; cap 2003; benefit 2012. Wellington 2008-09. IPL: MI 2009. MCC 2004. F-c Tour (Eng A): I 2003-04. HS 196 v Surrey (Croydon) 2011, hitting a then world record-equalling 16 sixes and being dismissed just 28 balls after reaching his century. Won 2008 Walter Lawrence Trophy with 44-ball hundred v Sussex (Chelmsford). Won 2012 Walter Lawrence Trophy with 48-ball hundred v Cambridge MCCU (Cambridge). 50 wkts (2); most – 52 (2014). BB 7-21 v Cambridge MCCU (Cambridge) 2014. CC BB 7-90 v Leics (Leicester) 2013. LO HS 79 Essex CB v Lancs CB (Chelmsford) 2000 (NWT). LO BB 7-32 v Surrey (Chelmsford) 2013 (Y40). T20 HS 152* v Sussex (Chelmsford) 2008 – Ex record. T20 BB 4-10.

NIJJAR, Aron Stuart Singh (Ilford County HS), b Goodmayes 24 Sep 1994. LHB, SLA. Squad No 19. Debut (Essex) 2015. Essex 2nd XI debut 2013. Suffolk 2014. HS 53 v Northants (Chelmsford) 2015. BB 2-33 v Lancs (Chelmsford) 2015. LO HS 21 v Yorks (Chelmsford) 2015 (RLC). LO BB 1-39 v Sussex (Hove) 2015 (RLC).

PORTER, James Alexander (Oak Park HS, Newbury Park; Epping Forest C), b Leytonstone 25 May 1993. 5'11½". RHB, RMF. Squad No 44. Debut (Essex) 2014, taking a wkt with his 5th ball; cap 2015. MCC YCs 2011-13. Essex 2nd XI debut 2014. HS 34 v Glamorgan (Cardiff) 2015. 50 wkts (1): 56 (2015). BB 4-28 v Derbys (Chelmsford) 2015. LO HS 5* v Yorks (Chelmsford) 2015 (RLC). LO BB 3-39 v Hants (Southampton) 2015 (RLC).

‡**NQ QUINN, Matthew** Richard, b Auckland, New Zealand 28 Feb 1993. RHB, RMF. Squad No 94. Auckland 2012-13 to date. Joins Essex in 2016. UK passport. HS 50 v Auckland v Canterbury (Auckland) 2013-14. BB 4-41 Auckland v Wellington (Wellington) 2014-15 and 4-41 Auckland v CD (Auckland) 2014-15. LO HS 36 Auckland v CD (Auckland) 2013-14. LO BB 3-19 Auckland v ND (Mt Maunganui) 2014-15. T20 HS 4*. T20 BB 3-35.

NQ RYDER, Jesse Daniel (Napier BHS), b Masterton, Wairarapa, New Zealand 6 Aug 1984. LHB, RM. Squad No 77. C Districts 2002-03 to 2003-04. Wellington 2004-05 to 2012-13. Otago 2013-14 to 2014-15. Essex debut/cap 2014. IPL: RCB 2009. PW 2011-12. **Tests** (NZ): 18 (2008-09 to 2011-12); HS 201 v I (Napier) 2008-09; BB 2-7 v A (Brisbane) 2008-09. **LOI** (NZ): 48 (2007-08 to 2013-14); HS 107 v P (Auckland) 2010-11; BB 3-29 v I (Auckland) 2008-09. **IT20** (NZ): 22 (2007-08 to 2013-14); HS 62 v WI (Hamilton) 2008-09; BB 1-2 v E (Auckland) 2007-08. F-c Tours (NZ): A 2008-09, 2011-12; I 2010-11; SL 2005-06 (NZ A), 2009; B 2008-09. HS 236 Wellington v CD (Palmerston N) 2004-05. Ex HS 133 v Glos (Chelmsford) 2014. BB 6-47 (10-100 match) v Glamorgan (Chelmsford) 2015. LO HS 136 CD v Canterbury (Christchurch) 2015-16. LO BB 4-39 Wellington v ND (Wellington) 2005-06. T20 HS 107*. T20 BB 5-27.

TAYLOR, Callum John (Cromer Ac; Eastern C, Norwich), b Norwich, Norfolk 26 Jun 1997. 5'11". RHB, RM. Squad No 12. Debut (Essex) 2015. Essex 2nd XI debut 2013. Norfolk 2013. England U19 2014-15 to 2015. HS 26 v Glamorgan (Cardiff) 2015. T20 HS 2.

NQ Ten DOESCHATE, Ryan Neil (Fairbairn C; Cape Town U), b Port Elizabeth, South Africa 30 Jun 1980. 5'10½". RHB, RMF. Squad No 27. Debut (Essex) 2003; cap 2006; captain (l-o) 2014-15; captain 2016. EU passport – Dutch ancestry. Netherlands 2005 to 2009-10. Otago 2012-13. IPL: KKR 2011-15. Big Bash: AS 2014-15. **LOI** (Ne): 33 (2006 to 2010-11); HS 119 v E (Nagpur) 2010-11; BB 4-31 v Canada (Nairobi) 2006-07. **IT20** (Ne): 9 (2008 to 2009-10); HS 56 v Kenya (Belfast) 2008; BB 3-23 v Scotland (Belfast) 2008. F-c Tours (Ne): SA 2006-07, 2007-08; K 2005-06, 2009-10; Ireland 2005. HS 259* and BB 6-20 (9-112 match) Netherlands v Canada (Pretoria) 2006. Ex HS 164 v Sri Lankans (Chelmsford) 2011. CC HS 159* v Surrey (Guildford) 2009. Ex BB 6-57 v New Zealanders (Chelmsford) 2008. CC BB 5-13 v Hants (Chelmsford) 2010. LO HS 180 v Scotland (Chelmsford) 2013 (Y40) – Ex 40-over record, inc 15 sixes. LO BB 5-50 v Glos (Bristol) 2007 (FPT). T20 HS 121*. T20 BB 4-24.

VELANI, Kishen Shailesh (Brentwood S), b Newham, London 2 Sep 1994. 5'10". RHB, RM. Squad No 8. Debut (Essex) 2013. Essex 2nd XI debut 2012. England U19s 2012-13. HS 58 v Glos (Chelmsford) 2015. BB – . LO HS 27 v Northants (Northampton) 2014 (RLC). T20 HS 34.

‡^{NQ}**WAHAB RIAZ**, b Lahore, Pakistan 28 Jun 1985. RHB, LFM. Squad No 47. Lahore 2001-02 to 2006-07. Karachi Port Trust 2003-04. Hyderabad 2003-04 to 2004-05. National Bank 2007-08 to 2014-15. Kent 2011. Lahore Shalimar 2012-13. Joins Essex in 2016 for T20 only. **Tests** (P): 15 (2010 to 2015-16); HS 27 and BB 5-63 v E (Oval) 2010. **LOI** (P): 69 (2007-08 to 2015-16); HS 54* v Z (Brisbane) 2014-15; BB 5-46 v I (Mohali) 2010-11. **IT20** (P): 17 (2007-08 to 2015-16); HS 30* v NZ (Auckland) 2010-11; BB 3-34 v NZ (Auckland) 2015-16. F-c Tours (P): E 2010; A 2009 (P A); WI 2011; NZ 2010-11; SL 2009 (P A), 2014, 2015; B 2014-15; UAE 2015-16. HS 84 NBP v WAPDA (Lahore) 2011-12. CC HS 34 K v Surrey (Canterbury) 2011. 50 wkts (0+2); most – 68 (2007-08). BB 9-59 (12-120 match) Lahore S v Lahore Ravi (Lahore) 2012-13. CC BB 4-94 K v Leics (Leicester) 2011. LO HS 77 NBP v PT (Rawalpindi) 2013-14. LO BB 5-24 NBP v SNGPL (Sargodha) 2008-09. T20 HS 32*. T20 BB 5-17.

WESTLEY, Thomas (Linton Village C; Hills Road SFC), b Cambridge 13 March 1989. 6'2". RHB, OB. Squad No 21. Debut (Essex) 2007; cap 2013. MCC 2007, 2009. Durham MCCU 2010-11. Cambridgeshire 2005. HS 185 v Glamorgan (Colchester) 2012. BB 4-55 DU v Durham (Durham) 2010. CC BB 4-75 v Surrey (Colchester) 2015. LO HS 111* v Yorks (Scarborough) 2014 (RLC). LO BB 4-60 v Northants (Northampton) 2014 (RLC). T20 HS 109*. T20 BB 2-27.

WINSLADE, Jack Robert (Whitgift S, Croydon), b Epsom 12 Apr 1995. Younger brother of T.S.Winslade (Loughborough MCCU 2010). 5'10". RHB, RMF. Debut (Essex) 2015. Surrey 2nd XI debut 2011, aged 16y 6d. LHB. BB 4-20 v Derbys (Derby) 2015 – on debut. LO HS – . LO BB 1-61 v Durham (Chester-le-St) 2014 (RLC).

RELEASED/RETIRED

(Having made a County 1st XI appearance in 2015)

^{NQ}**ADEEL MALIK** (Sialkot S), b Sialkot, Pakistan 17 Oct 1985. Younger brother of Shoaib Malik (*see DURHAM*). RHB, LB. Sialkot 2002-03 to 2009-10. Essex 2015. HS 79 Sialkot v Karachi Blues (Karachi) 2009-10. Ex HS 25 v Glos (Chelmsford) 2015. BB 3-39 v Glamorgan (Cardiff) 2015. LO HS 70 Sialkot Stallions v Lahore Lions (Sialkot) 2009-10. LO BB 3-39 Sialkot Stallions v Quetta Bears (Mirpur Khas) 2012-13. T20 HS 70*. T20 BB 4-15.

PANESAR, Mudhsuden Singh ('**Monty**') (Stopsley HS; Bedford Modern S; Loughborough U), b Luton, Beds 25 Apr 1982. 6'0". LHB, SLA. Northamptonshire 2001-09; cap 2006. British U 2002-05. Loughborough UCCE 2004. Lions 2009-10. Sussex 2010-13; cap 2010. Essex 2013-15. MCC 2006, 2014. Bedfordshire 1998-99. *Wisden* 2007. **Tests**: 50 (2005-06 to 2013-14); HS 26 v SL (Nottingham) 2006; BB 6-37 v NZ (Manchester) 2008. **LOI**: 26 (2006-07 to 2007-08); HS 13 v WI (Nottingham) 2007; BB 3-25 v B (Bridgetown) 2006-07. **IT20**: 1 (2006-07); HS 1 and BB 2-40 v A (Sydney) 2006-07. F-c Tours: A 2006-07, 2010-11, 2013-14; WI 2008-09; NZ 2007-08, 2012-13; I 2005-06, 2008-09, 2012-13; SL 2002-03 (ECB Acad), 2007-08, 2011-12; UAE 2011-12 (v P). HS 46* Sx v Middx (Hove) 2010. Ex HS 38 v Worcs (Chelmsford) 2014. 50 wkts (6); most – 71 (2006). BB 7-60 (13-137 match) Sx v Somerset (Taunton) 2012. Ex BB 6-111 v Leics (Chelmsford) 2014. LO HS 17* Nh v Leics (Northampton) 2008 (FPT). LO BB 5-20 ECB Acad v SL Acad XI (Colombo) 2002-03. T20 HS 3*. T20 BB 3-14.

PETTINI, M.L. – *see LEICESTERSHIRE*.

RELEASED/RETIRED continued on p 110

ESSEX 2015

RESULTS SUMMARY

	Place	Won	Lost	Tied	Drew	NR
LV= County Championship (2nd Division)	3rd	6	5		5	
All First-Class Matches		6	6		5	
Royal London One-Day Cup (Group B)	QF	4	3			2
NatWest t20 Blast (South Group)	QF	7	7			1

LV= COUNTY CHAMPIONSHIP AVERAGES
BATTING AND FIELDING

Cap		M	I	NO	HS	Runs	Avge	100	50	Ct/St
2006	M.L.Pettini	5	7	3	134	402	100.50	2	1	5
	L.A.Dawson	2	4	1	99	169	56.33	–	1	2
2006	R.N.ten Doeschate	12	19	4	88	832	55.46	–	7	6
2015	N.L.J.Browne	16	29	2	151*	1157	42.85	5	3	16
2014	J.D.Ryder	14	24	5	124	806	42.42	2	3	14
2013	T.Westley	12	21	1	179	782	39.10	1	4	6
	D.W.Lawrence	7	12	1	161	409	37.18	1	1	8
	A.S.S.Nijjar	6	8	4	53	129	32.25	–	1	–
2001	J.S.Foster	16	23	2	98	671	31.95	–	5	44/3
2005	R.S.Bopara	12	21	1	99	565	28.25	–	4	3
	K.S.Velani	4	7	–	58	190	27.14	–	1	3
2005	A.N.Cook	3	5	–	80	135	27.00	–	1	4
2003	G.R.Napier	13	17	1	73	363	22.68	–	2	5
2013	J.C.Mickleburgh	10	18	–	61	398	22.11	–	2	6
	G.M.Smith	4	5	1	50*	76	19.00	–	1	3
2008	D.D.Masters	7	10	3	28	85	12.14	–	–	3
	M.E.T.Salisbury	4	6	–	24	56	9.33	–	–	2
	Adeel Malik	3	6	–	25	48	8.00	–	–	1
2015	J.A.Porter	15	19	5	34	98	7.00	–	–	5

Also played: T.C.Moore (2 matches) 0* (1 ct); M.S.Panesar (3) 11, 11*, 2* (1 ct); R.H.Patel (1) 0*, 0; C.J.Taylor (1) 26, 22; R.J.W.Topley (2 – cap 2013) 0, 4*, 0 (1 ct); J.R.Winslade (2) did not bat.

BOWLING

	O	M	R	W	Avge	Best	5wI	10wM
R.S.Bopara	148.2	24	505	20	25.25	4- 29	–	–
J.D.Ryder	333.4	70	1120	44	25.45	6- 47	3	1
G.R.Napier	281	39	979	35	27.97	4- 27	–	–
J.A.Porter	393.5	64	1418	50	28.36	4- 28	–	–
D.D.Masters	224.2	54	606	20	30.30	4- 45	–	–
A.S.S.Nijjar	83.3	10	332	10	33.20	2- 33	–	–
Also bowled:								
G.M.Smith	33.2	5	110	5	22.00	3- 22	–	–
R.N.ten Doeschate	40	5	144	6	24.00	3- 15	–	–
R.J.W.Topley	53	10	206	7	29.42	3- 90	–	–
M.S.Panesar	75.1	17	270	7	38.57	4-112	–	–
T.Westley	98.4	7	310	6	51.66	4- 75	–	–

Adeel Malik 46.5-2-224-4; N.L.J.Browne 2.5-1-7-0; L.A.Dawson 27.2-6-73-4; T.C.Moore 24-6-95-3; R.H.Patel 18-2-92-1; M.E.T.Salisbury 32-3-125-1; J.R.Winslade 21-2-97-4.

The First-Class Averages (pp 227–243) give the records of Essex players in all first-class county matches (Essex's other opponents being the Australians), with the exception of A.N.Cook, L.A.Dawson and R.H.Patel, whose first-class figures for Essex are as above.

ESSEX RECORDS

FIRST-CLASS CRICKET

Highest Total	For	761-6d		v	Leics	Chelmsford	1990
	V	803-4d		by	Kent	Brentwood	1934
Lowest Total	For	20		v	Lancashire	Chelmsford	2013
	V	14		by	Surrey	Chelmsford	1983
Highest Innings	For	343*	P.A.Perrin	v	Derbyshire	Chesterfield	1904
	V	332	W.H.Ashdown	for	Kent	Brentwood	1934

Highest Partnership for each Wicket

1st	316	G.A.Gooch/P.J.Prichard	v	Kent	Chelmsford	1994
2nd	403	G.A.Gooch/P.J.Prichard	v	Leics	Chelmsford	1990
3rd	347*	M.E.Waugh/N.Hussain	v	Lancashire	Ilford	1992
4th	314	Salim Malik/N.Hussain	v	Surrey	The Oval	1991
5th	339	J.C.Mickleburgh/J.S.Foster	v	Durham	Chester-le-St[2]	2010
6th	253	A.J.A.Wheater/J.S.Foster	v	Northants	Chelmsford	2011
7th	261	J.W.H.T.Douglas/J.Freeman	v	Lancashire	Leyton	1914
8th	263	D.R.Wilcox/R.M.Taylor	v	Warwicks	Southend	1946
9th	251	J.W.H.T.Douglas/S.N.Hare	v	Derbyshire	Leyton	1921
10th	218	F.H.Vigar/T.P.B.Smith	v	Derbyshire	Chesterfield	1947

Best Bowling	For	10- 32	H.Pickett	v	Leics	Leyton	1895
(Innings)	V	10- 40	E.G.Dennett	for	Glos	Bristol	1906
Best Bowling	For	17-119	W.Mead	v	Hampshire	Southampton	1895
(Match)	V	17- 56	C.W.L.Parker	for	Glos	Gloucester	1925

Most Runs – Season	2559	G.A.Gooch	(av 67.34)		1984
Most Runs – Career	30701	G.A.Gooch	(av 51.77)		1973-97
Most 100s – Season	9	J.O'Connor			1929, 1934
	9	D.J.Insole			1955
Most 100s – Career	94	G.A.Gooch			1973-97
Most Wkts – Season	172	T.P.B Smith	(av 27.13)		1947
Most Wkts – Career	1610	T.P.B.Smith	(av 26.68)		1929-51
Most Career W-K Dismissals	1231	B.Taylor	(1040 ct; 191 st)		1949-73
Most Career Catches in the Field	519	K.W.R.Fletcher			1962-88

LIMITED-OVERS CRICKET

Highest Total	50ov	391-5		v	Surrey	The Oval	2008
	40ov	368-7		v	Scotland	Chelmsford	2013
	T20	242-3		v	Sussex	Chelmsford	2008
Lowest Total	50ov	57		v	Lancashire	Lord's	1996
	40ov	69		v	Derbyshire	Chesterfield	1974
	T20	74		v	Middlesex	Chelmsford	2013
Highest Innings	50ov	201*	R.S.Bopara	v	Leics	Leicester	2008
	40ov	180	R.N.ten Doeschate	v	Scotland	Chelmsford	2013
	T20	152*	G.R.Napier	v	Sussex	Chelmsford	2008
Best Bowling	50ov	5- 8	J.K.Lever	v	Middlesex	Westcliff	1972
		5- 8	G.A.Gooch	v	Cheshire	Chester	1995
	40ov	8-26	K.D.Boyce	v	Lancashire	Manchester	1971
	T20	6-16	T.G.Southee	v	Glamorgan	Chelmsford	2011

GLAMORGAN

Formation of Present Club: 6 July 1888
Inaugural First-Class Match: 1921
Colours: Blue and Gold
Badge: Gold Daffodil
County Champions: (3) 1948, 1969, 1997
Pro 40/National League (Div 1) Winners: (2) 2002, 2004
Sunday League Winners: (1) 1993
Twenty20 Cup Winners: (0); best – Semi-Finalist 2004

GLAMORGAN

Chief Executive: Hugh Morris, The SSE SWALEC, Cardiff, CF11 9XR • Tel: 02920 409380 • Fax: 02920 419389 • email: info@glamorgancricket.co.uk • Web: www.glamorgancricket.com • Twitter: @GlamCricket (22,430 followers)

Head Coach: Robert Croft. **2nd XI Coach**: Steve Watkin. **Player Development Manager**: Richard Almond. **Captain**: J.A.Rudolph. **Vice-Captain**: M.A.Wallace. **Overseas Players**: J.A.Rudolph. **2016 Beneficiary**: None. **Head Groundsman**: Robin Saxton. **Scorer**: Andrew K.Hignell. ‡ New registration. NQ Not qualified for England.

BRAGG, William David (Rougemont S, Newport; UWIC), b Newport, Monmouthshire 24 Oct 1986. 5'9". LHB, RM. Squad No 22. Debut (Glamorgan) 2007; cap 2015. No f-c appearances in 2008. Wales MC 2004-09. 1000 runs (2); most – 1033 (2011). HS 120 v Leics (Leicester) 2015. BB 2-10 v Worcs (Cardiff) 2013. LO HS 88 v Surrey (Guildford) 2014 (RLC). LO BB 1-11 v Glos (Cardiff) 2013 (Y40). T20 HS 15.

BULL, Kieran Andrew (Q Elizabeth HS, Haverfordwest; Cardiff Met U), b Haverfordwest 5 Apr 1995. 6'2". RHB, OB. Squad No 11. Debut (Glamorgan) 2014. Cardiff MCCU 2015. Wales MC 2012-13. HS 31 v Glos (Swansea) 2015. BB 4-62 v Kent (Canterbury) 2014. LO HS – . LO BB 1-40 v Middx (Lord's) 2015 (RLC).

COOKE, Christopher Barry (Bishops S, Cape Town; U of Cape Town), b Johannesburg, South Africa 30 May 1986. 5'11". RHB, WK. Squad No 46. W Province 2009-10. Glamorgan debut 2013. Glamorgan 2nd XI debut 2010. HS 171 v Kent (Canterbury) 2014. LO HS 137* v Somerset (Taunton) 2012 (CB40). T20 HS 65*.

COSKER, Dean Andrew (Millfield S), b Weymouth, Dorset 7 Jan 1978. 5'11". RHB, SLA. Squad No 23. Debut (Glamorgan) 1996; cap 2000; benefit 2010. MCC 2010. F-c Tours (Eng A): SA 1998-99; SL 1997-98; Z 1998-99; K 1997-98. HS 69 v Kent (Canterbury) 2015. 50 wkts (1): 51 (2010). BB 6-91 (11-126 match) v Essex (Cardiff) 2009. LO HS 50* v Northants (Northampton) 2009 (FPT). LO BB 5-54 v Essex (Chelmsford) 2003 (NL). T20 HS 21*. T20 BB 4-25.

DONALD, Aneurin Henry Thomas (Pontarddulais CS), b Swansea 20 Dec 1996. RHB, OB. Squad No 12. Debut (Glamorgan) 2014. Glamorgan 2nd XI debut 2012, aged 15y 189d. Wales MC 2012. HS 98 v Glos (Bristol) 2015. LO HS 37 v Essex (Cardiff) 2015 (RLC). T20 HS 6.

HOGAN, Michael Garry, b Newcastle, New South Wales, Australia 31 May 1981. British passport. 6'5". RHB, RFM. Squad No 31. W Australia 2009-10 to date. Glamorgan debut/cap 2013. Big Bash: HH 2011-13. HS 57 v Lancs (Colwyn Bay) 2015. 50 wkts (2); most – 67 (2013). BB 7-92 v Glos (Bristol) 2013. LO HS 27 WA v Vic (Melbourne) 2011-12. LO BB 5-44 WA v Vic (Melbourne) 2010-11. T20 HS 5*. T20 BB 4-26.

NO **INGRAM, Colin** Alexander, b Port Elizabeth, South Africa 3 Jul 1985. LHB, LB. Squad No 41. Free State 2004-05 to 2005-06. Eastern Province 2005-06 to 2008-09. Warriors 2006-07 to date. Somerset 2014. Glamorgan debut 2015 (Kolpak signing). IPL: DD 2011. **LOI** (SA): 31 (2010-11 to 2013-14); HS 124 v Z (Bloemfontein) 2010-11 – on debut; BB – . **IT20** (SA): 9 (2010-11 to 2011-12); HS 78 v I (Johannesburg) 2011-12. HS 190 EP v KZN (Port Elizabeth) 2008-09. Gm HS 105 v Kent (Cardiff) 2015. BB 4-16 EP v Boland (Port Elizabeth) 2005-06. Gm BB 3-90 v Essex (Chelmsford) 2015. LO HS 130 v Essex (Cardiff) 2015. LO BB 2-13 EP v Boland (Port Elizabeth) 2005-06. T20 HS 96. T20 BB 2-20.

KETTLEBOROUGH, James Michael (Bedford S), b Huntingdon 22 Oct 1992. 5'11". RHB, OB. Squad No 3. Northamptonshire 2014. Glamorgan debut 2015. Northamptonshire 2nd XI debut 2012. Middlesex 2nd XI 2011-12. Bedfordshire 2009-13. HS 81 v Glos (Bristol) 2015. LO HS 26 Nh v Lancs (Manchester) 2014 (RLC).

LAWLOR, Jeremy Lloyd (Monmouth S; Cardiff Met U), b Cardiff 4 Nov 1995. Son of P.J.Lawlor (Glamorgan 1981). 6'0". RHB, RM. Squad No 6. Cardiff MCCU 2015. Glamorgan debut 2015. Glamorgan 2nd XI debut 2012. Wales MC 2013. HS 3 CfU v Glamorgan (Cardiff) 2015. Gm HS 0. BB – .

LLOYD, David Liam (Darland HS; Shrewsbury S), b St Asaph, Denbighs 15 May 1992. 5'9". RHB, RM. Squad No 14. Debut (Glamorgan) 2012. Glamorgan 2nd XI debut 2008. Wales MC 2010-11. HS 92 v Northants (Northampton) 2015. BB 3-68 v Surrey (Guildford) 2015. LO HS 33 v Hants (Cardiff) 2015 (RLC). BB 4-10 v Durham (Cardiff) 2014 (RLC). T20 HS 18. T20 BB 2-13.

MESCHEDE, Craig Anthony Joseph (King's C, Taunton), b Johannesburg, South Africa 21 Nov 1991. 6'1". RHB, RMF. Squad No 44. Somerset 2011-14. Glamorgan debut 2015. Somerset 2nd XI debut 2008, aged 16y 244d. HS 107 v Northants (Cardiff) 2015. BB 4-43 Sm v Surrey (Taunton) 2013. Gm BB 4-89 v Glos (Swansea) 2015. LO HS 40* Sm v Glamorgan (Taunton) 2013 (Y40). LO BB 4-5 Sm v Leics (Taunton) 2013 (Y40). T20 HS 53. T20 BB 3-9.

MURPHY, Jack Roger (Greenhill S, Tenby; Cardiff Met U), b Haverfordwest 15 Jul 1995. LHB, LFM. Squad No 7. Debut (Cardiff MCCU) 2015. Glamorgan 2nd XI debut 2011. Wales MC 2011-13. Awaiting 1st XI debut. HS 22 and BB 2-90 CfU v Glamorgan (Cardiff) 2015.

PENRHYN JONES, Dewi (Ellesmere S), b Wrexham, Denbighs 9 Sep 1994. 6'1". RHB, RFM. Squad No 30. Debut (Glamorgan) 2015. Glamorgan 2nd XI debut 2013. Wales MC 2012-14. HS 17 and BB 3-55 v Nhants (Northampton) 2015. LO HS 0* v Middx (Lord's) 2015 (RLC). LO BB 1-22 v Middx (Cardiff) 2014 (RLC).

‡PODMORE, Harry William (Twyford HS), b Hammersmith, London 23 Jul 1994. 6'3". RHB, RM. Squad No 17. Joins from Middlesex on two-month loan. Middlesex 2nd XI debut 2011. MCC YC 2013. Awaiting f-c debut. LO HS 1* M v Notts (Lord's) 2014 (RLC). LO BB 2-46 M v Somerset (Lord's) 2014 (RLC). T20 HS 9. T20 BB 3-13.

^{NQ}**RUDOLPH**, Jacobus Andries ('**Jacques**') (Afrikaanse Hoer Seunskool), b Springs, Transvaal, South Africa 4 May 1981. Elder brother of G.J.Rudolph (Limpopo and Namibia 2006-07 to 2012-13). 5'11". LHB, LBG. Squad No 4. Northerns 1997-98 to 2003-04. Titans 2004-05 to 2014-15. Eagles 2005-06 to 2007-08. Yorkshire 2007-11 (Kolpak registration); scored 122 v Surrey (Oval) on debut; cap 2007. Surrey 2012. Glamorgan debut/cap 2014; captain 2015 to date. **Tests** (SA): 48 (2003 to 2012-13); HS 222* v B (Chittagong) 2003 – on debut; BB 1-1 v E (Leeds) 2003. **LOI** (SA): 45 (2003 to 2005-06); HS 81 v B (Dhaka) 2003. **IT20** (SA): 1 (2005-06); HS 6* v A (Brisbane) 2005-06. F-c Tours (SA): E 2003, 2012; A 2001-02, 2005-06, 2012-13; WI 2004-05; NZ 2003-04, 2011-12; I 2004-05; SL 2004, 2005-06, 2006; B 2003. 1000 runs (4+1); most – 1375 (2010). HS 228* Y v Durham (Leeds) 2010. Gm HS 139 and Gm BB 1-25 v Glos (Bristol) 2014. BB 5-80 Eagles v Cape Cobras (Cape Town) 2007-08. CC BB 1-13 Y v Somerset (Scarborough) 2008. LO HS 169* v Sussex (Hove) 2014 – Gm record. LO BB 4-41 SA A v New Zealand A (Colombo) 2005-06. T20 HS 101*. T20 BB 3-16.

SALTER, Andrew Graham (Milford Haven SFC; Cardiff Met U), b Haverfordwest 1 Jun 1993. 5'9". RHB, OB. Squad No 21. Cardiff MCCU 2012-14. Glamorgan debut 2013. Glamorgan 2nd XI debut 2010. Wales MC 2010-11. HS 73 v Glos (Swansea) 2015. BB 3-5 v Northants (Cardiff) 2015. LO HS 36* v Notts (Cardiff) 2014 (RLC). LO BB 2-41 v Notts (Nottingham) 2012 (CB40) and 2-41 v Notts (Lord's) 2013 (Y40). T20 HS 17*. T20 BB 2-19.

‡**SELMAN, Nicholas** James (Matthew Flinders Anglican C, Buderim), b Brisbane, Australia 18 Oct 1995. RHB, RM. Squad No 9. Kent 2nd XI debut 2014. Gloucestershire 2nd XI 2015. Awaiting 1st XI debut.

SMITH, Ruaidhri Alexander James (Llandaff Cathedral S; Shrewsbury S; Bristol U), b Glasgow, Scotland 5 Aug 1994. 6'1". RHB, RM. Squad No 20. Debut (Glamorgan) 2013. Wales MC 2010-11. Glamorgan 2nd XI debut 2011. Scotland (l-o only) 2013. HS 57* v Glos (Bristol) 2014. BB 3-23 v Derbys (Chesterfield) 2015. LO HS 9 v Middx (Lord's) 2015 (RLC). LO BB 3-48 Scot v Surrey (Oval) 2013 (Y40). T20 HS 16*. T20 BB 1-11.

‡**van der GUGTEN, Timm**, b Hornsby, Sydney, Australia 25 Feb 1991. 6'1½". RHB, RFM. Squad No 64. New South Wales 2011-12. Netherlands 2012 to date. Big Bash: HH 2014-15. **LOI** (Neth): 4 (2011-12 to 2013); HS 2 (twice); BB 5-24 v Canada (King City, NW) 2013. **IT20** (Neth): 20 (2011-12 to 2015-16); HS 12* v Nepal (Rotterdam) 2015; BB 3-18 v B (The Hague) 2012. HS 57 Neth v Papua New Guinea (Amstelveen) 2015. BB 7-68 (10-121 match) Neth v Namibia (Windhoek) 2013. LO HS 23 Neth v Namibia (Windhoek) 2013; LO BB 5-24 (*see LOI*). T20 HS 12*. T20 BB 5-21.

WAGG, Graham Grant (Ashlawn S, Rugby), b Rugby, Warwks 28 Apr 1983. 6'0". RHB, LM. Squad No 8. Warwickshire 2002-04. Derbyshire 2006-10; cap 2007. Glamorgan debut 2011; cap 2013. F-c Tour (Eng A): I 2003-04. HS 200 v Surrey (Guildford) 2015. 50 wkts (2); most – 59 (2008). BB 6-29 v Surrey (Oval) 2014. LO HS 62* v Essex (Cardiff) 2015 (RLC). LO BB 4-35 De v Durham (Derby) 2008 (FPT). T20 HS 62. T20 BB 5-14 v Worcs (Worcester) 2013 – Gm record.

WALLACE, Mark Alexander (Crickhowell HS), b Abergavenny, Monmouthshire 19 Nov 1981. 5'9". LHB, WK. Squad No 18. Debut (Glamorgan) 1999; cap 2003; captain 2012-14; benefit 2013. F-c Tour (ECB Acad): SL 2002-03. 1000 runs (1): 1020 (2011). HS 139 v Surrey (Oval) 2009, sharing Gm record 6th wkt partnership of 240 with J.Allenby. LO HS 118* v Glos (Cardiff) 2013 (Y40). T20 HS 69*.

(Having made a County 1st XI appearance in 2015)

^{NQ}**PARNELL, Wayne** Dillon (Grey HS), b Port Elizabeth, South Africa 30 Jul 1989. 6'1". LHB, LFM. E Province 2006-07 to 2010-11. Warriors 2008-09 to 2014-15. Kent 2009. Sussex 2011. Glamorgan 2015 (T20 only). Cape Cobras 2015-16. IPL: PW 2011-13. DD 2014. **Tests** (SA): 4 (2009-10 to 2013-14); HS 22 v I (Kolkata) 2009-10; BB 2-17 v E (Johannesburg) 2009-10. **LOI** (SA): 46 (2008-09 to 2014-15); HS 56 v P (Sharjah) 2013-14; BB 5-48 v E (Cape Town) 2009-10. **IT20** (SA): 35 (2008-09 to 2015); HS 29* v A (Johannesburg) 2011-12; BB 4-13 v WI (Oval) 2009. F-c Tour (SA): I 2009-10; Ire 2012 (SA A). HS 91 SA A v India A (Pretoria) 2013. CC HS 90 K v Glamorgan (Canterbury) 2009. BB 7-56 SA A v Ireland (Oak Hill) 2012. CC BB 4-78 K v Essex (Chelmsford) 2009. LO HS 129 Warriors v Lions (Potchefstroom) 2013-14. LO BB 6-51 Warriors v Knights (Kimberley) 2013-14. T20 HS 99. T20 BB 4-13.

WRIGHT, Ben James (Cowbridge CS), b Preston, Lancs 5 Dec 1987. 5'9". RHB, RM. Glamorgan 2006-15; cap 2011. No f-c appearances in 2008. HS 172 v Glos (Cardiff) 2010. BB 1-14 v Essex (Chelmsford) 2007. LO HS 79 v Lancs (Colwyn Bay) 2010 (CB40). LO BB 1-19 v Derbys (Derby) 2009 (FPT). T20 HS 63*. T20 BB 1-16.

W.T.Owen left the staff without making a County 1st XI appearance in 2015.

ESSEX RELEASED/RETIRED (continued from p 104)

SALISBURY, Matthew Edward Thomas (Shenfield HS; Anglia Ruskin U), b Chelmsford 18 Apr 1993. 6'0½". RHB, RMF. Cambridge MCCU 2012-13. Essex 2014-15. Essex 2nd XI debut 2011. HS 24 v Leics (Chelmsford) 2015. BB 4-50 v Worcs (Worcester) 2014. LO HS 5* v Leics (Chelmsford) 2014 (RLC). LO BB 4-55 v Lancs (Chelmsford) 2014 (RLC). T20 HS 1*. T20 BB 2-19.

^{NQ}**SMITH, Gregory** Marc (St Stithins C), b Johannesburg, South Africa 20 Apr 1983. 5'9". RHB, RM/OB. Debut (SA Academy) 2003-04. Griqualand West 2003-04. Derbyshire 2006-11 (Kolpak registration); cap 2009; captain 2010 (*part*). Mountaineers 2010-11. Essex 2012-15. HS 177 v Glos (Bristol) 2013. BB 5-42 v Leics (Chelmsford) 2013. LO HS 89 Abahani v KKC (Savar) 2013-14. LO BB 4-53 De v Lancs (Derby) 2009 (P40). T20 HS 100*. T20 BB 5-17.

^{NQ}**TAIT, Shaun** William (Oakwood Area State S, S Aus), b Bedford Park, Adelaide, S Australia 22 Feb 1983. 6'4". RHB, RF. S Aus 2002-03 to 2008-09. Durham 2004. Essex 2013-15 (T20 only). IPL: RR 2009-13. Big Bash: MR 2011-12. AS 2012-13 to 2014-15. HH 2015-16. **Tests** (A): 3 (2005 to 2007-08); HS 8 v I (Perth) 2007-08; BB 3-97 v E (Nottingham) 2005. **LOI** (A): 35 (2006-07 to 2010-11); HS 11 v E (Sydney) 2006-07; BB 4-39 v SA (Gros Islet) 2006-07. **IT20** (A): 21 (2007-08 to 2015-16); HS 6 v P (Birmingham) 2010; BB 3-13 v P (Melbourne) 2009-10. F-c Tour (A): E 2005. HS 68 S Aus v Vic (Adelaide) 2005-06. CC HS 4. BB 7-29 (10-98 match) S Aus v Q (Brisbane) 2007-08. CC BB – . LO HS 22* Aus A v Z (Perth) 2003-04. LO BB 8-43 inc hat-trick S Aus v Tas (Adelaide) 2003-04, 8th best analysis in all l-o cricket. T20 HS 26. T20 BB 5-32.

TOPLEY, R.J.W. – *see HAMPSHIRE.*

GLAMORGAN 2015

RESULTS SUMMARY

	Place	Won	Lost	Tied	Drew	NR
LV= County Championship (2nd Division)	4th	4	4		8	
All First-Class Matches		4	4		9	
Royal London One-Day Cup (Group B)	8th	2	2			4
NatWest t20 Blast (South Group)	6th	7	7			

LV= COUNTY CHAMPIONSHIP AVERAGES

BATTING AND FIELDING

Cap		M	I	NO	HS	Runs	Avge	100	50	Ct/St
2000	D.A.Cosker	5	6	3	69	146	48.66	–	1	6
	D.L.Lloyd	12	19	5	92	547	39.07	–	3	4
2014	J.A.Rudolph	14	26	2	111	927	38.62	1	7	13
	C.A.Ingram	16	28	3	105*	931	37.24	2	4	10
2013	G.G.Wagg	16	23	–	200	838	36.43	1	4	6
	C.B.Cooke	15	27	5	102*	772	35.09	1	5	18
	A.H.T.Donald	5	10	1	98	288	32.00	–	1	3
	C.A.J.Meschede	16	23	3	107	635	31.75	2	2	5
2015	W.D.Bragg	13	23	1	120	588	26.72	2	1	3
	J.M.Kettleborough	8	15	1	81	364	26.00	–	3	4
2013	M.G.Hogan	14	19	8	57	271	24.63	–	1	11
	A.G.Salter	12	19	2	73	411	24.17	–	2	5
2003	M.A.Wallace	15	23	2	92	507	24.14	–	3	42/3
	A.Carter	4	4	2	21*	42	21.00	–	–	–
2011	B.J.Wright	4	6	–	68	115	19.16	–	1	2

Also batted: K.A.Bull (2 matches) 31, 7; J.L.Lawlor (1) 0, 0; D.Penrhyn Jones (2) 17, 9* (1 ct); R.A.J.Smith (2) 49*, 6*.

BOWLING

	O	M	R	W	Avge	Best	5wI	10wM
A.Carter	121.1	23	373	16	23.31	4-53	–	–
M.G.Hogan	482.1	126	1297	48	27.02	5-44	2	–
G.G.Wagg	459.4	71	1656	45	36.80	5-54	1	–
C.A.J.Meschede	429.3	66	1591	40	39.77	4-89	–	–
C.A.Ingram	103.3	9	398	10	39.80	3-90	–	–
A.G.Salter	339.1	42	1150	25	46.00	3- 5	–	–
D.L.Lloyd	206.2	22	912	19	48.00	3-68	–	–
Also bowled:								
R.A.J.Smith	33	5	134	5	26.80	3-23	–	–
D.Penrhyn Jones	32	1	190	5	38.00	3-55	–	–
D.A.Cosker	168	20	637	6	106.16	2-81	–	–

W.D.Bragg 23.4-3-86-1; K.A.Bull 21.5-4-104-0; J.L.Lawlor 4-1-11-0; J.A.Rudolph 3-0-11-0.

The First-Class Averages (pp 227–243) give the records of Glamorgan players in all first-class county matches (Glamorgan's other opponents being Cardiff MCCU), with the exception of K.A.Bull, A. Carter and J.L.Lawlor, whose first-class figures for Glamorgan are as above.

GLAMORGAN RECORDS

FIRST-CLASS CRICKET

Highest Total	For 718-3d			v	Sussex	Colwyn Bay	2000
	V 712			by	Northants	Northampton	1998
Lowest Total	For 22			v	Lancashire	Liverpool	1924
	V 33			by	Leics	Ebbw Vale	1965
Highest Innings	For 309*	S.P.James		v	Sussex	Colwyn Bay	2000
	V 322*	M.B.Loye		for	Northants	Northampton	1998

Highest Partnership for each Wicket

1st	374	M.T.G.Elliott/S.P.James	v	Sussex	Colwyn Bay	2000
2nd	252	M.P.Maynard/D.L.Hemp	v	Northants	Cardiff	2002
3rd	313	D.E.Davies/W.E.Jones	v	Essex	Brentwood	1948
4th	425*	A.Dale/I.V.A.Richards	v	Middlesex	Cardiff	1993
5th	264	M.Robinson/S.W.Montgomery	v	Hampshire	Bournemouth	1949
6th	240	J.Allenby/M.A.Wallace	v	Surrey	The Oval	2009
7th	211	P.A.Cottey/O.D.Gibson	v	Leics	Swansea	1996
8th	202	D.Davies/J.J.Hills	v	Sussex	Eastbourne	1928
9th	203*	J.J.Hills/J.C.Clay	v	Worcs	Swansea	1929
10th	143	T.Davies/S.A.B.Daniels	v	Glos	Swansea	1982

Best Bowling	For 10- 51	J.Mercer	v	Worcs	Worcester	1936
(Innings)	V 10- 18	G.Geary	for	Leics	Pontypridd	1929
Best Bowling	For 17-212	J.C.Clay	v	Worcs	Swansea	1937
(Match)	V 16- 96	G.Geary	for	Leics	Pontypridd	1929

Most Runs – Season	2276	H.Morris	(av 55.51)		1990
Most Runs – Career	34056	A.Jones	(av 33.03)		1957-83
Most 100s – Season	10	H.Morris			1990
Most 100s – Career	54	M.P.Maynard			1985-2005
Most Wkts – Season	176	J.C.Clay	(av 17.34)		1937
Most Wkts – Career	2174	D.J.Shepherd	(av 20.95)		1950-72
Most Career W-K Dismissals	933	E.W.Jones	(840 ct; 93 st)		1961-83
Most Career Catches in the Field	656	P.M.Walker			1956-72

LIMITED-OVERS CRICKET

Highest Total	50ov	429		v	Surrey	The Oval	2002
	40ov	328-4		v	Lancashire	Colwyn Bay	2011
	T20	240-3		v	Surrey	The Oval	2015
Lowest Total	50ov	68		v	Lancashire	Manchester	1973
	40ov	42		v	Derbyshire	Swansea	1979
	T20	94-9		v	Essex	Cardiff	2010
Highest Innings	50ov	169*	J.A.Rudolph	v	Sussex	Hove	2014
	40ov	155*	J.H.Kallis	v	Surrey	Pontypridd	1999
	T20	116*	I.J.Thomas	v	Somerset	Taunton	2004
Best Bowling	50ov	6-20	S.D.Thomas	v	Comb Univs	Cardiff	1995
	40ov	7-16	S.D.Thomas	v	Surrey	Swansea	1998
	T20	5-14	G.G.Wagg	v	Worcs	Worcester	2013

GLOUCESTERSHIRE

Formation of Present Club: 1871
Inaugural First-Class Match: 1870
Colours: Blue, Gold, Brown, Silver, Green and Red
Badge: Coat of Arms of the City and County of Bristol
County Champions (since 1890): (0); best – 2nd 1930, 1931,
1947, 1959, 1969, 1986
Gillette/NatWest/C&G Trophy Winners: (5) 1973, 1999,
2000, 2003, 2004
Benson and Hedges Cup Winners: (3) 1977, 1999, 2000
Pro 40/National League (Div 1) Winners: (1) 2000
Royal London One-Day Cup Winners: (1) 2015
Twenty20 Cup Winners: (0); best – Finalist 2007

Chief Executive: Will Brown, County Ground, Nevil Road, Bristol BS7 9EJ •

Tel: 0117 910 8000 • Fax: 0117 924 1193 • Email: info@gloscc.co.uk • Web:
www.glosccc.co.uk • Twitter : @Gloscricket (20,118 followers)

Head Coach: Richard Dawson. **Asst Head Coach**: Ian Harvey. **Captain**: M.Klinger.
Overseas Players: C.T.Bancroft, M.Klinger and A.J.Tye (T20 only). **2016 Beneficiary**:
None. **Head Groundsman**: Sean Williams. **Scorer**: Adrian Bull. ‡ New registration. NQ Not
qualified for England.

*Gloucestershire revised their capping policy in 2004 and now award players with their
County Caps when they make their first-class debut.*

‡NQ**BANCROFT, Cameron** Timothy (Aquinas C, Perth), b Attadale, Perth, Australia
19 Nov 1992. 6'0''. RHB, RM, WK. W Australia 2013-14 to date. Big Bash: PS 2014-15 to
date. **IT20** (A): 1 (2015-16); HS 0* v I (Sydney) 2015-16. HS 211 WA v NSW (Perth)
2014-15. LO HS 176 WA v S Aus (Sydney) 2015-16. T20 HS 72.

COCKBAIN, Ian Andrew (Maghull HS), b Bootle, Liverpool 17 Feb 1987. Son of
I.Cockbain (Lancs and Minor Cos 1979-94). 6'0''. RHB, RM. Squad No 28. Debut
(Gloucestershire) 2011; cap 2011. MCC YC 2008-10. HS 151* v Surrey (Bristol) 2014. LO
HS 98* v Worcs (Worcester) 2014 (RLC). T20 HS 91*.

DENT, Christopher David James (Backwell CS; Alton C), b Bristol 20 Jan 1991. 5'9''.
LHB, WK, occ SLA. Squad No 15. Debut (Gloucestershire) 2010; cap 2010. 1000 runs (2);
most – 1128 (2013). HS 268 v Glamorgan (Bristol) 2015. BB 1-4 v Kent (Bristol) 2015. LO
HS 151* v Glamorgan (Cardiff) 2013 (Y40). LO BB 4-43 v Leics (Bristol) 2012 (CB40).
T20 HS 63*. T20 BB 1-4.

GILMOUR, Brandon S. (Park House S), b Bulawayo, Zimbabwe 11 Apr 1996. 5'10''.
LHB, RM. Squad No 55. Gloucestershire 2nd XI debut 2014. Awaiting 1st XI debut.

HAMMOND, Miles Arthur Halhead (St Edward's S, Oxford), b Cheltenham 11 Jan 1996.
5'11''. LHB, OB. Squad No 88. Debut (Gloucestershire) 2013; cap 2013. England U19
2012-13. Gloucestershire 2nd XI debut 2010, aged 14y 120d. HS 30 v Glamorgan
(Swansea) 2015. BB 1-96 v Glamorgan (Bristol) 2013. LO HS 0. LO BB 2-18 v Northants
(Northampton) 2015 (RLC). T20 HS and BB – .

HAMPTON, Thomas Robert Garth (John Hampden S, High Wycombe), b Kingston-upon-Thames, Surrey 5 Oct 1990. 6'0". RHB, RMF. Squad No 16. Middlesex 2010. Gloucestershire debut/cap 2015. MCC YCs 2011-12. Buckinghamshire 2014-15. HS 1* and BB 1-15 M v Oxford MCCU (Oxford) 2010. CC HS 0* and CC BB 1-109 v Glamorgan (Bristol) 2015.

HANKINS, George Thomas (Millfield S), b Bath, Somerset 4 Jan 1997. 6'1½". RHB, OB. Squad No 21. Gloucestershire 2nd XI debut 2014. Awaiting 1st XI debut.

HOWELL, Benny Alexander Cameron (The Oratory S), b Bordeaux, France 5 Oct 1988. Son of J.B.Howell (Warwickshire 2nd XI 1978). 5'11". RHB, RM. Squad No 13. Hampshire 2011. Gloucestershire debut/cap 2012. Berkshire 2007. HS 102 v Leics (Cheltenham) 2015. BB 5-57 v Leics (Leicester) 2013. LO HS 122 v Surrey (Croydon) 2011 (CB40). LO BB 3-37 v Yorks (Leeds) 2015 (RLC). T20 HS 57. T20 BB 4-26.

[NQ]KLINGER, Michael (Scopus Memorial C, Kew), b Kew, Melbourne, Australia 4 Jul 1980. 5'10½". RHB. Squad No 7. Victoria 1999-00 to 2007-08. S Australia 2008-09 to 2013-14. Worcestershire 2012; cap 2012. Gloucestershire debut/cap 2015; captain 2013 to date. W Australia 2014-15 to date. Big Bash: AS 2011-12 to 2013-14. PS 2014-15 to date. 1000 runs (1+2); most – 1203 (2008-09). HS 255 S Aus v WA (Adelaide) 2008-09. Gs HS 163 v Hants (Bristol) 2013. LO HS 140* S Aus v Tas (Sydney) 2013-14. T20 HS 126* v Essex (Bristol) 2015 – Gs record.

‡LIDDLE, Christopher John (Nunthorpe CS; Teesside Tertiary C), b Middlesbrough, Yorks 1 Feb 1984. 6'5". RHB, LFM. Squad No 11. Leicestershire 2005-06. Sussex 2007-15. Missed entire 2009 season with a stress fracture of the right ankle. HS 53 Sx v Worcs (Hove) 2007. BB 3-42 Le v Somerset (Leicester) 2006. LO HS 18 Sx v Warwks (Rugby) 2015 (RLC). LO BB 5-18 v Netherlands (Amstelveen) 2011 (CB40). T20 HS 16. T20 BB 5-17.

MARSHALL, Hamish John Hamilton (Mahurangi C, Warkworth; King C, Auckland), b Warkworth, New Zealand 15 Feb 1979. Twin brother of J.A.H.Marshall (ND and NZ 1997-98 to 2011-12). Irish passport, qualified to play in April 2017. RHB, RM. Squad No 9. N Districts 1998-99 to 2011-12. Gloucestershire debut 2006 (scoring 102 v Worcs on UK debut); cap 2006; benefit 2015. MCC 2012. Buckinghamshire 2003. **Tests** (NZ): 13 (2000-01 to 2005-06); HS 160 v SL (Napier) 2004-05. **LOI** (NZ): 66 (2003-04 to 2006-07); HS 101* v P (Faisalabad) 2003-04. **IT20** (NZ): 3 (2004-05 to 2005-06); HS 8 v A (Auckland) 2004-05. F-c Tours (NZ): A 2004-05; SA 2000-01, 2005-06; Z 2005; B 2004-05. 1000 runs (2); most – 1218 (2006). HS 170 ND v Canterbury (Rangiora) 2009-10. Gs HS 168 v Leics (Leicester) 2009. LO HS 162 v Leics (Leicester) 2009. LO HS 162 v Sussex (Hove) 2007 (P40). LO BB 2-21 v Hants (Southampton) 2009 (P40). T20 HS 102.

MILES, Craig Neil (Bradon Forest S, Swindon; Filton C, Bristol), b Swindon, Wilts 20 July 1994. Brother of A.J.Miles (Cardiff MCCU 2012). 6'4". RHB, RMF. Squad No 34. Debut (Gloucestershire) 2011; cap 2011. Gloucestershire 2nd XI debut 2009, aged 14y 318d. HS 62* v Worcs (Cheltenham) 2014. 50 wkts (1): 50 (2015). BB 6-63 v Northants (Northampton) 2015. LO HS 12 v Northants (Cheltenham) 2014 (RLC). LO BB 4-29 v Yorks (Scarborough) 2015 (RLC). T20 HS 3*. T20 BB 3-25.

[NQ]NOEMA-BARNETT, Kieran, b Dunedin, New Zealand 4 Jun 1987. 6'1". LHB, RM. Squad No 11. Central Districts 2008-09 to 2014-15. HS 107 CD v Auckland (Auckland) 2011-12. Gs HS 61 v Leics (Cheltenham) 2015. BB 4-20 CD v Otago (Dunedin) 2010-11. Gs BB 3-28 v Glamorgan (Swansea) 2015. LO HS 67 CD v Wellington (Wellington) 2012-13. LO BB 3-42 CD v Auckland (Auckland) 2013-14. T20 HS 57*. T20 BB 2-13.

NORWELL, Liam Connor (Redruth SS), b Bournemouth, Dorset 27 Dec 1991. 6'3". RHB, RMF. Squad No 24. Debut (Gloucestershire) 2011, taking 6-46 v Derbys (Bristol); cap 2011. Gloucestershire 2nd XI debut 2009. HS 78 v Worcs (Cheltenham) 2014. 50 wkts (1): 68 (2015). BB 6-33 (10-65 match) v Essex (Chelmsford) 2015. LO HS 6 v Surrey (Bristol) 2015 (RLC). LO BB 6-52 v Leics (Leicester) 2012 (CB40). T20 HS 1*. T20 BB 3-27.

PAYNE, David Alan (Lytchett Minster S), b Poole, Dorset, 15 Feb 1991. 6'2". RHB, LMF. Squad No 14. Debut (Gloucestershire) 2011; cap 2011. Dorset 2009. HS 62 v Glamorgan (Bristol) 2011. BB 6-26 v Leics (Bristol) 2011. LO HS 18 v Leics (Leicester) 2013 (Y40). LO BB 7-29 v Essex (Chelmsford) 2010 (CB40), inc 4 wkts in 4 balls and 6 wkts in 9 balls – Gs record. T20 HS 10. T20 BB 5-24 v Middx (Richmond) 2015 – Gs record.

[NQ]RODERICK, Gareth Hugh (Maritzburg C), b Durban, South Africa 29 Aug 1991. 6'0". RHB, WK. Squad No 27. UK passport. KZN 2010-11 to 2011-12. Gloucestershire debut/cap 2013. Gloucestershire 2nd XI debut 2012. Northamptonshire 2nd XI 2011. HS 171 v Leics (Bristol) 2014. LO HS 104 v Leics (Leicester) 2015 (RLC). T20 HS 32.

‡SHAW, Joshua (Crofton HS, Wakefield; Skills Exchange C), b Wakefield, Yorks 3 Jan 1996. Son of C.Shaw (Yorkshire 1984-88). 6'1". RHB, RMF. Yorkshire 2nd XI debut 2012. England U19 2012-13 to 2014. Joins from Yorkshire on loan. T20 HS 0*. T20 BB – .

SMITH, Thomas Michael John (Seaford Head Community C; Sussex Downs C), b Eastbourne, Sussex 29 Aug 1987. 5'9". RHB, SLA. Squad No 6. Sussex 2007-09. No f-c appearances in 2008. Surrey 2009 (l-o only). Middlesex 2010-13. Gloucestershire debut/cap 2013. HS 80 v Surrey (Bristol) 2014. BB 4-35 v Kent (Canterbury) 2014. LO HS 65 Sy v Leics (Leicester) 2009 (P40). LO BB 3-26 M v Derbys (Lord's) 2010 (CB40). T20 HS 36*. T20 BB 5-24.

TAVARÉ, William Andrew (Bristol GS; Loughborough U), b Bristol 1 Jan 1990. Nephew of C.J.Tavaré (Kent, Somerset & England 1974-93). 6'0". RHB, RM. Squad No 4. Loughborough MCCU 2010-12. Gloucestershire debut/cap 2014. 1000 runs (1): 1014 (2014). HS 139 v Hants (Bristol) 2014 – on CC debut. BB – . LO HS 77 v Hants (Bristol) 2014 (RLC) – on l-o debut.

TAYLOR, Jack Martin Robert (Chipping Norton S), b Banbury, Oxfordshire 12 Nov 1991. Elder brother of M.D.Taylor (*see below*). 5'11". RHB, OB. Squad No 10. Debut (Gloucestershire) 2010; cap 2010. Gloucestershire 2nd XI debut 2007, aged 15y 191d. Oxfordshire 2009-11. HS 156 v Northants (Cheltenham) 2015. BB 4-125 v Essex (Chelmsford) 2014. LO HS 53 v Derbys (Derby) 2014 (RLC). LO BB 4-38 v Hants (Bristol) 2014 (RLC). T20 HS 38. T20 BB 4-16.

TAYLOR, Matthew David (Chipping Norton S), b Banbury, Oxfordshire 8 Jul 1994. Younger brother of J.M.R.Taylor (*see above*). 6'0". RHB, LM. Squad No 36. Debut (Gloucestershire) 2013; cap 2013. Gloucestershire 2nd XI debut 2011. Oxfordshire 2011-12. HS 32* v Essex (Chelmsford) 2014. BB 5-75 v Hants (Bristol) 2014. LO HS 7* and LO BB 2-43 v Notts (Cheltenham) 2011 (CB40). T20 HS 5*. T20 BB 1-30.

‡[NQ]TYE, Andrew James (Padbury Senior HS, WA), b Perth, Australia 12 Dec 1986. 6'4". RHB, RMF. Squad No 68. W Australia 2014-15 to date. Big Bash: ST 2013-14. PS 2014-15 to date. Somerset 2nd XI 2010. Durham 2nd XI 2010-11. Northamptonshire 2nd XI 2012. Joins Gloucestershire for T20 in 2016. **IT20** (A): 3 (2015-16); HS 4 and BB 1-28 v I (Melbourne) 2015-16. HS 10 WA v Tas (Hobart) 2014-15. BB 3-47 WA v Q (Brisbane) 2014-15. LO HS 28* WA v NSW (Sydney) 2013-14. LO BB 5-46 WA v Tas (Sydney) 2013-14. T20 HS 16*. T20 BB 4-18.

RELEASED/RETIRED continued on p 142

GLOUCESTERSHIRE 2015

RESULTS SUMMARY

	Place	Won	Lost	Tied	Drew	NR
LV= County Championship (2nd Division)	6th	5	5		6	
All First-Class Matches		5	5		6	
Royal London One-Day Cup (Group A)	**Winners**	8	2			1
NatWest t20 Blast (South Group)	5th	7	7			

LV= COUNTY CHAMPIONSHIP AVERAGES
BATTING AND FIELDING

Cap†		M	I	NO	HS	Runs	Avge	100	50	Ct/St
2013	M.Klinger	6	11	1	103	468	46.80	2	2	5
2015	P.S.P.Handscomb	6	11	2	76	401	44.55	–	4	8
2010	C.D.J.Dent	16	28	4	268	1062	44.25	3	6	23
2006	H.J.H.Marshall	13	18	2	92	588	36.75	–	6	7
2013	T.M.J.Smith	5	5	2	47*	98	32.66	–	–	1
2010	J.M.R.Taylor	11	14	–	156	414	29.57	2	–	4
2014	W.A.Tavaré	15	26	2	66	708	29.50	–	5	9
2013	G.H.Roderick	15	24	1	76	663	28.82	–	6	48
2014	G.O.Jones	9	15	–	88	400	26.66	–	3	10
2011	J.K.Fuller	10	13	1	73	300	25.00	–	2	5
2012	B.A.C.Howell	11	16	–	102	395	24.68	1	1	8
2015	K.Noema-Barnett	11	15	3	61	272	22.66	–	1	4
2011	D.A.Payne	9	10	3	23	138	19.71	–	–	4
2011	C.N.Miles	11	18	1	41	237	13.94	–	–	3
2011	I.A.Cockbain	6	10	–	28	139	13.90	–	–	2
2011	L.C.Norwell	14	19	9	19	83	8.30	–	–	5
2013	M.D.Taylor	5	8	3	8	24	4.80	–	–	–

Also batted: M.A.H.Hammond (1 match – cap 2013) 30; T.R.G.Hampton (2 – cap 2015) 0*.

BOWLING

	O	M	R	W	Avge	Best	5wI	10wM
L.C.Norwell	480.3	102	1525	61	25.00	6- 33	3	1
C.N.Miles	350.4	70	1155	46	25.10	6- 63	4	1
B.A.C.Howell	163.3	31	538	20	26.90	3- 28	–	–
D.A.Payne	260.4	60	838	31	27.03	4- 50	–	–
K.Noema-Barnett	190.5	53	598	17	35.17	3- 28	–	–
J.K.Fuller	265.5	51	918	24	38.25	4- 35	–	–
M.D.Taylor	157.1	36	544	13	41.84	5- 93	1	–
J.M.R.Taylor	159	29	466	10	46.60	3-119	–	–

Also bowled:
C.D.J.Dent 40-5-168-2; T.R.G.Hampton 33-4-171-1; P.S.P.Handscomb 2-0-21-0; H.J.H.Marshall 14-5-31-3; T.M.J.Smith 85.4-7-329-3; W.A.Tavaré 7-0-24-0.

The First-Class Averages (pp 227–243) give the records of Gloucestershire players in all first-class county matches (Gloucestershire's other opponents being Cardiff MCCU).

† Gloucestershire revised their capping policy in 2004 and now award players with their County Caps when they make their first-class debut.

GLOUCESTERSHIRE RECORDS

FIRST-CLASS CRICKET

Highest Total	For	695-9d		v	Middlesex	Gloucester	2004
	V	774-7d		by	Australians	Bristol	1948
Lowest Total	For	17		v	Australians	Cheltenham	1896
	V	12		by	Northants	Gloucester	1907
Highest Innings	For	341	C.M.Spearman	v	Middlesex	Gloucester	2004
	V	319	C.J.L.Rogers	for	Northants	Northampton	2006

Highest Partnership for each Wicket

1st	395	D.M.Young/R.B.Nicholls	v	Oxford U	Oxford	1962
2nd	256	C.T.M.Pugh/T.W.Graveney	v	Derbyshire	Chesterfield	1960
3rd	392	G.H.Roderick/A.P.R.Gidman	v	Leics	Bristol	2014
4th	321	W.R.Hammond/W.L.Neale	v	Leics	Gloucester	1937
5th	261	W.G.Grace/W.O.Moberley	v	Yorkshire	Cheltenham	1876
6th	320	G.L.Jessop/J.H.Board	v	Sussex	Hove	1903
7th	248	W.G.Grace/E.L.Thomas	v	Sussex	Hove	1896
8th	239	W.R.Hammond/A.E.Wilson	v	Lancashire	Bristol	1938
9th	193	W.G.Grace/S.A.P.Kitcat	v	Sussex	Bristol	1896
10th	137	C.N.Miles/L.C.Norwell	v	Worcs	Cheltenham	2014

Best Bowling	For	10-40	E.G.Dennett	v	Essex	Bristol	1906
(Innings)	V	10-66	A.A.Mailey	for	Australians	Cheltenham	1921
		10-66	K.Smales	for	Notts	Stroud	1956
Best Bowling	For	17-56	C.W.L.Parker	v	Essex	Gloucester	1925
(Match)	V	15-87	A.J.Conway	for	Worcs	Moreton-in-M	1914

Most Runs – Season	2860	W.R.Hammond	(av 69.75)	1933
Most Runs – Career	33664	W.R.Hammond	(av 57.05)	1920-51
Most 100s – Season	13	W.R.Hammond		1938
Most 100s – Career	113	W.R.Hammond		1920-51
Most Wkts – Season	222	T.W.J.Goddard	(av 16.80)	1937
	222	T.W.J.Goddard	(av 16.37)	1947
Most Wkts – Career	3170	C.W.L.Parker	(av 19.43)	1903-35
Most Career W-K Dismissals	1054	R.C.Russell	(950 ct; 104 st)	1981-2004
Most Career Catches in the Field	719	C.A.Milton		1948-74

LIMITED-OVERS CRICKET

Highest Total	50ov	401-7		v	Bucks	Wing	2003
	40ov	344-6		v	Northants	Cheltenham	2001
	T20	254-3		v	Middlesex	Uxbridge	2011
Lowest Total	50ov	82		v	Notts	Bristol	1987
	40ov	49		v	Middlesex	Bristol	1978
	T20	68		v	Hampshire	Bristol	2010
Highest Innings	50ov	177	A.J.Wright	v	Scotland	Bristol	1997
	40ov	153	C.M.Spearman	v	Warwicks	Gloucester	2003
	T20	126*	M.Klinger	v	Essex	Bristol	2015
Best Bowling	50ov	6-13	M.J.Procter	v	Hampshire	Southampton	1977
	40ov	7-29	D.A.Payne	v	Essex	Chelmsford	2010
	T20	5-24	D.A.Payne	v	Middlesex	Richmond	2015

HAMPSHIRE

HAMPSHIRE
CRICKET

Formation of Present Club: 12 August 1863
Inaugural First-Class Match: 1864
Colours: Blue, Gold and White
Badge: Tudor Rose and Crown
County Champions: (2) 1961, 1973
NatWest/C&G/FP Trophy Winners: (3) 1991, 2005, 2009
Benson and Hedges Cup Winners: (2) 1988, 1992
Sunday League Winners: (3) 1975, 1978, 1986
Clydesdale Bank Winners: (1) 2012
Twenty20 Cup Winners: (2) 2010, 2012

Chairman: Rod Bransgrove, The Ageas Bowl, Botley Road, West End, Southampton SO30
3XH • Tel: 023 8047 2002 • Fax: 023 8047 2122 • Email: enquiries@ageasbowl.com • Web:
www.ageasbowl.com Twitter: @hantscricket (27,967 followers)

CEO: David Mann. **Cricket Operations Manager**: Tim Tremlett. **Director of Cricket**:
Giles White. **1st XI Coach**: Dale Benkenstein. **Batting Coach**: Tony Middleton. **Assistant
Coach**: Craig White. **2nd XI Coach**: Charlie Freeston. **Captain**: J.M.Vince. **Vice-Captain**:
tbc. **Overseas Players**: R.McLaren and Shahid Afridi (T20 only). **2016 Beneficiary**:
S.M.Ervine. **Head Groundsman**: Karl McDermott. **Scorer**: Kevin Baker. ‡ New registra-
tion. NQ Not qualified for England.

ADAMS, James Henry Kenneth (Sherborne S; University C, London; Loughborough U), b
Winchester 23 Sep 1980. 6'2". LHB, LM. Squad No 4. British U 2002-04. Hampshire debut
2002; cap 2006; captain 2012-15; benefit 2015. Loughborough UCCE 2003-04 – scoring
107 v Somerset (Taunton) on debut. MCC 2013. Dorset 1998. F-c Tour (EL): WI 2010-11.
1000 runs (5); most – 1351 (2009). HS 262* v Notts (Nottingham) 2006. BB 2-16 v Durham
(Chester-le-St). 2004. LO HS 131 v Warwks (Birmingham) 2010 (CB40). LO BB 1-34 v
Essex (Chelmsford) 2007 (FPT). T20 HS 101*. T20 BB – .

ALSOP, Thomas Philip (Lavington S), b High Wycombe, Bucks 26 Nov 1995. Younger
brother of O.J.Alsop (Wiltshire 2010-12). 5'11". LHB, WK. Squad No 9. Debut (Hampshire) 2014. Hampshire 2nd XI debut 2013. England U19 2014 to 2015. No 1st XI
appearances in 2015. HS 33 v Kent (Southampton) 2014. LO HS 0.

BERG, Gareth Kyle (South African College S), b Cape Town, South Africa 18 Jan 1981.
6'0". RHB, RMF. Squad No 13. England qualified through residency. Middlesex 2008-14;
cap 2010. Hampshire debut 2015. Italy (T20 only) 2011-12 to date. HS 130* M v Leics
(Leicester) 2011, sharing M record 9th wkt partnership of 172 with T.J.Murtagh. H HS 99 v
Sussex (Hove) 2015. BB 6-58 M v Glamorgan (Cardiff) 2011. H BB 4-64 v Somerset
(Southampton) 2015. LO HS 75 M v Glamorgan (Lord's) 2013 (Y40). LO BB 4-24 M v
Worcs (Worcester) 2011 (CB40). T20 HS 90. T20 BB 4-20.

CARBERRY, Michael Alexander (St John Rigby Catholic C), b Croydon, Surrey 29 Sep
1980. 6'0". LHB, RM. Squad No 15. Surrey 2001-02. Kent 2003-05. Hampshire debut/cap
2006. MCC 2008, 2015. Big Bash: PS 2014-15. **Tests**: 6 (2009-10 to 2013-14); HS 60 v A
(Adelaide) 2013-14. **LOI**: 6 (2013 to 2014); HS 63 v A (Cardiff) 2013. **IT20**: 1 (2014); HS
7 v SL (Oval) 2014. F-c Tours: A 2013-14; B 2006-07 (Eng A), 2009-10. 1000 runs (4);
most – 1275 (2015). HS 300* v Yorks (Southampton) 2011, sharing in UK 3rd highest and
UK record 3rd-wkt partnership of 523 with N.D.McKenzie. BB 2-85 v Durham (Chester-le-
St) 2006. LO HS 150* v Lancs (Southampton) 2013 (Y40). LO BB 3-37 v Derbys (Derby)
2013 (Y40). T20 HS 100*. T20 BB 1-16.

CRANE, Mason Sydney (Lancing C), b Shoreham-by-Sea, Sussex 18 Feb 1997. RHB, LB. Squad No 32. Debut (Hampshire) 2015. Hampshire 2nd XI debut 2013. HS 13 and BB 5-35 v Warwks (Southampton) 2015. LO HS 16* v Kent (Canterbury) 2015 (RLC). LO BB 4-30 v Middx (Southampton) 2015 (RLC). T20 HS – . T20 BB 2-35.

DAWSON, Liam Andrew (John Bentley S, Calne), b Swindon, Wilts 1 Mar 1990. 5'8". RHB, SLA. Squad No 8. Debut (Hampshire) 2007; cap 2013. Mountaineers 2011-12. Essex 2015 (on loan). Wiltshire 2006-07. HS 169 v Somerset (Southampton) 2011. BB 7-51 Mountaineers v ME (Mutare) 2011-12 (also scored 110* in same match). BB 5-29 v Leics (Southampton) 2012. LO HS 113* SJD v Kalabagan (Savar) 2014-15. LO BB 6-47 v Sussex (Southampton) 2015 (RLC). T20 HS 45*. T20 BB 4-19.

^{NQ}**EDWARDS, Fidel** Henderson, b Gays, St Peter, Barbados 6 Feb 1982. RHB, RF. Squad No 82. Half-brother of P.T.Collins (Barbados, Surrey, Middlesex & West Indies 1996-97 to 2011-12). Barbados 2001-02 to 2013-14. Hampshire debut 2015. Kolpak signing. IPL: DC 2009. Big Bash: ST 2011-12. **Tests** (WI): 55 (2003 to 2012-13); HS 30 v I (Roseau) 2011; BB 7-87 v NZ (Napier) 2008-09. **LOI** (WI): 50; HS 13 v NZ (Wellington) 2008-09; BB 6-22 v Z (Harare) 2003-04 – on debut. **IT20** (WI): 20 (2007-08 to 2012-13); HS 7* v E (Oval) 2011; BB 3-23 v A (Bridgetown) 2011-12. F-c Tours (WI): E 2004, 2007, 2009, 2012; A 2005-06; SA 2003-04, 2007-08; NZ 2005-06, 2008-09; I 2011-12, 2013-14 (WI A); P 2006-07; Z 2003-04; B 2011-12, 2012-13. HS 40 Bar v Jamaica (Bridgetown) 2007-08. H HS 17* v Warwks (Southampton) 2015. BB 7-87 (see *Tests*). H BB 6-88 (10-145 match) v Notts (Nottingham) 2015. LO HS 21* Bar v Jamaica (Providence) 2007-08. LO BB 6-22 (see *LOI*). T20 HS 11*. T20 BB 5-22.

ERVINE, Sean Michael (Lomagundi C, Chinhoyi), b Harare, Zimbabwe 6 Dec 1982. Elder brother of C.R.Ervine (Midlands, SR 2003-04 to date); son of R.M.Ervine (Rhodesia 1977-78); grandson of M.A.Den (Rhodesia 1935-36); nephew of N.B.Ervine (Rhodesia 1977-78) and G.M.Den (Rhodesia and Eastern Province 1963-64 to 1969-70). 6'2". LHB, RMF. Squad No 7. CFX Academy 2000-01 to 2001. Midlands 2001-02 to 2003-04. Hampshire debut/cap 2005; qualified for England in 2013 season; benefit 2016. W Australia 2006-07 to 2007-08. Southern Rocks 2009-10. Matabeleland Tuskers 2011-12 to 2012-13. **Tests** (Z): 5 (2003 to 2003-04); HS 86 v B (Harare) 2003-04; BB 4-146 v A (Perth) 2003-04. **LOI** (Z): 42 (2001-02 to 2003-04); HS 100 v I (Adelaide) 2003-04; BB 3-29 v P (Sharjah) 2001-02. F-c Tours (Z): E 2003; A 2003-04. HS 237* v Somerset (Southampton) 2010. BB 6-82 Midlands v Mashonaland (Kwekwe) 2002-03. H BB 5-60 v Glamorgan (Cardiff) 2005. LO HS 167* v Ireland (Southampton) 2009 (FPT). LO BB 5-50 v Glamorgan (Cardiff) 2005 (CGT). T20 HS 82. T20 BB 4-12.

^{NQ}**McLAREN, Ryan** (Grey C, Bloemfontein; Free State U), b Kimberley, South Africa 9 Feb 1983. 6'4". Son of P.McLaren (GW 1977-78 to 1994-95), nephew of Keith McLaren (GW 1971-72 to 1984-85), cousin of A.P.McLaren (GW 1998-99 to 2011-12, Eagles 2007-08 to 2008-09, Knights 2010-11, SW Districts 2012-13 to 2013-14, Warriors 2012-13). LHB, RFM. Squad No 24. FS 2003-04 to 2004-05. Eagles 2004-05 to 2009-10. Kent 2007-09 (Kolpak registration); cap 2007. Knights 2010-11 to 2013-14. Dolphins 2014-15. Hampshire debut 2015. IPL: MI 2009-10, KXIP 2011, KKR 2013. **Tests** (SA): 2 (2009-10 to 2013-14); HS 33* v E (Johannesburg) 2009-10; BB 2-72 v A (Centurion) 2013-14. **LOI** (SA): 54 (2009-10 to 2014-15); HS 71* v I (Cardiff) 2013; BB 4-19 v P (Birmingham) 2013. **IT20** (SA): 12 (2009-10 to 2014-15); HS 6* and BB 5-19 (SA record analysis) v WI (North Sound) 2009-10. F-c Tour (SA A): Ire 2012. HS 140 Eagles v Warriors (Bloemfontein) 2005-06. UK HS 65* K v Durham (Canterbury) 2008. H HS 52 v Notts (Nottingham) 2015. 50 wkts (1+1); most – 54 (2006-07). BB 8-38 Eagles v Cape Cobras (Stellenbosch) 2006-07. UK BB 6-75 K v Notts (Nottingham) 2008. H BB 4-60 v Durham (Chester-le-St) 2015. LO HS 88 Knights v Cape Cobras (Bloemfontein) 2013-14. LO BB 5-38 Knights v Warriors (Kimberley) 2012-13. T20 HS 51*. T20 BB 5-19.

McMANUS, Lewis David (Clayesmore S, Bournemouth), b Poole, Dorset 9 Oct 1994. 5'10". RHB, WK. Squad No 18. Debut (Hampshire) 2015. Hampshire 2nd XI debut 2011. Dorset 2011-13. HS 53* v Durham (Southampton) 2015.

‡^{NQ}**SHAHID KHAN AFRIDI**, Sahibzada Mohammad (Ibrahim Alibhai S; Islamia Science C, Karachi) b Kohat, Pakistan, 1 Mar 1980. Brother of Tariq Afridi (Karachi 1999-00) and Ashfaq Afridi (Karachi Blues 2008-09). RHB, LBG. Squad No 10. Debut Combined XI v Eng A 1995-96. Karachi 1995-96 to 2003-04. HB 1997-98 to date. Leicestershire 2001; cap 2001. Derbyshire 2003. GW 2003-04. Sind 2007-08 to 2008-09. MCC 2001. Joins Hampshire in 2016 for T20 only. IPL: DC 2007-08. Big Bash: MR 2011-12. **Tests** (P): 27 (1998-99 to 2010, 1 as captain); HS 156 v I (Faisalabad) 2005-06; BB 5-52 v A (Karachi) 1998-99 – on debut. **LOI** (P): 398 (1996-97 to 2014-15, 38 as captain); HS 124 v B (Dambulla) 2010; BB 7-12 v WI (Providence) 2013, 2nd best analysis in all LOIs. Scored a 37-ball hundred which included then joint record 11 sixes v SL (Nairobi) 1996-97 in his first LOI innings. **IT20** (P): 94 (2006-07 to 2015-16, 39 as captain); HS 54* v SL (Lord's) 2009; BB 4-11 v Netherlands (Lord's) 2009. F-c Tours (P): E 2006, 2010; A 1996-97, 2004-05; WI 1999-00, 2005; I 1998-99, 2004-05; SL 2005-06; Z 2002-03; B 1998-99. HS 164 Le v Northants (Northampton) 2001. BB 6-101 HB v KRL (Rawalpindi) 1997-98. UK BB 5-84 Le v Essex (Chelmsford) 2001. LO HS 124 (see LOI). LO BB 7-12 (see LOI). T20 HS 80. T20 BB 5-7.

SMITH, William Rew (Bedford S; Collingwood C, Durham U), b Luton, Beds 28 Sep 1982. 5'9". RHB, OB. Squad No 2. Nottinghamshire 2002-06. Durham UCCE 2003-05; captain 2004-05. British U 2004-05. Durham 2007-13; captain 2009-10 (part). Hampshire debut 2014; cap 2015. Bedfordshire 1999-2002. 1000 runs (1): 1187 (2014). HS 201* Du v Surrey (Guildford) 2008. H HS 151* v Essex (Southampton) 2014. BB 3-34 DU v Leics (Leicester) 2005. H BB 2-27 v Kent (Southampton) 2014. LO HS 120* Du v Surrey (Chester-le-St) 2013 (Y40). LO BB 2-19 Du v Derbys (Derby) 2013 (Y40). T20 HS 55. T20 BB 3-15.

STEVENSON, Ryan Anthony (King Edward VI Community C), b Torquay, Devon 2 Apr 1992. RHB, RMF. Squad No 47. Debut (Hampshire) 2015. Devon 2015. HS 30 v Durham (Chester-le-St) 2015. BB 1-15 v Notts (Nottingham) 2015.

TAYLOR, Bradley Jacob (Eggar's S, Alton), b Winchester 14 Mar 1997. 5'11". RHB, OB. Squad No 93. Debut (Hampshire) 2013. Hampshire 2nd XI debut 2013. England U19 2014 to 2014-15. No 1st XI appearances in 2015. HS 20 and BB 4-64 v Lancs (Southport) 2013. LO HS 2* and LO BB 2-23 v Bangladesh A (Southampton) 2013. T20 HS – .

TOMLINSON, James Andrew (Harrow Way S, Andover; Cardiff U), b Winchester 12 Jun 1982. 6'1". LHB, LMF. Squad No 21. British U 2002-03. Hampshire debut 2002; cap 2008. Wiltshire 2001. HS 51 v Glos (Southampton) 2014. 50 wkts (2); most – 67 (2008). BB 8-46 (10-194 match) v Somerset (Taunton) 2008. LO HS 14 v Durham (Chester-le-St) 2010 (CB40). LO BB 4-47 v Glamorgan (Southampton) 2006 (CGT). T20 HS 5. T20 BB 1-20.

‡**TOPLEY, Reece** James William (Royal Hospital S, Ipswich), b Ipswich, Suffolk 21 February 1994. Son of T.D.Topley (Surrey, Essex, GW 1985-94) and nephew of P.A.Topley (Kent 1972-75). 6'7". RHB, LMF. Squad No 6. Essex 2011-15; cap 2013. Took 5-46 on CC debut. Essex 2nd XI debut 2010, aged 16y 156d. England U19 2012-13. **LOI**: 10 (2015 to 2015-16); HS 6 v A (Manchester) 2015. BB 4-50 v SA (Pt Elizabeth) 2015-16. **IT20**: 4 (2015 to 2015-16); HS 1* v SA (Johannesburg) 2015-16; BB 3-24 v P (Dubai, DSC) 2015-16. F-c Tour (EL): SL 2013-14. HS 12 Ex v Hants (Southampton) 2014. BB 6-29 (11-85 match) Ex v Worcs (Chelmsford) 2013. LO HS 19 Ex v Somerset (Taunton) 2011 (CB40). LO BB 4-26 Ex v Derbys (Colchester) 2013 (Y40). T20 HS 5*. T20 BB 4-26.

VINCE, James Michael (Warminster S), b Cuckfield, Sussex 14 Mar 1991. 6'2". RHB, RM. Squad No 14. Debut (Hampshire) 2009; cap 2013; captain 2016. Wiltshire 2007-08. **LOI**: 1 (2015); HS – . **IT20**: 3 (2015-16); HS 46 v P (Sharjah) 2015-16. F-c Tours (EL): SA 2014-15; SL 2013-14. 1000 runs (2); most – 1525 (2014). HS 240 v Essex (Southampton) 2014. BB 5-41 v Loughborough MCCU (Southampton) 2013. CC BB 2-2 v Lancs (Southport) 2013. LO HS 131 v Scotland (Southampton) 2011 (CB40). LO BB 1-18 EL v Australia A (Sydney) 2012-13. T20 HS 107*. T20 BB 1-5.

‡**WEATHERLEY, Joe** James (King Edward VI S, Southampton), b Winchester 19 Jan 1997. RHB, OB. Squad No 5. Hampshire 2nd XI debut 2014. England U19 2014-15. Awaiting 1st XI debut.

WHEAL, Bradley Thomas James (Clifton C), b Durban, South Africa 28 Aug 1996. 5'9". RHB, RMF. Squad No 58. Debut (Hampshire) 2015. **LOI** (Scot): 1 (2015-16); HS 2* and BB 1-44 v Hong Kong (Mong Kok) 2015-16. **IT20** (Scot): 2 (2015-16); HS 2* and BB 3-20 v Hong Kong (Mong Kok) 2015-16. HS 10 v Worcs (Worcester) 2015. BB 4-101 v Middx (Lord's) 2015. LO HS 2* (see LOI). LO BB 1-44 (see LOI). T20 HS 2*. T20 BB 3-20.

WHEATER, Adam Jack Aubrey (Millfield S), b Whipps Cross, Essex 13 Feb 1990. 5'6". RHB, WK. Squad No 31. Essex 2008-12. Cambridge MCCU 2010. Matabeleland Tuskers 2010-11 to 2012-13. Badureliya Sports Club 2011-12. Northern Districts 2012-13. Hampshire debut 2013. HS 164 Ex v Northants (Chelmsford) 2011, sharing Ex record 6th wkt partnership of 253 with J.S.Foster. H HS 140 v Lancs (Southport) 2013. BB 1-86 Ex v Leics (Leicester) 2012 – in contrived circumstances. LO HS 135 v Essex (Chelmsford) 2014 (RLC). T20 HS 78.

WOOD, Christopher Philip (Alton C), b Basingstoke 27 June 1990. 6'2". RHB, LM. Squad No 25. Debut (Hampshire) 2010. HS 105* v Leics (Leicester) 2012. BB 5-39 v Kent (Canterbury) 2014. LO HS 41 v Essex (Southampton) 2013 (Y40). LO BB 5-22 v Glamorgan (Cardiff) 2012 (CB40). T20 HS 27. T20 BB 4-16.

NO**YASIR ARAFAT** Satti (Gordon C, Rawalpindi), b Rawalpindi, Pakistan 12 Mar 1982. 5'9½". RHB, RFM. Squad No 99. Rawalpindi 1997-98 to date. Pakistan Reserves 1999-00. KRL 2000-01 to 2014-15. NBP 2005-06. Sussex 2006-10; cap 2006. Kent 2007-08; cap 2007. Federal Areas 2007-08 to 2008-09. Surrey 2011. Joined Hampshire in 2015 (l-o only); UK passport. Big Bash: PS 2013 to 2014-15. **Tests** (P): 3 (2007-08 to 2008-09); HS 50* v SL (Karachi) 2008-09; BB 5-161 v I (Bangalore) 2007-08 – on debut. **LOI** (P): 11 (1999-00 to 2009); HS 27 v SA (Chandigarh) 2006-07; BB 1-28 v SL (Karachi) 1999-00. **IT20** (P): 13 (2007-08 to 2012-13); HS 17 v Scotland (Durban) 2007-08; BB 3-18 v SL (Hambantota) 2012. F-c Tours (P): WI 2010-11 (Pak A); I 2007-08; SL 2001 (Pak A), 2004-05 (Pak A). HS 170 KRL v Multan (Multan) 2011-12. CC HS 122 K v Sussex (Canterbury) 2007. 50 wkts (0+4); most – 91 (2001-02). BB 9-35 KRL v SSGC (Rawalpindi) 2008-09. CC BB 6-86 K v Hants (Canterbury) 2008. LO HS 110* Otago v Auckland (Oamaru) 2009-10. LO BB 6-24 Pakistan A v England A (Colombo) 2004-05. T20 HS 49. T20 BB 4-5.

RELEASED/RETIRED

(Having made a County 1st XI appearance in 2015)

NQADAMS, Andre Ryan (Westlake BHS, Auckland), b Mangere, Auckland, New Zealand 17 Jul 1975. 5'9". RHB, RMF. Auckland 1997-98 to 2011-12. Essex 2004-06, scoring 124 on debut (*see below*); cap 2004. Nottinghamshire 2007-14; cap 2007. Hampshire 2015 (Kolpak registration). MCC 2014. Herefordshire 2001. **Tests** (NZ): 1 (2001-02); HS 11 and BB 3-44 v E (Auckland) 2001-02. **LOI** (NZ): 42 (2000-01 to 2006-07); HS 45 v P (Rawalpindi) 2001-02; BB 5-22 v I (Queenstown) 2002-03. **IT20** (NZ): 4 (2004-05 to 2005-06); HS 7 v A (Auckland) 2004-05; BB 2-20 v SL (Auckland) 2006-07. HS 124 Ex v Leics (Leicester) 2004 (91 balls, 7 sixes, 13 fours; 100 off 80 balls) on UK debut. H HS 31 v Notts (Southampton) 2015. 50 wkts (3); most – 68 (2010). BB 7-32 (10-50 match) Nt v Lancs (Manchester) 2012. H BB 3-68 v Yorks (Leeds) 2015. Hat-trick Ex v Somerset (Taunton) 2005. LO HS 90* North Is Selection XI v Sri Lankans (New Plymouth) 2000-01. LO BB 5-7 Auckland v ND (Auckland) 1999-00. T20 HS 54*. T20 BB 5-20.

BIRD, J.M. – *see NOTTINGHAMSHIRE.*

BRIGGS, D.R. – *see SUSSEX.*

GATTING, Joe Stephen (Cardinal Newman C; Brighton C), b Brighton 25 Nov 1987. Son of S.P.Gatting (Middlesex 2nd XI, football for Arsenal, Brighton & Hove Albion, Charlton Athletic), nephew of M.W.Gatting (Middlesex and England 1975-98). 6'0". RHB, OB. Sussex 2009-13, scoring 152 v Cambridge UCCE (Cambridge) on debut. Hampshire 2014-15. HS 152 (*see above*). CC HS 116* Sx v Worcs (Worcester) 2011. H HS 67 v Derbys (Derby) 2014. BB 1-8 Sx v Notts (Nottingham) 2011. H BB – . LO HS 122 Sx v Worcs (Horsham) 2011 (CB40). LO BB – . T20 HS 45*. LO BB 1-12.

SHAH, Owais Alam (Isleworth & Syon S), b Karachi, Pakistan 22 Oct 1978. 6'0". RHB, OB. Middlesex 1996-2010; cap 2000; captain 2004 (*part*); benefit 2008. Cape Cobras 2010-11. Essex 2011-13; cap 2013. MCC 2002-08. YC 2001. Hampshire T20 only 2014-15. **Tests**: 6 (2005-06 to 2008-09); HS 88 v I (Bombay) 2005-06; BB – . **LOI**: 71 (2001 to 2009-10); HS 107* v I (Oval) 2007; BB 3-15 v Ire (Belfast) 2009. **IT20**: 17 (2007 to 2009); HS 55* v WI (Oval) 2007. F-c Tours (Eng A): A: 1996-97; WI 2005-06 (*part*), 2008-09 (Eng); I 2005-06 (Eng – *part*); SL 1997-98, 2004-05, 2007-08 (Eng). 1000 runs (8); most – 1728 (2005). HS 203 M v Derbys (Southgate) 2001. BB 3-33 M v Glos (Bristol) 1999. LO HS 134 M v Sussex (Arundel) 1999 (NL). LO BB 4-11 M v Leics (Lord's) 2009 (P40). T20 HS 84. T20 BB 2-26.

TERRY, Sean Paul (Aquinas C, Perth; Notre Dame U, Perth, Australia), b Southampton 1 Aug 1991. Son of V.P.Terry (Hampshire and England 1978-96). 5'11". RHB, OB. Hampshire 2012-15. Hampshire 2nd XI debut 2011. HS 62* v Sussex (Hove) 2015. LO HS 63 v Leics (Southampton) 2014 (RLC). T20 HS 1.

B.M.R.Akram and T.E.Barber left the staff without making a County 1st XI appearance in 2015.

HAMPSHIRE 2015

RESULTS SUMMARY

	Place	Won	Lost	Tied	Drew	NR
LV= County Championship (1st Division)	7th	4	6		6	
All First-Class Matches		4	6		7	
Royal London One-Day Cup (Group B)	QF	3	4			2
NatWest t20 Blast (South Group)	SF	9	7			

LV= COUNTY CHAMPIONSHIP AVERAGES

BATTING AND FIELDING

Cap		M	I	NO	HS	Runs	Avge	100	50	Ct/St
	J.S.Gatting	4	8	2	64*	280	46.66	–	2	1
	L.D.McManus	2	4	1	53*	120	40.00	–	1	4
2006	M.A.Carberry	16	30	1	97	1129	38.93	–	10	4
2013	L.A.Dawson	13	23	3	140	695	34.75	1	1	11
2015	W.R.Smith	16	30	5	93	859	34.36	–	6	19
2005	S.M.Ervine	12	19	4	102	508	33.86	1	1	14
	G.K.Berg	16	24	3	99	672	32.00	–	5	11
	R.McLaren	4	4	–	52	123	30.75	–	1	1
2013	J.M.Vince	15	28	2	125*	743	28.57	1	5	22
2006	J.H.K.Adams	15	29	1	136	760	27.14	1	5	4
	A.J.A.Wheater	14	22	1	111	563	26.80	1	4	26/2
	S.P.Terry	5	10	1	62*	232	25.77	–	2	4
2012	D.R.Briggs	8	13	2	48	231	21.00	–	–	1
	A.R.Adams	3	5	1	31	58	14.50	–	–	3
	F.H.Edwards	8	8	5	17*	32	10.66	–	–	1
	M.S.Crane	3	4	2	13	18	9.00	–	–	1
	J.M.Bird	6	10	2	12	54	6.75	–	–	1
2008	J.A.Tomlinson	8	13	3	17	52	5.20	–	–	1
	B.T.J.Wheal	4	6	1	10	17	3.40	–	–	1

Also batted: R.A.Stevenson (3 matches) 30, 4, 0; C.P.Wood (1) 48, 30.

BOWLING

	O	M	R	W	Avge	Best	5wI	10wM
F.H.Edwards	240.5	38	940	45	20.88	6- 88	3	1
G.K.Berg	429.1	94	1181	42	28.11	4- 64	–	–
M.S.Crane	77	11	336	10	33.60	5- 35	1	–
D.R.Briggs	251.3	64	711	19	37.42	4- 74	–	–
R.McLaren	128.5	24	419	11	38.09	4- 60	–	–
L.A.Dawson	271.2	52	850	22	38.63	5-139	1	–
J.M.Bird	207.2	34	755	19	39.73	4-146	–	–
J.A.Tomlinson	241	57	754	18	41.88	4- 37	–	–

Also bowled:

A.R.Adams	120	26	359	9	39.88	3- 68	–	–
B.T.J.Wheal	94	10	393	8	49.12	4-101	–	–
S.M.Ervine	125.2	31	443	8	55.37	3- 37	–	–

M.A.Carberry 7.4-4-22-0; J.S.Gatting 3-1-7-0; W.R.Smith 46.4-13-111-3; R.A.Stevenson 56.5-9-215-3; J.M.Vince 19-2-74-1; C.P.Wood 29-5-101-2.

The First-Class Averages (pp 227–243) give the records of Hampshire players in all first-class county matches (Hampshire's other opponents being Loughborough MCCU), with the exception of:
L.A.Dawson 14-24-4-140-753-37.65-1-2-11ct. 273.2-52-853-25-34.12-5/139-1-0.

HAMPSHIRE RECORDS

FIRST-CLASS CRICKET

Highest Total	For 714-5d		v	Notts	Southampton	2005
	V 742		by	Surrey	The Oval	1909
Lowest Total	For 15		v	Warwicks	Birmingham	1922
	V 23		by	Yorkshire	Middlesbrough	1965
Highest Innings	For 316	R.H.Moore	v	Warwicks	Bournemouth	1937
	V 303*	G.A.Hick	for	Worcs	Southampton	1997

Highest Partnership for each Wicket

1st	347	V.P.Terry/C.L.Smith	v	Warwicks	Birmingham	1987
2nd	373	J.H.K.Adams/M.A.Carberry	v	Somerset	Taunton	2011
3rd	523	M.A.Carberry/N.D.McKenzie	v	Yorkshire	Southampton	2011
4th	278	J.H.K.Adams/J.M.Vince	v	Yorkshire	Scarborough	2010
5th	235	G.Hill/D.F.Walker	v	Sussex	Portsmouth	1937
6th	411	R.M.Poore/E.G.Wynyard	v	Somerset	Taunton	1899
7th	325	G.Brown/C.H.Abercrombie	v	Essex	Leyton	1913
8th	257	N.Pothas/A.J.Bichel	v	Glos	Cheltenham	2005
9th	230	D.A.Livingstone/A.T.Castell	v	Surrey	Southampton	1962
10th	192	H.A.W.Bowell/W.H.Livsey	v	Worcs	Bournemouth	1921

Best Bowling	For 9-25	R.M.H.Cottam	v	Lancashire	Manchester	1965
(Innings)	V 10-46	W.Hickton	for	Lancashire	Manchester	1870
Best Bowling	For 16-88	J.A.Newman	v	Somerset	Weston-s-Mare	1927
(Match)	V 17-103	W.Mycroft	for	Derbyshire	Southampton	1876

Most Runs – Season	2854	C.P.Mead	(av 79.27)	1928
Most Runs – Career	48892	C.P.Mead	(av 48.84)	1905-36
Most 100s – Season	12	C.P.Mead		1928
Most 100s – Career	138	C.P.Mead		1905-36
Most Wkts – Season	190	A.S.Kennedy	(av 15.61)	1922
Most Wkts – Career	2669	D.Shackleton	(av 18.23)	1948-69
Most Career W-K Dismissals	700	R.J.Parks	(630 ct; 70 st)	1980-92
Most Career Catches in the Field	629	C.P.Mead		1905-36

LIMITED-OVERS CRICKET

Highest Total	50ov	371-4		v	Glamorgan	Southampton	1975
	40ov	353-8		v	Middlesex	Lord's	2005
	T20	225-2		v	Middlesex	Southampton	2006
Lowest Total	50ov	50		v	Yorkshire	Leeds	1991
	40ov	43		v	Essex	Basingstoke	1972
	T20	85		v	Sussex	Southampton	2008
Highest Innings	50ov	177	C.G.Greenidge	v	Glamorgan	Southampton	1975
	40ov	172	C.G.Greenidge	v	Surrey	Southampton	1987
	T20	124*	M.J.Lumb	v	Essex	Southampton	2009
Best Bowling	50ov	7-30	P.J.Sainsbury	v	Norfolk	Southampton	1965
	40ov	6-20	T.E.Jesty	v	Glamorgan	Cardiff	1975
	T20	5-14	A.D.Mascarenhas	v	Sussex	Hove	2004

KENT

Formation of Present Club: 1 March 1859
Substantial Reorganisation: 6 December 1870
Inaugural First-Class Match: 1864
Colours: Maroon and White
Badge: White Horse on a Red Ground
County Champions: (6) 1906, 1909, 1910, 1913, 1970, 1978
Joint Champions: (1) 1977
Gillette Cup Winners: (2) 1967, 1974
Benson and Hedges Cup Winners: (3) 1973, 1976, 1978
Pro 40/National League (Div 1) Winners: (1) 2001
Sunday League Winners: (4) 1972, 1973, 1976, 1995
Twenty20 Cup Winners: (1) 2007

Cricket Chief Executive: Jamie Clifford, The Spitfire Ground, Old Dover Road, Canterbury, CT1 3NZ • Tel: 01227 456886 • Fax: 01227 762168 • Email: feedback.kent@ecb.co.uk • Web: www.kentcricket.co.uk • Twitter : @kentcricket (26,279 followers)

Head Coach: Jimmy Adams. **High Performance Director**: Simon Willis. **Assistant Coach**: Matt Walker. **Captain**: S.A.Northeast. **Overseas Players**: T.W.M.Latham and K.Rabada. **2016 Beneficiary**: D.I.Stevens. **Head Groundsman**: Simon Williamson. **Scorer**: Lorne Hart. ‡ New registration. NQ Not qualified for England.

BALL, Adam James (Beths GS, Bexley) b Greenwich, London 1 March 1993. 6'2". RHB, LFM. Squad No 24. Debut (Kent) 2011. No f-c appearances in 2012. Kent 2nd XI debut 2009, aged 16y 117d. England U19s 2010 to 2010-11. HS 69 v Lancs (Canterbury) 2013. BB 3-36 v Leics (Leicester) 2011. LO HS 28 v Warwks (Birmingham) 2013 (Y40). LO BB 3-36 v Sussex (Horsham) 2013 (Y40). T20 HS 18. T20 BB 2-18.

BELL-DRUMMOND, Daniel James (Millfield S), b Lewisham, London 4 Aug 1993. 5'10". RHB, RMF. Squad No 23. Debut (Kent) 2011; cap 2015. MCC 2014. Kent 2nd XI debut 2009, aged 16y 21d. England U19 2010 to 2010-11. 1000 runs (1): 1058 (2014). HS 153 v Hants (Southampton) 2014. BB – . LO HS 83 v Sussex (Canterbury) 2014 (RLC). T20 HS 77.

BERNARD, Hugh Robert (Archbishop's S, Canterbury), Canterbury 14 Sep 1996. 5'10". RHB, RMF. Squad No 27. Kent 2nd XI debut 2014. Awaiting 1st XI debut.

BILLINGS, Samuel William (Haileybury S; Loughborough U), b Pembury 15 Jun 1991. 5'11". RHB, WK. Squad No 20. Loughborough MCCU 2011, scoring 131 v Northants (Loughborough) on f-c debut. Kent debut 2011; cap 2015. MCC 2015. Kent 2nd XI debut 2007, aged 15y 349d. LOI: 5 (2015); HS 41 v NZ (Chester-le-St) 2015. IT20: 6 (2015 to 2015-16); HS 53 v P (Dubai, DSC) 2015-16. HS 131 (*see above*). K HS 100 v Essex (Tunbridge W) 2015. LO HS 143 v Derbys (Canterbury) 2012 (CB40). T20 HS 61*.

BLAKE, Alexander James (Hayes SS; Leeds Met U), b Farnborough 25 Jan 1989. 6'1". LHB, RMF. Squad No 10. Debut (Kent) 2008. Leeds/Bradford UCCE 2009-11 (not f-c). HS 105* v Yorks (Leeds) 2010. BB 2-9 v Pakistanis (Canterbury) 2010. CC BB 1-60 v Hants (Southampton) 2010. LO HS 89 v Lancs (Canterbury) 2015 (RLC). LO BB 2-13 v Yorks (Leeds) 2011 (CB40). T20 HS 71*.

CLAYDON, Mitchell Eric (Westfield Sports HS, Sydney), b Fairfield, NSW, Australia 25 Nov 1982. 6'4". LHB, RMF. Squad No 8. Yorkshire 2005-06. Durham 2007-13. Canterbury 2010-11. Kent debut 2013 (on loan). HS 77 v Leics (Leicester) 2014. 50 wkts (1): 59 (2014). BB 6-104 Du v Somerset (Taunton) 2011. K BB 5-61 v Glos (Canterbury) 2014. LO HS 19 Du v Glos (Bristol) 2009 (FPT). LO BB 4-39 Cant v Otago (Timaru) 2010-11. T20 HS 19. T20 BB 5-26.

COLES, Matthew Thomas (Maplesden Noakes S; Mid-Kent C), b Maidstone 26 May 1990. 6'3". LHB, RFM. Squad No 26. Debut (Kent) 2009; cap 2012. Hampshire 2013-14. HS 103* v Yorks (Leeds) 2012. 50 wkts (2); most – 67 (2015). BB 6-51 v Northants (Northampton) 2012. LO HS 100 v Surrey (Oval) 2014 (RLC). LO BB 6-32 v Yorks (Leeds) 2012 (CB40). T20 HS 54. T20 BB 3-14.

COWDREY, Fabian Kruuse (Tonbridge S), b Canterbury 30 Jan 1993. Son of C.S.Cowdrey (Kent, Glamorgan, England 1977-92), grandson of M.C.Cowdrey (Kent, Oxford U, England 1950-76), nephew of G.R.Cowdrey (Kent 1984-97). 6'0". RHB, SLA. Squad No 30. Cardiff MCCU 2013. Kent debut 2014. Kent 2nd XI debut 2009, aged 16y 207d. HS 62 CfU v Glamorgan (Cardiff) 2013. K HS 54 v Glamorgan (Canterbury) 2015. BB 3-59 v Hants (Canterbury) 2014. LO HS 75 v Surrey (Oval) 2014 (RLC). LO BB 3-32 v Hants (Canterbury) 2015 (RLC). T20 HS 55. T20 BB 2-15.

CRAWLEY, Zak (Tonbridge S), b Bromley 3 Feb 1998. 6'6". RHB, RM. Squad No 16. Kent 2nd XI debut 2013, aged 15y 199d. Awaiting 1st XI debut.

DENLY, Joseph Liam (Chaucer TC), b Canterbury 16 Mar 1986. 6'0". RHB, LB. Squad No 6. Kent debut 2004; cap 2008. Middlesex 2012-14; cap 2012. MCC 2013. **LOI**: 9 (2009 to 2009-10); HS 67 v Ireland (Belfast) 2009 – on debut. **IT20**: 5 (2009 to 2009-10); HS 14 and BB 1-9 v SA (Centurion) 2009-10. F-c Tours (Eng A): NZ 2008-09; I 2007-08. 1000 runs (3); most – 1081 (2015). HS 199 v Derbys (Derby) 2011. BB 3-43 v Surrey (Oval) 2011. LO HS 115 v Warwks (Birmingham) 2009 (FPT). LO BB 3-19 Brothers v Abahani (Fatullah) 2014-15. T20 HS 100. T20 BB 1-9.

NO DICKSON, Sean Robert, b Johannesburg, South Africa 2 Sep 1991. 5'10". RHB, RM. Squad No 58. Northerns 2013-14 to date. Kent debut 2015. UK passport holder. Somerset 2nd XI 2010. HS 173 Northerns v NW (Potchefstroom) 2013-14. K HS 59 v Glamorgan (Cardiff) 2015. BB 1-15 Northerns v GW (Centurion) 2014-15. LO HS 47 Northerns v SW Districts (Oudtshoorn) 2014-15. T20 HS 53. T20 BB 1-9.

GRIFFITHS, David Andrew (Sandown HS, IoW), b Newport, IoW 10 Sep 1985. 6'1". LHB, RFM. Squad No 18. Hampshire 2006-13. Kent debut 2014. HS 31* H v Surrey (Southampton) 2007. K HS 12 and BB 6-63 v Glos (Canterbury) 2014. LO HS 12* v Warwks (Birmingham) 2014 (RLC). LO BB 4-29 H v Glos (Southampton) 2009 (P40). T20 HS 18*. T20 BB 4-22.

HAGGETT, Calum John (Millfield S), b Taunton, Somerset 30 Oct 1990. 6'3". LHB, RMF. Squad No 25. Debut (Kent) 2013. HS 80 v Surrey (Oval) 2015. BB 4-43 v Essex (Tunbridge W) 2015. LO HS 36 and LO BB 2-54 v Durham (Canterbury) 2014 (RLC). T20 HS 11. T20 BB 2-12.

HARTLEY, Charles Frederick (Millfield S), b Redditch, Worcs 4 Jan 1994. 6'2". RHB, RMF. Squad No 22. Debut (Kent) 2014. Kent 2nd XI debut 2013. No 1st XI appearances in 2015. HS 2 and BB 2-40 v Leics (Leicester) 2014. LO HS 5 v Sri Lankans (Canterbury) 2014. LO BB 1-51 v New Zealand A (Canterbury) 2014.

HUNN, Matthew David (St Joseph's C, Ipswich), b Colchester, Essex 22 Mar 1994. 6'4". RHB, RMF. Squad No 14. Debut (Kent) 2013. Essex 2nd XI debut 2012. Kent 2nd XI debut 2013. Suffolk 2011-13. HS 23* v Derbys (Derby) 2015. BB 5-99 v Australians (Canterbury) 2015. CC BB 4-47 v Essex (Tunbridge W) 2015. LO HS 5* v Lancs (Canterbury) 2015 (RLC). LO BB 2-31 v Sussex (Canterbury) 2015 (RLC). T20 HS – . T20 BB 3-30.

KEY, Robert William Trevor (Colfe's S), b East Dulwich, London 12 May 1979. 6'1". RHB, RM/OB. Squad No 4. Debut (Kent) 1998; cap 2001; captain 2006-12, 2014-15; benefit 2011. MCC 2002-04, 2009. *Wisden* 2004. **Tests**: 15 (2002 to 2004-05); HS 221 v WI (Lord's) 2004. **LOI**: 5 (2003 to 2004); HS 19 v WI (Lord's) 2004. **IT20**: 1 (2009); HS 10* v Netherlands (Lord's) 2009. F-c Tours: A 2002-03; SA 1998-99 (Eng A), 2004-05; NZ 2008-09 (EL – captain); SL 2002-03 (ECB Acad); Z 1998-99 (Eng A). 1000 runs (7); most – 1896 (2004). HS 270* v Glamorgan (Cardiff) 2009. BB 2-31 v Somerset (Canterbury) 2010. LO HS 144* v Netherlands (Tunbridge W) 2013 (Y40). T20 HS 98*.

‡^{NQ}**LATHAM, Thomas** William Maxwell, b Christchurch, New Zealand 2 Apr 1992. Son of R.T.Latham (Canterbury and New Zealand 1980-81 to 1994-95). 5'9". LHB, RM, WK. Squad No 48. Canterbury 2010-11 to date. **Tests** (NZ): 18 (2013-14 to 2015-16); HS 137 v P (Dubai, DSC) 2014-15. **LOI** (NZ): 38 (2011-12 to 2015-16); HS 110* v Z (Harare) 2015. **IT20** (NZ): 12 (2012 to 2015); HS 26 v P (Dubai, DSC) 2014-15. F-c Tours (NZ): E 2013, 2014 (NZ A), 2015; A 2015-16; WI 2014; I 2013-14 (NZ A); SL 2013-14 (NZ A); UAE 2014-15 (v P). HS 261 Cant v CD (Napier) 2013-14. BB 1-7 NZ v Cricket Australia (Sydney) 2015-16. LO HS 130 Cant v Wellington (Wellington) 2011-12. T20 HS 64.

NORTHEAST, Sam Alexander (Harrow S), b Ashford 16 Oct 1989. 5'11". RHB, LB. Squad No 17. Debut (Kent) 2007; cap 2012; captain 2016. MCC 2013. 1000 runs (1): 1204 (2015). HS 176 v Loughborough MCCU (Canterbury) 2011. CC HS 165 v Derbys (Canterbury) 2012. BB 1-60 v Glos (Cheltenham) 2013. LO HS 132 v Somerset (Taunton) 2014 (RLC). T20 HS 114 v Somerset (Taunton) 2015 – K record.

QAYYUM, Imran (Villiers HS, Southall; Greenford SFC; City U), b Ealing, Middx 23 May 1993. 6'0". RHB, SLA. Squad No 1. Kent 2nd XI debut 2013. Northamptonshire 2nd XI 2013. Awaiting 1st XI debut.

‡^{NQ}**RABADA, Kagiso**, b Johannesburg, South Africa 25 May 1995. 6'3". LHB, RF. Gauteng 2013-14. Lions 2013-14 to date. **Tests** (SA): 6 (2015-16); HS 24 v E (Johannesburg) 2015-16; BB 7-112 (13-144 match) v E (Centurion) 2015-16. **LOI** (SA): 14 (2015 to 2015-16); HS 19* v I (Indore) 2015-16; BB 6-16 v B (Dhaka) 2015 – on debut. **IT20** (SA): 13 (2014-15 to 2015-16); HS 5* and BB 3-30 v NZ (Centurion) 2015. F-c Tours (SA): A 2014 (SA A); I 2015-16. HS 48* Lions v Titans (Johannesburg) 2014-15. BB 9-33 (14-105 match) Lions v Dolphins (Johannesburg) 2014-15. LO HS 22 Lions v Knights (Johannesburg) 2014-15. LO BB 6-16 (*see LOI*).

RILEY, Adam Edward Nicholas (Beths GS, Bexley; Loughborough U), b Sidcup 23 Mar 1992. 6'2". RHB, OB. Squad No 33. Debut (Kent) 2011. Loughborough MCCU 2012-14. MCC 2015. Kent 2nd XI debut 2010. F-c Tour (EL): SA 2014-15. HS 34 v Derbys (Canterbury) 2015. 50 wkts (1): 57 (2014). BB 7-150 v Hants (Southampton) 2013. LO HS 5* v New Zealand A (Canterbury) 2014. LO BB 2-32 v Sussex (Hove) 2011 (CB40). T20 HS 5*. T20 BB 4-22.

ROUSE, Adam Paul (Perrins Community Sports C; Peter Symonds C, Winchester), b Harare, Zimbabwe 30 Jun 1992. 5'10". RHB, WK. Squad No 12. Hampshire 2013. Gloucestershire 2014; cap 2014. Hampshire 2nd XI debut 2008, aged 15y 331d. England U19 2010. HS 49 Gs v Essex (Chelmsford) 2014. LO HS 7 H v Bangladesh A (Southampton) 2013. T20 HS 35*.

STEVENS, Darren Ian (Hinckley C), b Leicester 30 Apr 1976. 5'11". RHB, RM. Squad No 3. Leicestershire 1997-2004; cap 2002. MCC 2002. Kent debut/cap 2005; benefit 2016. F-c Tour (ECB Acad): SL 2002-03. 1000 runs (3); most – 1304 (2013). HS 208 v Glamorgan (Canterbury) 2005 and 208 v Middx (Uxbridge) 2009. 50 wkts (2); most – 61 (2015). BB 7-21 (11-70 match) v Surrey (Canterbury) 2011. LO HS 133 Le v Northumb (Jesmond) 2000 (NWT). LO BB 5-32 v Scotland (Edinburgh) 2005 (NL). T20 HS 90. T20 BB 4-14.

THOMAS, Ivan Alfred Astley (John Roan S, Blackheath; Leeds U), b Greenwich, London 25 Sep 1991. 6'4". RHB, RMF. Squad No 5. Leeds/Bradford MCCU 2012-14. Kent debut 2012. Kent 2nd XI debut 2011. HS 13 v Australians (Canterbury) 2015. CC HS 7* v Glos (Bristol) 2015. BB 4-48 v Leics (Canterbury) 2015. LO HS 1 v New Zealand A (Canterbury) 2014. LO BB 2-64 v Glamorgan (Cardiff) 2015 (RLC). T20 HS 0. T20 BB 1-21.

TREDWELL, James Cullum (Southlands Community CS, New Romney), b Ashford 27 Feb 1982. 6'0". LHB, OB. S quad No 15. Debut (Kent) 2001; cap 2007; captain 2013. Sussex (on loan) 2014. MCC 2004, 2008. **Tests**: 2 (2009-10 to 2014-15); HS 37 v B (Dhaka) 2009-10; BB 4-47 v WI (North Sound) 2014-15. **LOI**: 45 (2009-10 to 2014-15); HS 30 v I (Nottingham) 2014; BB 4-41 v Scotland (Aberdeen) 2014. **IT20**: 17 (2012-13 to 2014); HS 22 and BB 1-16 v WI (Bridgetown) 2013-14. F-c Tours: WI 2014-15; NZ 2012-13 (*part*); I 2003-04 (Eng A, captain); B 2009-10. HS 123* v New Zealanders (Canterbury) 2008. CC HS 116* v Yorks (Tunbridge W) 2007. 50 wkts (1): 69 (2009). BB 8-66 (11-120 match) v Glamorgan (Canterbury) 2009. LO HS 88 v Surrey (Oval) 2007 (FPT). LO BB 6-27 v Middx (Southgate) 2009 (FPT). T20 HS 34*. T20 BB 4-21.

WELLER, Sam David (Millfield S; Oxford Brookes U), b Chislehurst 21 Nov 1994. 6'2". RHB, RFM. Squad No 19. Oxford MCCU 2014-15. Kent 2nd XI debut 2011. Awaiting 1st XI debut. HS 18* OU v Warwks (Oxford) 2014. BB 3-26 OU v Middlesex (Oxford) 2015.

RELEASED/RETIRED

(Having made a County 1st XI appearance in 2015)

DAVIES, R.C. – *see SOMERSET*.

HARMISON, Ben William (Ashington HS), b Ashington, Northumb 9 Jan 1986. Younger brother of S.J.Harmison (Durham, Yorkshire and England 1996-2012). 6'5". LHB, RMF. Durham 2006-10, scoring 110 v Oxford U (Oxford) on debut. Scored 105 in his second match (v West Indies A) to emulate A.Fairbairn (Middlesex 1947) in scoring hundreds in first two f-c matches, those matches being in England. Kent 2012-15. HS 125 v Glos (Bristol) 2014. BB 4-27 Du v Surrey (Guildford) 2008. K BB 2-26 v Essex (Canterbury) 2014. LO HS 67 Du v Notts (Chester-le-St) 2009 (P40). LO BB 3-40 v Glos (Canterbury) 2014 (RLC). T20 HS 24. T20 BB 3-20.

NQNASH, Brendan Paul (St Joseph's C, Nudgee), b Attadale, Western Australia 14 Dec 1977. 5'8". LHB, LM. Queensland 2000-01 to 2006-07. Jamaica 2007-08 to 2011-12. Kent 2012-15; cap 2013. Kolpak signing. **Tests** (WI): 21 (2008-09 to 2011); HS 114 v SA (Basseterre) 2010; BB 1-21 v SL (Galle) 2010-11. **LOI** (WI): 9 (2008 to 2008-09); HS 39* and BB 3-56 v Canada (King City) 2008. F-c Tours (WI): E 2009; A 2009-10; NZ 2008-09; SL 2010-11; B 2010 (WI A). 1000 runs (2): 1110 (2013). HS 207 Jamaica v T&T (St Augustine) 2010-11. K HS 199* v Glos (Cheltenham) 2013. BB 2-7 Jamaica v CC&C (Kingston) 2007-08. K BB 1-2 v Glamorgan (Canterbury) 2012. LO HS 98* v Warwks (Birmingham) 2013 (Y40). LO BB 4-20 Jamaica v Guyana (Bridgetown) 2007-08. T20 HS 26. T20 BB 1-32.

KENT 2015

RESULTS SUMMARY

	Place	Won	Lost	Tied	Drew	NR
LV= County Championship (2nd Division)	7th	4	7		5	
All First-Class Matches		4	8		5	
Royal London One-Day Cup (Group B)	QF	3	4			2
NatWest t20 Blast (South Group)	QF	9	5			1

LV= COUNTY CHAMPIONSHIP AVERAGES
BATTING AND FIELDING

Cap		M	I	NO	HS	Runs	Avge	100	50	Ct/St
	S.R.Dickson	3	4	2	59	113	56.50	–	1	–
2012	S.A.Northeast	16	28	3	139	1168	46.72	1	9	11
2008	J.L.Denly	16	29	4	161*	1023	40.92	2	7	8
2001	R.W.T.Key	12	22	–	158	857	38.95	2	4	1
2015	S.W.Billings	11	17	2	100*	447	29.80	1	1	31/1
2013	B.P.Nash	4	8	–	49	229	28.62	–	–	–
2005	D.I.Stevens	15	23	–	92	635	27.60	–	6	5
	B.W.Harmison	6	9	–	123	247	27.44	1	1	6
2015	D.J.Bell-Drummond	16	29	–	123	767	26.44	2	2	8
	C.J.Haggett	11	16	2	80	345	24.64	–	2	4
	F.K.Cowdrey	5	9	–	54	169	18.77	–	1	4
	M.E.Claydon	6	9	4	24	88	17.60	–	–	–
2012	M.T.Coles	14	22	3	66	277	14.57	–	1	15
	A.E.N.Riley	8	11	4	34	97	13.85	–	–	7
	M.D.Hunn	7	6	4	23*	26	13.00	–	–	3
	A.J.Ball	3	5	–	32	53	10.60	–	–	4
2007	J.C.Tredwell	7	11	–	53	107	9.72	–	1	13
	R.C.Davies	5	6	–	17	35	5.83	–	–	9
	I.A.A.Thomas	10	16	8	7*	27	3.37	–	–	1

Also played: A.J.Blake (1 match) did not bat.

BOWLING

	O	M	R	W	Avge	Best	5wI	10wM
D.I.Stevens	419.1	100	1242	61	20.36	5- 58	2	–
M.T.Coles	433	82	1574	67	23.49	6- 55	2	1
I.A.A.Thomas	248.4	53	755	27	27.96	4- 48	–	–
C.J.Haggett	268	60	792	28	28.28	4- 43	–	–
M.D.Hunn	163	31	555	18	30.83	4- 47	–	–
M.E.Claydon	138.5	11	520	13	40.00	4-103	–	–
J.C.Tredwell	164.5	45	443	11	40.27	3- 59	–	–

Also bowled:

	O	M	R	W	Avge	Best		
A.E.N.Riley	108.5	13	424	8	53.00	4- 47		

A.J.Ball 4-0-13-0; J.L.Denly 17-2-50-1.

The First-Class Averages (pp 227–243) give the records of Kent players in all first-class county matches (Kent's other opponents being the Australians).

KENT RECORDS

FIRST-CLASS CRICKET

Highest Total	For 803-4d		v	Essex	Brentwood	1934
	V 676		by	Australians	Canterbury	1921
Lowest Total	For 18		v	Sussex	Gravesend	1867
	V 16		by	Warwicks	Tonbridge	1913
Highest Innings	For 332	W.H.Ashdown	v	Essex	Brentwood	1934
	V 344	W.G.Grace	for	MCC	Canterbury	1876

Highest Partnership for each Wicket

1st	300	N.R.Taylor/M.R.Benson	v	Derbyshire	Canterbury	1991
2nd	366	S.G.Hinks/N.R.Taylor	v	Middlesex	Canterbury	1990
3rd	323	R.W.T.Key/M.van Jaarsveld	v	Surrey	Tunbridge Wells	2005
4th	368	P.A.de Silva/G.R.Cowdrey	v	Derbyshire	Maidstone	1995
5th	277	F.E.Woolley/L.E.G.Ames	v	N Zealanders	Canterbury	1931
6th	315	P.A.de Silva/M.A.Ealham	v	Notts	Nottingham	1995
7th	248	A.P.Day/E.Humphreys	v	Somerset	Taunton	1908
8th	177	G.O.Jones/Yasir Arafat	v	Warwicks	Canterbury	2007
9th	171	M.A.Ealham/P.A.Strang	v	Notts	Nottingham	1997
10th	235	F.E.Woolley/A.Fielder	v	Worcs	Stourbridge	1909

Best Bowling	For	10- 30	C.Blythe	v	Northants	Northampton	1907
(Innings)	V	10- 48	C.H.G.Bland	for	Sussex	Tonbridge	1899
Best Bowling	For	17- 48	C.Blythe	v	Northants	Northampton	1907
(Match)	V	17-106	T.W.J.Goddard	for	Glos	Bristol	1939

Most Runs – Season	2894	F.E.Woolley	(av 59.06)	1928
Most Runs – Career	47868	F.E.Woolley	(av 41.77)	1906-38
Most 100s – Season	10	F.E.Woolley		1928, 1934
Most 100s – Career	122	F.E.Woolley		1906-38
Most Wkts – Season	262	A.P.Freeman	(av 14.74)	1933
Most Wkts – Career	3340	A.P.Freeman	(av 17.64)	1914-36
Most Career W-K Dismissals	1253	F.H.Huish	(901 ct; 352 st)	1895-1914
Most Career Catches in the Field	773	F.E.Woolley		1906-38

LIMITED-OVERS CRICKET

Highest Total	50ov	384-6		v	Berkshire	Finchampstead	1994
	40ov	337-7		v	Sussex	Canterbury	2013
	T20	231-7		v	Surrey	The Oval	2015
Lowest Total	50ov	60		v	Somerset	Taunton	1979
	40ov	83		v	Middlesex	Lord's	1984
	T20	72		v	Hampshire	Southampton	2011
Highest Innings	50ov	143	C.J.Tavaré	v	Somerset	Taunton	1985
	40ov	146	A.Symonds	v	Lancashire	Tunbridge Wells	2004
	T20	114	S.A.Northeast	v	Somerset	Taunton	2015
Best Bowling	50ov	8-31	D.L.Underwood	v	Scotland	Edinburgh	1987
	40ov	6- 9	R.A.Woolmer	v	Derbyshire	Chesterfield	1979
	T20	5-17	Wahab Riaz	v	Glos	Beckenham	2011

LANCASHIRE

Formation of Present Club: 12 January 1864
Inaugural First-Class Match: 1865
Colours: Red, Green and Blue
Badge: Red Rose
County Champions (since 1890): (8) 1897, 1904, 1926, 1927, 1928, 1930, 1934, 2011
Joint Champions: (1) 1950
Gillette/NatWest Trophy Winners: (7) 1970, 1971, 1972, 1975, 1990, 1996, 1998
Benson and Hedges Cup Winners: (4) 1984, 1990, 1995, 1996
Pro 40/National League (Div 1) Winners: (1) 1999.
Sunday League Winners: (4) 1969, 1970, 1989, 1998
Twenty20 Cup Winners: (1) 2015

Chief Executive: Daniel Gidney, Emirates Old Trafford, Talbot Road, Manchester M16 0PX • Tel: 0161 868 6700 • Email: enquiries@lccc.co.uk • Web: www.lccc.co.uk • Twitter: @LancsCCC (42,494 followers)

Cricket Director/Head Coach: Ashley Giles. **Player/Coach**: Glen Chapple. **Batting Coach**: Mark Chilton. **Academy Director**: Gary Yates. **Captain**: T.C.Smith. **Overseas Player**: N.Wagner. **2016 Beneficiary**: None. **Head Groundsman**: Matthew Merchant. **Scorer**: Chris Rimmer. ‡ New registration. NQ Not qualified for England.

ANDERSON, James Michael (St Theodore RC HS and SFC, Burnley), b Burnley 30 Jul 1982. 6'2". LHB, RFM. Squad No 9. Debut (Lancashire) 2002; cap 2003; benefit 2012. YC 2003. *Wisden* 2008. **ECB central contract 2015-16. Tests**: 113 (2003 to 2015-16); HS 81 v I (Nottingham) 2014, sharing a world Test record 10th wkt partnership of 198 with J.E.Root; 50 wkts (2); most – 57 (2010); BB 7-43 v NZ (Nottingham) 2008. **LOI**: 194 (2002-03 to 2014-15); HS 28 v NZ (Southampton) 2013; BB 5-23 v SA (Port Elizabeth) 2009-10. Hat-trick v P (Oval) 2003 – 1st for E in 373 LOI. **IT20**: 19 (2006-07 to 2009-10); HS 1* v A (Sydney) 2006-07; BB 3-23 v Netherlands (Lord's) 2009. F-c Tours: A 2006-07, 2010-11, 2013-14; SA 2004-05, 2009-10, 2015-16; WI 2003-04, 2005-06 (Eng A) (*part*), 2008-09, 2014-15; NZ 2007-08, 2012-13; I 2005-06 (*part*), 2008-09, 2012-13; SL 2003-04, 2007-08, 2011-12; UAE 2011-12 (v P), 2015-16 (v P). HS 81 (*see Tests*). La HS 42 v Surrey (Manchester) 2015. 50 wkts (3); most – 60 (2005). BB 7-43 (*see Tests*). La BB 7-77 v Essex (Chelmsford) 2015. Hat-trick v Essex (Manchester) 2003. LO HS 28 (*see LOI*). LO BB 5-23 (*see LOI*). T20 HS 16. T20 BB 3-23.

BAILEY, Thomas Ernest (Our Lady's Catholic HS, Preston), b Preston 21 Apr 1991. 6'4". RHB, RMF. Squad No 8. Debut (Lancashire) 2012. Lancashire 2nd XI debut 2011. HS 34 v Northants (Northampton) 2015 and 34 v Surrey (Oval) 2015. BB 5-12 v Leics (Leicester) 2015. LO HS 5* and LO BB 3-31 v Middx (Blackpool) 2015 (RLC). T20 HS 0*. T20 BB 2-24.

BROWN, Karl Robert (Hesketh Fletcher HS, Atherton), b Bolton 17 May 1988. 5'10". RHB, RMF. Squad No 14. Debut (Lancashire) 2006; cap 2015. Moors Sports Club 2011-12. HS 132 v Glamorgan (Manchester) 2015. BB 2-30 v Notts (Nottingham) 2009. LO HS 129 v Yorks (Manchester) 2014 (RLC). T20 HS 69.

131

BUCK, Nathan Liam (Newbridge HS; Ashby S), b Leicester 26 Apr 1991. 6'2" RHB, RMF. Squad No 11. Leicestershire 2009-14; cap 2011. Lancashire debut 2015. F-c Tour (EL): WI 2010-11. HS 29* Le v Worcs (Worcester) 2014. La HS 25 and La BB 3-64 v Leics (Leicester) 2015. BB 5-76 Le v Essex (Chelmsford) 2014. LO HS 21 Le v Glamorgan (Leicester) 2009 (P40). LO BB 4-39 EL v Sri Lanka A (Dambulla) 2011-12. T20 HS 8*. T20 BB 3-16.

BUTTLER, Joseph Charles (King's C, Taunton), b Taunton, Somerset 8 Sep 1990. 6'0". RHB, WK. Squad No 6. Somerset 2009-13; cap 2013. Lancashire debut 2014. Big Bash: MR 2013-14. **ECB Central Contract 2015-16. Tests**: 15 (2014 to 2015-16); HS 85 v I (Southampton) 2014. **LOI**: 70 (2011-12 to 2015-16); HS 129 v NZ (Birmingham) 2015. **IT20**: 42 (2011 to 2015-16); HS 67 v WI (Bridgetown) 2013-14. HS 144 Sm v Hants (Southampton) 2010. La HS 100* v Durham (Chester-le-St) 2014. BB – . LO HS 129 (*see LOI*). T20 HS 72*.

CHAPPLE, Glen (West Craven HS; Nelson & Colne C), b Skipton, Yorks 23 Jan 1974. 6'1". RHB, RMF. Squad No 3. Debut (Lancashire) 1992; cap 1994; benefit 2004; captain 2009-14. *Wisden* 2011. **LOI**: 1 (2006); HS 14 and BB – v Ireland (Belfast) 2006. F-c Tours (Eng A): A 1996-97; WI 1995-96 (La); I 1994-95. HS 155 v Somerset (Manchester) 2001. Scored 100 off 27 balls in contrived circumstances v Glamorgan (Manchester) 1993. 50 wkts (7); most – 57 (2011). BB 7-53 v Durham (Blackpool) 2007. LO HS 81* v Derbys (Manchester) 2002 (CGT). LO BB 6-18 v Essex (Lord's) 1996 (NWT) – La record. T20 HS 55*. T20 BB 3-36.

CLARK, Jordan (Sedbergh S), b Whitehaven, Cumbria 14 Oct 1990. Elder brother of G.Clark (*see DURHAM*). 6'4". RHB, RM, occ WK. Squad No 16. Debut (Lancashire) 2015. HS 63 v Surrey (Oval) 2015. BB 4-101 v Northants (Northampton) 2015. LO HS 72 v Durham (Chester-le-St) 2013 (Y40). LO BB 2-27 v Kent (Canterbury) 2015 (RLC). T20 HS 44. T20 BB 4-22.

CROFT, Steven John (Highfield HS, Blackpool; Myerscough C), b Blackpool 11 Oct 1984. 5'10". RHB, OB. Squad No 15. Debut (Lancashire) 2005; cap 2010. Auckland 2008-09. HS 156 v Northants (Manchester) 2014. BB 6-41 v Worcs (Manchester) 2012. LO HS 107 v Somerset (Taunton) 2011 (CB40). LO BB 4-24 v Scotland (Manchester) 2008 (FPT). T20 HS 94*. T20 BB 3-6.

DAVIES, Alexander Luke (Queen Elizabeth GS, Blackburn), b Darwen 23 Aug 1994. 5'7". RHB, WK. Squad No 17. Debut (Lancashire) 2012, without batting or bowling. Lancashire 2nd XI debut 2011. HS 99 v Kent (Manchester) 2015. LO HS 73* v Warwks (Manchester) 2015 (RLC). T20 HS 47.

EDWARDS, George Alexander (St Joseph C, Croydon), b King's College H, Camberwell, London 29 Jul 1992. 6'3". RHB, RMF. Squad No 22. Surrey 2011-13. Joined Lancashire in 2015, awaiting f-c and l-o debut. Surrey 2nd XI debut 2009, aged 16y 322d. HS 19 Sy v Cambridge MCCU (Cambridge) 2011. CC HS 17 and BB 4-44 Sy v Worcs (Worcester) 2012. LO HS 8* Sy v Glamorgan (Guildford) 2014 (RLC). LO BB 1-29 Sy v Durham (Chester-le-St) 2014 (RLC). T20 HS 1*. T20 BB 4-20.

GRIFFITHS, Gavin Timothy (St Mary's C, Crosby), b Ormskirk 19 Nov 1993. 6'2". RHB, RMF. Squad No 18. Lancashire 2nd XI debut 2011. Awaiting f-c debut. England U19 2012-13. LO HS 5* v Kent (Canterbury) 2015 (RLC). LO BB 3-41 v Notts (Liverpool) 2015 (RLC). T20 HS – . T20 BB 2-23.

HAMEED, Haseeb (Bolton S), b Bolton 17 Jan 1997. 6'2". RHB, LB. Squad No 23. Debut (Lancashire) 2015. Lancashire 2nd XI debut 2013. England U19 2014-15 to 2015. HS 91 v Surrey (Manchester) 2015. BB – .

^{NO}**JARVIS, Kyle** Malcolm (St John's C, Harare), b Harare, Zimbabwe 16 Feb 1989. Son of M.P.Jarvis (Zimbabwe 1979-80 to 1994-95). 6'4". RHB, RFM. Squad No 27. Mashonaland Eagles 2009-10 to 2012-13. C Districts 2011-12 to 2012-13. Lancashire debut 2013; cap 2015. **Tests** (Z): 8 (2011 to 2013); HS 25* v P (Bulawayo) 2011; BB 5-54 v WI (Bridgetown) 2012-13. **LOI** (Z): 24 (2009-10 to 2013); HS 13 v SA (Centurion) 2009-10; BB 3-36 v Kenya (Harare) 2009-10. **IT20** (Z): 9 (2011 to 2012-13); HS 9* v SA (Hambantota) 2012-13; BB 3-15 v P (Harare) 2011. F-c Tour (Z): WI 2012-13. HS 48 ME v MWR (Harare) 2012-13. La HS 47 v Surrey (Oval) 2015. 50 wkts (1): 62 (2015). BB 7-35 ME v MT (Bulawayo) 2012-13. La BB 5-13 v Derbys (Derby) 2015. LO HS 33* MWR v Mountaineers (Kwekwe) 2014-15. LO BB 4-35 ME v Mountaineers (Mutare) 2011-12. T20 HS 10. T20 BB 3-15.

JONES, Robert Peter (Bridgewater HS), b Warrington, Cheshire 3 Nov 1995. Lancashire 2nd XI debut 2013. Cheshire 2014. England U19 2014. RHB, LB. Awaiting 1st XI debut.

KERRIGAN, Simon Christopher (Corpus Christi RC HS, Preston), b Preston 10 May 1989. 5'9". RHB, SLA. Squad No 10. Debut (Lancashire) 2010; cap 2013. MCC 2013. **Tests**: 1 (2013); HS 1* and BB – v A (Oval) 2013. F-c Tour (EL): SL 2013-14. HS 62* v Hants (Southport) 2013. 50 wkts (2); most – 58 (2013). BB 9-51 (12-192 match) v Hants (Liverpool) 2011. LO HS 10 v Middx (Lord's) 2012 (CB40). LO BB 3-21 EL v Sri Lanka A (Northampton) 2011. T20 HS 4*. T20 BB 3-17.

LAMB, Daniel John (St Michael's HS, Chorley; Cardinal Newman C, Preston), b Preston 7 Sep 1995. RHB, RM. Lancashire 2nd XI debut 2013. Awaiting 1st XI debut.

LESTER, Toby James (Rossall S; Loughborough U), b Blackpool 5 Apr 1993. 6'4". LHB, LFM. Loughborough MCCU 2012-14. Lancashire debut 2015. MCC Univs 2012-14. Worcestershire 2nd XI 2014. Lancashire 2nd XI debut 2014. HS 2* LU v Sussex (Hove) 2014. La HS 0*. BB 3-50 v Essex (Manchester) 2015.

LILLEY, Arron Mark (Mossley Hollins HS; Ashton SFC), b Tameside 1 Apr 1991. 6'1". RHB, OB. Squad No 19. Debut (Lancashire) 2013. HS 63 and BB 5-23 v Derbys (Southport) 2015. LO HS 10 v Hants (Manchester) 2013 (Y40). LO BB 4-30 v Derbys (Manchester) 2013 (Y40). T20 HS 22*. T20 BB 3-31.

LIVINGSTONE, Liam Stephen (Chetwynde S, Barrow-in-Furness), b Barrow-in-Furness, Cumberland 4 Aug 1993. 6'1". RHB, LB. Squad No 7. Lancashire 2nd XI debut 2012. Cumberland 2011. Awaiting f-c debut. LO HS 91 v Kent (Canterbury) 2015 (RLC) – only 1-o game. T20 HS 27.

MAHMOOD, Saqib (Matthew Moss HS, Rochdale), b Birmingham 25 Feb 1997. 6'3". RHB, RFM. Squad No 25. England U19 2014. Awaiting f-c debut. T20 HS – . T20 BB 1-14.

PARKINSON, Matthew William (Bolton S), b Bolton 24 Oct 1996. 6'0". RHB, LB. Squad No 28. Lancashire 2nd XI debut 2013. Staffordshire 2014. England U19 2015. Awaiting 1st XI debut.

133

PARRY, Stephen David (Audenshaw HS), b Manchester 12 Jan 1986. 6'0". RHB, SLA. Squad No 4. Debut (Lancashire) 2007, taking 5-23 v Durham U (Durham); cap 2015. No 1st XI appearances in 2008. Cumberland 2005-06. Big Bash: BH 2014-15. **LOI**: 2 (2013-14); HS – ; BB 3-32 v WI (North Sound) 2013-14. **IT20**: 5 (2013-14 to 2015-16); HS 1 v Netherlands (Chittagong) 2013-14; BB 2-33 v P (Dubai, DSC) 2015-16. HS 37 v Durham (Manchester) 2014. CC BB 3-51 v Kent (Canterbury) 2013. BB 5-23 (see above). LO HS 31 v Essex (Chelmsford) 2009 (FPT). LO BB 5-17 v Surrey (Manchester) 2013 (Y40). T20 HS 11*. T20 BB 4-16.

NQ**PETERSEN, Alviro** Nathan, b Port Elizabeth, South Africa 25 November 1980. RHB, RM/OB. Squad No 73. Northerns 2000-01 to 2005-06. Titans 2004-05 to 2005-06. Lions 2005-06 to date. North West 2008-09. Glamorgan 2011; cap/captain 2011. Essex 2012. Somerset 2013-14; cap 2013. Lancashire debut 2015. **Tests** (SA): 36 (2009-10 to 2014-15); HS 182 v E (Leeds) 2012; scored 100 v I (Kolkata) on debut; BB 1-2 v WI (Port of Spain) 2010. **LOI** (SA): 21 (2006-07 to 2013); HS 80 v Z (Potchefstroom) 2006-07; BB – . **IT20** (SA): 2 (2010); HS 8 v WI (North Sound) 2010. F-c Tours (SA): E 2012; A 2012-13; WI 2010; NZ 2011-12; I 2007-08 (SA A), 2009-10; SL 2014; Z 2007 (SA A), 2014; B 2010 (SA A); UAE (v P) 2010-11, 2013-14. 1000 runs (1+2); most – 1376 (2008-09). HS 286 v Glamorgan (Colwyn Bay) 2015, sharing La record partnership of 501 with A.G.Prince. BB 3-58 Lions v Warriors (Port Elizabeth) 2013-14. CC BB 1-27 Sm v Sussex (Taunton) 2013. LO HS 145* Lions v Dolphins (Potchefstroom) 2011-12. LO BB 2-48 Lions v Cape Cobras (Johannesburg) 2011-12. T20 HS 84*. T20 BB 1-4.

PROCTER, Luke Anthony (Counthill S, Oldham), b Oldham 24 June 1988. 5'11". LHB, RM. Squad No 2. Debut (Lancashire) 2010. Cumberland 2007. HS 106 v Glos (Bristol) 2013. BB 7-71 v Surrey (Liverpool) 2012. LO HS 97 v West Indies A (Manchester) 2010. LO BB 3-29 v Unicorns (Colwyn Bay) 2010 (CB40). T20 HS 25*. T20 BB 3-22.

REECE, Luis Michael (St Michael's HS, Chorley; Leeds Met U), b Taunton, Somerset 4 Aug 1990. 6'1". LHB, LM. Squad No 21. Leeds/Bradford MCCU 2012-13. Lancashire debut 2014. MCC 2014. Unicorns 2011-12. HS 114* and BB 4-28 LBU v Leics (Leicester) 2013. La HS 97 v Glos (Bristol) 2013. La BB 1-20 v Hants (Southport) 2013. LO HS 59 Unicorns v Derbys (Chesterfield) 2012 (CB40). LO BB 4-35 Unicorns v Glos (Exmouth) 2011 (CB40).

SMITH, Thomas Christopher (Parkland HS, Chorley; Runshaw C, Leyland), b Liverpool 26 Dec 1985. 6'3". LHB, RMF. Squad No 24. Debut (Lancashire) 2005; cap 2010; captain 2015 to date. Leicestershire (on loan) 2008. F-c Tour (Eng A): B 2006-07. HS 128 v Hants (Southampton) 2010. 50 wkts (1): 54 (2014). BB 6-46 v Yorks (Manchester) 2009. LO HS 117 and LO BB 4-48 v Notts (Nottingham) 2011 (CB40). T20 HS 92*. T20 BB 3-12.

‡NQ**WAGNER, Neil**, b Pretoria, South Africa 13 Mar 1986. LHB, LMF. Northerns 2005-06 to 2007-08. Titans 2006-07 to 2007-08. Otago 2008-09 to date. Northamptonshire 2014. **Tests** (NZ): 19 (2012 to 2015-16); HS 37 v WI (Dunedin) 2013-14; BB 6-106 v A (Christchurch) 2015-16. F-c Tours (NZ): E 2013, 2015; SA 2012-13; WI 2012, 2014; Z 2007 (SA Acad); B 2013-14. HS 70 Otago v Wellington (Queenstown) 2009-10. CC HS 18 Nh v Warwks (Birmingham) 2014. 50 wkts (0+2); most – 51 (2010-11, 2012-13). BB 7-46 Otago v Wellington (Dunedin) 2011-12. CC BB 5-104 Nh v Durham (Chester-le-St) 2014. LO HS 42 Otago v CD (Dunedin) 2014-15. LO BB 5-34 Otago v Wellington (Wellington) 2008-09. T20 HS 14. T20 BB 4-33.

RELEASED/RETIRED

(Having made a County 1st XI appearance in 2015)

NQFAULKNER, James Peter, b Launceston, Tasmania, Australia 29 Apr 1990. Son of P.I.Faulkner (Tasmania 1982-83 to 1989-90). 6'1''. RHB, LMF. Tasmania 2008-09 to date. Lancashire 2015. IPL: PW 2011. KXIP 2012. RR 2013 to date. Big Bash: MS 2011-12 to date. **Tests** (A): 1 (2013); HS 23 and BB 4-51 (Oval) 2013. **LOI** (A): 50 (2012-13 to 2015-16); HS 116 v I (Bangalore) 2013-14; BB 4-48 v WI (Canberra) 2012-13. **IT20** (A): 15 (2011-12 to 2015-16); HS 41* v SA (Adelaide) 2014-15; BB 3-25 v SA (Melbourne) 2014-15. F-c Tour (A): E 2013. HS 121 v Surrey (Oval) 2015. BB 5-5 Tas v S Aus (Hobart) 2010-11. La BB 5-39 v Essex (Manchester) 2015. LO HS 116 (*see LOI*). LO BB 4-20 Tas v Vic (Melbourne) 2010-11. T20 HS 73. T20 BB 5-16.

HORTON, P.J. – *see LEICESTERSHIRE*.

NQPRINCE, Ashwell Gavin (St Thomas Senior SS, UPE), b Port Elizabeth, South Africa, 28 May 1977. 5'8''. LHB, OB. E Province 1995-96 to 1997-98. W Province 1997-98 to 2003-04. W Province-Boland 2004-05. Cape Cobras 2005-06 to 2007-08. Nottinghamshire 2008. Warriors 2008-09 to 2013-14. Lancashire 2009-15; cap 2010. **Tests** (SA): 66 (2001-02 to 2011-12, 2 as captain); HS 162* v B (Centurion) 2008-09; BB 1-2 v NZ (Cape Town) 2006. **LOI** (SA): 52 (2002-03 to 2007); HS 89* v WI (Port of Spain) 2005; BB – . **IT20** (SA): 1 (2005-06); HS 5 v NZ (Johannesburg) 2005-06. F-c Tours (SA): E 2008; A 2005-06; WI 2000 (SA A), 2005, 2010; I 2007-08, 2009-10; P 2007-08; SL 2006; Z 2007 (SA A); B 2007-08; UAE 2010-11 (v P). 1000 runs (4+1): 1478 (2015). HS 261 v Glamorgan (Colwyn Bay) 2015, sharing La record partnership of 501 with A.N.Petersen. BB 2-11 SA v Middx (Uxbridge) 2008. CC BB – . LO HS 128 Warriors v Dolphins (East London) 2009-10. LO BB – . T20 HS 78. T20 BB – .

NQSIDDLE, Peter Matthew, b Traralgon, Victoria, Australia 25 Nov 1984. 6'1½''. RHB, RFM. Victoria 2005-06 to date. Nottinghamshire 2014; cap 2014. Lancashire 2015. Big Bash: MR 2013-14 to 2014-15. **Tests** (A): 61 (2008-09 to 2015-16); HS 51 v I (Delhi) 2012-13; BB 6-54 v E (Brisbane) 2010-11. **LOI** (A): 17 (2008-09 to 2010-11); HS 9* v SL (Sydney) 2010-11; BB 3-55 v E (Centurion) 2009-10. **IT20** (A): 2 (2008-09 to 2010-11); HS 1* and BB 2-24 v NZ (Sydney) 2008-09. F-c Tours (A): E 2009, 2013, 2015; SA 2008-09, 2011-12, 2013-14; WI 2011-12; NZ 2015-16; I 2008-09 (Aus A), 2008-09, 2012-13; SL 2011; Z 2011 (Aus A); UAE 2014-15 (v P). HS 103* Aus A v Scotland (Edinburgh) 2013. La HS 89 v Northants (Northampton) 2015. 50 wkts (0+1): 54 (2011-12). BB 8-54 Vic v S Aus (Adelaide) 2014-15. La BB 4-39 v Glos (Manchester) 2015. LO HS 25* Vic v Tas (Hobart) 2010-11. LO BB 4-27 Vic v Tas (Hobart) 2008-09. T20 HS 9*. T20 BB 4-29.

LANCASHIRE 2015

RESULTS SUMMARY

		Place	Won	Lost	Tied	Drew	NR
LV= County Championship (2nd Division)		2nd	7	1		8	
All First-Class Matches			7	1		8	
Royal London One-Day Cup (Group B)		5th	3	3			2
NatWest t20 Blast (North Group)		Winners	10	6			1

LV= COUNTY CHAMPIONSHIP AVERAGES
BATTING AND FIELDING

Cap		M	I	NO	HS	Runs	Avge	100	50	Ct/St
2010	A.G.Prince	16	23	1	261	1478	67.18	5	5	13
2015	K.R.Brown	12	17	–	132	766	45.05	1	7	12
	A.N.Petersen	14	21	1	286	861	43.05	3	1	6
	H.Hameed	4	6	–	91	257	42.83	–	2	2
2010	S.J.Croft	16	23	2	122	874	41.61	2	6	21
	A.L.Davies	14	19	1	99	730	40.55	–	7	46/4
	A.M.Lilley	7	8	2	63	230	38.33	–	2	3
2007	P.J.Horton	12	18	1	168	611	35.94	1	5	16
	J.P.Faulkner	7	9	–	121	310	34.44	1	2	3
	P.M.Siddle	4	6	–	89	204	34.00	–	1	1
	J.Clark	12	17	2	63	419	27.93	–	1	3
2015	K.M.Jarvis	13	15	9	47	139	23.16	–	–	3
	L.M.Reece	5	8	–	82	142	17.75	–	1	1
	T.E.Bailey	12	16	3	34	224	17.23	–	–	2
1994	G.Chapple	5	5	1	29*	51	12.75	–	–	2
2013	S.C.Kerrigan	14	15	5	34*	110	11.00	–	–	6

Also played: J.M.Anderson (2 matches – cap 2003) 42, 6* (5 ct); N.L.Buck (2) 4, 17, 25 (1 ct); T.J.Lester (2) 0* (2 ct); P.Mustard (2) 43, 8, 5 (3 ct); T.C.Smith (1 – cap 2010) 38, 1 (2 ct).

BOWLING

	O	M	R	W	Avge	Best	5wI	10wM
J.M.Anderson	73.5	17	207	11	18.81	7- 77	1	–
P.M.Siddle	139.4	32	370	18	20.55	4- 39	–	–
J.P.Faulkner	186	44	501	23	21.78	5- 39	1	–
K.M.Jarvis	450.5	87	1533	62	24.72	5- 13	4	–
S.J.Croft	96.1	13	286	10	28.60	4- 35	–	–
A.M.Lilley	234.3	44	751	26	28.88	5- 23	1	–
S.C.Kerrigan	460.2	100	1321	41	32.21	4- 28	–	–
T.E.Bailey	347.3	64	1192	35	34.05	5- 12	1	–
J.Clark	244.4	38	880	19	46.31	4-101	–	–
G.Chapple	166	44	489	10	48.90	4- 62	–	–

Also bowled:

N.L.Buck	45.3	3	210	6	35.00	3- 64		

K.R.Brown 1-0-16-0; H.Hameed 1-0-9-0; P.J.Horton 2-0-7-0; T.J.Lester 44-8-172-3; A.N.Petersen 4-2-9-0; L.M.Reece 17-0-97-0; T.C.Smith 17-2-75-0.

Lancashire played no first-class fixtures outside the County Championship in 2015. The First-Class Averages (pp 227–243) give the records of their players in all first-class county matches, with the exception of J.M.Anderson, P.Mustard and P.M.Siddle, whose first-class figures for Lancashire are as above.

LANCASHIRE RECORDS

FIRST-CLASS CRICKET

Highest Total	For 863		v	Surrey	The Oval	1990
	V 707-9d		by	Surrey	The Oval	1990
Lowest Total	For 25		v	Derbyshire	Manchester	1871
	V 20		by	Essex	Chelmsford	2013
Highest Innings	For 424	A.C.MacLaren	v	Somerset	Taunton	1895
	V 315*	T.W.Hayward	for	Surrey	The Oval	1898

Highest Partnership for each Wicket

1st	368	A.C.MacLaren/R.H.Spooner	v	Glos	Liverpool	1903
2nd	371	F.B.Watson/G.E.Tyldesley	v	Surrey	Manchester	1928
3rd	501	A.N.Petersen/A.G.Prince	v	Glamorgan	Colwyn Bay	2015
4th	358	S.P.Titchard/G.D.Lloyd	v	Essex	Chelmsford	1996
5th	360	S.G.Law/C.L.Hooper	v	Warwicks	Birmingham	2003
6th	278	J.Iddon/H.R.W.Butterworth	v	Sussex	Manchester	1932
7th	248	G.D.Lloyd/I.D.Austin	v	Yorkshire	Leeds	1997
8th	158	J.Lyon/R.M.Ratcliffe	v	Warwicks	Manchester	1979
9th	142	L.O.S.Poidevin/A.Kermode	v	Sussex	Eastbourne	1907
10th	173	J.Briggs/R.Pilling	v	Surrey	Liverpool	1885

Best Bowling	For	10-46	W.Hickton	v	Hampshire	Manchester	1870
(Innings)	V	10-40	G.O.B.Allen	for	Middlesex	Lord's	1929
Best Bowling	For	17-91	H.Dean	v	Yorkshire	Liverpool	1913
(Match)	V	16-65	G.Giffen	for	Australians	Manchester	1886

Most Runs – Season	2633	J.T.Tyldesley	(av 56.02)	1901
Most Runs – Career	34222	G.E.Tyldesley	(av 45.20)	1909-36
Most 100s – Season	11	C.Hallows		1928
Most 100s – Career	90	G.E.Tyldesley		1909-36
Most Wkts – Season	198	E.A.McDonald	(av 18.55)	1925
Most Wkts – Career	1816	J.B.Statham	(av 15.12)	1950-68
Most Career W-K Dismissals	925	G.Duckworth	(635 ct; 290 st)	1923-38
Most Career Catches in the Field	556	K.J.Grieves		1949-64

LIMITED-OVERS CRICKET

Highest Total	50ov	381-3		v	Herts	Radlett	1999
	40ov	324-4		v	Worcs	Worcester	2012
	T20	231-4		v	Yorkshire	Manchester	2015
Lowest Total	50ov	59		v	Worcs	Worcester	1963
	40ov	68		v	Yorkshire	Leeds	2000
		68		v	Surrey	The Oval	2002
	T20	91		v	Derbyshire	Manchester	2003
Highest Innings	50ov	162*	A.R.Crook	v	Bucks	Wormsley	2005
	40ov	143	A.Flintoff	v	Essex	Chelmsford	1999
	T20	102*	L.Vincent	v	Derbyshire	Manchester	2008
Best Bowling	50ov	6-10	C.E.H.Croft	v	Scotland	Manchester	1982
	40ov	6-25	G.Chapple	v	Yorkshire	Leeds	1998
	T20	5-29	M.J.McClenaghan	v	Notts	Manchester	2013

LEICESTERSHIRE

Formation of Present Club: 25 March 1879
Inaugural First-Class Match: 1894
Colours: Dark Green and Scarlet
Badge: Gold Running Fox on Green Ground
County Champions: (3) 1975, 1996, 1998
Benson and Hedges Cup Winners: (3) 1972, 1975, 1985
Sunday League Champions: (2) 1974, 1977
Twenty20 Cup Winners: (3) 2004, 2006, 2011

Chief Executive: Wasim Khan, Fischer County Ground, Grace Road, Leicester LE2 8EB • Tel: 0116 283 2128 • Fax: 0116 244 0363 • Email: enquiries@leicestershireccc.co.uk • Web: www.leicestershireccc.co.uk • Twitter: @leicsccc (17,857 followers)

Elite Performance Director: Andrew McDonald. **Elite Development Coach**: Keith Piper. **Captains**: M.J.Cosgrove (f-c) and M.L.Pettini (l-o). **Vice-Captains**: P.J.Horton (f-c) and C.J.McKay (l-o). **Overseas Players**: C.J.McKay and Umar Akmal (T20 only). **2016 Beneficiary**: None. **Head Groundsman**: Andy Ward. **Scorer**: Paul Rogers. ‡ New registration. [NQ] Not qualified for England.

ALI, Aadil Masud (Lancaster S, Leicester; Q Elizabeth C), b Leicester 29 Dec 1994. 5'11". RHB, OB. Squad No 14. Debut (Leicestershire) 2015. Leicestershire 2nd XI debut 2013. HS 80 v Glos (Leicester) 2015. BB – . LO HS 84 v Glos (Leicester) 2015 (RLC). LO BB – . T20 HS 26.

BURGESS, Michael Gregory Kerran (Cranleigh S; Loughborough U), b Epsom, Surrey 8 Jul 1994. RHB, RM, occ WK. Squad No 20. Loughborough MCCU 2014-15. Surrey 2nd XI 2011-13. HS 49 LU v Sussex (Hove) 2014. LO HS 49 v Glos (Leicester) 2015 (RLC).

CHAPPELL, Zachariah John ('**Zak**') (Stamford S), b Grantham, Lincs 21 Aug 1996. 6'4". RHB, RFM. Squad No 32. Debut (Leicestershire) 2015. HS 96 and BB 1-35 v Derbys (Derby) 2015. LO HS 31 and LO BB 1-28 v Worcs (Worcester) 2015 (RLC).

[NQ]**COSGROVE, Mark** James, b Elizabeth, Adelaide, S Australia 14 Jun 1984. 5'9". LHB, RM. Squad No 55. S Australia 2002-03 to date. Glamorgan 2006-10; cap 2006. Tasmania 2010-11 to 2013-14. Leicestershire debut/cap 2015; captain 2015 to date. Big Bash: HH 2011-12. ST 2012-13 to 2014-15. SS 2013-14. **LOI** (A): 3 (2005-06 to 2006-07); HS 74 v B (Fatullah) 2005-06 – on debut; BB 1-1 v WI (Kuala Lumpur) 2006-07. 1000 runs (2); most – 1187 (2010). HS 233 Gm v Derbys (Derby) 2006. Le HS 156 v Derbys (Derby) 2015. BB 3-3 S Aus v Tas (Adelaide) 2006-07. CC BB Gm 3-30 v Derbys (Derby) 2009. Le BB 1-5 v Glos (Cheltenham) 2015. LO HS 121 S Aus v WA (Perth) 2005-06. LO BB 2-21 S Aus v Q (Brisbane) 2005-06. T20 HS 89. T20 BB 2-11.

‡**DEXTER, Neil** John (Northwood HS, Durban; Varsity C; U of South Africa), b Johannesburg, South Africa 21 Aug 1984. 6'0". RHB, RM. Squad No 17. Kent 2005-08. Essex 2008. Middlesex 2009-15; cap 2010; captain 2010 (*part*) to 2013. Qualified for England in 2010. HS 163* M v Northants (Northampton) 2014. Le BB 6-63 M v Lancs (Lord's) 2014. LO HS 135* K v Glamorgan (Cardiff) 2006 (CGT). LO BB 3-17 K v Leics (Canterbury) 2006 (P40). T20 HS 73. T20 BB 4-21.

‡**ECKERSLEY**, Edmund John Holden ('**Ned**') (St Benedict's GS, Ealing), b Oxford 9 Aug 1989. 6'0". RHB, WK, occ OB. Squad No 33. Debut (Leicestershire) 2011; cap 2013. Mountaineers 2011-12. MCC 2013. 1000 runs (1): 1302 (2013). HS 147 v Essex (Chelmsford) 2013 and 147 v Glamorgan (Leicester) 2015. BB 2-29 v Lancs (Manchester) 2013. LO HS 108 v Yorks (Leicester) 2013 (Y40). T20 HS 43.

138

FRECKINGHAM, Oliver Henry (K Edward S, Melton Mowbray), b Oakham, Rutland 12 Nov 1988. 6'1". RHB, RFM. Squad No 24. Debut (Leicestershire) 2013. HS 34* v Derbys (Derby) 2015. BB 6-125 v Northants (Northampton) 2013. LO HS 3* v Durham (Leicester) 2015 (RLC). LO BB 2-38 v Worcs (Leicester) 2014 (RLC). T20 HS 4*. T20 BB 2-21.

HILL, Lewis John (Hastings HS, Hinckley; John Cleveland C), b Leicester 5 Oct 1990. 5'7½". RHB, WK, occ RM. Squad No 23. Debut (Leicestershire) 2015. Unicorns 2012-13. HS 126 v Surrey (Oval) 2015. LO HS 86 v Durham (Leicester) 2015 (RLC). T20 HS – .

‡**HORTON, Paul** James (St Margaret's HS, Liverpool), b Sydney, Australia 20 Sep 1982. 5'10". RHB, RM. Squad No 2. UK resident since 1997. Lancashire 2003-15; cap 2007. Matabeleland Tuskers 2010-11 to 2011-12. 1000 runs (3); most – 1116 (2007). HS 209 MT v SR (Masvingo) 2010-11. CC HS 173 La v Somerset (Taunton) 2009. LO HS 111* La v Derbys (Manchester) 2009 (FPT). T20 HS 71*.

HURT, Liam Jack (Balshaw's CE HS, Leyland), b Preston, Lancs 15 Mar 1994. RHB, RMF. Lancashire 2nd XI 2013-14. Derbyshire 2nd XI 2015. Awaiting f-c debut. LO HS 15 and LO BB 2-59 v Durham (Leicester) 2015 (RLC).

[NQ]**McKAY, Clinton** James, b Melbourne, Australia 22 Feb 1983. 6'4". RHB, RFM. Squad No 27. Victoria 2006-07 to date. Leicestershire debut/cap 2015. IPL: MI 2012. Big Bash: MS 2011-12 to 2014-15. ST 2015-16. **Tests** (A): 1 (2009-10); HS 10 and BB 1-56 v WI (Perth) 2009-10. **LOI** (A): 59 (2009-10 to 2013-14); HS 30 v SL (Oval) 2013; BB 5-28 v SL (Adelaide) 2011-12. **IT20** (A): 6 (2010-11 to 2013-14); HS 7 and BB 2-24 v WI (Bridgetown) 2011-12. HS 65 Vic v WA (Melbourne) 2012-13. Le HS 51* v Northants (Northampton) 2015. 50 wkts (1): 58 (2015). BB 6-40 Vic v Tas (Melbourne) 2011-12. Le BB 6-54 v Kent (Canterbury) 2015. LO HS 57 Vic v Tas (Brisbane) 2014-15. LO BB 5-28 (see LOI). T20 HS 21*. T20 BB 4-24.

NAIK, Jigar Kumar Hakumatrai (Rushey Mead SS; Gateway SFC; Nottingham Trent U; Loughborough U), b Leicester 10 Aug 1984. 6'2". RHB, OB. Squad No 22. Debut (Leicestershire) 2006; cap 2013. Loughborough UCCE 2007. Colombo CC 2010-11. HS 109* v Derbys (Leicester) 2009. BB 8-179 v Lancs (Manchester) 2015. LO HS 36* v Derbys (Leicester) 2014 (RLC). LO BB 3-21 v Lancs (Leicester) 2009 (P40). T20 HS 16*. T20 BB 3-3.

‡[NQ]**O'BRIEN, Kevin** Joseph (Marian C, Dublin; Tallaght I of Tech), b Dublin, Ireland 4 Mar 1984. RHB, RM. Squad No 31. Son of B.A.O'Brien (Ireland 1966-81) and younger brother of N.J.O'Brien (see below). Ireland 2006-07 to date. Nottinghamshire 2009. Surrey 2014. **LOI** (Ire): 94 (2006 to 2015-16); HS 142 v Kenya (Nairobi) 2006-07; BB 4-13 v Netherlands (Amstelveen) 2013. **IT20** (Ire): 49 (2008 to 2015-16); HS 42* v Netherlands (Sylhet) 2013-14; BB 3-8 v Nepal (Belfast) 2015. HS 171* Ire v Kenya (Nairobi) 2008-09. CC HS 17 Sy v Hants (Oval) 2014. BB 5-39 Ire v Canada (Toronto) 2010. LO HS 142 (see LOI). LO BB 4-13 (see LOI). T20 HS 119. T20 BB 4-22.

[NQ]**O'BRIEN, Niall** John (Marian C, Dublin), b Dublin, Ireland 8 Nov 1981. Son of B.A.O'Brien (Ireland 1966-81); elder brother of K.J.O'Brien (see above). RHB, WK. Squad No 81. Kent 2004-06. Ireland 2005-06 to date. Northamptonshire 2007-12; cap 2011. Leicestershire debut 2013. MCC 2012. **LOI** (Ire): 74 (2006 to 2015-16); HS 80* v Scotland (Dubai, DSC) 2014-15. **IT20** (Ire): 20 (2008 to 2015-16); HS 50 v Canada (Colombo, SSC) 2009-10. HS 182 Nh v Glamorgan (Cardiff) 2012. Le HS 133 v Glamorgan (Leicester) 2013. BB 1-4 K v Cambridge UCCE (Cambridge) 2006. LO HS 121 Nh v Hants (Southampton) 2011 (CB40). T20 HS 84.

‡**PETTINI, Mark** Lewis (Comberton Village C; Hills Road SFC, Cambridge; Cardiff U), b Brighton, Sussex 7 Aug 1983. 5'10". RHB, RM. Squad No 6. Essex 2001-15; cap 2006; captain 2007 (*part*) to 2010 (*part*). Mountaineers 2011-12 to 2014-15. Mashonaland Eagles 2015-16. Joins Leicestershire in 2016 as l-o captain. MCC 2005. 1000 runs (1): 1218 (2006). HS 209 Mountaineers v MT (Bulawayo) 2013-14. CC HS 208* Ex v Derbys (Chelmsford) 2006. BB 1-72 Ex v Leics (Leicester) 2012 – in contrived circumstances. LO HS 144 Ex v Surrey (Oval) 2007 (FPT). T20 HS 95*.

RAINE, Benjamin Alexander (St Aidan's RC SS, Sunderland) b Sunderland, Co Durham 14 Sep 1991. 6'0". LHB, RMF. Squad No 44. Durham 2011. Leicestershire debut 2013. Durham 2nd XI debut 2010. HS 72 v Lancs (Manchester) 2013. 50 wkts (1): 61 (2015). BB 5-43 v Glamorgan (Cardiff) 2015. LO HS 43 v Yorks (Leicester) 2014 (RLC). LO BB 2-48 v Yorks (Leeds) 2013 (RLC). T20 HS 32*. T20 BB 3-12.

ROBSON, Angus James (Marcellin C, Randwick; Australian C of PE), b Darlinghurst, Sydney, Australia 19 Feb 1992. Younger brother of S.D.Robson (*see MIDDLESEX*). 5'9". RHB, LB. Squad No 8. Debut (Leicestershire) 2013. Leicestershire 2nd XI debut 2013. 1000 runs (2); most – 1086 (2014). HS 120 v Essex (Chelmsford) 2015. BB – . LO HS 90 v Yorks (Leeds) 2015 (RLC).

SAYER, Robert John (Ramsey Abbey C; Leeds Beckett U), b Huntingdon, Cambridgeshire 25 Jan 1995. 6'3". RHB, OB. Squad No 12. Debut (Leicestershire) 2015. Leicestershire 2nd XI debut 2013. Cambridgeshire 2013. Summer contract to end of 2016. HS 34 v Glos (Leicester) 2015. BB 2-59 v Derbys (Leicester) 2015. LO HS 22* v New Zealanders (Leicester) 2015. LO BB 1-46 v Northants (Northampton) 2015 (RLC). T20 HS 9. T20 BB 2-16.

SHEIKH, Atif (Bluecoat S), b Nottingham 18 Feb 1991. 6'0". RHB, LFM. Squad No 3. Derbyshire 2010. Leicestershire debut 2014. HS 12 v Essex (Leicester) 2014. BB 4-97 v Glos (Bristol) 2014, inc hat-trick. LO HS 22 and LO BB 3-49 v Australians (Leicester) 2015. T20 HS 14. T20 BB 2-11.

SHRECK, Charles Edward (Truro S), b Truro, Cornwall 6 Jan 1978. 6'7". RHB, RFM. Squad No 4. Nottinghamshire 2003-11; cap 2006. Wellington 2005-06 to 2007-08. Kent 2012-13. Leicestershire debut 2014. MCC 2008. Cornwall 1997-2002. HS 56 v Surrey (Oval) 2014. 50 wkts (4); most – 61 (2006, 2008). BB 8-31 (12-129 match) Nt v Middx (Nottingham) 2006. Le BB 5-71 v Essex (Chelmsford) 2015. Hat-trick Nt v Middx (Lord's) 2006. LO HS 9* Wellington v CD (Palmerston N) 2005-06. LO BB 5-19 Cornwall v Worcs (Truro) 2002 (CGT). T20 HS 10. T20 BB 4-22.

SYKES, James Stuart (St Ives S, Huntingdon), b Hinchingbrooke, Cambs 26 Apr 1992. 6'2". LHB, SLA. Squad No 60. Debut (Leicestershire) 2013. Leicestershire 2nd XI debut 2009. Cambridgeshire 2010. HS 34 v Lancs (Manchester) 2013. BB 4-176 v Essex (Chelmsford) 2013 – on debut. LO HS 15 v Glos (Bristol) 2013 (Y40). LO BB 3-34 v Hants (Southampton) 2014 (RLC). T20 HS 2*. T20 BB 2-24.

NQ**TAYLOR, Robert** Meadows Lombe (Harrow S; Loughborough U), b Northampton 21 Dec 1989. 6'3". LHB, LMF. Squad No 10. Leicestershire MCCU 2010-12. Leicestershire debut 2011. **LOI** (Scot): 15 (2012-13 to 2015-16); HS 46* v Kenya (Christchurch) 2013-14; BB 3-39 v Kenya (Aberdeen) 2013. **IT20** (Scot): 8 (2013-14 to 2015-16); HS 41* v Netherlands (Dubai) 2013-14; BB 3-17 v Hong Kong (Dublin) 2015. HS 101* LU v Leics (Leicester) 2011. Le HS 98 v Kent (Leicester) 2014. BB 5-55 v Glos (Leicester) 2014. LO HS 48* v Yorks (Scarborough) 2013 (Y40). LO BB 3-39 (*see LOI*). T20 HS 41*. T20 BB 4-11.

[NQ]**UMAR AKMAL**, b Lahore, Pakistan 26 May 1990. Younger brother of Kamran Akmal (Lahore City, NBP, Lahore Whites & Pakistan 1997-98 to date) and Adnan Akmal (ZTB, Lahore, Multan, SNGPL & Pakistan 2003-04 to date). RHB, WK, occ OB. Squad No 96. SNGPL 2007-08 to date. Lahore Shalimar 2012-13. Leicestershire debut/cap 2013. **Tests** (P): 16 (2009-10 to 2011); HS 129 v NZ (Dunedin) 2009-10 – on debut. **LOI** (P): 111 (2009 to 2014-15); HS 102* v SL (Colombo, RPS) 2009 and 102* v Afghan (Fatullah) 2013-14. **IT20** (P): 75 (2009 to 2015-16); HS 94 v A (Dhaka) 2013-14. F-c Tours (P): E 2010; A 2009 (Pak A), 2009-10; WI 2011; NZ 2009-10; Z 2011; UAE 2010-11 (v SA). HS 248 SNGPL v Karachi Blues (Karachi) 2007-08. Le HS 20 v James (Manchester) 2015. BB 2-24 Lahore S v Hyderabad (Lahore) 2012-13. LO HS 104 Pak A v Aus A (Brisbane) 2009. LO BB 1-7 SNGPL v WAPDA (Faisalabad) 2013-14. T20 HS 95*. T20 BB 1-36.

WELLS, Thomas Joshua (Gartree HS; Beauchamp C, Leicester), b Grantham, Lincs 15 Mar 1993. Father, John Wells, played rugby for Leicester. 6'2". RHB, RMF. Squad No 48. Debut (Leicestershire) 2013. Leicestershire 2nd XI debut 2010. HS 82 v Hants (Leicester) 2013. BB 3-68 v Lancs (Leicester) 2015. LO HS 32* v Glamorgan (Swansea) 2013 (Y40). LO BB 2-45 v Glos ((Leicester) 2015 (RLC). T20 HS 64*. T20 BB 1-17.

WHITE, Wayne Andrew (John Port S, Etwall; Nottingham Trent U), b Derby 22 Apr 1985. 6'2". RHB, RMF. Squad No 35. Derbyshire 2005-15. Leicestershire debut 2009; cap 2012. Lancashire 2013-14. HS 101* v Derbys (Derby) 2010. BB 6-25 De v Kent (Canterbury) 2015. Le BB 5-51 v Northants (Northampton) 2015. De BB 5-87 v Northants (Northampton) 2007. LO HS 46* v Glamorgan (Leicester) 2009 (P40). LO BB 6-29 v Notts (Leics) 2010 (CB40). T20 HS 26. T20 BB 3-21.

RELEASED/RETIRED

(Having made a County 1st XI appearance in 2015)

AGATHANGELOU, Andrea Peter (Fields C, Rustenburg), b Rustenburg, South Africa 16 Nov 1989. 6'3". RHB, LB. North West 2007-08 to 2010-11. Lions 2008-09. Lancashire 2011-14. Leicestershire 2015. HS 158 NW v KZN (Potchefstroom) 2009-10. CC HS 121 La v Hants (Southampton) 2013. Le HS 54 v Lancs (Manchester) 2015. BB 2-18 La v Glos (Liverpool) 2013. Le BB 1-7 v Surrey (Leics) 2015. LO HS 94 NW v EP (Port Elizabeth) 2010-11. LO BB – . T20 HS 40.

BOYCE, Matthew Andrew Golding (Oakham S; Nottingham U), b Cheltenham, Glos 13 Aug 1985. 5'9". LHB, RM. Leicestershire 2006-15; cap 2013. HS 135 v Kent (Leicester) 2013. BB – . LO HS 80 v Hants (Leicester) 2009 (FPT). T20 HS 63*.

[NQ]**ELLIOTT, Grant** David (St Stithians) b Johannesburg, South Africa 21 Mar 1979. 6'1". RHB, RMF. Debut Transvaal B 1996-97. Griqualand West 1999-00 to 2000-01. Gauteng 2001-02 to 2002-03. Wellington 2005-06 to date. Surrey 2009 (one f-c match). Leicestershire (T20 only) 2015. Qualified for NZ in 2007. **Tests** (NZ): 5 (2007-08 to 2009-10); HS 25 v P (Dunedin) 2009-10. BB 2-9 v P (Wellington) 2009-10. **LOI** (NZ): 83 (2008 to 2015-16); HS 115 v A (Sydney) 2008-09; BB 4-31 v E (Johannesburg) 2009-10. **IT20** (NZ): 11 (2008-09 to 2015-16); HS 23* v A (Sydney) 2008-09; BB 4-22 v SL (Auckland) 2015-16. F-c Tours (NZ): E 2008; A 2008-09; B 2008-09. HS 196* Wellington v Auckland (Wellington) 2007-08. CC HS 22 Sy v Middx (Oval) 2009. BB 5-33 Wellington v ND (Whangarei) 2013-14. LO HS 115 (see LOI). LO BB 5-34 Wellington v Otago (Wellington) 2007-08. T20 HS 70. T20 BB 4-15.

PINNER, Neil Douglas (RGS Worcester), b Wordsley, Stourbridge, Worcs 29 Sep 1990. 5'11". RHB, OB. Worcestershire 2011-13. Leicestershire 2015. HS 165* v Cambridge MCCU (Cambridge) 2015. CC HS 82 Wo v Lancs (Worcester) 2012. BB – . LO HS 37 Wo v Kent (Canterbury) 2011 (CB40). LO BB – . T20 HS – . T20 BB – .

141

REDFERN, Daniel James (Adam's GS, Newport, Shropshire), b Shrewsbury, Shrops 18 Apr 1990. 5'9". LHB, OB. Derbyshire 2007-13; cap 2012. Leicestershire 2014-15. HS 133 De v Hants (Southampton) 2012. Le HS 74 v Glos (Leicester) 2015. BB 3-33 De v Durham (Chester-le-St) 2013. Le BB 2-20 v Worcs (Worcester) 2014. LO HS 57* De v Yorks (Derby) 2007 (P40). LO BB 2-10 De v Kent (Chesterfield) 2009 (P40). T20 HS 43. T20 BB 2-17.

A.C.F.Wyatt left the staff without making a 1st XI appearance in 2015.

GLOUCESTERSHIRE RELEASED/RETIRED (continued from p 115)

(Having made a County 1st XI appearance in 2015)

FULLER, J.K. – *see MIDDLESEX*.

NQ**HANDSCOMB, Peter** Stephen Patrick (Mt Waverley SC; Deakin U, Melbourne), b Melbourne, Australia 26 Apr 1991. RHB, WK. British passport (English parents). Victoria 2011-12 to date. Gloucestershire 2015; cap 2015. Leicestershire 2nd XI 2011. Big Bash: MS 2012-13 to date. HS 137 Vic v Q (Melbourne) 2015-16. Gs HS 76 v Lancs (Manchester) 2015. LO HS 72 Vic v Q (Sydney) 2014-15. T20 HS 103*.

JONES, Geraint Owen (Harristown State HS, Toowoomba and MacGregor State HS, Brisbane, Australia), b Kundiawa, Papua New Guinea 14 Jul 1976. Welsh parents. 5'10". RHB, WK. Kent 2001-13; cap 2003; benefit 2012. Gloucestershire 2014-15; cap 2014; captain 2015. MBE 2005. Papua New Guinea (l-o and T20). **Tests**: 34 (2003-04 to 2006-07); HS 100 v NZ (Leeds) 2004. **LOI** (E/PNG): 51 (49 for E 2004 to 2006; 2 for PNG 2014-15); HS 80 v Z (Bulawayo) 2004-05. **IT20**: 2 (2005 to 2006); HS 19 v A (Southampton) 2005. F-c Tours: A 2006-07; SA 2004-05; WI 2003-04; v I 2005-06; P 2005-06; SL 2003-04. 1000 runs (2); most – 1345 (2009). HS 178 K v Somerset (Canterbury) 2010. Gs HS 93 v Leics (Leicester) 2014. LO HS 87 v Leics (Leicester) 2015 (RLC). T20 HS 56.

C.L.Herring and R.J.Montgomery left the staff without making a County 1st XI appearance in 2015.

MIDDLESEX RELEASED/RETIRED (continued from p 149)

NQ**JUNAID KHAN**, Mohammad, b Matra, NW Frontier, Pakistan 24 Dec 1989. RHB, LMF. Abbottabad 2006-07 to 2011-12. NW Frontier Province 2008-09. KRL 2008-09. Lancashire 2011-14. WAPDA 2012-13 to date. **Tests** (P): 22 (2011 to 2015); HS 17 v Z (Harare) 2013; BB 5-38 v SL (Abu Dhabi) 2011-12. **LOI** (P): 52 (2011 to 2015); HS 25 v SA (Benoni) 2012-13; BB 4-12 v Ireland (Belfast) 2011. **IT20** (P): 9 (2011 to 2013-14); HS 3* v WI (Gros Islet) 2011; BB 3-24 v Afghanistan (Sharjah) 2013-14. F-c Tours (P): SA 2012-13; WI 2010-11; SL 2010 (P A), 2012, 2014, 2015; Z 2011, 2013; B 2015; UAE 2011-12 (v E), 2013-14 (v SA), 2013-14 (v SL). HS 71 Abbottabad v Rawalpindi (Abbottabad) 2007-08. CC HS 16 La v Durham (Liverpool) 2014. BB 7-46 (13-77 match) Abbottabad v Peshawar (Peshawar) 2007-08. CC BB 3-84 La v Middx (Manchester) 2014. LO HS 32 P A v South Africa A (Colombo, PSS) 2010. LO BB 5-45 Fighters v Warriors (Karachi) 2014-15. T20 HS 36. T20 BB 4-12.

PODMORE, H.W. – *see GLAMORGAN*.

SANDHU, Gurjit Singh (Isleworth & Syon S; Heathland S), b W Middlesex Hospital 24 Mar 1992. 6'4". RHB, LMF. Middlesex 2011-14 – no f-c appearances in 2015. HS 8 v Sri Lankans (Uxbridge) 2011. CC HS 6* v Somerset (Taunton) 2014. BB 4-49 v Cambridge MCCU (Cambridge) 2013. CC BB 2-54 v Sussex (Hove) 2013. LO HS 3 v Notts (Lord's) 2015 (RLC). LO BB 3-28 v Essex (Lord's) 2012 (CB40). T20 HS 2*. T20 BB 2-15.

142

LEICESTERSHIRE 2015

RESULTS SUMMARY

	Place	Won	Lost	Tied	Drew	NR
LV= County Championship (2nd Division)	9th	2	9		5	
All First-Class Matches		3	9		5	
Royal London One-Day Cup (Group A)	9th		7			1
NatWest t20 Blast (North Group)	7th	4	7	1		2

LV= COUNTY CHAMPIONSHIP AVERAGES

BATTING AND FIELDING

Cap		M	I	NO	HS	Runs	Avge	100	50	Ct/St
2015	M.J.Cosgrove	15	28	1	156	1093	40.48	4	4	8
	A.M.Ali	7	12	1	80	412	37.45	–	3	2
	N.J.O'Brien	12	22	2	95	693	34.65	–	7	51/4
	A.J.Robson	16	32	1	120	967	31.19	1	8	13
	R.M.L.Taylor	8	15	7	42	221	27.62	–	–	4
2013	E.J.H.Eckersley	16	31	–	147	798	25.74	2	2	9
2015	C.J.McKay	12	22	4	51*	452	25.11	–	1	2
	D.J.Redfern	5	10	1	74	226	25.11	–	1	1
	L.J.Hill	9	18	2	126	356	22.25	1	1	15
2013	M.A.G.Boyce	6	12	–	60	260	21.66	–	2	4
	O.H.Freckingham	4	7	4	34*	65	21.66	–	–	–
2012	W.A.White	3	4	–	43	84	21.00	–	–	–
	A.P.Agathangelou	6	12	1	54	225	20.45	–	1	12
	B.A.Raine	16	28	2	57	502	19.30	–	2	3
	N.D.Pinner	5	10	1	68	168	18.66	–	1	7
2013	J.K.H.Naik	7	13	3	30	111	11.10	–	–	1
	T.J.Wells	5	8	–	18	71	8.87	–	–	3
	G.P.Smith	2	4	–	20	24	6.00	–	–	1
	C.E.Shreck	14	22	7	15	41	2.73	–	–	5

Also batted: Z.J.Chappell (1 match) 96, 7; R.J.Sayer (4) 23, 1, 34 (1 ct); A.Sheikh (2) 1, 5, 0* (1 ct); Umar Akmal (1 – cap 2015) 13, 20.

BOWLING

	O	M	R	W	Avge	Best	5wI	10wM
C.J.McKay	480.5	122	1439	58	24.81	6- 54	3	
B.A.Raine	521.1	121	1673	59	28.35	5- 43	2	
C.E.Shreck	512.4	116	1691	57	29.66	5- 71	2	
O.H.Freckingham	113	13	458	14	32.71	4- 91	–	
R.M.L.Taylor	167.4	24	720	18	40.00	3- 41	–	
J.K.H.Naik	173	33	661	16	41.31	8-179	1	

Also bowled:

	O	M	R	W	Avge	Best	5wI	10wM
W.A.White	74.2	8	289	9	32.11	5- 51	1	
T.J.Wells	85.5	12	369	7	52.71	3- 68	–	

A.P.Agathangelou 9-1-33-1; A.M.Ali 4-0-19-0; Z.J.Chappell 26-1-106-2; M.J.Cosgrove 60.2-14-192-3; L.J.Hill 2-0-6-0; D.J.Redfern 38.1-8-100-2; R.J.Sayer 86-7-352-4; A.Sheikh 38.1-6-186-3.

The First-Class Averages (pp 227–243) give the records of Leicestershire players in all first-class county matches (Leicestershire's other opponents being Cambridge MCCU), with the exception of G.P.Smith and W.A.White, whose first-class figures for Leicestershire are as above.

LEICESTERSHIRE RECORDS

FIRST-CLASS CRICKET

Highest Total	For 701-4d		v Worcs	Worcester	1906
	V 761-6d		by Essex	Chelmsford	1990
Lowest Total	For 25		v Kent	Leicester	1912
	V 24		by Glamorgan	Leicester	1971
	24		by Oxford U	Oxford	1985
Highest Innings	For 309*	H.D.Ackerman	v Glamorgan	Cardiff	2006
	V 355*	K.P.Pietersen	for Surrey	The Oval	2015

Highest Partnership for each Wicket

1st	390	B.Dudleston/J.F.Steele	v Derbyshire	Leicester	1979
2nd	289*	J.C.Balderstone/D.I.Gower	v Essex	Leicester	1981
3rd	436*	D.L.Maddy/B.J.Hodge	v L'boro UCCE	Leicester	2003
4th	360*	J.W.A.Taylor/A.B.McDonald	v Middlesex	Leicester	2010
5th	330	J.W.A.Taylor/S.J.Thakor	v L'boro MCCU	Leicester	2011
6th	284	P.V.Simmons/P.A.Nixon	v Durham	Chester-le-St[2]	1996
7th	219*	J.D.R.Benson/P.Whitticase	v Hampshire	Bournemouth	1991
8th	195	J.W.A.Taylor/J.K.H.Naik	v Derbyshire	Leicester	2009
9th	160	R.T.Crawford/W.W.Odell	v Worcs	Leicester	1902
10th	228	R.Illingworth/K.Higgs	v Northants	Leicester	1977

Best Bowling	For 10- 18	G.Geary	v Glamorgan	Pontypridd	1929
(Innings)	V 10- 32	H.Pickett	for Essex	Leyton	1895
Best Bowling	For 16- 96	G.Geary	v Glamorgan	Pontypridd	1929
(Match)	V 16-102	C.Blythe	for Kent	Leicester	1909

Most Runs – Season	2446	L.G.Berry	(av 52.04)	1937
Most Runs – Career	30143	L.G.Berry	(av 30.32)	1924-51
Most 100s – Season	7	L.G.Berry		1937
	7	W.Watson		1959
	7	B.F.Davison		1982
Most 100s – Career	45	L.G.Berry		1924-51
Most Wkts – Season	170	J.E.Walsh	(av 18.96)	1948
Most Wkts – Career	2131	W.E.Astill	(av 23.18)	1906-39
Most Career W-K Dismissals	905	R.W.Tolchard	(794 ct; 111 st)	1965-83
Most Career Catches in the Field	426	M.R.Hallam		1950-70

LIMITED-OVERS CRICKET

Highest Total	50ov	406-5	v Berkshire	Leicester	1996
	40ov	344-4	v Durham	Chester-le-St[2]	1996
	T20	221-3	v Yorkshire	Leeds	2004
Lowest Total	50ov	56	v Northants	Leicester	1964
		56	v Minor Cos	Wellington	1982
	40ov	36	v Sussex	Leicester	1973
	T20	90	v Notts	Nottingham	2014
Highest Innings	50ov	201	V.J.Wells	v Berkshire	Leicester	1996
	40ov	154*	B.J.Hodge	v Sussex	Horsham	2004
	T20	111	D.L.Maddy	v Yorkshire	Leeds	2004
Best Bowling	50ov	6-16	C.M.Willoughby	v Somerset	Leicester	2005
	40ov	6-17	K.Higgs	v Glamorgan	Leicester	1973
	T20	5-13	A.B.McDonald	v Notts	Nottingham	2010

MIDDLESEX

Formation of Present Club: 2 February 1864
Inaugural First-Class Match: 1864
Colours: Blue
Badge: Three Seaxes
County Champions (since 1890): (10) 1903, 1920, 1921, 1947, 1976, 1980, 1982, 1985, 1990, 1993
Joint Champions: (2) 1949, 1977
Gillette/NatWest Trophy Winners: (4) 1977, 1980, 1984, 1988
Benson and Hedges Cup Winners: (2) 1983, 1986
Sunday League Winners: (1) 1992
Twenty20 Cup Winners: (1) 2008

Chief Executive: Richard Goatley, Lord's Cricket Ground, London NW8 8QN • Tel: 020 7289 1300 • Fax: 020 7289 5831 • Email: enquiries@middlesexccc.com • Web: www.middlesexccc.com • Twitter: @Middlesex_CCC (22,638 followers)

Managing Director of Cricket: Angus Fraser. **Head Coach**: Richard Scott. **Assistant Coach**: Richard Johnson. **Captains**: A.C.Voges (f-c), J.E.C.Franklin (l-o), D.J.Malan (T20). **Overseas Players**: M.J.McClenaghan (T20 only), B.B.McCullum (T20 only) and A.C.Voges. **2016 Beneficiary**: None. **Head Groundsman**: Mick Hunt. **Scorer**: Don Shelley. ‡ New registration. NQ Not qualified for England.

ANDERSSON, Martin Kristoffer (Reading Blue Coat S), b Reading, Berks 6 Sep 1996. RHB, RM. Squad No 24. Middlesex 2nd XI debut 2013. Berkshire 2015. Awaiting 1st XI debut.

NQ**BALBIRNIE, Andrew** (St Andrew's C, Dublin; UWIC), b Dublin, Ireland 28 Dec 1990. 6'2". RHB, OB. Squad No 15. Cardiff MCCU 2012-13. Ireland 2012. Middlesex debut 2012. MCC YCs 2010. **LOI** (Ire): 22 (2010 to 2015-16); HS 97 v Z (Hobart) 2014-15; BB 1-26 v Afghanistan (Dubai, DSC) 2014-15. **IT20** (Ire): 10 (2015 to 2015-16); HS 31 v Scotland (Bready) 2015 and 31 v Netherlands (Dublin) 2015. HS 44 Ire v Zimbabwe A (Harare) 2015-16. M HS 14 v Surrey (Oval) 2012. BB 1-5 Ire v Netherlands (Deventer) 2013. LO HS 129 Ire v NZ A (Dubai, CA) 2014-15. LO BB 1-26 (*see LOI*). T20 HS 44.

COMPTON, Nicholas Richard Denis (Harrow S; Durham U), b Durban, South Africa 26 Jun 1983. Son of R.Compton (Natal 1978-79 to 1980-81); grandson of D.C.S.Compton (Middlesex, England, Holkar, Europeans, Commonwealth and Cavaliers 1936-64); great-nephew of L.H.Compton (Middlesex 1938-56). 6'1". RHB, OB. Squad No 3. Middlesex debut 2004; cap 2006. Somerset 2010-14; cap 2011. Mashonaland Eagles 2010-11. Worcestershire (1 game) 2013. MCC 2007, 2015. PCA 2012. *Wisden* 2012. **Tests**: 13 (2012-13 to 2015-16); HS 117 v NZ (Dunedin) 2012-13. F-c Tours: SA 2015-16; NZ 2012-13; I 2012-13; B 2006-07 (Eng A). 1000 runs (6); most – 1494 (2012). Scored 685 runs in April 2012 – a record for April. HS 254* Sm v Durham (Chester-le-St) 2011. M HS 190 v Durham (Lord's) 2006. BB 1-1 Sm v Hants (Southampton) 2010. M BB 1-94 v Sussex (Southgate) 2007. LO HS 131 v Kent (Canterbury) 2009 (FPT). LO BB 1-0 v Scotland (Lord's) 2009 (FPT). T20 HS 78.

NQ**ESKINAZI, Stephen** Sean (Christ Church GS, Claremont; U of WA), b Johannesburg, South Africa 28 Mar 1994. 6'2". RHB, WK. Squad No 28. Debut (Middlesex) 2015. Middlesex 2nd XI debut 2013. UK passport. HS 22 v Yorks (Lord's) 2015 – only 1st XI appearance.

FINN, Steven Thomas (Parmiter's S, Garston), b Watford, Herts 4 Apr 1989. 6'7½". RHB, RF. Squad No 9. Debut (Middlesex) 2005; cap 2009. Otago 2011-12. YC 2010. **ECB central contract 2015-16. Tests**: 29 (2009-10 to 2015-16); HS 56 v NZ (Dunedin) 2012-13; BB 6-79 v A (Birmingham) 2015. **LOI**: 65 (2010-11 to 2015); HS 35 v A (Brisbane) 2010-11; BB 5-33 v I (Brisbane) 2014-15. **IT20**: 21 (2011 to 2015); HS 8* v I (Colombo, RPS) 2012-13; BB 3-16 v NZ (Pallekele) 2012-13. F-c Tours: A 2010-11, 2013-14; SA 2015-16; NZ 2012-13; I 2012-13; SL 2011-12; B 2009-10; UAE 2011-12 (v P). HS 56 (*see Tests*). M HS 41* v Oxford MCCU (Oxford) 2015. CC HS 37* v Warwks (Birmingham) 2014. 50 wkts (2); most – 64 (2010). BB 9-37 (14-106 match) v Worcs (Worcester) 2010. LO HS 42* v Glamorgan (Cardiff) 2014 (RLC). LO BB 5-33 v Derbys (Lord's) 2011 (CB40). T20 HS 8*. T20 BB 4-28.

[NQ]**FRANKLIN, James** Edward Charles (Wellington C; Victoria U), Wellington, New Zealand 7 Nov 1980. 6'4½". LHB, LM. Squad No 74. Irish passport. Wellington 1998-99 to date. Gloucestershire 2004-10; cap 2004. Glamorgan 2006; cap 2006. Nottinghamshire 2014; cap 2014. Middlesex debut/cap 2015; captain (l-o) 2016. IPL: MI 2011-12. Big Bash: AS 2011-12. **Tests** (NZ): 31 (2000-01 to 2012-13); HS 122* v SA (Cape Town) 2006-07; BB 6-119 v A (Auckland) 2004-05. Hat-trick v B (Dhaka) 2004-05. **LOI** (NZ): 110 (2000-01 to 2013); HS 98* v I (Bangalore) 2010-11; BB 5-42 v E (Chester-le-St) 2004. **IT20** (NZ): 38 (2005-06 to 2013); HS 60 v Z (Hamilton) 2011-12; BB 4-15 v E (Hamilton) 2012-13. F-c Tours (NZ): E 2004; A 2004-05; SA 2004-05 (NZ A), 2005-06, 2012-13; I 2012; SL 2012-13; Z 2005, 2010-11 (NZ A); B 2004-05. HS 219 Wellington v Auckland (Auckland) 2008-09. HS 135 v Worcs (Uxbridge) 2015. BB 7-14 Gs v Derbys (Bristol) 2010. M BB 3-41 v Notts (Nottingham) 2015. Hat-tricks (*see above*) and Gs v Derbys (Cheltenham) 2009, also scoring 109 in same match. LO HS 133* Gs v Derbys (Bristol) 2010 (CB40). LO BB 5-42 (*see LOI*). T20 HS 90. T20 BB 5-21.

‡[NQ]**FULLER, James** Kerr (Otago U, NZ), b Cape Town, South Africa 24 Jan 1990. UK passport. 6'3". RHB, RFM. Squad No 26. Otago 2009-10 to 2012-13. Gloucestershire 2011-15; cap 2011. HS 73 Gs v Glamorgan (Bristol) 2015. BB 6-24 (10-79 match) Otago v Wellington (Dunedin) 2012-13. CC BB 6-47 Gs v Surrey (Oval) 2014. Hat-trick v Worcs (Cheltenham) 2013. LO HS 45 Gs v Surrey (Bristol) 2015 (RLC). LO BB 6-35 v Netherlands (Amstelveen) 2012 (CB40). T20 HS 36. T20 BB 4-24.

GUBBINS, Nicholas Richard Trail (Radley C; Leeds U), b Richmond, Surrey 31 Dec 1993. 6'0½". LHB, LB. Squad No 18. Leeds/Bradford MCCU 2013-15. Middlesex debut 2014. Middlesex 2nd XI debut 2012. HS 95 v Somerset (Uxbridge) 2014. LO HS 141 v Sussex (Hove) 2015 (RLC). T20 HS 46.

HARRIS, James Alexander Russell (Pontardulais CS; Gorseinon C), b Morriston, Swansea, Glamorgan 16 May 1990. 6'0". RHB, RMF. Squad No 5. Glamorgan 2007-12, making debut aged 16y 351d – youngest Glamorgan player to take an f-c wicket; cap 2010. Middlesex debut 2013; cap 2015. Loaned to Glamorgan during 2014. Wales MC 2005-06. F-c Tours (EL): WI 2010-11; SL 2013-14. HS 87* Gm v Notts (Swansea) 2007. M HS 73 v Notts (Nottingham) 2015. 50 wkts (2); most – 73 (2015). BB 9-34 (13-103 match) v Durham (Lord's) 2015 – record innings and match analysis v Durham. Took 12-118 in match for Gm v Glos (Bristol) 2007 – youngest (17y 3d) to take 10 wickets in any CC match. LO HS 32 v Hants (Southampton) 2015 (RLC). LO BB 4-38 v Glamorgan (Lord's) 2015 (RLC). T20 HS 18. T20 BB 4-23.

HELM, Thomas George (Misbourne S, Gt Missenden), b Stoke Mandeville Hospital, Bucks 7 May 1994. 6'4". RHB, RMF. Squad No 7. Debut (Middlesex) 2013. Glamorgan 2014 (on loan). Middlesex 2nd XI debut 2011. Buckinghamshire 2011. HS 27 v Oxford MCCU (Oxford) 2015. CC HS 18 and BB 3-46 v Yorks (Leeds) 2013. LO HS – . LO BB 3-27 v Unicorns (Southend) 2013 (Y40).

HIGGINS, Ryan Francis (Bradfield C), b Harare, Zimbabwe 6 Jan 1995. 5'10". RHB, OB. Squad No 11. Middlesex 2nd XI debut 2012. Awaiting f-c debut. LO HS 27 v Somerset (Lord's) 2014 (RLC). T20 HS 44*.

HOLDEN, Max David Edward (Sawston Village C; Hills Road SFC, Cambridge), b Cambridge 18 Dec 1997. 5'11". LHB, OB. Squad No 4. Middlesex 2nd XI debut 2013. England U19 2014-15 to 2015. Awaiting 1st XI debut.

‡^{NQ}**McCLENAGHAN, Mitchell** John, b Hastings, Hawke's Bay, New Zealand 11 Jun 1986. LHB, LMF. Squad No 81. C Districts 2007-08 to 2010-11. Auckland 2011-12 to date. Worcestershire 2014. IPL: MI 2015. **LOI** (NZ): 48 (2012-13 to 2015-16); HS 34* v SA (Mt Maunganui) 2014-15; BB 5-58 v WI (Auckland) 2013-14. **IT20** (NZ): 24 (2012-13 to 2015-16); HS 6* v E (Auckland) 2012-13; BB 2-23 v P (Hamilton) 2015-16. HS 34 v Auckland v CD (Napier) 2011-12. CC HS 27 and CC BB 5-78 Wo v Derbys (Derby) 2014. BB 8-23 Auckland v Otago (Auckland) 2011-12. LO HS 34* (see *LOI*). LO BB 6-41 Auckland v Wellington (Auckland) 2011-12. T20 HS 16. T20 BB 5-29.

‡^{NQ}**McCULLUM, Brendon** Barrie, b Dunedin, New Zealand 27 Sep 1981. Son of S.J.McCullum (Otago 1976-77 to 1990-91); younger brother of N.L.McCullum (Otago and Glamorgan 1999-00 to date). RHB, RM, WK. Squad No 42. Otago 1999-00 to 2014-15. Canterbury 2003-04 to 2006-07. Glamorgan 2006; cap 2006. Joins Middlesex in 2016 for T20 only. IPL: KKR 2007-08 to 2013. CSK 2014 to 2015. Big Bash: BH 2011-12. **Tests** (NZ): 101 (2003-04 to 2015-16, 31 as captain); 1000 runs (1): 1164 (2014); HS 302 v I (Wellington) 2013-14 – NZ record; BB 1-1 v P (Dubai) 2014-15. Scored fastest Test century (54 balls) in final Test, v A (Christchurch) 2015-16. **LOI** (NZ): 260 (2001-02 to 2015-16, 62 as captain); HS 166 v Ireland (Aberdeen) 2008. **IT20** (NZ): 71 (2004-05 to 2015, 28 as captain); HS 123 v B (Pallekele) 2012-13. F-c Tours (NZ)(C=Captain): E 2004, 2008, 2013C, 2015C; A 2004-05, 2008-09, 2011-12, 2015-16C; SA 2005-06, 2007-08, 2012-13C; WI 2012, 2014C; I 2010-11, 2012; SL 2009, 2012-13; Z 2005, 2011-12; B 2004-05, 2008-09, 2013-14C; UAE (v P) 2014-15C. HS 302 (see *Tests*). CC HS 160 Gm v Leics (Cardiff) 2006 – on Gm debut. BB 1-1 (see *Tests*). LO HS 170 Otago v Auckland (Auckland) 2007-08. T20 HS 158* Wa v Derbys (Birmingham) 2015 – UK record & joint 2nd highest score in all T20 cricket, and 158* KKR v RCB (Bangalore) 2007-08.

MALAN, Dawid Johannes (Paarl HS), b Roehampton, Surrey 3 Sep 1987. Son of D.J.Malan (WP B and Transvaal B 1978-79 to 1981-82), elder brother of C.C.Malan (Loughborough MCCU 2009-10). 6'0". LHB, LB. Squad No 29. Boland 2005-06. MCC YC 2006-07. Middlesex debut 2008, scoring 132* v Northants (Uxbridge); cap 2010; T20 captain 2016. MCC 2010-11, 2013. 1000 runs (2); most – 1137 runs (2014). HS 182* v Notts (Nottingham) 2015. BB 5-61 v Lancs (Liverpool) 2012. LO HS 156* v Glamorgan (Lord's) 2015 (RLC). LO BB 4-25 PDSC v Partex (Savar) 2014-15. T20 HS 115*. T20 BB 2-10.

MORGAN, Eoin Joseph Gerard (Catholic University S), b Dublin, Ireland 10 Sep 1986. 6'0". LHB, RM. Squad No 16. UK passport. Ireland 2004 to 2007-08. Middlesex debut 2006; cap 2008; l-o captain 2014-15. IPL: RCB 2009-10. KKR 2011-13. SH 2015. Big Bash: ST 2013-14 to 2014-15. *Wisden* 2010. **ECB Central Contract 2015-16. Tests**: 16 (2010 to 2011-12); HS 130 v P (Nottingham) 2010. **LOI** (E/Ire): 160 (23 for Ire 2006 to 2008-09; 137 for E 2009 to 2015-16, 38 as captain). HS 124* v Ireland (Dublin) 2013. **IT20**: 56 (2009 to 2015-16, 13 as captain). HS 85* v SA (Johannesburg) 2009-10. F-c Tours (Ire): A 2010-11 (E); NZ 2008-09 (Eng A); Namibia 2005-06; UAE 2006-07, 2007-08, 2011-12 (v P). 1000 runs (1): 1085 (2008). HS 209* Ire v UAE (Abu Dhabi) 2006-07. M HS 191 v Notts (Nottingham) 2014. BB 2-24 v Notts (Lord's) 2007. LO HS 161 v Kent (Canterbury) 2009 (FPT). LO BB – . T20 HS 85*.

NQMURTAGH, Timothy James (John Fisher S; St Mary's C), b Lambeth, London 2 Aug 1981. Elder brother of C.P.Murtagh (Loughborough UCCE and Surrey 2005-09); nephew of A.J.Murtagh (Hampshire and EP 1973-77). 6'0". LHB, RFM. Squad No 34. British U 2000-03. Surrey 2001-06. Middlesex debut 2007; cap 2008; benefit 2015. Ireland 2012-13 to date. MCC 2010. **LOI** (Ire): 14 (2012 to 2015-16); HS 23* v Scotland (Belfast) 2013; BB 4-32 v Z (Harare) 2015-16. **IT20** (Ire): 13 (2012 to 2015-16); HS 12* v UAE (Abu Dhabi) 2015-16; BB 3-23 v PNG (Townsville) 2015-16. HS 74* Sy v Middx (Oval) 2004 and 74* Sy v Warwks (Croydon) 2005. M HS 55 v Leics (Leicester) 2011, sharing M record 9th wkt partnership of 172 with G.K.Berg. 50 wkts (6); most – 85 (2011). BB 7-82 v Derbys (Derby) 2009. LO HS 35* v Surrey (Lord's) 2008 (FPT). LO BB 4-14 Sy v Derbys (Derby) 2005 (NL). T20 HS 40*. T20 BB 6-24 Sy v Middx (Lord's) 2005 – Sy record and 4th best UK figs.

PATEL, Ravi Hasmukh (Merchant Taylors' S, Northwood; Loughborough U), b Harrow 4 Aug 1991. 5'8". RHB, SLA. Squad No 36. Debut (Middlesex) 2010. No 1st XI appearances in 2011. Loughborough MCCU 2011. Essex (on loan) 2015. Middlesex 2nd XI debut 2008. HS 26* v Warwks (Uxbridge) 2013. BB 5-69 v Cambridge MCCU (Cambridge) 2013. CC BB 4-42 v Sussex (Lord's) 2015. LO HS 0*. LO BB 3-71 EL v Sri Lanka A (Taunton) 2014. T20 HS 11*. T20 BB 4-18.

RAYNER, Oliver Philip (St Bede's S, Upper Dicker), b Fallingbostel, W Germany, 1 Nov 1985. 6'5". RHB, OB. Squad No 2. Sussex 2006-11, scoring 101 v Sri Lankans (Hove) – first hundred on debut for Sussex since 1920. Middlesex debut 2011; cap 2015. MCC 2014. F-c Tour (EL): SL 2013-14. HS 143* v Notts (Nottingham) 2012. BB 8-46 (15-118 match) v Surrey (Oval) 2013. LO HS 61 Sx v Lancs (Hove) 2006 (P40). LO BB 4-35 v Notts (Lord's) 2015 (RLC). T20 HS 41*. T20 BB 5-18.

ROBSON, Sam David (Marcellin C, Randwick), b Paddington, Sydney, Australia 1 Jul 1989. Elder brother of A.J.Robson (*see LEICESTERSHIRE*). 6'0". RHB, LB. Squad No 12. Qualified for England in April 2013. Debut (Middlesex) 2009; cap 2013. **Tests**: 7 (2014); HS 127 v SL (Leeds) 2014. F-c Tours (EL): SA 2014-15; SL 2013-14. 1000 runs (2); most – 1180 (2013). HS 215* v Warwks (Birmingham) (2013). BB 1-4 EL v Sri Lanka A (Dambulla) 2013-14. M BB – . LO HS 88 v Notts (Lord's) 2015 (RLC). T20 HS 28*.

ROLAND-JONES, Tobias Skelton (**'Toby'**) (Hampton S; Leeds U), b Ashford 29 Jan 1988. 6'4". RHB, RMF. Squad No 21. Debut (Middlesex) 2010; cap 2012. MCC 2011. Leeds/Bradford UCCE 2009 (not f-c). HS 103* v Yorks (Lord's) 2015. 50 wkts (1): 64 (2012). BB 6-50 (12-105 match) v Northants (Northampton) 2014. Hat-trick v Derbys (Lord's) 2013. LO HS 31* v Kent (Radlett) 2015. LO BB 4-42 v Sussex (Hove) 2014 (RLC). T20 HS 30. T20 BB 4-25.

SCOTT, George Frederick Buchan (Beechwood Park S; St Albans S; Leeds U), b Hemel Hempstead, Herts 6 Nov 1995. Younger brother of J.E.B.Scott (Hertfordshire 2013 to date). 6'2". RHB, RM. Squad No 17. Leeds/Bradford MCCU 2015. Middlesex 2nd XI debut 2013. Hertfordshire 2011-14. Awaiting Middlesex f-c debut. HS 11 LBU v Yorks (Leeds) 2015. BB 2-67 v Sussex (Hove) 2015. LO HS 4 v Notts (Lord's) 2015 (RLC). LO BB – . T20 HS 20.

SIMPSON, John Andrew (St Gabriel's RC HS), b Bury, Lancs 13 Jul 1988. 5'10". LHB, WK. Squad No 20. Debut (Middlesex) 2009; cap 2011. Cumberland 2007. MCC YCs 2008. HS 143 v Surrey (Lord's) 2011. LO HS 82 v Glos (Cheltenham) 2010 (CB40). T20 HS 84*.

NQSOWTER, Nathan Adam (Hill Sport HS, NSW), b Penrith, NSW, Australia 12 Oct 1992. RHB, LB. Squad No 72. Middlesex 2nd XI debut 2014. Signed l-o contract for 2016. Awaiting f-c debut. T20 HS 1*. T20 BB 2-2.

^{NQ}**STEEL, Cameron** Tate (Scotch C, Perth, Australia; Durham U), b San Francisco, USA 13 Sep 1995. 5'10". RHB, LB. Squad No 22. Durham MCCU 2014-15. Middlesex 2nd XI debut 2013. Somerset 2nd XI 2013. Awaiting 1st XI debut. HS 80 DU v Somerset (Taunton Vale) 2015. BB 1-39 DU v Durham (Chester-le-St) 2014.

^{NQ}**STIRLING, Paul** Robert (Belfast HS), b Belfast, N Ireland 3 Sep 1990. Father Brian Stirling was an international rugby referee. 5'10". RHB, OB. Squad No 39. Ireland 2007-08 to date. Middlesex debut 2013. **LOI** (Ire): 62 (2008 to 2015-16); HS 177 v Canada (Toronto) 2010; BB 4-11 v Netherlands (Amstelveen) 2010. **IT20** (Ire): 36 (2009 to 2015-16); HS 79 v Afghanistan (Dubai, DSC) 2011-12; BB 3-21 v B (Belfast) 2012. F-c Tours (Ire): WI 2009-10; Kenya 2011-12; Z 2015-16; UAE 2013-14. HS 115 Ire v UAE (Dublin) 2015. M HS 66* v Notts (Nottingham) 2014. BB 2-27 Ire v Namibia (Windhoek) 2015-16. M BB 2-31 v Oxford MCCU (Oxford) 2015. CC BB 2-43 v Surrey (Lord's) 2013. LO HS 177 (*see LOI*). LO BB 4-11 (*see LOI*). T20 HS 90. T20 BB 4-10.

^{NQ}**VOGES, Adam** Charles (Edith Cowan U, Perth), b Perth, Australia 4 Oct 1979. 6'0". RHB, SLA. Squad No 32. W Australia 2002-03 to date. Nottinghamshire 2008-12; cap 2008. Middlesex debut 2013; captain 2015 to date. IPL: RR 2009-10. Big Bash: MS: 2011-12. PS 2012-13 to date. **Tests** (A): 15 (2015 to 2015-16); 1000 runs 1: 1028 (2015) – becoming only the 3rd batsman to score 1000 runs in the year of his debut; HS 269* v WI (Hobart) 2015-16; scored a record 614 Test runs between dismissals (269*, 106* and 239 v WI); BB – . **LOI** (A): 31 (2006-07 to 2013-14); HS 112* v WI (Melbourne) 2012-13. BB 1-3 v E (Birmingham) 2013. **IT20** (A): 7 (2007-08 to 2012-13); HS 51 v WI (Brisbane) 2012-13; BB 2-5 v I (Melbourne) 2007-08. F-c Tours (A): E 2015; WI 2015; NZ 2015-16; I 2008-09 (Aus A); P 2007-08 (Aus A). 1000 runs (0+1): 1132 (2014-15). HS 269* (*see Tests*). UK HS 165 Nt v Oxford MCCU (Oxford) 2011. M HS 150 v Warwks (Uxbridge) 2013. BB 4-92 WA v S Aus (Adelaide) 2006-07. UK BB 3-21 Nt v Durham (Nottingham) 2008. M BB 2-20 v Durham (Lord's) 2015. LO HS 112* (*see LOI*). LO BB 3-20 WA v Q (Sydney) 2015-16. T20 HS 82*. T20 BB 2-4.

WHITE, Robert George (Harrow S; Loughborough U), b 15 Sep 1995. RHB, WK, occ RM. Squad No 14. Loughborough MCCU 2015. Middlesex 2nd XI debut 2013. Awaiting 1st XI debut. HS 4 LU v Hants (Southampton) 2015.

RELEASED/RETIRED

(Having made a County 1st XI appearance in 2015)

ABBOTT, K.J. – *see WORCESTERSHIRE.*

^{NQ}**BURNS, Joseph** Antony, b Herston, Brisbane, Australia 6 Sep 1989. RHB, RMF. Queensland 2010-11 to date. Leicestershire 2013. Middlesex 2015. Big Bash: BH 2012-13 to date. **Tests** (A): 10 (2014-15 to 2015-16); HS 170 v NZ (Christchurch) 2015-16. F-c Tours (A): E 2012 (Aus A); NZ 2015-16; I 2015 (Aus A). HS 183 Q v NSW (Brisbane) 2014-15. M HS 87 v Worcs (Uxbridge) 2015. BB – . LO HS 154 Aus A v India A (Chennai) 2015. T20 HS 81*.

DEXTER, N.J. – *see LEICESTERSHIRE.*

RELEASED/RETIRED continued on p 142

MIDDLESEX 2015

RESULTS SUMMARY

	Place	Won	Lost	Tied	Drew	NR
LV= County Championship (1st Division)	2nd	7	2		7	
All First-Class Matches		8	2		7	
Royal London One-Day Cup (Group B)	7th	3	4			1
NatWest t20 Blast (South Group)	9th	4	9			1

LV= COUNTY CHAMPIONSHIP AVERAGES

BATTING AND FIELDING

Cap		M	I	NO	HS	Runs	Avge	100	50	Ct/St
	A.C.Voges	4	8	–	132	451	56.37	1	3	7
2010	D.J.Malan	9	15	2	182*	629	48.38	2	3	3
2006	N.R.D.Compton	16	31	2	149	1123	38.72	2	6	5
2013	S.D.Robson	16	31	2	178	891	30.72	1	4	12
	J.A.Burns	7	11	–	87	320	29.09	–	3	1
2011	J.A.Simpson	16	29	7	64	619	28.13	–	3	50/2
2010	N.J.Dexter	10	19	2	112	473	27.82	1	1	2
2015	J.E.C.Franklin	15	27	3	135	667	27.79	2	3	15
2012	T.S.Roland-Jones	13	19	4	103*	416	27.73	1	1	7
	N.R.T.Gubbins	7	13	–	92	354	27.23	–	2	2
2015	J.A.R.Harris	16	25	5	73	462	23.10	–	3	4
2015	O.P.Rayner	14	23	2	52	360	17.14	–	1	30
	P.R.Stirling	7	14	–	41	224	16.00	–	–	3
2008	T.J.Murtagh	13	18	6	24	180	15.00	–	–	4
2009	S.T.Finn	7	9	4	21*	73	14.60	–	–	3
2008	E.J.G.Morgan	4	6	–	44	61	10.16	–	–	1

Also batted: S.S.Eskinazi (1 match) 4, 22 (1 ct); T.G.Helm (1) 0, 5; R.H.Patel (1) 6*, 3.

BOWLING

	O	M	R	W	Avge	Best	5wI	10wM
N.J.Dexter	163.2	35	485	21	23.09	5-64	1	
J.A.R.Harris	460.2	66	1776	69	25.73	9-34	3	1
T.S.Roland-Jones	471	112	1298	48	27.04	5-27	1	
S.T.Finn	252.3	49	752	27	27.85	4-41	–	
T.J.Murtagh	385.2	85	1127	40	28.17	4-55	–	
O.P.Rayner	273	71	780	24	32.50	3-44	–	
Also bowled:								
R.H.Patel	28	10	84	5	16.80	4-42	–	
A.C.Voges	30	3	132	6	22.00	2-20	–	
J.E.C.Franklin	104	12	381	7	54.42	3-41	–	

J.A.Burns 5-0-14-0; N.R.D.Compton 1-0-4-0; N.R.T.Gubbins 3-1-10-0; T.G.Helm
28-4-101-3; D.J.Malan 8-0-25-1; S.D.Robson 5-0-26-1; P.R.Stirling 33-5-127-3.

The First-Class Averages (pp 227–243) give the records of Middlesex players in all
first-class county matches (Middlesex's other opponents being Oxford MCCU), with the
exception of R.H.Patel and A.C.Voges, whose first-class figures for Middlesex are as above,
and:
S.T.Finn 8-10-5-41*-114-22.80-0-0-3ct. 275.3-56-801-31-25.83-4/41-0-0.
N.R.T.Gubbins 8-15-0-92-403-26.86-0-2-3ct. 3-1-10-0.

MIDDLESEX RECORDS

FIRST-CLASS CRICKET

Highest Total	For 642-3d		v	Hampshire	Southampton	1923
	V 850-7d		by	Somerset	Taunton	2007
Lowest Total	For 20		v	MCC	Lord's	1864
	V 31		by	Glos	Bristol	1924
Highest Innings	For 331*	J.D.B.Robertson	v	Worcs	Worcester	1949
	V 341	C.M.Spearman	for	Glos	Gloucester	2004

Highest Partnership for each Wicket

1st	372	M.W.Gatting/J.L.Langer	v	Essex	Southgate	1998
2nd	380	F.A.Tarrant/J.W.Hearne	v	Lancashire	Lord's	1914
3rd	424*	W.J.Edrich/D.C.S.Compton	v	Somerset	Lord's	1948
4th	325	J.W.Hearne/E.H.Hendren	v	Hampshire	Lord's	1919
5th	338	R.S.Lucas/T.C.O'Brien	v	Sussex	Hove	1895
6th	270	J.D.Carr/P.N.Weekes	v	Glos	Lord's	1994
7th	271*	E.H.Hendren/F.T.Mann	v	Notts	Nottingham	1925
8th	182*	M.H.C.Doll/H.R.Murrell	v	Notts	Lord's	1913
9th	172	G.K.Berg/T.J.Murtagh	v	Leics	Leicester	2011
10th	230	R.W.Nicholls/W.Roche	v	Kent	Lord's	1899

Best Bowling	For 10- 40	G.O.B.Allen	v	Lancashire	Lord's	1929
(Innings)	V 9- 38	R.C.R-Glasgow†	for	Somerset	Lord's	1924
Best Bowling	For 16-114	G.Burton	v	Yorkshire	Sheffield	1888
(Match)	16-114	J.T.Hearne	v	Lancashire	Manchester	1898
	V 16-100	J.E.B.B.P.Q.C.Dwyer	for	Sussex	Hove	1906

Most Runs – Season	2669	E.H.Hendren	(av 83.41)	1923
Most Runs – Career	40302	E.H.Hendren	(av 48.81)	1907-37
Most 100s – Season	13	D.C.S.Compton		1947
Most 100s – Career	119	E.H.Hendren		1907-37
Most Wkts – Season	158	F.J.Titmus	(av 14.63)	1955
Most Wkts – Career	2361	F.J.Titmus	(av 21.27)	1949-82
Most Career W-K Dismissals	1223	J.T.Murray	(1024 ct; 199 st)	1952-75
Most Career Catches in the Field	561	E.H.Hendren		1907-37

LIMITED-OVERS CRICKET

Highest Total	50ov	367-6		v	Sussex	Hove	2015
	40ov	350-6		v	Lancashire	Lord's	2012
	T20	221-2		v	Sussex	Hove	2015
Lowest Total	50ov	41		v	Essex	Westcliff	1972
	40ov	23		v	Yorkshire	Leeds	1974
	T20	92		v	Surrey	Lords	2013
Highest Innings	50ov	163	A.J.Strauss	v	Surrey	The Oval	2008
	40ov	147*	M.R.Ramprakash	v	Worcs	Lord's	1990
	T20	129	D.T.Christian	v	Kent	Canterbury	2014
Best Bowling	50ov	7-12	W.W.Daniel	v	Minor Cos E	Ipswich	1978
	40ov	6- 6	R.W.Hooker	v	Surrey	Lord's	1969
	T20	5-13	M.Kartik	v	Essex	Lord's	2007

† R.C.Robertson-Glasgow

NORTHAMPTONSHIRE

Formation of Present Club: 31 July 1878
Inaugural First-Class Match: 1905
Colours: Maroon
Badge: Tudor Rose
County Champions: (0); best – 2nd 1912, 1957, 1965, 1976
Gillette/NatWest/C&G/FP Trophy Winners: (2) 1976, 1992
Benson and Hedges Cup Winners: (1) 1980
Twenty20 Cup Winners: (1) 2013

Chief Executive: Ray Payne, County Ground, Abington Avenue, Northampton, NN1 4PR • Tel: 01604 514455 • Fax: 01604 609288 • Email: post@nccc.co.uk • Web: www.nccc.co.uk • Twitter: @NorthantsCCC (22,932 followers)

Head Coach: David Ripley. **Captain**: A.G.Wakely. **Overseas Player**: R.K.Kleinveldt. **2016 Beneficiary**: None. **Head Groundsman**: Paul Marshall. **Scorer**: Tony Kingston. ‡ New registration. NQ Not qualified for England.

AZHARULLAH, Mohammad, b Burewala, Punjab, Pakistan 25 Dec 1983. 5'7''. RHB, RFM. Squad No 92. Multan 2004-05 to 2006-07. WAPDA 2004-05 to 2012-13. Quetta 2005-06. Baluchistan 2007-08 to 2008-09. Northamptonshire debut 2013; cap 2015. UK qualified through residency and British wife. HS 58* v Kent (Canterbury) 2015. BB 7-74 Quetta v Lahore Ravi (Quetta) 2005-06. Nh BB 7-76 (10-158 match) v Sussex (Northampton) 2014. LO HS 9 (twice). LO BB 5-38 v Hants (Southampton) 2014 (RLC). T20 HS 5*. T20 BB 4-14.

COBB, Joshua James (Oakham S), b Leicester 17 Aug 1990. Son of R.A.Cobb (Leics and N Transvaal 1980-89). 5'11½''. RHB, LB. Squad No 4. Leicestershire 2007-14; l-o captain 2014. Northamptonshire debut 2015. HS 148* Le v Middx (Lord's) 2008. Nh HS 95 v Derbys (Derby) 2015. BB 2-11 Le v Glos (Leicester) 2008. Nh BB 1-20 v Leics (Leicester) 2015. LO HS 137 Le v Lancs (Manchester) 2012 (CB40). LO BB 3-34 Le v Glos (Leicester) 2013 (Y40). T20 HS 84. T20 BB 4-22.

CROOK, Steven Paul (Rostrevor C; Magill U), b Modbury, S Australia 28 May 1983. Younger brother of A.R.Crook (S Australia, Aus Academy, Lancashire, Northamptonshire 1998-99 to 2008). 5'11''. RHB, RFM. Squad No 25. British passport. Lancashire 2003-05. Northamptonshire debut 2005; cap 2013. Middlesex 2011-12. Aus Academy 2001-02. HS 142* v Australians (Northampton) 2015. CC HS 131 v Middx (Lord's) 2014. BB 5-48 M v Lancs (Lord's) 2012. Nh BB 5-71 v Essex (Northampton) 2009. LO HS 100 SJD v PDSC (Savar) 2013-14. LO BB 5-36 v Warwks (Northampton) 2013 (Y40). T20 HS 63. T20 BB 3-19.

DUCKETT, Ben Matthew (Stowe S), b Farnborough, Kent 17 Oct 1994. LHB, WK, occ OB. Squad No 17. Debut (Northamptonshire) 2013. Northamptonshire 2nd XI debut 2011. England U19 2012-13. 1000 runs (1): 1002 (2015). HS 154 v Derbys (Northampton) 2015. LO HS 69 v Durham (Northampton) 2015 (RLC). T20 HS 40*.

GLEESON, Richard James, b Blackpool, Lancs 2 Dec 1987. RHB, RM. Squad No 33. Debut (Northamptonshire) 2015. Cumberland 2010 to date. HS 6 v Australians (Northampton) 2015. CC HS 2 and BB 2-35 v Glamorgan (Northampton) 2015.

152

KEOGH, Robert Ian (Queensbury S; Dunstable C), b Luton, Beds 21 Oct 1991. 5'11". RHB, OB. Squad No 14. Debut (Northamptonshire) 2009. Northamptonshire 2nd XI debut 2009. Bedfordshire 2009-10. HS 221 v Hants (Southampton) 2013. BB 3-35 v Essex (Northampton) 2015. LO HS 61 v Warwks (Birmingham) 2013 (Y40). LO BB 1-49 v Somerset (Northampton) 2015 (RLC). T20 HS 28. T20 BB – .

^{NQ}**KLEINVELDT, Rory** Keith, b Cape Town, South Africa 15 Mar 1983. Cousin of M.C.Kleinveldt (W Province 2010-11 to date). Nephew of J.Kleinveldt (W Province and Transvaal 1979-80 to 1982-83). RHB, RFM. Squad No 6. W Province 2002-03 to 2005-06. Cape Cobras 2005-06 to date. Hampshire 2008 (1 game). Northamptonshire debut 2015. **Tests** (SA): 4 (2012-13); HS 17* v A (Brisbane) 2012-13; BB 3-65 v A (Adelaide) 2012-13. **LOI** (SA): 10 (2012-13 to 2013); HS 43 v E (Oval) 2013; BB 4-22 v P (Bloemfontein) 2012-13. **IT20** (SA): 6 (2008-09 to 2012-13); HS 22 v P (Centurion) 2012-13; BB 3-18 v NZ (Durban) 2012-13. F-c Tours (SA A): A 2012-13 (SA); I 2007-08; SL 2010. HS 115* WP v KZN (Chatsworth) 2005-06. Nh HS 56 v Leics (Leicester) 2015. 50 wkts (1): 57 (2015). BB 8-47 Cobras v Warriors (Stellenbosch) 2005-06. Nh BB 5-41 v Kent (Northampton) 2015. LO HS 55 WP v KZN (Durban) 2010-11. LO BB 4-22 (*see LOI*). T20 HS 46. T20 BB 3-18.

^{NQ}**LEVI, Richard** Ernst, b Johannesburg, South Africa 14 Jan 1988. RHB, RM. Squad No 88. W Province 2006-07 to 2013-14. Cape Cobras 2008-09 to date. Northamptonshire debut 2014 (Kolpak signing). **IT20** (SA): 13 (2011-12 to 2012-13); HS 117* v NZ (Hamilton) 2011-12. HS 168 v Essex (Northampton) 2015. LO HS 166 Cobras v Titans (Paarl) 2012-13. T20 HS 117*.

^{NQ}**MURPHY, David** (Richard Hale S, Hertford; Loughborough U), b Welwyn Garden City, Herts 24 June 1989. 5'11". RHB, WK. Squad No 19. Loughborough MCCU 2009-11. Northamptonshire debut 2009. **LOI** (Scot): 8 (2012-13 to 2013); HS 20* v Ireland (Belfast) 2013. **IT20** (Scot): 4 (2012-13 to 2013-14); HS 20 v Kenya (Dubai) 2013-14. HS 135* v Surrey (Oval) 2015. LO HS 31* v Netherlands (Northampton) 2010 (CB40). T20 HS 20.

NEWTON, Robert Irving (Framlingham C), b Taunton, Somerset 18 Jan 1990. 5'8". RHB, OB. Squad No 21. Debut (Northamptonshire) 2010. HS 119* v Derbys (Northampton) 2012. BB – . LO HS 88* v Kent (Tunbridge W) 2013 (Y40). T20 HS 38.

ROSSINGTON, Adam Matthew (Mill Hill S), b Edgware, Middx 5 May 1993. 5'11". RHB, WK. Squad No 7. Middlesex 2010-14. Northamptonshire debut 2014. Middlesex 2nd XI debut 2010. England U19s 2010-11, scoring 113 v SL on debut. HS 116 v Surrey (Oval) 2015. Won 2013 Walter Lawrence Trophy with 55-ball century v Cambridge MCCU (Cambridge). LO HS 82 v Glos (Cheltenham) 2014 (RLC). T20 HS 74.

SANDERSON, Ben William (Ecclesfield CS; Sheffield C), b Sheffield, Yorks 3 Jan 1989. RHB, RMF. Squad No 29. Yorkshire 2008-10. Northamptonshire debut 2015. Shropshire 2013-15. HS 42 and CC BB 4-44 v Kent (Canterbury) 2015. BB 5-50 Y v Loughborough MCCU (Leeds) 2010. LO HS 12* Y v Essex (Leeds) 2010 (CB40). LO BB 2-17 Y v Derbys (Leeds) 2010 (CB40). T20 HS – . T20 BB 4-21.

STONE, Oliver Peter (Thorpe St Andrew HS), b Norwich, Norfolk 9 Oct 1993. 6'1". RHB, RFM. Squad No 9. Debut (Northamptonshire) 2012. Northamptonshire 2nd XI debut 2010. Norfolk 2011. Captained England U19 2012-13. HS 38 v Lancs (Northampton) 2015. BB 5-44 v Kent (Northampton) 2015. LO HS 24* v Derbys (Derby) 2015 (RLC). LO BB 3-34 v Glos (Northampton) 2015 (RLC). T20 HS 6*. T20 BB 2-18.

153

WAKELY, Alexander George (Bedford S), b Hammersmith, London 3 Nov 1988. 6'2". RHB, RM. Squad No 8. Debut (Northamptonshire) 2007; cap 2012; captain 2015 to date. Missed entire 2014 season due to ruptured Achilles. Bedfordshire 2004-05. HS 123 v Leics (Northampton) 2015. BB 2-62 v Somerset (Taunton) 2007. LO HS 102 v Kent (Tunbridge W) 2013 (Y40). LO BB 2-14 v Lancs (Northampton) 2007 (P40). T20 HS 62. T20 BB – .

WHITE, Graeme Geoffrey (Stowe S), b Milton Keynes, Bucks 18 Apr 1987. 5'11". RHB, SLA. Squad No 87. Debut (Northamptonshire) 2006. Nottinghamshire 2010-13. HS 65 v Glamorgan (Colwyn Bay) 2007. BB 4-72 Nt v Durham (Nottingham) 2011. Nh BB 3-81 v Surrey (Oval) 2015. LO HS 39* v Somerset (Taunton) 2012 (CB40). LO BB 5-35 v Scotland (Edinburgh) 2010 (CB40). T20 HS 34. T20 BB 5-22 Nt v Lancs (Nottingham) 2013 – Nt record.

ZAIB, Saif Ali (RGS High Wycombe), b High Wycombe, Bucks 22 May 1998. LHB, SLA. Squad No 5. Debut (Northamptonshire) 2015. Northamptonshire 2nd XI debut 2013, aged 15y 90d. HS 21 v Australians (Northampton) 2015. CC HS 0. LO HS 16 v Leics (Northampton) 2015 (RLC). LO BB – .

RELEASED/RETIRED

(Having made a County 1st XI appearance in 2015)

CHAMBERS, Maurice Anthony (Homerton TC; Sir George Monoux C), b Port Antonio, Portland, Jamaica 14 Sep 1987. 6'3". RHB, RFM. Essex 2005-13. No f-c appearances 2006-07 – stress fracture of the back. Warwickshire 2013 (on loan). Northamptonshire 2014-15. MCC YC 2004. F-c Tour (EL): WI 2010-11. HS 58 Wa v Derbys (Derby) 2013. Nh HS 20 v Middx (Lord's) 2014. BB 6-68 (10-123 match) Ex v Notts (Chelmsford) 2010. Nh BB 3-44 v Surrey (Oval) 2015. LO HS 2 Ex v Lancs (Chelmsford) 2012 (CB40). LO BB 3-29 v Lancs (Manchester) 2014 (RLC). T20 HS 10*. T20 BB 3-31.

[NQ]**COETZER, Kyle** James (Aberdeen GS), b Aberdeen, Scotland 14 Apr 1984. 5'11". RHB, RM. Durham 2004-10. Northamptonshire 2011-15; cap 2013. Scotland 2004 to date. LOI (Scot): 27 (2008 to 2015-16); HS 156 v B (Nelson) 2014-15; BB 1-35 v Netherlands (Aberdeen) 2011. IT20 (Scot): 34 (2008 to 2015-16); HS 70 v Hong Kong (Mong Kok) 2015-16; BB 3-25 v Afghanistan (Abu Dhabi) 2009-10. F-c Tour (Scot): Kenya 2009-10. HS 219 v Leics (Leicester) 2013. BB 2-16 Scot v Kenya (Nairobi) 2009-10. CC BB 1-8 v Glamorgan (Cardiff) 2015. LO HS 156 (see *LOI*). LO BB 1-2 v Notts (Nottingham) 2013 (Y40). T20 HS 71*. T20 BB 3-25.

PETERS, Stephen David (Coopers Coborn & Co S), b Harold Wood, Essex 10 Dec 1978. 5'11". RHB, occ LB. Essex 1996-2001, scoring 110 and 12* v Cambridge U (Cambridge) on debut. Worcestershire 2002-05. Northamptonshire 2006-15; cap 2007; captain 2013-14. MCC 2011, 2012. 1000 runs (4); most – 1320 (2010). HS 222 v Glamorgan (Swansea) 2011. BB 1-19 Ex v Oxford U (Chelmsford) 1999. LO HS 107 v Yorks (Leeds) 2007 (FPT). T20 HS 61*.

SHAHID AFRIDI – *see HAMPSHIRE*.

WILLEY, D.J. – *see YORKSHIRE*.

NORTHAMPTONSHIRE 2015

RESULTS SUMMARY

	Place	Won	Lost	Tied	Drew	NR
LV= County Championship (1st Division)	5th	3	3		10	
All First-Class Matches		3	3		12	
Royal London One-Day Cup (Group A)	5th	4	3			1
NatWest t20 Blast (North Group)	Finalist	9	6			2

LV= COUNTY CHAMPIONSHIP AVERAGES

BATTING AND FIELDING

Cap		M	I	NO	HS	Runs	Avge	100	50	Ct/St
	D.Murphy	5	8	2	135*	324	54.00	1	1	15
2013	D.J.Willey	5	9	1	104*	407	50.87	2	2	3
	B.M.Duckett	11	19	1	154	851	47.27	4	2	8
	R.E.Levi	11	18	3	168	663	44.20	1	5	5
2013	S.P.Crook	8	12	1	102*	445	40.45	1	1	3
2012	A.G.Wakely	15	26	2	123	853	35.54	2	4	12
	A.M.Rossington	13	23	1	116	738	33.54	1	7	34
	R.I.Keogh	16	29	2	163*	850	31.48	2	2	5
	J.J.Cobb	16	28	5	95	678	29.47	—	5	8
2007	S.D.Peters	9	16	—	82	440	27.50	—	4	4
	R.I.Newton	11	20	—	107	534	26.70	1	3	3
	R.K.Kleinveldt	13	21	3	56	391	21.72	—	2	9
2015	M.Azharullah	14	19	9	58*	189	18.90	—	1	5
	O.P.Stone	12	17	4	38	231	17.76	—	—	6
	B.W.Sanderson	3	5	2	42	48	16.00	—	—	1
	G.G.White	3	6	—	24	43	7.16	—	—	1
2013	K.J.Coetzer	4	7	—	13	37	5.28	—	—	—
	M.A.Chambers	5	8	—	14	22	2.75	—	—	1

Also batted: R.J.Gleeson (1 match) 2 (2 ct); S.A.Zaib (1) 0.

BOWLING

	O	M	R	W	Avge	Best	5wI	10wM
B.W.Sanderson	65	16	202	10	20.20	4-44	—	—
R.K.Kleinveldt	407.5	69	1547	57	27.14	5-41	5	—
M.A.Chambers	94.3	16	340	12	28.33	3-44	—	—
M.Azharullah	419.5	95	1329	44	30.20	5-31	2	—
O.P.Stone	344.4	60	1148	38	30.21	5-44	1	—
D.J.Willey	148.1	24	511	14	36.50	4-72	—	—
S.P.Crook	154.1	19	630	15	42.00	3-28	—	—
R.I.Keogh	296	40	1019	19	53.63	3-35	—	—
Also bowled:								
G.G.White	67.4	13	240	8	30.00	3-81	—	—

J.J.Cobb 103.5-12-363-4; K.J.Coetzer 3-0-12-1; R.J.Gleeson 12-0-67-2; R.I.Newton 1-0-6-0; A.M.Rossington 1-0-6-0; A.G.Wakely 4-0-17-0; S.A.Zaib 1-0-4-0.

The First-Class Averages (pp 227–243) give the records of Northamptonshire players in all first-class county matches (Northamptonshire's other opponents being Cambridge MCCU and the Australians).

NORTHAMPTONSHIRE RECORDS

FIRST-CLASS CRICKET

Highest Total	For 781-7d		v	Notts	Northampton	1995
	V 673-8d		by	Yorkshire	Leeds	2003
Lowest Total	For 12		v	Glos	Gloucester	1907
	V 33		by	Lancashire	Northampton	1977
Highest Innings	For 331*	M.E.K.Hussey	v	Somerset	Taunton	2003
	V 333	K.S.Duleepsinhji	for	Sussex	Hove	1930

Highest Partnership for each Wicket

1st	375	R.A.White/M.J.Powell	v	Glos	Northampton	2002
2nd	344	G.Cook/R.J.Boyd-Moss	v	Lancashire	Northampton	1986
3rd	393	A.Fordham/A.J.Lamb	v	Yorkshire	Leeds	1990
4th	370	R.T.Virgin/P.Willey	v	Somerset	Northampton	1976
5th	401	M.B.Loye/D.Ripley	v	Glamorgan	Northampton	1998
6th	376	R.Subba Row/A.Lightfoot	v	Surrey	The Oval	1958
7th	293	D.J.G.Sales/D.Ripley	v	Essex	Northampton	1999
8th	179	A.J.Hall/J.D.Middlebrook	v	Surrey	The Oval	2011
9th	156	R.Subba Row/S.Starkie	v	Lancashire	Northampton	1955
10th	148	B.W.Bellamy/J.V.Murdin	v	Glamorgan	Northampton	1925

Best Bowling	For	10-127	V.W.C.Jupp	v	Kent	Tunbridge W	1932
(Innings)	V	10- 30	C.Blythe	for	Kent	Northampton	1907
Best Bowling	For	15- 31	G.E.Tribe	v	Yorkshire	Northampton	1958
(Match)	V	17- 48	C.Blythe	for	Kent	Northampton	1907

Most Runs – Season	2198	D.Brookes	(av 51.11)		1952
Most Runs – Career	28980	D.Brookes	(av 36.13)		1934-59
Most 100s – Season	8	R.A.Haywood			1921
Most 100s – Career	67	D.Brookes			1934-59
Most Wkts – Season	175	G.E.Tribe	(av 18.70)		1955
Most Wkts – Career	1102	E.W.Clark	(av 21.26)		1922-47
Most Career W-K Dismissals	810	K.V.Andrew	(653 ct; 157 st)		1953-66
Most Career Catches in the Field	469	D.S.Steele			1963-84

LIMITED-OVERS CRICKET

Highest Total	50ov	360-2		v	Staffs	Northampton	1990
	40ov	324-6		v	Warwicks	Birmingham	2013
	T20	224-5		v	Glos	Milton Keynes	2005
Lowest Total	50ov	62		v	Leics	Leicester	1974
	40ov	41		v	Middlesex	Northampton	1972
	T20	47		v	Durham	Chester-le-St[2]	2011
Highest Innings	50ov	161	D.J.G.Sales	v	Yorkshire	Northampton	2006
	40ov	172*	W.Larkins	v	Warwicks	Luton	1983
	T20	111*	L.Klusener	v	Worcs	Kidderminster	2007
Best Bowling	50ov	7-10	C.Pietersen	v	Denmark	Brondby	2005
	40ov	7-39	A.Hodgson	v	Somerset	Northampton	1976
	T20	6-21	A.J.Hall	v	Worcs	Northampton	2008

NOTTINGHAMSHIRE

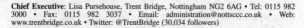

Formation of Present Club: March/April 1841
Substantial Reorganisation: 11 December 1866
Inaugural First-Class Match: 1864
Colours: Green and Gold
Badge: Badge of City of Nottingham
County Champions (since 1890): (6) 1907, 1929, 1981, 1987, 2005, 2010
NatWest Trophy Winners: (1) 1987
Benson and Hedges Cup Winners: (1) 1989
Sunday League Winners: (1) 1991
Yorkshire Bank 40 Winners: (1) 2013
Twenty20 Cup Winners: (0); best – Finalist 2006

Chief Executive: Lisa Pursehouse, Trent Bridge, Nottingham NG2 6AG • Tel: 0115 982 3000 • Fax: 0115 982 3037 • Email: administration@nottsccc.co.uk • Web: www.trentbridge.co.uk • Twitter: @TrentBridge (30,034 followers)

Director of Cricket: Mick Newell. **Assistant Coach**: Wayne Noon. **Bowling Coach**: Andy Pick. **Captains**: C.M.W.Read (f-c & l-o) and D.T.Christian (T20). **Vice-Captain**: J.W.A.Taylor. **Overseas Players**: J.M.Bird and D.T.Christian (T20 only). **2016 Beneficiary**: None. **Head Groundsman**: Steve Birks. **Scorer**: Roger Marshall. ‡ New registration. NQ Not qualified for England.

BALL, Jacob Timothy (**'Jake'**) (Meden CS), b Mansfield 14 Mar 1991. Nephew of B.N.French (Notts and England 1976-95). 6'0". RHB, RM. Squad No 28. Debut (Nottinghamshire) 2011. HS 49* v Warwks (Nottingham) 2015. BB 6-49 v Sussex (Nottingham) 2015. LO HS 19* v Sri Lanka A (Nottingham) 2011. BB 4-25 v Somerset (Nottingham) 2013 (Y40). T20 HS 8*. T20 BB 3-36.

‡NQ**BIRD, Jackson** Munro (St Pius X C, Sydney; St Ignatius C, Riverview), b Paddington, Sydney, Australia 11 Dec 1986. RHB, RFM. Squad No 22. Tasmania 2011-12 to date. Hampshire 2015. Big Bash: MS 2011-12 to 2014-15. SS 2015-16. **Tests** (A): 5 (2012-13 to 2013); HS 6* v SL (Sydney) 2012-13; BB 5-59 v NZ (Christchurch) 2015-16. F-c Tours (A): E 2012 (Aus A), 2013, 2013; NZ 2015-16. HS 26 Tas v WA (Hobart) 2012-13. 50 wkts (1): 53 (2011-12). BB 7-45 (10-92 match) Tas v NSW (Hobart) 2015-16. CC BB 4-146 H v Worcs (Worcester) 2015. LO HS 5* Tas v Q (Hobart) 2012-13. LO BB 3-39 Tas v S Aus (Adelaide) 2011-12. T20 HS 14*. T20 BB 4-31.

BROAD, Stuart Christopher John (Oakham S), b Nottingham 24 Jun 1986. 6'6". LHB, RFM. Squad No 16. Son of B.C.Broad (Glos, Notts, OFS and England 1979-94). Debut (Leicestershire) 2005; cap 2007. Nottinghamshire debut/cap 2008. YC 2006. *Wisden* 2009. **ECB central contract 2015-16. Tests**: 91 (2007-08 to 2015-16); HS 169 v P (Lord's) 2010, sharing in record Test and UK f-c 8th-wkt partnership of 332 with I.J.L.Trott; 50 wkts (2); most – 62 (2013); BB 8-15 v A (Nottingham) 2015. Hat-tricks (2) v I (Nottingham) 2011, and v SL (Leeds) 2014. **LOI**: 121 (2006 to 2015-16, 3 as captain); HS 45* v I (Manchester) 2007; BB 5-23 v SA (Nottingham) 2008. **IT20**: 56 (2006 to 2013-14, 27 as captain); HS 18* v SA (Chester-le-St) 2012 and 18* v A (Melbourne) 2013-14; BB 4-24 v NZ (Auckland) 2012-13. F-c Tours: A 2010-11, 2013-14; SA 2009-10, 2015-16; WI 2005-06 (Eng A), 2008-09, 2014-15; NZ 2007-08, 2012-13; I 2008-09, 2012-13; SL 2007-08, 2011-12; B 2006-07 (Eng A), 2009-10; UAE 2011-12 (v P), 2015-16 (v P). HS 169 (*see Tests*). CC HS 91* Le v Derbys (Leicester) 2007. Nt HS 60 v Worcs (Nottingham) 2009. BB 8-15 (*see Tests*). CC BB 8-52 (11-131 match) Nt v Warwks (Birmingham) 2010. LO HS 45* (*see LOI*). LO BB 5-23 (*see LOI*). T20 HS 18*. T20 BB 4-24.

CARTER, Matthew (Branston S), b Lincoln 26 May 1996. Younger brother of A.Carter (see *DERBYSHIRE*). RHB, OB. Debut (Nottinghamshire) 2015, taking 7-56 v Somerset (Taunton) – the best debut figures for Nt since 1914. Nottinghamshire 2nd XI debut 2015. Lincolnshire 2013-14. HS 11 and BB 7-56 (10-195 match) v Somerset (Taunton) 2015 – only 1st XI appearance.

NQ**CHRISTIAN, Daniel** Trevor, b Camperdown, NSW, Australia 4 May 1983. RHB, RFM. S Australia 2007-08 to 2012-13. Hampshire 2010. Gloucestershire 2013; cap 2013. Victoria 2013-14 to date. Joined Nottinghamshire in 2015 for l-o and T20 only; captain 2016 (T20 only). IPL: DC 2011-12. RCB 2013. Big Bash BH 2011-12 to 2014-15. HH 2015-16. **LOI** (A): 19 (2011-12 to 2013-14); HS 39 v I (Adelaide) 2011-12; BB 5-31 v SL (Melbourne) 2011-12. **IT20** (A): 15 (2009-10 to 2013-14); HS 6* v E (Hobart) 2013-14; BB 3-27 v WI (Gros Islet) 2011-12. HS 131* S Aus v NSW (Adelaide) 2011-12. CC HS 36 and CC BB 2-115 H v Somerset (Taunton) 2010. BB 5-24 (9-87 match) S Aus v WA (Perth) (2009-10). LO HS 117 Vic v NSW (Sydney) 2013-14. LO BB 6-48 S Aus v Vic (Geelong) 2010-11. T20 HS 129 M v Kent (Canterbury) 2014 – M record. T20 BB 5-26.

FLETCHER, Luke Jack (Henry Mellish S, Nottingham), b Nottingham 18 Sep 1988. 6'6". RHB, RMF. Squad No 19. Debut (Nottinghamshire) 2008; cap 2014. Surrey 2015 (on loan). HS 92 v Hants (Southampton) 2009. BB 5-52 v Warwks (Nottingham) 2013. LO HS 40* v Durham (Chester-le-St) 2009 (P40). LO BB 4-44 v Warwks (Nottingham) 2014 (RLC). T20 HS 8. T20 BB 4-30.

GIDMAN, William Robert Simon (Wycliffe C; Berkshire C of Agriculture), b High Wycombe, Bucks 14 Feb 1985. Younger brother of A.P.R.Gidman (see *WORCESTERSHIRE*). 6'2". LHB, RM. Squad No 24. Durham 2007. No f-c appearances in 2008-10. Gloucesterhire 2011-14; cap 2011, becoming first player for Gs to score 1000 runs and take 50 wkts in debut season. Nottinghamshire debut 2015. MCC YC 2004-06. 1000 runs (1): 1006 (2011). HS 143 and BB 6-15 (10-43 match) Gs v Leics (Bristol) 2013 – only the fifth Gs player to score a century and take ten wkts in a match. Nt HS v Sussex (Nottingham) 2015. 50 wkts (2); most – 55 (2013). Nt BB 2-29 v Somerset (Taunton) 2015. LO HS 76 Gs v Worcs (Worcester) 2012 (CB40). LO BB 4-36 Du v Hants (Chester-le-St) 2010 (CB40). T20 HS 40*. T20 BB 2-23.

GURNEY, Harry Frederick (Garendon HS; Loughborough GS; Leeds U), b Nottingham 25 Oct 1986. 6'2". RHB, LFM. Squad No 11. Leicestershire 2007-11. Nottinghamshire debut 2012; cap 2014. MCC 2014. Bradford/Leeds UCCE 2006-07 (not f-c). **LOI**: 10 (2014 to 2014-15); HS 6* v SL (Colombo, RPS) 2014-15; BB 4-55 v SL (Lord's) 2014. HS 24* Le v Middx (Leicester) 2009. Nt HS 22* v Somerset (Taunton) 2015. BB 5-43 v Sussex (Nottingham) 2015. Hat-trick v Sussex (Hove) 2013. LO HS 13* v Durham (Chester-le-St) 2012 (CB40). LO BB 5-24 Le v Hants (Leicester) 2010 (CB40). T20 HS 5*. T20 BB 3-21.

HALES, Alexander Daniel (Chesham HS), b Hillingdon, Middx 3 Jan 1989. 6'5". RHB, OB, occ WK. Squad No 10. Debut (Nottinghamshire) 2008; cap 2011. Worcestershire 2014 (1 game, on loan). Buckinghamshire 2006-07. MCC YCs 2006-07. Big Bash: MR 2012-13. AS 2013-14. HH 2014-15. **Tests**: 4 (2015-16); HS 60 v SA (Cape Town) 2015-16; BB – . **LOI**: 29 (2014 to 2015-16); HS 112 v SA (Cape Town) 2015-16. **IT20**: 39 (2011 to 2015-16); HS 116* v SL (Chittagong) 2013-14, E record. 1000 runs (3); most – 1127 (2011). HS 236 v Notts (Nottingham) 2015. BB 2-63 v Yorks (Nottingham) 2009. LO HS 150* v Worcs (Nottingham) 2009 (P40) – Nt record. T20 HS 116*.

HUTTON, Brett Alan (Worksop C), b Doncaster, Yorks 6 Feb 1993. 6'2". RHB, RM. Squad No 26. Debut (Nottinghamshire) 2011. Nottinghamshire 2nd XI debut 2010. No 1st XI appearances in 2014. HS 72 v Middx (Nottingham) 2015. BB 5-29 (10-106 match) v Durham (Nottingham) 2015. LO HS 33* v Lancs (Liverpool) 2015 (RLC). LO BB 3-72 v Kent (Nottingham) 2015 (RLC).

LIBBY, Jacob ('**Jake**') Daniel (Plymouth C; UWIC), b Plymouth, Devon 3 Jan 1993. 5'9". RHB, OB. Squad No 2. Cardiff MCCU 2014. Nottinghamshire debut 2014. Cornwall 2011-14. HS 108 v Sussex (Nottingham) 2014 – on Nt debut. BB 1-18 CfU v Glamorgan (Cardiff) 2014.

LUMB, Michael John (St Stithians C, Johannesburg), b Johannesburg, South Africa 12 Feb 1980. Son of R.G.Lumb (Yorkshire 1970-84); nephew of A.J.S.Smith (SAU and Natal 1972-73 to 1983-84). 6'0". LHB, RM. Squad No 45. Yorkshire 2000-06; ECB qualified and CC debut 2001; cap 2003. Hampshire 2007-11; cap 2008. Nottinghamshire debut/cap 2012. IPL: RR 2009-10. DC 2011. Big Bash: SS 2011-12 to date. **LOI**: 3 (2013-14); HS 106 v WI (North Sound) 2013-14, becoming only the 2nd England player after D.L.Amiss to score a century on LOI debut. **IT20**: 27 (2009-10 to 2013-14); HS 63 v WI (Bridgetown) 2013-14. F-c Tour (Eng A): I 2003-04. 1000 runs (3); most – 1120 (2013). HS 221* v Derbys (Nottingham) 2013. BB 2-10 Y v Kent (Canterbury) 2001. LO HS 110 EL v Pakistan A (Dubai) 2009-10. LO BB – . T20 HS 124* H v Essex (Southampton) 2009 – H record. T20 BB 3-32.

MULLANEY, Steven John (St Mary's RC S, Astley), b Warrington, Cheshire 19 Nov 1986. 5'9". RHB, RM. Squad No 5. Lancashire 2006-08. No f-c appearances in 2009. Nottinghamshire debut 2010, scoring 100* v Hants (Southampton); cap 2013. HS 165* La v Durham UCCE (Durham) 2007. Nt HS 125 v Middx (Lord's) 2013. BB 4-31 v Essex (Nottingham) 2010. LO HS 63* v Glamorgan (Cardiff) 2013 (RLC). LO BB 4-29 v Kent (Nottingham) 2013 (Y40). T20 HS 53. T20 BB 4-19.

PATEL, Samit Rohit (Worksop C), b Leicester 30 Nov 1984. Elder brother of A.Patel (Derbyshire and Notts 2007-11). 5'8". RHB, SLA. Squad No 21. Debut Nottinghamshire 2002; cap 2008. MCC 2014. Nottinghamshire 2nd XI debut 1999, aged 14y 274d. **Tests**: 6 (2011-12 to 2015-16); HS 42 v P (Sharjah) 2015-16; BB 2-27 v SL (Galle) 2011-12. **LOI**: 36 (2008 to 2012-13); HS 70* v I (Mohali) 2011-12; BB 5-41 v SA (Oval) 2008. **IT20**: 18 (2011 to 2012-13); HS 67 v SL (Pallekele) 2012-13; BB 2-6 v Afghanistan (Colombo, RPS) 2012-13. F-c Tours: NZ 2008-09 (Eng A); I 2012-13; SL 2011-12; UAE 2015-16 (v P). 1000 runs (1): 1125 (2014). HS 256 v Durham MCCU (Nottingham) 2013. CC HS 176 v Glos (Nottingham) 2007. BB 7-68 (11-111 match) v Hants (Southampton) 2011. LO HS 129* v Warwks (Nottingham) 2013 (Y40). LO BB 6-13 v Ireland (Dublin) 2009 (FPT). T20 HS 90*. T20 BB 3-11.

READ, Christopher Mark Wells (Torquay GS; Bath U), b Paignton, Devon 10 Aug 1978. 5'8". RHB, WK. Squad No 7. Gloucestershire (l-o only) 1997. Debut 1997-98 for England A in Kenya. Nottinghamshire debut 1998; cap 1999; captain 2008 to date; benefit 2009. MCC 2002. Devon 1995-97. *Wisden* 2010. **Tests**: 15 (1999 to 2006-07); HS 55 v P (Leeds) 2006. Made six dismissals twice in successive innings 2006-07 to establish an Ashes record. **LOI**: 36 (1999-00 to 2006-07); HS 30* v SA (Manchester) 2003. **IT20**: 1 (2006); HS 13 v P (Bristol) 2006. F-c Tours: A 2006-07; SA 1998-99 (Eng A), 1999-00; WI 2000-01 (Eng A), 2003-04, 2005-06 (Eng A); SL 1997-98 (Eng A), 2002-03 (ECB Acad), 2003-04; Z 1998-99 (Eng A); B 2003-04; K 1997-98 (Eng A). 1000 runs (3); most – 1203 (2009). HS 240 v Essex (Chelmsford) 2007. BB – . LO HS 135 v Durham (Nottingham) 2006 (CGT). T20 HS 58*.

ROOT, William Thomas (Worksop C; Leeds Beckett U), b Sheffield, Yorks 5 Aug 1992. Younger brother of J.E.Root (see *YORKSHIRE*). LHB, OB. Leeds/Bradford MCCU 2015. Nottinghamshire debut 2015. Yorkshire 2nd XI 2009-11. Nottinghamshire 2nd XI debut 2011. Suffolk 2014. Nt HS 37 v Hants (Nottingham) 2015.

SMITH, Gregory Philip (Oundle S; St Hild & St Bede C, Durham U), b Leicester 16 Nov 1988. 6'0". RHB, LBG. Squad No 22. Leicestershire 2008-14, returned in 2015 on loan. Durham MCCU 2009-11. Badureliya 2013-14. Colombo CC 2014-15. Nottinghamshire debut 2015. HS 158* Le v Glos (Leicester) 2010. Nt HS 14 v Sussex (Nottingham) 2015. BB 1-64 Le v Glos (Leicester) 2008. LO HS 135* Le v Somerset (Leicester) 2013 (Y40). T20 HS 102.

159

NQTAYLOR, Brendan Ross Murray, b Harare, Zimbabwe 6 Feb 1986. RHB, WK, OB. Mashonaland 2001-02 to 2004-05. Northerns (Zim) 2007-08 to 2008-09. MRW 2009-10 to 2013-14. Nottinghamshire debut/cap 2015. **Tests** (Z): 23 (2004 to 2014-15, 13 as captain); HS 171 v B (Harare) 2013; BB – . **LOI** (Z): 167 (2004 to 2014-15, 34 as captain); HS 145* v SA (Bloemfontein) 2010-11; BB 3-54 v B (Dhaka) 2004-05. **IT20** (Z): 26 (2006-07 to 2013-14, 17 as captain); HS 75* v NZ (Hamilton) 2011-12; BB 1-16 v SA (Kimberley) 2010-11. F-c Tours (Z) (C=Captain): SA 2004-05, 2007-08; WI 2010, 2012-13C; NZ 2011-12C; I 2005-06; P 2004-05, 2007-08; B 2003-04 (ZA), 2004-05, 2014-15C. 1000 runs (1+1); most – 1070 (2015). HS 217 MWR v SR (Masvingo) 2009-10. Nt HS 152 v Somerset (Taunton) 2015. BB 2-36 Mashonaland v Manicaland (Mutare) 2003-04. LO HS 145* (*see LOI*). LO BB 5-28 Zim A v India A (Harare) 2004. T20 HS 101*. T20 BB 3-38.

TAYLOR, James William Arthur (Shrewsbury S), b Nottingham 6 Jan 1990. 5'6". RHB, LB. Squad No 4. Leicestershire 2008-11; cap 2009. Nottinghamshire debut/cap 2012; l-o captain 2014-15. Sussex (1 game) 2013. MCC 2010. Shropshire 2007. YC 2009. **Tests**: 7 (2012); HS 76 v P (Sharjah) 2015-16. **LOI**: 27 (2011 to 2015-16); HS 101 v A (Manchester) 2015. F-c Tours: SA 2015-16; WI 2010-11 (EL); SL 2013-14 (EL); UAE 2015-16 (v P). 1000 runs (5); most – 1602 (2011). HS 291 v Sussex (Horsham) 2015. BB – . LO HS 146* v Derbys (Nottingham) 2014 (RLC). LO BB 4-61 Le v Warwks (Leicester) 2010 (CB40). T20 HS 62*. T20 BB 1-10.

NQWESSELS, Mattheus Hendrik ('Riki') (Woodridge C, Pt Elizabeth; Northampton U), b Marogudoore, Queensland, Australia 12 Nov 1985. Left Australia when 2 months old. Son of K.C.Wessels (OFS, Sussex, WP, NT, Q, EP, GW, Australia and South Africa 1973-74 to 1999-00). 5'11". RHB, WK. Squad No 9. MCC 2004. Northamptonshire 2005-09. Nondescripts 2007-08. MWR 2009-10 to 2011-12. Nottinghamshire debut 2011; cap 2014. Big Bash: SS 2014-15. 1000 runs (2); most – 1213 (2014). HS 199 v Sussex (Hove) 2012. BB 1-10 MWR v MT (Bulawayo) 2009-10. LO HS 132 v Middx (Lord's) 2015 (RLC). LO BB 1-0 MWR v MT (Bulawayo) 2009-10. T20 HS 97 v Durham (Chester-le-St) 2015 – Nt record.

WOOD, Luke (Portland CS, Worksop), b Sheffield, Yorks 2 Aug 1995. 5'9". LHB, LM. Squad No 14. Debut (Nottinghamshire) 2014. Nottinghamshire 2nd XI debut 2012. England U19s 2014. HS 100 v Sussex (Nottingham) 2015. BB 3-27 v Sussex (Horsham) 2015.

WOOD, Samuel Kenneth William (Colonel Frank Seely S, Nottingham), b Nottingham 3 Apr 1993. 5'11". LHB, OB. Squad No 23. Debut (Nottinghamshire) 2011. Nottinghamshire 2nd XI debut 2008, aged 15y 40d. England U19s 2010-11. HS 45 and BB 3-64 v Surrey (Oval) 2012. LO HS 32 v Bangladesh A (Nottingham) 2013. LO BB 2-24 v Lancs (Manchester) 2011 (CB40). T20 HS 13*. T20 BB 2-21.

RELEASED/RETIRED

(Having made a County 1st XI appearance in 2015)

CARTER, A. – *see* DERBYSHIRE.

NQHILFENHAUS, Benjamin William, b Ulverston, Tasmania, Australia 15 Mar 1983. 6'1". RHB, RFM. Squad No 20. Tasmania 2005-06 to date. Nottinghamshire 2015; cap 2015. IPL: CSK 2012-14. Big Bash: HH 2011-12 to 2014-15. MS 2015-16. **Tests** (A): 27 (2008-09 to 2012-13); HS 56* v P (Lord's) 2010; BB 5-75 v I (Melbourne) 2011-12. **LOI** (A): 25 (2006-07 to 2012); HS 16 v I (Nagpur) 2009-10; BB 5-33 v I (Brisbane) 2011-12. **IT20** (A): 7 (2008-09 to 2012); HS 2 v P (Dubai, DSC) 2009; BB 2-15 v SA (Melbourne) 2008-09. F-c Tours (A): E 2009, 2010 (v P); SA 2008-09; WI 2011-12; I 2010-11; Z 2011 (v A). HS 56* (*see Tests*). Nt HS 28* v Yorks (Leeds) 2015. 50 wkts (1): 60 (2006-07). BB 7-58 (10-87 match) Tas v NSW (Hobart) 2005-06. Nt BB 4-67 v Worcs (Nottingham) 2015. LO HS 18* Tas v Q (Hobart) 2008-09. LO BB 5-33 (*see LOI*). T20 HS 38*. T20 BB 4-27.

^{NQ}**IMRAN TAHIR**, Mohammad (Government Pakistan Angels HS and MAO College, Lahore), b Lahore, Pakistan 4 Jun 1979. 5'11". RHB, LB. Lahore City 1996-97 to 1997-98. WAPDA 1998-99. REDCO 1999-00. Lahore Whites 2000-01. SNGPL 2001-02 to 2003-04. Sialkot 2002-03. Middlesex 2003. Lahore Blues 2004-05. PIA 2004-05 to 2006-07. Lahore Ravi 2005-06. Yorkshire (1 match) 2007. Titans 2007-08 to 2009-10. Hampshire 2008-14; cap 2009. Easterns 2008-09 to 2009-10. Warwickshire 2010; cap 2010. Dolphins 2010-11 to date. Lions 2012-13 to 2013-14. Nottinghamshire 2015; cap 2015. Staffordshire 2004-05. Qualified for SA on 1 Apr 2009. IPL: DD 2014 to 2015. **Tests** (SA): 20 (2011-12 to 2015-16); HS 29* v SL (Centurion) 2011-12; BB 5-32 v P (Dubai) 2013-14. **LOI** (SA): 54 (2010-11 to 2015-16); HS 23* v Z (Harare) 2014; LO BB 5-45 v WI (Sydney) 2014-15. **IT20** (SA): 23 (2013 to 2015-16); HS 9* and 4-21 v E (Cape Town) 2015-16. F-c Tours (SA): E 2012; A 2012-13; NZ 2011-12; I 2015-16; SL 2004-05 (Pak A), 2012; UAE 2013-14 (v P). HS 77* H v Somerset (Southampton) 2009. 50 wkts (2+2); most – 74 (2004-05). BB 8-42 (12-133 match) Dolphins v Knights (Kimberley) 2015-16. UK BB 7-66 (12-189 match) H v Lancs (Manchester) 2008. Nt HS 2 and BB 2-65 v Worcs (Worcester) 2015. LO HS 41* Staffs v Lancs (Stone) 2004 (CGT). LO BB 5-27 v Sussex (Southampton) 2008 (P40). T20 HS 17*. T20 BB 4-21.

KEEDY, Gary (Garforth CS), b Wakefield, Yorks 27 Nov 1974. 6'0". LHB, SLA. Squad No 3. Yorkshire 1994 (one match). Lancashire 1995-2012; cap 2000; benefit 2009. Surrey 2013. Nottinghamshire 2014-15. MCC 2011. F-c Tour: WI 1995-96 (La). HS 64 La v Sussex (Hove) 2008. Nt HS 15* v Durham (Chester-le-St) 2014. 50 wkts (4); most – 72 (2004). BB 7-68 (10-128 match) La v Durham (Manchester) 2010. Nt BB 5-163 v Yorks (Nottingham) 2014. LO HS 33 La v Derbys (Derby) 2008. LO BB 5-30 La v Sussex (Manchester) 2000 (NL). T20 HS 9*. T20 BB 4-15.

^{NQ}**PHILANDER, Vernon** Darryl, b Bellville, Cape Province, South Africa 24 Jun 1985. RHB, RMF. Western Province 2003-04 to 2009-10. WP Boland 2004-05. Cape Cobras 2005-06 to date. Middlesex 2008. Somerset 2012. Kent 2013. Nottinghamshire 2015; cap 2015. Devon 2004. **Tests** (SA): 32 (2011-12 to 2015-16); HS 74 v P (Centurion) 2012-13; BB 6-44 (10-114 match) v NZ (Hamilton) 2011-12. **LOI** (SA): 30 (2007 to 2015); HS 30* v NZ (Potchefstroom) 2015; BB 4-12 v Ireland (Belfast) 2007 – on debut. **IT20** (SA): 7 (2007-08); HS 6 v E (Cape Town) 2007-08; BB 2-23 v B (Cape Town) 2007-08. F-c Tours (SA): E 2012; A 2012-13; NZ 2011-12; I 2015-16; SL 2010 (SA A), 2014; Z 2014; B 2010 (SA A), 2015; UAE (v P) 2013-14. HS 168 WP v GW (Kimberley) 2004-05. CC HS 41 Nt v Durham (Chester-le-St) 2015. 50 wkts (0+2); most – 59 (2009-10). BB 7-61 Cobras v Knights (Cape Town) 2011-12. CC BB 5-43 Sm v Middx (Taunton) 2012. Nt BB 4-56 v Somerset (Nottingham) 2015. LO HS 79* SA A v Bangladesh A (East London) 2010-11. LO BB 4-12 (see LOI). T20 HS 56*. T20 BB 5-17.

^{NQ}**SAMMY, Darren** Julius Garvey, b Micoud, St Lucia, 20 Dec 1983. RHB, RM. Windward Is 2002-03 to 2012-13. Nottinghamshire (T20 only) 2015. IPL: SH 2013-14. RCB 2015. Big Bash: HH 2014-15 to date. **Tests** (WI): 38 (2007 to 2013-14, 30 as captain); HS 106 v E (Nottingham) 2012; BB 7-66 v E (Manchester) 2007. **LOI** (WI): 126 (2004 to 2015-16, 51 as captain); HS 89 v Ireland (Nelson) 2014-15; BB 4-26 v Z (Kingstown) 2009-10. **IT20** (WI): 60 (2007 to 2015-16, 39 as captain); HS 42* v P (Dhaka) 2013-14; BB 5-26 v Z (Port of Spain) 2009-10. F-c Tours (WI)(C=Captain): E 2006 (WI A), 2007, 2009, 2012C; A 2009-10; SA 2007-08; NZ 2013-14C; I 2011-12C, 2013-14C; SL 2005 (WI A), 2010-11C; B 2011-12C, 2012-13C. HS 121 Windward Is v Barbados (Bridgetown) 2008-09. BB 7-66 (see Tests). LO HS 89 (see LOI). LO BB 4-16 WI A v Sri Lanka A (Gros Islet) 2006-07. T20 HS 60. T20 BB 5-26.

P.J.Franks left the staff without making a County 1st XI appearance in 2015.

NOTTINGHAMSHIRE 2015

RESULTS SUMMARY

		Place	Won	Lost	Tied	Drew	NR
LV= County Championship	(1st Division)	3rd	6	5		5	
All First-Class Matches			6	5		6	
Royal London One-Day Cup	(Group B)	SF	6	2			2
NatWest t20 Blast	(North Group)	5th	7	6			1

LV= COUNTY CHAMPIONSHIP AVERAGES
BATTING AND FIELDING

Cap		M	I	NO	HS	Runs	Avge	100	50	Ct/St
1999	C.M.W.Read	13	21	4	121	873	51.35	3	6	36/1
2011	A.D.Hales	11	18	–	236	892	49.555	3	2	2
2012	J.W.A.Taylor	12	21	1	291	991	49.55	2	5	6
2014	M.H.Wessels	16	28	2	117	1033	39.73	2	6	18
2015	B.W.Hilfenhaus	3	6	4	28*	76	38.00	–	–	1
2015	B.R.M.Taylor	16	28	–	152	956	34.14	3	3	12
2013	S.J.Mullaney	15	26	–	112	819	31.50	1	4	22
2008	S.C.J.Broad	2	4	–	50	123	30.75	–	1	1
	L.Wood	11	16	2	100	420	30.00	1	2	2
2015	V.D.Philander	5	9	2	41	177	25.28	–	–	1
	B.A.Hutton	9	13	2	72	278	25.27	–	1	5
2008	S.R.Patel	16	28	1	100	650	24.07	2	2	8
2012	M.J.Lumb	5	9	–	73	195	21.66	–	1	3
	W.R.S.Gidman	6	11	–	57	185	16.81	–	1	3
	J.T.Ball	13	20	3	49*	235	13.82	–	–	1
	G.P.Smith	3	6	–	14	60	10.00	–	–	2
	J.D.Libby	2	4	–	34	37	9.25	–	–	1
2014	H.F.Gurney	11	14	8	8	15	2.50	–	–	1

Also played: A.Carter (1 match) 24*, 17* (1 ct); M.Carter (1) 0, 11 (1 ct); L.J.Fletcher (2 – cap 2014) 5, 7, 24*; Imran Tahir (1 – cap 2015) 2; G.Keedy (1) did not bat (1 ct); W.T.Root (1) 37, 15.

BOWLING

	O	M	R	W	Avge	Best	5wI	10wM
M.Carter	49.4	6	195	10	19.50	7-56	1	1
V.D.Philander	154.3	40	384	16	24.00	4-56	–	–
H.F.Gurney	305.5	58	1000	41	24.39	5-43	2	–
B.A.Hutton	262.1	51	912	37	24.64	5-29	2	1
J.T.Ball	314.3	59	1121	39	28.74	6-49	1	–
L.Wood	247.2	53	907	30	30.23	3-27	–	–
S.R.Patel	302.1	83	891	26	34.26	4-23	–	–
S.J.Mullaney	120.3	25	436	12	36.33	3-44	–	–

Also bowled:

A.Carter	20	2	91	5	18.20	4-46	–	–
G.Keedy	40	12	107	5	21.40	3-45	–	–
S.C.J.Broad	51.3	8	201	9	22.33	7-84	1	–
B.W.Hilfenhaus	97	22	294	7	42.00	4-67	–	–

L.J.Fletcher 12-2-42-2; W.R.S.Gidman 92-26-259-4; Imran Tahir 36-5-145-4; W.T.Root 5-2-6-0; B.R.M.Taylor 3-0-12-0.

The First-Class Averages (pp 227–243) give the records of Nottinghamshire players in all first-class county matches (Nottinghamshire's other opponents being Loughborough MCCU), with the exception of S.C.J.Broad, A.Carter, W.T.Root and G.P.Smith, whose first-class figures for Nottinghamshire are as above, and:
L.J.Fletcher 3-4-1-24*-39-13.00-0-0-0ct. 12-1-10-98-3-32.66-2/40-0-0.

NOTTINGHAMSHIRE RECORDS

FIRST-CLASS CRICKET

Highest Total	For	791	v	Essex	Chelmsford	2007
	V	781-7d	by	Northants	Northampton	1995
Lowest Total	For	13	v	Yorkshire	Nottingham	1901
	V	16	by	Derbyshire	Nottingham	1879
		16	by	Surrey	The Oval	1880
Highest Innings	For	312*	W.W.Keeton	v	Middlesex	The Oval	1939
	V	345	C.G.Macartney	for	Australians	Nottingham	1921

Highest Partnership for each Wicket

1st	406*	D.J.Bicknell/G.E.Welton	v	Warwicks	Birmingham	2000
2nd	398	A.Shrewsbury/W.Gunn	v	Sussex	Nottingham	1890
3rd	367	W.Gunn/J.R.Gunn	v	Leics	Nottingham	1903
4th	361	A.O.Jones/J.R.Gunn	v	Essex	Leyton	1905
5th	359	D.J.Hussey/C.M.W.Read	v	Essex	Nottingham	2007
6th	372*	K.P.Pietersen/J.E.Morris	v	Derbyshire	Derby	2001
7th	301	C.C.Lewis/B.N.French	v	Durham	Chester-le-St[2]	1993
8th	220	G.F.H.Heane/R.Winrow	v	Somerset	Nottingham	1935
9th	170	J.C.Adams/K.P.Evans	v	Somerset	Taunton	1994
10th	152	E.B.Alletson/W.Riley	v	Sussex	Hove	1911
	152	U.Afzaal/A.J.Harris	v	Worcs	Nottingham	2000

Best Bowling	For	10-66	K.Smales	v	Glos	Stroud	1956
(Innings)	V	10-10	H.Verity	for	Yorkshire	Leeds	1932
Best Bowling	For	17-89	F.C.L.Matthews	v	Northants	Nottingham	1923
(Match)	V	17-89	W.G.Grace	for	Glos	Cheltenham	1877

Most Runs – Season	2620	W.W.Whysall	(av 53.46)	1929
Most Runs – Career	31592	G.Gunn	(av 35.69)	1902-32
Most 100s – Season	9	W.W.Whysall		1928
	9	M.J.Harris		1971
	9	B.C.Broad		1990
Most 100s – Career	65	J.Hardstaff jr		1930-55
Most Wkts – Season	181	B.Dooland	(av 14.96)	1954
Most Wkts – Career	1653	T.G.Wass	(av 20.34)	1896-1920
Most Career W-K Dismissals	957	T.W.Oates	(733 ct; 224 st)	1897-1925
Most Career Catches in the Field	466	A.O.Jones		1892-1914

LIMITED-OVERS CRICKET

Highest Total	50ov	368-2		v	Middlesex	Lord's	2014
	40ov	296-7		v	Somerset	Taunton	2002
	T20	220-4		v	Leics	Leicester	2014
Lowest Total	50ov	74		v	Leics	Leicester	1987
	40ov	57		v	Glos	Nottingham	2009
	T20	91		v	Lancashire	Manchester	2006
Highest Innings	50ov	167*	P.Johnson	v	Kent	Nottingham	1993
	40ov	150*	A.D.Hales	v	Worcs	Nottingham	2009
	T20	97	M.H.Wessels	v	Durham	Chester-le-St[2]	2015
Best Bowling	50ov	6-10	K.P.Evans	v	Northumb	Jesmond	1994
	40ov	6-12	R.J.Hadlee	v	Lancashire	Nottingham	1980
	T20	5-22	G.G.White	v	Lancashire	Nottingham	2013

SOMERSET

Formation of Present Club: 18 August 1875
Inaugural First-Class Match: 1882
Colours: Black, White and Maroon
Badge: Somerset Dragon
County Champions: (0); best – 2nd (Div 1) 2001, 2010, 2012
Gillette/NatWest/C&G Trophy Winners: (3) 1979, 1983, 2001
Benson and Hedges Cup Winners: (2) 1981, 1982
Sunday League Winners: (1) 1979
Twenty20 Cup Winners: (1) 2005

Chief Executive: Guy Lavender, Cooper Associates County Ground, Taunton TA1 1JT. Tel: 0845 337 1875 • Fax: 01823 332395 • Email: enquiries@somersetcountyycc.co.uk • Web: www.somersetcricketclub.co.uk • Twitter: @SomersetCCC (36,429 followers)

Director of Cricket: Matt Maynard. **Assistant Coach**: Jason Kerr. **Academy/2nd XI Coach**: Steve Snell. **Captains**: C.J.L.Rogers (f-c) and J.Allenby (l-o). **Vice-Captain**: tbc. **Overseas Players**: C.H.Gayle (T20 only) and C.J.L.Rogers. **2016 Beneficiary**: None. **Groundsman**: Simon Lee. **Scorer**: Gerald Stickley. ‡ New registration. NQ Not qualified for England.

ABELL, Thomas Benjamin (Taunton S; Exeter U), b Taunton 5 Mar 1994. 5'10". RHB, RM. Squad No 28. Debut (Somerset) 2014. Somerset 2nd XI debut 2010. HS 131 v Hants (Taunton) 2015. BB 1-11 v Yorks (Taunton) 2015. LO HS 80 v Yorks (Scarborough) 2015 (RLC).

ALLENBY, James (Christ Church GS, Perth), b Perth, W Australia 12 Sep 1982. 6'0". RHB, RM. Squad No 6. Leicestershire 2006-09. Glamorgan 2009-14; cap 2010; captain (T20) 2014. Somerset debut 2015; captain (l-o) 2016. 1000 runs (1): 1202 (2013). HS 138* Le v Bangladesh A (Leicester) 2008 and 138* Gm v Leics (Leicester) 2013. Sm HS 64 v Notts (Nottingham) 2015. 50 wkts (1): 54 (2014). BB 6-54 (10-128 match) Gm v Hants (Cardiff) 2014. Sm BB 3-36 v New Zealanders (Taunton) 2015. LO HS 91* Le v Middx (Lord's) 2007 (P40). LO BB 5-43 Le v Derbys (Leicester) 2007 (FPT). T20 HS 110. T20 BB 5-21 Le v Lancs (Manchester) 2008, inc 4 wkts in 4 balls.

BARROW, Alexander William Rodgerson (King's C, Taunton), b Frome 6 May 1992. 5'7". RHB, RM/OB. Squad No 18. Debut (Somerset) 2011. Somerset 2nd XI debut 2009. HS 88 v Northants (Taunton) 2014. BB 1-4 v Hants (Southampton) 2011. LO HS 72 v Durham (Chester-le-St) 2012 (CB40).

NODAVEY, Joshua Henry (Culford S), b Aberdeen, Scotland 3 Aug 1990. RHB, RMF. Squad No 38. Middlesex 2010-12. Scotland 2011-12 to date. Somerset 2015. Somerset 2nd XI debut 2013. Suffolk 2014. **LOI** (Scot): 25 (2010 to 2015-16); HS 64 v Afghanistan (Sharjah) 2012-13; BB 6-28 v Afghanistan (Abu Dhabi) 2014-15. **IT20** (Scot): 10 (2012 to 2015-16); HS 24 v Z (Nagpur) 2015-16; BB 3-23 v B (The Hague) 2012. HS 72 M v Oxford MCCU (Oxford) 2010 – on debut. CC HS 61 M v Glos (Bristol) 2010. Sm HS 15 v New Zealanders (Taunton) 2015. BB 4-53 Scot v Afghanistan (Abu Dhabi) 2012-13. CC BB – . LO HS 91 Scot v Warwks (Birmingham) 2011 (CB40). LO BB 6-28 (see LOI). T20 HS 24. T20 BB 3-23.

‡DAVIES, Ryan Christopher (Sandwich TS), b Thanet, Kent 5 Nov 1996. 5'9". RHB, WK. Kent 2015. Kent 2nd XI debut 2013. England U19 2014-15 to 2015. HS 17 v Lancs (Canterbury) 2015. T20 HS 6.

^{NQ}**GAYLE, Chris**topher Henry, b Kingston, Jamaica 21 Sep 1979. LHB, OB. Jamaica 1998-99 to 2012-13. Worcestershire 2005. Somerset T20 debut 2015. IPL: KKR 2009 to 2009-10. RCB 2011 to date. Big Bash: ST 2011-12 to 2012-13. MR 2015-16. **Tests** (WI): 103 (1999-00 to 2014, 20 as captain); HS 333 v SL (Galle) 2010-11; BB 5-34 v E (Birmingham) 2004. **LOI** (WI): 266+3 for ICC (1999 to 2014-15, 53 as captain); HS 215 v Z (Canberra) 2014-15 – WI record and 4th highest in all LOI; BB 5-46 v A (St George's) 2003. **IT20** (WI): 45 (2005-06 to 2014-15, 17 as captain); HS 117 v SA (Johannesburg) 2007; BB 2-15 v A (Hobart) 2009-10. F-c Tours (WI)(C=captain): E 2000, 2002 (WI A), 2004, 2007, 2009C; A 2005-06, 2009-10C; SA 2003-04, 2007-08C; NZ 2005-06, 2008-09C; I 1998-99 (WI A), 2002-03, 2013-14; P 2006-07; SL 2001-02, 2010-11; Z 2001, 2003-04; B 2002-03, 2012-13; UAE 2001-02. 1000 runs (0+1): 1271 (2000-01). HS 333 (*see Tests*). CC HS 57 and CC BB 2-18 Wo v Leics (Worcester) 2005. BB 5-34 (*see Tests*). LO HS 215 (*see LOI*). LO BB 5-46 (*see LOI*). T20 HS 175* RCB v PW (Bangalore) 2013 – world record T20 score. T20 BB 4-22.

GREGORY, Lewis (Hele's S, Plympton), b Plymouth, Devon 24 May 1992. 6'0''. RHB, RMF. Squad No 24. Debut (Somerset) 2011; cap 2015. Somerset 2nd XI debut 2008, aged 16y 87d. Devon 2008. England U19 2010 to 2010-11. HS 69 v Yorks (Taunton) 2014. BB 6-47 (11-122 match) v Northants (Northampton) 2014. LO HS 105* v Durham (Taunton) 2014 (RLC). LO BB 4-27 v Glos (Taunton) 2011 (CB40). T20 HS 27. T20 BB 4-15.

GROENEWALD, Timothy Duncan (Maritzburg C; South Africa U), b Pietermaritzburg, South Africa 10 Jan 1984. 6'0''. RHB, RFM. Squad No 5. Debut Cambridge UCCE 2006. Warwickshire 2006-08. Derbyshire 2009-14; cap 2011. Somerset debut 2014. HS 78 Wa v Bangladesh A (Birmingham) 2008. CC HS 76 Wa v Durham (Chester-le-St) 2006. Sm HS 47 and Sm BB 5-65 v New Zealanders (Taunton) 2015. BB 6-50 De v Surrey (Croydon) 2009. Hat-trick De v Essex (Chelmsford) 2014. LO HS 57 v Warwicks (Birmingham) 2014 (RLC). LO BB 4-22 De v Worcs (Worcester) 2011 (CB40). T20 HS 41. T20 BB 4-21.

HILDRETH James Charles (Millfield S), b Milton Keynes, Bucks 9 Sep 1984. 5'10'', RHB, RMF. Squad No 25. Debut (Somerset) 2003; cap 2007. MCC 2015. F-c Tour (EL): WI 2010-11. 1000 runs (6); most – 1620 (2015). HS 303* v Warwks (Taunton) 2009. BB 2-39 v Hants (Taunton) 2004. LO HS 151 v Scotland (Taunton) 2009 (FPT). LO BB 2-26 v Worcs (Worcester) 2008 (FPT). T20 HS 107*. T20 BB 3-24.

HOSE, Adam John (Carisbrooke S), b Newport, IoW 25 Oct 1992. RHB, RMF. MCC YC 2011-14. Glamorgan 2nd XI 2012. Hampshire 2nd XI 2014. Kent 2nd XI 2014. Awaiting f-c debut. LO HS 46 v Worcs (Taunton) 2015 (RLC). T20 HS 20.

LEACH, Matthew Jack (Bishop Fox's Community S, Taunton; Richard Huish C; UWIC), b Taunton 22 Jun 1991. 6'0''. LHB, SLA. Squad No 17. Cardiff MCCU 2012. Somerset debut 2012. Somerset 2nd XI debut 2009. Dorset 2011. HS 43 v Yorks (Leeds) 2014. BB 7-106 (11-180 match) v Warwks (Taunton) 2015. LO HS 18 v Surrey (Oval) 2014 (RLC). LO BB 3-52 v Worcs (Taunton) 2015 (RLC).

^{NQ}**LEASK, Michael** Alexander, b Aberdeen, Scotland 29 Oct 1990. RHB, OB. Northamptonshire (l-o only) 2014. Somerset 2nd XI debut 2015. Awaiting f-c debut. **LOI** (Scot): 10 (2013-14 to 2014-15); HS 50 and BB 1-26 v Ireland (Dublin) 2014. **IT20** (Scot): 13 (2013 to 2015-16); HS 58 v Netherlands (Abu Dhabi) 2013-14; BB 3-20 v UAE (Edinburgh) 2015. LO HS 50 (*see LOI*). LO BB 2-23 Scot v Nepal (Ayr) 2015. T20 HS 58. T20 BB 3-20.

[NQ]**MYBURGH, Johannes** Gerhardus (Pretoria BHS; U of SA), b Pretoria, South Africa 22 Oct 1980. 5'7". Elder brother of S.J.Myburgh (Northerns, KZN and Netherlands 2005-06 to date); brother-in-law of F.de Wet (Northerns, NW, Lions, Hampshire, Dolphins and South Africa 2001-02 to 2011-12). RHB, OB. Squad No 9. Northerns 1997-98 to 2006-07. Titans 2004-05. Canterbury 2007-08 to 2009-10. Hampshire 2011. Durham 2012. Somerset debut 2014. EU qualified through wife's visa. HS 203 Northerns B v Easterns (Pretoria) 1997-98. Sm HS 150 v Durham MCCU (Taunton Vale) 2015. CC HS 118 v Durham (Taunton) 2015. BB 4-56 Canterbury v ND (Hamilton) 2008-09. Sm BB 3-57 v Yorks (Taunton) 2015. LO HS 112 Canterbury v Auckland (Christchurch) 2009-10. LO BB 2-22 Canterbury v CD (Christchurch) 2009-10. T20 HS 88. T20 BB 3-16.

OVERTON, Craig (West Buckland S), b Barnstaple, Devon 10 Apr 1994. 6'5". RHB, RMF. Squad No 12. Debut (Somerset) 2012. Somerset 2nd XI debut 2011. Devon 2010-11. HS 99 v Lancs (Taunton) 2014. BB 6-74 v Warwks (Birmingham) 2015. LO HS 49 v Durham (Taunton) 2015 (RLC). LO BB 3-37 v Surrey (Taunton) 2015 (RLC). T20 HS 15. T20 BB 1-23.

OVERTON, Jamie (West Buckland S), b Barnstaple, Devon 10 Apr 1994. 6'5". RHB, RFM. Squad No 11. Debut (Somerset) 2012. Somerset 2nd XI debut 2011. Devon 2011. HS 56 v Warwks (Birmingham) 2014. BB 6-95 v Middx (Taunton) 2013. LO HS 16* v Durham (Taunton) 2015 (RLC). LO BB 4-42 v Durham (Chester-le-St) 2012 (CB40). T20 HS 31. T20 BB 3-26.

‡[NQ]**ROGERS, Christopher** John Llewellyn (Wesley C, Perth; Curtin U, Perth), b St George, Sydney, Australia 31 Aug 1977. Son of W.J.Rogers (NSW 1968-69 to 1969-70). 5'10". LHB, LBG. W Australia 1998-99 to 2007-08. Derbyshire 2004-10; cap 2008; captain 2008 (*part*) to 2010 (*part*). Leicestershire 2005. Northamptonshire 2006-07. Victoria 2008-09 to 2014-15. Middlesex 2011-14; cap 2011; captain 2013-14. Joins Somerset in 2016 as f-c captain. MCC 2011. Big Bash: ST 2012-13. **Tests** (A): 25 (2007-08 to 2015); HS 173 v E (Lord's) 2015. F-c Tours (A): E 2013, 2015; SA 2013-14; P 2007-08 (Aus A); UAE 2014-15 (v P). 1000 runs (8+2); most – 1536 (2013). HS 319 Nh v Glos (Northampton) 2006. BB 1-16 Nh v Leics (Northampton) 2006. LO HS 140 Vic v S Aus (Melbourne) 2009-10. LO BB 2-22 Nh v Durham (Northampton) 2006. T20 HS 58.

TREGO, Peter David (Wyvern CS, W-s-M), b Weston-super-Mare 12 Jun 1981. 6'0". RHB, RMF. Squad No 7. Somerset 2000-02, 2006 to date; cap 2007; benefit 2015. Kent 2003. Middlesex 2005. C Districts 2013-14. MCC 2013. Herefordshire 2005. HS 141 CD v Auckland (Napier) 2013-14. Sm HS 140 v West Indies A (Taunton) 2002. CC HS 135 v Derbys (Taunton) 2006. 50 wkts (1): 50 (2012). BB 7-84 (11-153 match) v Yorks (Leeds) 2014. LO HS 147 v Glamorgan (Taunton) 2010 (CB40). LO BB 5-40 EL v West Indies A (Worcester) 2010. T20 HS 94*. T20 BB 4-27.

TRESCOTHICK, Marcus Edward (Sir Bernard Lovell S), b Keynsham 25 Dec 1975. 6'2". LHB, RM, occ WK. Squad No 2. Debut (Somerset) 1993; cap 1999; joint captain 2002; benefit 2008; captain 2010-15. PCA 2000, 2009, 2011. *Wisden* 2004. MBE 2005. **Tests**: 76 (2000 to 2006, 2 as captain); HS 219 v SA (Oval) 2003; BB 1-34 v P (Karachi) 2000-01. **LOI**: 123 (2000 to 2006, 10 as captain); HS 137 v P (Lord's) 2001; BB 2-7 v Z (Manchester) 2000. **IT20**: 3 (2005 to 2006); HS 72 v SL (Southampton) 2006. F-c Tours: A 2002-03; SA 2004-05; WI 2003-04; NZ 1999-00 (Eng A), 2001-02; I 2001-02, 2005-06 (*part*); P 2000-01, 2005-06; SL 2000-01, 2003-04; B 1999-00 (Eng A), 2003-04. 1000 runs (7); most – 1817 (2009). HS 284 v Northants (Northampton) 2007. BB 4-36 (inc hat-trick) v Young A (Taunton) 1995. CC BB 4-82 v Yorks (Leeds) 1998. Hat-trick 1995 (*see above*). LO HS 184 v Glos (Taunton) 2008 (P40) – Sm l-o record. LO BB 4-50 v Northants (Northampton) 2000 (NL). T20 HS 108*.

‡^{NQ}**VAN DER MERWE, Roelof** Erasmus, b Johannesburg, South Africa 31 Dec 1984. RHB, SLA. Northerns 2006-07 to 2013-14. Titans 2007-08 to 2014-15. Netherlands 2015 to date. IPL: RCB: 2009 to 2009-10. DD 2011-13. Big Bash: BH 2011-12. **LOI** (SA): 13 (200809 to 2010); HS 12 v I (Gwalior) 2009-10; BB 3-27 v Z (Centurion) 2009-10. **IT20** (SA/Neth): 20 (13 for SA 2008-09 to 2010; 7 for Neth 2015 to 2015-16); HS 48 v A (Centurion) 2008-09; BB 2-10 v UAE (Edinburgh) 2015. HS 205* Titans v Warriors (Benoni) 2014-15. BB 4-59 Northerns v FS (Bloemfontein) 2008-09. LO HS 93 Titans v Lions (Centurion) 2010-11. LO BB 5-26 Titans v Knights (Centurion) 2012-13. T20 HS 89*. T20 BB 3-18.

WALLER, Maximilian Thomas Charles (Millfield S; Bournemouth U), b Salisbury, Wiltshire 3 March 1988. 6'0". RHB, LB. Squad No 10. Debut (Somerset) 2009. Dorset 2007-08. No f-c appearances in 2013 and 2014. HS 28 v Hants (Southampton) 2009. BB 3-33 v Cardiff MCCU (Taunton Vale) 2012. CC BB 2-27 v Sussex (Hove) 2009. LO HS 25* v Glamorgan (Taunton) 2013 (Y40). LO BB 3-39 v Middx (Taunton) 2010 (Y40). T20 HS 7*. T20 BB 4-16.

RELEASED/RETIRED

(Having made a County 1st XI appearance in 2015)

^{NQ}**ABDUR REHMAN**, b Sialkot, Pakistan 1 Mar 1980. LHB, SLA. Gujranwala 1997-98 to 2001-02. HB 1999-00 to date. Sialkot 2003-04 to 2012-13. Somerset 2012-15. **Tests** (P): 22 (2007-08 to 2014); HS 60 v SA (Abu Dhabi) 2010-11; BB 6-25 v E (Abu Dhabi) 2011-12. **LOI** (P): 31 (2006-07 to 2013-14); HS 31 v SA (Multan) 2007-08; BB 4-48 v Ireland (Dublin) 2013. **IT20** (P): 8 (2006-07 to 2013-14); HS 7* v SA (Dubai, DSC) 2013-14; BB 2-7 v Kenya (Nairobi) 2007. F-c Tours (P): E 2010; A 2006 (Pak A), 2009 (Pak A); WI 2011; NZ 2010-11; SA 2009 (Pak A), 2012, 2014; Z 2013; B 2011-12; UAE 2010-11 (v SA), 2011-12 (v SL and E), 2013-14 (v SL). HS 96 HB v NBP (Multan) 2005-06. Sm HS 55* v Durham (Taunton) 2015. 50 wkts (1): 88 (2009-10). BB 9-65 (14-101 match) v Worcs (Taunton) 2012. LO HS 50 HB v KRL (Rawalpindi) 2007-08. LO BB 6-16 v Notts (Taunton) 2012 (CB40) – Sm record. T20 HS 30*. T20 BB 3-17.

BATES, Michael David (Lord Wandsworth C, Hook), b Frimley, Surrey 10 Oct 1990. 5'10". RHB, WK. Hampshire 2010-14. Somerset 2015. Berkshire 2009. HS 103 H v Yorks (Leeds) 2012. Sm HS 16 v Warwks (Birmingham) 2015. LO HS 24* H v Warwks (Birmingham) 2011 (CB40). T20 HS 15.

^{NQ}**COOPER, Tom** Lexley William, b Wollongong, NSW, Australia 26 Nov 1986. 6'1½". RHB, OB. S Australia 2008-09 to date. Netherlands 2011-13. Somerset 2015. Big Bash: AS 2011-12. MR 2012-13 to date. **LOI** (Neth): 23 (2010 to 2013); HS 101 v Afghanistan (Hague) 2010; BB 3-11 v Afghanistan (Sharjah) 2011-12. **IT20** (Neth): 17 (2011-12 to 2015-16); HS 72* v Z (Sylhet) 2013-14; BB 2-18 v UAE (Sylhet) 2013-14. HS 203* S Aus v NSW (Sydney) 2011-12. Sm HS 118 v Hants (Taunton) 2015. BB 5-76 v Warwks (Taunton) 2015. LO HS 126* Neth v Middx (Lord's) 2011 (CB40). LO BB 3-11 (see LOI). T20 HS 84*. T20 BB 2-7.

DIBBLE, Adam John (Taunton S), b Exeter, Devon 9 Mar 1991. 6'4". RHB, RMF. Somerset 2011-15. No 1st XI appearances in 2014. Devon 2009. HS 43 and BB 3-42 v Warwks (Birmingham) 2012. LO HS 15 v Glamorgan (Cardiff) 2013 (Y40). LO BB 4-52 v Yorks (Taunton) 2013 (Y40). T20 HS – . T20 BB 1-20.

[NQ]**RONCHI, Luke**, b Dannevirke, Manawatu, New Zealand 23 Apr 1981. RHB, WK. W Australia 2002-03 to 2011-12. Wellington 2011-12 to date. Somerset 2015. IPL: MI 2007-08 to 2009. PS 2011-12 to 2012-13. **Tests** (NZ): 1 (2015); HS 88 v E (Leeds) 2015. **LOI** (A/NZ): 70 (4 for A 2008; 66 for NZ 2013 to 2015-16); HS 170* v SL (Dunedin) 2014-15. **IT20** (A/NZ): 24 (3 for A 2008 to 2008-09; 21 for NZ 2013-14 to 2015-16); HS 51* v WI (Wellington) 2013-14. F-c Tours: E 2015 (NZ); I 2008-09 (Aus A), 2013 (NZ A); P 2007-08 (Aus A); SL 2013-14 (NZ A). HS 148 WA v NSW (Sydney) 2009-10. Sm HS 51 v Warwks (Taunton) 2015. LO HS 170* (*see LOI*). T20 HS 76.

[NQ]**SOHAIL TANVIR**, b Rawalpindi, Pakistan 12 Dec 1984. LHB, LMF. Rawalpindi 2004-05 to date. KRL 2007-08 to 2008-09. Federal Areas 2007-08 to 2011-12. ZTB 2009-10 to 2014-15. Hampshire 2013. Somerset (T20 only) 2015. IPL: RR 2007-09. **Tests** (P): 2 (2007-08); HS 13 and BB 3-83 v I (Delhi) 2007-08. **LOI** (P): 62 (2007-08 to 2014-15); HS 59 v Hong Kong (Karachi) 2008; BB 5-48 v SL (Karachi) 2008. **IT20** (P): 50 (2007 to 2015-16); HS 41 v SL (Dubai) 2013-14; BB 3-12 v SL (Hambantota) 2012. F-c Tour (P): I 2007-08. HS 163 ZTB v Lahore Lions (Lahore) 2014-15. CC HS 38 and CC BB 3-62 H v Glamorgan (Cardiff) 2013. BB 8-54 (15-174 match) KRL v PIA (Mirpur) 2008-09. LO HS 93 KRL v SSGC (Rawalpindi) 2008-09. LO BB 7-34 KRL v WAPDA (Lahore) 2007-08. T20 HS 60*. T20 BB 6-14.

[NQ]**THOMAS, Alfonso** Clive (Ravensmead SS; Parow HS), b Cape Town, South Africa 9 Feb 1977. 5'10". RHB, RFM. W Province 1998-99. North West 2000-01 to 2002-03. Northerns 2003-04 to 2005-06. Titans 2004-05 to 2007-08. Warwickshire 2007. Somerset 2008-15; cap 2008 (Kolpak registration). **IT20** (SA): 1 (2006-07); HS – and BB 3-25 v P (Johannesburg) 2006-07. F-c Tour (SA A): Z 2004. HS 119* NW v Northerns (Pretoria) 2002-03. UK HS 94 v Hants (Taunton) 2011. 50 wkts (1): 57 (2014). BB 7-54 Titans v Cobras (Cape Town) 2005-06. UK BB 6-60 (10-88 match) v Sussex (Taunton) 2011 and 6-60 v Warwks (Taunton) 2012. LO HS 49* v Kent (Taunton) 2014 (RLC). LO BB 4-18 v Glos (Bristol) 2009 (P40). T20 HS 30*. T20 BB 5-24.

G.H.Dockrell and J.A.Regan left the staff without making a County 1st XI appearance in 2015.

SOMERSET 2015

RESULTS SUMMARY

	Place	Won	Lost	Tied	Drew	NR
LV= County Championship (1st Division)	6th	4	6		6	
All First-Class Matches		4	6		8	
Royal London One-Day Cup (Group A)	6th	4	4			
NatWest t20 Blast (South Group)	8th	4	8			2

LV= COUNTY CHAMPIONSHIP AVERAGES

BATTING AND FIELDING

Cap		M	I	NO	HS	Runs	Avge	100	50	Ct/St
2007	J.C.Hildreth	16	27	1	220*	1390	53.46	3	8	7
1999	M.E.Trescothick	16	29	1	210*	1284	45.85	3	8	28
	T.B.Abell	13	24	4	131	726	36.30	1	5	5
2007	P.D.Trego	16	27	3	130*	871	36.29	2	4	7
	C.Overton	11	14	3	55	320	29.09	–	3	9
	T.L.W.Cooper	13	22	–	118	581	26.40	1	2	6
	L.Ronchi	4	5	–	51	121	24.20	–	1	14/3
	J.G.Myburgh	10	19	2	118	411	24.17	1	2	6
	J.Allenby	16	27	1	64	568	21.84	–	4	15
	J.Overton	8	10	3	50	146	20.85	–	1	–
	Abdur Rehman	8	13	4	55*	153	17.00	–	1	1
	M.J.Leach	5	5	2	21*	43	14.33	–	–	1
2015	L.Gregory	12	19	1	32	242	13.44	–	–	11
	A.W.R.Barrow	6	11	2	28	120	13.33	–	–	12
2008	A.C.Thomas	7	10	4	32*	79	13.16	–	–	6
	T.D.Groenewald	9	16	2	34	142	10.14	–	–	4
	M.D.Bates	6	9	3	16	53	8.83	–	–	13

BOWLING

	O	M	R	W	Avge	Best	5wI	10wM
C.Overton	282.2	55	933	43	21.69	6- 74	1	–
A.C.Thomas	237.4	54	735	29	25.34	5- 73	1	–
M.J.Leach	145.1	37	391	15	26.06	7-106	1	1
T.D.Groenewald	272	47	976	30	32.53	4- 41	–	–
L.Gregory	341.1	47	1314	38	34.57	6-101	3	–
P.D.Trego	268.3	52	946	26	36.38	4- 73	–	–
J.Allenby	261	70	657	18	36.50	3- 54	–	–
J.Overton	179.5	32	612	16	38.25	4- 37	–	–
Abdur Rehman	206.2	34	719	10	71.90	2- 60	–	–

Also bowled:
T.L.W.Cooper	65	6	226	6	37.66	5- 76	1	–

T.B.Abell 4.4-0-11-1; J.G.Myburgh 55-13-162-3.

The First-Class Averages (pp 227–243) give the records of Somerset players in all first-class county matches (Somerset's other opponents being Durham MCCU and the New Zealanders), with the exception of L.Ronchi, whose first-class figures for Somerset are as above.

SOMERSET RECORDS

FIRST-CLASS CRICKET

Highest Total	For 850-7d		v	Middlesex	Taunton	2007
	V 811		by	Surrey	The Oval	1899
Lowest Total	For 25		v	Glos	Bristol	1947
	V 22		by	Glos	Bristol	1920
Highest Innings	For 342	J.L.Langer	v	Surrey	Guildford	2006
	V 424	A.C.MacLaren	for	Lancashire	Taunton	1895

Highest Partnership for each Wicket

1st	346	L.C.H.Palairet / H.T.Hewett	v	Yorkshire	Taunton	1892
2nd	450	N.R.D.Compton / J.C.Hildreth	v	Cardiff MCCU	Taunton Vale	2012
3rd	319	P.M.Roebuck / M.D.Crowe	v	Leics	Taunton	1984
4th	310	P.W.Denning / I.T.Botham	v	Glos	Taunton	1980
5th	320	J.D.Francis / I.D.Blackwell	v	Durham UCCE	Taunton	2005
6th	265	W.E.Alley / K.E.Palmer	v	Northants	Northampton	1961
7th	279	R.J.Harden / G.D.Rose	v	Sussex	Taunton	1997
8th	172	I.V.A.Richards / I.T.Botham	v	Leics	Leicester	1983
	172	A.R.K.Pierson / P.S.Jones	v	N Zealanders	Taunton	1999
9th	183	C.H.M.Greetham / H.W.Stephenson	v	Leics	Weston-s-Mare	1963
	183	C.J.Tavaré / N.A.Mallender	v	Sussex	Hove	1990
10th	163	I.D.Blackwell / N.A.M.McLean	v	Derbyshire	Taunton	2003

Best Bowling	For	10- 49	E.J.Tyler	v	Surrey	Taunton	1895
(Innings)	V	10- 35	A.Drake	for	Yorkshire	Weston-s-Mare	1914
Best Bowling	For	16- 83	J.C.White	v	Worcs	Bath	1919
(Match)	V	17-137	W.Brearley	for	Lancashire	Manchester	1905

Most Runs – Season	2761	W.E.Alley	(av 58.74)		1961
Most Runs – Career	21142	H.Gimblett	(av 36.96)		1935-54
Most 100s – Season	11	S.J.Cook			1991
Most 100s – Career	49	H.Gimblett			1935-54
Most Wkts – Season	169	A.W.Wellard	(av 19.24)		1938
Most Wkts – Career	2165	J.C.White	(av 18.03)		1909-37
Most Career W-K Dismissals	1007	H.W.Stephenson	(698 ct; 309 st)		1948-64
Most Career Catches in the Field	381	J.C.White			1909-37

LIMITED-OVERS CRICKET

Highest Total	50ov	413-4		v	Devon	Torquay	1990
	40ov	377-9		v	Sussex	Hove	2003
	T20	250-3		v	Glos	Taunton	2006
Lowest Total	50ov	58		v	Middlesex	Southgate	2000
	40ov	58		v	Essex	Chelmsford	1977
	T20	82		v	Kent	Taunton	2010
Highest Innings	50ov	177	S.J.Cook	v	Sussex	Hove	1990
	40ov	184	M.E.Trescothick	v	Glos	Taunton	2008
	T20	151*	C.H.Gayle	v	Kent	Taunton	2015
Best Bowling	50ov	8-66	S.R.G.Francis	v	Derbyshire	Derby	2004
	40ov	6-16	Abdur Rehman	v	Notts	Taunton	2012
	T20	6- 5	A.V.Suppiah	v	Glamorgan	Cardiff	2011

SURREY

Formation of Present Club: 22 August 1845
Inaugural First-Class Match: 1864
Colours: Chocolate
Badge: Prince of Wales' Feathers
County Champions (since 1890): (18) 1890, 1891, 1892, 1894, 1895, 1899, 1914, 1952, 1953, 1954, 1955, 1956, 1957, 1958, 1971, 1999, 2000, 2002
Joint Champions: (1) 1950
NatWest Trophy Winners: (1) 1982
Benson and Hedges Cup Winners: (3) 1974, 1997, 2001
Pro 40/National League (Div 1) Winners: (1) 2003
Sunday League Winners: (1) 1996
Clydesdale Bank 40 Winners: (1) 2011
Twenty20 Cup Winners: (1) 2003

Chief Executive: Richard Gould, The Kia Oval, London, SE11 5SS • Tel: 0844 376 1845 • Fax: 020 7820 5601 • E-mail: enquiries@surreycricket.com • Web: www.kiaoval.com • Twitter: @surreycricket (45,030 followers)

Director of Cricket: Alec Stewart. **Head Coach**: Michael Di Venuto. **Player/Coach**: Azhar Mahmood. **Captain**: G.J.Batty. **Vice-Captain**: tba. **Overseas Players**: D.J.Bravo (T20 only), A.J.Finch, C.Morris (T20 only), K.C.Sangakkara. **2016 Beneficiary**: None. **Head Groundsman**: Lee Fortiss. **Scorer**: Keith Booth. ‡ New registration. ᴺᑫ Not qualified for England.

ANSARI, Zafar Shahaan (Hampton S; Trinity Hall, Cambridge), b Ascot, Berks 10 Dec 1991. Younger brother of A.S.Ansari (Cambridge U 2008-13). 5'11". LHB, SLA. Squad No 22. Cambridge MCCU 2011-13. Surrey debut 2011; cap 2014. MCC 2015. Surrey 2nd XI debut 2008, aged 16y 133d. **LOI**: 1 (2015) did not bat or bowl. 1000 runs (1): 1029 (2014). HS 112 v Glamorgan (Colwyn Bay) 2014. BB 6-30 v Glos (Oval) 2015. LO HS 66* v Yorks (Oval) 2013 (RLC). LO BB 4-42 v Scotland (Oval) 2013 (Y40). T20 HS 67*. T20 BB 3-17.

ᴺᑫ**AZHAR MAHMOOD** Sagar (F.G. No. 1 HS, Islamabad), b Rawalpindi, Pakistan 28 Feb 1975. 6'0". RHB, RMF. Islamabad 1993-94 to 2006-07. United Bank 1995-96 to 1996-97. Rawalpindi 1998-99 to 2004-05. PIA 2001-02. Surrey debut 2002; cap 2004. HB 2006-07 to 2010-11. Kent 2008-12, (British passport holder) scoring 116 v Notts (Canterbury) on debut; cap 2008. MCC 2001. Returned to Surrey in 2015 for l-o and T20 only. IPL: KXIP 2012-13. Big Bash: ST 2012-13. **Tests** (P): 21 (1997-98 to 2001); HS 136 v SA (Johannesburg) 1997-98; BB 4-50 v E (Lord's) 2001. Scored 128* and 50* v SA (Rawalpindi) 1997-98 on debut. **LOI** (P): 143 (1996-97 to 2006-07); HS 67 v I (Adelaide) 1999-00; BB 6-18 v WI (Sharjah) 1999-00. F-c Tours (P): E 1997 (Pak A), 2001; A 1999-00; SA 1997-98; I 1998-99; SL 2000; Z 1997-98. HS 204* v Middx (Oval) 2005. 50 wkts (0+1): 59 (1996-97). BB 8-61 v Lancs (Oval) 2002. LO HS 101* v Glamorgan (Oval) 2006 (CGT). LO BB 6-18 (*see LOI*). T20 HS 106*. T20 BB 5-24.

BATTY, Gareth Jon (Bingley GS), b Bradford, Yorks 13 Oct 1977. Younger brother of J.D.Batty (Yorkshire and Somerset 1989-96). 5'11". RHB, OB. Squad No 13. Yorkshire 1997. Surrey 1999-2001, rejoined in 2010; cap 2011; captain 2015. Worcestershire 2002-09. MCC 2012. **Tests**: 7 (2003-04 to 2005); HS 38 v SL (Kandy) 2003-04; BB 3-55 v SL (Galle) 2003-04. Took wicket with his third ball in Test cricket. **LOI**: 10 (2002-03 to 2008-09); HS 17 v WI (Bridgetown) 2008-09; BB 2-40 v WI (Gros Islet, St Lucia) 2003-04. **IT20**: 1 (2008-09); HS 4 v WI (Port of Spain) 2008-09. F-c Tours: WI 2003-04 (Eng A); NZ 2008-09 (Eng A); WI 2002-03 (ECB Acad); SL 2003-04; B 2003-04. HS 133 Wo v Surrey (Oval) 2004. Sy HS 79 v Essex (Croydon) 2011. 50 wkts (2); most – 60 (2003). BB 8-68 v Essex (Chelmsford) 2014. LO HS 83* v Yorks (Oval) 2001 (NL). LO BB 5-35 Wo v Hants (Southampton) 2009 (FPT). T20 HS 87. T20 BB 4-13.

‡NOBRAVO, Dwayne John, b Santa Cruz, Trinidad 7 Oct 1983. Older half-brother of D.M.Bravo (Trinidad & Tobago, Nottinghamshire and WI 2006-07 to date). RHB, RMF. Trinidad & Tobago 2001-02 to 2012-13. Kent 2006. IPL: MI 2007-08 to 2009-10. CSK 2011 to date. Big Bash: SS 2011-12. MR 2013-14 to date. Joins Surrey in 2016 for T20 only. **Tests** (WI): 40 (2004 to 2010-11, 1 as captain); HS 113 v A (Hobart) 2005-06; BB 6-55 v E (Manchester) 2004. **LOI** (WI): 164 (2004 to 2014-15, 37 as captain); HS 112* v E (Ahmedabad) 2006-07; BB 6-43 v Z (St George's) 2012-13. **IT20** (WI): 55 (2005-06 to 2015-16, 6 as captain); HS 66* v I (Lord's) 2009; BB 4-28 v SL (Colombo, RPS) 2015-16. F-c Tours (WI): E 2002 (WI A), 2004, 2007; A 2005-06, 2009-10; SA 2007-08; NZ 2005-06; P 2006-07; SL 2010-11. The 197 T&T v West Indies B (Couva) 2003-04. CC HS 76 K v Lancs (Canterbury) 2006. BB 6-11 T&T v Windward Is (St George's) 2002-03. CC BB 6-112 K v Notts (Nottingham) 2006. LO HS 112* (see LOI). LO BB 6-43 (see LOI). T20 HS 70*. T20 BB 5-23.

BURKE, James Edward (Plymouth C), b Plymouth, Devon 25 Jan 1991. 6'2". RHB, RMF. Squad No 8. Somerset 2012. Surrey debut 2015. Devon 2008-13. HS 79 v Derbys (Oval) 2015. BB 4-19 v Leics (Leicester) 2015. LO HS 26* v Northants (Oval) 2015 (RLC). LO BB 5-28 v Derbys (Guildford) 2015 (RLC). T20 HS 8. T20 BB 3-23.

BURNS, Rory Joseph (City of London Freemen's S), b Epsom 26 Aug 1990. 5'10". LHB, WK, occ RM. Squad No 17. Debut (Surrey) 2011; cap 2014. MCC Univs 2010. 1000 runs (2); most – 1055 (2014). HS 199 v Glos (Bristol) 2014. BB 1-18 v Middx (Lord's) 2013. LO HS 95 v Glos (Bristol) 2015 (RLC). T20 HS 46*.

CURRAN, Samuel Matthew (Wellington C), b Northampton 3 Jun 1998. Son of K.M.Curran (Glos, Natal, Northants, Boland and Zimbabwe 1980-81 to 1999); grandson of K.P.Curran (Rhodesia 1947-48 to 1954-55); younger brother of T.K.Curran (see below). 5'8". LHB, LMF. Squad No 58. Debut (Surrey) 2015, taking 5-101 v Kent (Oval). Surrey 2nd XI debut 2013. HS 61* v Northants (Oval) 2015. BB 5-67 v Lancs (Manchester) 2015. LO HS 42 v Glos (Bristol) 2015 (RLC). LO BB 4-32 v Northants (Oval) 2015 (RLC). T20 HS 17*. T20 BB 3-17.

CURRAN, Thomas Kevin (Hilton C, Durban), b Cape Town, South Africa 12 Mar 1995. Son of K.M.Curran (Glos, Natal, Northants, Boland and Zimbabwe 1980-81 to 1999); grandson of K.P.Curran (Rhodesia 1947-48 to 1954-55); elder brother of S.M.Curran (see above). 6'0". RHB, RMF. Squad No 59. Debut (Surrey) 2014. Surrey 2nd XI debut 2013. YC 2015. HS 60 v Leics (Leicester) 2015. 50 wkts (1): 76 (2015). BB 7-20 v Glos (Oval) 2015. LO HS 44 v Yorks (Oval) 2015 (RLC). LO BB 5-34 v Scotland (Oval) 2013 (Y40). T20 HS 41. T20 BB 4-35.

DAVIES, Steven Michael (King Charles I S, Kidderminster), b Bromsgrove, Worcs 17 Jun 1986. 5'10". LHB, WK. Squad No 9. Worcestershire 2005-09. Surrey debut 2010; cap 2011. MCC 2006-07, 2011. **LOI**: 8 (2009-10 to 2010-11); HS 87 v P (Chester-le-St) 2010. **IT20**: 5 (2008-09 to 2010-11); HS 33 v P (Cardiff) 2010. F-c Tours: A 2010-11; B 2006-07 (Eng A); UAE 2011-12 (v P). 1000 runs (5); most – 1090 (2010). HS 200* v Glamorgan (Cardiff) 2015. LO HS 127* v Hants (Oval) 2013 (Y40). T20 HS 99*.

DERNBACH, Jade Winston (St John the Baptist S), b Johannesburg, South Africa 3 Mar 1986. 6'1½". RHB, RFM. Squad No 16. Italian passport. UK resident since 1998. Debut (Surrey) 2003; cap 2011. **LOI**: 24 (2011 to 2013); HS 5 v SL (Leeds) 2011; BB 4-45 v P (Dubai) 2011-12. **IT20**: 34 (2011 to 2013-14); HS 12 v I (Colombo, RPS) 2012-13; BB 4-22 v I (Manchester) 2011. F-c Tour (EL): WI 2010-11. HS 56* v Northants (Northampton) 2010. 50 wkts (1): 51 (2010). BB 6-47 v Leics (Leicester) 2009. LO HS 31 v Somerset (Taunton) 2010 (CB40). LO BB 6-35 v Glos (Lord's) 2015 (RLC). T20 HS 24*. T20 BB 4-22.

DUNN, Matthew Peter (Bearwood C, Wokingham), b Egham 5 May 1992. 6'1''. LHB, RFM. Squad No 4. Debut (Surrey) 2010. MCC 2015. Surrey 2nd XI debut 2009. England U19s 2010. HS 31* v Kent (Guildford) 2014. BB 5-48 v Glos (Oval) 2014. LO HS – . LO BB 2-32 England Dev XI v Sri Lanka A (Manchester) 2011. T20 HS 2. BB 3-8.

‡^{NQ}**FINCH, Aaron** James, b Colac, Victoria, Australia 17 Nov 1986. 5'9''. RHB, SLA. Victoria 2007-08 to date. Yorkshire 2014-15. IPL: RR: 2009-10. DD 2011-12. PW 2013. SH 2014. MI 2015. Big Bash: MR 2011-12 to date. **LOI** (A): 57 (2012-13 to 2015-16); HS 148 v Scotland (Edinburgh) 2013; BB 1-2 v I (Pune) 2013-14. **IT20** (A): 26 (2010-11 to 2015-16); HS 156 v E (Southampton) 2013 – world record IT20 score. F-c Tours (Aus A): SA/Z 2013; Z 2011. HS 122 Cricket A v New Zealanders (Sydney) 2015-16. CC HS 110 Y v Warwks (Birmingham) 2014. BB 1-0 Vic v WA (Perth) 2013-14. CC BB 1-20 Y v Sussex (Arundel) 2014. LO HS 154 Vic v Q (Brisbane) 2012-13. LO BB 2-44 Aus A v EL (Hobart) 2012-13. T20 HS 156. T20 BB 1-9.

FOAKES, Benjamin Thomas (Tendring TC), b Colchester, Essex 15 Feb 1993. 6'1''. RHB, WK. Squad No 7. Essex 2011-14. Surrey debut 2015. Essex 2nd XI debut 2008, aged 15y 172d. England U19 2010-11. F-c Tour (EL): SL 2013-14. HS 140* v Glos (Bristol) 2015. LO HS 56 EL v Australia A (Hobart) 2012-13. T20 HS 49.

‡**FOOTITT, Mark** Harold Alan (Carlton le Willows S; West Notts C), b Nottingham 25 Nov 1985. 6'2''. RHB, LFM. Nottinghamshire 2005-09. MCC 2006. No f-c appearances in 2008. Derbyshire 2010-15; cap 2014. F-c Tour: SA 2015-16. HS 34 De v Leics (Leicester) 2015. 50 wkts (2); most – 84 (2014). BB 7-71 De v Leics (Derby) 2015. LO HS 11* v Notts (Nottingham) 2014 (RLC). LO BB 5-28 De v Scotland (Edinburgh) 2013 (Y40). T20 HS 2*. T20 BB 3-22.

HARINATH, Arun (Tiffin Boys GS; Loughborough U), b Sutton 26 Mar 1987. 5'11''. LHB, OB. Squad No 10. Loughborough UCCE 2007-09. Surrey debut 2009. MCC 2008. Buckinghamshire 2007-08. HS 154 v Derbys (Derby) 2013. BB 2-1 v Glamorgan (Colwyn Bay) 2014. LO HS 52 v Derbys (Oval) 2013 (Y40). LO BB – .

KAPIL, Aneesh (Denstone C), b Wolverhampton 3 Aug 1993. 5'10''. RHB, RFM. Squad No 47. Worcestershire 2011-13. Surrey debut 2014. Worcestershire 2nd XI debut 2008, aged 15y 10d. HS 104* v New Zealand A (Oval) 2013. CC HS 54 Wo v Sussex (Horsham) 2011. BB 3-17 Wo v Notts (Worcester) 2012. Sy BB 2-23 v Kent (Canterbury) 2014. LO HS 59 v Somerset (Oval) 2014 (RLC). LO BB 1-18 Wo v Netherlands (Worcester) 2011 (CB40). T20 HS 13. T20 BB 3-9.

‡**McKERR, Conor** (St John's C, Johannesburg), b 19 Jan 1998. 6'6''. RHB, RFM. SA U19 ODI 2014-15 to 2015. UK passport. Awaiting senior debut.

MEAKER, Stuart Christopher (Cranleigh S), b Durban, South Africa 21 Jan 1989. Moved to UK in 2001. 5'11''. RHB, RFM. Squad No 18. Debut (Surrey) 2008; cap 2012. **LOI**: 2 (2011-12); HS 1 and BB 1-45 v I (Mumbai) 2011-12. **IT20**: 2 (2012-13); HS – ; BB 1-28 v I (Pune) 2012-13. F-c Tour: I 2012-13. HS 94 v Bangladeshis (Oval) 2010. CC HS 72 v Essex (Colchester) 2009. 50 wkts (1): 51 (2012). BB 8-52 (11-167 match) v Somerset (Oval) 2012. LO HS 21* v Glamorgan (Oval) 2012 (CB40). LO BB 4-47 EL v Bangladesh A (Chittagong) 2011-12. T20 HS 17. T20 BB 4-30.

‡^{NQ}**MORRIS, Chris**topher Henry, b Pretoria, South Africa 20 Apr 1987. Son of W.F.Morris (N Transvaal 1979-80 to 1991-92). RHB, RFM. North West 2009-10 to 2011-12. Lions 2011-12 to 2014-15. Titans 2015-16. IPL: CSK 2013. RR 2015. Joins Surrey in 2016 for T20 only. **Tests** (SA): 2 (2015-16); HS 69 v E (Cape Town) 2015-16 – on debut; BB 1-8 v E (Johannesburg) 2015-16. **LOI** (SA): 11 (2013 to 2015-16); HS 62 v E (Johannesburg) 2015-16; BB 3-74 v E (Bloemfontein) 2015-16. **IT20** (SA): 8 (2012-13 to 2015-16); HS 17* v E (Cape Town) 2015-16; BB 2-16 v I (Cuttack) 2015-16. HS 154 NW v Easterns (Potchefstroom) 2010-11. BB 8-44 (12-101 match) Lions v Dolphins (Johannesburg) 2012-13. LO HS 90* NW v SW Districts (Potchefstroom) 2010-11. LO BB 4-30 NW v KZN (Durban) 2010-11. T20 HS 41. T20 BB 4-9.

‡^{NQ}**PILLANS, Mathew** William (Pretoria BHS; U of Pretoria), b Durban, South Africa 4 Jul 1991. 6'4". RHB, RF. Northerns 2012-13. KwaZula Natal Inland 2013-14 to date. Dolphins 2013-14 to date. Somerset 2nd XI 2014. HS 49 KZN v Easterns (Benoni) 2015-16. BB 6-67 (10-129 match) Dolphins v Knights (Durban) 2014-15. LO HS 20* KZN v NW (Pietermaritzburg) 2013-14. LO BB 3-14 KZN v Namibia (Pietermaritzburg) 2015-16. T20 HS 23. T20 BB 3-15.

ROY, Jason Jonathan (Whitgift S), b Durban, South Africa 21 Jul 1990. 6'0". RHB, RM. Squad No 20. Debut (Surrey) 2010; cap 2014. LOI: 20 (2015 to 2015-16); HS 102 v P (Dubai, DSC) 2015-16. **IT20**: 8 (2014 to 2015-16); HS 29 v P (Dubai, DSC) 2015-16. 1000 runs (1): 1078 (2014). HS 143 v Lancs (Oval) 2015. BB 3-9 v Glos (Bristol) 2014. LO HS 141 EL v SA A (Kimberley) 2014-15. LO BB – . T20 HS 122* v Somerset (Oval) 2015 – Sy record. T20 BB 1-23.

^{NQ}**SANGAKKARA, Kumar** Chokshanada (Trinity C, Kandy; Colombo U), b Matale, Sri Lanka, 27 Oct 1977. 5'11". LHB, WK, occ OB. Squad No 11. Nondescripts 1997-98 to 2007-08. Central Province 2003-04 to 2004-05. Warwickshire 2007; cap 2007. Durham 2014. Surrey debut/cap 2015. IPL: KXIP 2007-10. DC 2011-12. SH 2013. Big Bash: HH 2015-16. *Wisden* 2011. **Tests** (SL): 134 (2000 to 2015, 15 as captain); 1000 runs (5); most – 1438 (2014); HS 319 v B (Chittagong) 2013-14 (also scored 105 to become only the 2nd man, after G.A.Gooch, to score a treble century and a century in the same match). Scored 287 v SA (Colombo, SSC) 2006, sharing in world record f-c partnership for any wkt of 624 with D.P.M.D.Jayawardena; BB – . **LOI** (SL): 397 (2000 to 2014-15, 45 as captain; +4 for Asia XI, 2 for ICC World XI); 1000 runs (6); most – 1333 (2006); HS 169 v SA (Colombo, RPS) 2013. **IT20** (SL): 56 (2006 to 2013-14, 22 as captain); HS 78 v I (Nagpur) 2009-10. F-c Tours (SL) (C=Captain): E 2002, 2006, 2011, 2014; A 2004, 2007-08, 2012-13; SA 1999-00 (SL A), 2000-01, 2002-03, 2011-12; WI 2003, 2007-08; NZ 2004-05, 2006-07, 2014-15; I 2005-06, 2009-10C; P 2001-02, 2004-05, 2008-09; Z 2004, 2008-09; B 2005-06, 2008-09, 2013-14; UAE 2011-12 (v P), 2013-14 (v P). 1000 runs (v P): 1191 (2003-04). HS 319 (*see Tests*). CC HS 159 Du v Sussex (Hove) 2014. Sy HS 149 v Glamorgan (Cardiff) 2015. BB 1-13 SL v Zim A (Harare) 2004. LO HS 169 (*see LOI*). T20 HS 94.

SIBLEY, Dominic Peter (Whitgift S, Croydon), b Epsom 5 Sep 1995. 6'0". RHB, LB. Squad No 45. Debut (Surrey) 2013. Surrey 2nd XI debut 2011, aged 15y 302d. England U19s 2012-13 to 2014. HS 242 v Yorks (Oval) 2013. LO HS 37 v Durham (Chester-le-St) 2013 (Y40).

VAN DEN BERGH, Frederick Oliver Edward (Whitgift S, Croydon; Hatfield C, Durham U), b Farnborough, Kent 14 Jun 1992. 6'0". RHB, SLA. Squad No 5. Debut (Surrey) 2011. Durham MCCU 2013-14. Surrey 2nd XI debut, aged 16y 326d. Summer contract. No 1st XI appearances in 2015. HS 34 and BB 4-84 DU v Notts (Nottingham) 2013. Sy HS 16* v Leeds/Bradford MCCU (Oval) 2012. Sy BB 3-79 v Cambridge MCCU (Cambridge) 2011. LO HS 29* v Sussex (Oval) 2014 (RLC). LO BB – .

NQWILSON, Gary Craig (Methodist C, Belfast; Manchester Met U), b Dundonald, N Ireland 5 Feb 1986. 5'10". RHB, WK. Squad No 14. Ireland 2005 to date. Surrey debut 2010; cap 2014. MCC YC 2005. LOI (Ire): 63 (2007 to 2015-16); HS 113 v Netherlands (Dublin) 2010. IT20 (Ire): 45 (2008 to 2015-16); HS 45 v PNG (Townsville) 2015-16. HS 160* v Leics (Oval) 2014. BB - . LO HS 113 (*see LOI*). T20 HS 63*.

RELEASED/RETIRED

(Having made a County 1st XI appearance in 2015)

NQELGAR, Dean, b Welkom, OFS, South Africa 11 Jun 1987. LHB, SLA. Free State 2005-06 to 2010-11. Eagles 2006-07 to 2009-10. Knights 2010-11 to 2013-14. Somerset 2013. Titans 2014-15 to date. Surrey 2015. Tests (SA): 25 (2012-13 to 2015-16); HS 121 v WI (Pt Elizabeth) 2014-15; BB 4-22 v I (Mohali) 2015-16. LOI (SA): 5 (2012); HS 42 v E (Oval) 2012; BB 1-11 v E (Southampton) 2012. F-c Tours (SA): A 2012-13; I 2015-16; SL 2010 (SA A), 2014; Z 2014; B 2010 (SA A), 2015; UAE (v P) 2013-14; Ire 2012 (SA A). 1000 runs (0+1): 1193 (2009-10). HS 268 SA A v Australia A (Pretoria) 2013. Sy HS 98 v Glos (Oval) 2015. CC BB 1-26 Sm v Durham (Taunton) 2013. BB 4-22 (*see Tests*). LO HS 117 Knights v Dolphins (Pietermaritzburg) 2011-12. LO BB 3-43 Titans v Dolphins (Durban) 2014-15. T20 HS 72. T20 BB 4-23.

NQHENRIQUES, Moises Constantino, b Funchal, Madeira, Portugal 1 Feb 1987. 6'1½". RHB, RFM. New South Wales 2006-07 to date. Glamorgan 2012. Surrey 2015 (T20 only). IPL: KKR 2009. DD 2009-10. RCB 2013. SH 2014-15. Big Bash: SS 2011-12 to date. Tests (A): 3 (2012-13); HS 81* and BB 1-48 v I (Chennai) 2012-13. LOI (A): 6 (2009-10 to 2014-15); HS 12 v I (Delhi) 2009-10; BB 3-32 v SL (Hobart) 2012-13. IT20 (A): 4 (2009-10 to 2013-14); HS 12 v I (Rajkot) 2013-14; BB 2-35 v E (Hobart) 2013-14. F-c Tours (A): SA/Z 2013 (Aus A); I 2012-13; Scot/Ire 2013 (Aus A). HS 161* NSW v Tas (Sydney) 2012-13. BB 5-17 NSW v Q (Brisbane) 2006-07. LO HS 131 NSW v Vic (Sydney) 2014-15. LO BB 4-17 NSW v Tas (Sydney) 2013-14. T20 HS 77. T20 BB 3-11.

LINLEY, Timothy Edward (St Mary's RC CS, Menston; Notre Dame SFC; Oxford Brookes U), b Leeds, Yorks 23 Mar 1982. 6'2". RHB, RFM. Squad No 12. Oxford UCCE 2003-05. British U 2004. Sussex 2006 (1 match) and 2015 (on loan). Surrey 2009-15. HS 42 OU v Derbys (Oxford) 2005. Sy HS 36 v Kent (Canterbury) 2009. 50 wkts (1): 73 (2011). BB 6-57 v Leics (Leicester) 2011. LO HS 20* v Warwks (Oval) 2009 (P40). LO BB 3-50 v Hants (Croydon) 2011 (CB40). T20 HS 8. T20 BB 4-45.

PIETERSEN, Kevin Peter (Maritzburg C; Natal U), b Pietermaritzburg, South Africa 27 Jun 1980. British passport (English mother) – qualified for England Oct 2004. 6'4". RHB, OB. Natal/KZN 1997-98 to 1999-00. Nottinghamshire 2001-04; cap 2002. Hampshire 2005-08; cap 2005 (no f-c appearances 2006-07, 2009-10). Surrey 2010-15. Dolphins 2010-11. MCC 2004. IPL: RCB 2009-10. DD 2012-14. Big Bash: MS 2014-15 to date. MBE 2005. Wisden 2005. Tests: 104 (2005 to 2013-14, 3 as captain); 1000 runs (4); most – 1343 (2006); HS 227 v A (Adelaide) 2010-11; BB 3-52 v SA (Leeds) 2012. LOI: 134 (2004-05 to 2013, 12 as captain; +2 for ICC World XI); HS 130 v P (Dubai) 2011-12; BB 2-22 v SA (Leeds) 2008. IT20: 37 (2005 to 2013); HS 79 v Z (Cape Town) 2007-08; BB 1-27 v SA (Centurion) 2009-10. F-c Tours: A 2006-07, 2010-11, 2013-14; SA 2009-10; WI 2008-09; NZ 2007-08, 2012-13; I 2003-04 (Eng A), 2005-06, 2008-09 (Captain), 2012-13; P 2005-06; SL 2007-08, 2011-12; B 2009-10; UAE 2011-12 (v P). 1000 runs (3); most – 1546 (2003). HS 355* v Leics (Oval) 2015 – record score v Le. BB 4-31 Nt v Durham U (Nottingham) 2003. CC BB 3-72 Nt v Hants (Nottingham) 2004. Sy BB 2-24 v Notts (Oval) 2012. LO HS 147 Nt v Somerset (Taunton) 2002 (NL). LO BB 3-14 Nt v Middx (Lord's) 2004 (NL). T20 HS 115*. T20 BB 3-33.

175

SOLANKI, Vikram Singh (Regis S, Wolverhampton), b Udaipur, India 1 Apr 1976. 6'0''. RHB, OB, occ WK. Worcestershire 1995-2012; cap 1998; captain 2005-10; benefit 2007. Rajasthan 2006-07. Surrey 2013-15; cap 2014. **LOI**: 51 (1999-00 to 2006); HS 106 v SA (Oval) 2003; BB 1-17 v SL (Leeds) 2006. **IT20**: 3 (2005 to 2007-08); HS 43 v I (Durban) 2007-08. F-c Tours (Eng A): SA 1998-99, 1999-00 (Eng – *part*); WI 2000-01, 2005-06 (Captain); NZ 1999-00; SL 2004-05; Z 1996-97 (Wo), 1998-99; B 1999-00. 1000 runs (6); most – 1339 (1999). HS 270 Wo v Glos (Cheltenham) 2008, sharing Wo 2nd wkt record partnership of 316 with S.C.Moore. Sy HS 162 v Warwks (Birmingham) 2013. Won Walter Lawrence Trophy in 2009 with 49-ball hundred v Glamorgan (Worcester). BB 5-40 Wo v Middx (Lord's) 2004. Sy BB 2-20 v Hants (Oval) 2014. LO HS 164* Wo v Worcs CB (Worcester) 2003 (CGT). LO BB 4-14 Wo v Somerset (Taunton) 2006 (P40). T20 HS 100. T20 BB 1-6.

TREMLETT, Christopher Timothy (Thornden S, Chandler's Ford; Taunton's C, South-ampton), b Southampton, Hants 2 Sep 1981. Son of T.M.Tremlett (Hampshire 1976-91); grandson of M.F.Tremlett (Somerset, CD and England 1947-60). 6'7''. RHB, RFM. Hampshire 2000-09, taking wicket of M.H.Richardson (NZ A) with his first ball; cap 2004. Surrey 2010-15; cap 2014. **Tests**: 12 (2007 to 2013-14); HS 25* v I (Oval) 2007; BB 6-48 v SL (Southampton) 2011. **LOI**: 15 (2005 to 2010-11); HS 19* v I (Birmingham) 2007; BB 4-32 v B (Nottingham) 2005 – on debut (hat-trick ball hit stump without dislodging bails). **IT20**: 1 (2007-08); BB 2-45 v I (Durban) 2007-08. F-c Tours: A 2010-11, 2013-14; SL 2002-03 (ECB Acad); UAE 2011-12 (v P). HS 90 v Leics (Oval) 2014. BB 8-96 v Durham (Chester-le-St) 2013. Hat-trick: H v Notts (Nottingham) 2005. LO HS 38* H v Cheshire (Alderley Edge) 2004 (CGT). LO BB 4-25 H v Essex (Southend) 2002 (NL). T20 HS 13. T20 BB 4-16.

NQ**WAHAB RIAZ**, b Lahore, Pakistan 28 Jun 1985. RHB, LFM. Lahore Whites 2001-02 to 2002-03. Karachi Port Trust 2003-04. Hyderabad 2003-04 to 2004-05. Lahore Ravi 2005-06 to 2006-07. NBP 2007-08 to 2014-15. Kent 2011. Lahore Shalimar 2012-13. Surrey 2015 (T20 only). **Tests** (P): 15 (2010 to 2015-16); HS 27 and BB 5-63 v E (Oval) 2010 – on debut. **LOI** (P): 69 (2007-08 to 2015-16); HS 54* v Z (Brisbane) 2014-15; BB 5-46 v I (Mohali) 2010-11. **IT20** (P): 17 (2008 to 2015-16); HS 30* v NZ (Auckland) 2010-11; BB 3-34 v NZ (Auckland) 2015-16. F-c Tours (P): E 2010; A 2009 (P A); WI 2011; NZ 2010-11; SL 2009 (P A), 2014, 2015; B 2015; UAE 2010-11 (v SA), 2015-16 (v E). HS 84 NBP v WAPDA (Lahore) 2011-12. CC HS 34 K v Surrey (Canterbury) 2011. 50 wkts (0+2); most – 68 (2007-08). BB 9-59 (12-120 match) L Shalimar v L Ravi (Lahore) 2012-13. CC BB 4-94 K v Leics (Leicester) 2011. LO HS 77 NBP v PT (Rawalpindi) 2013-14. LO BB 5-24 NBP v SNGP (Sheikhupura) 2006-07. T20 HS 32*. T20 BB 5-17.

D.J.Balcombe left the staff without making a County 1st XI appearance in 2015.

SURREY 2015

RESULTS SUMMARY

	Place	Won	Lost	Tied	Drew	NR
LV= County Championship (2nd Division)	**1st**	8	1		7	
All First-Class Matches		8	1		7	
Royal London One-Day Cup (Group A)	Finalist	8	2			1
NatWest t20 Blast (South Group)	7th	5	6			3

LV= COUNTY CHAMPIONSHIP AVERAGES

BATTING AND FIELDING

Cap		M	I	NO	HS	Runs	Avge	100	50	Ct/St
	K.P.Pietersen	4	6	3	355*	469	156.33	1	1	1
	B.T.Foakes	10	16	4	140*	617	51.41	2	2	20/3
2011	S.M.Davies	12	19	3	200*	819	51.18	2	2	4
2014	R.J.Burns	14	24	3	158	1019	48.52	2	5	11
	S.M.Curran	6	8	3	61*	239	47.80	–	1	1
2014	G.C.Wilson	14	23	6	74*	811	47.70	–	6	40/1
2014	J.J.Roy	12	19	2	143	810	47.64	2	4	19
2015	K.C.Sangakkara	11	19	–	149	870	45.78	5	1	7
	A.Harinath	8	13	–	120	568	43.69	2	1	1
2014	Z.S.Ansari	14	22	1	106	771	36.71	1	4	8
2011	G.J.Batty	15	18	5	50*	388	29.84	–	2	5
	J.E.Burke	7	10	1	79	232	25.77	–	2	5
	D.P.Sibley	6	10	–	74	242	24.20	–	1	6
2014	C.T.Tremlett	3	5	1	30	85	21.25	–	–	1
	T.K.Curran	16	18	2	60	297	18.56	–	1	5
	M.P.Dunn	9	10	2	13	45	5.62	–	–	1

Also batted: J.W.Dernbach (4 matches – cap 2011) 0*, 1 (3 ct); D.Elgar (2) 44, 19, 98 (2 ct); L.J.Fletcher (3) 23, 2*, 14; A.Kapil (1) 21, 0; T.E.Linley (1) 0, 2*; S.C.Meaker (3 – cap 2012) 13, 0, 0; V.S.Solanki (1 – cap 2014) 1, 33 (2 ct).

BOWLING

	O	M	R	W	Avge	Best	5wI	10wM
J.E.Burke	104	19	347	16	21.68	4-19	–	–
T.K.Curran	544.4	129	1754	76	23.07	7-20	5	1
S.M.Curran	145.2	21	575	22	26.13	5-67	2	–
G.J.Batty	400	77	1127	40	28.17	6-51	2	–
Z.S.Ansari	425.3	71	1363	44	30.97	6-30	3	–
M.P.Dunn	253.4	37	984	28	35.14	4-72	–	–
Also bowled:								
L.J.Fletcher	54	10	155	8	19.37	4-58		
C.T.Tremlett	68	14	219	6	36.50	2-38		
S.C.Meaker	61.2	8	281	5	56.20	3-92		

R.J.Burns 6-1-12-0; J.W.Dernbach 80.2-27-204-2; A.Harinath 25.1-3-85-1; A.Kapil 12-1-68-2; T.E.Linley 20-6-67-1; K.P.Pietersen 2-0-8-0; J.J.Roy 24.4-2-115-3.

Surrey played no first-class fixtures outside the County Championship in 2015. The First-Class Averages (pp 227–243) give the records of Surrey players in all first-class county matches, with the exception of L.J.Fletcher and T.E.Linley, whose first-class figures for Surrey are as above.

SURREY RECORDS

FIRST-CLASS CRICKET

Highest Total	For 811		v	Somerset	The Oval	1899
	V 863		by	Lancashire	The Oval	1990
Lowest Total	For 14		v	Essex	Chelmsford	1983
	V 16		by	MCC	Lord's	1872
Highest Innings	For 357*	R.Abel	v	Somerset	The Oval	1899
	V 366	N.H.Fairbrother	for	Lancashire	The Oval	1990

Highest Partnership for each Wicket

1st	428	J.B.Hobbs/A.Sandham	v	Oxford U	The Oval	1926
2nd	371	J.B.Hobbs/E.G.Hayes	v	Hampshire	The Oval	1909
3rd	413	D.J.Bicknell/D.M.Ward	v	Kent	Canterbury	1990
4th	448	R.Abel/T.W.Hayward	v	Yorkshire	The Oval	1899
5th	318	M.R.Ramprakash/Azhar Mahmood	v	Middlesex	The Oval	2005
6th	298	A.Sandham/H.S.Harrison	v	Sussex	The Oval	1913
7th	262	C.J.Richards/K.T.Medlycott	v	Kent	The Oval	1987
8th	205	I.A.Greig/M.P.Bicknell	v	Lancashire	The Oval	1990
9th	168	E.R.T.Holmes/E.W.J.Brooks	v	Hampshire	The Oval	1936
10th	173	A.Ducat/A.Sandham	v	Essex	Leyton	1921

Best Bowling	For	10-43	T.Rushby	v	Somerset	Taunton	1921
(Innings)	V	10-28	W.P.Howell	for	Australians	The Oval	1899
Best Bowling	For	16-83	G.A.R.Lock	v	Kent	Blackheath	1956
(Match)	V	15-57	W.P.Howell	for	Australians	The Oval	1899

Most Runs – Season	3246	T.W.Hayward	(av 72.13)		1906
Most Runs – Career	43554	J.B.Hobbs	(av 49.72)		1905-34
Most 100s – Season	13	T.W.Hayward			1906
	13	J.B.Hobbs			1925
Most 100s – Career	144	J.B.Hobbs			1905-34
Most Wkts – Season	252	T.Richardson	(av 13.94)		1895
Most Wkts – Career	1775	T.Richardson	(av 17.87)		1892-1904
Most Career W-K Dismissals	1221	H.Strudwick	(1035 ct; 186 st)		1902-27
Most Career Catches in the Field	605	M.J.Stewart			1954-72

LIMITED-OVERS CRICKET

Highest Total	50ov	496-4		v	Glos	The Oval	2007
	40ov	386-3		v	Glamorgan	The Oval	2010
	T20	224-5		v	Glos	Bristol	2006
Lowest Total	50ov	74		v	Kent	The Oval	1967
	40ov	64		v	Worcs	Worcester	1978
	T20	88		v	Kent	The Oval	2012
Highest Innings	50ov	268	A.D.Brown	v	Glamorgan	The Oval	2002
	40ov	203	A.D.Brown	v	Hampshire	Guildford	1997
	T20	122*	J.J.Roy	v	Somerset	The Oval	2015
Best Bowling	50ov	7-33	R.D.Jackman	v	Yorkshire	Harrogate	1970
	40ov	7-30	M.P.Bicknell	v	Glamorgan	The Oval	1999
	T20	6-24	T.J.Murtagh	v	Middlesex	Lord's	2005

SUSSEX

Formation of Present Club: 1 March 1839
Substantial Reorganisation: August 1857
Inaugural First-Class Match: 1864
Colours: Dark Blue, Light Blue and Gold
Badge: County Arms of Six Martlets
County Champions: (3) 2003, 2006, 2007
Gillette/NatWest/C&G Trophy Winners: (5) 1963, 1964, 1978, 1986, 2006
Pro 40/National League (Div 1) Winners: (2) 2008, 2009
Sunday League Winners: (1) 1982
Twenty20 Cup Winners: (1) 2009

Chief Executive: Zac Toumazi, The BrightonandHoveJobs.com County Ground, Eaton Road, Hove BN3 3AN • Tel: 0844 264 0202 • Fax: 01273 771549 • Email: info@sussexcricket.co.uk • Web: www.sussexcricket.co.uk • Twitter: @SussexCCC (27,636 followers)

Director of Cricket: Keith Greenfield. **Head Coach**: Mark J.G.Davis. **Asst Head Coach/ Bowling Coach**: Jon Lewis. **Academy Director**: Carl Hopkinson. **Captain**: L.J.Wright. **Vice-Captain**: B.C.Brown. **Overseas Players**: Mustafizur Rahman (T20 only) and L.R.P.L.Taylor. **2016 Beneficiary**: Sussex Cricket Foundation. **Head Groundsman**: Andy Mackay. **Scorer**: M.J. (Mike) Charman. ‡ New registration. ^{NQ} Not qualified for England.

ANYON, James Edward (Garstang HS; Preston C; Loughborough U), b Lancaster, Lancs 5 May 1983. 6'1". LHB, RFM. Squad No 30. Loughborough U 2003-04. Warwickshire 2005-09. Surrey 2009 (on loan). Sussex debut 2010; cap 2011. No 1st XI appearances in 2015. Cumberland 2003. HS 64* v Surrey (Horsham) 2012. 50 wkts (1): 55 (2011). BB 6-82 Wa v Glamorgan (Cardiff) 2008. Sx BB 5-14 v Loughborough MCCU (Hove) 2014. LO HS 12 Wa v Worcs (Birmingham) 2006 (CGT). LO BB 3-6 Wa v Notts (Nottingham) 2008 (FPT). T20 HS 8*. T20 BB 3-6.

BEER, William Andrew Thomas (Reigate GS; Collyer's C, Horsham), b Crawley 8 Oct 1988. RHB, LB. Squad No 18. Debut (Sussex) 2008. HS 39 v Middx (Lord's) 2013. BB 3-31 v Worcs (Worcester) 2010. LO HS 45* v Durham (Hove) 2014 (RLC). LO BB 3-27 v Warwks (Hove) 2012 (CB40). T20 HS 37. T20 BB 3-14.

‡BRIGGS, Danny Richard (Isle of Wight C), b Newport, IoW, 30 Apr 1991. 6'2". RHB, SLA. Hampshire 2009-15; cap 2012. **LOI**: 1 (2011-12); HS – ; BB 2-39 v P (Dubai) 2011-12. **IT20**: 7 (2012 to 2013-14); HS 0*; BB 2-25 v A (Chester-le-St) 2013. F-c Tour (EL): WI 2010-11. HS 54 H v Glos (Bristol) 2013. BB 6-45 EL v Windward Is (Roseau) 2010-11. CC BB 6-65 H v Notts (Southampton) 2011. LO HS 25 and LO BB 4-32 H v Glamorgan (Cardiff) 2012 (CB40). T20 HS 10. T20 BB 5-19.

BROWN, Ben Christopher (Ardingly C), b Crawley 23 Nov 1988. RHB, WK. Squad No 26. Debut (Sussex) 2007; cap 2014. 1000 runs (1): 1031 (2015). HS 163 v Durham (Hove) 2014. BB – . LO HS 60 v Yorks (Scarborough) 2011 (CB40). T20 HS 68.

CACHOPA, Craig (West Lake BHS), b Welkom, OFS, South Africa 17 Jan 1992. Younger brother of Carl Cachopa (Auckland, C Districts 2004-05 to 2014-15) and B.Cachopa (Auckland, Canterbury 2010-11 to date). RHB, RM, occ WK. Squad No 12. Wellington 2011-12 to date. Auckland 2012-13 to 2014-15. Sussex debut 2014. Portuguese passport holder. HS 203 Auckland v Wellington (Auckland) 2013-14. Sx HS 84 v Warwks (Horsham) 2014 – on Sx debut. BB – . LO HS 121 Auckland v Canterbury (Christchurch) 2012-13. T20 HS 89*.

179

FINCH, Harry Zachariah (St Richard's Catholic C, Bexhill; Eastbourne C), b Hastings 10 Feb 1995. RHB, RMF. Squad No 6. Debut (Sussex) 2013. Sussex 2nd XI debut 2011, aged 16y 69d. England U19 2012-13. HS 22 v Durham (Chester-le-St) 2015. BB – . LO HS 92* v Glamorgan (Hove) 2014 (RLC). LO BB – . T20 HS 35*.

GARTON, George Henry Simmons (Hurstpierpoint C), b Brighton 15 Apr 1997. LHB, LMF. Sussex 2nd XI debut 2014. Awaiting 1st XI debut.

HATCHETT, Lewis James (Steyning GS), b Shoreham-by-Sea 21 Jan 1990. 6'3''. LHB, LMF. Squad No 5. Debut (Sussex) 2010. HS 25 v Yorks (Leeds) 2015. BB 5-47 v Leics (Leicester) 2010. LO HS 5 v Kent (Canterbury) 2014 (RLC). LO BB 3-44 v Surrey (Oval) 2014 (RLC). T20 HS 0*. T20 BB 3-23.

HUDSON-PRENTICE, Fynn Jake (Warden Park S, Cuckfield; Bede's S, Upper Dicker), b Haywards Heath 12 Jan 1996. RHB, RMF. Squad No 14. Debut (Sussex) 2015. Sussex 2nd XI debut 2012. HS 15 v Hants (Hove) 2015 – only f-c appearance. BB – . LO BB – .

JORDAN, Christopher James (Comber Mere S, Barbados; Dulwich C), b Christ Church, Barbados 4 Oct 1988. 6'0''. RHB, RFM. Squad No 8. Surrey 2007-12. Barbados 2011-12 to 2012-13. Sussex debut 2013; cap 2014. **ECB central contract 2014-15. Tests**: 8 (2014 to 2014-15); HS 35 v SL (Lord's) 2014; BB 4-18 v I (Oval) 2014. **LOI**: 27 (2013 to 2015-16); HS 38* v SL (Oval) 2014; BB 5-29 v SL (Manchester) 2014. **IT20**: 11 (2013-14 to 2015-16); HS 27* v WI (Bridgetown) 2013-14; BB 3-23 v SA (Cape Town) 2015-16. F-c Tour: WI 2014-15. HS 92 v Derbys (Derby) 2014. 50 wkts (1): 61 (2013). BB 7-43 Barbados v CC&C (Bridgetown) 2012-13. Sx BB 6-48 v Yorks (Leeds) 2013. LO HS 38* *(see LOI)*. LO BB 5-29 *(see LOI)*. T20 HS 37. T20 BB 3-23.

[NO]**JOYCE, Edmund** Christopher (Presentation C, Bray, Co Wicklow; Trinity C, Dublin), b Dublin, Ireland 22 Sep 1978. Brother of four Ireland cricketers: Augustine (2000), Dominick (2004-06), Cecilia (2001-07) and Isobel, her twin (1999-2007). 5'11''. LHB, RM. Squad No 24. Ireland 1997-98 to date. Middlesex 1999-2008; cap 2002. Sussex debut/cap 2009; captain 2013-15. MCC 2006, 2008. **LOI** (E/Ire): 56 (17 for E 2006 to 2006-07; 39 for Ire 2010-11 to 2015-16); HS 116* Ire v P (Dublin) 2013. **IT20** (E/Ire): 18 (2 for E 2006 to 2006-07; 16 for Ire 2011-12 to 2013-14); HS 78* Ire v Scotland (Dubai, DSC) 2011-12. F-c Tour (Eng A): WI 2005-06. 1000 runs (8); most – 1668 (2005). HS 231 Ire v UAE (Dublin) 2015. Sx HS 204* v Notts (Nottingham) 2013. BB M 2-34 v Cambridge U (Cambridge) 2004. CC BB 1-4 M v Glamorgan (Cardiff) 2005. Sx BB 1-9 v Hants (Southampton) 2009. LO HS 146 v Glos (Hove) 2009 (FPT). LO BB 2-10 M v Notts (Nottingham) 2003 (NL). T20 HS 78*.

MACHAN, Matthew William (Brighton C), b Brighton 15 Feb 1991. 5'8''. LHB, RM. Squad No 15. Debut (Sussex) 2010. Scotland 2012-13 to date. **LOI** (Scot): 23 (2012-13 to 2015-16); HS 114 and BB 3-31 v Kenya (Aberdeen) 2013. **IT20** (Scot): 13 (2012-13 to 2015-16); HS 67* v Netherlands (Dubai) 2013-14; BB 3-23 v Afghanistan (Sharjah) 2012-13. HS 192 v Somerset (Taunton) 2015. BB 1-36 Sc v Australia A (Edinburgh) 2013. LO HS 126* v Unicorns (Hove) 2012 (CB40). BB 3-31 *(see LOI)*. T20 HS 90*. T20 BB 3-23.

[NO]**MAGOFFIN, Stephen** James (Indooroopilly HS; Curtin U, Perth), b Corinda, Queensland, Australia 17 Dec 1979. 6'3''. LHB, RFM. Squad No 64. W Australia 2004-05 to 2010-11. Surrey 2007 (one f-c match). Worcestershire 2008. Queensland 2011-12. Sussex debut 2012; cap 2013. HS 79 WA v Tas (Perth) 2008-09. UK HS 51 v Northants (Northampton) 2014. 50 wkts (4); most – 73 (2015). BB 8-20 (12-31 match) v Somerset (Horsham) 2013. LO HS 24* Wo v Hants (Southampton) 2008 (FPT). LO BB 4-58 Sy v Kent (Oval) 2007 (FPT). T20 HS 11*. T20 BB 2-15.

180

MILLS, Tymal Solomon (Mildenhall TC), b Dewsbury, Yorks 12 Aug 1992. 6'1". RHB, LF. Squad No 7. Essex 2011-14. Sussex debut 2015. Essex 2nd XI debut 2010. England U19 2010-11. F-c Tour (EL): SL 2013-14. HS 31* EL v Sri Lanka A (Colombo, RPS) 2013-14. CC HS 30 Ex v Kent (Canterbury) 2014. Sx HS 8 v Worcs (Hove) 2015. BB 4-25 Ex v Glamorgan (Cardiff) 2012. Sx BB 2-28 v Hants (Southampton) 2015. LO HS 3* v Notts (Hove) 2015 (RLC). LO BB 3-23 Ex v Durham (Chelmsford) 2013 (Y40). T20 HS 8*. T20 BB 4-22.

‡NQ**MUSTAFIZUR RAHMAN**, b Khulna, Bangladesh 6 Sep 1995. 5'11". LHB, LMF. Squad No 90. Khulna 2013-14 to date. South Zone 2013-14 to 2014-15. Joins Sussex in 2016 for T20 only. **Tests** (B): 2 (2015); HS 3 and BB 4-37 v SA (Chittagong) 2015. **LOI** (B): 9 (2015 to 2015-16); HS 9 v I (Dhaka) 2015; BB 6-43 v I (Dhaka) 2015. **IT20** (B): 10 (2015 to 2015-16); HS 1* v Z (Dhaka) 2015-16; BB 2-13 v UAE (Dhaka) 2015-16. HS 14 South Zone v East Zone (Chittagong) 2015. BB 5-28 Khulna v Chittagong (Savar) 2014-15. LO HS 9 (*see LOI*). LO BB 6-43 (*see LOI*). T20 HS 1*. T20 BB 3-14.

NASH, Christopher David (Collyer's SFC; Loughborough U), b Cuckfield 19 May 1983. 5'11". RHB, OB. Squad No 23. Debut (Sussex) 2002; cap 2008. Loughborough UCCE 2003-04. British U 2004. 1000 runs (3); most – 1321 (2009). HS 184 v Leics (Leicester) 2010. BB 4-12 v Glamorgan (Cardiff) 2010. LO HS 124* v Kent (Canterbury) 2011 (CB40). LO BB 4-40 v Yorks (Hove) 2009 (FPT). T20 HS 88. T20 BB 4-7.

ROBINSON, Oliver Edward (King's S, Canterbury), b Margate, Kent 1 Dec 1993. RHB, RM. Squad No 25. Debut (Sussex) 2015. Kent 2nd XI 2011-12. Leicestershire 2nd XI 2013. Yorkshire 2nd XI 2013-14. HS 110 v Durham (Chester-le-St) 2015, on debut, sharing Sx record 10th wkt partnership of 164 with M.E.Hobden. BB 6-33 v Warwks (Hove) 2015. LO HS 30 v Kent (Canterbury) 2015 (RLC). LO BB 2-61 v Middx (Hove) 2015 (RLC). T20 HS 10. T20 BB 3-16.

SALT, Philip Dean (Reed's S, Cobham), b Bodelwyddan, Denbighs 28 Aug 1996. RHB, OB. Sussex 2nd XI debut 2014. Awaiting f-c debut. LO HS 22 v Essex (Hove) 2015 (RLC) – only 1st XI appearance.

SHAHZAD, Ajmal (Woodhouse Grove S; Bradford U), b Huddersfield, Yorkshire 27 Jul 1985. 6'0". RHB, RFM. Squad No 4. Yorkshire 2006-12 (first British-born Asian to play for Yorkshire); cap 2010. Lancashire 2012 (on loan). Nottinghamshire 2013-14. Sussex debut 2015. **Tests**: 1 (2010); HS 5 and BB 3-45 v B (Manchester) 2010. **LOI**: 11 (2009-10 to 2010-11); HS 9 v A (Brisbane) 2010-11; BB 3-41 v B (Bristol) 2010. **IT20**: 3 (2009-10 to 2010-11); HS 0*; BB 2-38 v P (Dubai) 2009-10. F-c Tours: A 2010-11; B 2009-10. HS 88 Y v Sussex (Hove) 2009. Sx HS 45* and BB 5-46 v Worcs (Hove) 2015. LO HS 59* Y v Kent (Leeds) 2011 (CB40). LO BB 5-51 Y v Sri Lanka A (Leeds) 2007. T20 HS 20. T20 BB 3-30.

‡NQ**TAYLOR**, Luteru Ross Poutoa Lote, b Lower Hutt, Wellington, New Zealand 8 Mar 1984. 6'0". RHB, OB. Central Districts 2002-03 to date. IPL: RCB 2007-08 to 2009-10. RR 2011. DD 2012-14. PW 2013. **Tests** (NZ): 69 (2007-08 to 2015-16, 13 as captain); HS 290 v A (Perth) 2015-16; BB 2-4 v I (Ahmedabad) 2010-11. **LOI** (NZ): 171 (2005-06 to 2015-16, 20 as captain); 1000 runs (1): 1046 (2015); HS 131* v P (Pallekele) 2010-11; BB – . **IT20** (NZ): 68 (2006-07 to 2015-16, 13 as captain); HS 63 v WI (Auckland) 2008-09. F-c Tours (NZ) (C=Captain): E 2008, 2013, 2015; A 2008-09, 2011-12C, 2015-16; SA 2004 (NZ A), 2007-08; WI 2012C; I 2010-11, 2012C, 2014; SL 2009, 2012-13C; Z 2011-12C; B 2008-09, 2013-14; UAE 2014-15 (v P). HS 290 (*see Tests*). BB 2-4 (*see Tests*). LO HS 132* CD v Otago (Dunedin) 2003-04. LO BB 1-13 CD v Canterbury (Christchurch) 2005-06. T20 HS 111*. T20 BB 3-28.

WELLS, Luke William Peter (St Bede's S, Upper Dicker), b Eastbourne 29 Dec 1990. Son of A.P.Wells (Border, Kent, Sussex and England 1981-2000); nephew of C.M.Wells (Border, Derbyshire, Sussex and WP 1979-96). 6'4". LHB, LB. Squad No 31. Debut (Sussex) 2010. Colombo CC 2011-12. 1000 runs (1): 1016 (2014). HS 208 v Surrey (Oval) 2013. BB 3-35 v Durham (Arundel) 2015. LO HS 23 v Notts (Horsham) 2014 (RLC). BB 3-19 v Netherlands (Amstelveen) 2011 (CB40). T20 HS 11.

WHITTINGHAM, Stuart Gordon (Christ's Hospital, Horsham; Loughborough U), b Derby 10 Feb 1994. RHB, RFM. Loughborough MCCU 2015. Sussex 2nd XI debut 2014. MCC Universities 2013. Awaiting 1st XI debut. HS 0. BB 1-77 LU v Hants (Southampton) 2015.

WRIGHT, Luke James (Belvoir HS; Ratcliffe C; Loughborough U), b Grantham, Lincs 7 Mar 1985. Younger brother of A.S.Wright (Leicestershire 2001-02). 5'11". RHB, RMF. Squad No 10. Leicestershire 2003 (one f-c match). Sussex debut 2004; cap 2007; T20 captain & benefit 2015; captain 2016. IPL: PW 2012-13. Big Bash: MS 2011-12 to date. **LOI:** 50 (2007 to 2013-14); HS 52 v NZ (Birmingham) 2008; BB 2-34 v NZ (Bristol) 2008 and 2-34 v A (Southampton) 2010. **IT20:** 51 (2007-08 to 2013-14); HS 99* v Afghanistan (Colombo, RPS) 2012-13; BB 2-24 v NZ (Hamilton) 2012-13. F-c Tour (EL): NZ 2008-09. 1000 runs (1): 1220 (2015). HS 226* v Worcs (Worcester) 2015, sharing Sx record 6th wkt partnership of 335 with B.C.Brown. Big Bash 5-65 v Derbys (Derby) 2010. LO HS 143* EL v Bangladesh A (Bristol) 2013. LO BB 4-12 v Middx (Hove) 2004 (NL). T20 HS 153* v Essex (Chelmsford) 2014 – Sx record. T20 BB 3-17.

RELEASED/RETIRED

(Having made a County 1st XI appearance in 2015)

ASHAR ZAIDI – *see ESSEX.*

NQ**BAILEY, George** John, b Launceston, Tasmania, Australia 7 Sep 1982. 5'10". RHB, RM. Tasmania 2004-05 to date. Hampshire 2013. Sussex 2015 (L-o and T20 only) IPL: CSK 2009 to 2009-10. KXIP 2014-15. Big Bash: MS 2011-12. HH 2012-13 to date. **Tests** (A): 5 (2013-14); HS 53 v E (Adelaide) 2013-14. **LOI** (A): 71 (2011-12 to 2015-16); HS 156 v I (Nagpur) 2013-14. **IT20** (A): 28 (2011-12 to 2013-14); HS 63 v WI (Colombo, RPS) 2012-13. F-c Tours (Aus A): E 2012; I 2008-09. HS 160* Tas v Vic (Hobart) 2010-11. UK HS 93 H v Leics (Southampton) 2013. BB – . LO HS 156 (*see LOI*). LO BB 1-19 Tas v Vic (Melbourne) 2004-05. T20 HS 71.

BURGOYNE, Peter Ian (St John Houghton S, Ilkeston; Derby SFC), b Nottingham 11 Nov 1993. RHB, OB. Debut Southern Rocks 2012-13, scoring 102* v ME (Harare). Derbyshire 2013. Sussex 2015. HS 104 and BB 3-27 SR v MWR (Kwekwe) 2012-13. CC HS 62* De v Sussex (Hove) 2013. Sx HS 15 v Notts (Horsham) 2015. CC BB 3-66 De v Middx (Derby) 2013. Sx BB 1-113 v Warwks (Birmingham) 2015. LO HS 43 SR v MWR (Masvingo) 2012-13. LO BB 3-31 De v Northants (Derby) 2012 (CB40). T20 HS 38. T20 BB 2-13.

HOBDEN, Matthew Edward (Eastbourne C; UWIC), b Eastbourne 27 Mar 1993; d Scotland 2 Jan 2016. RHB, RFM. Cardiff MCCU 2012-13. Sussex 2014-15. HS 65* v Durham (Chester-le-St) 2015, sharing Sx record 10th wkt partnership of 164 with O.E.Robinson. BB 5-62 CfU v Warwks (Birmingham) 2012. Sx BB 4-48 v Warwks (Hove) 2015. LO HS 3* v Warwks (Rugby) 2015 (RLC). LO BB 1-39 v Notts (Nottingham) 2013 (Y40). T20 BB – .

JACKSON, Callum Frederick (St Bede's S, Upper Dicker), b Eastbourne 7 Sep 1994. 5'11". RHB, WK. Sussex 2013. Sussex 2nd XI debut 2011, aged 16y 225d. England U19s 2012-13. No f-c appearances in 2014-15. HS 26 v Australians (Hove) 2013. LO HS 34* v Essex (Hove) 2015 (RLC). T20 HS 3.

^{NQ}**JAYAWARDENA**, Denagamage Proboth **Mahela** De Silva (Nalanda C, Colombo), b Colombo, Sri Lanka 27 May 1977. 5'9". RHB, RM. Sinhalese SC 1996-97 to 2012-13. Sussex 2015 (T20 only). IPL: KXIP 2007-10. DD 2012-13. Big Bash: AS 2015-16. *Wisden* 2006. **Tests** (SL): 149 (1997 to 2014, 38 as captain); 1000 runs (3); most – 1194 (2009); HS 374 v SA (Colombo) 2006; BB 2-32 v P (Galle) 2000-01. **LOI** (SL): 448 (1997-98 to 2014-15, 129 as captain); 1000 runs (4); most – 1260 (2001); HS 144 v E (Leeds) 2011; BB 2-56 v K (Southampton) 1999. **IT20** (SL): 55 (2006 to 2013-14); HS 100 v Z (Providence) 2010. F-c Tours (SL) (C=captain): E 1998, 2002, 2006C, 2011, 2014; A 2004, 2007-08C, 2012-13; SA 1997-98, 2000-01, 2002-03, 2011-12; WI 2003, 2007-08C; NZ 2004-05, 2006-07C; I 1997-98, 2005-06, 2009-10; P 1998-99, 1999-00, 2001-02, 2004-05, 2008-09C; Z 1999-00, 2004; B 1998-99, 2005-06C, 2008-09C, 2013-14; UAE 2011-12 (v P), 2013-14 (v P). 1000 runs (0+2); most 1426 (2001-02). HS 374 (*see Tests*). BB 5-72 Sinhalese v Colts (Colombo) 1996-97. LO HS 163* Sinhalese v Bloomfield (Colombo) 2010-11. LO BB 3-25 Sinhalese v Sebastianites (Colombo) 1998-99. T20 HS 110*. T20 BB 2-22.

LIDDLE, C.J. – *see GLOUCESTERSHIRE*.

PIOLET, Steffan Andrew (Warden Park S; Central Sussex C), b Redhill, Surrey 8 Aug 1988. 6'1". RHB, RM. Warwickshire 2009-13. Sussex 2014. No f-c appearances in 2015. HS 103* v Loughborough MCCU (Hove) 2014 – on Sx debut. CC HS 32 v Yorks (Scarborough) 2014. BB 6-17 (10-43 match) Wa v Durham UCCE (Durham) 2009 – on debut. Sx BB 2-61 v Somerset (Taunton) 2014. LO HS 63* v Notts (Horsham) 2014 (RLC). LO BB 4-31 Wa v Derbys (Derby) 2012 (CB40). T20 HS 26*. T20 BB 3-14.

YARDY, Michael Howard (William Parker S, Hastings), b Pembury, Kent 27 Nov 1980. 6'0". LHB, LM/SLA. Sussex 2000-15; cap 2005; captain 2009-12; benefit 2014. **LOI**: 28 (2006 to 2010-11); HS 60* v A (Perth) 2010-11; BB 3-24 v P (Nottingham) 2006 – on debut. **IT20**: 14 (2006 to 2010-11); HS 35* v P (Cardiff) 2010; BB 2-19 v P (Bridgetown) 2009-10. F-c Tours (Eng A) (C=Captain): WI 2005-06; I 2007-08C; B 2006-07C. 1000 runs (2); most – 1520 (2005). HS 257 (record Sx score v touring team) and BB 5-83 v Bangladeshis (Hove) 2005. CC HS 179 v Middx (Lord's) 2005. CC BB 3-15 v Yorks (Leeds) 2009. LO HS 98* v Surrey (Oval) 2008 (CGT). LO BB 6-27 v Warwks (Birmingham) 2005 (NL). T20 HS 76*. T20 BB 3-21.

M.J.Prior left the staff without making a County 1st XI appearance in 2015.

SUSSEX 2015

RESULTS SUMMARY

	Place	Won	Lost	Tied	Drew	NR
LV= County Championship (1st Division)	8th	4	8		4	
All First-Class Matches		4	8		5	
Royal London One-Day Cup (Group B)	9th		5			3
NatWest t20 Blast (South Group)	QF	7	6			2

LV= COUNTY CHAMPIONSHIP AVERAGES

BATTING AND FIELDING

Cap		*M*	*I*	*NO*	*HS*	*Runs*	*Avge*	*100*	*50*	*Ct/St*
2007	L.J.Wright	16	28	2	226*	1210	46.53	2	8	11
2014	B.C.Brown	16	27	4	144*	1031	44.82	4	4	45/1
	M.W.Machan	14	24	–	192	955	39.79	3	3	3
	Ashar Zaidi	7	10	1	106	354	39.33	1	1	3
2005	M.H.Yardy	10	17	–	124	606	35.64	2	3	14
2008	C.D.Nash	15	26	1	142*	833	33.32	2	3	15
2009	E.C.Joyce	14	25	–	100	786	31.44	1	3	22
2014	C.J.Jordan	6	8	2	56*	177	29.50	–	1	18
	L.W.P.Wells	13	22	–	108	615	27.95	1	4	6
	A.Shahzad	5	10	2	45*	182	22.75	–	–	1
	O.E.Robinson	11	17	3	110	282	20.14	1	–	3
	Craig Cachopa	8	16	–	54	220	13.75	–	1	5
	H.Z.Finch	2	4	–	22	46	11.50	–	–	3
2013	S.J.Magoffin	16	24	4	41	208	10.40	–	–	2
	M.E.Hobden	10	17	8	65*	84	9.33	–	1	3
	C.J.Liddle	4	4	2	10*	18	9.00	–	–	1
	T.S.Mills	2	4	–	8	18	4.50	–	–	–

Also batted: P.I.Burgoyne (2 matches) 13, 13; G.H.Dockrell (1) 37*, 0; L.J.Hatchett (2) 2*, 25, 8* (1 ct); F.J.Hudson-Prentice (1) 15, 0; T.E.Linley (1) 10, 21*.

BOWLING

	O	*M*	*R*	*W*	*Avge*	*Best*	*5wI*	*10wM*
A.Shahzad	111.2	17	411	22	18.68	5-46	1	–
S.J.Magoffin	582	140	1660	69	24.05	6-50	4	1
O.E.Robinson	320.1	66	1137	46	24.71	6-33	1	–
C.J.Jordan	197.4	28	686	24	28.58	5-68	1	–
L.W.P.Wells	226	27	862	23	37.47	3-35	–	–
C.J.Liddle	110	15	391	10	39.10	3-49	–	–
Ashar Zaidi	188.1	42	461	11	41.90	3-55	–	–
M.E.Hobden	252.3	36	1088	23	47.30	4-48	–	–
Also bowled:								
T.E.Linley	41.4	8	156	8	19.50	5-63	1	–

B.C.Brown 8-0-31-0; P.I.Burgoyne 52-5-215-1; G.H.Dockrell 44-2-180-0; L.J.Hatchett 58-9-206-4; F.J.Hudson-Prentice 8-0-51-0; E.C.Joyce 4-0-8-0; M.W.Machan 6-0-28-0; T.S.Mills 38.3-7-135-3; C.D.Nash 64-3-282-0; L.J.Wright 9-0-39-0; M.H.Yardy 8-1-41-1.

The First-Class Averages (pp 227–243) give the records of Sussex players in all first-class county matches (Sussex's other opponents being Leeds/Bradford MCCU), with the exception of T.E.Linley, whose first-class figures for Sussex are as above.

SUSSEX RECORDS
FIRST-CLASS CRICKET

Highest Total	For 742-5d		v	Somerset	Taunton	2009
	V 726		by	Notts	Nottingham	1895
Lowest Total	For 19		v	Surrey	Godalming	1830
	19		v	Notts	Hove	1873
	V 18		by	Kent	Gravesend	1867
Highest Innings	For 344*	M.W.Goodwin	v	Somerset	Taunton	2009
	V 322	E.Paynter	for	Lancashire	Hove	1937

Highest Partnership for each Wicket

1st	490	E.H.Bowley/J.G.Langridge	v	Middlesex	Hove	1933
2nd	385	E.H.Bowley/M.W.Tate	v	Northants	Hove	1921
3rd	385*	M.H.Yardy/M.W.Goodwin	v	Warwicks	Hove	2006
4th	363	M.W.Goodwin/C.D.Hopkinson	v	Somerset	Taunton	2009
5th	297	J.H.Parks/H.W.Parks	v	Hampshire	Portsmouth	1937
6th	335	L.J.Wright/B.C.Brown	v	Durham	Hove	2014
7th	344	K.S.Ranjitsinhji/W.Newham	v	Essex	Leyton	1902
8th	291	R.S.C.Martin-Jenkins/M.J.G.Davis	v	Somerset	Taunton	2002
9th	178	H.W.Parks/A.F.Wensley	v	Derbyshire	Horsham	1930
10th	164	O.E.Robinson/M.E.Hobden	v	Durham	Chester-le-St^2	2015

Best Bowling	For 10- 48	C.H.G.Bland	v	Kent	Tonbridge	1899
(Innings)	V 9- 11	A.P.Freeman	for	Kent	Hove	1922
Best Bowling	For 17-106	G.R.Cox	v	Warwicks	Horsham	1926
(Match)	V 17- 67	A.P.Freeman	for	Kent	Hove	1922

Most Runs – Season	2850	J.G.Langridge	(av 64.77)	1949
Most Runs – Career	34150	J.G.Langridge	(av 37.69)	1928-55
Most 100s – Season	12	J.G.Langridge		1949
Most 100s – Career	76	J.G.Langridge		1928-55
Most Wkts – Season	198	M.W.Tate	(av 13.47)	1925
Most Wkts – Career	2211	M.W.Tate	(av 17.41)	1912-37
Most Career W-K Dismissals	1176	H R Butt	(911 ct; 265 st)	1890-1912
Most Career Catches in the Field	779	J.G.Langridge		1928-55

LIMITED-OVERS CRICKET

Highest Total	50ov	384-9		v	Ireland	Belfast	1996
	40ov	399-4		v	Worcs	Horsham	2011
	T20	239-5		v	Glamorgan	Hove	2010
Lowest Total	50ov	49		v	Derbyshire	Chesterfield	1969
	40ov	59		v	Glamorgan	Hove	1996
	T20	67		v	Hampshire	Hove	2004
Highest Innings	50ov	158*	M.W.Goodwin	v	Essex	Chelmsford	2006
	40ov	163	C.J.Adams	v	Middlesex	Arundel	1999
	T20	153*	L.J.Wright	v	Essex	Chelmsford	2014
Best Bowling	50ov	6- 9	A.I.C.Dodemaide	v	Ireland	Downpatrick	1990
	40ov	7-41	A.N.Jones	v	Notts	Nottingham	1986
	T20	5-11	Mushtaq Ahmed	v	Essex	Hove	2005

WARWICKSHIRE

Formation of Present Club: 8 April 1882
Substantial Reorganisation: 19 January 1884
Inaugural First-Class Match: 1894
Colours: Dark Blue, Gold and Silver
Badge: Bear and Ragged Staff
County Champions: (7) 1911, 1951, 1972, 1994, 1995, 2004, 2012
Gillette/NatWest Trophy Winners: (5) 1966, 1968, 1989, 1993, 1995
Benson and Hedges Cup Winners: (2) 1994, 2002
Sunday League Winners: (3) 1980, 1994, 1997
Clydesdale Bank 40 Winners: (1) 2010
Twenty20 Cup Winners: (1) 2014

Chief Executive: Neil Snowball, County Ground, Edgbaston, Birmingham, B5 7QU • Tel: 0844 635 1902 • Fax: 0121 446 4544 • Email: info@edgbaston.com • Web: www.edgbaston.com • Twitter: @CricketingBears (27,352 followers)

Director of Cricket: Dougie Brown. **Batting Coach**: Tony Frost. **Bowling Coach**: Alan Richardson. **Fielding Coach**: Jim Troughton. **Captain**: I.R.Bell. **Vice-Captain**: tba. **Overseas Player**: J.S.Patel. **2016 Beneficiary**: T.R.Ambrose. **Head Groundsman**: Gary Barwell. **Scorer**: Mel Smith. New registration. ^{NQ} Not qualified for England.

ADAIR, Mark Richard (Sullivan Upper S, Hollywood), b Belfast, N Ireland 27 Mar 1996. RHB, RFM. Squad No 27. Debut (Warwickshire) 2015. Warwickshire 2nd XI debut 2013. HS 24* and BB 1-61 v Somerset (Taunton) 2015 – only 1st XI appearance.

AMBROSE, Timothy Raymond (Merewether HS, NSW; TAFE C), b Newcastle, NSW, Australia 1 Dec 1982. ECB qualified – British/EU passport. 5'7". RHB, WK. Squad No 11. Sussex 2001-05; cap 2003. Warwickshire debut 2006; cap 2007; benefit 2016. **Tests**: 11 (2007-08 to 2008-09); HS 102 v NZ (Wellington) 2007-08. **LOI**: 5 (2008); HS 6 v NZ (Oval) 2008. **IT20**: 1 (2008); HS – . F-c Tours: WI 2008-09; NZ 2007-08. HS 251* v Worcs (Worcester) 2007. LO HS 135 v Durham (Birmingham) 2007 (FPT). T20 HS 77.

BARKER, Keith Hubert Douglas (Moorhead HS; Fulwood C, Preston), b Manchester 21 Oct 1986. Son of K.H.Barker (British Guiana 1960-61 to 1963-64). Played football for Blackburn Rovers and Rochdale. 6'3". LHB, LMF. Squad No 13. Debut (Warwickshire) 2009; cap 2013. HS 125 v Surrey (Guildford) 2013. 50 wkts (2); most – 56 (2012). BB 6-40 v Somerset (Taunton) 2012. LO HS 56 v Scotland (Birmingham) 2011 (CB40). LO BB 4-33 v Scotland (Birmingham) 2010 (CB40). T20 HS 46. T20 BB 4-19.

BELL, Ian Ronald (Princethorpe C), b Walsgrave-on-Sowe 11 Apr 1982. 5'9". RHB, RM. Squad No 4. Debut (Warwickshire) 1999; cap 2001; benefit 2011; captain 2016. MCC 2004. YC 2004. MBE 2005. *Wisden* 2007. **ECB central contract 2015-16**. **Tests**: 118 (2004 to 2015-16); 1000 runs (1): 1005 (2013); 1000 runs (1): 1080 (2007); HS 235 v I (Oval) 2011; BB 1-33 v P (Faisalabad) 2005-06. **LOI**: 161 (2004-05 to 2014-15); HS 141 v A (Hobart) 2014-15; BB 3-9 v Z (Bulawayo) 2004-05 – taking a wicket with his third ball in LOI. **IT20**: 8 (2006 to 2014); HS 60* v NZ (Manchester) 2008. F-c Tours: A 2006-07, 2010-11, 2013-14; SA 2009-10; WI 2000-01 (Eng A – *part*), 2008-09, 2014-15; NZ 2007-08, 2012-13; I 2005-06, 2008-09, 2012-13; P 2005-06; SL 2002-03 (ECB Acad), 2004-05, 2007-08, 2011-12; B 2009-10; UAE 2011-12 (v P), 2015-16 (v P). 1000 runs (4); most – 1714 (2004). HS 262* v Sussex (Horsham) 2004. BB 4-4 v Middx (Lord's) 2004. LO HS 158 EL v India A (Worcester) 2010. LO BB 5-41 v Essex (Chelmsford) 2003 (NL). T20 HS 90. T20 BB 1-12.

CHOPRA, Varun (Ilford County HS), b Barking, Essex 21 Jun 1987. 6'1". RHB, LB. Squad No 3. Essex 2006-09, scoring 106 v Glos (Chelmsford) on CC debut. Warwickshire debut 2010; cap 2012; captain 2015-16. Tamil Union 2011-12. F-c Tour (EL): SL 2013-14. 1000 runs (3); most – 1203 (2011). HS 233* TU v Sinhalese (Colombo, PSS) 2011-12. Wa HS 228 v Worcs (Worcester) 2011 (in 2nd CC game of season, having scored 210 v Somerset in 1st). BB – . LO HS 115 v Leics (Birmingham) 2011 (CB40). T20 HS 86*.

186

CLARKE, Rikki (Broadwater SS; Godalming C), b Orsett, Essex 29 Sep 1981. 6'4". RHB, RFM. Squad No 81. Surrey 2002-07, scoring 107* v Cambridge U (Cambridge) on debut; cap 2005. Derbyshire cap/captain 2008. Warwickshire debut 2008; cap 2011. MCC 2006. YC 2002. **Tests**: 2 (2003-04); HS 55 and BB 2-7 v B (Chittagong) 2003-04. **LOI**: 20 (2003 to 2006); HS 39 v P (Lord's) 2006; BB 2-28 v B (Dhaka) 2003-04. F-c Tours: WI 2003-04, 2005-06; SL 2002-03 (ECB Acad), 2004-05; B 2003-04. 1000 runs (1): 1027 (2006). HS 214 Sy v Somerset (Guildford) 2006. Wa HS 140 v Lancs (Liverpool) 2012. BB 6-63 v Kent (Canterbury) 2010. Took seven catches in an innings v Lancs (Liverpool) 2011 to equal world record. Lo HS 98* Sy v Derbys (Derby) 2002 (NL). LO BB 4-28 v Northants (Birmingham) 2011 (CB40). T20 HS 79*. T20 BB 3-11.

COLEMAN, Frederick Robert John (Strathallan S; Oxford Brookes U), b Edinburgh, Scotland 15 Dec 1991. RHB, WK, occ OB. Squad No 21. Scotland 2011-12 to date. Oxford MCCU 2012-13. Warwickshire debut 2015. Warwickshire 2nd XI debut 2010. **LOI** (Scot): 16 (2013 to 2014-15); HS 70 v SL (Hobart) 2014-15. **IT20** (Scot): 1 (2013); HS 9 v Kenya (Aberdeen) 2013. HS 110 OU v Worcs (Oxford) 2012 – on UK debut. Wa HS 0. LO HS 70 (*see LOI*). T20 HS 20*.

EVANS, Laurie John (Whitgift S; The John Fisher S; St Mary's C, Durham S), b Lambeth, London 12 Oct 1987. 6'0". RHB, OB. Squad No 32. Durham UCCE 2007. MCC 2007. Surrey 2009-10. Warwickshire debut 2010. HS 213* and BB 1-29 v Sussex (Birmingham) 2015, sharing Wa 6th wkt record of 327 with T.R.Ambrose. LO HS 50 v Somerset (Birmingham) 2014 (RLC). LO BB – . T20 HS 69*. T20 BB 1-5.

GORDON, Recordo Olton (Aston Manor S; Hamstead Hall SFC), b St Elizabeth, Jamaica 12 Oct 1991. RHB, RFM. Squad No 44. Debut (Warwickshire) 2013. Warwickshire 2nd XI debut 2011. No f-c appearances in 2015. HS 14* and BB 4-53 v Somerset (Taunton) 2014. LO HS 9* v Notts (Mkt Warsop) 2015 (RLC). LO BB 3-25 v Surrey (Birmingham) 2014 (RLC). T20 HS 18. T20 BB 4-20.

HAIN, Samuel Robert (Southport S, Gold Coast), b Hong Kong 16 July 1995. RHB, OB. Squad No 16. Debut (Warwickshire) 2014. Warwickshire 2nd XI debut 2011. UK passport (British parents). HS 208 v Northants (Birmingham) 2014. LO HS 1 v Worcs (Worcester) 2013 (Y40).

HANNON-DALBY, Oliver James (Brooksbank S, Leeds Met U), b Halifax, Yorkshire 20 Jun 1989. 6'7". LHB, RMF. Squad No 20. Yorkshire 2008-12. Warwickshire debut 2013. HS 40 v Somerset (Taunton) 2014. BB 5-68 Y v Warwks (Birmingham) and 5-68 Y v Somerset (Leeds) 2010 – in consecutive matches. Wa BB 4-50 v Oxford MCCU (Oxford) 2013. LO HS 21* Y v Warwks (Scarborough) 2012 (CB40). LO BB 5-27 v Glamorgan (Birmingham) 2015 (RLC). T20 HS 9. T20 BB 4-29.

JAVID, Ateeq (Aston Manor S), b Birmingham 15 Oct 1991. RHB, OB. Squad No 17. Debut (Warwickshire) 2009. Warwickshire 2nd XI debut 2008. England U19 2010 to 2010-11. HS 133 v Somerset (Birmingham) 2013. BB 1-1 v Lancs (Manchester) 2014. LO HS 43 v Kent (Canterbury) 2013 (Y40). LO BB 3-48 v Glamorgan (Swansea) 2014 (RLC). T20 HS 51*. T20 BB 4-17.

JONES, Richard Alan (Grange HS and King Edward VI C, Stourbridge; Loughborough U), b Wordsley, Stourbridge, Worcs 6 Nov 1986. 6'2". RHB, RMF. Squad No 25. Worcestershire 2007-13; cap 2007. Matabeleland Tuskers 2011-12. Warwickshire debut 2014. Leicestershire 2014 (on loan). HS 62 MT v SR (Bulawayo) 2011-12. UK HS 53* Wo v Durham (Worcester) 2009. Wa HS 35 v Somerset (Taunton) 2014. BB 7-115 Wo v Sussex (Hove) 2010. Wa BB 4-48 v Durham (Birmingham) 2015. LO HS 11* Wo v Sussex (Worcester) 2010 (CB40). LO BB 1-25 MT v ME (Bulawayo) 2011-12. T20 HS 9. T20 BB 5-34.

MELLOR, Alexander James (Westwood C, Leek; Staffordshire U), b Stoke-on-Trent, Staffs 22 Jul 1991. LHB, WK. Squad No 15. Somerset 2nd XI 2012-14. Warwickshire 2nd XI 2015. Staffordshire 2014-15. Awaiting 1st XI debut.

NQ**PATEL, Jeetan** Shashi, b Wellington, New Zealand 7 May 1980. RHB, OB. Squad No 5. Wellington 1999-00 to date. Warwickshire debut 2009; cap 2012. *Wisden* 2014. **Tests** (NZ): 19 (2006-07 to 2012-13); HS 27* v SA (Cape Town) 2006-07; BB 5-110 v WI (Napier) 2008-09. **LOI** (NZ): 39 (2005 to 2009-10); HS 34 v SL (Kingston) 2006-07; BB 3-11 v SA (Mumbai, BS) 2006-07. **IT20** (NZ): 11 (2005-06 to 2008-09); HS 5 v E (Auckland) 2007-08; BB 3-20 v SA (Johannesburg) 2006-07. F-c Tours (NZ): E 2008; SA 2005-06, 2012-13; I 2010-11, 2012; SL 2009, 2012-13; Z 2010-11, 2011-12; B 2008-09. HS 120 v Yorks (Birmingham) 2009. 50 wkts (4); most – 59 (2014). BB 7-38 v Somerset (Taunton) 2015. LO HS 50 v Kent (Birmingham) 2013 (Y40). LO BB 4-16 NZ A v Aus A (Hyderabad) 2008-09. T20 HS 34*. T20 BB 4-11.

NQ**PORTERFIELD, William** Thomas Stuart (Strabane GS; Leeds Met U), b Londonderry, N.Ireland 6 Sep 1984. 5'11''. LHB, OB. Squad No 10. Ireland 2006-07 to 2008-09. Gloucestershire 2008-10; cap 2008. Warwickshire debut 2011; cap 2014. MCC 2007. **LOI** (Ire): 84 (2006 to 2015-16, 61 as captain); HS 112* v Bermuda (Nairobi) 2006-07. **IT20** (Ire): 48 (2008 to 2015-16, 48 as captain); HS 72 v UAE (Abu Dhabi) 2015-16. HS 186 Ire v Namibia (Windhoek) 2015-16. CC HS 175 Gs v Worcs (Cheltenham) 2010. Wa HS 118 v Somerset (Birmingham) 2014. BB 1-29 Ire v Jamaica (Spanish Town) 2009-10. UK BB 1-57 Gs v Loughborough UCCE (Bristol) 2008. LO HS 112* (*see LOI*). T20 HS 127*.

POYSDEN, Joshua Edward (Cardinal Newman S, Hove; Anglia RU), b Shoreham-by-Sea, Sussex 8 Aug 1991. LHB, LB. Squad No 14. Cambridge MCCU 2011-13. Warwickshire debut 2015. Unicorns (l-o) 2013. HS 47 and BB 3-20 CU v Surrey (Cambridge) 2011. Wa BB 1-165 v Sussex (Birmingham) 2015. LO HS 10* Unicorns v Glos (Wormsley) 2013 (Y40). LO BB 3-33 Unicorns v Middx (Lord's) 2013 (Y40). T20 BB 1*. T20 BB 4-51.

NQ**RANKIN, William Boyd** (Strabane GS; Harper Adams UC), b Londonderry, Co Derry, N Ireland 5 Jul 1984. Brother of R.J.Rankin (Ireland U19 2003-04). 6'8''. LHB, RFM. Squad No 30. Ireland 2006-07 to 2008. Derbyshire 2007. Warwickshire debut 2008; cap 2013. Middlesex summer contract 2004-05. Became available for England in 2012, before rejoining Ireland in 2015-16. **Tests**: 1 (2013-14); HS 13 and BB 1-47 v A (Sydney) 2013-14. **LOI** (E/Ire): 44 (37 for Ire 2006-07 to 2011-12, 7 for E 2013 to 2013-14); HS 7* Ire v SL (St George's) 2006-07; BB 4-46 E v Ire (Dublin) 2013. **IT20** (E/Ire): 22 (20 for Ire 2009 to 2015-16, 2 for E 2013); HS 16* Ire v UAE (Abu Dhabi) 2015-16; BB 3-17 Ire v UAE (Abu Dhabi) 2015-16. F-c Tour: A 2013-14. HS 56* v Worcs (Birmingham) 2015. 50 wkts (1): 55 (2011). BB 6-55 v Yorks (Leeds) 2015. LO HS 18* v Northants (Northampton) 2013 (Y40). LO BB 4-34 v Kent (Birmingham) 2010 (CB40). T20 HS 16*. T20 BB 4-9.

THOMASON, Aaron Dean (Barr Beacon S, Walsall), b Birmingham 26 Jun 1997. RHB, RMF. Squad No 26. Warwickshire 2nd XI debut 2014. England U19 2015. Awaiting f-c debut. LO HS 0* and LO BB – v Middx (Lord's) 2014 (RLC) – only 1st XI appearance.

TROTT, Ian Jonathan Leonard (Rondebosch BHC; Stellenbosch U), b Cape Town, South Africa 22 Apr 1981. Stepbrother of K.C.Jackson (WP and Boland 1988-89 to 2001-02). 6'0''. RHB, RM. Squad No 9. Boland 2000-01. W Province 2001-02. EU/British passport. Warwickshire debut 2003, scoring 134 v Sussex (Birmingham); cap 2005; benefit 2014. Otago 2005-06. *Wisden* 2010. **Tests**: 52 (2009 to 2014-15); 1000 runs (2); most – 1325 (2010); HS 226 v B (Lord's) 2010; scored 119 v A (Oval) 2009 on debut. BB 1-5 v SL (Lord's) 2011. **LOI**: 68 (2009 to 2013); 1000 runs (1): 1315 (2011); HS 137 v A (Sydney) 2010-11; BB 2-31 v A (Adelaide) 2010-11. **IT20**: 7 (2007 to 2009-10); HS 51 v SA (Centurion) 2009-10. F-c Tours: A 2010-11, 2013-14 (*part*); SA 2009-10, 2014-15 (EL); WI 2014-15; NZ 2008-09 (EL), 2012-13; I 2007-08 (EL), 2012-13; SL 2011-12; B 2009-10; UAE 2011-12 (v P). 1000 runs (6); most – 1400 (2009). HS 226 (*see Tests*). CC HS 210 v Sussex (Birmingham) 2005. BB 7-39 v Kent (Canterbury) 2003. LO HS 137 (*see LOI*). LO BB 4-55 v Hants (Lord's) 2005 (CGT). T20 HS 86*. T20 BB 2-19.

UMEED, Andrew Robert Isaac (High School of Glasgow), b Glasgow 19 Apr 1996. 6'1". RHB, LB. Squad No 23. Scotland 2015. Warwickshire 2nd XI debut 2014. Awaiting 1st XI debut. HS 7 Scot v Afghanistan (Stirling) 2015.

WEBB, Jonathon Patrick (Bromsgrove S; Leeds U), b Solihull 12 Jan 1992. RHB, RM. Squad No 12. Leeds/Bradford MCCU 2012-13. Warwickshire debut 2015. Warwickshire 2nd XI debut 2008, aged 16y 200d. HS 38 LBU v Surrey (Oval) 2012. Wa HS 14 v Middx (Lord's) 2015. LO HS 11 v Notts (Market Warsop) 2015 (RLC). T20 HS 50.

WESTWOOD, Ian James (Wheelers Lane S; Solihull SFC), b Birmingham 13 Jul 1982. 5'7½". LHB, OB. Squad No 22. Debut (Warwickshire) 2003; cap 2008; captain 2009-10; benefit 2015. HS 196 v Yorks (Leeds) 2015. BB 2-39 v Hants (Southampton) 2009. LO HS 65 v Northants (Northampton) 2008 (FPT). BB 1-28 Wa CB v Cambs (March) 2001 (CGT). T20 HS 49*. T20 BB 3-29.

WOAKES, Christopher Roger (Barr Beacon Language S, Walsall), b Birmingham 2 March 1989. 6'2". RHB, RFM. Squad No 19. Debut (Warwickshire) 2006; cap 2009. MCC 2009. Herefordshire 2006-07. **Tests**: 6 (2013 to 2015-16); HS 26* v I (Manchester) 2014; BB 3-30 v I (Oval) 2014. **LOI**: 43 (2010-11 to 2015-16); HS 42* v B (Adelaide) 2014-15; BB 6-45 v A (Brisbane) 2010-11. **IT20**: 8 (2010-11 to 2015-16); HS 37 v P (Sharjah) 2015-16; BB 2-40 v P (Dubai, DSC) 2015-16. F-c Tours: SA 2015-16; WI 2010-11 (EL); SL 2013-14 (EL); UAE 2015-16 (v P). HS 152* v Derbys (Derby) 2013. 50 wkts (2); most – 58 (2010). BB 7-20 (10-123 match) v Hants (Birmingham) 2011. LO HS 49* v Leics (Birmingham) 2010 (CB40). LO BB 6-45 (*see LOI*). T20 HS 55*. T20 BB 4-21.

WRIGHT, Christopher Julian Clement (Eggars S, Alton; Anglia Ruskin U), b Chipping Norton, Oxon 14 Jul 1985. 6'3". RHB, RFM. Squad No 31. Cambridge UCCE 2004-05. Middlesex 2004-07. Tamil Union 2005-06. Essex 2008-11. Warwickshire debut 2011; cap 2013. HS 77 Ex v Cambridge MCCU (Cambridge) 2011. Wa HS 65 v Notts (Birmingham) 2014 and 65 v Sussex (Birmingham) 2015. 50 wkts (1): 67 (2012). BB 6-22 Ex v Leics (Leicester) 2008. Wa BB 6-31 v Durham (Birmingham) 2013. LO HS 42 Ex v Glos (Cheltenham) 2011 (CB40). LO BB 4-20 Ex v Unicorns (Chelmsford) 2011 (CB40). T20 HS 6*. T20 BB 4-24.

RELEASED/RETIRED

(Having made a County 1st XI appearance in 2015)

LEWIS, Thomas Peter (Princethorpe C, Rugby; Castle SFC, Kenilworth), b Coventry 7 Mar 1991. Younger brother of M.F.Lewis (Oxford UCCE 2009). LHB, RM. Warwickshire 2nd XI debut 2008. MCC YC 2010-12. T20 HS 27.

McCULLUM, B.B. – *see MIDDLESEX*.

McKAY, Peter John (Polesworth Int Language C, Tamworth), b Staffs 12 Oct 1994. LHB, WK. Warwickshire 2013-15. Warwickshire 2nd XI debut 2012. HS 33 v Notts (Nottingham) 2013. LO HS 22* v Essex (Chelmsford) 2014 (RLC). T20 HS 2*.

MILNES, T.P. – *see DERBYSHIRE*.

WARWICKSHIRE 2015

RESULTS SUMMARY

	Place	Won	Lost	Tied	Drew	NR
LV= County Championship (1st Division)	5th	5	5		6	
All First-Class Matches		5	5		6	
Royal London One-Day Cup (Group B)	6th	3	3			2
NatWest t20 Blast (North Group)	SF	11	5			

LV= COUNTY CHAMPIONSHIP AVERAGES

BATTING AND FIELDING

Cap		M	I	NO	HS	Runs	Avge	100	50	Ct/St
	S.R.Hain	10	17	2	106	547	36.46	2	3	8
2008	I.J.Westwood	14	25	1	196	856	35.66	1	4	6
	L.J.Evans	15	27	3	213*	826	34.41	1	4	16
2013	K.H.D.Barker	13	20	3	102*	516	30.35	1	2	2
2013	C.J.C.Wright	11	16	6	65	300	30.00	–	2	2
2007	T.R.Ambrose	14	22	–	153	651	29.59	2	1	34/5
2012	V.Chopra	15	25	1	119*	658	27.41	2	2	20
2012	J.S.Patel	16	23	2	98	543	25.85	–	2	10
2005	I.J.L.Trott	11	18	–	87	451	25.05	–	2	6
2011	R.Clarke	16	26	3	67	535	23.26	–	2	22
2014	W.T.S.Porterfield	6	11	–	61	196	17.81	–	1	7
2009	C.R.Woakes	3	5	–	42	83	16.60	–	–	1
2013	W.B.Rankin	13	18	8	56*	155	15.50	–	1	4
	A.Javid	4	6	–	27	64	10.66	–	–	4
	P.J.McKay	2	4	–	17	24	6.00	–	–	6/1
	O.J.Hannon-Dalby	4	6	1	8	24	4.80	–	–	1
	J.P.Webb	2	4	–	14	18	4.50	–	–	1

Also played: M.R.Adair (1 match) 24*, 10*; I.R.Bell (2 – cap 2001) 111, 12, 55 (4 ct); F.R.J.Coleman (1) 0, 0 (2 ct); R.A.Jones (1) 3; T.P.Milnes (1) 12*, 14*; J.E.Poysden (1) did not bat.

BOWLING

	O	M	R	W	Avge	Best	5wI	10wM
C.R.Woakes	74	20	217	11	19.72	3-48	–	–
J.S.Patel	497.5	113	1466	58	25.27	7-38	3	–
R.Clarke	387.3	83	1206	47	25.65	5-62	1	–
W.B.Rankin	273.2	28	1127	43	26.20	6-55	2	–
K.H.D.Barker	424.4	91	1274	46	27.69	5-68	2	–
C.J.C.Wright	274.2	36	1033	31	33.32	5-40	1	–

Also bowled:

| O.J.Hannon-Dalby | 116 | 23 | 406 | 8 | 50.75 | 3-80 | – | – |

M.R.Adair 15-3-61-1; L.J.Evans 5-0-31-1; A.Javid 21-2-74-0; R.A.Jones 17-1-68-4; T.P.Milnes 30-3-120-4; J.E.Poysden 40.4-4-165-1; I.J.L.Trott 34-6-108-1; I.J.Westwood 4-0-18-0.

Warwickshire played no first-class fixtures outside the County Championship in 2015. The First-Class Averages (pp 227–243) give the records of Warwickshire players in all first-class county matches, with the exception of I.R.Bell and T.P.Milnes, whose first-class figures for Warwickshire are as above.

WARWICKSHIRE RECORDS

FIRST-CLASS CRICKET

Highest Total	For	810-4d		v	Durham	Birmingham	1994
	V	887		by	Yorkshire	Birmingham	1896
Lowest Total	For	16		v	Kent	Tonbridge	1913
	V	15		by	Hampshire	Birmingham	1922
Highest Innings	For	501*	B.C.Lara	v	Durham	Birmingham	1994
	V	322	I.V.A.Richards	for	Somerset	Taunton	1985

Highest Partnership for each Wicket

1st	377*	N.F.Horner/K.Ibadulla	v	Surrey	The Oval	1960
2nd	465*	J.A.Jameson/R.B.Kanhai	v	Glos	Birmingham	1974
3rd	327	S.P.Kinneir/W.G.Quaife	v	Lancashire	Birmingham	1901
4th	470	A.I.Kallicharran/G.W.Humpage	v	Lancashire	Southport	1982
5th	335	J.O.Troughton/T.R.Ambrose	v	Hampshire	Birmingham	2009
6th	327	L.J.Evans/T.R.Ambrose	v	Sussex	Birmingham	2015
7th	289*	I.R.Bell/T.Frost	v	Sussex	Horsham	2004
8th	228	A.J.W.Croom/R.E.S.Wyatt	v	Worcs	Dudley	1925
9th	233	I.J.L.Trott/J.S.Patel	v	Yorkshire	Birmingham	2009
10th	214	N.V.Knight/A.Richardson	v	Hampshire	Birmingham	2002

Best Bowling	For	10-41	J.D.Bannister	v	Comb Servs	Birmingham	1959
(Innings)	V	10-36	H.Verity	for	Yorkshire	Leeds	1931
Best Bowling	For	15-76	S.Hargreave	v	Surrey	The Oval	1903
(Match)	V	17-92	A.P.Freeman	for	Kent	Folkestone	1932

Most Runs – Season	2417	M.J.K.Smith	(av 60.42)	1959
Most Runs – Career	35146	D.L.Amiss	(av 41.64)	1960-87
Most 100s – Season	9	A.I.Kallicharran		1984
	9	B.C.Lara		1994
Most 100s – Career	78	D.L.Amiss		1960-87
Most Wkts – Season	180	W.E.Hollies	(av 15.13)	1946
Most Wkts – Career	2201	W.E.Hollies	(av 20.45)	1932-57
Most Career W-K Dismissals	800	E.J.Smith	(662 ct; 138 st)	1904-30
Most Career Catches in the Field	422	M.J.K.Smith		1956-75

LIMITED-OVERS CRICKET

Highest Total	50ov	392-5		v	Oxfordshire	Birmingham	1984
	40ov	321-7		v	Leics	Birmingham	2010
	T20	242-2		v	Derbyshire	Birmingham	2015
Lowest Total	50ov	94		v	Glos	Bristol	2000
	40ov	59		v	Yorkshire	Leeds	2001
	T20	73		v	Somerset	Taunton	2013
Highest Innings	50ov	206	A.I.Kallicharran	v	Oxfordshire	Birmingham	1984
	40ov	137	I.R.Bell	v	Yorkshire	Birmingham	2005
	T20	158*	B.B.McCullum	v	Derbyshire	Birmingham	2015
Best Bowling	50ov	7-32	R.G.D.Willis	v	Yorkshire	Birmingham	1981
	40ov	6-15	A.A.Donald	v	Yorkshire	Birmingham	1995
	T20	5-19	N.M.Carter	v	Worcs	Birmingham	2005

WORCESTERSHIRE

Formation of Present Club: 11 March 1865
Inaugural First-Class Match: 1899
Colours: Dark Green and Black
Badge: Shield Argent a Fess between three Pears Sable
County Championships: (5) 1964, 1965, 1974, 1988, 1989
NatWest Trophy Winners: (1) 1994
Benson and Hedges Cup Winners: (1) 1991
Pro 40/National League (Div 1) Winners: (1) 2007
Sunday League Winners: (3) 1971, 1987, 1988
Twenty20 Cup Winners: (0); best – Quarter-Finalist 2004, 2007, 2012, 2014, 2015

Interim Chief Executive: Tom Scott, County Ground, New Road, Worcester, WR2 4QQ •
Tel: 01905 748474 • Fax: 01905 748005 • Email: info@wccc.co.uk • Web: www.wccc.co.uk
• Twitter : @WorcsCCC (25,647 followers)

Director of Cricket: Steve Rhodes. **Bowling/Assistant Coach**: Matt Mason. **Captain**:
D.K.H.Mitchell. **Vice-Captain**: tba. **Overseas Players**: K.J.Abbott, M.J.Henry and
M.J.Santner (T20 only). **2016 Beneficiary**: D.K.H.Mitchell. **Head Groundsman**: Tim
Packwood. **Scorer**: Sue Drinkwater. ‡ New registration. ^{NQ} Not qualified for England.

*Worcestershire revised their capping policy in 2002 and now award players with their
County Colours when they make their Championship debut.*

‡^{NQ}**ABBOTT, Kyle** John, b Empangeni, South Africa 18 Jun 1987. RHB, RFM. KwaZulu-
Natal 2008-09 to 2009-10. Dolphins 2008-09 to date. Hampshire 2014. Joins Worcestershire
for second half of 2016. **Tests** (SA): 7 (2012-13 to 2015-16); HS 16 v E (Centurion) 2015-16;
BB 7-29 v P (Centurion) 2012-13. **LOI** (SA): 24 (2012-13 to 2015-16); HS 23 v Z (Bulawayo)
2014; BB 4-21 v Ireland (Canberra) 2014-15. **IT20** (SA): 18 (2012-13 to 2015-16); HS 9* v
NZ (Centurion) 2015; BB 3-20 v B (Dhaka) 2015. HS 80 Dolphins v Titans (Benoni) 2010-11.
CC HS 40 H v Leics (Leicester) 2014. BB 8-45 (12-96 match) Dolphins v Cobras (Cape Town)
2012-13. CC BB 5-44 H v Essex (Southampton) 2014. LO HS 45* Dolphins v Titans (Durban)
2013-14. LO BB 4-21 (*see LOI*). T20 HS 16*. T20 BB 5-14.

ALI, Moeen Munir (Moseley S), b Birmingham, Warwks 18 Jun 1987. Brother of A.K.Ali
(Worcs, Glos and Leics 2000-12); cousin of Kabir Ali (Worcs, Rajasthan, Hants and Lancs
1999-2014). 6'0". LHB, OB. Squad No 8. Warwickshire 2005-06. Worcestershire debut
2007. Moors SC 2011-12. MT 2012-13. MCC 2012. PCA 2013. *Wisden* 2014. **ECB
Central Contract 2015-16**. **Tests**: 23 (2014 to 2015-16); HS 108* v SL (Leeds) 2014; BB
6-67 v I (Southampton) 2014. **LOI**: 36 (2013-14 to 2015-16); HS 128 v Scotland
(Christchurch) 2014-15; BB 3-32 v A (Manchester) 2015. **IT20**: 12 (2013-14 to 2015-16);
HS 72* v A (Cardiff) 2015; BB 2-22 v SA (Cape Town) 2015-16. F-c Tours: SA 2015-16;
WI 2014-15; SL 2013-14 (EL); UAE 2015-16 (v P). 1000 runs (2); most – 1420 (2013). HS
250 v Glamorgan (Worcester) 2013. BB 6-29 (12-96 match) v Lancs (Manchester) 2012. LO
HS 158 v Sussex (Horsham) 2011 (CB40). LO BB 3-28 v Notts (Nottingham) 2013 (Y40).
T20 HS 90. T20 BB 5-34.

BARNARD, Edward George (Shrewsbury S), b Shrewsbury, Shrops 20 Nov 1995. Younger
brother of M.R.Barnard (Oxford MCCU 2010). 6'1". RHB, RMF. Squad No 30. Debut
(Worcestershire) 2015. Shropshire 2012. England U19 2012-13 to 2014. HS 17 and BB 3-63
v Durham (Chester-le-St) 2015. LO HS 51 v Somerset (Taunton) 2015 (RLC). LO BB 3-59
v Yorks (Worcester) 2015 (RLC). T20 HS 10. T20 BB 2-18.

CLARKE, Joe Michael (Llanfyllin HS), b Shrewsbury, Shrops 26 May 1996. 5'11". RHB, WK. Squad No 33. Debut (Worcestershire) 2015. Worcestershire 2nd XI debut 2013. Shropshire 2012-13. England U19s 2014. HS 104* v Sussex (Worcester) 2015. LO HS 131* v Glos (Worcester) 2015 (RLC). T20 HS 16.

COX, Oliver Ben (Bromsgrove S), b Wordsley, Stourbridge 2 Feb 1992. 5'10". RHB, WK. Squad No 10. Debut (Worcestershire) 2009. Worcestershire 2nd XI debut 2009. HS 109 v Somerset (Worcester) 2015. LO HS 39 v Derbys (Worcester) 2014 (RLC). T20 HS 46.

D'OLIVEIRA, Brett Louis (Worcester SFC), b Worcester 28 Feb 1992. Son of D.B.D'Oliveira (Worcs 1982-95), grandson of B.L.D'Oliveira (Worcs, EP and England 1964-80). 5'9". RHB, LB. Squad No 15. Debut (Worcestershire) 2012. Worcestershire 2nd XI debut 2010. HS 49 and BB 5-48 v Durham (Chester-le-St) 2015. LO HS 42 v Yorks (Worcester) 2015 (RLC). LO BB 3-35 v Warwks (Worcester) 2013 (Y40). T20 HS 56*. T20 BB 3-20.

FELL, Thomas Charles (Oakham S; Oxford Brookes U), b Hillingdon, Middx 17 Oct 1993. 6'1". RHB, WK, occ OB. Squad No 29. Oxford MCCU 2013. Worcestershire debut 2013. Worcestershire 2nd XI debut 2010. 1000 runs (1): 1127 (2015). HS 171 v Middx (Worcester) 2015. LO HS 89 v Glos (Worcester) 2014 (RLC).

‡NOHENRY, Matthew James, b Christchurch, New Zealand 14 Dec 1991. RHB, RFM. Canterbury 2010-11 to date. Joins Worcestershire for first half of 2016. **Tests** (NZ): 4 (2015 to 2015-16); HS 66 v A (Christchurch) 2015-16; BB 4-93 v E (Lord's) 2015. **LOI** (NZ): 25 (2013-14 to 2015-16); HS 48* v P (Wellington) 2015-16; BB 5-30 v P (Abu Dhabi) 2014-15. **IT20** (NZ): 5 (2014-15 to 2015-16); HS 10 v P (Auckland) 2015-16; BB 3-44 v SL (Mt Maunganui) 2015-16. F-c Tours (NZ): E 2014 (NZ A), 2015; A 2015-16 SL 2013-14 (NZ A). HS 75* Canterbury v CD (Rangiora) 2015-16. BB 5-18 NZ A v Surrey (Oval) 2014. LO HS 48* (*see LOI*). LO BB 6-45 Canterbury v Auckland (Auckland) 2012-13. T20 HS 42. T20 BB 4-43.

HEPBURN, Alex (Aquinas C, Perth), b Subiaco, W Australia 21 Dec 1995. RHB, RM. Squad No 26. Worcestershire 2nd XI debut 2013. Awaiting f-c debut. LO HS 32 v Derbys (Derby) 2015 (RLC). LO BB 4-34 v Leics (Worcester) 2015 (RLC).

KERVEZEE, Alexei Nicolaas (Duneside HS, Namibia; Grenoobi HS, SA; Segbroek C, Holland), b Walvis Bay, Namibia 11 Sep 1989. 5'8". RHB, OB. Squad No 5. Netherlands 2005 to 2009-10. Worcestershire debut 2008. Now qualified for England. **LOI** (Neth): 39 (2006 to 2011-12); HS 92 v Kenya (Voorburg) 2010; BB – . **IT20** (Neth): 10 (2009 to 2011-12); HS 58* v Afghanistan (Dubai, DSC) 2011-12. 1000 runs (1): 1190 (2010). HS 155 v Derbys (Derby) 2010. BB 3-72 v Sussex (Hove) 2015. LO HS 121* Netherlands v Denmark (Potchefstroom) 2008-09. LO BB – . T20 HS 58*.

KOHLER-CADMORE, Tom (Malvern C), b Chatham, Kent 19 Aug 1994. 6'2". RHB, OB. Squad No 32. Debut (Worcestershire) 2014. Worcestershire 2nd XI debut 2010, aged 15y 342d. HS 130* v Middx (Worcester) 2015. LO HS 71 v Derbys (Worcester) 2014 (RLC). T20 HS 75.

LEACH, Joseph (Shrewsbury S; Leeds U), b Stafford 30 Oct 1990. 6'1". RHB, RMF. Squad No 23. Leeds/Bradford MCCU 2012. Worcestershire debut 2012. Worcestershire 2nd XI debut 2008. Staffordshire 2008-09. HS 114 v Glos (Cheltenham) 2013. 50 wkts (1): 59 (2015). BB 6-73 v Warwks (Birmingham) 2015. LO HS 45* v Essex (Worcester) 2014 (RLC). LO BB 4-30 v Northants (Worcester) 2015 (RLC). T20 HS 20. T20 BB 3-20.

MITCHELL, Daryl Keith Henry (Prince Henry's HS; University C, Worcester), b Badsey, near Evesham 25 Nov 1983. 5'10". RHB, RM. Squad No 27. Debut (Worcestershire) 2005; captain 2011 to date; benefit 2016. Mountaineers 2011-12. MCC 2015. 1000 runs (3); most – 1334 (2014). HS 298 v Somerset (Taunton) 2009. BB 4-49 v Yorks (Leeds) 2009. LO HS 107 v Sussex (Hove) 2013 (Y40). LO BB 4-19 v Northants (Milton Keynes) 2014 (RLC). T20 HS 68*. T20 BB 5-28 v Northants (Northampton) 2014 – Wo record.

MORRIS, Charles Andrew John (King's C, Taunton; Oxford Brookes U), b Hereford 6 Jul 1992. 6'0". RHB, RMF. Squad No 31. Oxford MCCU 2012-14. Worcestershire debut 2013. Worcestershire 2nd XI debut 2012. Kent 2nd XI 2011. MCC Univs 2012. Devon 2011-12. HS 33* OU v Warwks (Oxford) 2013. Wo HS 25* v Australians (Worcester) 2013. CC HS 24 v Glos (Worcester) 2014 and 24 v Sussex (Hove) 2015. 50 wkts (2); most – 56 (2014). BB 5-54 v Derbys (Derby) 2014. LO HS 16* v Northants (Milton Keynes) 2014 (RLC). LO BB 3-46 v Derbys (Derby) 2015 (RLC). T20 HS 2*. T20 BB 2-44.

OLIVER, Richard Kenneth (Grove HS, Mkt Drayton; Wrekin C), b Stoke-on-Trent, Staffs 14 Nov 1989. 6'1". LHB, RM. Squad No 43. Debut (Worcestershire) 2014. Shropshire 2008-14. HS 179 v Glos (Worcester) 2014. LO HS 14 v Northants (Milton Keynes) 2014 (RLC) and 14 v Glos (Worcester) 2015 (RLC). T20 HS 77.

RUSSELL, Christopher James (Medina HS), b Newport, IoW 16 Feb 1989. 6'1". RHB, RMF. Squad No 18. Debut (Worcestershire) 2012. HS 22 v Middx (Worcester) 2012. BB 4-43 v Warwks (Birmingham) 2012. LO HS 1* (twice). LO BB 4-32 v Netherlands (Rotterdam) 2013 (Y40). T20 HS 3*. T20 BB 4-40.

‡NQ**SANTNER, Mitchell** Josef, b Hamilton, New Zealand 5 Feb 1992. LHB, SLA. N Districts 2011-12 to date. **Tests** (NZ): 3 (2015-16); HS 45 v A (Adelaide) 2015-16; BB 2-37 v SL (Dunedin) 2015-16. **LOI** (NZ): 14 (2015 to 2015-16); HS 48 v P (Wellington) 2015-16; BB 3-31 v E (Chester-le-St) 2015. **IT20** (NZ): 5 (2015 to 2015-16); HS 9 v E (Manchester) 2015; BB 2-14 v P (Auckland) 2015-16. F-c Tour (NZ): A 2015-16. HS 118 ND v Canterbury (Gisborne) 2013-14. BB 3-51 ND v Auckland (Whangarei) 2014-15. LO HS 86 ND v CD (New Plymouth) 2014-15. LO BB 4-38 NZ A v Sri Lanka A (Christchurch) 2015-16. T20 HS 19. T20 BB 2-14.

SHANTRY, Jack David (Priory SS; Shrewsbury SFC; Liverpool U), b Shrewsbury, Shrops 29 Jan 1988. Son of B.K.Shantry (Gloucestershire 1978-79); brother of A.J.Shantry (Northants, Warwicks, Glamorgan 2003-11). 6'4". LHB, LM. Squad No 11. Debut (Worcestershire) 2009. Shropshire 2007-09. HS 101* v Surrey (Worcester) 2014. 50 wkts (2); most – 67 (2015). BB 7-60 v Oxford MCCU (Oxford) 2013. CC BB 7-69 v Essex (Worcester) 2013. LO HS 31 v Somerset (Taunton) 2013 (RLC). LO BB 4-29 v Northants (Worcester) 2015 (RLC). T20 HS 12*. T20 BB 4-33.

TONGUE, Joshua Charles (King's S, Worcester; Worcester SFC), b Redditch 15 Nov 1997. RHB, RM. Worcestershire 2nd XI debut. Awaiting 1st XI debut.

TWOHIG, Benjamin Jake (Malvern C), b Dewsbury, Yorks 13 Apr 1998. RHB, SLA. Worcestershire 2nd XI debut. Awaiting 1st XI debut.

WHITELEY, Ross Andrew (Repton S), b Sheffield, Yorks 13 Sep 1988. 6'2". LHB, LM. Squad No 44. Derbyshire 2008-13. Worcestershire debut 2013. No f-c appearances in 2009-10. HS 130* De v Kent (Derby) 2011. Wo HS 101 v Yorks (Scarborough) 2015. BB 2-6 De v Hants (Derby) 2012. Wo BB 1-23 v Hants (Worcester) 2013. LO HS 77 v Yorks (Worcester) 2015 (RLC). LO BB 1-17 De v Unicorns (Wormsley) 2012 (CB40). T20 HS 91*. T20 BB 1-12.

RELEASED/RETIRED

(Having made a County 1st XI appearance in 2015)

ANDREW, Gareth Mark (Ansford Community S; Richard Huish C), b Yeovil, Somerset 27 Dec 1983. 6'0". LHB, RMF. Somerset 2003-05. Worcestershire 2008-15. Canterbury 2012-13. HS 180* Canterbury v Auckland (Auckland) 2012-13. Wo HS 92* v Notts (Worcester) 2009. 50 wkts (1): 52 (2011). BB 5-40 v Glamorgan (Cardiff) 2014. LO HS 104 v Surrey (Oval) 2010 (CB40). LO BB 5-31 v Yorks (Worcester) 2009 (P40). T20 HS 65*. T20 BB 4-22.

NQGABRIEL, Shannon Terry, b Trinidad 28 Apr 1988. RHB, RFM. Trinidad & Tobago 2009-10 to date. Worcestershire 2015. **Tests** (WI): 16 (2012 to 2015-16); HS 20* v E (St George's) 2015; BB 3-10 v Z (Bridgetown) 2012-13. **IT20** (WI): 2 (2012-13 to 2013); HS – ; BB 3-44 v P (Kingstown) 2013. F-c Tours (WI): E 2012; A 2015-16; SA 2014-15; NZ 2013-14; I 2013-14; SL 2014-15 (WI A), 2015-16. HS 20* (*see Tests*). BB 5-29 WI A v SL A (Matara) 2014-15. Wo BB 5-31 v Middx (Worcester) 2015. LO HS 6* Sagicor HP Centre v Guyana (Kingston) 2010-11. LO BB 4-34 T&T v Jamaica (Kingston) 2012-13. T20 HS 2*. T20 BB 3-19.

GIDMAN, Alex Peter Richard (Wycliffe C), b High Wycombe, Bucks 22 Jun 1981. Elder brother of W.R.S.Gidman (*see NOTTINGHAMSHIRE*). 6'3". RHB, RM. Gloucestershire 2002-14; cap 2004; captain 2009-12; benefit 2012. Worcestershire 2015. MCC YC 2001. MCC 2004, 2007, 2010. F-c Tour (Eng A): SL 2004-05. 1000 runs (6); most – 1278 (2014). HS 264 Gs v Leics (Bristol) 2014, sharing Gs record 3nd wkt partnership of 392 with G.H.Roderick. Wo HS 78 v Somerset (Worcester) 2015. BB 4-47 Gs v Glamorgan (Cardiff) 2005. Wo BB 1-11 v Sussex (Hove) 2015. LO HS 116 Gs v Sussex (Hove) 2009 (FPT). LO BB 5-42 Eng A v Bangladesh A (Mirpur) 2006-07. T20 HS 64. T20 BB 2-24.

NQMUNRO, Colin, b Durban, South Africa 11 Mar 1987. LHB, RM. Auckland 2006-07 to date. Worcestershire 2015. **Tests** (NZ): 1 (2012-13); HS 15 and BB 2-40 v SA (Port Elizabeth) 2012-13. **LOI** (NZ): 12 (2012-13 to 2015); HS 85 v B (Fatullah) 2013-14; BB – . **IT20** (NZ): 23 (2012-13 to 2015-16); HS 73* v B (Dhaka) 2013-14. F-c Tours (NZ): SA 2012-13; SL 2013-14. HS 281 Auckland v CD (Napier) 2014-15, inc world record 23 sixes. Wo HS 34 v Hants (Southampton) 2015. BB 4-36 Auckland v CD (Auckland) 2010-11. LO HS 151 Auckland v Canterbury (Auckland) 2012-13. LO BB 3-45 Auckland v Otago (Oamaru) 2010-11. T20 HS 89. T20 BB 2-26.

NQSAEED AJMAL, b Faisalabad, Pakistan 14 Oct 1977. 5'4". RHB, OB. Faisalabad 1996-97 to 2006-07. KRL 2000-01 to 2008-09. Islamabad 2001-02. Federal Areas 2007-08. ZTB 2009-10 to date. Worcestershire 2011-15. Big Bash: AS 2012-13. **Tests** (P): 35 (2009 to 2014); HS 50 v E (Birmingham) 2010; 50 wkts (1): 50 (2011); BB 7-55 (10-97 match) v E (Dubai) 2011-12. **LOI** (P): 113 (2008 to 2014-15); HS 33 v NZ (Abu Dhabi) 2009-10; 50 wkts (1): 62 (2013); BB 5-24 v I (Delhi) 2012-13. **IT20** (P): 64 (2009 to 2014-15); HS 21* v WI (Gros Islet) 2010-11; BB 4-19 v Ireland (Oval) 2009. F-c Tours (P): E 2010; A 2009-10; SA 2012-13; WI 2011; NZ 2009-10; SL 2009, 2012; Z 2011, 2013, 2014; B 2011-12; UAE 2010-11 (v SA), 2011-12 (v SL), 2011-12 (v E), 2013-14 (v SA), 2013-14 (v SL). HS 53* v Leics (Worcester) 2014. 50 wkts (1+1); most – 63 (2014). BB 7-19 (13-94 match) v Essex (Worcester) 2014. LO HS 33 (*see LOI*). LO BB 5-18 Faisalabad v Karachi (Karachi) 2003-04. T20 HS 21*. T20 BB 4-14.

RELEASED/RETIRED continued on p 202

WORCESTERSHIRE 2015

RESULTS SUMMARY

	Place	Won	Lost	Tied	Drew	NR
LV= County Championship (1st Division)	9th	3	10		3	
All First-Class Matches		4	10		3	
Royal London One-Day Cup (Group A)	8th	1	6			1
NatWest t20 Blast (North Group)	QF	9	5			1

LV= COUNTY CHAMPIONSHIP AVERAGES

BATTING AND FIELDING

Cap†		M	I	NO	HS	Runs	Avge	100	50	Ct/St
2014	T.Kohler-Cadmore	5	8	1	130*	294	42.00	1	1	5
2013	T.C.Fell	16	26	–	171	1084	41.69	3	4	20
2008	G.M.Andrew	2	4	–	70	152	38.00	–	2	–
2009	O.B.Cox	16	26	5	109	778	37.04	1	5	43/2
2013	R.A.Whiteley	8	13	1	101	436	36.33	1	3	6
2015	J.M.Clarke	11	16	1	104*	530	35.33	1	4	3
2005	D.K.H.Mitchell	15	25	3	206*	768	34.90	2	1	18
2008	M.M.Ali	4	8	1	62	227	32.42	–	2	1
2012	J.Leach	14	19	2	95	498	29.29	–	3	4
2012	B.L.D'Oliveira	7	11	–	49	267	24.27	–	–	4
2015	A.P.R.Gidman	12	19	2	78	397	23.35	–	3	11
2009	A.N.Kervezee	4	7	–	93	162	23.14	–	1	–
2014	R.K.Oliver	12	21	–	101	452	21.52	1	1	8
2011	Saeed Ajmal	8	12	2	37	162	16.20	–	–	5
2015	S.M.S.M.Senanayake	5	9	–	32	120	13.33	–	–	3
2009	J.D.Shantry	16	22	4	41*	221	12.27	–	–	4
2015	E.G.Barnard	4	4	1	17	35	11.66	–	–	2
2014	C.A.J.Morris	14	21	10	24	85	7.72	–	–	2

Also played: S.T.Gabriel (2 matches – cap 2015) did not bat; C.Munro (1 – cap 2015) 34.

BOWLING

	O	M	R	W	Avge	Best	5wI	10wM
J.D.Shantry	515.2	130	1430	57	25.08	5-48	3	–
E.G.Barnard	100.1	20	345	12	28.75	3-63	–	–
J.Leach	467	74	1772	59	30.03	6-73	2	–
C.A.J.Morris	470	90	1510	44	34.31	5-71	1	–
B.L.D'Oliveira	103.4	17	407	11	37.00	5-48	1	–
Saeed Ajmal	272.3	42	890	16	55.62	5-28	1	–

Also bowled:

	O	M	R	W	Avge	Best	5wI	10wM
S.T.Gabriel	40	3	183	9	20.33	5-31	1	–
G.M.Andrew	50.1	5	220	8	27.50	5-85	1	–
S.M.S.M.Senanayake	137	18	381	9	42.33	4-50	–	–

M.M.Ali 85-6-272-3; T.C.Fell 1-0-7-0; A.P.R.Gidman 3-1-11-1; A.N.Kervezee 23-1-86-3; D.K.H.Mitchell 7-0-24-0; C.Munro 8-2-29-1; R.A.Whiteley 42-1-234-1.

The First-Class Averages (pp 227–243) give the records of Worcestershire players in all first-class county matches (Worcestershire's other opponents being Oxford MCCU), with the exception of M.M.Ali, whose first-class figures for Worcestershire are as above.

† Worcestershire revised their capping policy in 2002 and now award players with their County Colours when they make their Championship debut.

WORCESTERSHIRE RECORDS

FIRST-CLASS CRICKET

Highest Total	For 701-6d		v	Surrey	Worcester	2007
	V 701-4d		by	Leics	Worcester	1906
Lowest Total	For 24		v	Yorkshire	Huddersfield	1903
	V 30		by	Hampshire	Worcester	1903
Highest Innings	For 405*	G.A.Hick	v	Somerset	Taunton	1988
	V 331*	J.D.B.Robertson	for	Middlesex	Worcester	1949

Highest Partnership for each Wicket

1st	309	H.K.Foster/F.L.Bowley	v	Derbyshire	Derby	1901
2nd	316	S.C.Moore/V.S.Solanki	v	Glos	Cheltenham	2008
3rd	438*	G.A.Hick/T.M.Moody	v	Hampshire	Southampton	1997
4th	330	B.F.Smith/G.A.Hick	v	Somerset	Taunton	2006
5th	393	E.G.Arnold/W.B.Burns	v	Warwicks	Birmingham	1909
6th	265	G.A.Hick/S.J.Rhodes	v	Somerset	Taunton	1988
7th	256	D.A.Leatherdale/S.J.Rhodes	v	Notts	Nottingham	2002
8th	184	S.J.Rhodes/S.R.Lampitt	v	Derbyshire	Kidderminster	1991
9th	181	J.A.Cuffe/R.D.Burrows	v	Glos	Worcester	1907
10th	119	W.B.Burns/G.A.Wilson	v	Somerset	Worcester	1906

Best Bowling	For 9- 23	C.F.Root	v	Lancashire	Worcester	1931
(Innings)	V 10- 51	J.Mercer	for	Glamorgan	Worcester	1936
Best Bowling	For 15- 87	A.J.Conway	v	Glos	Moreton-in-M	1914
(Match)	V 17-212	J.C.Clay	for	Glamorgan	Swansea	1937

Most Runs – Season	2654	H.H.I.H.Gibbons	(av 52.03)	1934
Most Runs – Career	34490	D.Kenyon	(av 34.18)	1946-67
Most 100s – Season	10	G.M.Turner		1970
	10	G.A.Hick		1988
Most 100s – Career	106	G.A.Hick		1984-2008
Most Wkts – Season	207	C.F.Root	(av 17.52)	1925
Most Wkts – Career	2143	R.T.D.Perks	(av 23.73)	1930-55
Most Career W-K Dismissals	1095	S.J.Rhodes	(991 ct; 104 st)	1985-2004
Most Career Catches in the Field	528	G.A.Hick		1984-2008

LIMITED-OVERS CRICKET

Highest Total	50ov	404-3	v	Devon	Worcester	1987
	40ov	376-6	v	Surrey	Oval	2010
	T20	227-6	v	Northants	Kidderminster	2007
Lowest Total	50ov	58	v	Ireland	Worcester	2009
	40ov	86	v	Yorkshire	Leeds	1969
	T20	86	v	Northants	Worcester	2006
Highest Innings	50ov	180* T.M.Moody	v	Surrey	The Oval	1994
	40ov	160 T.M.Moody	v	Kent	Worcester	1991
	T20	116* G.A.Hick	v	Northants	Luton	2004
Best Bowling	50ov	7-19 N.V.Radford	v	Beds	Bedford	1991
	40ov	6-16 Shoaib Akhtar	v	Glos	Worcester	2005
	T20	5-28 D.K.H.Mitchell	v	Northants	Northampton	2014

YORKSHIRE

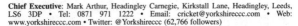

Formation of Present Club: 8 January 1863
Substantial Reorganisation: 10 December 1891
Inaugural First-Class Match: 1864
Colours: Dark Blue, Light Blue and Gold
Badge: White Rose
County Championships (since 1890): (32) 1893, 1896, 1898, 1900, 1901, 1902, 1905, 1908, 1912, 1919, 1922, 1923, 1924, 1925, 1931, 1932, 1933, 1935, 1937, 1938, 1939, 1946, 1959, 1960, 1962, 1963, 1966, 1967, 1968, 2001, 2014, 2015
Joint Champions: (1) 1949
Gillette/C&G Trophy Winners: (3) 1965, 1969, 2002
Benson and Hedges Cup Winners: (1) 1987
Sunday League Winners: (1) 1983
Twenty20 Cup Winners: (0); best – Finalist 2012

Chief Executive: Mark Arthur, Headingley Carnegie, Kirkstall Lane, Headingley, Leeds, LS6 3DP • Tel: 0871 971 1222 • Email: cricket@yorkshireccc.com • Web: www.yorkshireccc.com • Twitter: @Yorkshireccc (62,766 followers)

Director of Professional Cricket: Martyn Moxon. **Senior 1st XI Coach**: Jason Gillespie. **2nd XI Coach**: Ian Dews. **Captains**: A.W.Gale (f-c) and A.Z.Lees (l-o). **Overseas Players**: T.M.Head and K.S.Williamson. **2016 Beneficiary**: A.W.Gale. **Head Groundsman**: Andy Fogarty. **Scorer**: John Potter. ‡ New registration. ^{NQ} Not qualified for England.

BAIRSTOW, Jonathan Marc (St Peter's S, York; Leeds Met U), b Bradford 26 Sep 1989. Son of D.L.Bairstow (Yorkshire, GW and England 1970-90); brother of A.D.Bairstow (Derbyshire 1995). 6'0". RHB, WK, occ RM. Squad No 21. Debut (Yorkshire) 2009; cap 2011. Inaugural winner of Young Wisden Schools Cricketer of the Year 2008. YC 2011. **Tests**: 24 (2012 to 2015-16); HS 150* v SA (Cape Town) 2015-16. **LOI**: 12 (2011 to 2015); HS 83* v NZ (Chester-le-St) 2015. **IT20**: 19 (2011 to 2015); HS 60* v P (Dubai) 2011-12. F-c Tours: A 2013-14; SA 2014-15 (EL), 2015-16; I 2012-13; WI 2010-11 (EL); SL 2013-14 (EL); UAE 2015-16 (v P). 1000 runs (2); most – 1226 (2015). HS 219* v Durham (Chester-le-St) 2015, sharing Y record 7th wkt partnership of 366* with T.T.Bresnan. LO HS 123 EL v New Zealand A (Bristol) 2014. T20 HS 102*.

BALLANCE, Gary Simon (Peterhouse S, Marondera, Zimbabwe; Harrow S; Leeds Met U), b Harare, Zimbabwe 22 Nov 1989. Nephew of G.S.Ballance (Rhodesia B 1978-79) and D.L.Houghton (Rhodesia/Zimbabwe 1978-79 to 1997-98). 6'0". LHB, LB. Squad No 19. Debut (Yorkshire) 2008; cap 2012. MWR 2010-11 to 2011-12. *Wisden* 2014. **Tests**: 15 (2013-14 to 2015); HS 156 v I (Southampton) 2014; BB – . **LOI**: 16 (2013 to 2014-15); HS 79 v A (Melbourne) 2013-14. F-c Tours: A 2013-14; WI 2014-15. 1000 runs (1+1); most – 1363 (2013). HS 210 MWR v SR (Masvingo) 2011-12. Y HS 174 v Northants (Leeds) 2014. BB – . LO HS 139 v Unicorns (Leeds) 2013. T20 HS 68.

BRESNAN, Timothy Thomas (Castleford HS and TC; Pontefract New C), b Pontefract 28 Feb 1985. 6'0". RHB, RFM. Squad No 16. Debut (Yorkshire) 2003; cap 2006; benefit 2014. MCC 2006, 2009. Big Bash: HH 2014-15. *Wisden* 2011. **Tests**: 23 (2009 to 2013-14); HS 91 v B (Dhaka) 2009-10; BB 5-48 v I (Nottingham) 2011. **LOI**: 84 (2006 to 2013-14); HS 80 v SA (Centurion) 2009-10; BB 5-48 v I (Bangalore) 2010-11. **IT20**: 34 (2006 to 2013-14); HS 47* v WI (Bridgetown) 2013-14; BB 3-10 v P (Cardiff) 2010. F-c Tours: A 2010-11, 2013-14; I 2012-13; SL 2011-12; B 2006-07 (Eng A), 2009-10. HS 169* v Durham (Chester-le-St) 2015, sharing Y record 7th wkt partnership of 366* with J.M.Bairstow. BB 5-42 v Worcs (Worcester) 2005. LO HS 80 (*see LOI*). BB 5-48 (*see LOI*). T20 HS 51. T20 BB 3-10.

BROOKS, Jack Alexander (Wheatley Park S), b Oxford 4 Jun 1984. 6'2". RHB, RFM. Squad No 70. Northamptonshire 2009-12; cap 2012. Yorkshire debut 2013; cap 2013. Oxfordshire 2004-09. F-c Tour (EL): SA 2014-15. HS 53 Nh v Glos (Bristol) 2010. Y HS 50* v Middx (Lord's) 2015. 50 wkts (2); most – 71 (2014). BB 5-23 Nh v Leics (Leicester) 2011. Y BB 5-35 v Somerset (Leeds) 2015. LO HS 10 Nh v Middx (Uxbridge) 2009 (P40). LO BB 3-30 v Hants (Southampton) 2014 (RLC). T20 HS 33*. T20 BB 5-21.

CARVER, Karl (Thirsk S & SFC), b Northallerton 26 Mar 1996. 5'10". LHB, SLA. Squad No 29. Debut (Yorkshire) 2014. Yorkshire 2nd XI debut 2013; cap 2013. CC HS 16 and BB 2-6 v Leeds/Bradford MCCU (Leeds) 2015. CC CC HS 5 v Worcs (Worcester) 2015. CC BB – . LO HS 35* v Somerset (Scarborough) 2015 (RLC). LO BB 2-40 v Surrey (Oval) 2015 (RLC). T20 HS 2. T20 BB – .

COAD, Benjamin Oliver (Thirsk S & SFC), b Harrogate 10 Jan 1994. 6'2". RHB, RMF. Squad No 10. Yorkshire 2nd XI debut 2012. Awaiting f-c debut. LO HS 2* v Sri Lanka A (Leeds) 2014. LO BB 1-34 v Glos (Bristol) 2013 (Y40). T20 HS 2*. T20 BB 2-24.

FISHER, Matthew David (Easingwold SS), b York 9 Nov 1997. 6'1". RHB, RFM. Squad No 7. Debut (Yorkshire) 2015. Yorkshire 2nd XI debut 2013, aged 15y 201d. England U19 2014. HS 0*. BB 2-61 v Hants (Southampton). 2015. LO HS 34 v Somerset (Scarborough) 2015 (RLC). LO BB 3-32 v Leics (Leeds) 2015 (RLC). T20 HS 0*. T20 BB 5-22.

GALE, Andrew William (Whitcliffe Mount S; Heckmondwike GS), b Dewsbury 28 Nov 1983. 6'2". LHB, LB. Squad No 26. Debut (Yorkshire) 2004, 2006 to date; cap 2008; captain 2010 to date; benefit 2016. F-c Tour (EL): WI 2010-11. 1000 runs (2); most – 1076 (2013). HS 272 v Notts (Scarborough) 2013. BB 1-33 v Loughborough UCCE (Leeds) 2007. LO HS 125* v Essex (Chelmsford) 2010 (CB40). T20 HS 91.

GIBSON, Ryan (Fylinghall S), b Middlesbrough 22 Jan 1996. 6'4". RHB, RM. Squad No 24. Yorkshire 2nd XI debut 2012. Awaiting f-c debut. LO HS 9 v Sri Lanka A (Leeds) 2014. LO BB 1-17 v Bangladesh A (Leeds) 2013. T20 HS 18. T20 BB – .

‡**NQHEAD, Travis** Michael, b Adelaide, Australia 29 Dec 1993. LHB, OB. S Australia 2011-12 to date. Big Bash: AS 2012-13 to date. MCC YC 2013. **IT20** (A): 2 (2015-16); HS 26 v I (Sydney) 2015-16; BB – . F-c Tour (Aus A): I 2015. HS 134 S Aus v WA (Perth) 2015-16. BB 3-42 S Aus v NSW (Adelaide) 2015-16. LO HS 202 S Aus v WA (Sydney) 2015-16. LO BB 2-9 S Aus v NSW (Brisbane) 2014-15. T20 HS 101*. T20 BB 3-16.

HODD, Andrew John (Bexhill C; Loughborough U), b Chichester, Sussex 12 Jan 1984. 5'9". RHB, WK. Squad No 4. Sussex 2003-11. Surrey 2005 (1 match). Yorkshire debut 2012 (on loan). HS 123 Sx v Yorks (Hove) 2007. Y HS 68* v Somerset (Taunton) 2013. LO HS 91 Sx v Lancs (Hove) 2010 (CB40). T20 HS 70.

LEANING, Jack Andrew (Archbishop Holgate's S, York; York C), b Bristol, Glos 18 Oct 1993. 5'10". RHB, RMF. Squad No 34. Debut (Yorkshire) 2013. Yorkshire 2nd XI debut 2011. HS 123 v Somerset (Taunton) 2014. BB 1-82 v Notts (Nottingham) 2015. LO HS 111* v Essex (Scarborough) 2014 (RLC). LO BB 5-22 v Unicorns (Leeds) 2013 (Y40). T20 HS 60*. T20 BB – .

LEES, Alexander Zak (Holy Trinity SS, Halifax), b Halifax 14 Apr 1993. 6'3". LHB, LB. Squad No 14. Debut (Yorkshire) 2010; cap 2014; captain (l-o) 2016. Yorkshire 2nd XI debut 2010. YC 2014. 1000 runs (1): 1018 (2014). HS 275* v Derbys (Chesterfield) 2013 (Y40). LO HS 102 v Northants (Northampton) 2014 (RLC). T20 HS 67*.

LYTH, Adam (Caedmon S, Whitby; Whitby Community C), b Whitby 25 Sep 1987. 5'8". LHB, RM. Squad No 9. Debut (Yorkshire) 2007; cap 2010. PCA 2014. *Wisden* 2014. **Tests**: 7 (2015); HS 107 v NZ (Leeds) 2015. F-c Tours (EL): SA 2014-15; WI 2010-11. 1000 runs (2); most – 1619 (2014). HS 251 v Lancs (Manchester) 2014, sharing in Y record 6th wicket partnership of 296 with A.U.Rashid. BB 2-15 v Somerset (Taunton) 2013. LO HS 109* v Sussex (Scarborough) 2009 (P40). LO BB 1-6 v Middx (Leeds) 2013 (Y40). T20 HS 78. T20 BB 2-5.

PATTERSON, Steven Andrew (Malet Lambert CS; St Mary's SFC, Hull; Leeds U), b Hull 3 Oct 1983. 6'4". RHB, RMF. Squad No 17. Debut (Yorkshire) 2005; cap 2012. Bradford/ Leeds UCCE 2003 (not f-c). HS 53 v Sussex (Hove) 2011. 50 wkts (2); most – 53 (2012). BB 5-11 v Worcs (Worcester) 2015. LO HS 25* v Worcs (Leeds) 2006 (P40). LO BB 6-32 v Derbys (Leeds) 2010. T20 HS 3*. T20 BB 4-30.

PLUNKETT, Liam Edward (Nunthorpe SS; Teesside Tertiary C), b Middlesbrough, Yorks 6 Apr 1985. 6'3". RHB, RFM. Squad No 28. Durham 2003-12. Dolphins 2007-08. Yorkshire debut 2013; cap 2013. **Tests**: 13 (2005-06 to 2014); HS 55* v I (Lord's) 2014; BB 5-64 v SL (Leeds) 2014. **LOI**: 34 (2005-06 to 2015); HS 56 v P (Lahore) 2005-06; BB 3-24 v A (Sydney) 2006-07. **IT20**: 3 (2006 to 2015-15); HS 1 v P (Dubai, DSC) 2015-16; BB 3-21 v P (Dubai, DSC) 2015-16. F-c Tours (SL): SA 2014-15; WI 2010-11; NZ 2008-09; I 2005-06 (E), 2007-08; P 2005-06 (E); SL 2013-14. HS 114 EL v Sri Lanka A (Colombo) 2013-14. CC HS 94* Du v Sussex (Hove) 2009. Y HS 86 v Warwks (Leeds) 2014. 50 wkts (3); most – 60 (2009). BB 6-33 v Leeds/Bradford MCCU (Leeds) 2013 on Y debut. CC BB 6-63 (11-119 match) Du v Worcs (Chester-le-St) 2009. LO HS 72 Du v Somerset (Chester-le-St) 2008 (P40). LO BB 4-15 Du v Essex (Chester-le-St) 2007 (FPT). T20 HS 41. T20 BB 5-31.

RASHID, Adil Usman (Belle Vue S, Bradford), b Bradford 17 Feb 1988. 5'8". RHB, LBG. Squad No 3. Debut (Yorkshire) 2006; cap 2008. MCC 2007-09. Big Bash: AS 2015-16. YC 2007. Match double (114, 48, 8-157 and 2-45) for England U19 v India U19 (Taunton) 2006. **Tests**: 3 (2015-16); HS 61 v P (Dubai, DSC) 2015-16; BB 5-64 v P (Abu Dhabi) 2015-16 – on debut. **LOI**: 25 (2009 to 2015-16); HS 69 and BB 4-55 v NZ (Birmingham) 2015. **IT20**: 12 (2009 to 2015-16); HS 9* v SA (Nottingham) 2009; BB 2-18 v P (Dubai, DSC) 2015-16. F-c Tours: WI 2010-11 (EL); I 2007-08 (EL); B 2006-07 (Eng A); UAE 2015-16 (v P). HS 180 v Somerset (Leeds) 2013. 50 wkts (2); most – 65 (2008). BB 7-107 v Hants (Southampton) 2008. LO HS 71 v Glos (Leeds) 2014 (RLC). LO BB 5-33 v Hants (Southampton) 2014 (RLC). T20 HS 36*. T20 BB 4-20.

RHODES, William Michael Henry (Cottingham HS, Cottingham SFC, Hull), b Notting-ham 2 Mar 1995. 6'2". LHB, RMF. Squad No 35. Debut (Yorkshire) 2014-15. Yorkshire 2nd XI debut 2012. England U19 2014. HS 79 v Warwks (Birmingham) 2015. BB 3-42 v Middx (Leeds) 2015. LO HS 46 v Leics (Leeds) 2015 (RLC). LO BB 2-22 v Essex (Chelmsford) 2015 (RLC). T20 HS 13. T20 BB 3-27.

ROOT, Joseph Edward (King Ecgbert S, Sheffield; Worksop C), b Sheffield 30 Dec 1990. Elder brother of W.T.Root (see *NOTTINGHAMSHIRE*). 6'0". RHB, OB. Squad No 5. Debut (Yorkshire) 2010; cap 2012. YC 2012. **ECB central contract 2015-16. Tests**: 39 (2012-13 to 2015-16); 1000 runs (1): 1385 (2015); HS 200* v SL (Lord's) 2014; BB 2-9 v A (Lord's) 2013. **LOI**: 68 (2012-13 to 2015-16); HS 125 v SA (Centurion) 2015-16; BB 2-15 v WI (North Sound) 2013-14. **IT20**: 14 (2012-13 to 2015-16); HS 90* v A (Southampton) 2013; BB 1-13 v A (Sydney) 2013-14. F-c Tours: A 2013-14; SA 2015-16; WI 2014-15; NZ 2012-13; I 2012-13; UAE 2015-16 (v P). 1000 runs (3); most – 1228 (2013). HS 236 v Derbys (Leeds) 2013. BB 3-33 v Warwks (Leeds) 2011. LO HS 125 (see *LOI*). LO BB 2-10 EL v Bangladesh A (Sylhet) 2011-12. T20 HS 90*. T20 BB 1-12.

SIDEBOTTOM, Ryan Jay (King James's GS, Almondbury), b Huddersfield 15 Jan 1978. Son of A.Sidebottom (Yorkshire, OFS and England 1973-91). 6'3". LHB, LFM. Squad No 11. Debut (Yorkshire) 1997; cap 2000. Returned to Yorkshire in 2011. Nottinghamshire 2004-10; cap 2004; benefit 2010. *Wisden* 2007. **Tests**: 22 (2001 to 2009-10); HS 31 v SL (Kandy) 2007-08; BB 7-47 v NZ (Napier) 2007-08. Hat-trick v NZ (Hamilton) 2007-08. **LOI**: 25 (2001-02 to 2009-10); HS 24 v A (Southampton) 2009; BB 3-19 v SL (Dambulla) 2007-08. **IT20**: 18 (2007 to 2010); HS 5* and BB 3-16 v NZ (Auckland) 2007-08. F-c Tours: SA 2009-10; WI 2000-01 (Eng A), 2008-09; NZ 2007-08; SL 2007-08. HS 61 v Worcs (Worcester) 2011. 50 wkts (4); most - 62 (2011). BB 7-37 (11-98 match) v Somerset (Leeds) 2011. LO HS 32 Nt v Middx (Nottingham) 2005 (NL). LO BB 6-40 v Glamorgan (Cardiff) 1998 (SL). T20 HS 17*. T20 BB 4-25.

WAINMAN, James Charles (Leeds GS), b Harrogate 25 Jan 1993. 6'4". RHB, LMF. Squad No 15. Yorkshire 2nd XI debut 2010. Awaiting f-c debut. LO HS 33 and LO BB 3-51 v Sri Lanka A (Leeds) 2014 – only 1st XI appearance.

WAITE, Matthew James (Brigshaw HS), b Leeds 24 Dec 1995. 6'0". RHB, RFM. Squad No 6. Yorkshire 2nd XI debut 2014. Awaiting f-c debut. LO HS 12 v Sri Lanka A (Leeds) 2014. LO BB – . T20 HS 14*. T20 BB – .

WARNER, Jared David (Kettleborough Park HS; Silcoates SFC), b Wakefield 14 Nov 1995. 6'1". RHB, RFM. Squad No 45. Yorkshire 2nd XI debut 2015. England U19 2014-15 to 2015. Awaiting 1st XI debut.

‡**WILLEY, David** Jonathan (Northampton S), b Northampton 28 Feb 1990. Son of P.Willey (Northants, Leics and England 1966-91). 6'1". LHB, LFM. Squad No 72. Northamptonshire 2009-15; cap 2013. Bedfordshire 2008. **LOI**: 13 (2015 to 2015-16); HS 13* v SA (Centurion) 2015-16; BB 3-25 v P (Abu Dhabi) 2015-16. **IT20**: 5 (2015 to 2015-16); HS 7* v SA (Cape Town) 2015-16; BB 3-22 v NZ (Manchester) 2015. HS 104* Nh v Glos (Northampton) 2015. BB 5-29 (10-75 match) Nh v Glos (Northampton) 2011. LO HS 167 Nh v Warwks (Birmingham) 2013 (Y40). LO BB 5-62 EL v New Zealand A (Bristol) 2014. T20 HS 100. T20 BB 4-9.

NQ**WILLIAMSON, Kane** Stuart (Tauranga Boys' C), b Tauranga, New Zealand 8 Aug 1990. Cousin of D.Cleaver (C Districts 2010-11 to date). 5'8". RHB, OB. Squad No 8. N Districts 2007-08 to date. Gloucestershire 2011-12; cap 2011. Yorkshire debut 2013. IPL: SH 2015. **Tests** (NZ): 48 (2010-11 to 2015-16); 1000 runs (1): 1172 (2015); HS 242* v SL (Wellington) 2014-15; scored 131 v I (Ahmedabad) 2010-11 on debut; BB 4-44 v E (Auckland) 2012-13. **LOI** (NZ): 93 (2010 to 2015-16); 1000 runs (1): 1376 (2015); HS 145* v SA (Kimberley) 2012-13; BB 4-22 v SA (Paarl) 2012-13. **IT20** (NZ): 30 (2011-12 to 2015-16); HS 72* v P (Hamilton) 2015-16; BB 1-6 v Z (Auckland) 2011-12. F-c Tours (NZ): E 2013, 2015; A 2011-12, 2015-16; SA 2012-13; WI 2012, 2014; I 2010-11, 2012; SL 2012-13; Z 2011-12; B 2013-14; UAE 2014-15 (v P). HS 284* ND v Wellington (Lincoln) 2011-12). Y HS 189 v Sussex (Scarborough) 2014. BB 5-75 ND v Canterbury (Christchurch) 2008-09. CC BB 3-58 Gs v Northants (Northampton) 2012. Y BB 2-44 v Sussex (Hove) 2013. LO HS 145* (*see LOI*). LO BB 5-51 ND v Auckland (Auckland) 2009-10. T20 HS 101*. T20 BB 3-33.

RELEASED/RETIRED

(Having made a County 1st XI appearance in 2015)

FINCH, A.J. – *see SURREY*.

HODGSON, Daniel Mark (Richmond S; Leeds U), b Northallerton 26 Feb 1990. RHB, WK. Leeds/Bradford MCCU 2012, scoring 64 v Surrey (Oval) on debut. Mountaineers 2012-13. Yorkshire 2014-15. Derbyshire 2014 (on loan). HS 94* Mountaineers v SR (Mutare) 2012-13. Y HS 35 v Leeds/Bradford MCCU (Leeds) 2015. CC HS 1 De v Worcs (Worcester) 2014. LO HS 90 v Glamorgan (Leeds) 2013 (Y40). T20 HS 52*.

201

NQMAXWELL, Glenn James, b Kew, Melbourne, Australia 14 Oct 1988. RHB, OB. Victoria 2010-11 to date. Hampshire 2014. Yorkshire 2015. IPL: DD 2012. MI 2013. KXIP 2014-15. Big Bash: MR 2011-12. MS 2012-13 to date. **Tests** (A): 3 (2012-13 to 2014-15); HS 37 v P (Abu Dhabi) 2014-15; BB 4-127 v I (Hyderabad) 2012-13. **LOI** (A): 62 (2012 to 2015-16); HS 102 v SL (Sydney) 2014-15; BB 4-46 v E (Perth) 2014-15. **IT20** (A): 30 (2012 to 2015-16); HS 75 v SA (Johannesburg) 2015-16; BB 3-13 v P (Dubai, DSC) 2014-15. F-c Tours (A): I 2012-13; SA/Z 2013 (Aus A); UAE 2014-15 (v P). HS 155* Aus A v South Africa A (Pretoria) 2013. CC HS 140 Y v Durham (Scarborough) 2015. BB 4-42 Vic v S Aus (Melbourne) 2012-13. CC BB 3-55 Y v Middx (Leeds) 2015. LO HS 146 H v Lancs (Manchester) 2014 (RLC). LO BB 4-46 (*see LOI*). T20 HS 95. T20 BB 3-13.

MIDDLEBROOK, James Daniel (Pudsey Crawshaw S), b Leeds, Yorks 13 May 1977. 6'1". RHB, OB. Yorkshire 1998-2015. Essex 2002-09; cap 2003. Northamptonshire 2010-14, cap 2011. MCC 2010, 2013. HS 127 Ex v Middx (Lord's) 2007. Y HS 84 v Essex (Chelmsford) 2001. 50 wkts (1): 56 (2003). BB 6-78 Nh v Kent (Northampton) 2013. Y BB 6-82 (10-170 match) v Hants (Southampton) 2000, inc 4 wkts in 5 balls. Hat-trick Ex v Kent (Canterbury) 2003. LO HS 57* Nh v Derbys (Derby) 2010 (CB40). LO BB 4-27 Ex v Somerset (Taunton) 2006 (CGT). T20 HS 43. T20 BB 3-13.

NQPUJARA, Cheteshwar Arvindbhai, b Rajkot, India 25 Jan 1988. RHB, LB. Son of A.S.Pujara (Saurashtra 1976-77 to 1979-80), nephew of B.S.Pujara (Saurashtra 1983-84 to 1996-97). Saurashtra 2005-06 to date. Derbyshire 2014. Yorkshire 2015. IPL: KKR 2009-10. RCB 2011-13. KXIP 2014. **Tests** (I): 32 (2010-11 to 2015-16); HS 206* v E (Ahmedabad) 2012-13. **LOI** (I): 5 (2013 to 2014); HS 27 v B (Dhaka) 2014. F-c Tours (I): E 2010 (IA), 2014; A 2006 (IA), 2014-15; SA 2010-11, 2013 (IA), 2013-14; WI 2012 (IA); NZ 2013-14; SL 2015; Z/Ken 2007-08 (IA). 1000 runs (0+2); most – 1585 (2012-13). HS 352 Saur v Karnataka (Rajkot) 2012-13. CC HS 133* v Hants (Leeds) 2015. BB 2-4 Saur v Rajasthan (Jaipur) 2007-08. LO HS 158* Ind B v India A (Rajkot) 2012-13. T20 HS 81.

PYRAH, Richard Michael (Ossett S; Wakefield C), b Dewsbury 1 Nov 1982. 6'0". RHB, RM. Yorkshire 2004-15; cap 2010; benefit 2015. HS 134* v Loughborough MCCU (Leeds) 2010. CC HS 117 v Lancs (Leeds) 2011. BB 5-58 v Notts (Leeds) 2011. LO HS 69 v Netherlands (Leeds) 2011 (CB40). LO BB 5-50 Yorks CB v Somerset (Scarborough) 2002 (CGT). T20 HS 42. T20 BB 5-16 v Durham (Scarborough) 2011 – Y record.

SHAW, J. – *see GLOUCESTERSHIRE.*

M.A.Ashraf, B.P.Gibson and J.A.Tattersall left the staff without making a County 1st XI appearance in 2015.

WORCESTERSHIRE RELEASED/RETIRED (continued from p 195)

NQSENANAYAKE, Senanayake Mudiyanselage **Sachithra** Madhushanka (Ananda C), b Colombo, Sri Lanka 9 Feb 1985. 6'0". RHB, OB. Sinhalese SC 2006-07 to date. Ruhuna 2008-09 to 2009-10. Worcestershire 2015. IPL: KKR 2013. Big Bash: SS 2012-13. **Tests** (SL): 1 (2013-14); HS 5 and BB – v P (Abu Dhabi) 2013-14. **LOI** (SL): 49 (2011-12 to 2015-16); HS 42 v P (Sharjah) 2013-14; BB 4-13 v E (Chester-le-St) 2014. **IT20** (SL): 22 (2012 to 2015-16); HS 17 v NZ (Chittagong) 2013-14; BB 4-46 v WI (Pallekele) 2015-16. F-c Tours (SL): E 2011; A 2010; UAE 2013-14 (SL v P). HS 89 Ruhuna v Wayamba (Colombo, CCC) 2009-10. Wo HS 32 and Wo BB 4-50 v Sussex (Hove) 2015. 50 wkts (0+3); most – 72 (2009-10). BB 8-70 (11-180 match) SL A v Australia A (Brisbane) 2010. LO HS 51* Ruhuna v Kandurata (Moratuwa) 2009-10. LO BB 5-23 SSC v Chilaw Marians (Colombo, CCC) 2011-12. T20 HS 20. T20 BB 4-26.

S.H.Choudhry left the staff without making a County 1st XI appearance in 2015.

YORKSHIRE 2015

RESULTS SUMMARY

	Place	Won	Lost	Tied	Drew	NR
LV= County Championship (1st Division)	**1st**	11	1		4	
All First-Class Matches		11	1		5	
Royal London One-Day Cup (Group A)	SF	5	3			2
NatWest t20 Blast (North Group)	8th	5	8	1		

LV= COUNTY CHAMPIONSHIP AVERAGES

BATTING AND FIELDING

Cap		M	I	NO	HS	Runs	Avge	100	50	Ct/St
2011	J.M.Bairstow	9	15	3	219*	1108	92.33	5	5	29
	C.A.Pujara	4	6	1	133*	264	52.80	1	1	2
2006	T.T.Bresnan	16	22	5	169*	849	49.94	2	4	13
2000	R.J.Sidebottom	10	12	10	28	95	47.50	–	–	3
	A.J.Finch	3	4	1	73*	124	41.33	–	1	3
	G.J.Maxwell	4	7	1	140	244	40.66	1	–	3
2008	A.W.Gale	15	25	–	164	1006	40.24	3	3	4
	J.A.Leaning	15	25	2	123	922	40.08	3	3	19
2012	G.S.Ballance	8	13	–	165	458	35.23	1	2	7
2008	A.U.Rashid	7	10	–	127	347	34.70	1	2	3
2014	A.Z.Lees	16	27	3	100	795	33.12	1	5	20
	W.M.H.Rhodes	9	15	2	79	388	29.84	–	1	3
2010	A.Lyth	7	12	–	67	315	26.25	–	3	10
	A.J.Hodd	8	10	2	54*	180	22.50	–	1	21/2
2012	S.A.Patterson	15	17	4	44*	272	20.92	–	–	4
2013	J.A.Brooks	14	15	1	50*	185	13.21	–	1	4
2013	L.E.Plunkett	5	8	–	28	96	12.00	–	–	4
	J.D.Middlebrook	6	7	–	23	49	7.00	–	–	1

Also batted: K.Carver (1 match) 5; M.D.Fisher (3) 0, 0* (1 ct); R.M.Pyrah (2 – cap 2010) 43, 37.

BOWLING

	O	M	R	W	Avge	Best	5wI	10wM
R.J.Sidebottom	248	65	734	41	17.90	6-34	3	1
J.A.Brooks	420.5	83	1480	65	22.76	5-35	3	–
S.A.Patterson	431.1	142	1128	45	25.06	5-11	2	–
J.D.Middlebrook	126.3	22	441	17	25.94	5-82	1	–
A.U.Rashid	212.2	31	813	29	28.03	4-48	–	–
T.T.Bresnan	422.5	112	1390	45	30.88	5-85	1	–
L.E.Plunkett	115.1	17	459	14	32.78	4-61	–	–
Also bowled:								
W.M.H.Rhodes	80.5	17	271	8	33.87	3-42	–	–
M.D.Fisher	73.5	18	243	5	48.60	2-61	–	–

K.Carver 6-0-36-0; A.J.Finch 2-1-1-0; J.A.Leaning 23-3-141-1; A.Z.Lees 3-0-12-0; A.Lyth 27.5-3-76-4; G.J.Maxwell 29-2-144-4; C.A.Pujara 1-0-5-0; R.M.Pyrah 10-2-40-0.

The First-Class Averages (pp 227–243) give the records of Yorkshire players in all first-class county matches (Yorkshire's other opponents being Leeds/Bradford MCCU), with the exception of J.M.Bairstow, G.S.Ballance and A.Lyth, whose first-class figures for Yorkshire are as above.

YORKSHIRE RECORDS

FIRST-CLASS CRICKET

Highest Total	For	887	v	Warwicks	Birmingham	1896
	V	681-7d	by	Leics	Bradford	1996
Lowest Total	For	23	v	Hampshire	Middlesbrough	1965
	V	13	by	Notts	Nottingham	1901
Highest Innings	For	341	G.H.Hirst	v	Leics	Leicester	1905
	V	318*	W.G.Grace	for	Glos	Cheltenham	1876

Highest Partnership for each Wicket

1st	555	P.Holmes/H.Sutcliffe	v	Essex	Leyton	1932
2nd	346	W.Barber/M.Leyland	v	Middlesex	Sheffield	1932
3rd	346	J.J.Sayers/A.McGrath	v	Warwicks	Birmingham	2009
4th	358	D.S.Lehmann/M.J.Lumb	v	Durham	Leeds	2006
5th	340	E.Wainwright/G.H.Hirst	v	Surrey	The Oval	1899
6th	296	A.Lyth/A.U.Rashid	v	Lancashire	Manchester	2014
7th	366*	J.M.Bairstow/T.T.Bresnan	v	Durham	Chester-le-St²	2015
8th	292	R.Peel/Lord Hawke	v	Warwicks	Birmingham	1896
9th	246	T.T.Bresnan/J.N.Gillespie	v	Surrey	The Oval	2007
10th	149	G.Boycott/G.B.Stevenson	v	Warwicks	Birmingham	1982

Best Bowling	For	10-10	H.Verity	v	Notts	Leeds	1932
(Innings)	V	10-37	C.V.Grimmett	for	Australians	Sheffield	1930
Best Bowling	For	17-91	H.Verity	v	Essex	Leyton	1933
(Match)	V	17-91	H.Dean	for	Lancashire	Liverpool	1913

Most Runs – Season	2883	H.Sutcliffe	(av 80.08)	1932
Most Runs – Career	38558	H.Sutcliffe	(av 50.20)	1919-45
Most 100s – Season	12	H.Sutcliffe		1932
Most 100s – Career	112	H.Sutcliffe		1919-45
Most Wkts – Season	240	W.Rhodes	(av 12.72)	1900
Most Wkts – Career	3597	W.Rhodes	(av 16.02)	1898-1930
Most Career W-K Dismissals	1186	D.Hunter	(863 ct; 323 st)	1888-1909
Most Career Catches in the Field	665	J.Tunnicliffe		1891-1907

LIMITED-OVERS CRICKET

Highest Total	50ov	411-6		v	Devon	Exmouth	2004
	40ov	352-6		v	Notts	Scarborough	2001
	T20	213-7		v	Worcs	Leeds	2010

Lowest Total	50ov	76		v	Surrey	Harrogate	1970
	40ov	54		v	Essex	Leeds	2003
	T20	90-9		v	Durham	Chester-le-St²	2009

Highest Innings	50ov	160	M.J.Wood	v	Devon	Exmouth	2004
	40ov	191	D.S.Lehmann	v	Notts	Scarborough	2001
	T20	109	I.J.Harvey	v	Derbyshire	Leeds	2005

Best Bowling	50ov	7-27	D.Gough	v	Ireland	Leeds	1997
	40ov	7-15	R.A.Hutton	v	Worcs	Leeds	1969
	T20	5-16	R.M.Pyrah	v	Durham	Scarborough	2011

204

FIRST-CLASS UMPIRES 2016

† New appointment. See page 87 for key to abbreviations.

BAILEY, Robert John (Biddulph HS), b Biddulph, Staffs 28 Oct 1963. 6'3". RHB, OB. Northamptonshire 1982-99; cap 1985; benefit 1993; captain 1996-97. Derbyshire 2000-01; cap 2000. Staffordshire 1980. YC 1984. **Tests:** 4 (1988 to 1989-90); HS 43 v WI (Oval) 1988. **LOI:** 4 (1984-85 to 1989-90); HS 43* v SL (Oval) 1988. F-c Tours: SA 1991-92 (Nh); WI 1989-90; Z 1994-95 (Nh). 1000 runs (13); most – 1987 (1990). HS 224* Nh v Glamorgan (Swansea) 1986. BB 5-54 Nh v Notts (Northampton) 1993. F-c career: 374 matches; 21844 runs @ 40.52, 47 hundreds; 121 wickets @ 42.51; 272 ct. Appointed 2006. Umpired 12 LOI (2011 to 2015). **ICC International Panel 2011 to date.**

BAINTON, Neil Laurence, b Romford, Essex 2 October 1970. No f-c appearances. Appointed 2006.

BALDWIN, Paul Kerr, b Epsom, Surrey 18 Jul 1973. No f-c appearances. Umpired 18 LOI (2006 to 2009). Reserve List 2010-14. Appointed 2015.

BENSON, Mark Richard (Sutton Valence S), b Shoreham, Sussex 6 Jul 1958. 5'10". LHB, OB. Kent 1980-95; cap 1981; captain 1991-96 (did not play in 1996); benefit 1991. **Tests:** 1 (1986); HS 30 v I (Birmingham) 1986. **LOI:** 1 (1986); HS 24 v NZ (Leeds) 1986. 1000 runs (11); most – 1725 (1987). HS 257 K v Hants (Southampton) 1991. BB 2-55 K v Surrey (Dartford) 1986. F-c career: 292 matches; 18387 runs @ 40.23, 48 hundreds; 5 wickets @ 98.60; 140 ct. Appointed 2000. Umpired 27 Tests (2004-05 to 2009-10) and 72 LOI (2004 to 2008-09). **ICC Elite Panel 2006-09.**

†BURNS, Michael (Walney CS), b Barrow-in-Furness, Lancs 6 Feb 1969. 6'0". RHB, RM, WK. Warwickshire 1992-96. Somerset 1997-2005; cap 1999; captain 2003-04. 1000 runs (2); most – 1133 (2003). HS 221 Sm v Yorks (Bath) 2001. BB 6-54 Sm v Leics (Taunton) 2001. F-c career: 154 matches; 7648 runs @ 32.68, 8 hundreds; 68 wickets @ 42.42; 142 ct, 7 st. Appointed 2016.

COOK, Nicholas Grant Billson (Lutterworth GS), b Leicester 17 Jun 1956. 6'0". RHB, SLA. Leicestershire 1978-85; cap 1982. Northamptonshire 1986-94; cap 1987; benefit 1995. **Tests:** 15 (1983 to 1989); HS 31 v A (Oval) 1989; BB 6-65 (11-83 match) v P (Karachi) 1983-84. **LOI:** 3 (1983-84 to 1989-90); HS – ; BB 2-18 v P (Peshawar) 1987-88. F-c Tours: NZ 1979-80 (DHR), 1983-84; P 1983-84, 1987-88; SL 1985-86 (Eng B); Z 1980-81 (Le), 1984-85 (EC). HS 75 Le v Somerset (Taunton) 1980. 50 wkts (8); most – 90 (1982). BB 7-34 (10-97 match) Nh v Essex (Chelmsford) 1992. F-c career: 356 matches; 3137 runs @ 11.66; 879 wickets @ 29.01; 197 ct. Appointed 2009.

COWLEY, Nigel Geoffrey Charles (Dutchy Manor SS, Mere), b Shaftesbury, Dorset 1 Mar 1953. 5'7". RHB, OB. Dorset 1972. Hampshire 1974-89; cap 1978; benefit 1988. Glamorgan 1990. 1000 runs (1): 1042 (1984). HS 109* H v Somerset (Taunton) 1977. BB 6-48 H v Leics (Southampton) 1982. F-c career: 271 matches; 7309 runs @ 23.35, 2 hundreds; 437 wickets @ 34.04; 105 ct. Appointed 2000.

EVANS, Jeffery Howard, b Llanelli, Carms 7 Aug 1954. No f-c appearances. Appointed 2001. Umpired in Indian Cricket League 2007-08.

EVANS, Russell John (Colonel Frank Seely S), b Calverton, Notts 1 Oct 1965. Younger brother of K.P.Evans (Nottinghamshire 1984-99). 6'0". RHB, RM. Nottinghamshire 1987-90. Minor Cos 1994. Lincolnshire 1994-97. HS 59 MC v South Africans (Torquay) 1994. BB 3-40 Nt v OU (Oxford) 1988. F-c career: 7 matches; 201 runs @ 25.12; 3 wickets @ 32.33; 5 ct. Reserve List 2011-14. Appointed 2015.

GALE, Stephen Clifford, b Shrewsbury, Shropshire 3 Jun 1952. RHB, LB. No f-c appearances. Shropshire (list A only) 1976-85. Reserve List 2008-10. Appointed 2011.

GARRATT, Steven Arthur, b Nottingham 5 Jul 1953. No f-c appearances. Reserve List 2003-07. Appointed 2008.

GOUGH, Michael Andrew (English Martyrs RCS; Hartlepool SFC), b Hartlepool, Co Durham 18 Dec 1979. Son of M.P.Gough (Durham 1974-77). 6'5". RHB, OB. Durham 1998-2003. F-c Tours (Eng A): NZ 1999-00; B 1999-00. HS 123 Du v CU (Cambridge) 1998. CC HS 103 Du v Essex (Colchester) 2002. BB 5-56 Du v Middx (Chester-le-St) 2001. F-c career: 67 matches; 2952 runs @ 25.44, 2 hundreds; 30 wickets @ 45.00; 57 ct. Reserve List 2006-08. Appointed 2009. Umpired 25 LOI (2013 to 2015-16). **ICC International Panel 2012 to date.**

GOULD, Ian James (Westgate SS, Slough), b Taplow, Bucks 19 Aug 1957. 5'8". LHB, WK. Middlesex 1975 to 1980-81, 1996; cap 1977. Auckland 1979-80. Sussex 1981-90; cap 1981; captain 1987; benefit 1990. MCC YC. **LOI:** 18 (1982-83 to 1983); HS 42 v A (Sydney) 1982-83. F-c Tours: A 1982-83; P 1980-81 (Int); Z 1980-81 (M). HS 128 M v Worcs (Worcester) 1978. BB 3-10 Sx v Surrey (Oval) 1989. Middlesex coach 1991-2000. Reappeared in one match (v OU) 1996. F-c career: 298 matches; 8756 runs @ 26.05, 4 hundreds; 7 wickets @ 52.14; 603 dismissals (536 ct, 67 st). Appointed 2002. Umpired 49 Tests (2008-09 to 2015-16) and 111 LOI (2006 to 2015-16), including 2010-11 and 2014-15 World Cups. **ICC Elite Panel 2009 to date.**

HARTLEY, Peter John (Greenhead GS; Bradford C), b Keighley, Yorks 18 Apr 1960. 6'0". RHB, RMF. Warwickshire 1982. Yorkshire 1985-97; cap 1987; benefit 1996. Hampshire 1998-2000; cap 1998. F-c Tours (Y): SA 1991-92; WI 1986-87; Z 1995-96. HS 127* Y v Lancs (Manchester) 1988. 50 wkts (7); most – 81 (1995). BB 9-41 (inc hat-trick, 4 wkts in 5 balls and 5 in 9; 11-68 match) Y v Derbys (Chesterfield) 1995. Hat-trick 1995. F-c career: 232 matches; 4321 runs @ 19.91, 2 hundreds; 683 wickets @ 30.21; 68 ct. Appointed 2003. Umpired 6 LOI (2007 to 2009). **ICC International Panel 2006-09.**

ILLINGWORTH, Richard Keith (Salts GS), b Bradford, Yorks 23 Aug 1963. 5'11". RHB, SLA. Worcestershire 1982-2000; cap 1986; benefit 1997. Natal 1988-89. Derbyshire 2001. Wiltshire 2005. **Tests:** 9 (1991 to 1995-96); HS 28 v SA (Pt Elizabeth) 1995-96; BB 4-96 v WI (Nottingham) 1995. Took wicket of P.V.Simmons with his first ball in Tests – v WI (Nottingham) 1991. **LOI:** 25 (1991 to 1995-96); HS 14 v P (Melbourne) 1991-92; BB 3-33 v Z (Albury) 1991-92. F-c Tours: SA 1995-96; NZ 1991-92; P 1990-91 (Eng A); SL 1990-91 (Eng A); Z 1989-90 (Eng A), 1990-91 (Wo), 1993-94 (Wo), 1996-97 (Wo). HS 120* Wo v Warwks (Worcester) 1987 – as night-watchman. Scored 106 for England A v Z (Harare) 1989-90 – also as night-watchman. 50 wkts (5); most – 75 (1990). BB 7-50 Wo v OU (Oxford) 1985. F-c career: 376 matches; 7027 runs @ 22.45, 4 hundreds; 831 wickets @ 31.54; 161 ct. Appointed 2006. Umpired 20 Tests (2012-13 to 2015-16) and 44 LOI (2010 to 2015-16), including 2014-15 World Cup. **ICC Elite Panel 2013 to date.**

KETTLEBOROUGH, Richard Allan (Worksop C), b Sheffield, Yorks 15 Mar 1973. 6'0". LHB, RM. Yorkshire 1994-97. Middlesex 1998-99. F-c Tour (Y): Z 1995-96. HS 108 Y v Essex (Leeds) 1996. BB 2-26 Y v Notts (Scarborough) 1996. F-c career: 33 matches; 1258 runs @ 25.16, 1 hundred; 3 wickets @ 81.00; 20 ct. Appointed 2006. Umpired 35 Tests (2010-11 to 2015-16) and 62 LOI (2009 to 2015-16), including 2010-11 and 2014-15 World Cups. **ICC Elite Panel 2011 to date.**

LLONG, Nigel James (Ashford North S), b Ashford, Kent 11 Feb 1969. 6'0". LHB, OB. Kent 1990-98; cap 1993. F-c Tour (K): Z 1992-93. HS 130 K v Hants (Canterbury) 1996. BB 5-21 K v Middx (Canterbury) 1996. F-c career: 68 matches; 3024 runs @ 31.17, 6 hundreds; 35 wickets @ 35.97; 59 ct. Appointed 2002. Umpired 35 Tests (2007-08 to 2015-16) and 100 LOI (2006 to 2015-16), including 2010-11 and 2014-15 World Cups. **ICC Elite Panel 2012 to date.**

LLOYD, Graham David (Hollins County HS), b Accrington, Lancs 1 Jul 1969. Son of D.Lloyd (Lancs and England 1965-83). 5'9". RHB, RM. Lancashire 1988-2002; cap 1992; benefit 2001. **LOI:** 6 (1996 to 1998-99); HS 22 v A (Oval) 1997. F-c Tours: A 1992-93 (Eng A); WI 1995-96 (La). 1000 runs (5); most – 1389 (1992). HS 241 La v Essex (Chelmsford) 1996. BB 1-4. F-c career: 203 matches; 11279 runs @ 38.23, 24 hundreds; 2 wickets @ 220.00; 140 ct. Reserve List 2009-13. Appointed 2014.

LLOYDS, Jeremy William (Blundell's S), b Penang, Malaya 17 Nov 1954. 6'0". LHB, OB. Somerset 1979-84; cap 1982. Gloucestershire 1985-91; cap 1985. OFS 1983-84 to 1987-88. F-c Tour (Gl): SL 1986-87. 1000 runs (3); most – 1295 (1986). HS 132* Sm v Northants (Northampton) 1982. BB 7-88 Sm v Essex (Chelmsford) 1982. F-c career: 267 matches; 10679 runs @ 31.04, 10 hundreds; 333 wickets @ 38.86; 229 ct. Appointed 1998. Umpired 5 Tests (2003-04 to 2004-05) and 18 LOI (2000 to 2005-06). **ICC International Panel 2003-06.**

MALLENDER, Neil Alan (Beverley GS), b Kirk Sandall, Yorks 13 Aug 1961. 6'0". RHB, RFM. Northamptonshire 1980-86 and 1995-96; cap 1984. Somerset 1987-94; cap 1987; benefit 1994. Otago 1983-84 to 1992-93; captain 1990-91 to 1992-93. **Tests:** 2 (1992); HS 4 v P (Oval) 1992; BB 5-50 v P (Leeds) 1992 – on debut. F-c Tour (Nh): Z 1994-95. HS 100* Otago v CD (Palmerston N) 1991-92. UK HS 87* Sm v Sussex (Hove) 1990. 50 wkts (6); most – 56 (1983). BB 7-27 Otago v Auckland (Auckland) 1984-85. UK BB 7-41 Nh v Derbys (Northampton) 1982. F-c career: 345 matches; 4709 runs @ 17.18, 1 hundred; 937 wickets @ 26.31; 111 ct. Appointed 1999. Umpired 3 Tests (2003-04) and 22 LOI (2001 to 2003-04), including 2002-03 World Cup. **ICC Elite Panel 2004.**

MILLNS, David James (Garibaldi CS; N Notts C; Nottingham Trent U), b Clipstone, Notts 27 Feb 1965. 6'3". LHB, RF. Nottinghamshire 1988-89, 2000-01; cap 2000. Leicestershire 1990-99; cap 1994; benefit 1999. Tasmania 1994-95. Boland 1996-97. F-c Tours: A 1992-93 (Eng A); SA 1996-97 (Le). HS 121 Le v Northants (Northampton) 1997. 50 wkts (4); most – 76 (1994). BB 9-37 (12-91 match) Le v Derbys (Derby) 1991. F-c career: 171 matches; 3082 runs @ 22.01, 3 hundreds; 553 wickets @ 27.35; 76 ct. Reserve List 2007-08. Appointed 2009.

O'SHAUGHNESSY, Steven Joseph (Harper Green SS, Franworth), b Bury, Lancs 9 Sep 1961. 5'10½". RHB, RM. Lancashire 1980-87; cap 1985. Worcestershire 1988-89. Scored 100 in 35 min to equal world record for La v Leics (Manchester) 1983. 1000 runs (1): 1167 (1984). HS 159* La v Somerset (Bath) 1984. BB 4-66 La v Notts (Nottingham) 1982. F-c career: 112 matches; 3720 runs @ 24.31, 5 hundreds; 114 wickets @ 36.03; 57 ct. Reserve List 2009-10. Appointed 2011.

ROBINSON, Robert Timothy (Dunstable GS; High Pavement SFC; Sheffield U), b Sutton in Ashfield, Notts 21 Nov 1958. 6'0". RHB, RM. Nottinghamshire 1978-99; cap 1983; captain 1988-95; benefit 1992. *Wisden* 1985. **Tests:** 29 (1984-85 to 1989); HS 175 v A (Leeds) 1985. **LOI:** 26 (1984-85 to 1988); HS 83 v P (Sharjah) 1986-87. F-c Tours: A 1987-88; SA 1989-90 (Eng XI), 1996-97 (Nt); NZ 1987-88; WI 1985-86; I/SL 1984-85; P 1987-88. 1000 runs (14) inc 2000 (1): 2032 (1984). HS 220* Nt v Yorks (Nottingham) 1990. BB 1-22. F-c career: 425 matches; 27571 runs @ 42.15, 63 hundreds; 4 wickets @ 72.25; 257 ct. Appointed 2007. Umpired 7 LOI (2013 to 2015). **ICC International Panel (Third Umpire) 2012 to date.**

SAGGERS, Martin John (Springwood HS, King's Lynn; Huddersfield U), b King's Lynn, Norfolk 23 May 1972. 6'2". RHB, RMF. Durham 1996-98. Kent 1999-2009; cap 2001; benefit 2009. MCC 2004. Essex 2007 (on loan). Norfolk 1995-96. **Tests:** 3 (2003-04 to 2004); HS 1 and BB 2-29 v B (Chittagong) 2003-04 – on debut. F-c Tour: B 2003-04. HS 64 K v Worcs (Canterbury) 2004. 50 wkts (4); most – 83 (2002). BB 7-79 K v Durham (Chester-le-St) 2000. F-c career: 119 matches; 1165 runs @ 11.20; 415 wickets @ 25.33; 27 ct. Reserve List 2010-11. Appointed 2012.

WHARF, Alexander George (Buttershaw Upper S; Thomas Danby C), b Bradford, Yorks 4 Jun 1975. 6'5". RHB, RMF. Yorkshire 1994-97. Nottinghamshire 1998-99. Glamorgan 2000-08, scoring 100* v OU (Oxford) on debut; cap 2000; benefit 2008. **LOI:** 13 (2004 to 2004-05); HS 9 v India (Lord's) 2004; BB 4-24 v Z (Harare) 2004-05. F-c Tour (Eng A): WI 2005-06. HS 128* Gm v Glos (Bristol) 2007. 50 wkts (1): 52 (2003). BB 6-59 Gm v Glos (Bristol) 2005. F-c career: 121 matches; 3570 runs @ 23.03, 6 hundreds; 293 wickets @ 37.34; 63 ct. Reserve List 2011-13. Appointed 2014.

RESERVE FIRST-CLASS LIST: Ian D.Blackwell, Ben J.Debenham, Tom Lungley, Paul R.Pollard, Billy V.Taylor, Russell J.Warren, Christopher M.Watts.

Test Match and LOI statistics to 23 February 2016.

TOURING TEAMS REGISTER 2015

AUSTRALIA

Full Names	Birthdate	Birthplace	Team	Type	F-C Debut
CLARKE, Michael John	02.04.81	Liverpool	NSW	RHB/SLA	1999-00
CUMMINS, Patrick James	08.05.93	Sydney	NSW	RHB/RF	2010-11
FAWAD AHMED	05.02.82	Marghuz, Pak	Victoria	RHB/LB	2005-06
HADDIN, Bradley James	23.10.77	Cowra	NSW	RHB/WK	1999-00
HARRIS, Ryan James	11.10.79	Sydney	Queensland	RHB/RF	2001-02
HAZLEWOOD, Josh Reginald	08.01.91	Tamworth	NSW	LHB/RFM	2008-09
JOHNSON, Mitchell Guy	02.11.81	Townsville	W Australia	LHB/LF	2001-02
LYON, Nathan Michael	20.11.87	Young	NSW	RHB/OB	2010-11
MARSH, Mitchell Ross	20.10.91	Perth	W Australia	RHB/RFM	2009-10
MARSH, Shaun Edward	09.07.83	Narrogin	W Australia	LHB/SLA	2000-01
NEVILL, Peter Michael	13.10.85	Melbourne	NSW	RHB/WK	2008-09
ROGERS, Christopher John Llewellyn	31.08.77	Sydney	Victoria	LHB/LBG	1998-99
SIDDLE, Peter Matthew	25.11.84	Traralgon	Victoria	RHB/RFM	2005-06
SMITH, Steven Peter Devereux	02.06.89	Sydney	NSW	RHB/LBG	2007-08
STARC, Mitchell Aaron	30.01.90	Sydney	NSW	LHB/LF	2008-09
VOGES, Adam Charles	04.10.79	Perth	W Australia	RHB/SLA	2002-03
WARNER, David Andrew	27.10.86	Paddington	NSW	LHB/RM	2008-09
WATSON, Shane Robert	17.06.81	Ipswich	NSW	RHB/RMF	2000-01

NEW ZEALAND

Full Names	Birthdate	Birthplace	Team	Type	F-C Debut
ANDERSON, Corey James	13.12.90	Christchurch	N Districts	LHB/LMF	2006-07
BOULT, Trent Alexander	22.07.89	Rotorua	N Districts	RHB/LFM	2008-09
BRACEWELL, Douglas Andrew John	28.09.90	Tauranga	C Districts	RHB/RMF	2008-09
CRAIG, Mark Donald	23.03.87	Auckland	Otago	LHB/OB	2010-11
DUFFY, Jacob Andrew	02.08.94	Lumsden	Otago	RHB/RFM	2011-12
GUPTILL, Martin James	30.09.86	Auckland	Auckland	RHB/OB	2005-06
HENRY, Matthew James	14.12.91	Christchurch	Canterbury	RHB/RFM	2010-11
LATHAM, Thomas William Maxwell	02.04.92	Christchurch	Canterbury	LHB/RM	2010-11
McCULLUM, Brendon Barrie	27.09.81	Dunedin	Otago	RHB/WK	1999-00
RONCHI, Luke	23.04.81	Manawatu	Wellington	RHB/WK	2002-03
RUTHERFORD, Hamish Duncan	27.04.89	Dunedin	Otago	LHB/SLA	2008-09
SANTNER, Mitchell Josef	05.02.92	Hamilton	N Districts	LHB/SLA	2011-12
SOUTHEE, Timothy Grant	11.12.88	Whangarei	N Districts	RHB/RMF	2006-07
TAYLOR, Luteru Ross Poutoa Lote	08.03.84	Lower Hutt	C Districts	RHB/OB	2002-03
WAGNER, Neil	13.03.86	Pretoria, SA	Otago	LHB/LMF	2005-06
WATLING, Bradley-John	09.07.85	Durban, SA	N Districts	RHB/WK	2004-05
WHEELER, Ben Matthew	10.11.91	Blenheim	C Districts	RHB/LMF	2009-10
WILLIAMSON, Kane Stuart	08.08.90	Tauranga	N Districts	RHB/OB	2007-08

UNIVERSITIES REGISTER 2015

CAMBRIDGE († = Blue)

Full Names	Birthdate	Birthplace	College	Bat/Bowl	F-C Debut
†ABBOTT, James Barrington	25.05.94	Hammersmith	Magdalene	RHB/WK	2014
ARIF, Adil Tahir	06.11.94	Sharjah, UAE	Anglia RU	RHB/RM	2014
ARKSEY, Joshua Benjamin Thomas	20.12.94	Cambridge	Anglia RU	RHB/SLA	2015
†BLOFIELD, Alexander David	28.10.91	Shrewsbury	Darwin	RHB/OB	2015
†CHOHAN, Darshan	04.11.95	Singapore	St Catharine's	LHB/SLA	2015
†CRICHARD, Ruari James	09.01.95	Hammersmith	St John's	RHB/RM	2015
ELLISON, Harry Richard Clive	22.02.93	Canterbury	Anglia RU	RHB/OB	2014
†HEARNE, Alexander Gordon	23.09.93	Kensington	St John's	RHB/LB	2013
†HUGHES, Philip Heywood	17.06.91	Southampton	Downing	RHB/RM	2010
†HUNT, Alexander Patrick	04.04.92	Stanford, USA	Queens'	RHB/RM	2015
†PATEL, Avish Rasiklal	31.07.94	Leicester	Robinson	RHB/LB	2015
†POLLOCK, Alasdair William	24.10.93	High Wycombe	Robinson	RHB/RMF	2015
TETLEY, Joseph William	14.04.95	Sheffield	Anglia RU	LHB/WK	2015
†TICE, Patrick James Aikman	30.06.94	Basingstoke	Fitzwilliam	RHB/WK	2015
WRIGHT, Andrew R.	08.03.94	????	Anglia RU	RHB/WK	
†WYLIE, Benjamin Alexander	24.04.94	Belfast	St Catharine's	LHB/SLA	2013
ZAIN SHAHZAD	20.09.91	Sialkot, Pakistan	Anglia RU	RHB/RMF	2014

CARDIFF

Full Names	Birthdate	Birthplace	College	Bat/Bowl	F-C Debut
BRACEY, Samuel Nicholas	19.05.94	Bristol	Cardiff Met	RHB/WK	2014
BRAND, Neil	12.04.96	Johannesburg, SA	Cardiff Met	LHB/SLA	2015
BULL, Kieran Andrew	05.04.95	Haverfordwest	Cardiff Met	RHB/OB	2014
CULLEN, Thomas N.	04.01.92	Perth, Australia	Cardiff Met	RHB/WK	2015
GEORGE, Jacob	05.05.94	Ealing	Cardiff	RHB/OB	2014
GRIFFITHS, Sean William	16.05.95	Neath	Cardiff Met	RHB/RM	2015
LAWLOR, Jeremy Lloyd	04.11.95	Cardiff	Cardiff Met	RHB/RM	2015
LEVEROCK, Kamau Sadiki	19.10.94	Bermuda	Cardiff Met	LHB/RFM	2015
LEWIS-WILLIAMS, Daniel Evan	12.10.93	Yeovil	Cardiff Met	RHB/LM	2015
MURPHY, Jack Roger	15.07.95	Haverfordwest	Cardiff Met	LHB/LMF	2015
NORRIS, Matthew Jonathan	18.12.92	Cape Town, SA	Cardiff Met	LHB/SLA	2015
ROUSE, Timothy David	09.04.96	Sheffield	Cardiff	RHB/OB	2015
SCRIVEN, Bradley	08.12.93	High Wycombe	Cardiff Met	RHB/RM	2015
WESTPHAL, Andrew Alexander	28.07.94	London	Cardiff Met	RHB/RMF	2014

DURHAM

Full Names	Birthdate	Birthplace	College	Bat/Bowl	F-C Debut
BISHNOI, Chaitanya	25.08.94	Delhi, India	Hatfield	LHB/SLA	2013
GIBSON, Robert Andrew Max	11.03.94	Emsworth		RHB/LB	2015
JENKINS, William Henry	04.07.94	Yeovil		RHB/RM	2014
MacDONELL, Charles Michael	23.02.95	Basingstoke		RHB/RFM	
McINLEY, Harry Peter Stuart	10.08.93	Redhill	Hatfield	RHB/RM	2015
PHILLIPS, William David Beauclerk	12.04.93	Auckland, NZ		RHB/RM	2015
POLLOCK, Edward John	10.07.95	High Wycombe		LHB/OB	2015
RATNAYAKE, Dimitri Eranga Mahen	09.03.90	Kandy, Sri Lanka		RHB/RM	2011
STEEL, Cameron Tate	13.09.95	California, USA		RHB/LB	2014
STEELE, Oliver James	15.10.93	Worcester	Collingwood	RHB/WK	2013
WILLIAMS, Benjamin Peter Robert	28.10.93	Plymouth		RHB/LMF	2015
WILLIAMS, Darrel Ryan	21.09.95	Banbury		RHB/LB	2015
WOOD, Jack Michael	04.11.94	Reading		RHB/RM	2015

LEEDS/BRADFORD

Full Names	Birthdate	Birthplace	College	Bat/Bowl	F-C Debut
BULLEN, Steven Frank Gregory	12.07.92	Watford	Leeds Beckett	RHB/WK	2015
DAVIS, Christian Arthur Linghorne	11.10.92	Milton Keynes	Leeds	RHB/LFM	2014
ELLIS-GREWAL, Joe Sukhdev Edwin	18.02.92	Walthamstow	Leeds	LHB/SLA	2015
GUBBINS, Nicholas Richard Trail	31.12.93	Richmond, Surrey	Leeds	LHB/LB	2012
LILLEY, Alexander Edward	17.04.92	Halifax	Leeds Beckett	RHB/LM	2011
PRATT, Douglas Thomas Piers	14.04.93	Cambridge	Leeds	RHB/RMF	2015
ROOT, William Thomas	05.08.92	Sheffield	Leeds Beckett	LHB/OB	2015
ROUSE, Harry Philip	20.10.93	Sheffield	Leeds	RHB/RFM	2013
SCOTT, George Frederick Buchan	06.11.95	Hemel Hempstead	Leeds	RHB/RM	2015
THOMPSON, Henry Lester	01.12.92	Preston	Leeds	RHB/OB	2013
WAKEFIELD, Christopher Francis	11.10.91	Hammersmith	Leeds Beckett	RHB/WK	2015
WATKINSON, Liam	27.07.91	Bolton	Leeds Beckett	RHB/RM	2015
WESTON, Logan Patrick	03.07.92	Bradford	Leeds Beckett	RHB/OB	2015

LOUGHBOROUGH

Full Names	Birthdate	Birthplace	College	Bat/Bowl	F-C Debut
AKRAM, Basil Mohammad Ramzan	23.02.93	Waltham Forest	Loughborough	RHB/RMF	2014
BEST, Mark Treloar	29.11.94	Nuneaton	Loughborough	LHB/RM	2014
BURGESS, Michael Gregory Kerran	08.07.94	Epsom	Loughborough	RHB/WK	2014
GAMBLE, Robert Neil	25.01.95	Nottingham	Loughborough	RHB/RMF	2015
GRANT, Samuel Edward	30.08.95	Shoreham-by-Sea	Loughborough	LHB/LMF	2014
HASAN AZAD, Mohammad	07.01.94	Karachi, Pakistan	Loughborough	LHB/OB	2015
KUMAR, Nitish Roenik	21.05.94	Scarborough, Can	Loughborough	RHB/OB	2009
McKINLEY, George Kenneth Robert	03.11.93	Larne, N.Ireland	Loughborough	RHB/RM	2015
NUGENT, Thomas Michael	11.07.94	Bath	Loughborough	RHB/RFM	2014
PATEL, Anish Kirtesh	26.05.90	Manchester	Loughborough	RHB/OB	2013
PROWSE, Ian	31.01.91	Lisburn, N.Ireland	Loughborough	RHB/RM	2015
WHITE, Robert George	15.09.95	Ealing	Loughborough	RHB/RM	2015
WHITTINGHAM, Stuart Gordon	10.02.94	Derby	Loughborough	RHB/RFM	2015

OXFORD († = Blue)

Full Names	Birthdate	Birthplace	College	Bat/Bowl	F-C Debut
†CATO, Samuel John	23.11.92	Chiswick	New	RHB/OB	2013
†CLAUGHTON, Thomas Hugh	24.01.96	Slough	Magdalen	RHB/OB	2015
ELLIS, Edward John	09.05.95	Ascot	Brookes U	RHB/WK	2015
†GNODDE, James Spencer D.	.11.95	Westminster	Pembroke		2015
GRUNDY, Jack Oliver	25.06.94	Warwick	Brookes U	RHB/LMF	2015
HUGHES, Henry Christopher David	11.09.92	Manchester	Brookes U	RHB	2015
†HUGHES, Matthew Stephen Turner	17.04.96	Manchester	Hertford	RHB	2015
†JONES, Owain James	24.09.92	Brighton	St Edmund Hall	LHB/RM	2015
KIDD, Matthew James Lewis	22.10.92	Cambridge	Brookes U	RHB/RM	2014
LAKE, Malcolm Blair	03.08.94	Harare, Zimbabwe	Brookes U	LHB/RM	2014
LEACH, Stephen Geoffrey	19.11.93	Stafford	Brookes U	LHB/LB	2014
McIVER, Jack Nathan	26.04.92	Hammersmith	Brookes U	RHB/OB	2015
†MARSDEN, Jonathan	07.04.93	Sevenoaks	St Hilda's	RHB/RFM	2013
†MYLAVARAPU, Sachin Venkata S.	21.06.91	Singapore	St Hugh's	RHB/SLA	2015
†O'GRADY, Richard James	21.01.95	Westminster	Merton	RHB/RM	2014
PATERNOTT, Lloyd Christopher	15.01.92	Watford	Brookes U	RHB/OB	2013
SABIN, Lloyd Michael	22.06.94	Banbury	Brookes U	RHB/OB	2015
†SAKANDE, Abidine	22.09.94	Chester	St John's	RHB/RM	2015
WEBB, Luke Alexander	31.12.95	Stoke Mandeville	Brookes U	RHB/OB	2015
WELLER, Sam David	21.11.94	Chislehurst	Brookes U	RHB/RFM	2014
†WESTAWAY, Samuel Alexander	29.07.92	Welwyn Garden Green	Templeton	RHB/WK	2011
†WINTER, Matthew James	08.11.93	Crewe	Lady Margaret	RHB	2013

THE 2015 FIRST-CLASS SEASON
STATISTICAL HIGHLIGHTS

FIRST TO INDIVIDUAL TARGETS

1000 RUNS	A.G.Prince	Lancashire	30 June
2000 RUNS	–	Most – 1620 J.C.Hildreth (Somerset)	
50 WICKETS	K.M.Jarvis	Lancashire	14 June
100 WICKETS	–	Most – 88 C.Rushworth (Durham)	

TEAM HIGHLIGHTS
HIGHEST INNINGS TOTALS

698-5d	Lancashire v Glamorgan	Colwyn Bay
633-8d	Kent v Essex	Tunbridge Wells
630-9d	Somerset v Hampshire	Taunton
612-6d	Warwickshire v Sussex	Birmingham
610-8d	Essex v Surrey	The Oval
601-6d	Sussex v Warwickshire	Birmingham
600	Nottinghamshire v Warwickshire	Nottingham

HIGHEST FOURTH INNINGS TOTAL

390-9	Northamptonshire (set 427) v Derbyshire	Derby

LOWEST INNINGS TOTALS († One man short)

60	Australia v England (4th Test)	Nottingham
69	Warwickshire v Yorkshire	Birmingham
71	Durham v Middlesex	Lord's
78	Leicestershire v Lancashire	Leicester
80	Worcestershire v Warwickshire	Worcester
86	Derbyshire v Kent	Canterbury
89	Middlesex v Durham	Lord's
90	Somerset v Worcestershire	Worcester
94†	Derbyshire v Essex	Derby
95	Oxford MCCU v Worcestershire	Oxford
95	Cardiff MCCU v Gloucestershire	Bristol
98	Middlesex v Worcestershire	Worcester
99	Kent v Surrey	The Oval

MATCH AGGREGATES OF 1500 RUNS

1610-40	England (389 & 478) v New Zealand (523 & 220) (1st Test)	Lord's
1547-33	Leicestershire (292 & 480) v Surrey (557 & 218-3)	The Oval

BATSMEN'S MATCH (Qualification: 1200 runs, average 60 per wicket)

101.08 (1213-12)	Sussex (601-6d) v Warwickshire (612-6d)	Birmingham
62.14 (1305-21)	Surrey (563-7d & 207-4d) v Glamorgan (419 & 116-0)	Cardiff

LARGE MARGINS OF VICTORY

405 runs	Australia (566-8d & 254-2d) beat England (312 & 103) (2nd Test)	Lord's
379 runs	Durham (448-4d & 260-7d) beat Durham MCCU (159 & 170)	Chester-le-Street
Inns & 207 runs	Kent (633-8d) beat Essex (260 & 166)	Tunbridge Wells

NARROW MARGINS OF VICTORY

1 wkt	Sussex (191 & 190-9) beat Warwickshire (180 & 200)	Hove
17 runs	Somerset (438 & 110) beat Warwickshire (324 & 207)	Taunton
20 runs	Middlesex (234 & 331) beat Sussex (300 & 245)	Lord's

ALL ELEVEN SCORING DOUBLE FIGURES

| Gloucestershire (416, lowest score 11) v Glamorgan | Swansea |
| Surrey (560, lowest score 10) v Derbyshire | The Oval |

FOUR HUNDREDS IN AN INNINGS

| Sussex (601-6d) v Warwickshire | Birmingham |

SIX FIFTIES IN AN INNINGS

| Essex (610-8d) v Surrey | The Oval |
| Kent (633-8d) v Essex | Tunbridge Wells |

ELEVEN BOWLERS IN AN INNINGS

| Sussex v Warwickshire (612-6d) | Birmingham |

MOST EXTRAS IN AN INNINGS

B	LB	W	NB		
67	26	34	6	1	New Zealand (523) v England (*1st Test*)	Lord's
62	9	22	1	30	Middlesex (269) v Sussex	Hove
61	1	11	5	44	Glamorgan (513-9d) v Leicestershire	Leicester
61	12	20	3	26	Surrey (315) v Derbyshire	Derby

Under ECB regulations, Test matches excluded, two penalty extras were scored for each no-ball.

BATTING HIGHLIGHTS
TRIPLE HUNDREDS

| K.P.Pietersen | 355* | Surrey v Leicestershire | The Oval |

DOUBLE HUNDREDS

J.M.Bairstow	219*	Yorkshire v Durham	Chester-le-Street
S.M.Davies	200*	Surrey v Glamorgan	Cardiff
C.D.J.Dent	268	Gloucestershire v Glamorgan	Bristol
L.J.Evans	213*	Warwickshire v Sussex	Birmingham
M.J.Guptill	227	Derbyshire v Gloucestershire	Bristol
A.D.Hales	236	Nottinghamshire v Yorkshire	Nottingham
J.C.Hildreth	220*	Somerset v Worcestershire	Taunton
D.K.H.Mitchell	206*	Worcestershire v Hampshire	Worcester
A.N.Petersen	286	Lancashire v Glamorgan	Colwyn Bay
A.G.Prince (2)	230	Lancashire v Derbyshire	Southport
	261	Lancashire v Glamorgan	Colwyn Bay
S.P.D.Smith	215	Australia v England (*2nd Test*)	Lord's
J.W.A.Taylor	291	Nottinghamshire v Sussex	Horsham
M.E.Trescothick	210*	Somerset v Sussex	Hove
G.G.Wagg	200	Glamorgan v Surrey	Guildford
L.J.Wright	226*	Sussex v Worcestershire	Worcester

HUNDREDS IN THREE CONSECUTIVE INNINGS

| B.A.Godleman | | 101 | Derbyshire v Leicestershire | Leicester |
| | 108 | 105* | Derbyshire v Kent | Derby |

HUNDRED IN EACH INNINGS OF A MATCH

A.Harinath	120	104	Surrey v Glamorgan	Guildford
B.A.Godleman	108	105*	Derbyshire v Kent	Derby

FASTEST HUNDRED AGAINST GENUINE BOWLING

S.M.Davies (115*)   57 balls Surrey v Leicestershire   The Oval

MOST SIXES IN AN INNINGS

15	K.P.Pietersen (355*)	Surrey v Leicestershire	The Oval
11	M.J.Guptill (227)	Derbyshire v Gloucestershire	Bristol
11	G.G.Wagg (200)	Glamorgan v Surrey	Guildford

150 OR MORE RUNS FROM BOUNDARIES IN AN INNINGS

Runs	6s	4s			
234	15	36	K.P.Pietersen	Surrey v Leicestershire	The Oval
182	11	29	M.J.Guptill	Derbyshire v Gloucestershire	Bristol
182	7	35	A.G.Prince	Lancashire v Glamorgan	Colwyn Bay
168	2	39	J.W.A.Taylor	Nottinghamshire v Sussex	Horsham
158	1	38	A.D.Hales	Nottinghamshire v Yorkshire	Nottingham
154	7	28	L.J.Wright	Sussex v Worcestershire	Worcester
152	2	35	A.N.Petersen	Lancashire v Glamorgan	Colwyn Bay
150	11	21	G.G.Wagg	Glamorgan v Surrey	Guildford

HUNDRED ON FIRST-CLASS DEBUT

M.S.T.Hughes	116	Oxford U v Cambridge U	Cambridge
O.E.Robinson	110	Sussex v Durham	Chester-le-Street

HUNDRED ON FIRST-CLASS DEBUT IN BRITAIN

M.R.Marsh	101	Australians v Kent	Canterbury
S.E.Marsh	114	Australians v Kent	Canterbury
B.R.M.Taylor	105	Nottinghamshire v Loughborough MCCU	Nottingham

CARRYING BAT THROUGH COMPLETED INNINGS

T.B.Abell (2)	76*	Somerset (200) v Nottinghamshire	Taunton
	88*	Somerset (170) v Warwickshire	Birmingham
D.K.H.Mitchell	206*	Worcestershire (478) v Hampshire	Worcester

LONG INNINGS (Qualification 600 mins and/or 400 balls)

Mins	Balls		
542	413	D.K.H.Mitchell (206*) Worcestershire v Hampshire	Worcester

UNUSUAL DISMISSAL – HANDLED THE BALL

C.A.Pujara   Derbyshire v Leicestershire   Derby

NOTABLE PARTNERSHIPS († *Team record*)

Qualifications: 1st-4th wkts: 250 runs; 5th-6th: 225; 7th: 200; 8th: 175; 9th: 150; 10th: 100.

First Wicket

272	M.E.Trescothick/T.B.Abell	Somerset v Hampshire	Taunton

Second Wicket

284	C.J.L.Rogers/S.P.D.Smith	Australia v England (*2nd Test*)	Lord's
257	A.D.Hales/S.J.Mullaney	Nottinghamshire v Warwickshire	Nottingham

Third Wicket

501†	A.N.Petersen/A.G.Prince	Lancashire v Glamorgan	Colwyn Bay
290	M.W.Machan/C.D.Nash	Sussex v Somerset	Taunton
261	M.E.Trescothick/J.C.Hildreth	Somerset v Middlesex	Taunton
258	A.N.Petersen/A.G.Prince	Lancashire v Derbyshire	Southport

Fourth Wicket

294	K.C.Sangakkara/S.M.Davies	Surrey v Glamorgan	Cardiff
282	L.J.Wright/B.C.Brown	Sussex v Worcestershire	Worcester
	(A further 13 runs were added for the 4th wkt between C.D.Nash, retd hurt, and L.J.Wright)		
258	T.Westley/J.D.Ryder	Essex v Northamptonshire	Northampton
255	A.W.Gale/J.A.Leaning	Yorkshire v Nottinghamshire	Leeds
254	A.W.Gale/J.M.Bairstow	Yorkshire v Worcestershire	Scarborough

Fifth Wicket

236	S.M.Davies/J.J.Roy	Surrey v Lancashire	The Oval

Sixth Wicket

365	J.W.A.Taylor/C.M.W.Read	Nottinghamshire v Sussex	Horsham
327†	L.J.Evans/T.R.Ambrose	Warwickshire v Sussex	Birmingham
248	G.J.Maxwell/A.U.Rashid	Yorkshire v Durham	Scarborough

Seventh Wicket

366*†	J.M.Bairstow/T.T.Bresnan	Yorkshire v Durham	Chester-le-Street

Eighth Wicket

175	D.J.Malan/J.A.R.Harris	Middlesex v Nottinghamshire	Nottingham

Tenth Wicket

164†	O.E.Robinson/M.E.Hobden	Sussex v Durham	Chester-le-Street
139	K.P.Pietersen/M.P.Dunn	Surrey v Leicestershire	The Oval
105	G.G.Wagg/M.G.Hogan	Glamorgan v Surrey	Guildford
100	A.L.Davies/K.M.Jarvis	Lancashire v Derbyshire	Derby

BOWLING HIGHLIGHTS
EIGHT OR MORE WICKETS IN AN INNINGS

S.C.J.Broad	8- 15	England v Australia *(4th Test)*	Nottingham
J.A.R.Harris	9- 34	Middlesex v Durham	Lord's
J.K.H.Naik	8-179	Leicestershire v Lancashire	Manchester

TEN OR MORE WICKETS IN A MATCH

M.Carter	10-195	Nottinghamshire v Somerset	Taunton
On f-c debut			
M.T.Coles	10- 98	Kent v Leicestershire	Leicester
T.K.Curran	10-176	Surrey v Northamptonshire	The Oval
F.H.Edwards	10-145	Hampshire v Nottinghamshire	Nottingham
M.H.A.Footitt	10-155	Derbyshire v Leicestershire	Derby
J.A.R.Harris	13-103	Middlesex v Durham	Lord's
B.A.Hutton	10-106	Nottinghamshire v Durham	Nottingham
M.J.Leach	11-180	Somerset v Warwickshire	Taunton
S.J.Magoffin	12-159	Sussex v Nottinghamshire	Nottingham
C.N.Miles	10-121	Gloucestershire v Lancashire	Bristol
L.C.Norwell	10- 65	Gloucestershire v Essex	Chelmsford
J.D.Ryder	10-100	Essex v Glamorgan	Chelmsford
J.D.Shantry	10- 26	Worcestershire v Oxford MCCU	Oxford
R.J.Sidebottom	11- 76	Yorkshire v Warwickshire	Birmingham

BOWLING UNCHANGED THROUGHOUT INNINGS

J.A.R.Harris (12.1-2-34-9)/S.T.Finn (12-4-35-1) Middlesex v Durham Lord's

HAT-TRICKS

C.Rushworth   Durham v Hampshire   Southampton
Hat-trick off last two balls of 1st innings and first ball of 2nd innings
G.J.Batty   Surrey v Derbyshire   The Oval

MOST RUNS CONCEDED IN AN INNINGS

J.K.H.Naik   44.3-7-179-8 Leicestershire v Lancashire   Manchester

MOST OVERS BOWLED IN AN INNINGS

Z.S.Ansari   51.1-12-152-6 Surrey v Essex   The Oval

ALL-ROUND HIGHLIGHTS

MATCH DOUBLE (CENTURY AND FIVE WICKETS IN AN INNINGS)

K.H.D.Barker (102* & 5-103)   Warwickshire v Durham   Birmingham
P.D.Collingwood (109* & 5-57) Durham v Somerset   Taunton
T.S.Roland-Jones (103* & 5-27) Middlesex v Yorkshire   Lord's

WICKET-KEEPING HIGHLIGHTS

SIX OR MORE WICKET-KEEPING DISMISSALS IN AN INNINGS

L.Ronchi   7ct   Somerset v Hampshire   Taunton
S.W.Billings   6ct   Kent v Lancashire   Manchester
G.H.Roderick   6ct   Gloucestershire v Northamptonshire   Northampton

NINE OR MORE WICKET-KEEPING DISMISSALS IN A MATCH

N.J.O'Brien   9ct   Leicestershire v Glamorgan   Leicester

NO BYES CONCEDED IN AN INNINGS OF 600 OR MORE

J.S.Foster   Essex v Kent (633-8d)   Tunbridge Wells

FIELDING HIGHLIGHTS

SIX OR MORE CATCHES IN THE FIELD IN A MATCH

M.H.Yardy   6ct   Sussex v Middlesex   Hove

COUNTY CHAMPIONSHIP 2015
LV= FINAL TABLES

DIVISION 1

	P	W	L	D	Bonus Points Bat	Bonus Points Bowl	Deduct Points	Total Points
1 YORKSHIRE (1)	16	11	1	4	45	45	–	286
2 Middlesex (7)	16	7	2	7	29	43	1	218
3 Nottinghamshire (4)	16	6	5	5	45	45	–	211
4 Durham (6)	16	7	8	1	26	45	–	188
5 Warwickshire (2)	16	5	5	6	31	45	–	186
6 Somerset (5)	16	4	6	6	46	43	–	183
7 Hampshire (-)	16	4	6	6	31	38	–	163
8 Sussex (3)	16	4	8	4	36	41	–	161
9 Worcestershire (-)	16	3	10	3	44	44	–	151

DIVISION 2

	P	W	L	D	Bonus Points Bat	Bonus Points Bowl	Deduct Points	Total Points
1 Surrey (5)	16	8	1	7	56	45	–	264
2 Lancashire (-)	16	7	1	8	58	44	–	254
3 Essex (3)	16	6	5	5	37	42	–	200
4 Glamorgan (8)	16	4	4	8	42	37	–	183
5 Northamptonshire (-)	16	3	3	10	38	46	2	180
6 Gloucestershire (7)	16	5	5	6	31	36	–	177
7 Kent (6)	16	4	7	5	28	44	–	161
8 Derbyshire (4)	16	3	7	6	34	42	1	153
9 Leicestershire (9)	16	2	9	5	36	41	16	118

Middlesex and Derbyshire deducted 1 point for slow over rate.
Northamptonshire deducted 2 points for slow over rate.
Leicestershire deducted 16 points for poor onfield behaviour.

SCORING OF CHAMPIONSHIP POINTS 2015

(a) For a win, 16 points, plus any points scored in the first innings.

(b) In a tie, each side to score eight points, plus any points scored in the first innings.

(c) In a drawn match, each side to score five points, plus any points scored in the first innings (see also paragraph (e) below).

(d) If the scores are equal in a drawn match, the side batting in the fourth innings to score eight points plus any points scored in the first innings, and the opposing side to score three points plus any points scored in the first innings.

(e) **First Innings Points** (awarded only for performances **in the first 110 overs** of each first innings and retained whatever the result of the match).
   (i) A maximum of five batting points to be available as under:
      200 to 249 runs – 1 point; 250 to 299 runs – 2 points; 300 to 349 runs – 3 points; 350 to 399 runs – 4 points; 400 runs and over – 5 points.
   (ii) A maximum of three bowling points to be available as under:
      3 to 5 wickets taken – 1 point; 6 to 8 wickets taken – 2 points; 9 to 10 wickets taken – 3 points.

(f) If a match is abandoned without a ball being bowled, each side to score five points.

(g) The side which has the highest aggregate of points gained at the end of the season shall be the Champion County of their respective Division. Should any sides in the Championship table be equal on points, the following tie-breakers will be applied in the order stated: most wins, fewest losses, team achieving most points in contests between teams level on points, most wickets taken, most runs scored. At the end of the season, the top two teams from the Second Division will be promoted and the bottom two teams from the First Division will be relegated.

COUNTY CHAMPIONS

The English County Championship was not officially constituted until December 1889. Prior to that date there was no generally accepted method of awarding the title; although the 'least matches lost' method existed, it was not consistently applied. Rules governing playing qualifications were agreed in 1873 and the first unofficial points system 15 years later.

Research has produced a list of champions dating back to 1826, but at least seven different versions exist for the period from 1864 to 1889 (see *The Wisden Book of Cricket Records*). Only from 1890 can any authorised list of county champions commence.

That first official Championship was contested between eight counties: Gloucestershire, Kent, Lancashire, Middlesex, Nottinghamshire, Surrey, Sussex and Yorkshire. The remaining counties were admitted in the following seasons: 1891 – Somerset, 1895 – Derbyshire, Essex, Hampshire, Leicestershire and Warwickshire, 1899 – Worcestershire, 1905 – Northamptonshire, 1921 – Glamorgan, and 1992 – Durham.

The Championship pennant was introduced by the 1951 champions, Warwickshire, and the Lord's Taverners' Trophy was first presented in 1973. The first sponsors, Schweppes (1977-83), were succeeded by Britannic Assurance (1984-98), PPP Healthcare (1999-2000), CricInfo (2001), Frizzell (2002-05), Liverpool Victoria (2006-15) and Specsavers (from 2016). Based on their previous season's positions, the 18 counties were separated into two divisions in 2000. From 2000 to 2005 the bottom three Division 1 teams were relegated and the top three Division 2 sides promoted. This was reduced to two teams from the end of the 2006 season.

1890	Surrey	1935	Yorkshire	1979	Essex
1891	Surrey	1936	Derbyshire	1980	Middlesex
1892	Surrey	1937	Yorkshire	1981	Nottinghamshire
1893	Yorkshire	1938	Yorkshire	1982	Middlesex
1894	Surrey	1939	Yorkshire	1983	Essex
1895	Surrey	1946	Yorkshire	1984	Essex
1896	Yorkshire	1947	Middlesex	1985	Middlesex
1897	Lancashire	1948	Glamorgan	1986	Essex
1898	Yorkshire	1949 {	Middlesex	1987	Nottinghamshire
1899	Surrey		Yorkshire	1988	Worcestershire
1900	Yorkshire	1950 {	Lancashire	1989	Worcestershire
1901	Yorkshire		Surrey	1990	Middlesex
1902	Yorkshire	1951	Warwickshire	1991	Essex
1903	Middlesex	1952	Surrey	1992	Essex
1904	Lancashire	1953	Surrey	1993	Middlesex
1905	Yorkshire	1954	Surrey	1994	Warwickshire
1906	Kent	1955	Surrey	1995	Warwickshire
1907	Nottinghamshire	1956	Surrey	1996	Leicestershire
1908	Yorkshire	1957	Surrey	1997	Glamorgan
1909	Kent	1958	Surrey	1998	Leicestershire
1910	Kent	1959	Yorkshire	1999	Surrey
1911	Warwickshire	1960	Yorkshire	2000	Surrey
1912	Yorkshire	1961	Hampshire	2001	Yorkshire
1913	Kent	1962	Yorkshire	2002	Surrey
1914	Surrey	1963	Yorkshire	2003	Sussex
1919	Yorkshire	1964	Worcestershire	2004	Warwickshire
1920	Middlesex	1965	Worcestershire	2005	Nottinghamshire
1921	Middlesex	1966	Yorkshire	2006	Sussex
1922	Yorkshire	1967	Yorkshire	2007	Sussex
1923	Yorkshire	1968	Yorkshire	2008	Durham
1924	Yorkshire	1969	Glamorgan	2009	Durham
1925	Yorkshire	1970	Kent	2010	Nottinghamshire
1926	Lancashire	1971	Surrey	2011	Lancashire
1927	Lancashire	1972	Warwickshire	2012	Warwickshire
1928	Lancashire	1973	Hampshire	2013	Durham
1929	Nottinghamshire	1974	Worcestershire	2014	Yorkshire
1930	Lancashire	1975	Leicestershire	2015	Yorkshire
1931	Yorkshire	1976	Middlesex		
1932	Yorkshire	1977 {	Kent		
1933	Yorkshire		Middlesex		
1934	Lancashire	1978	Kent		

COUNTY CHAMPIONSHIP RESULTS 2015

DIVISION 1

	DURHAM	HANTS	MIDDX	NOTTS	SOM'T	SUSSEX	WARWKS	WORCS	YORKS
DURHAM	—	C-le-St H 7w	C-le-St M 71	C-le-St D 6w	C-le-St D 120	C-le-St D 6w	C-le-St Wa 2w	C-le-St D 3w	C-le-St Y I/47
HANTS	So'ton Drawn	—	So'ton Drawn	So'ton Drawn	So'ton Sm 9w	So'ton Sx 92	So'ton H 216	So'ton Drawn	So'ton Y 5w
MIDDX	Lord's M 187	Lord's M 9w	—	Lord's Drawn	N'wood Drawn	Lord's M 20	Lord's Drawn	Uxbridge Drawn	Lord's M 246
NOTTS	N'ham N 52	N'ham H 8w	N'ham Drawn	—	N'ham Sm 133	N'ham N 159	N'ham N I/123	N'ham N 113	N'ham Drawn
SOM'T	Taunton D 7w	Taunton Drawn	Taunton M 5w	Taunton Sm 2w	—	Taunton Drawn	Taunton Sm 17	Taunton Drawn	Taunton Drawn
SUSSEX	Arundel D 178	Hove H 6w	Hove M 79	Horsham N I/103	Hove Drawn	—	Hove Sx 1w	Hove Sx 61	Hove Drawn
WARWKS	B'ham Wa 8w	B'ham Drawn	B'ham Drawn	B'ham Drawn	B'ham Wa 7w	B'ham Drawn	—	B'ham Wa 181	B'ham Y 174
WORCS	Worcs D 6w	Worcs Wo I/33	Worcs Wo I/128	Worcs N 5w	Worcs Wo I/92	Worcs Sx I/63	Worcs Wa I/17	—	Worcs Y 10w
YORKS	Scar Y 183	Leeds Y 305	Leeds Y 4w	Leeds Y I/8	Leeds Y I/126	Leeds Y 100	Leeds Drawn	Scar Y 7w	—

DIVISION 2

	DERBYS	ESSEX	GLAM	GLOS	KENT	LANCS	LEICS	N'HANTS	SURREY
DERBYS	—	Derby E I/188	C'field Drawn	Derby Drawn	Derby Drawn	Derby La 250	Derby Drawn	Derby Drawn	Derby S 222
ESSEX	C'ford E I/31	—	C'ford E 248	C'ford Gs 9w	C'ford E 5w	C'ford Drawn	C'ford Le 6w	C'ford Drawn	Colch'r S 3w
GLAM	Cardiff Drawn	Cardiff Gm 89	—	Swansea Gs 7w	Cardiff K 316	Col B La I/157	Cardiff Drawn	Cardiff Gm 10w	Cardiff Drawn
GLOS	Bristol D 7w	Bristol E 5w	Bristol Drawn	—	Bristol K 8w	Bristol La 91	Chelt'm Gs 155	Chelt'm Gs 9w	Bristol Drawn
KENT	Cant D 8w	Tun W K I/207	Cant Drawn	Cant Drawn	—	Cant Drawn	Cant Drawn	Cant N I/23	Beck S 3w
LANCS	S'port La I/15	Man Drawn	Man Drawn	Man Gs 91	Man La 9w	—	Man La I/157	Man Drawn	Man Drawn
LEICS	Leics Le 3w	Leics E 5w	Leics Drawn	Leics Drawn	Leics K 8w	Leics La 244	—	Leics N 92	Leics S 178
N'HANTS	No'ton D 7w	No'ton Drawn	No'ton Drawn	No'ton Drawn	No'ton N 8w	No'ton Drawn	No'ton Drawn	—	No'ton Drawn
SURREY	Oval S I/98	Oval Drawn	G'ford Gm 7w	Oval S I/180	Oval S 6w	Oval Drawn	Oval S 7w	Oval Drawn	—

COUNTY CHAMPIONSHIP FIXTURES 2016

KEEP YOUR OWN RECORD (see page 218)

DIVISION 1

	DURHAM	HANTS	LANCS	MIDDX	NOTTS	SOM'T	SURREY	WARWKS	YORKS
DURHAM	–	C-le-St	C-le-St	C-le-St	C-le-St	C-le-St	C-le-St	C-le-St	C-le-St
HANTS	So'ton	–	So'ton	So'ton	So'ton	So'ton	So'ton	So'ton	So'ton
LANCS	S'port	Man	–	Man	Man	Man	Man	Man	Man
MIDDX	Lord's	N'wood	Lord's	–	Lord's	Lord's	Lord's	Lord's	Lord's
NOTTS	N'ham	N'ham	N'ham	N'ham	–	N'ham	N'ham	N'ham	N'ham
SOM'T	Taunton	Taunton	Taunton	Taunton	Taunton	–	Taunton	Taunton	Taunton
SURREY	Oval	Oval	Oval	Oval	Oval	Oval	–	G'ford	Oval
WARWKS	B'ham	B'ham	B'ham	B'ham	B'ham	B'ham	B'ham	–	B'ham
YORKS	Leeds	Leeds	Leeds	Scar	Scar	Leeds	Leeds	Leeds	–

DIVISION 2

	DERBYS	ESSEX	GLAM	GLOS	KENT	LEICS	N'HANTS	SUSSEX	WORCS
DERBYS	–	Derby	Derby	Derby	Derby	Derby	C'field	Derby	Derby
ESSEX	C'ford	–	C'ford	C'ford	C'ford	C'ford	C'ford	Colch'r	C'ford
GLAM	Col B	Cardiff	–	Cardiff	Cardiff	Cardiff	Swansea	Cardiff	Cardiff
GLOS	Bristol	Chelt'm	Bristol	–	Bristol	Chelt'm	Bristol	Bristol	Bristol
KENT	Cant	Cant	Cant	Cant	–	Cant	Beck	Tun W	Cant
LEICS	Leics	Leics	Leics	Leics	Leics	–	Leics	Leics	Leics
N'HANTS	No'ton	No'ton	No'ton	No'ton	No'ton	No'ton	–	No'ton	No'ton
SUSSEX	Hove	Hove	Hove	Hove	Hove	Hove	Arundel	–	Hove
WORCS	Worcs	Worcs	Worcs	Worcs	Worcs	Worcs	Worcs	Worcs	–

ROYAL LONDON ONE-DAY CUP 2015

This latest format of limited-overs competition was launched in 2014, and is now the only List-A tournament played in the UK. The top four from each group went through to the quarter-finals, with the top team from each group having a home draw against the fourth team in the other group, and the second team in each group having a home draw against the third team in the other group. The winner is decided in the final at Lord's.

GROUP A	P	W	L	T	NR	Pts	Net RR
1 Surrey	8	6	1	–	1	13	+1.07
2 Gloucestershire	8	5	2	–	1	11	+0.06
3 Yorkshire	8	4	2	–	2	10	+0.53
4 Durham	8	4	3	–	1	9	+0.40
5 Northamptonshire	8	4	3	–	1	9	–0.45
6 Somerset	8	4	4	–	–	8	+0.81
7 Derbyshire	8	4	4	–	–	8	+0.15
8 Worcestershire	8	1	6	–	1	3	–0.62
9 Leicestershire	8	–	7	–	1	1	–1.91

GROUP A	P	W	L	T	NR	Pts	Net RR
1 Nottinghamshire	8	5	1	–	2	12	+0.75
2 Essex	8	4	2	–	2	10	+0.48
3 Hampshire *	8	3	3	–	2	9	+0.55
4 Kent	8	3	3	–	2	8	+0.03
5 Lancashire	8	3	3	–	2	8	–0.03
6 Warwickshire	8	3	3	–	2	8	–0.76
7 Middlesex	8	3	4	–	1	7	–0.22
8 Glamorgan †	8	2	2	–	4	3	+0.16
9 Sussex	8	–	5	–	3	3	–1.06

Win = 2 points. Tie (T)/No Result (NR) = 1 point.

* Hampshire awarded 2 points in the match against Glamorgan, abandoned due to a bad pitch, for which Glamorgan were fined a further 2 points.

† Glamorgan deducted 2 points for a poor pitch v Durham in 2014 competition.

Positions of counties finishing equal on points are decided by most wins or, if equal, the team with the higher net run rate (ie deducting from the average runs per over scored by that team in matches where a result was achieved, the average runs per over scored against that team); if still equal, the team that achieved the most points in the matches played between them. In the even the teams still cannot be separated, the winner will be decided by drawing lots.

Statistical Highlights in 2015

Highest total	367-6		Middlesex v Sussex	Hove
Biggest victory (runs)	220		Surrey beat Northamptonshire	The Oval
Biggest victory (wkts)	10		Hampshire beat Middlesex	Southampton
Most runs	531 (ave 106.20)	M.Klinger	Gloucestershire	
Highest innings	166	K.C.Sangakkara	Surrey v Notts	The Oval
Highest partnership	268	D.J.Malan/N.R.T.Gubbins	Middlesex v Sussex	Hove
Most wickets	20 (ave 17.95)	R.J.W.Topley	Essex	
Best bowling	6-35	J.W.Dernbach	Surrey v Gloucestershire	Lord's
Most economical	10-2-19-2	C.Overton	Somerset v Yorkshire	Scarborough
Most expensive	9-0-92-1	O.H.Freckingham	Leics v Durham	Leicester
Most w/k dismissals	19	G.C.Wilson	Surrey	
Most dismissals inns	6	C.M.W.Read	Notts v Sussex	Hove
Most catches	9	J.M.R.Taylor	Gloucestershire	

2015 ROYAL LONDON ONE-DAY CUP FINAL
GLOUCESTERSHIRE v SURREY

At Lord's, London, on 19 September.
Result: **GLOUCESTERSHIRE** won by 6 runs.
Toss: Surrey. Award: J.M.R.Taylor.

GLOUCESTERSHIRE		Runs	Balls	4/6	Fall
* M.Klinger	c Wilson b Dernbach	0	3	–	1- 0
C.D.J.Dent	c Mahmood b Dernbach	22	20	4	2- 40
† G.H.Roderick	b Mahmood	39	64	3	5-108
H.J.H.Marshall	st Wilson b Batty	18	35	1	3- 79
B.A.C.Howell	b Mahmood	9	17	1	4-100
G.O.Jones	b Dernbach	50	65	4/1	8-220
T.M.J.Smith	run out	20	51	–	6-160
J.M.R.Taylor	c S.M.Curran b Dernbach	35	26	2/2	7-209
J.K.Fuller	not out	3	4	–	
C.N.Miles	c Wilson b Dernbach	0	1	–	9-220
D.A.Payne	lbw b Dernbach	0	1	–	10-220
Extras	(B 2, LB 9, W 11, NB 2)	24			
Total	(47.4 overs)	220			

SURREY		Runs	Balls	4/6	Fall
J.J.Roy	c Smith b Fuller	11	23	2	1- 13
S.M.Davies	b Fuller	13	31	–	2- 42
K.C.Sangakkara	c sub (W.A.Tavaré) b Taylor	60	87	3	3-143
R.J.Burns	st Roderick b Taylor	56	72	5	4-148
† G.C.Wilson	c Klinger b Smith	8	15	–	5-165
S.M.Curran	c Howell b Payne	37	39	5	9-214
Azhar Mahmood	st Roderick b Smith	5	12	–	6-191
T.K.Curran	lbw b Taylor	0	4	–	7-192
J.E.Burke	run out	11	13	1	8-214
* G.J.Batty	c Taylor b Payne	0	2	–	10-214
J.W.Dernbach	not out	0	0	–	
Extras	(B 2, LB 4, W 5, NB 2)	13			
Total	(49.3 overs)	214			

SURREY	O	M	R	W	GLOUCESTERSHIRE	O	M	R	W
Dernbach	8.4	0	35	6	Payne	8.3	0	36	2
S.M.Curran	6	0	32	0	Fuller	10	2	34	2
T.K.Curran	9	1	51	0	Miles	3	0	24	0
Batty	10	0	43	1	Taylor	10	0	43	3
Azhar Mahmood	10	0	28	2	Howell	8	0	29	0
Burke	4	0	20	0	Smith	10	0	42	2

Umpires: R.J.Bailey and N.G.B.Cook.

SEMI-FINALS

At Headingley, Leeds, on 6 September. Toss: Gloucestershire. **GLOUCESTERSHIRE** won by eight wickets. Yorkshire 263-9 (50; A.Lyth 96, B.A.C.Howell 3-37). Gloucestershire 267-2 (46.5; M.Klinger 137*, H.J.H.Marshall 78*). Award: M.Klinger.

At The Oval, London, on 7 September. Toss: Surrey. **SURREY** won by 4 runs. Surrey 300-5 (50; K.C.Sangakkara 166). Nottinghamshire 296-7 (50; G.P.Smith 124, D.T.Christian 54, S.R.Patel 51). Award: K.C.Sangakkara.

PRINCIPAL LIST A RECORDS 1963-2015

These records cover all the major limited-overs tournaments played by the counties since the inauguration of the Gillette Cup in 1963.

Highest Totals	496-4		Surrey v Glos	The Oval	2007
	438-5		Surrey v Glamorgan	The Oval	2002
Highest Total Batting Second	429		Glamorgan v Surrey	The Oval	2002
Lowest Totals	23		Middlesex v Yorks	Leeds	1974
	36		Leics v Sussex	Leicester	1973
Largest Victory (Runs)	346		Somerset beat Devon	Torquay	1990
	304		Sussex beat Ireland	Belfast	1996
Highest Scores	268		A.D.Brown	Surrey v Glamorgan	The Oval	2002
	206		A.I.Kallicharran	Warwicks v Oxfords	Birmingham	1984
	203		A.D.Brown	Surrey v Hampshire	Guildford	1997
	201*		R.S.Bopara	Essex v Leics	Leicester	2008
	201		V.J.Wells	Leics v Berkshire	Leicester	1996
Fastest Hundred	36 balls	G.D.Rose	Somerset v Devon	Torquay	1990
	44 balls	M.A.Ealham	Kent v Derbyshire	Maidstone	1995
	44 balls	T.C.Smith	Lancashire v Worcs	Worcester	2012
	44 balls	D.I.Stevens	Kent v Sussex	Canterbury	2013
Most Sixes (Inns)	15	R.N.ten Doeschate	Essex v Scotland	Chelmsford	2013

Highest Partnership for each Wicket

1st	311	A.J.Wright/N.J.Trainor	Glos v Scotland	Bristol	1997
2nd	302	M.E.Trescothick/C.Kieswetter	Somerset v Glos	Taunton	2008
3rd	309*	T.S.Curtis/T.M.Moody	Worcs v Surrey	The Oval	1994
4th	234*	D.Lloyd/C.H.Lloyd	Lancashire v Glos	Manchester	1978
5th	221*	R.R.Sarwan/M.A.Hardinges	Glos v Lancashire	Manchester	2005
6th	226	N.J.Llong/M.V.Fleming	Kent v Cheshire	Bowdon	1999
7th	170	D.R.Brown/A.F.Giles	Warwicks v Essex	Birmingham	2003
8th	174	R.W.T.Key/J.C.Tredwell	Kent v Surrey	The Oval	2007
9th	155	C.M.W.Read/A.J.Harris	Notts v Durham	Nottingham	1984
10th	82	G.Chapple/P.J.Martin	Lancashire v Worcs	Manchester	1996

Best Bowling	8-21	M.A.Holding	Derbyshire v Sussex	Hove	1988
	8-26	K.D.Boyce	Essex v Lancashire	Manchester	1971
	8-31	D.L.Underwood	Kent v Scotland	Edinburgh	1987
	8-66	S.R.G.Francis	Somerset v Derbys	Derby	2004
Four Wkts in Four Balls		A.Ward	Derbyshire v Sussex	Derby	1970
		V.C.Drakes	Notts v Derbyshire	Nottingham	1999
		D.A.Payne	Gloucestershire v Essex	Chelmsford	2010
		G.R.Napier	Essex v Surrey	Chelmsford	2013

Most Economical Analyses

8-8-0-0	B.A.Langford	Somerset v Essex	Yeovil	1969
8-7-1-1	D.R.Doshi	Notts v Northants	Northampton	1977
12-9-3-1	J.Simmons	Lancashire v Suffolk	Bury St Eds	1985
8-6-2-3	F.J.Titmus	Middlesex v Northants	Northampton	1972

Most Expensive Analyses

9-0-108-3	S.D.Thomas	Glamorgan v Surrey	The Oval	2002
10-0-107-0	J.W.Dernbach	Surrey v Essex	The Oval	2008
11-0-103-0	G.Welch	Warwicks v Lancs	Birmingham	1995
8-0-100-0	D.S.Harrison	Glamorgan v Somerset	Taunton	2010

Century and Five Wickets in an Innings

154*, 5-26	M.J.Procter	Glos v Somerset	Taunton	1972
206, 6-32	A.I.Kallicharran	Warwicks v Oxfords	Birmingham	1984
103, 5-41	C.L.Hooper	Kent v Essex	Maidstone	1993
125, 5-41	I.R.Bell	Warwicks v Essex	Chelmsford	2003

Most Wicket-Keeping Dismissals in an Innings

8 (8 ct)	D.J.S.Taylor	Somerset v British Us	Taunton	1982
8 (8 ct)	D.J.Pipe	Worcs v Herts	Hertford	2001

Most Catches in an Innings by a Fielder

5	J.M.Rice	Hampshire v Warwicks	Southampton	1978
5	D.J.G.Sales	Northants v Essex	Northampton	2007

NATWEST t20 BLAST 2015

In 2015, the Twenty20 competition was sponsored by NatWest. Between 2003 and 2009, three regional leagues competed to qualify for the knockout stages, but this was reduced to two leagues in 2010, before returning to the three-division format in 2012. In 2014, the competition reverted to two regional leagues. (2014's positions in brackets.)

NORTH GROUP

	P	W	L	T	NR	Pts	Net RR
Warwickshire (4)	14	10	4	–	–	20	+0.20
Worcestershire (3)	14	9	4	–	1	19	+0.68
Northamptonshire (7)	14	7	5	–	2	16	+0.11
Lancashire (1)	14	7	6	–	1	15	+0.46
Nottinghamshire (2)	14	7	6	–	1	15	+0.01
Durham (6)	14	5	8	–	1	11	–0.14
Leicestershire (8)	14	4	7	1	2	11	–0.30
Yorkshire (5)	14	5	8	1	–	11	–0.32
Derbyshire (9)	14	4	10	–	–	8	–0.66

SOUTH GROUP

	P	W	L	T	NR	Pts	Net RR
Kent (6)	14	9	4	–	1	19	+0.16
Sussex (7)	14	7	5	–	2	16	+0.20
Hampshire (3)	14	8	6	–	–	16	–0.12
Essex (1)	14	7	6	–	1	15	+0.20
Gloucestershire (8)	14	7	7	–	–	14	+0.35
Glamorgan (4)	14	7	7	–	–	14	–0.52
Surrey (2)	14	5	6	–	3	13	+0.04
Somerset (5)	14	4	8	–	2	10	–0.18
Middlesex (9)	14	4	9	–	1	9	+0.03

QUARTER-FINALS: NORTHAMPTONSHIRE beat Sussex by seven wickets at Hove.
WARWICKSHIRE beat Essex by 24 runs at Birmingham.
HAMPSHIRE beat Worcestershire by 17 runs (D/L) at Worcester.
LANCASHIRE beat Kent by losing fewer wickets at Canterbury.

SEMI-FINALS: NORTHANTS beat Warwickshire by five wickets at Birmingham.
LANCASHIRE beat Hampshire by six wickets at Birmingham.

LEADING AGGREGATES AND RECORDS 2015

BATTING (600 runs)

	M	I	NO	HS	Runs	Avg	100	50	R/100b	Sixes
J.M.Vince (Hampshire)	16	16	4	107*	710	59.16	1	5	134.4	14
M.Klinger (Glos)	12	12	4	126*	654	81.75	3	4	142.1	21
S.A.Northeast (Kent)	14	14	1	114	641	49.30	1	4	152.9	16

BOWLING (25 wkts)

		O	M	R	W	Avge	BB	4w	R/Over
J.P.Faulkner	(Lancashire)	50.3	1	316	25	12.64	3-19	–	6.25
S.D.Parry	(Lancashire)	57.0	–	392	25	15.68	4-16	1	6.87

Highest total	242-2		Warwickshire v Derbyshire	Birmingham
Highest innings	158*	B.B.McCullum	Warwickshire v Derbyshire	Birmingham
Highest partnership	187	D.J.Malan/P.R.Stirling	Middlesex v Sussex	Hove
Best bowling	5-14	K.J.Abbott	Middlesex v Sussex	Hove
Most economical	4-0-10-1	R.Clarke	Warwickshire v Leics	Leicester
Most expensive	4-0-62-0	G.R.Napier	Essex v Gloucestershire	Bristol
Most w/k dismissals	16	A.J.A.Wheater	Hampshire	
Most catches	14	S.J.Croft	Lancashire	
Most catches (inns)	4	E.J.G.Morgan	Middlesex v Sussex	Hove

2015 NATWEST t20 BLAST FINAL
NORTHAMPTONSHIRE v LANCASHIRE

At Edgbaston, Birmingham, on 29 August (floodlit).

Result: LANCASHIRE won by 13 runs.

Toss: Northamptonshire. Award: A.L.Davies.

LANCASHIRE		Runs	Balls	4/6	Fall
A.G.Prince	c Levi b Willey	43	45	4	4-125
A.L.Davies	b Cobb	47	26	6/1	1- 77
K.R.Brown	c Duckett b Afridi	0	3	–	2- 78
† J.C.Buttler	c Cobb b Willey	27	15	1/2	3-123
* S.J.Croft	run out	9	10	–	7-156
J.P.Faulkner	c Levi b Afridi	5	3	1	5-130
L.S.Livingstone	b Afridi	0	1	–	6-130
A.M.Lilley	not out	22	17	1/1	
S.D.Parry	not out	1	1	–	
G.T.Griffiths					
G.A.Edwards					
Extras	(LB 8, W 2, NB 2)	12			
Total	(7 wkts; 20 overs)	166			

NORTHAMPTONSHIRE		Runs	Balls	4/6	Fall
R.E.Levi	c Davies b Faulkner	16	12	3	1- 32
D.J.Willey	c Lilley b Faulkner	24	21	3/1	2- 45
J.J.Cobb	not out	44	37	2/1	
† B.M.Duckett	lbw b Parry	20	16	3	3- 74
S.P.Crook	c Lilley b Croft	2	6	–	4- 81
Shahid Afridi	c Livingstone b Griffiths	26	18	2/1	5-133
R.K.Kleinveldt	c Croft b Griffiths	11	8	2	6-148
* A.G.Wakely	not out	4	2	1	
G.G.White					
O.P.Stone					
M.Azharullah					
Extras	(LB 4, W 2)	6			
Total	(6 wkts; 20 overs)	153			

NORTHAMPTONSHIRE	O	M	R	W	LANCASHIRE	O	M	R	W
Kleinveldt	3	0	29	0	Croft	3	0	24	1
Willey	4	0	21	2	Griffiths	3	0	23	2
Stone	2	0	20	0	Edwards	3	0	34	0
Azharullah	3	0	27	0	Faulkner	4	0	25	2
White	2	0	31	0	Parry	4	0	23	1
Shahid Afridi	4	0	13	3	Lilley	3	0	20	0
Cobb	2	0	16	1					

Umpires: M.A.Gough and R.K.Illingworth

TWENTY20 CUP WINNERS

2003	Surrey	2008	Middlesex	2013	Northamptonshire
2004	Leicestershire	2009	Sussex	2014	Warwickshire
2005	Somerset	2010	Hampshire	2015	Lancashire
2006	Leicestershire	2011	Leicestershire		
2007	Kent	2012	Hampshire		

PRINCIPAL TWENTY20 CUP RECORDS 2003-15

Highest Total	254-3		Gloucestershire v Middx Uxbridge	2011
Highest Total Batting 2nd	226-3		Sussex v Essex Chelmsford	2014
Lowest Total	47		Northants v Durham Chester-le-St	2011
Largest Victory (Runs)	143		Somerset v Essex Chelmsford	2011
Largest Victory (Balls)	75		Hampshire v Glos Bristol	2010
Highest Scores	158*	B.B.McCullum	Warwickshire v Derbys Birmingham	2015
	153*	L.J.Wright	Sussex v Essex Chelmsford	2014
	152*	G.R.Napier	Essex v Sussex Chelmsford	2008
	151*	C.H.Gayle	Somerset v Kent Taunton	2015
Fastest Hundred	34 balls	A.Symonds	Kent v Middlesex Maidstone	2004
Most Sixes (Innings)	16	G.R.Napier	Essex v Sussex Chelmsford	2008
Most Runs in Career	3033	D.I.Stevens	Kent, Leicestershire	2003-15

Highest Partnership for each Wicket

1st	192	K.J.O'Brien/H.J.H.Marshall	Gloucestershire v Middx Uxbridge	2011
2nd	186	J.L.Langer/C.L.White	Somerset v Glos Taunton	2006
3rd	144*	J.H.K.Adams/S.M.Ervine	Hampshire v Surrey Southampton	2010
4th	159*	L.J.Wright/M.W.Machan	Sussex v Essex Chelmsford	2014
5th	117*	M.N.W.Spriegel/G.C.Wilson	Surrey v Middlesex Lord's	2012
6th	126*	C.S.MacLeod/J.W.Hastings	Durham v Northants Chester-le-St	2014
7th	80	D.T.Christian/T.S.Roland-Jones	Middlesex v Kent Canterbury	2014
8th	71*	M.Klinger/J.K.Fuller	Gloucestershire v Essex Chelmsford	2015
9th	59*	G.Chapple/P.J.Martin	Lancashire v Leics Leicester	2003
9th	59*	D.J.Willey/J.A.Brooks	Northants v Warwickshire Birmingham	2011
10th	59	H.H.Streak/J.E.Anyon	Warwickshire v Worcs Birmingham	2005

Best Bowling	6- 5	A.V.Suppiah	Somerset v Glamorgan Cardiff	2011
	6-16	T.G.Southee	Essex v Glamorgan Chelmsford	2011
	6-21	A.J.Hall	Northants v Worcs Northampton	2008
	6-24	T.J.Murtagh	Surrey v Middlesex Lord's	2005
Most Wkts in Career	153	Yasir Arafat	Hants, Kent, Lancs, Somerset, Surrey, Sussex	2006-15

Most Economical Innings Analyses (Qualification: 4 overs)

4-2-5-2	A.C.Thomas	Somerset v Hampshire Southampton	2010
4-0-5-3	D.R.Briggs	Hampshire v Kent Canterbury	2010
4-1-6-2	J.Louw	Northants v Warwicks Birmingham	2004
4-0-6-1	M.W.Alleyne	Glos v Worcs Worcester	2005

Most Maiden Overs in an Innings

4-2-9-1	M.Morkel	Kent v Surrey Beckenham	2007
4-2-5-2	A.C.Thomas	Somerset v Hampshire Southampton	2010

Most Expensive Innings Analyses

4-0-67-1	R.J.Kirtley	Sussex v Essex Chelmsford	2008
4-0-65-2	M.J.Hoggard	Yorkshire v Lancs Leeds	2005
4-0-64-0	Abdul Razzaq	Hampshire v Somerset Taunton	2010
4-0-63-1	R.J.Kirtley	Sussex v Surrey Hove	2004

Most Wicket-Keeping Dismissals in an Innings

5 (5 ct)	M.J.Prior	Sussex v Middlesex Richmond	
5 (4 ct, 1 st)	G.L.Brophy	Yorkshire v Durham Chester-le-St	2008
5 (3 ct, 2 st)	B.J.M.Scott	Worcs v Yorkshire Worcester	2011
5 (4 ct, 1 st)	G.C.Wilson	Surrey v Hampshire The Oval	2014
5 (5 ct)	N.J.O'Brien	Leics v Northants Leicester	2014
5 (3 ct, 2 st)	J.A.Simpson	Middlesex v Surrey Lord's	2015

Most Catches in an Innings by a Fielder

4	D.Pretorius	Warwicks v Glamorgan Swansea	2005
4	W.R.Smith	Notts v Surrey Nottingham	2006
4	D.J.G.Sales	Northants v Worcs Northampton	2008
4	G.D.Elliott	Surrey v Kent The Oval	2009
4	G.R.Breese	Durham v Yorkshire Scarborough	2011
4	A.J.Finch	Yorkshire v Durham Chester-le-St	2014
4	D.K.H.Mitchell	Worcs v Nothants Northampton	2014
4	E.J.G.Morgan	Middlesex v Sussex Hove	2015

YOUNG CRICKETER OF THE YEAR

This annual award, made by The Cricket Writers' Club, is currently restricted to players qualified for England, Andrew Symonds meeting that requirement at the time of his award, and under the age of 23 on 1st May. In 1986 their ballot resulted in a dead heat. Up to 7 April 2016 their selections have gained a tally of 2,484 international Test match caps (shown in brackets).

1950	R.Tattersall (16)	1973	M.Hendrick (30)	1995	A.Symonds (26 – Australia)
1951	P.B.H.May (66)	1974	P.H.Edmonds (51)	1996	C.E.W.Silverwood (6)
1952	F.S.Trueman (67)	1975	A.Kennedy	1997	B.C.Hollioake (2)
1953	M.C.Cowdrey (114)	1976	G.Miller (34)	1998	A.Flintoff (79)
1954	P.J.Loader (13)	1977	I.T.Botham (102)	1999	A.J.Tudor (10)
1955	K.F.Barrington (82)	1978	D.I.Gower (117)	2000	P.J.Franks
1956	B.Taylor	1979	P.W.G.Parker (1)	2001	O.A.Shah (6)
1957	M.J.Stewart (8)	1980	G.R.Dilley (41)	2002	R.Clarke (2)
1958	A.C.D.Ingleby-Mackenzie	1981	M.W.Gatting (79)	2003	J.M.Anderson (113)
1959	G.Pullar (28)	1982	N.G.Cowans (19)	2004	I.R.Bell (118)
1960	D.A.Allen (39)	1983	N.A.Foster (29)	2005	A.N.Cook (126)
1961	P.H.Parfitt (37)	1984	R.J.Bailey (4)	2006	S.C.J.Broad (91)
1962	P.J.Sharpe (12)	1985	D.V.Lawrence (5)	2007	A.U.Rashid (3)
1963	G.Boycott (108)	1986 {	A.A.Metcalfe	2008	R.S.Bopara (13)
1964	J.M.Brearley (39)		J.J.Whitaker (1)	2009	J.W.A.Taylor (7)
1965	A.P.E.Knott (95)	1987	R.J.Blakey (2)	2010	S.T.Finn (29)
1966	D.L.Underwood (86)	1988	M.P.Maynard (4)	2011	J.M.Bairstow (24)
1967	A.W.Greig (58)	1989	N.Hussain (96)	2012	J.E.Root (39)
1968	R.M.H.Cottam (4)	1990	M.A.Atherton (115)	2013	B.A.Stokes (23)
1969	A.Ward (5)	1991	M.R.Ramprakash (52)	2014	A.Z.Lees
1970	C.M.Old (46)	1992	I.D.K.Salisbury (15)	2015	T.K.Curran
1971	J.Whitehouse	1993	M.N.Lathwell (2)		
1972	D.R.Owen-Thomas	1994	J.P.Crawley (37)		

THE PROFESSIONAL CRICKETERS' ASSOCIATION

PLAYER OF THE YEAR

Founded in 1967, the Professional Cricketers' Association introduced this award, decided by their membership, in 1970. The NatWest-sponsored award is presented at the PCA's Annual Awards Dinner in London.

1970 {	M.J.Procter	1985	N.V.Radford	2001	D.P.Fulton
	J.D.Bond	1986	C.A.Walsh	2002	M.P.Vaughan
1971	L.R.Gibbs	1987	R.J.Hadlee	2003	Mushtaq Ahmed
1972	A.M.E.Roberts	1988	G.A.Hick	2004	A.Flintoff
1973	P.G.Lee	1989	S.J.Cook	2005	A.Flintoff
1974	B.Stead	1990	G.A.Gooch	2006	M.R.Ramprakash
1975	Zaheer Abbas	1991	Waqar Younis	2007	O.D.Gibson
1976	P.G.Lee	1992	C.A.Walsh	2008	M.van Jaarsveld
1977	M.J.Procter	1993	S.L.Watkin	2009	M.E.Trescothick
1978	J.K.Lever	1994	B.C.Lara	2010	N.M.Carter
1979	J.K.Lever	1995	D.G.Cork	2011	M.E.Trescothick
1980	R.D.Jackman	1996	P.V.Simmons	2012	N.R.D.Compton
1981	R.J.Hadlee	1997	S.P.James	2013	M.M.Ali
1982	M.D.Marshall	1998	M.B.Loye	2014	A.Lyth
1983	K.S.McEwan	1999	S.G.Law	2015	C.Rushworth
1984	R.J.Hadlee	2000	M.E.Trescothick		

2015 FIRST-CLASS AVERAGES

These averages involve the 501 players who appeared in the 168 first-class matches played by 27 teams in England and Wales during the 2015 season.

'Cap' denotes the season in which the player was awarded a 1st XI cap by the county he represented in 2015. If he played for more than one county in 2015, the county(ies) who awarded him his cap is (are) underlined. Durham abolished both their capping and 'awards' system after the 2005 season. Glamorgan's capping system is based on a player's number of appearances. Gloucestershire now cap players on first-class debut. Worcestershire now award county colours when players make their Championship debut.

Team abbreviations: A – Australia(ns); CU – Cambridge University/Cambridge MCCU; CfU – Cardiff MCCU; De – Derbyshire; DU – Durham; DU – Durham MCCU; E – England; Ex – Essex; Gm – Glamorgan; Gs – Gloucestershire; H – Hampshire; K – Kent; La – Lancashire; LBU – Leeds/Bradford MCCU; Le – Leicestershire; LU – Loughborough MCCU; M – Middlesex; Nh – Northamptonshire; Nt – Nottinghamshire; NZ – New Zealand(ers); OU – Oxford University/Oxford MCCU; Sm – Somerset; Sy – Surrey; Sx – Sussex; Wa – Warwickshire; Wo – Worcestershire; Y – Yorkshire.

† Left-handed batsman. Cap: a dash (–) denotes a non-county player. A blank denotes uncapped by his current county.

BATTING AND FIELDING

	Cap	M	I	NO	HS	Runs	Avge	100	50	Ct/St
J.B.Abbott (CU)	–	3	5	–	19	55	11.00	–	–	5
† Abdur Rehman (Sm)		9	15	5	55*	177	17.70	–	1	1
T.B.Abell (Sm)		15	27	4	131	770	33.47	1	5	7
M.R.Adair (Wa)		1	2	2	24*	34	–	–	–	
A.R.Adams (H)		3	5	1	31	58	14.50	–	–	3
† J.H.K.Adams (H)	2006	16	31	1	136	868	28.93	1	6	4
Adeel Malik (Ex)		3	6	–	25	48	8.00	–	–	1
A.P.Agathangelou (Le)		6	12	1	54	225	20.45	–	1	12
B.M.R.Akram (LU)		1	1	–	0	0	0.00	–	–	–
A.M.Ali (Le)		7	12	1	80	412	37.45	–	3	2
† M.M.Ali (E/Wo)	2007	11	20	1	77	624	32.84	–	5	5
J.Allenby (Sm)		18	30	2	64	654	23.35	–	5	19
T.R.Ambrose (Wa)	2007	14	22	–	153	651	29.59	2	1	34/5
H.M.Amla (De)		2	4	–	69	101	25.25	–	1	2
† C.J.Anderson (NZ)	–	1	2	–	67	76	38.00	–	1	–
J.M.Anderson (E/La)	2003	7	11	4	42	88	12.57	–	–	11
† G.M.Andrew (Wo)	2008	3	4	–	70	152	38.00	–	2	–
† Z.S.Ansari (Sy)	2014	14	22	1	106	771	36.71	1	4	8
A.T.Arif (CU)	–	2	2	–	39	56	28.00	–	–	1
J.B.T.Arksey (CU)	–	1								1
U.Arshad (De)		3	4	–	60	111	27.75	–	1	3
† Ashar Zaidi (Sx)		7	10	1	106	354	39.33	1	1	3
M.Azharullah (Nh)	2015	15	19	9	58*	189	18.90	–	1	5
T.E.Bailey (La)		12	16	3	34	224	17.23	–	–	2
J.M.Bairstow (E/Y)	2011	12	19	3	219*	1226	76.62	5	6	29
A.Balbirnie (M)		1	1	–	5	5	5.00	–	–	1
A.J.Ball (K)		4	7	–	45	99	14.14	–	–	1
J.T.Ball (Nt)		14	21	3	49*	244	13.55	–	–	1
† G.S.Ballance (E/Y)	2012	12	21	–	165	592	28.19	1	3	12
† K.H.D.Barker (Wa)	2013	13	20	3	102*	516	30.35	1	2	2
E.G.Barnard (Wo)	2015	4	4	1	17	35	11.66	–	–	2
A.W.R.Barrow (Sm)		8	13	2	32	157	14.27	–	–	21
M.D.Bates (Sm)		6	9	3	16	53	8.83	–	–	13

227

	Cap	M	I	NO	HS	Runs	Avge	100	50	Ct/St
G.J.Batty (Sy)	2011	15	18	5	50*	388	29.84	–	2	5
I.R.Bell (E/Wa)	2001	9	16	1	111	436	29.06	1	4	12
D.J.Bell-Drummond (K)	2015	17	31	–	127	894	28.83	3	2	9
G.K.Berg (H)		17	25	3	99	674	30.63	–	5	11
† M.T.Best (LU)	–	2	3	–	42	69	23.00	–	–	–
S.W.Billings (K)	2015	12	19	2	100*	474	27.88	1	1	33/1
J.M.Bird (H)		6	10	2	12	54	6.75	–	–	–
† C.Bishnoi (DU)	–	2	3	–	27	37	12.33	–	–	–
† A.J.Blake (K)	–	1			–	–	–	–	–	–
A.D.Blofield (CU)	–	3	5	3	105	211	105.50	1	1	4
R.S.Bopara (Ex)	2005	13	23	1	107	714	32.45	1	4	4
S.G.Borthwick (Du)		17	33	2	104	1390	44.83	2	11	19
T.A.Boult (NZ)	–	2	3	–	15	25	8.33	–	–	1
† M.A.G.Boyce (Le)	2013	6	12	–	60	260	21.66	–	2	4
D.A.J.Bracewell (NZ)	–	1	2	–	20	36	18.00	–	–	1
S.N.Bracey (CfU)	–	1	1	1	0*	0	–	–	–	1
W.D.Bragg (Gm)	2015	14	24	1	120	659	28.65	2	3	3
† N.Brand (CfU)	–	2	3	–	46	94	31.33	–	–	1
T.T.Bresnan (Y)	2006	17	24	5	169*	895	47.10	2	4	14
D.R.Briggs (H)	2012	9	14	3	48	256	23.27	–	–	1
† S.C.J.Broad (E/Nt)	2008	9	16	1	50	339	22.60	–	1	2
J.A.Brooks (Y)	2013	15	17	3	50*	223	15.92	–	1	4
B.C.Brown (Sx)	2014	17	28	4	144*	1031	42.95	4	4	46/1
† K.R.Brown (La)	2015	12	17	–	132	766	45.05	1	7	12
† N.L.J.Browne (Ex)	2015	17	29	2	151*	1157	42.85	5	3	17
N.L.Buck (La)		2	3	–	25	46	15.33	–	–	1
K.A.Bull (CfU/Gm)		4	4	1	31	38	12.66	–	–	1
S.F.G.Bullen (LBU)	–	1	2	–	36	61	30.50	–	–	–
M.G.K.Burgess (LU)	–	2	2	1	43	77	77.00	–	–	3
P.I.Burgoyne (Sx)		2	2	–	13	26	13.00	–	–	–
J.E.Burke (Sy)		7	10	1	79	232	25.77	–	2	5
J.T.A.Burnham (Du)		4	8	–	50	115	14.37	–	1	2
J.A.Burns (M)		7	11	–	87	320	29.09	–	3	1
† R.J.Burns (Sy)	2014	14	24	3	158	1019	48.52	2	5	11
J.C.Buttler (E)		7	12	–	73	286	23.83	–	2	20
Craig Cachopa (Sx)		9	17	–	54	270	15.88	–	2	6
† M.A.Carberry (H)	2006	17	31	1	146	1275	42.50	1	10	4
A.Carter (Gm/Nt)		5	6	4	24*	83	41.50	–	–	1
M.Carter (Nt)		1	2	–	11	11	5.50	–	–	1
† K.Carver (Y)		2	3	1	16	28	14.00	–	–	–
S.J.Cato (OU)	–	1	2	1	12*	14	14.00	–	–	1
M.A.Chambers (Nh)		6	9	–	14	22	2.44	–	–	–
Z.J.Chappell (Le)		1	2	–	96	103	51.50	–	1	–
G.Chapple (La)	1994	5	5	1	29*	51	12.75	–	–	2
† D.Chohan (CU)	–	1	2	–	6	6	3.00	–	–	–
V.Chopra (Wa)	2012	15	25	1	119*	658	27.41	2	2	20
J.L.Clare (De)	2012	1	1	–	4	4	4.00	–	–	–
G.Clark (Du)		3	6	–	36	65	10.83	–	–	2
J.Clark (La)		12	17	2	63	419	27.93	–	1	3
J.M.Clarke (Wo)	2015	11	16	1	104*	530	35.33	1	4	3
M.J.Clarke (A)	–	8	15	2	77	372	28.61	–	2	7
R.Clarke (Wa)	2011	16	26	3	67	535	23.26	–	2	22

	Cap	M	I	NO	HS	Runs	Avge	100	50	Ct/St
T.H.Claughton (OU)	–	1	2	–	29	48	24.00	–	–	–
† M.E.Claydon (K)		7	11	4	53	151	21.57	–	1	–
J.J.Cobb (Nh)		18	30	5	95	688	27.52	–	5	8
I.A.Cockbain (Gs)	2011	7	12	1	66*	244	22.18	–	1	2
† K.J.Coetzer (Nh)	2013	5	8	–	86	123	15.37	–	1	–
F.R.J.Coleman (Wa)		1	2	–	0	0	0.00	–	–	2
M.T.Coles (K)	2012	14	22	3	66	277	14.57	–	1	15
P.D.Collingwood (Du)	1998	16	29	5	127	807	33.62	2	3	25
N.R.D.Compton (M)	2006	17	33	2	149	1171	37.77	2	6	5
† A.N.Cook (E/Ex)	2005	10	18	–	182	774	43.00	1	5	13
C.B.Cooke (Gm)		16	28	5	112	884	38.43	2	5	18
T.L.W.Cooper (Sm)		14	24	–	118	590	24.58	1	2	7
† M.J.Cosgrove (Le)	2015	16	29	1	156	1185	42.32	4	5	10
D.A.Cosker (Gm)	2000	6	7	4	69	148	49.33	–	1	6
B.D.Cotton (De)		8	12	3	43	126	14.00	–	–	2
P.Coughlin (Du)		7	11	1	64	232	23.20	–	2	1
F.K.Cowdrey (K)		5	9	–	54	169	18.77	–	1	4
O.B.Cox (Wo)	2009	17	27	5	109	793	36.04	1	5	48/3
† M.D.Craig (NZ)	–	3	6	2	58*	130	32.50	–	1	4
M.S.Crane (H)		3	4	2	13	18	9.00	–	–	1
R.J.Crichard (CU)	–	3	3	1	21	32	16.00	–	–	2
M.J.J.Critchley (De)		6	8	2	137*	246	41.00	1	–	2
S.J.Croft (La)	2010	16	23	2	122	874	41.61	2	6	21
S.P.Crook (Nh)	2013	10	14	3	142*	597	54.27	2	1	4
T.N.Cullen (CfU)	–	1	2	–	26	30	15.00	–	–	1
P.J.Cummins (A)		2	2	2	82*	103	–	–	1	–
† S.M.Curran (Sy)		6	8	3	61*	239	47.80	–	1	1
T.K.Curran (Sy)		16	18	2	60	297	18.56	–	1	5
J.H.Davey (Sm)		1	2	–	15	20	10.00	–	–	–
A.L.Davies (La)		14	19	1	99	730	40.55	–	7	46/4
R.C.Davies (K)		5	6	–	17	35	5.83	–	–	9
† S.M.Davies (Sy)	2011	12	19	3	200*	819	51.18	2	2	4
C.A.L.Davis (LBU)	–	1	1	–	59	59	59.00	–	1	–
W.S.Davis (De)		1	1	1	8*	8	–	–	–	–
L.A.Dawson (Ex/H)	2013	16	28	5	140	922	40.08	1	3	13
J.L.Denly (K)	2008	17	31	4	161*	1081	40.03	2	7	9
† C.D.J.Dent (Gs)	2010	17	29	4	268	1112	44.48	3	7	23
J.W.Dernbach (Sy)	2011	4	2	1	1	1	1.00	–	–	3
N.J.Dexter (M)	2010	10	19	2	112	473	27.82	1	1	2
A.J.Dibble (Sm)		1	–	–	–	–	–	–	–	–
S.R.Dickson (K)		3	4	2	59	113	56.50	–	1	–
T.M.Dilshan (De)		3	6	2	27*	69	17.25	–	–	1
G.H.Dockrell (Sx)		1	2	1	37*	37	37.00	–	–	1
B.L.D'Oliveira (Wo)	2012	8	12	1	49	297	27.00	–	–	4
A.H.T.Donald (Gm)		5	10	1	98	288	32.00	–	2	4
† B.M.Duckett (Nh)		13	21	2	154	1002	52.73	5	3	9
J.A.Duffy (NZ)	–	1	2	1	1*	1	1.00	–	–	–
† M.P.Dunn (Sy)		9	10	2	13	45	5.62	–	–	1
W.J.Durston (De)	2012	11	21	5	85	451	28.18	–	2	12
E.J.H.Eckersley (Le)	2013	17	33	–	147	814	24.66	2	2	9
F.H.Edwards (H)		8	8	5	17*	32	10.66	–	–	1
† D.Elgar (Sy)		2	3	–	98	161	53.66	–	1	2

229

	Cap	M	I	NO	HS	Runs	Avge	100	50	Ct/St
E.J.Ellis (OU)	–	2	4	–	8	26	6.50	–	–	5/1
† J.S.E.Ellis-Grewal (LBU)	–	2	2	–	42	44	22.00	–	–	–
H.R.C.Ellison (CU)	–	1	2	–	24	26	13.00	–	–	–
S.L.Elstone (De)		8	13	1	103*	253	21.08	1	–	3
† S.M.Ervine (H)	2005	13	20	4	102	518	32.37	1	1	15
S.S.Eskinazi (M)		1	2	–	22	26	13.00	–	–	1
L.J.Evans (Wa)		15	27	3	213*	826	34.41	1	4	16
J.P.Faulkner (La)		7	9	–	121	310	34.44	1	2	3
Fawad Ahmed (A)	–	3	2	2	4*	8	–	–	–	–
T.C.Fell (Wo)	2013	17	27	–	171	1127	41.74	3	4	22
A.J.Finch (Y)		3	4	1	73*	124	41.33	–	1	3
H.Z.Finch (Sx)		2	4	–	22	46	11.50	–	–	3
S.T.Finn (E/M)	2009	11	14	9	41*	123	24.60	–	–	3
M.D.Fisher (Y)		3	2	1	0*	0	0.00	–	–	1
L.J.Fletcher (Nt/Sy)	2014	6	7	2	24*	78	15.60	–	–	–
B.T.Foakes (Sy)		10	16	4	140*	617	51.41	2	2	20/3
M.H.A.Footitt (De)	2014	16	21	6	34	110	7.33	–	–	3
J.S.Foster (Ex)	2001	17	25	2	98	694	30.17	–	5	46/3
† J.E.C.Franklin (M)	2015	15	27	3	135	667	27.79	2	3	15
O.H.Freckingham (Le)		5	8	4	34*	80	20.00	–	–	–
J.K.Fuller (Gs)	2011	11	14	2	73	343	28.58	–	2	6
S.T.Gabriel (Wo)	2015	2								–
† A.W.Gale (Y)	2008	16	27	–	164	1045	38.70	3	3	4
R.N.Gamble (LU)	–	2	2	–	5	5	2.50	–	–	1
J.S.Gatting (H)		4	8	2	64*	280	46.66	–	2	1
J.George (CfU)	–	2	3	–	14	27	9.00	–	–	–
R.A.M.Gibson (DU)	–	2	3	–	24	47	15.66	–	–	–
A.P.R.Gidman (Wo)	2015	13	20	2	78	440	24.44	–	3	13
† W.R.S.Gidman (Nt)		7	12	1	57	213	19.36	–	1	3
R.J.Gleeson (Nh)		2	2	–	6	8	4.00	–	–	2
J.S.D.Gnodde (OU)	–	1	2	–	3	6	3.00	–	–	–
† B.A.Godleman (De)	2015	14	28	4	108	1069	44.54	3	7	12
† S.E.Grant (LU)	–	1	1	–	0	0	0.00	–	–	–
L.Gregory (Sm)	2015	13	19	1	32	242	13.44	–	–	11
S.W.Griffiths (CfU)	–	2	3	–	34	60	20.00	–	–	1
T.D.Groenewald (Sm)		10	18	3	47	192	12.80	–	–	5
J.O.Grundy (OU)	–	2	4	2	21*	36	18.00	–	–	–
† N.R.T.Gubbins (LBU/M)		9	16	–	92	417	26.06	–	2	3
M.J.Guptill (De/NZ)		4	8	1	227	430	61.42	1	2	6
H.F.Gurney (Nt)	2014	12	15	8	8	15	2.14	–	–	1
B.J.Haddin (A)	–	3	5	1	35	107	26.75	–	–	9
† C.J.Haggett (K)		11	16	2	80	345	24.64	–	2	4
S.R.Hain (Wa)		10	17	2	106	547	36.46	2	3	8
A.D.Hales (Nt)	2011	12	20	–	236	1021	51.05	3	3	2
H.Hameed (La)		4	6	–	91	257	42.83	–	2	2
† M.A.H.Hammond (Gs)	2013	1	1	–	30	30	30.00	–	–	–
T.R.G.Hampton (Gs)	2015	2	1	1	0*	0		–	–	–
P.S.P.Handscomb (Gs)	2015	7	13	2	76	443	40.27	–	4	10
† O.J.Hannon-Dalby (Wa)		4	6	1	8	24	4.80	–	–	–
† A.Harinath (Sy)		8	13	–	120	568	43.69	2	2	1
† B.W.Harmison (K)		7	11	–	123	283	25.72	1	1	7
J.A.R.Harris (M)	2015	17	26	5	73	467	22.23	–	3	4

	Cap	M	I	NO	HS	Runs	Avge	100	50	Ct/St
R.J.Harris (A)	–	1	1	–	9	9	9.00	–	–	1
J.Harrison (Du)		5	10	–	53	99	9.90	–	1	–
Hasan Azad (LU)	–	2	3	1	99	149	74.50	–	1	1
J.W.Hastings (Du)		15	25	–	91	487	19.48	–	3	6
† L.J.Hatchett (Sx)		2	3	2	25	35	35.00	–	–	1
† J.R.Hazlewood (A)	–	5	8	4	14*	57	14.25	–	–	1
A.G.Hearne (CU)		1	2	–	43	72	36.00	–	–	–
T.G.Helm (M)		2	3	–	27	32	10.66	–	–	–
M.J.Henry (NZ)	–	2	4	2	27	59	29.50	–	–	1
J.C.Hildreth (Sm)	2007	18	30	1	220*	1620	55.86	5	8	7
B.W.Hilfenhaus (Nt)	2015	3	4	2	28*	76	38.00	–	–	1
L.J.Hill (Le)		9	18	2	126	356	22.25	1	1	15
M.E.Hobden (Sx)		11	17	8	65*	84	9.33	–	1	3
A.J.Hodd (Y)		9	12	2	54*	239	23.90	–	2	24/2
D.M.Hodgson (Y)		1	2	–	35	54	27.00	–	–	1
M.G.Hogan (Gm)	2013	14	19	8	57	271	24.63	–	1	11
P.J.Horton (La)	2007	12	18	1	168	611	35.94	1	5	16
H.R.Hosein (De)		12	18	2	61	273	17.06	–	1	32/1
B.A.C.Howell (Gs)	2012	12	17	–	102	409	24.05	1	1	8
F.J.Hudson-Prentice (Sx)		1	2	–	15	15	7.50	–	–	–
A.L.Hughes (De)		7	11	3	111*	279	34.87	1	–	2
† C.F.Hughes (De)		13	26	1	104	816	32.64	2	4	6
H.C.D.Hughes (OU)		2	4	–	4	7	1.75	–	–	1
M.S.T.Hughes (OU)		1	2	–	116	157	78.50	1	–	2
P.H.Hughes (CU)		3	5	1	55*	104	26.00	–	1	1
M.D.Hunn (K)		8	8	6	23*	59	29.50	–	–	3
A.P.Hunt (CU)		1	1	1	19*	19	–	–	–	1
B.A.Hutton (Nt)		9	13	2	72	278	25.27	–	1	5
Imran Tahir (Nt)	2015	1	1	–	2	2	2.00	–	–	–
† C.A.Ingram (Gm)		16	28	3	105*	931	37.24	2	4	10
K.M.Jarvis (La)	2015	13	15	9	47	139	23.16	–	–	3
A.Javid (Wa)		4	6	–	27	64	10.66	–	–	4
W.H.Jenkins (DU)	–	2	3	–	12	17	5.66	–	–	–
† K.K.Jennings (Du)		11	21	1	177*	650	32.50	1	3	6
† M.G.Johnson (A)	–	6	10	2	77	200	25.00	–	1	3
G.O.Jones (Gs)	2014	10	16	1	88	472	31.46	–	4	13
† O.J.Jones (OU)	–	1	2	–	32	56	28.00	–	–	1
R.A.Jones (Wa)		1	1	–	3	3	3.00	–	–	–
C.J.Jordan (Sx)	2014	6	8	2	56*	177	29.50	–	1	18
† E.C.Joyce (Sx)	2009	15	26	–	100	855	32.88	1	4	25
A.Kapil (Sy)		1	2	–	21	21	10.50	–	–	–
† G.Keedy (Nt)		1	–	–	–	–	–	–	–	1
R.I.Keogh (Nh)		18	31	2	163*	876	30.20	2	6	6
S.C.Kerrigan (La)	2013	14	15	5	34*	110	11.00	–	–	6
A.N.Kervezee (Wo)	2009	5	8	–	93	169	21.12	–	1	–
J.M.Kettleborough (Gm)		9	16	1	81	413	27.53	–	3	4
R.W.T.Key (K)	2001	13	24	–	158	958	39.91	2	5	4
M.J.L.Kidd (OU)	–	1	2	1	4*	5	5.00	–	–	–
R.K.Kleinveldt (Nh)		13	21	3	56	391	21.72	–	2	9
M.Klinger (Gs)	2013	6	11	1	103	468	46.80	2	2	5
T.C.Knight (De)		2	3	1	25	42	21.00	–	–	2
T.Kohler-Cadmore (Wo)	2014	6	9	2	130*	357	51.00	1	2	8

	Cap	M	I	NO	HS	Runs	Avge	100	50	Ct/St
N.R.Kumar (LU)	–	2	3	1	28	39	19.50	–	–	–
† M.B.Lake (OU)	–	2	4	–	66	82	20.50	–	1	1
† T.W.M.Latham (NZ)	–	3	6	–	84	209	34.83	–	3	7
J.L.Lawlor (CfU/Gm)	–	2	3	–	3	3	1.00	–	–	–
D.W.Lawrence (Ex)	–	7	12	1	161	409	37.18	1	1	8
J.Leach (Wo)	2012	14	19	2	95	498	29.29	–	3	4
† M.J.Leach (Sm)	–	6	5	2	21*	43	14.33	–	–	3
† S.G.Leach (OU)	–	2	4	–	41	88	22.00	–	–	–
J.A.Leaning (Y)	–	16	27	2	123	961	38.44	3	3	20
† A.Z.Lees (Y)	2014	17	29	3	100	866	33.30	1	6	20
† T.J.Lester (La)	–	2	1	1	0*	0	–	–	–	2
† K.S.Leverock (CfU)	–	1	2	–	25	34	17.00	–	–	–
R.E.Levi (Nh)	–	11	18	3	168	663	44.20	1	5	5
D.E.Lewis-Williams (CfU)	–	1	1	–	0	0	0.00	–	–	–
J.D.Libby (Nt)	–	2	4	–	34	37	9.25	–	–	–
C.J.Liddle (Sx)	–	4	4	2	10*	18	9.00	–	–	1
A.E.Lilley (LBU)	–	2	2	1	13*	19	19.00	–	–	1
A.M.Lilley (La)	–	7	8	2	63	230	38.33	–	2	3
T.E.Linley (Sy/Sx)	–	2	4	2	21*	33	16.50	–	–	–
D.L.Lloyd (Gm)	–	13	20	6	92	589	42.07	–	3	4
† M.J.Lumb (Nt)	2012	5	9	–	73	195	21.66	–	1	3
N.M.Lyon (A)	–	7	10	3	41	129	18.42	–	–	4
† A.Lyth (E/Y)	2010	14	25	–	107	580	23.20	1	3	18
B.J.McCarthy (Du)	–	2	4	2	38*	55	27.50	–	–	2
B.B.McCullum (NZ)	–	2	4	–	55	138	34.50	–	1	–
† C.M.MacDonell (DU)	–	2	3	–	37	56	18.66	–	–	–
H.P.S.McInley (DU)	–	2	2	–	8	12	6.00	–	–	3
J.N.McIver (DU)	–	2	4	–	41	49	12.25	–	–	1
C.J.McKay (Le)	2015	12	22	4	51*	452	25.11	–	1	2
† P.J.McKay (Wa)	–	2	4	–	17	24	6.00	–	–	6/1
G.K.R.McKinley (LU)	–	2	2	–	39	39	19.50	–	–	–
† R.McLaren (H)	–	4	4	–	52	123	30.75	–	1	1
C.S.MacLeod (Du)	–	8	15	3	67	271	22.58	–	1	6
L.D.McManus (H)	–	2	4	1	53*	120	40.00	–	1	4
† M.W.Machan (Sx)	–	14	24	–	192	955	39.79	3	3	3
W.L.Madsen (De)	2011	14	27	5	172*	1033	46.95	2	6	13
† S.J.Magoffin (Sx)	2013	17	24	4	41	208	10.40	–	–	2
† D.J.Malan (M)	2010	10	17	3	182*	690	49.28	2	4	5
J.Marsden (OU)	–	1	2	1	9*	13	13.00	–	–	1
M.R.Marsh (A)	–	7	11	1	169	506	50.60	2	2	4
† S.E.Marsh (A)	–	4	6	–	114	271	45.16	2	–	4
H.J.H.Marshall (Gs)	2006	13	18	2	92	588	36.75	–	6	7
D.D.Masters (Ex)	2008	7	10	3	28	85	12.14	–	–	3
G.J.Maxwell (Y)	–	4	7	1	140	244	40.66	1	–	3
S.C.Meaker (Sy)	2012	3	3	–	13	13	4.33	–	–	–
C.A.J.Meschede (Gm)	–	17	24	3	107	655	31.19	2	2	6
J.C.Mickleburgh (Ex)	2013	11	20	–	61	431	21.55	–	2	6
J.D.Middlebrook (Y)	–	6	7	1	23	49	7.00	–	–	1
C.N.Miles (Gs)	2011	12	18	1	41	237	13.94	–	–	4
T.S.Mills (Sx)	–	3	4	1	8	14	4.50	–	–	–
T.P.Milnes (De/Wa)	–	3	6	2	23	63	15.75	–	–	–
D.K.H.Mitchell (Wo)	2005	16	26	3	206*	832	36.17	2	2	20

	Cap	M	I	NO	HS	Runs	Avge	100	50	Ct/St
T.C.Moore (Ex)		3	3	2	16*	16	16.00	–	–	1
† E.J.G.Morgan (M)	2008	4	6	–	44	61	10.16	–	–	1
C.A.J.Morris (Wo)	2014	15	21	10	24	85	7.72	–	–	2
G.J.Muchall (Du)	2005	11	21	2	145	693	36.47	2	2	10
S.J.Mullaney (Nt)	2013	16	27	–	118	937	34.70	2	4	23
† C.Munro (Wo)	2015	1	1	–	34	34	34.00	–	–	–
† H.G.Munsey (Nh)		1	1	–	27	27	27.00	–	–	–
D.Murphy (Nh)		6	9	2	135*	344	49.14	1	1	16/1
J.R.Murphy (CfU)	–	2	3	–	22	39	13.00	–	–	1
† T.J.Murtagh (M)	2008	14	19	6	24	185	14.23	–	–	4
† P.Mustard (Du/La)		8	11	–	43	146	13.27	–	–	24
J.G.Myburgh (Sm)		12	22	3	150*	568	29.89	2	2	6
S.V.S.Mylavarapu (OU)	–	1	2	–	4	4	2.00	–	–	1
J.K.H.Naik (Le)	2013	8	14	3	73	184	16.72	–	1	1
G.R.Napier (Ex)	2003	13	17	1	73	363	22.68	–	2	5
B.P.Nash (K)	2013	4	8	–	49	229	28.62	–	–	–
C.D.Nash (Sx)	2008	16	27	1	142*	866	33.30	2	3	15
P.M.Nevill (A)	–	7	10	–	78	259	25.90	–	2	20
R.I.Newton (Nh)		12	21	–	107	628	29.90	1	4	3
† A.S.S.Nijjar (Ex)		7	10	5	53	155	31.00	–	1	1
† K.Noema-Barnett (Gs)	2015	11	15	3	61	272	22.66	–	1	4
† M.J.Norris (CfU)	–	2	3	–	32	63	21.00	–	–	1
S.A.Northeast (K)	2012	17	30	3	139	1204	44.59	1	9	11
L.C.Norwell (Gs)	2011	15	19	9	19	83	8.30	–	–	5
T.M.Nugent (LU)	–	1	1	1	4*	4	–	–	–	1
† N.J.O'Brien (Le)	2011	13	24	2	95	718	32.63	–	7	54/4
R.J.O'Grady (OU)	–	1	2	–	15	26	13.00	–	–	–
† R.K.Oliver (Wo)	2014	13	22	–	101	494	22.45	1	1	8
G.Onions (Du)		6	25	15	36	141	14.10	–	–	3
C.Overton (Sm)		12	16	3	55	369	238	–	3	9
J.Overton (Sm)		9	10	3	50	146	20.85	–	1	–
A.P.Palladino (De)	2012	13	17	3	82	255	18.21	–	1	4
† M.S.Panesar (Ex)		3	3	2	11*	24	24.00	–	–	1
A.K.Patel (LU)	–	2	3	–	83	104	24.66	–	1	–
A.R.Patel (CU)	–	1	1	–	61	61	61.00	–	1	–
J.S.Patel (Wa)	2012	16	23	2	98	543	25.85	–	2	10
R.H.Patel (Ex/M)		2	4	2	6*	9	4.50	–	–	–
S.R.Patel (Nt)	2008	17	29	1	100	681	24.32	2	2	9
L.C.Paternott (OU)	–	2	4	–	40	56	14.00	–	–	2
S.A.Patterson (Y)	2012	16	19	4	44*	343	22.86	–	–	3
D.A.Payne (Gs)	2011	10	10	3	23	138	19.71	–	–	4
D.Penrhyn Jones (Gm)		2	2	1	17	26	26.00	–	–	1
S.D.Peters (Nh)	2007	10	17	–	82	464	27.29	–	4	4
A.N.Petersen (La)		14	21	1	286	861	43.05	3	1	6
M.L.Pettini (Ex)	2006	4	7	3	134	402	100.50	2	1	5
V.D.Philander (Nt)	2015	5	9	2	41	177	25.28	–	–	–
W.D.P.Phillips (DU)	–	1	2	–	14	15	7.50	–	–	–
K.P.Pietersen (Sy)		4	6	3	355*	469	156.33	1	1	1
N.D.Pinner (Le)		6	12	2	165*	365	36.50	1	1	10
L.E.Plunkett (Y)	2013	5	8	–	28	96	12.00	–	–	4
A.W.Pollock (CU)	–	3	4	–	15	24	6.00	–	–	1
† E.J.Pollock (DU)	–	1	1	–	15	15	15.00	–	–	–

	Cap	M	I	NO	HS	Runs	Avge	100	50	Ct/St
J.A.Porter (Ex)	2015	16	21	5	34	98	6.12	–	–	5
† W.T.S.Porterfield (Wa)	2014	6	11	–	61	196	17.81	–	1	7
T.Poynton (De)		5	9	–	19	47	5.22	–	–	11/3
† J.E.Poysden (Wa)		1	–	–	–	–	–	–	–	–
D.T.P.Pratt (LBU)	–	2	2	2	2*	2	–	–	–	–
† A.G.Prince (La)	2010	16	23	1	261	1478	67.18	5	5	13
R.D.Pringle (Du)		9	17	1	99	427	26.68	–	3	3
I.Prowse (LU)	–	2	2	–	15	23	11.50	–	–	–
C.A.Pujara (Y)		4	6	1	133*	264	52.80	1	1	2
R.M.Pyrah (Y)	2010	3	4	–	84	204	51.00	–	1	–
B.A.Raine (Le)		17	29	2	57	546	20.22	–	2	4
† W.B.Rankin (Wa)	2013	13	18	8	56*	155	15.50	–	1	4
A.U.Rashid (Y)	2008	7	10	–	127	347	34.70	1	2	3
D.E.M.Ratnayake (DU)	–	2	3	1	8	8	4.00	–	–	2
O.P.Rayner (M)	2015	14	23	2	52	360	17.14	–	1	30
C.M.W.Read (Nt)	1999	14	23	5	121	937	52.05	3	6	37/2
† D.J.Redfern (Le)		6	12	1	74	229	20.81	–	1	2
† L.M.Reece (La)		5	8	–	82	142	17.75	–	1	1
† W.M.H.Rhodes (Y)		10	17	2	79	408	27.20	–	1	3
M.J.Richardson (Du)		17	34	5	96*	1007	34.72	–	6	46/3
A.E.N.Riley (K)		9	13	4	34	106	11.77	–	–	7
O.E.Robinson (Sx)		11	17	3	110	282	20.14	1	–	3
A.J.Robson (Le)		17	34	1	120	1079	32.69	1	9	16
S.D.Robson (M)	2013	17	33	2	178	917	29.58	1	4	14
G.H.Roderick (Gs)	2013	16	26	2	100*	791	32.95	1	6	55
† C.J.L.Rogers (A)	–	7	13	1	173	662	55.16	1	4	3
T.S.Roland-Jones (M)	2012	13	19	4	103*	416	27.73	1	1	7
L.Ronchi (NZ/Sm)		6	9	–	88	255	28.33	–	2	22/3
J.E.Root (E)	–	7	13	1	134	643	53.58	2	4	14
† W.T.Root (LBU/Nt)		3	5	–	37	80	16.00	–	–	–
A.M.Rossington (Nh)		14	24	1	116	776	33.73	1	7	35
H.P.Rouse (LBU)	–	1	2	1	23	28	28.00	–	–	–
T.D.Rouse (CfU)	–	2	3	–	22	38	12.66	–	–	2
J.J.Roy (Sy)	2014	12	19	2	143	810	47.64	2	4	19
† J.A.Rudolph (Gm)	2014	15	27	2	111	962	38.48	1	7	13
C.Rushworth (Du)		17	27	4	43	387	16.82	–	–	6
† H.D.Rutherford (De/NZ)		5	9	–	108	335	37.22	1	2	1
J.D.Ryder (Ex)	2014	15	26	5	124	853	40.61	2	3	15
L.M.Sabin (OU)	–	2	4	–	26	57	14.25	–	–	–
Saeed Ajmal (Wo)	2011	8	12	2	37	162	16.20	–	–	5
A.Sakande (OU)	–	2	4	–	33	39	9.75	–	–	3
M.E.T.Salisbury (Ex)		5	8	–	24	64	8.00	–	–	2
A.G.Salter (Gm)		12	19	2	73	411	24.17	–	2	5
B.W.Sanderson (Nh)		4	6	2	42	51	12.75	–	–	2
† K.C.Sangakkara (Sy)	2015	11	19	–	149	870	45.78	5	1	7
† M.J.Santner (NZ)		1	2	–	94	121	60.50	–	1	1
R.J.Sayer (Le)		4	3	–	34	58	19.33	–	–	1
G.F.B.Scott (LBU)	–	2	3	1	11	16	8.00	–	–	1
B.Scriven (CfU)	–	1	2	–	5	7	3.50	–	–	–
S.M.S.M.Senanayake (Wo)	2015	5	9	–	32	120	13.33	–	–	3
A.Shahzad (Sx)		6	10	2	45*	182	22.75	–	–	1
† J.D.Shantry (Wo)	2009	17	22	4	41*	221	12.27	–	–	4

	Cap	M	I	NO	HS	Runs	Avge	100	50	Ct/St
A.Sheikh (Le)		3	4	2	5	10	5.00	–	–	1
C.E.Shreck (Le)		14	22	7	15	41	2.73	–	–	5
D.P.Sibley (Sy)		6	10	–	74	242	24.20	–	1	6
P.M.Siddle (A/La)		9	11	1	89	272	27.20	–	1	3
† R.J.Sidebottom (Y)	2000	10	12	10	28	95	47.50	–	–	3
J.A.Simpson (M)	2011	17	30	7	64	628	27.30	–	3	55/2
† B.T.Slater (De)		15	29	–	94	799	27.55	–	7	4
G.M.Smith (Ex)		4	5	1	50*	76	19.00	–	1	3
G.P.Smith (Le/Nt)		5	10	–	20	84	8.40	–	–	3
R.A.J.Smith (Gm)		3	2	2	49*	55	–	–	–	–
S.P.D.Smith (A)	–	7	11	–	215	619	56.27	3	1	3
† T.C.Smith (La)	2010	1	2	–	38	39	19.50	–	–	2
T.M.J.Smith (Gs)	2013	5	5	2	47*	98	32.66	–	–	1
W.R.Smith (H)	2015	17	31	5	93	948	36.46	–	7	19
V.S.Solanki (Sy)	2014	2	2	–	33	34	17.00	–	–	2
T.G.Southee (NZ)	–	2	4	–	40	72	18.00	–	–	2
† M.A.Starc (A)	–	6	10	1	58	177	19.66	–	2	4
C.T.Steel (DU)	–	2	3	–	80	101	33.66	–	1	1
O.J.Steele (DU)	–	2	3	1	48*	84	42.00	–	–	2
D.I.Stevens (K)	2005	15	23	–	92	635	27.60	–	6	5
R.A.Stevenson (H)		3	3	–	30	34	11.33	–	–	–
P.R.Stirling (M)		8	16	1	41	254	16.93	–	–	5
B.A.Stokes (E)		7	12	–	101	429	35.75	1	3	7
O.P.Stone (Nh)		13	17	4	38	231	17.76	–	–	6
† M.D.Stoneman (Du)		17	34	–	131	1131	33.26	3	5	7
W.A.Tavaré (Gs)	2014	16	27	2	93	801	32.04	–	6	11
B.R.M.Taylor (Nt)	2015	17	30	–	152	1070	35.66	4	3	12
C.J.Taylor (Ex)		1	2	–	26	48	24.00	–	–	–
J.M.R.Taylor (Gs)	2010	11	14	–	156	414	29.57	2	–	4
J.W.A.Taylor (Nt)	2012	13	23	2	291	1078	51.33	2	6	6
L.R.P.L.Taylor (NZ)	–	3	6	–	62	180	30.00	–	1	4
M.D.Taylor (Gs)	2013	8	8	3	8	24	4.80	–	–	–
† R.M.L.Taylor (Le)		8	15	7	42	221	27.62	–	–	4
T.A.I.Taylor (De)		9	13	3	49	133	13.30	–	–	2
R.N.ten Doeschate (Ex)	2006	13	21	4	88	929	54.64	–	8	9
S.P.Terry (H)		5	10	1	62*	232	25.77	–	2	4
† J.W.Tetley (CU)	–	2	3	–	21	40	13.33	–	–	3/1
S.J.Thakor (De)		12	17	1	83	349	21.81	–	1	4
A.C.Thomas (Sm)	2008	7	10	4	32*	79	13.16	–	–	6
I.A.A.Thomas (K)		11	18	8	13	40	4.00	–	–	1
H.L.Thompson (LBU)	–	2	3	–	21	39	13.00	–	–	1
P.J.A.Tice (CU)	–	1	1	–	7	7	7.00	–	–	–/1
† J.A.Tomlinson (H)	2008	9	13	3	17	52	5.20	–	–	1
R.J.W.Topley (Ex)	2013	2	3	1	4*	4	2.00	–	–	1
† J.C.Tredwell (K)	2007	7	11	–	53	107	9.72	–	1	13
P.D.Trego (Sm)	2007	18	29	3	130*	913	35.11	2	4	8
C.T.Tremlett (Sy)	2014	3	5	1	30	85	21.25	–	–	1
† M.E.Trescothick (Sm)	1999	17	30	1	210*	1311	45.20	3	8	29
I.J.L.Trott (Wa)	2005	11	18	–	87	451	25.05	–	2	6
Umar Akmal (Le)	2015	1	2	–	20	33	16.50	–	–	–
K.S.Velani (Ex)		4	7	–	58	190	27.14	–	1	2
J.M.Vince (H)	2013	16	29	2	140	883	32.70	2	5	22

	Cap	M	I	NO	HS	Runs	Avge	100	50	Ct/St
A.C.Voges (A/M)		12	21	2	132	740	38.94	1	5	17
G.G.Wagg (Gm)	2013	17	24	–	200	842	35.08	1	4	6
† N.Wagner (NZ)	–	1	2	–	29	33	16.50	–	–	–
† D.J.Wainwright (De)	2012	3	4	1	38	61	20.33	–	–	–
C.F.Wakefield (LBU)	–	2	2	–	7	7	3.50	–	–	4
A.G.Wakely (Nh)	2012	16	27	2	123	876	35.04	2	4	12
† M.A.Wallace (Gm)	2003	16	24	2	92	522	23.72	–	3	43/3
† D.A.Warner (A)	–	8	13	–	101	623	47.92	1	6	5
L.Watkinson (LBU)	–	2	2	–	35	55	27.50	–	–	1
B.J.Watling (NZ)	–	3	6	1	120	365	73.00	1	3	3
S.R.Watson (A)	–	5	8	–	81	290	36.25	–	3	4
J.P.Webb (Wa)	–	2	4	–	14	18	4.50	–	–	1
L.A.Webb (OU)	–	2	4	–	32	68	17.00	–	–	–
W.J.Weighell (Du)	–	2	4	–	25	69	17.25	–	–	1
S.D.Weller (OU)	–	2	4	1	7	14	4.66	–	–	1
† L.W.P.Wells (Sx)		14	23	–	108	625	27.17	1	4	6
T.J.Wells (Le)		6	10	1	30*	102	11.33	–	–	3
M.H.Wessels (Nt)	2014	17	30	2	117	1093	39.03	2	7	19
S.A.Westaway (OU)	–	1	2	–	33	47	23.50	–	–	3
T.Westley (Ex)	2013	13	22	1	179	926	44.09	2	4	6
L.P.Weston (LBU)	–	2	3	–	7	8	2.66	–	–	5
A.A.Westphal (CfU)	–	2	2	1	5*	7	7.00	–	–	–
† I.J.Westwood (Wa)	2008	14	25	1	196	856	35.66	1	4	6
B.T.J.Wheal (H)		4	6	1	10	17	3.40	–	–	1
A.J.A.Wheater (H)		15	24	2	111	613	27.86	1	4	29/2
B.M.Wheeler (NZ)	–	1	2	1	33	35	35.00	–	–	–
G.G.White (Nh)		3	6	–	24	43	7.16	–	–	1
H.J.White (De)		1	1	–	3	3	3.00	–	–	–
R.G.White (LU)	–	2	2	–	4	4	2.00	–	–	1
W.A.White (De/Le)		6	9	1	43	155	19.37	–	–	–
R.A.Whiteley (Wo)	2013	8	13	1	101	436	36.33	1	3	6
S.C.Whittingham (LU)	–	1	1	–	0	0	0.00	–	–	–
D.J.Willey (Nh)	2013	6	10	1	104*	438	48.66	2	2	3
B.P.R.Williams (DU)	–	1	2	1	0*	0	0.00	–	–	–
D.R.Williams (DU)	–	1	–	–	–	–	–	–	–	1
K.S.Williamson (NZ)	–	2	4	–	132	165	41.25	1	–	1
G.C.Wilson (Sy)	2014	14	23	6	74*	811	47.70	–	6	40/1
J.R.Winslade (Ex)		2	–	–	–	–	–	–	–	–
M.J.Winter (OU)	–	1	2	–	56	56	28.00	–	–	1
C.R.Woakes (Wa)	2009	3	5	–	42	83	16.60	–	–	1
C.P.Wood (H)		2	3	1	52*	130	65.00	–	1	–
J.M.Wood (DU)	–	2	2	2	2*	2	–	–	–	–
† L.Wood (Nt)		11	16	2	100	420	30.00	1	2	2
M.A.Wood (Du/E)		7	13	5	66	218	27.25	–	1	2
A.R.Wright (CU)	–	2	3	–	8	8	2.66	–	–	1
B.J.Wright (Gm)	2011	5	7	–	68	178	25.42	–	2	3
C.J.C.Wright (Wa)	2013	11	16	6	65	300	30.00	–	2	2
L.J.Wright (Sx)	2007	17	29	3	226*	1220	46.92	2	8	12
† B.A.Wylie (CU)	–	3	4	1	26	33	11.00	–	–	3
† M.H.Yardy (Sx)	2005	11	18	–	124	694	38.55	2	4	14
† S.A.Zaib (Nh)		2	2	–	21	21	10.50	–	–	–
Zain Shahzad (CU)	–	2	2	–	0	0	0.00	–	–	–

BOWLING

See BATTING AND FIELDING section for details of matches and caps

	Cat	O	M	R	W	Avge	Best	5wI	10wM
Abdur Rehman (Sm)	SLA	219.2	35	766	10	76.60	2- 60	–	–
T.B.Abell (Sm)	RM	4.4	0	11	1	11.00	1- 11	–	–
M.R.Adair (Wa)	RMF	15	3	61	1	61.00	1- 61	–	–
A.R.Adams (H)	RMF	120	26	359	9	39.88	3- 68	–	–
Adeel Malik (Ex)	LB	46.5	2	224	4	56.00	3- 39	–	–
A.P.Agathangelou (Le)	LB	9	1	33	1	33.00	1- 7	–	–
B.M.R.Akram (LU)	RMF	21	1	154	0			–	–
A.M.Ali (Le)	OB	4	0	19	0			–	–
M.M.Ali (E/Wo)	OB	269.4	29	1068	20	53.40	3- 59	–	–
J.Allenby (Sm)	RM	288	78	728	23	31.65	3- 36	–	–
C.J.Anderson (NZ)	LMF	8	1	27	0			–	–
J.M.Anderson (E/La)	RFM	239.5	56	740	27	27.40	7- 77	2	–
G.M.Andrew (Wo)	RMF	78.1	12	311	10	31.10	5- 85	1	–
Z.S.Ansari (Sy)	SLA	425.3	71	1363	44	30.97	6- 30	3	–
A.T.Arif (CU)	RM	28	3	151	3	50.33	2- 55	–	–
J.B.T.Arksey (SLA)	SLA	3.5	0	32	1	32.00	1- 32	–	–
U.Arshad (Du)	RMF	46.2	4	196	5	39.20	3- 41	–	–
Ashar Zaidi (Sx)	SLA	188.1	42	461	11	41.90	3- 55	–	–
R.Ashwin (I)	OB	35.3	3	101	3	33.66	3- 72	–	–
T.D.Astle (NZA)	LB	15	1	83	4	20.75	4- 83	–	–
Azeem Rafiq (Y)	OB	38	6	110	1	110.00	1- 79	–	–
M.Azharullah (Nh)	RFM	425.5	97	1342	45	29.82	5- 31	2	–
T.E.Bailey (La)	RMF	347.3	64	1192	35	34.05	5- 12	1	–
J.M.Bairstow (Y)	RM	1	0	1	0			–	–
A.J.Ball (K)	LFM	25.4	0	139	1	139.00	1- 87	–	–
J.T.Ball (Nt)	RFM	339.3	63	1210	41	29.51	6- 49	1	–
K.H.D.Barker (Wa)	LMF	424.4	91	1274	46	27.69	5- 68	2	–
E.G.Barnard (Wo)	RMF	100.1	20	345	12	28.75	3- 63	–	–
G.J.Batty (Sy)	OB	400	77	1127	40	28.17	6- 51	2	–
G.K.Berg (H)	RMF	442.1	97	1218	43	28.32	4- 64	–	–
J.M.Bird (H)	RFM	207.2	34	755	19	39.73	4-146	–	–
C.Bishnoi (DU)	SLA	46.5	5	175	2	87.50	1- 38	–	–
A.D.Blofield (CU)	OB	51.2	2	235	3	78.33	2- 33	–	–
R.S.Bopara (Ex)	RM	154.2	25	524	21	24.95	4- 29	–	–
S.G.Borthwick (Du)	LBG	183.2	29	734	20	36.70	4- 46	–	–
T.A.Boult (NZ)	LFM	116	25	323	13	24.84	5- 85	1	–
D.A.J.Bracewell (NZ)	RMF	29	7	129	4	32.25	3- 62	–	–
W.D.Bragg (Gm)	RM	24.4	0	86	1	86.00	1- 14	–	–
N.Brand (CfU)	SLA	16	0	67	0			–	–
T.T.Bresnan (Y)	RFM	443.5	120	1428	47	30.38	5- 85	1	–
D.R.Briggs (H)	SLA	258	66	723	21	34.42	4- 74	–	–
S.C.J.Broad (E/Nt)	RFM	271	50	970	43	22.55	8- 15	3	–
J.A.Brooks (Y)	RFM	440.5	89	1535	69	22.24	5- 35	3	–
B.C.Brown (Sx)	(WK)	8	0	31	0			–	–
K.R.Brown (La)	RMF	1	0	16	0			–	–
N.L.J.Browne (Ex)	LB	3.5	1	10	0			–	–
N.L.Buck (La)	RMF	45.3	3	210	6	35.00	3- 64	–	–
K.A.Bull (CfU/Gm)	OB	79.3	9	315	2	157.50	1- 63	–	–
P.I.Burgoyne (Sx)	OB	52	5	215	1	215.00	1-113	–	–
J.E.Burke (Sy)	RMF	104	19	347	16	21.68	4- 19	–	–

237

	Cat	O	M	R	W	Avge	Best	5wI	10wM
J.A.Burns (M)	RMF	5	0	14	0			–	–
R.J.Burns (Sy)	RM	6	1	12	0			–	–
M.A.Carberry (H)	OB	7.4	4	22	0				
A.Carter (Gm/Nt)	RMF	141.1	25	464	21	22.09	4- 46	–	–
M.Carter (Nt)	OB	49.4	6	195	10	19.50	7- 56	1	1
K.Carver (Y)	SLA	31	16	75	4	18.75	2- 6	–	–
S.J.Cato (OU)	OB	19	3	70	3	23.33	2- 43	–	–
M.A.Chambers (Nh)	RFM	114.3	21	415	14	29.64	3- 44	–	–
Z.J.Chappell (Le)	RFM	26	1	106	2	53.00	1- 35	–	–
G.Chapple (La)	RMF	166	44	489	10	48.90	4- 62	–	–
J.L.Clare (De)	RMF	21	1	78	0			–	–
J.Clark (La)	RM	244.4	38	880	19	46.31	4-101	–	–
R.Clarke (Wa)	RFM	387.3	83	1206	47	25.65	5- 62	1	–
M.E.Claydon (K)	RMF	175.5	19	656	13	50.46	4-103	–	–
J.J.Cobb (Nh)	LB	103.5	12	363	4	90.75	1- 19	–	–
I.A.Cockbain (Gs)	RM	1	0	1	0				
K.J.Coetzer (Nh)	RM	3	0	12	1	12.00	1- 8	–	–
M.T.Coles (K)	RMF	433	82	1574	67	23.49	6- 55	2	1
P.D.Collingwood (Du)	RM	93.5	20	320	11	29.09	5- 57	1	–
N.R.D.Compton (M)	OB	1	0	4	0				
T.L.W.Cooper (Sm)	OB	65	6	226	6	37.66	5- 76	1	–
M.J.Cosgrove (Le)	RM	60.2	14	192	3	64.00	1- 5	–	–
D.A.Cosker (Gm)	SLA	175.5	20	651	8	81.37	2- 14	–	–
B.D.Cotton (De)	RMF	223.1	49	745	15	49.66	3- 26	–	–
P.Coughlin (Du)	RM	134	34	443	19	23.31	4- 10	–	–
M.D.Craig (NZ)	OB	120.4	32	359	13	27.61	5- 34	1	–
M.S.Crane (H)	LB	77	11	336	10	33.60	5- 35	1	–
R.J.Crichard (CU)	RM	53	5	243	7	34.71	5- 62	1	–
M.J.J.Critchley (De)	LB	76.1	6	363	4	90.75	3- 50	–	–
S.J.Croft (La)	RMF	96.1	13	286	10	28.60	4- 35	–	–
S.P.Crook (Nh)	RFM	172.1	23	678	19	35.68	3- 28	–	–
P.J.Cummins (A)	RF	37.4	9	120	4	30.00	3- 61	–	–
S.M.Curran (Sy)	LMF	145.2	21	575	22	26.13	5- 67	2	–
T.K.Curran (Sy)	RMF	544.4	129	1754	76	23.07	7- 20	5	1
J.H.Davey (Sm)	RM	32	8	117	2	58.50	2- 54	–	–
W.S.Davis (De)	RFM	22	4	81	3	27.00	3- 63	–	–
L.A.Dawson (Ex/H)	SLA	300.4	58	926	29	31.93	5-139	1	–
J.L.Denly (K)	LB	23	4	70	1	70.00	1- 16	–	–
C.D.J.Dent (Gs)	SLA	40	5	168	2	84.00	1- 4	–	–
J.W.Dernbach (Sy)	RFM	80.2	27	204	2	102.00	1- 24	–	–
N.J.Dexter (M)	RM	163.2	35	485	21	23.09	5- 64	1	–
A.J.Dibble (Sm)	RMF	5	1	21	0			–	–
T.M.Dilshan (De)	OB	17	1	76	1	76.00	1- 9	–	–
G.H.Dockrell (Sx)	SLA	44	2	180	0				
B.L.D'Oliveira (Wo)	LB	118.5	20	445	13	34.23	5- 48	1	–
J.A.Duffy (NZ)	RFM	19	4	75	1	75.00	1- 36	–	–
M.P.Dunn (Sy)	RFM	253.4	37	984	28	35.14	4- 72	–	–
W.J.Durston (De)	OB	203	23	753	24	31.37	6-109	1	–
F.H.Edwards (H)	RF	240.5	38	940	45	20.88	6- 88	3	1
J.S.E.Ellis-Grewal (LBU)	SLA	56.2	5	201	6	33.50	4-118	–	–
S.L.Elstone (De)	OB	56	7	222	4	55.50	3- 68	–	–
S.M.Ervine (H)	RM	131.2	32	472	9	52.44	3- 37	–	–
L.J.Evans (Wa)	OB	5	0	31	1	31.00	1- 29	–	–

	Cat	O	M	R	W	Avge	Best	5wI	10wM
J.P.Faulkner (La)	LMF	186	44	501	23	21.78	5- 39	1	–
Fawad Ahmed (A)	LB	52.5	6	272	7	38.85	3- 68	–	–
T.C.Fell (Wo)	OB	1	0	7	0				
A.J.Finch (Y)	LM	2	1	1	0				
S.T.Finn (E/M)	RF	353.4	71	1071	43	24.90	6- 79	1	–
M.D.Fisher (Y)	RMF	73.5	18	243	5	48.60	2- 61	–	–
L.J.Fletcher (Nt/Sy)	RMF	86.1	20	253	11	23.00	4- 58	–	–
M.H.A.Footitt (De)	LFM	537.4	113	1796	76	23.63	7- 71	5	1
J.E.C.Franklin (M)	LM	104	12	381	7	54.42	3- 41	–	–
O.H.Freckingham (Le)	RMF	131	17	520	21	24.76	5- 39	1	–
J.K.Fuller (Gs)	RFM	292.5	58	972	27	36.00	4- 35	–	–
S.T.Gabriel (Wo)	RFM	40	3	183	9	20.33	5- 31	1	–
R.N.Gamble (LU)	RMF	86	21	327	4	81.75	1- 41	–	–
J.S.Gatting (H)	OB	3	1	7	0				
A.P.R.Gidman (Wo)	RM	6	2	17	1	17.00	1- 11	–	–
W.R.S.Gidman (Nt)	RM	114	26	357	4	89.25	2- 29	–	–
R.J.Gleeson (Nh)	RM	32	4	137	4	34.25	2- 35	–	–
J.S.D.Gnodde (OU)		2	0	21	0				
S.E.Grant (LU)	LMF	27	1	138	0				
L.Gregory (Sm)	RMF	354.1	53	1351	41	32.95	6-101	3	–
S.W.Griffiths (CfU)	RMF	38	5	160	2	80.00	2- 63	–	–
T.D.Groenewald (Sm)	RFM	312.5	54	1112	39	28.51	5- 65	1	–
J.O.Grundy (OU)	LMF	38	5	136	3	45.33	2- 41	–	–
N.R.T.Gubbins (LBU/M)	LB	3	1	10	0				
H.F.Gurney (Nt)	LFM	326.5	63	1063	43	24.72	5- 43	2	–
C.J.Haggett (K)	RMF	268	60	792	28	28.28	4- 43	–	–
H.Hameed (La)	LB	1	0	9	0				
T.R.G.Hampton (Gs)	RMF	33	4	171	1	171.00	1-109	–	–
P.S.P.Handscomb (Gs)		2	0	21	0				
O.J.Hannon-Dalby (Wa)	RMF	116	23	406	8	50.75	3- 80	–	–
A.Harinath (Sy)	OB	25.1	3	85	1	85.00	1- 18	–	–
J.A.R.Harris (M)	RFM	489.2	75	1854	73	25.39	9- 34	3	1
R.J.Harris (A)	RF	30	6	110	4	27.50	2- 51	–	–
J.Harrison (Du)	LMF	115.4	15	436	10	43.60	2- 42	–	–
J.W.Hastings (Du)	RFM	425	88	1458	46	31.69	7- 60	2	–
L.J.Hatchett (Sx)	LMF	58	9	206	4	51.50	2- 47	–	–
J.R.Hazlewood (A)	RMF	141	27	527	20	26.35	4- 42	–	–
T.G.Helm (M)	RMF	54.2	12	177	6	29.50	2- 42	–	–
M.J.Henry (NZ)	RFM	86.1	12	340	8	42.50	4- 93	–	–
B.W.Hilfenhaus (Nt)	RFM	97	22	294	7	42.00	4- 67	–	–
L.J.Hill (Le)	RM	2	0	6	0				
M.E.Hobden (Sx)	RFM	261.3	37	1114	23	48.43	4- 48	–	–
M.G.Hogan (Gm)	RFM	482.1	126	1297	48	27.02	5- 99	2	–
P.J.Horton (La)	RM	2	0	7	0				
B.A.C.Howell (Gs)	RMF	180.2	36	582	23	25.30	3- 28	–	–
F.J.Hudson-Prentice (Sx)	RMF	8	0	51	0				
A.L.Hughes (De)	RM	81.5	12	281	5	56.20	2- 34	–	–
C.F.Hughes (De)	SLA	41.2	4	200	3	66.66	1- 4	–	–
M.D.Hunn (K)	RFM	199	35	704	23	30.60	5- 99	1	–
A.P.Hunt (CU)	RM	18	2	73	2	36.50	1- 35	–	–
B.A.Hutton (Nt)	RM	262.1	51	912	37	24.64	5- 29	2	1
Imran Tahir (Nt)	LB	36	5	145	4	36.25	2- 65	–	–
C.A.Ingram (Gm)	LB	103.3	9	398	10	39.80	3- 90	–	–

239

	Cat	O	M	R	W	Avge	Best	5wI	10wM
K.M.Jarvis (La)	RFM	450.5	87	1533	62	24.72	5- 13	4	–
A.Javid (Wa)	OB	21	2	74	0				
W.H.Jenkins (DU)	RM	14	0	88	2	44.00	2- 27	–	–
K.K.Jennings (Du)	RMF	12	0	51	0				
M.G.Johnson (A)	LF	170.1	37	609	20	30.45	4- 56	–	–
O.J.Jones (OU)	RM	36	16	91	7	13.00	4- 70	–	–
R.A.Jones (Wa)	RMF	17	1	68	4	17.00	4- 48	–	–
C.J.Jordan (Sx)	RFM	197.4	28	686	24	28.58	5- 68	1	–
E.C.Joyce (Sx)	RM	4	0	8	0				
A.Kapil (Sy)	RFM	12	1	68	2	34.00	1- 13	–	–
G.Keedy (Nt)	SLA	40	12	107	5	21.40	3- 45	–	–
R.I.Keogh (Nh)	OB	310	42	1069	20	53.45	3- 35	–	–
S.C.Kerrigan (La)	SLA	460.2	100	1321	41	32.21	4- 28	–	–
A.N.Kervezee (Wo)	RM	23	1	86	3	28.66	3- 72	–	–
M.J.L.Kidd (OU)	RM	16	0	77	0				
R.K.Kleinveldt (Nh)	RMF	407.5	69	1547	57	27.14	5- 41	5	–
T.C.Knight (De)	SLA	2	0	21	0				
N.R.Kumar (LU)	OB	29	0	195	4	48.75	1- 25	–	–
M.B.Lake (OU)	RM	31	5	114	4	28.50	2- 41	–	–
J.L.Lawlor (CfU/Gm)	OB	4	1	11	0				
J.Leach (Wo)	RMF	467	74	1772	59	30.03	6- 73	2	–
M.J.Leach (Sm)	SLA	152.1	41	408	16	25.50	7-106	1	1
S.G.Leach (OU)	LB	0.4	0	2	0				
J.A.Leaning (Y)	RMF	26	4	152	1	152.00	1- 82	–	–
A.Z.Lees (Y)	LB	4	1	12	0				
T.J.Lester (La)	LFM	44	8	172	3	57.33	3- 50	–	–
K.S.Leverock (CfU)	LM	22	2	92	1	92.00	1- 61	–	–
D.E.Lewis-Williams (CfU)	LM	27	4	98	1	98.00	1- 98	–	–
C.J.Liddle (Sx)	LFM	110	15	391	10	39.10	3- 49	–	–
A.E.Lilley (LBU)	LM	49	7	156	6	26.00	4- 65	–	–
A.M.Lilley (La)	OB	234.3	44	751	26	28.88	5- 23	1	–
T.E.Linley (Sy/Sx)	RFM	61.4	14	223	9	24.77	5- 63	1	–
D.L.Lloyd (Gm)	OB	215.2	23	942	21	44.85	3- 68	–	–
N.M.Lyon (A)	OB	190.5	30	745	20	37.25	4- 75	–	–
A.Lyth (E/Y)	RM	28.5	4	76	4	19.00	1- 4	–	–
B.J.McCarthy (Du)	RMF	39	4	154	4	38.50	2- 51	–	–
C.M.MacDonell (DU)	RFM	25	5	120	0				
H.P.S.McInley (DU)	RMF	28.4	3	153	1	153.00	1- 30	–	–
J.N.McIver (OU)	OB	30	1	118	3	39.33	3- 64	–	–
C.J.McKay Le)	RFM	480.5	122	1439	58	24.81	6- 54	3	–
G.K.R.McKinley (LU)	RM	39	1	201	4	50.25	3- 67	–	–
R.McLaren (H)	RMF	128.5	24	419	11	38.09	4- 60	–	–
C.S.MacLeod (Du)	RMF	5	1	16	0				
M.W.Machan (Sx)	RM	6	0	28	0				
W.L.Madsen (De)	OB	17.4	2	51	1	51.00	1- 27	–	–
S.J.Magoffin (Sx)	RFM	594	143	1677	73	22.97	6- 50	4	1
D.J.Malan (M)	LB	11	0	36	1	36.00	1- 21	–	–
J.Marsden (OU)	RFM	27	5	99	2	49.50	2- 72	–	–
M.R.Marsh (A)	RFM	104.1	22	381	20	19.05	4- 41	–	–
H.J.H.Marshall (Gs)	RM	14	5	31	3	10.33	3- 30	–	–
D.D.Masters (Ex)	RMF	224.2	54	606	20	30.30	4- 45	–	–
G.J.Maxwell (Y)	OB	29	2	144	4	36.00	3- 55	–	–
S.C.Meaker (Sy)	RMF	61.2	8	281	5	56.20	3- 92	–	–

	Cat	O	M	R	W	Avge	Best	5wI	10wM
C.A.J.Meschede (Gm)	RMF	438.3	69	1609	43	37.41	4- 89	–	–
J.D.Middlebrook (Y)	OB	126.3	22	441	17	25.94	5- 82	1	–
C.N.Miles (Gs)	RMF	373.4	76	1224	50	24.48	6- 63	4	1
T.S.Mills (Sx)	LFM	48.3	11	157	3	52.33	2- 28	–	–
T.P.Milnes (De/Wa)	RMF	71	6	302	5	60.40	3- 96	–	–
D.K.H.Mitchell (Wo)	RM	7	0	24	0			–	–
T.C.Moore (Ex)	RMF	50	11	187	6	31.16	3- 12	–	–
C.A.J.Morris (Wo)	RMF	494	99	1549	50	30.98	5- 71	1	–
G.J.Muchall (Du)	RM	2	0	7	0			–	–
S.J.Mullaney (Nt)	RM	129.5	27	464	15	30.93	3- 44	–	–
C.Munro (Wo)	RM	8	2	29	1	29.00	1- 10	–	–
J.R.Murphy (CfU)	LFM	40	5	135	2	67.50	2- 90	–	–
T.J.Murtagh (M)	RFM	413.2	91	1194	46	25.95	4- 55	–	–
J.G.Myburgh (Sm)	OB	57	14	165	3	55.00	3- 57	–	–
S.V.S.Mylavarapu (OU)	SLA	34	6	99	1	99.00	1- 71	–	–
J.K.H.Naik (Le)	OB	182.5	33	690	18	38.33	8-179	1	–
G.R.Napier (Ex)	RM	281	39	979	35	27.97	4- 27	–	–
C.D.Nash (Sx)	OB	69	5	289	1	289.00	1- 7	–	–
R.I.Newton (Nh)	OB	1	0	6	0			–	–
A.S.S.Nijjar (Ex)	SLA	121.3	12	489	12	40.75	2- 33	–	–
K.Noema-Barnett (Gs)	RM	190.5	52	598	17	35.17	3- 28	–	–
L.C.Norwell (Gs)	RMF	507.3	109	1592	68	23.41	6- 33	3	1
T.M.Nugent (LU)	RMF	25	5	107	3	35.66	2- 32	–	–
G.Onions (Du)	RFM	491.5	90	1799	69	26.07	7- 68	3	–
C.Overton (Sm)	RMF	313.3	62	1022	47	21.74	6- 74	1	–
J.Overton (Sm)	RFM	188.5	36	633	17	37.23	4- 37	–	–
A.P.Palladino (De)	RMF	382.4	110	993	32	31.03	3- 19	–	–
M.S.Panesar (Ex)	SLA	75.1	17	270	7	38.57	4-112	–	–
A.R.Patel (CU)		29.4	2	88	5	17.60	5- 88	1	–
J.S.Patel (Wa)	OB	497.5	113	1466	58	25.27	7- 38	3	–
R.H.Patel (Ex/M)	SLA	46	12	176	6	29.33	4- 42	–	–
S.R.Patel (Nt)	SLA	320.1	88	944	30	31.46	4- 23	–	–
S.A.Patterson (Y)	RMF	451.1	150	1172	47	24.93	5- 11	2	–
D.A.Payne (Gs)	LMF	290.3	65	921	34	27.08	4- 50	–	–
D.Penrhyn Jones (Gm)	RFM	32	1	190	5	38.00	3- 55	–	–
A.N.Petersen (La)	RM/OB	4	2	9	0				
V.D.Philander (Nt)	RMF	154.3	40	384	16	24.00	4- 56	–	–
W.D.Phillips (DU)	RM	19	3	93	2	46.50	2- 53	–	–
K.P.Pietersen (Sy)	OB	2	0	8	0				
L.E.Plunkett (Y)	RFM	115.1	17	459	14	32.78	4- 61	–	–
A.W.Pollock (CU)	RMF	83.5	24	254	8	31.75	4- 43	–	–
J.A.Porter (Ex)	RMF	431.3	66	1557	56	27.80	4- 28	–	–
J.E.Poysden (Wa)	LB	40.4	4	165	1	165.00	1-165	–	–
D.T.P.Pratt (LBU)	RM	53.2	8	155	5	31.00	2- 51	–	–
R.D.Pringle (Du)	OB	160.4	37	566	20	28.30	5- 63	1	–
I.Prowse (LU)	RM/OB	31	7	121	2	60.50	1- 12	–	–
C.A.Pujara (Y)	LB	1	0	5	0				
R.M.Pyrah (Y)	RM	21	3	73	0				
B.A.Raine (Le)	RMF	537.1	127	1698	61	27.83	5- 43	2	–
W.B.Rankin (Wa)	RFM	272.3	28	1127	43	26.20	6- 55	2	–
A.U.Rashid (Y)	LB	212.2	31	813	29	28.03	4- 48	–	–
D.E.M.Ratnayake (DU)	RM	29	1	130	4	32.50	3- 72	–	–
O.P.Rayner (M)	OB	273	71	780	24	32.50	3- 44	–	–

241

	Cat	O	M	R	W	Avge	Best	5wI	10wM
D.J.Redfern (Le)	OB	39.1	8	104	3	34.66	1- 0	–	–
L.M.Reece (La)	LM	17	0	97	0				
W.M.H.Rhodes (Y)	RMF	86.5	20	289	9	32.11	3- 42	–	–
A.E.N.Riley (K)	OB	153.5	18	634	12	52.83	4- 47	–	–
O.E.Robinson (Sx)	RM	320.1	66	1137	46	24.71	6- 33	1	–
S.D.Robson (M)	LB	5	0	26	1	26.00	1- 8	–	–
T.S.Roland-Jones (M)	RMF	471	112	1298	48	27.04	5- 27	1	–
J.E.Root (E)	OB	40.3	4	171	5	34.20	2- 28	–	–
W.T.Root (LBU/Nt)	OB	5	2	6	0				
A.M.Rossington (Nh)	(WK)	1	0	6	0				
H.P.Rouse (LBU)	RFM	27	3	105	4	26.25	3- 45	–	–
T.D.Rouse (CfU)	OB	15	0	64	2	32.00	1- 3	–	–
J.J.Roy (Sy)	RM	24.4	2	115	3	38.33	1- 6	–	–
J.A.Rudolph (Gm)	LBG	3	0	11	0				
C.Rushworth (Du)	RMF	613.4	145	1768	88	20.09	6- 39	7	–
J.D.Ryder (Ex)	RM	345.4	71	1176	45	26.13	6- 47	3	1
Saeed Ajmal (Wo)	OB	272.3	42	890	16	55.62	5- 28	1	–
A.Sakande (OU)	RFM	55.2	10	167	6	27.83	3- 38	–	–
M.E.T.Salisbury (Ex)	RMF	64	8	256	4	64.00	2- 29	–	–
A.G.Salter (Gm)	OB	339.1	42	1150	25	46.00	3- 5	–	–
B.W.Sanderson (Nh)	RMF	78	23	223	11	20.27	4- 44	–	–
M.J.Santner (NZ)	SLA	1	1	0	0				
R.J.Sayer (Le)	OB	86	7	352	4	88.00	2- 59	–	–
G.F.B.Scott (LBU)	RM	21	1	121	2	60.50	2- 67	–	–
S.M.S.M.Senanayake (Wo)	OB	137	18	381	9	42.33	4- 50	–	–
A.Shahzad (Sx)	RFM	129.2	19	461	26	17.73	5- 46	1	–
J.D.Shantry (Wo)	LM	546.5	149	1456	67	21.73	5- 8	5	1
A.Sheikh (Le)	LMF	58	9	276	8	34.50	3- 42	–	–
C.E.Shreck (Le)	RFM	512.4	116	1691	57	29.66	5- 71	2	–
P.M.Siddle (A/La)	RFM	257.2	76	662	28	23.64	4- 35	–	–
R.J.Sidebottom (Y)	LFM	248	65	734	41	17.90	6- 34	3	1
B.T.Slater (De)	LB	1	0	8	0				
G.M.Smith (Ex)	OB/RM	33.2	5	110	5	22.00	3- 22	–	–
R.A.J.Smith (Gm)	RM	42	5	155	6	25.83	3- 23	–	–
S.P.D.Smith (A)	LBG	11.4	0	77	4	19.25	3- 54	–	–
T.C.Smith (La)	RMF	17	2	75	0				
T.M.J.Smith (Gs)	SLA	85.4	7	329	3	109.66	1- 24	–	–
W.R.Smith (H)	OB	46.4	13	111	3	37.00	1- 8	–	–
T.G.Southee (NZ)	RMF	106	17	392	8	49.00	4- 83	–	–
M.A.Starc (A)	LF	170.4	30	626	27	23.18	6- 51	3	–
C.T.Steel (DU)	LB	6	0	53	0				
D.I.Stevens (K)	RM	419.1	100	1242	61	20.36	5- 58	2	–
R.A.Stevenson (H)	RFM	56.5	9	215	3	71.66	1- 15	–	–
P.R.Stirling (M)	OB	47.1	10	158	6	26.33	2- 31	–	–
B.A.Stokes (E)	RFM	166	36	642	15	42.80	6- 36	1	–
O.P.Stone (Nh)	RMF	350.4	62	1166	38	30.68	5- 44	1	–
M.D.Stoneman (Du)	RM	6	0	37	0				
W.A.Tavaré (Gs)	RM	9	0	30	0				
B.R.M.Taylor (Nt)	OB	3	0	12	0				
J.M.R.Taylor (Gs)	OB	159	29	466	10	46.60	3-119	–	–
M.D.Taylor (Gs)	LMF	157.1	36	544	13	41.84	5- 93	1	–
R.M.L.Taylor (Le)	LM	167.4	24	720	18	40.00	3- 41	–	–
T.A.I.Taylor (De)	RMF	241.2	34	946	28	33.78	6- 61	1	–

242

	Cat	O	M	R	W	Avge	Best	5wI	10wM
R.N.ten Doeschate (Ex)	RMF	60	5	249	9	27.66	3- 15	–	–
S.J.Thakor (De)	RM	188.4	33	667	13	51.30	2- 11	–	–
A.C.Thomas (Sm)	RFM	237.4	54	735	29	25.34	5- 73	1	–
I.A.A.Thomas (K)	RMF	289.4	57	923	27	34.18	4- 48	–	–
J.A.Tomlinson (H)	LMF	252	61	778	20	38.90	4- 37	–	–
R.J.W.Topley (Ex)	LMF	53	10	206	7	29.42	3- 90	–	–
J.C.Tredwell (K)	OB	164.5	45	443	11	40.27	3- 59	–	–
P.D.Trego (Sm)	RMF	298.3	62	1037	28	37.03	4- 73	–	–
C.T.Tremlett (Sy)	RFM	68	14	219	6	36.50	2- 38	–	–
I.J.L.Trott (Wa)	RM	34	6	108	1	108.00	1- 24	–	–
J.M.Vince (H)	RM	19	2	74	1	74.00	1- 7	–	–
A.C.Voges (A/M)	SLA	31	3	141	6	23.50	2- 20	–	–
G.G.Wagg (Gm)	LM	467.4	73	1681	45	37.35	5- 54	1	–
N.Wagner (NZ)	LMF	21.5	4	101	3	33.66	2- 41	–	–
D.J.Wainwright (De)	SLA	43.1	1	188	1	188.00	1-131	–	–
A.G.Wakely (Nh)	OB	4	0	17	0			–	–
D.A.Warner (A)	LB	6	0	34	0			–	–
L.Watkinson (LBU)	RM	38	4	137	2	68.50	1- 32	–	–
S.R.Watson (A)	RMF	53	11	163	1	163.00	1- 30	–	–
W.J.Weighell (Du)	RM	36.3	5	179	1	179.00	1-101	–	–
S.D.Weller (OU)	RFM	46	15	121	5	24.20	3- 26	–	–
L.W.P.Wells (Sx)	LB	226	27	862	23	37.47	3- 35	–	–
T.J.Wells (Le)	RMF	98.5	17	412	9	45.77	3- 68	–	–
T.Westley (Ex)	OB	109.4	8	373	6	62.16	4- 75	–	–
A.A.Westphal (CfU)	RMF	40	10	135	3	45.00	1- 20	–	–
I.J.Westwood (Wa)	OB	4	0	18	0			–	–
B.T.J.Wheal (H)	RM	94	10	393	8	49.12	4-101	–	–
B.M.Wheeler (NZ)	LMF	26	9	92	6	15.33	5- 18	1	–
G.G.White (Nh)	SLA	67.4	13	240	8	30.00	3- 81	–	–
H.J.White (De)	LM	24	3	116	2	58.00	2- 85	–	–
W.A.White (De/Le)	RMF	153.5	26	568	26	21.84	6- 25	3	–
R.A.Whiteley (Wo)	LMF	42	1	234	1	234.00	1- 51	–	–
S.G.Whittingham (LU)	RFM	18	0	109	1	109.00	1- 77	–	–
D.J.Willey (Nh)	LFM	155	25	547	15	36.46	4- 72	–	–
B.P.R.Williams (DU)	LMF	17	0	85	1	85.00	1- 66	–	–
D.R.Williams (DU)	LB	12	0	83	0			–	–
K.S.Williamson (NZ)	OB	10	2	22	3	7.33	3- 15	–	–
J.R.Winslade (Ex)	RMF	21	2	97	4	24.25	4- 20	–	–
C.R.Woakes (Wa)	RFM	74	20	217	11	19.72	3- 48	–	–
C.P.Wood (H)	LM	38	6	145	3	48.33	1- 30	–	–
J.M.Wood (DU)	RM	20	6	68	2	34.00	2- 32	–	–
L.Wood (Nt)	LM	247.2	53	907	30	30.23	3- 27	–	–
M.A.Wood (Du)	RFM	219.4	48	764	25	30.56	4- 39	–	–
C.J.C.Wright (Wa)	RFM	274.2	36	1033	31	33.32	5- 40	1	–
L.J.Wright (Sx)	RMF	9	0	39	0			–	–
B.A.Wylie (CU)	SLA	59	14	173	6	28.33	3- 14	–	–
M.H.Yardy (Sx)	LM	14	1	73	1	73.00	1- 17	–	–
S.A.Zaib (Nh)	SLA	11	0	56	0			–	–
Zain Shahzad (CU)	RMF	53	9	192	6	32.00	3- 49	–	–

FIRST-CLASS CAREER RECORDS

Compiled by Philip Bailey

The following career records are for all players who appeared in first-class cricket during the 2015 season, and are complete to the end of that season. Some players who did not appear in 2015 but may do so in 2016 are included.

BATTING AND FIELDING

'1000' denotes instances of scoring 1000 runs in a season. Where these have been achieved outside the British Isles they are shown after a plus sign.

	M	I	NO	HS	Runs	Avge	100	50	1000	Ct/St
Abbott, J.B.	4	7	–	41	104	14.85	–	–	–	6
Abbott, K.J.	61	85	17	80	1254	18.44	–	4	–	14
Abdur Rehman	149	205	25	96	3175	17.63	–	16	–	60
Abell, T.B.	19	34	4	131	1062	35.40	1	8	–	11
Adair, M.R.	1	2	2	24*	34	–	–	–	–	–
Adams, A.R.	173	237	24	124	4540	21.31	3	20	–	115
Adams, J.H.K.	191	339	28	262*	11893	38.24	21	63	5	146
Agathangelou, A.P.	53	96	6	158	2774	30.82	5	14	0+1	85
Akram, B.M.R.	2	3	–	36	37	12.33	–	–	–	–
Ali, A.M.	7	12	1	80	412	37.45	–	3	–	2
Ali, M.M.	137	234	19	250	8174	38.01	14	52	2	85
Allenby, J.	139	221	30	138*	7310	38.27	10	51	1	140
Ambrose, T.R.	195	296	26	251*	9089	33.66	14	53	–	498/33
Amla, H.M.	188	307	28	311*	14331	51.36	44	69	0+2	142
Anderson, C.J.	40	67	9	167	2052	35.37	3	9	–	23
Anderson, J.M.	184	232	83	81	1564	10.49	–	1	–	108
Andrew, G.M.	90	136	17	180*	2909	24.44	1	18	–	30
Ansari, Z.S.	56	91	14	112	2469	32.06	3	13	1	25
Arif, A.T.	4	6	–	39	72	12.00	–	–	–	–
Arksey, J.B.T.	1	–	–	–	–	–	–	–	–	1
Arshad, U.	14	18	1	83	429	25.23	–	2	–	5
Ashar Zaidi	107	172	13	202	5870	36.91	12	29	0+1	82
Azhar Mahmood	176	274	32	204*	7703	31.83	9	42	–	142
Azharullah, M.	91	124	68	58*	823	14.69	–	1	–	21
Bailey, G.J.	107	189	16	160*	6487	37.49	14	33	–	101
Bailey, T.E.	16	21	6	34	279	18.60	–	–	–	2
Bairstow, J.M.	116	186	26	219*	7362	46.01	16	42	2	273/10
Balbirnie, A.	11	15	1	38	196	14.00	–	–	–	8
Ball, A.J.	24	35	3	69	659	20.59	–	2	–	15
Ball, J.T.	21	32	4	49*	350	12.50	–	–	–	1
Ballance, G.S.	97	153	16	210	7085	51.71	26	33	2+1	91
Bancroft, C.T.	24	43	1	211	1570	37.38	4	6	–	25
Barker, K.H.D.	72	91	15	125	2176	28.63	5	5	–	23
Barnard, E.G.	4	4	1	17	35	11.66	–	–	–	2
Barrow, A.W.R.	38	63	5	88	1157	19.94	–	4	–	65
Bates, M.D.	52	69	10	103	1177	19.94	1	5	–	149/7
Batty, G.J.	221	329	54	133	6590	23.96	2	30	–	157
Beer, W.A.T.	9	12	2	39	219	21.90	–	–	–	3
Bell, I.R.	258	436	47	262*	17529	45.06	50	91	4	201
Bell-Drummond, D.J.	55	94	5	153	2871	32.25	7	14	1	26
Berg, G.K.	88	137	15	130*	3654	29.95	2	22	–	56
Best, M.T.	4	6	–	50	120	20.00	–	1	–	1

F-C	M	I	NO	HS	Runs	Avge	100	50	1000	Ct/St
Billings, S.W.	38	58	5	131	1653	31.18	2	9	–	99/8
Bird, J.M.	37	45	19	26	228	8.76	–	–	–	15
Bishnoi, C.	6	10	–	65	265	26.50	–	3	–	3
Blake, A.J.	29	47	2	105*	993	22.06	1	4	–	17
Blofield, A.D.	3	5	3	105	211	105.50	1	1	–	4
Bopara, R.S.	164	272	30	229	9915	40.97	26	38	1	86
Borthwick, S.G.	104	174	19	216	5563	35.89	10	32	3	134
Boult, T.A.	62	79	29	52*	687	13.74	–	1	–	26
Boyce, M.A.G.	104	184	9	135	4882	27.89	6	24	–	64
Bracewell, D.A.J.	63	99	12	105	2152	24.73	2	11	–	25
Bracey, S.N.	3	3	1	20	22	11.00	–	–	–	4
Bragg, W.D.	91	158	6	120	4482	29.48	4	27	2	34/1
Brand, N.	2	3	–	46	94	31.33	–	–	–	1
Bravo, D.J.	100	180	7	197	5302	30.64	8	30	–	89
Bresnan, T.T.	158	205	34	169*	5010	29.29	5	25	–	71
Briggs, D.R.	67	82	18	54	987	15.42	–	1	–	20
Broad, S.C.J.	143	196	29	169	3752	22.46	1	18	–	44
Brooks, J.A.	83	90	33	53*	853	14.96	–	3	–	22
Broom, N.T.	109	183	20	203*	6427	39.42	15	28	–	80
Brown, B.C.	84	132	19	163	4001	35.40	9	20	1	223/15
Brown, K.R.	73	119	6	132	3168	28.03	2	20	–	45
Browne, N.L.J.	29	49	6	151*	1833	42.62	8	5	1	27
Buck, N.L.	62	85	24	29*	659	10.80	–	–	–	9
Bull, K.A.	7	10	3	31	69	9.85	–	–	–	1
Bullen, S.F.G.	1	2	–	36	61	30.50	–	–	–	–
Burgess, M.G.K.	4	5	1	49	168	42.00	–	–	–	4
Burgoyne, P.I.	14	23	2	100	564	26.85	2	1	–	9
Burke, J.E.	8	10	1	79	232	25.77	–	2	–	5
Burnham, J.T.A.	4	8	–	50	115	14.37	–	1	–	2
Burns, J.A.	60	102	9	183	3807	40.93	8	24	–	45
Burns, R.J.	59	102	10	199	3767	40.94	8	18	2	57
Buttler, J.C.	71	108	10	144	3260	33.26	4	19	–	154/2
Cachopa, C.	36	63	2	203	2449	40.14	5	15	–	24
Carberry, M.A.	184	322	24	300*	12833	43.06	33	63	4	86
Carter, A.	29	33	13	24*	220	11.00	–	–	–	5
Carter, M.	1	2	–	11	11	5.50	–	–	–	1
Carver, K.	3	4	2	16	30	15.00	–	–	–	1
Cato, S.J.	3	5	2	33	100	33.33	–	–	–	1
Chambers, M.A.	64	86	24	58	410	6.61	–	1	–	19
Chappell, Z.J.	1	2	–	96	103	51.50	–	1	–	–
Chapple, G.	315	436	75	155	8725	24.16	6	37	–	104
Chohan, D.	1	2	–	6	3	3.00	–	–	–	–
Chopra, V.	151	249	17	233*	8473	36.52	18	41	3	172
Christian, D.T.	54	93	12	131*	2587	31.93	5	10	–	56
Clare, J.L.	57	82	9	130	1725	23.63	2	8	–	28
Clark, G.	3	6	–	36	65	10.83	–	–	–	2
Clark, J.	12	17	2	63	419	27.93	–	1	–	3
Clarke, J.M.	11	16	1	104*	530	35.33	1	4	–	3
Clarke, M.J.	188	327	33	329*	13826	47.02	45	48	0+1	203
Clarke, R.	193	296	34	214	8989	34.30	16	44	1	291
Claughton, T.H.	1	2	–	29	48	24.00	–	–	–	–
Claydon, M.E.	76	100	20	77	1258	15.72	–	3	–	9
Cobb, J.J.	95	165	16	148*	3821	25.64	3	24	–	46
Cockbain, I.A.	44	75	5	151*	1995	28.50	3	11	–	32
Coetzer, K.J.	90	152	11	219	4325	30.67	8	19	–	42
Coleman, F.R.J.	9	15	–	110	224	14.93	1	–	–	6

245

F-C	M	I	NO	HS	Runs	Avge	100	50	1000	Ct/St
Coles, M.T.	84	114	16	103*	1824	18.61	1	8	–	39
Collingwood, P.D.	266	458	44	206	14912	36.01	31	77	2	305
Compton, N.R.D.	157	275	33	254*	10408	43.00	24	51	6	76
Cook, A.N.	223	397	28	294	17312	46.91	49	86	5+1	224
Cooke, C.B.	42	71	8	171	2334	37.04	3	16	–	36/1
Cooper, T.L.W.	65	115	6	203*	3879	35.58	7	23	–	55
Cosgrove, M.J.	154	273	17	233	10834	42.32	28	63	2	106
Cosker, D.A.	248	329	96	69	3444	14.78	–	2	–	150
Cotton, B.D.	10	14	3	43	162	14.72	–	–	–	2
Coughlin, P.	14	22	4	85	469	26.05	–	3	–	6
Cowdrey, F.K.	11	19	1	62	354	19.66	–	2	–	5
Cox, O.B.	58	96	18	109	2116	27.12	2	12	–	147/9
Craig, M.D.	41	59	8	104	1403	27.50	1	8	–	40
Crane, M.S.	3	4	2	13	18	9.00	–	–	–	1
Crichard, R.J.	3	3	1	21	32	16.00	–	–	–	2
Critchley, M.J.J.	6	8	2	137*	246	41.00	1	–	–	2
Croft, S.J.	130	202	20	156	6167	33.88	10	37	–	125
Crook, S.P.	84	111	15	142*	3067	31.94	3	18	–	30
Cullen, T.N.	1	2	–	26	30	15.00	–	–	–	1
Cummins, P.J.	8	12	7	82*	142	28.40	–	1	–	2
Curran, S.M.	6	8	3	61*	239	47.80	–	1	–	1
Curran, T.K.	23	25	5	60	313	15.65	–	1	–	7
Davey, J.H.	9	17	1	72	333	20.81	–	3	–	5
Davies, A.L.	28	39	2	99	1257	33.97	–	10	–	67/5
Davies, R.C.	5	6	–	17	35	5.83	–	–	–	9
Davies, S.M.	166	271	28	200*	9731	40.04	18	45	5	397/20
Davis, C.A.L.	2	3	–	59	73	24.33	–	1	–	–
Davis, W.S.	1	1	1	8*	8	–	–	–	–	–
Dawson, L.A.	105	171	20	169	5165	34.20	7	26	1	124
Denly, J.L.	144	254	17	199	8033	33.89	17	42	3	60
Dent, C.D.J.	83	146	13	268	4677	35.16	8	27	2	105
Dernbach, J.W.	97	121	44	56*	725	9.41	–	1	–	15
Dexter, N.J.	117	195	24	163*	6032	35.27	13	30	–	82
Dibble, A.J.	4	6	2	43	84	21.00	–	–	–	–
Dickson, S.R.	12	21	3	173	592	32.88	1	3	–	4
Dilshan, T.M.	233	384	24	200*	13979	38.83	38	59	0+2	353/27
Dockrell, G.H.	41	50	20	53	481	16.03	–	1	–	15
D'Oliveira, B.L.	12	20	1	49	410	21.57	–	–	–	4
Donald, A.H.T.	6	12	1	98	351	31.90	–	3	–	5
Duckett, B.M.	31	51	4	154	1765	37.55	6	9	1	27/2
Duffy, J.A.	22	24	11	37	126	9.69	–	–	–	12
Dunn, M.P.	31	31	14	31*	115	6.76	–	–	–	5
Durston, W.J.	105	184	28	151	5283	33.86	6	32	1	110
Eckersley, E.J.H.	74	134	7	147	4127	32.49	10	13	1	101/3
Edwards, F.H.	95	141	52	40	635	7.13	–	–	–	19
Edwards, G.A.	4	5	1	19	56	14.00	–	–	–	1
Elgar, D.	112	191	20	268	7722	45.15	23	29	0+1	79
Elliott, G.D.	83	134	7	196*	3883	30.57	8	20	–	46
Ellis, E.J.	2	4	–	8	26	6.50	–	–	–	5/1
Ellis-Grewal, J.S.E.	2	2	–	42	44	22.00	–	–	–	–
Ellison, H.R.C.	2	4	–	32	58	14.50	–	–	–	–
Elstone, S.L.	14	22	1	103*	452	21.52	1	1	–	5
Ervine, S.M.	197	305	37	237*	9513	35.49	17	48	–	169
Eskinazi, S.S.	1	2	–	22	26	13.00	–	–	–	1
Evans, L.J.	51	86	6	213*	2753	34.41	5	14	–	39
Faulkner, J.P.	52	76	11	121	2097	32.26	1	14	–	25

F-C	M	I	NO	HS	Runs	Avge	100	50	1000	Ct/St
Fawad Ahmed	40	49	22	23	275	10.18	–	–	–	10
Fell, T.C.	39	63	3	171	2167	36.11	5	8	1	38
Finch, A.J.	49	81	2	122	2364	29.92	3	16	–	49
Finch, H.Z.	3	6	–	22	60	10.00	–	–	–	4
Finn, S.T.	115	141	48	56	815	8.76	–	1	–	38
Fisher, M.D.	3	2	1	0*	0	0.00	–	–	–	1
Fletcher, L.J.	71	104	21	92	1254	15.10	–	3	–	16
Foakes, B.T.	42	61	10	140*	1840	36.07	5	8	–	43/3
Footitt, M.H.A.	73	98	31	34	584	8.71	–	–	–	19
Foster, J.S.	257	386	49	212	12499	37.08	21	65	1	727/58
Franklin, J.E.C.	181	286	41	219	8843	36.09	21	39	–	92
Freckingham, O.H.	23	33	7	34*	296	11.38	–	–	–	4
Fuller, J.K.	38	46	5	73	730	17.80	–	3	–	14
Gabriel, S.T.	63	82	35	20*	238	5.06	–	–	–	16
Gale, A.W.	140	217	16	272	7640	38.00	20	29	2	47
Gamble, R.N.	2	2	–	5	5	2.50	–	–	–	1
Gatting, J.S.	47	70	7	152	1847	29.31	3	9	–	20
Gayle, C.H.	180	321	26	333	13226	44.83	32	64	0+1	158
George, J.	4	6	–	14	43	7.16	–	–	–	1
Gibson, R.A.M.	2	3	–	24	47	15.66	–	–	–	–
Gidman, A.P.R.	204	348	28	264	11622	36.31	24	60	6	141
Gidman, W.R.S.	63	97	17	143	2965	37.06	5	15	1	17
Gleeson, R.J.	2	2	–	6	8	4.00	–	–	–	2
Gnodde, J.S.D.	1	2	–	3	6	3.00	–	–	–	–
Godleman, B.A.	102	180	9	130	5276	30.85	9	29	1	74
Gordon, R.O.	6	5	2	14*	52	17.33	–	–	–	3
Grant, S.E.	2	2	1	14*	14	14.00	–	–	–	–
Gregory, L.	39	53	5	69	835	17.39	–	2	–	19
Griffiths, D.A.	38	52	19	31*	220	6.66	–	–	–	4
Griffiths, S.W.	4	5	–	40	121	24.20	–	–	–	1
Groenewald, T.D.	101	144	37	78	1896	17.71	–	6	–	38
Grundy, J.O.	2	4	2	21*	36	18.00	–	–	–	–
Gubbins, N.R.T.	17	31	1	95	747	24.90	–	5	–	5
Guptill, M.J.	85	155	10	227	5402	37.25	10	30	–	84
Gurney, H.F.	66	80	38	24*	206	4.90	–	–	–	8
Haddin, B.J.	184	300	39	169	9931	38.04	17	56	–	608/40
Haggett, C.J.	27	37	9	80	713	25.46	–	2	–	7
Hain, S.R.	22	35	4	208	1370	44.19	6	4	–	14
Hales, A.D.	85	146	6	236	5420	38.71	12	30	3	73
Hameed, H.	4	6	–	91	257	42.83	–	2	–	2
Hammond, M.A.H.	3	3	–	30	34	11.33	–	–	–	1
Hampton, T.R.G.	3	2	1	1*	1	–	–	–	–	–
Handscomb, P.S.P.	44	72	4	134	2441	35.89	4	17	–	64/4
Hannon-Dalby, O.J.	41	44	17	40	179	6.62	–	–	–	5
Harinath, A.	58	100	5	154	2952	31.07	5	16	–	14
Harmison, B.W.	85	134	10	125	3501	28.23	7	15	–	53
Harris, J.A.R.	102	141	29	87*	2344	20.92	–	10	–	28
Harris, R.J.	82	122	20	94	2056	20.15	–	11	–	41
Harrison, J.	18	30	5	65	436	17.44	–	2	–	4
Hasan Azad	2	3	1	99	149	74.50	–	1	–	1
Hastings, J.W.	66	96	6	93	1992	22.13	–	10	–	28
Hatchett, L.J.	24	32	11	25	204	9.71	–	–	–	9
Hazlewood, J.R.	38	45	16	43*	447	15.41	–	–	–	14
Head, T.M.	33	60	1	98	1886	31.96	–	17	–	10
Hearne, A.G.	5	9	1	88	246	30.75	–	1	–	–
Helm, T.G.	8	12	3	27	90	10.00	–	–	–	2

247

F-C	M	I	NO	HS	Runs	Avge	100	50	1000	Ct/St
Henriques, M.C.	58	95	11	161*	2730	32.50	4	15	–	24
Henry, M.J.	22	29	6	51	479	20.82	–	1	–	9
Hildreth, J.C.	203	332	25	303*	13481	43.91	35	64	5	172
Hilfenhaus, B.W.	103	147	40	56*	1392	13.00	–	3	–	30
Hill, L.J.	9	18	2	126	356	22.25	1	1	–	15
Hobden, M.E.	18	23	10	65*	121	9.30	–	1	–	3
Hodd, A.J.	85	117	20	123	2754	28.39	4	15	–	190/16
Hodgson, D.M.	13	24	2	94*	504	22.90	–	4	–	35/1
Hogan, M.G.	93	134	47	57	1462	16.80	–	2	–	50
Horton, P.J.	164	275	22	209	9521	37.63	21	51	3	168/1
Hosein, H.R.	14	20	2	61	290	16.11	–	–	–	47/1
Howell, B.A.C.	54	84	10	102	1933	26.12	1	11	–	29
Hudson-Prentice, F.J.	1	2	–	15	15	7.50	–	–	–	–
Hughes, A.L.	26	43	7	111*	863	23.97	1	3	–	10
Hughes, C.F.	57	105	4	270*	3128	30.97	7	13	–	41
Hughes, H.C.D.	2	4	–	4	7	1.75	–	–	–	1
Hughes, M.S.T.	1	2	–	116	157	78.50	1	–	–	2
Hughes, P.H.	11	20	3	92	500	29.41	–	4	–	2
Hunn, M.D.	11	12	8	23*	59	14.75	–	–	–	5
Hunt, A.P.	1	1	1	19*	19	–	–	–	–	1
Hutton, B.A.	11	17	3	72	349	24.92	–	1	–	6
Imran Tahir	175	217	54	77*	2343	14.37	–	4	–	74
Ingram, C.A.	92	163	15	190	5638	38.09	12	27	–	68
Jackson, C.F.	1	1	–	26	26	26.00	–	–	–	1
Jarvis, K.M.	47	64	26	48	533	14.02	–	–	–	14
Javid, A.	31	49	6	133	1068	24.83	2	3	–	16
Jayawardena, D.P.M.D.	237	383	24	374	17843	49.70	51	80	0+2	308
Jenkins, W.H.	4	6	–	19	36	6.00	–	–	–	–
Jennings, K.K.	55	98	4	177*	2670	28.40	5	13	–	21
Johnson, M.G.	114	167	31	123*	3135	23.05	2	15	–	37
Jones, G.O.	203	309	29	178	9087	32.45	15	50	2	599/36
Jones, O.J.	5	9	1	83	296	37.00	–	3	–	1
Jones, R.A.	50	76	13	62	723	11.47	–	2	–	18
Jordan, C.J.	78	105	16	92	1939	21.78	–	7	–	95
Joyce, E.C.	231	383	32	231	16505	47.02	41	85	8	213
Junaid Khan	69	94	30	71	700	10.93	–	2	–	11
Kapil, A.	14	24	2	104*	466	21.18	1	1	–	4
Keedy, G.	227	262	128	64	1448	10.80	–	2	–	57
Keogh, R.I.	36	58	5	221	1777	33.52	5	4	–	7
Kerrigan, S.C.	85	97	33	62*	656	10.25	–	1	–	27
Kervezee, A.N.	92	155	8	155	4411	30.00	6	26	1	45
Kettleborough, J.M.	18	32	1	81	811	26.16	–	6	–	10
Key, R.W.T.	299	517	37	270*	19419	40.45	54	76	7	154
Kidd, M.J.L.	2	3	2	4*	5	5.00	–	–	–	–
Kleinveldt, R.K.	111	152	17	115*	2604	19.28	1	12	–	48
Klinger, M.	155	275	26	255	9683	38.88	25	40	1+2	142
Knight, T.C.	4	6	2	25	57	14.25	–	–	–	3
Kohler-Cadmore, T.	19	32	2	130*	873	29.10	1	6	–	23
Kumar, N.R.	11	19	1	103	439	24.38	1	2	–	4
Lake, M.B.	2	4	–	66	82	20.50	–	1	–	1
Latham, T.W.M.	50	90	7	261	3532	42.55	6	23	–	65/1
Lawlor, J.L.	2	3	–	3	3	1.00	–	–	–	–
Lawrence, D.W.	7	12	1	161	409	37.18	1	1	–	8
Leach, J.	40	61	5	114	1419	25.33	1	10	–	9
Leach, M.J.	17	18	6	43	168	14.00	–	–	–	5
Leach, S.G.	4	7	–	41	131	18.71	–	–	–	2

F-C	M	I	NO	HS	Runs	Avge	100	50	1000	Ct/St
Leaning, J.A.	29	45	5	123	1466	36.65	3	7	–	24
Lees, A.Z.	51	82	7	275*	2819	37.58	7	12	1	35
Lester, T.J.	8	9	6	2*	5	1.66	–	–	–	2
Leverock, K.S.	1	2	–	25	34	17.00	–	–	–	–
Levi, R.E.	64	105	12	168	3639	39.12	6	25	–	43
Lewis-Williams, D.E.	1	1	–	0	0	0.00	–	–	–	–
Libby, J.D.	5	9	1	108	238	29.75	1	1	–	1
Liddle, C.J.	25	25	13	53	143	11.91	–	1	–	7
Lilley, A.E.	4	4	1	25	44	14.66	–	–	–	1
Lilley, A.M.	9	10	4	63	269	44.83	–	2	–	3
Linley, T.E.	64	89	20	42	569	8.24	–	–	–	21
Lloyd, D.L.	20	31	7	92	698	29.08	–	3	–	6
Lumb, M.J.	185	312	18	221*	10309	35.06	19	55	3	110
Lyon, N.M.	83	108	41	42	944	14.08	–	–	–	28
Lyth, A.	116	187	8	251	7244	40.46	16	43	2	141
McCarthy, B.J.	2	4	2	38*	55	27.50	–	–	–	2
McClenaghan, M.J.	32	39	13	34	273	10.50	–	–	–	6
McCullum, B.B.	142	248	12	302	8765	37.13	16	44	–	300/19
Macdonell, C.M.	2	3	–	37	56	18.66	–	–	–	–
McInley, H.P.S.	2	2	–	8	12	6.00	–	–	–	3
McIver, J.N.	2	4	–	41	49	12.25	–	–	–	1
McKay, C.J.	56	82	11	65	1404	19.77	–	5	–	16
McKay, P.J.	5	9	1	33	97	12.12	–	–	–	8/1
McKinley, G.K.R.	2	2	–	39	39	19.50	–	–	–	–
McLaren, R.	112	165	30	140	4318	31.98	5	21	–	54
MacLeod, C.S.	23	36	6	84	728	24.26	–	4	–	15
McManus, L.D.	2	4	1	53*	120	40.00	–	1	–	4
Machan, M.W.	35	56	4	192	1785	34.32	5	5	–	12
Madsen, W.L.	128	229	18	231*	8072	38.25	19	43	3	112
Magoffin, S.J.	136	189	49	79	2465	17.60	–	5	–	31
Malan, D.J.	120	204	16	182*	7012	37.29	14	35	2	143
Marsden, J.	5	6	3	9*	13	4.33	–	–	–	4
Marsh, M.R.	51	87	7	211	2546	31.82	4	14	–	28
Marsh, S.E.	110	194	24	166*	6570	38.64	16	30	–	103
Marshall, H.J.H.	238	392	28	170	13240	36.37	26	67	2	119
Masters, D.D.	193	236	35	119	2724	13.55	1	6	–	60
Maxwell, G.J.	35	58	4	155*	2183	40.42	5	12	–	26
Meaker, S.C.	63	82	13	94	1104	16.00	–	6	–	8
Meschede, C.A.J.	45	61	7	107	1312	24.29	2	6	–	17
Mickleburgh, J.C.	91	160	3	243	4328	27.56	6	20	–	62
Middlebrook, J.D.	226	327	43	127	7873	27.72	10	35	–	112
Miles, C.N.	30	40	3	62*	592	16.00	–	2	–	7
Mills, T.S.	32	38	15	31*	260	11.30	–	–	–	9
Milne, A.F.	13	18	9	97	257	28.55	–	1	–	5
Milnes, T.P.	16	19	4	52*	341	22.73	–	1	–	3
Mitchell, D.K.H.	148	266	32	298	9215	39.38	21	39	4	206
Moore, T.C.	7	7	4	17	43	14.33	–	–	–	2
Morgan, E.J.G.	93	153	16	209*	4791	34.97	11	22	1	71/1
Morris, C.A.J.	37	51	27	33*	242	10.08	–	–	–	11
Morris, C.H.	44	65	8	154	1747	30.64	3	8	–	39
Muchall, G.J.	160	279	17	219	7847	29.95	14	38	–	114
Mullaney, S.J.	82	137	6	165*	4144	31.63	7	24	–	71
Munro, C.	37	56	3	281	2671	50.39	9	10	–	20
Munsey, H.G.	1	1	–	27	27	27.00	–	–	–	–
Murphy, D.	59	80	18	135*	1769	28.53	1	11	–	162/14
Murphy, J.R.	2	3	–	22	39	13.00	–	–	–	1

249

F-C	M	I	NO	HS	Runs	Avge	100	50	1000	Ct/St
Murtagh, T.J.	173	232	68	74*	3369	20.54	–	10	–	51
Mustafizur Rahman	12	13	9	14	19	4.75	–	–	–	2
Mustard, P.	188	290	34	130	7613	29.77	6	46	–	625/19
Myburgh, J.G.	105	185	22	203	6607	40.53	15	37	–	61
Mylavarapu, S.V.S.	2	2	–	4	4	2.00	–	–	–	1
Naik, J.K.H.	74	116	27	109*	1854	20.83	1	5	–	40
Napier, G.R.	164	223	41	196	5435	29.86	6	31	–	60
Nash, B.P.	139	229	30	207	7752	38.95	18	32	1	50
Nash, C.D.	157	269	18	184	9590	38.20	19	47	3	82
Neesham, J.D.S.	32	55	5	147	1730	34.60	4	7	–	26
Nevill, P.M.	61	95	19	235*	3181	41.85	6	17	–	183/10
Newton, R.I.	57	98	8	119*	2938	32.64	7	11	–	17
Nijjar, A.S.S.	7	10	5	53	155	31.00	–	1	–	1
Noema-Barnett, K.	53	80	12	107	1975	29.04	2	11	–	22
Norris, M.J.	2	3	–	32	63	21.00	–	–	–	1
Northeast, S.A.	107	187	9	176	6109	34.32	11	37	1	59
Norwell, L.C.	43	56	26	78	377	12.56	–	1	–	10
Nugent, T.M.	1	1	1	4*	4	–	–	–	–	1
O'Brien, K.J.	31	42	4	171*	1214	31.94	1	7	–	28
O'Brien, N.J.	155	248	25	182	7934	35.57	14	42	–	427/44
O'Grady, R.J.	2	4	–	37	72	18.00	–	–	–	–
Oliver, R.K.	20	36	–	179	1052	29.22	2	5	–	10
Onions, G.	144	189	74	41	1557	13.53	–	–	–	30
Overton, C.	33	42	7	99	883	25.22	–	7	–	16
Overton, J.	33	43	14	56	498	17.17	–	3	–	1
Palladino, A.P.	118	162	34	106	2035	15.89	1	7	–	34
Panesar, M.S.	216	266	85	46*	1508	8.33	–	–	–	42
Parnell, W.D.	51	67	5	91	1410	22.74	–	8	–	18
Parry, S.D.	9	10	1	37	138	15.33	–	–	–	2
Patel, A.K.	6	9	–	83	218	24.22	–	1	–	1
Patel, A.R.	1	1	–	61	61	61.00	–	1	–	–
Patel, J.S.	201	254	60	120	4522	23.30	2	23	–	96
Patel, R.H.	20	27	13	26*	171	12.21	–	–	–	5
Patel, S.R.	164	264	15	256	9291	37.31	22	44	3	107
Paternott, L.C.	4	7	–	50	124	17.71	–	1	–	3
Patterson, S.A.	106	117	34	53	1369	16.49	–	1	–	17
Payne, D.A.	50	61	19	62	710	16.90	–	2	–	16
Penrhyn Jones, D.	2	2	1	17	26	26.00	–	–	–	1
Peters, S.D.	260	440	32	222	14231	34.87	31	71	4	192
Petersen, A.N.	205	355	18	286	13247	39.30	38	53	1+2	158
Pettini, M.L.	153	255	39	209	7934	36.73	12	46	1	114
Philander, V.D.	119	155	28	168	3299	25.97	2	10	–	29
Phillips, W.D.B.	1	2	–	14	15	7.50	–	–	–	–
Pietersen, K.P.	217	358	26	355*	16522	49.76	50	71	3	152
Pillans, M.W.	24	34	4	41*	404	13.46	–	–	–	13
Pinner, N.D.	19	31	2	165*	762	26.27	1	4	–	22
Piolet, S.A.	11	19	2	103*	361	21.23	1	–	–	8
Plunkett, L.E.	143	196	36	114	3820	23.87	2	19	–	83
Pollock, A.W.	8	12	2	45	158	15.80	–	–	–	2
Pollock, E.J.	1	1	–	15	15	15.00	–	–	–	–
Porter, J.A.	19	24	7	34	103	6.05	–	–	–	6
Porterfield, W.T.S.	114	188	7	175	5397	29.81	7	30	–	125
Poynton, T.	38	59	6	106	988	18.64	1	5	–	92/9
Poysden, J.E.	5	4	–	47	63	15.75	–	–	–	2
Pratt, D.T.P.	2	2	2	2*	2	–	–	–	–	–
Prince, A.G.	288	465	49	261	18484	44.43	45	90	4+1	221

250

F-C	M	I	NO	HS	Runs	Avge	100	50	1000	Ct/St
Pringle, R.D.	11	21	2	99	553	29.10	–	4	–	3
Procter, L.A.	46	69	5	106	1977	30.89	1	11	–	9
Prowse, I.	2	2	–	15	23	11.50	–	–	–	–
Pujara, C.A.	115	192	29	352	9252	56.76	30	31	0+2	75/1
Pyrah, R.M.	51	61	8	134*	1621	30.58	3	8	–	22
Quinn, M.R.	14	16	2	50	133	9.50	–	1	–	2
Rabada, K.	14	15	3	48*	172	14.33	–	–	–	5
Raine, B.A.	30	52	4	72	986	20.54	–	4	–	7
Rankin, W.B.	88	104	45	56*	551	9.33	–	1	–	23
Rashid, A.U.	139	192	33	180	5678	35.71	10	31	–	68
Ratnayake, D.E.M.	7	12	1	46	172	15.63	–	–	–	4
Rayner, O.P.	102	136	22	143*	2628	23.05	2	12	–	136
Read, C.M.W.	321	485	81	240	15128	37.44	24	85	3	957/50
Redfern, D.J.	85	145	9	133	3905	28.71	2	29	–	41
Reece, L.M.	29	51	5	114*	1503	32.67	1	12	–	17
Rhodes, W.M.H.	11	18	2	79	469	29.31	–	2	–	5
Richardson, M.J.	66	115	7	148	3354	31.05	4	18	2	124/4
Riley, A.E.N.	48	63	21	34	392	9.33	–	–	–	27
Rimmington, N.J.	33	45	13	102*	615	19.21	1	1	–	11
Robinson, O.E.	11	17	3	110	282	20.14	1	–	–	3
Robson, A.J.	36	68	1	120	2224	33.19	2	18	2	24
Robson, S.D.	101	182	15	215*	6325	37.87	14	25	2	100
Roderick, G.H.	45	70	11	171	2378	40.30	4	14	–	122/1
Rogers, C.J.L.	297	529	38	319	24460	49.81	73	116	8+2	236
Roland-Jones, T.S.	66	93	19	103*	1608	21.72	1	5	–	23
Ronchi, L.	88	137	13	148	4736	38.19	13	19	–	314/16
Root, J.E.	79	134	17	236	5904	50.46	15	26	3	57
Root, W.T.	3	5	–	37	80	16.00	–	–	–	–
Rossington, A.M.	29	49	3	116	1468	31.91	3	10	–	65/4
Rouse, A.P.	5	8	–	49	133	16.62	–	–	–	13/2
Rouse, H.P.	4	6	1	23	84	16.80	–	–	–	2
Rouse, T.D.	2	3	–	22	38	12.66	–	–	–	2
Roy, J.J.	62	101	10	143	3374	37.07	6	15	1	63
Rudolph, J.A.	266	457	28	228*	18503	43.13	49	89	4+1	231
Rushworth, C.	73	104	28	46	1034	13.60	–	–	–	14
Russell, C.J.	18	22	4	22	129	7.16	–	–	–	4
Rutherford, H.D.	56	100	1	239	3534	35.69	8	16	0+1	43
Ryder, J.D.	112	186	15	236	7691	44.97	22	34	–	107
Sabin, L.M.	6	11	–	50	190	17.27	–	1	–	2
Saeed Ajmal	142	194	52	53*	1773	12.48	–	4	–	49
Sakande, A.	3	5	–	33	68	13.60	–	–	–	3
Salisbury, M.E.T.	13	19	3	24	124	7.75	–	–	–	3
Salter, A.G.	24	36	6	73	584	19.46	–	2	–	9
Sammy, D.J.G.	96	158	9	121	3549	23.81	2	22	–	137
Sanderson, B.W.	7	8	3	42	57	11.40	–	–	–	2
Sandhu, G.S.	5	3	2	8	21	21.00	–	–	–	–
Sangakkara, K.C.	238	392	28	319	18381	50.49	55	77	0+1	356/33
Santner, M.J.	21	35	3	118	952	29.75	2	6	–	23
Sayer, R.J.	4	3	–	34	58	19.33	–	–	–	1
Scott, G.F.B.	2	3	1	11	16	8.00	–	–	–	1
Scriven, B.R.M.	3	4	1	44*	62	20.66	–	–	–	–
Senanayake, S.M.S.M.	76	95	25	89	1344	19.20	–	4	–	69
Shah, O.A.	252	428	38	203	16357	41.94	45	79	8	200
Shahid Afridi	112	184	4	164	5689	31.60	12	31	–	77
Shahzad, A.	86	118	30	88	2122	24.11	–	6	–	13
Shantry, J.D.	74	97	24	101*	1291	17.68	1	2	–	23

F-C	M	I	NO	HS	Runs	Avge	100	50	1000	Ct/St
Sheikh, A.	8	13	4	12	40	4.44	–	–	–	3
Shreck, C.E.	157	189	97	56	724	7.86	–	1	–	43
Sibley, D.P.	15	24	–	242	662	27.58	1	2	–	12
Siddle, P.M.	124	166	29	103*	2357	17.20	1	5	–	44
Sidebottom, R.J.	213	262	80	61	2552	14.02	–	3	–	61
Simpson, J.A.	99	158	24	143	3984	29.73	4	22	–	303/18
Slater, B.T.	38	72	1	119	2029	28.57	2	14	–	13
Smith, G.M.	124	202	18	177	5635	30.62	7	34	–	43
Smith, G.P.	94	176	8	158*	4542	27.03	8	19	–	75
Smith, R.A.J.	14	17	4	57*	260	20.00	–	1	–	2
Smith, S.P.D.	78	138	17	215	6438	53.20	21	29	–	86
Smith, T.C.	99	147	25	128	3555	29.13	3	22	–	103
Smith, T.M.J.	41	56	11	80	1024	22.75	–	2	–	12
Smith, W.R.	155	262	21	201*	8139	33.77	16	32	1	98
Sohail Tanvir	62	99	9	163	2669	29.65	5	13	–	28
Solanki, V.S.	325	546	33	270	18359	35.78	34	98	6	350
Southee, T.G.	72	103	9	156	1731	18.41	1	5	–	33
Starc, M.A.	53	64	19	99	1021	22.68	–	7	–	27
Steel, C.T.	4	6	–	80	222	37.00	–	2	–	3
Steele, O.J.	6	10	5	53*	175	35.00	–	1	–	4
Stevens, D.I.	250	399	23	208	13117	34.88	29	65	3	182
Stevenson, R.A.	3	3	–	30	34	11.33	–	–	–	–
Stirling, P.R.	35	59	3	146	1682	30.03	4	9	–	18
Stokes, B.A.	82	135	7	185	4370	34.14	10	20	–	47
Stone, O.P.	21	29	7	38	324	14.72	–	–	–	11
Stoneman, M.D.	118	209	5	187	6342	31.08	14	31	3	62
Sykes, J.S.	10	18	3	34	174	11.60	–	–	–	5
Tait, S.W.	50	70	29	68	509	12.41	–	2	–	15
Tavaré, W.A.	37	64	5	139	2077	35.20	4	12	1	23
Taylor, B.R.M.	103	188	10	217	7446	41.83	26	26	1+1	120/4
Taylor, C.J.	1	2	–	26	48	24.00	–	–	–	–
Taylor, J.M.R.	26	38	2	156	941	26.13	2	2	–	12
Taylor, J.W.A.	132	219	28	291	9017	47.20	20	45	5	84
Taylor, L.R.P.L.	119	205	13	217*	8025	41.79	18	43	–	161
Taylor, M.D.	18	23	10	32*	173	13.30	–	–	–	2
Taylor, R.M.L.	40	70	10	101*	1374	22.90	1	6	–	19
Taylor, T.A.I.	15	22	5	49	248	14.58	–	–	–	3
ten Doeschate, R.N.	128	190	28	259*	7638	47.14	21	34	–	76
Terry, S.P.	11	17	2	62*	440	29.33	–	5	–	9
Tetley, J.W.	2	3	–	21	40	13.33	–	–	–	3/1
Thakor, S.J.	36	56	7	134	1637	33.40	2	10	–	10
Thomas, A.C.	164	228	49	119*	4130	23.07	2	14	–	42
Thomas, I.A.A.	19	30	14	13	97	6.06	–	–	–	3
Thompson, H.L.	4	7	–	40	106	15.14	–	–	–	1
Tice, P.J.A.	1	1	–	7	7	7.00	–	–	–	–/1
Tomlinson, J.A.	123	153	69	51	870	10.35	–	1	–	25
Topley, R.J.W.	31	37	17	12	56	2.80	–	–	–	8
Tredwell, J.C.	157	224	25	123*	4250	21.35	3	16	–	175
Trego, P.D.	190	280	35	141	8137	33.21	13	46	–	80
Tremlett, C.T.	146	183	45	90	2462	17.84	–	10	–	38
Trescothick, M.E.	344	591	31	284	23531	42.01	58	118	7	479
Trott, I.J.L.	234	391	40	226	15468	44.06	37	75	6	198
Tye, A.J.	5	4	–	10	24	6.00	–	–	–	1
Umar Akmal	70	119	9	248	4936	44.87	10	29	–	58
van der Gugten, T.	5	7	2	57	77	15.40	–	1	–	1
van der Merwe, R.E.	48	78	12	205*	2422	36.69	3	18	–	38

F-C	M	I	NO	HS	Runs	Avge	100	50	1000	Ct/St
Velani, K.S.	9	14	1	58	310	23.84	–	1	–	3
Vince, J.M.	105	173	18	240	6379	41.15	17	26	2	98
Voges, A.C.	170	290	40	249	11290	45.16	26	60	0+1	235
Wagg, G.G.	130	187	18	200	4455	26.36	3	26	–	42
Wagner, N.	100	134	30	70	1742	16.75	–	6	–	29
Wahab Riaz	110	154	27	84	2185	17.20	–	8	–	34
Wainwright, D.J.	80	112	26	109	2234	25.97	3	9	–	28
Wakefield, C.F.	2	2	–	7	7	3.50	–	–	–	4
Wakely, A.G.	95	149	7	123	4263	30.02	4	25	–	55
Wallace, M.A.	249	395	31	139	10490	28.81	15	49	1	654/55
Waller, M.T.C.	8	9	1	28	91	11.37	–	–	–	5
Warner, D.A.	64	114	5	211	5362	49.19	18	25	–	43
Watkinson, L.	2	2	–	35	55	27.50	–	–	–	1
Watling, B.J.	106	188	23	164*	6444	39.05	13	39	–	220/5
Watson, S.R.	137	241	19	203*	9451	42.57	20	54	–	109
Webb, J.P.	6	12	–	38	95	7.91	–	–	–	4
Webb, L.A.	2	4	–	32	68	17.00	–	–	–	–
Weighell, W.J.	2	4	–	25	69	17.25	–	–	–	–
Weller, S.D.	4	7	2	18*	47	9.40	–	–	–	1
Wells, L.W.P.	81	138	8	208	4299	33.06	9	20	1	44
Wells, T.J.	12	20	1	82	307	16.15	–	1	–	6
Wessels, M.H.	157	262	22	199	8627	35.94	17	45	2	252/14
Westaway, S.A.	4	7	2	63*	167	33.40	–	1	–	20
Westley, T.	109	186	15	185	5614	32.83	10	27	–	73
Weston, L.P.	2	3	–	7	8	2.66	–	–	–	5
Westphal, A.A.	4	3	1	5*	11	5.50	–	–	–	–
Westwood, I.J.	144	242	21	196	7382	33.40	14	39	–	79
Wheal, B.T.J.	4	6	1	10	17	3.40	–	–	–	1
Wheater, A.J.A.	93	136	16	164	4373	36.44	8	25	–	142/7
Wheeler, B.M.	29	34	5	81*	527	18.17	–	3	–	15
White, G.G.	30	46	5	65	498	12.14	–	2	–	9
White, H.J.	1	1	–	3	3	3.00	–	–	–	–
White, R.G.	2	2	–	4	4	2.00	–	–	–	1
White, W.A.	82	130	18	101*	2666	23.80	1	13	–	24
Whiteley, R.A.	52	82	8	130*	2037	27.52	3	9	–	28
Whittingham, S.G.	1	1	–	0	0	0.00	–	–	–	–
Willey, D.J.	58	82	10	104*	2052	28.50	2	14	–	14
Williams, B.P.R.	1	2	1	0*	0	0.00	–	–	–	–
Williams, D.R.	1	–	–	–	–	–	–	–	–	1
Williamson, K.S.	99	172	12	284*	7492	46.82	20	37	–	93
Wilson, G.C.	76	112	19	160*	3366	36.19	3	20	–	144/5
Winslade, J.R.	2	–	–	–	–	–	–	–	–	–
Winter, M.J.	4	6	–	56	182	30.33	–	2	–	2
Woakes, C.R.	105	148	37	152*	4098	36.91	8	16	–	46
Wood, C.P.	36	51	5	105*	1169	25.41	1	6	–	12
Wood, J.M.	2	2	2	2*	2	–	–	–	–	–
Wood, L.	12	18	3	100	437	29.13	1	2	–	2
Wood, M.A.	30	48	12	66	772	21.44	–	2	–	9
Wood, S.K.W.	3	4	1	45	77	25.66	–	–	–	–
Wright, A.R.	2	3	–	8	8	2.66	–	–	–	1
Wright, B.J.	89	146	10	172	3684	27.08	6	16	–	47
Wright, C.J.C.	112	138	35	77	1909	18.53	–	9	–	18
Wright, L.J.	115	176	22	226*	6289	40.83	16	31	1	51
Wylie, B.A.	6	10	3	29*	78	11.14	–	–	–	5
Yardy, M.H.	193	320	27	257	10693	36.49	23	50	2	184
Yasir Arafat	200	291	41	170	6784	27.13	5	35	–	53

F-C	M	I	NO	HS	Runs	Avge	100	50	1000	Ct/St
Zaib, S.A.	2	2	–	21	21	10.50	–	–	–	–
Zain Shahzad	4	6	–	16	44	7.33	–	–	–	–

BOWLING

'50wS' denotes instances of taking 50 or more wickets in a season. Where these have been achieved outside the British Isles they are shown after a plus sign.

	Runs	Wkts	Avge	Best	5wI	10wM	50wS
Abbott, K.J.	4942	232	21.30	8-45	14	2	0+1
Abdur Rehman	14601	539	27.08	9-65	25	5	0+1
Abell, T.B.	22	1	22.00	1-11	–	–	–
Adair, M.R.	61	1	61.00	1-61	–	–	–
Adams, A.R.	16581	692	23.96	7-32	32	6	3
Adams, J.H.K.	718	13	55.23	2-16	–	–	–
Adeel Malik	573	12	47.75	3-39	–	–	–
Agathangelou, A.P.	469	10	46.90	2-18	–	–	–
Akram, B.M.R.	242	2	121.00	2-82	–	–	–
Ali, A.M.	19	0	–				
Ali, M.M.	7862	195	40.31	6-29	5	1	–
Allenby, J.	7279	277	26.27	6-54	5	1	1
Ambrose, T.R.	1	0	–				
Amla, H.M.	277	1	277.00	1-10	–	–	–
Anderson, C.J.	1450	35	41.42	5-22	1	–	–
Anderson, J.M.	19073	708	26.93	7-43	35	5	3
Andrew, G.M.	7793	231	33.73	5-40	6	–	1
Ansari, Z.S.	3513	100	35.13	6-30	5	–	–
Arif, A.T.	315	7	45.00	2-29	–	–	–
Arksey, J.B.T.	32	1	32.00	1-32	–	–	–
Arshad, U.	824	36	22.88	4-78	–	–	–
Ashar Zaidi	2699	89	30.32	4-50	–	–	–
Azhar Mahmood	15337	611	25.10	8-61	27	3	0+1
Azharullah, M.	8620	306	28.16	7-74	14	2	0+1
Bailey, G.J.	46	0	–				
Bailey, T.E.	1531	42	36.45	5-12	1	–	–
Bairstow, J.M.	1	0	–				
Balbirnie, A.	95	2	47.50	1- 5	–	–	–
Ball, A.J.	1233	26	47.42	3-36	–	–	–
Ball, J.T.	1630	58	28.10	6-49	1	–	–
Ballance, G.S.	143	0	–				
Barker, K.H.D.	6020	227	26.51	6-40	11	1	2
Barnard, E.G.	345	12	28.75	3-63	–	–	–
Barrow, A.W.R.	36	1	36.00	1- 4	–	–	–
Batty, G.J.	19313	584	33.07	8-68	24	2	2
Beer, W.A.T.	519	13	39.92	3-31	–	–	–
Bell, I.R.	1598	47	34.00	4- 4	–	–	–
Bell-Drummond, D.J.	54	0	–				
Berg, G.K.	5722	183	31.26	6-58	3	–	–
Billings, S.W.	4	0	–				
Bird, J.M.	3710	152	24.40	6-25	7	2	0+1
Bishnoi, C.	416	7	59.42	3-71	–	–	–
Blake, A.J.	129	3	43.00	2- 9	–	–	–
Blofield, A.D.	235	3	78.33	2-33	–	–	–
Bopara, R.S.	7107	181	39.26	5-75	1	–	–
Borthwick, S.G.	5682	163	34.85	6-70	2	–	–
Boult, T.A.	5660	219	25.84	6-40	11	1	–

F-C	Runs	Wkts	Avge	Best	5wI	10wM	50wS
Boyce, M.A.G.	72	0	–				
Bracewell, D.A.J.	6704	198	33.85	7- 35	6	–	–
Bragg, W.D.	430	5	86.00	2- 10	–	–	–
Brand, N.	67	0	–				
Bravo, D.J.	5918	177	33.43	6- 11	7	–	–
Bresnan, T.T.	13930	446	31.23	5- 42	7	–	–
Briggs, D.R.	6139	191	32.14	6- 45	6	–	–
Broad, S.C.J.	14757	531	27.79	8- 15	25	3	–
Brooks, J.A.	7991	300	26.63	5- 23	10	–	2
Broom, N.T.	394	5	78.80	1- 8	–	–	–
Brown, B.C.	45	0	–				
Brown, K.R.	65	2	32.50	2- 30	–	–	–
Browne, N.L.J.	163	0	–				
Buck, N.L.	5877	156	37.67	5- 76	4	–	–
Bull, K.A.	483	9	53.66	4- 62	–	–	–
Burgoyne, P.I.	1029	17	60.52	3- 27	–	–	–
Burke, J.E.	415	18	23.05	4- 19	–	–	–
Burns, J.A.	16	0	–				
Burns, R.J.	120	2	60.00	1- 18	–	–	–
Buttler, J.C.	11	0	–				
Cachopa, C.	73	0	–				
Carberry, M.A.	1069	17	62.88	2- 85	–	–	–
Carter, A.	2544	91	27.95	5- 40	2	–	–
Carter, M.	195	10	19.50	7- 56	1	1	–
Carver, K.	140	7	20.00	2- 6	–	–	–
Cato, S.J.	139	4	34.75	2- 43	–	–	–
Chambers, M.A.	5383	155	34.72	6- 68	3	1	–
Chappell, Z.J.	106	2	53.00	1- 35	–	–	–
Chapple, G.	26314	985	26.71	7- 53	39	3	7
Chopra, V.	116	0	–				
Christian, D.T.	4468	122	36.62	5- 24	2	–	–
Clare, J.L.	4268	154	27.71	7- 74	6	1	–
Clark, J.	880	19	46.31	4-101	–	–	–
Clarke, M.J.	1886	42	44.90	6- 9	2	–	–
Clarke, R.	11067	331	33.43	6- 63	3	–	–
Claydon, M.E.	6566	202	32.50	6-104	5	–	1
Cobb, J.J.	1179	13	90.69	2- 11	–	–	–
Cockbain, I.A.	1	0	–				
Coetzer, K.J.	414	7	59.14	2- 16	–	–	–
Coles, M.T.	7323	262	27.95	6- 51	9	2	2
Collingwood, P.D.	5943	154	38.59	5- 52	2	–	–
Compton, N.R.D.	227	3	75.66	1- 1	–	–	–
Cook, A.N.	211	7	30.14	3- 13	–	–	–
Cooper, T.L.W.	869	16	54.31	5- 76	1	–	–
Cosgrove, M.J.	2014	47	42.85	3- 3	–	–	–
Cosker, D.A.	21683	597	36.31	6- 91	12	1	1
Cotton, B.D.	856	23	37.21	4- 20	–	–	–
Coughlin, P.	830	29	28.62	4- 10	–	–	–
Cowdrey, F.K.	129	3	43.00	3- 59	–	–	–
Craig, M.D.	4152	102	40.70	7- 94	4	1	–
Crane, M.S.	336	10	33.60	5- 35	1	–	–
Crichard, R.J.	243	7	34.71	5- 62	1	–	–
Critchley, M.J.J.	363	4	90.75	3- 50	–	–	–
Croft, S.J.	2690	69	38.98	6- 41	1	–	–
Crook, S.P.	6968	181	38.49	5- 48	3	–	–
Cummins, P.J.	776	26	29.84	6- 79	1	–	–

F-C	Runs	Wkts	Avge	Best	5wI	10wM	50wS
Curran, S.M.	575	22	26.13	5- 67	2	–	–
Curran, T.K.	2280	95	24.00	7- 20	6	1	1
Davey, J.H.	382	15	25.46	4- 53	–	–	–
Davis, W.S.	81	3	27.00	3- 63	–	–	–
Dawson, L.A.	3995	110	36.31	7- 51	3	–	–
Denly, J.L.	1394	28	49.78	3- 43	–	–	–
Dent, C.D.J.	476	4	119.00	1- 4	–	–	–
Dernbach, J.W.	8734	267	32.71	6- 47	10	–	1
Dexter, N.J.	3611	105	34.39	6- 63	3	–	–
Dibble, A.J.	205	5	41.00	3- 42	–	–	–
Dickson, S.R.	40	2	20.00	1- 15	–	–	–
Dilshan, T.M.	3258	90	36.20	5- 49	1	–	–
Dockrell, G.H.	3743	126	29.70	6- 27	6	–	–
D'Oliveira, B.L.	716	14	51.14	5- 48	1	–	–
Duffy, J.A.	2097	65	32.26	6- 83	3	–	–
Dunn, M.P.	3143	94	33.43	5- 48	3	–	–
Durston, W.J.	4354	110	39.58	6-109	4	–	–
Eckersley, E.J.H.	58	2	29.00	2- 29	–	–	–
Edwards, F.H.	9914	314	31.57	7- 87	19	2	–
Edwards, G.A.	346	8	43.25	4- 44	–	–	–
Elgar, D.	2032	40	50.80	4- 25	–	–	–
Elliott, G.D.	3378	92	36.71	5- 33	1	–	–
Ellis-Grewal, J.S.E.	201	6	33.50	4-118	–	–	–
Elstone, S.L.	346	10	34.60	3- 68	–	–	–
Ervine, S.M.	11279	271	41.61	6- 82	5	–	–
Evans, L.J.	259	2	129.50	1- 29	–	–	–
Faulkner, J.P.	4039	170	23.75	5- 5	5	–	–
Fawad Ahmed	4112	134	30.68	8- 89	6	–	–
Fell, T.C.	7	0	–				
Finch, A.J.	247	4	61.75	1- 0	–	–	–
Finch, H.Z.	15	0	–				
Finn, S.T.	12081	428	28.22	9- 37	12	1	2
Fisher, M.D.	243	5	48.60	2- 61	–	–	–
Fletcher, L.J.	6163	213	28.93	5- 52	3	–	–
Foakes, B.T.	6	0	–				
Footitt, M.H.A.	7019	274	25.61	7- 71	16	1	2
Foster, J.S.	128	1	128.00	1-122	–	–	–
Franklin, J.E.C.	12503	456	27.41	7- 14	14	1	–
Freckingham, O.H.	2466	65	37.93	6-125	2	–	–
Fuller, J.K.	3424	101	33.90	6- 24	4	1	–
Gabriel, S.T.	4958	166	29.86	5- 29	3	–	–
Gale, A.W.	238	1	238.00	1- 33	–	–	–
Gamble, R.N.	327	4	81.75	1- 41	–	–	–
Gatting, J.S.	159	2	79.50	1- 8	–	–	–
Gayle, C.H.	5194	132	39.34	5- 34	2	–	–
Gidman, A.P.R.	4538	103	44.05	4- 47	–	–	–
Gidman, W.R.S.	4651	198	23.48	6- 15	9	1	2
Gleeson, R.J.	137	4	34.25	2- 35	–	–	–
Gnodde, J.S.D.	21	0	–				
Godleman, B.A.	35	0	–				
Gordon, R.O.	413	13	31.76	4- 53	–	–	–
Grant, S.E.	180	1	180.00	1- 42	–	–	–
Gregory, L.	3281	111	29.55	6- 47	7	1	–
Griffiths, D.A.	3828	113	33.87	6- 63	4	–	–
Griffiths, S.W.	340	3	113.33	2- 63	–	–	–
Groenewald, T.D.	9087	296	30.69	6- 50	12	–	–

256

F-C	Runs	Wkts	Avge	Best	5wI	10wM	50wS
Grundy, J.O.	136	3	45.33	2- 41	–	–	–
Gubbins, N.R.T.	10	0	–				
Guptill, M.J.	542	7	77.42	3- 37	–	–	–
Gurney, H.F.	5977	188	31.79	5- 43	4	–	–
Haggett, C.J.	2052	59	34.77	4- 43	–	–	–
Hales, A.D.	171	3	57.00	2- 63	–	–	–
Hameed, H.	9	0	–				
Hammond, M.A.H.	196	1	196.00	1- 96	–	–	–
Hampton, T.R.G.	213	2	106.50	1- 15	–	–	–
Handscomb, P.S.P.	21	0	–				
Hannon-Dalby, O.J.	3257	86	37.87	5- 68	2	–	–
Harinath, A.	131	5	26.20	2- 1	–	–	–
Harmison, B.W.	1512	37	40.86	4- 27	–	–	–
Harris, J.A.R.	9854	345	28.56	9- 34	12	2	2
Harris, R.J.	8045	303	26.55	7- 60	10	–	–
Harrison, J.	1573	52	30.25	5- 31	2	–	–
Hastings, J.W.	5672	209	27.13	7- 60	7	–	–
Hatchett, L.J.	2314	66	35.06	5- 47	2	–	–
Hazlewood, J.R.	3382	139	24.33	6- 50	3	–	–
Head, T.M.	343	5	68.60	3- 49	–	–	–
Helm, T.G.	605	20	30.25	3- 46	–	–	–
Henriques, M.C.	2844	96	29.62	5- 17	2	–	–
Henry, M.J.	2271	90	25.23	5- 18	5	–	–
Hildreth, J.C.	492	6	82.00	2- 39	–	–	–
Hilfenhaus, B.W.	11268	386	29.19	7- 58	13	1	0+1
Hill, L.J.	6	0	–				
Hobden, M.E.	1889	48	39.35	5- 62	2	–	–
Hodd, A.J.	7	0	–				
Hogan, M.G.	9055	365	24.80	7- 92	15	1	2
Horton, P.J.	23	0	–				
Howell, B.A.C.	2591	82	31.59	5- 57	1	–	–
Hudson-Prentice, F.J.	51	0	–				
Hughes, A.L.	951	21	45.28	4- 46	–	–	–
Hughes, C.F.	781	18	43.38	2- 9	–	–	–
Hunn, M.D.	977	29	33.68	5- 99	1	–	–
Hunt, A.P.	73	2	36.50	1- 35	–	–	–
Hutton, B.A.	1090	38	28.68	5- 29	2	1	–
Imran Tahir	18923	715	26.46	8- 76	48	10	2+2
Ingram, C.A.	1741	44	39.56	4- 16	–	–	–
Jarvis, K.M.	4981	197	25.28	7- 35	12	1	1
Javid, A.	340	3	113.33	1- 1	–	–	–
Jayawardena, D.P.M.D.	1629	52	31.32	5- 72	1	–	–
Jenkins, W.H.	249	3	83.00	2- 27	–	–	–
Jennings, K.K.	291	7	41.57	2- 8	–	–	–
Johnson, M.G.	12912	453	28.50	8- 61	17	4	–
Jones, G.O.	26	0	–				
Jones, O.J.	323	10	32.30	4- 70	–	–	–
Jones, R.A.	4602	150	30.68	7-115	5	–	–
Jordan, C.J.	7300	231	31.60	7- 43	8	–	1
Joyce, E.C.	1033	11	93.90	2- 34	–	–	–
Junaid Khan	7016	293	23.94	7- 46	20	3	0+1
Kapil, A.	408	14	29.14	3- 17	–	–	–
Keedy, G.	21851	696	31.39	7- 68	35	7	4
Keogh, R.I.	1304	25	52.16	3- 35	–	–	–
Kerrigan, S.C.	7842	270	29.04	9- 51	11	2	2
Kervezee, A.N.	265	5	53.00	3- 72	–	–	–

F-C	Runs	Wkts	Avge	Best	5wI	10wM	50wS
Key, R.W.T.	331	3	110.33	2- 31	–	–	–
Kidd, M.J.L.	154	1	154.00	1- 77	–	–	–
Kleinveldt, R.K.	9534	337	28.29	8- 47	15	1	1
Klinger, M.	3	0	–				
Knight, T.C.	164	2	82.00	2- 32	–	–	–
Kumar, N.R.	327	7	46.71	3- 58	–	–	–
Lake, M.B.	114	4	28.50	2- 41	–	–	–
Latham, T.W.M.	6	0	–				
Lawlor, J.L.	11	0	–				
Leach, J.	3292	110	29.92	6- 73	3	–	1
Leach, M.J.	1212	39	31.07	7-106	2	1	–
Leach, S.G.	2	0	–				
Leaning, J.A.	187	1	187.00	1- 82	–	–	–
Lees, A.Z.	26	0	–				
Lester, T.J.	702	9	78.00	3- 50	–	–	–
Leverock, K.S.	92	1	92.00	1- 61	–	–	–
Lewis-Williams, D.E.	98	1	98.00	1- 98	–	–	–
Libby, J.D.	104	1	104.00	1- 18	–	–	–
Liddle, C.J.	1736	34	51.05	3- 42	–	–	–
Lilley, A.E.	292	12	24.33	5- 41	1	–	–
Lilley, A.M.	963	28	34.39	5- 23	1	–	–
Linley, T.E.	5519	200	27.59	6- 57	6	1	1
Lloyd, D.L.	1068	25	42.72	3- 68	–	–	–
Lumb, M.J.	255	6	42.50	2- 10	–	–	–
Lyon, N.M.	9630	255	37.76	7- 94	7	1	–
Lyth, A.	750	18	41.66	2- 15	–	–	–
McCarthy, B.J.	154	4	38.50	2- 51	–	–	–
McClenaghan, M.J.	3722	95	39.17	8- 23	3	–	–
McCullum, B.B.	75	1	75.00	1- 1	–	–	–
Macdonell, C.M.	120	0	–				
McInley, H.P.S.	153	1	153.00	1- 30	–	–	–
McIver, J.N.	118	3	39.33	3- 64	–	–	–
McKay, C.J.	5536	200	27.68	6- 40	6	–	1
McKinley, G.K.R.	201	4	50.25	3- 67	–	–	–
McLaren, R.	9294	348	26.70	8- 38	13	1	1+1
MacLeod, C.S.	358	15	23.86	4- 66	–	–	–
Machan, M.W.	100	1	100.00	1- 36	–	–	–
Madsen, W.L.	581	11	52.81	3- 45	–	–	–
Magoffin, S.J.	12180	514	23.69	8- 20	21	3	4
Malan, D.J.	1823	43	42.39	5- 61	1	–	–
Marsden, J.	435	13	33.46	4- 65	–	–	–
Marsh, M.R.	2110	79	26.70	6- 84	1	–	–
Marsh, S.E.	138	2	69.00	2- 20	–	–	–
Marshall, H.J.H.	1865	42	44.40	4- 24	–	–	–
Masters, D.D.	16081	632	25.44	8- 10	30	–	4
Maxwell, G.J.	1922	49	39.22	4- 42	–	–	–
Meaker, S.C.	6218	215	28.92	8- 52	11	2	1
Meschede, C.A.J.	3302	92	35.89	4- 43	–	–	–
Mickleburgh, J.C.	50	0	–				
Middlebrook, J.D.	18123	475	38.15	6- 78	15	1	1
Miles, C.N.	2977	113	26.34	6- 63	8	1	1
Mills, T.S.	2008	55	36.50	4- 25	–	–	–
Milne, A.F.	1192	39	30.56	5- 47	1	–	–
Milnes, T.P.	1019	27	37.74	7- 39	1	–	–
Mitchell, D.K.H.	887	19	46.68	4- 49	–	–	–
Moore, T.C.	515	14	36.78	4- 78	–	–	–

258

F-C	Runs	Wkts	Avge	Best	5wI	10wM	50wS
Morgan, E.J.G.	90	2	45.00	2- 24	–	–	–
Morris, C.A.J.	3494	116	30.12	5- 54	2	–	2
Morris, C.H.	3434	145	23.68	8- 44	2	1	–
Muchall, G.J.	633	15	42.20	3- 26	–	–	–
Mullaney, S.J.	1922	49	39.22	4- 31	–	–	–
Munro, C.	1202	35	34.34	4- 36	–	–	–
Murphy, D.	3	0	–				
Murphy, J.R.	135	2	67.50	2- 90	–	–	–
Murtagh, T.J.	16016	592	27.05	7- 82	26	4	6
Mustafizur Rahman	649	32	20.28	5- 28	1	–	–
Mustard, P.	9	1	9.00	1- 9	–	–	–
Myburgh, J.G.	2138	45	47.51	4- 56	–	–	–
Mylavarapu, S.V.S.	209	9	23.22	5- 23	1	–	–
Naik, J.K.H.	6510	168	38.75	8-179	6	–	–
Napier, G.R.	13221	421	31.40	7- 21	12	–	2
Nash, B.P.	801	23	34.82	2- 7	–	–	–
Nash, C.D.	3115	75	41.53	4- 12	–	–	–
Neesham, J.D.S.	2202	70	31.45	5- 65	2	–	–
Nevill, P.M.	8	0	–				
Newton, R.I.	25	0	–				
Nijjar, A.S.S.	489	12	40.75	2- 33	–	–	–
Noema-Barnett, K.	2725	83	32.83	4- 20	–	–	–
Northeast, S.A.	145	1	145.00	1- 60	–	–	–
Norwell, L.C.	4330	145	29.86	6- 33	5	1	1
Nugent, T.M.	107	3	35.66	2- 32	–	–	–
O'Brien, K.J.	823	27	30.48	5- 39	1	–	–
O'Brien, N.J.	19	2	9.50	1- 4	–	–	–
Onions, G.	13895	528	26.31	9- 67	24	3	6
Overton, C.	2650	102	25.98	6- 74	2	–	–
Overton, J.	2831	69	41.02	6- 95	1	–	–
Palladino, A.P.	9473	322	29.41	7- 53	11	–	2
Panesar, M.S.	21710	704	30.83	7- 60	39	6	6
Parnell, W.D.	4447	135	32.94	7- 56	3	–	–
Parry, S.D.	650	18	36.11	5- 23	1	–	–
Patel, A.R.	88	5	17.60	5- 88	1	–	–
Patel, J.S.	19655	547	35.93	7- 38	19	1	4
Patel, R.H.	1942	56	34.67	5- 69	1	–	–
Patel, S.R.	9523	238	40.01	7- 68	3	1	–
Patterson, S.A.	7752	280	27.68	5- 11	5	–	2
Payne, D.A.	4271	127	33.62	6- 26	2	–	–
Penrhyn Jones, D.	190	5	38.00	3- 55	–	–	–
Peters, S.D.	31	1	31.00	1- 19	–	–	–
Petersen, A.N.	838	16	52.37	3- 58	–	–	–
Pettini, M.L.	263	1	263.00	1- 72	–	–	–
Philander, V.D.	9304	432	21.53	7- 61	20	2	0+2
Phillips, W.D.B.	93	2	46.50	2- 53	–	–	–
Pietersen, K.P.	3760	73	51.50	4- 31	–	–	–
Pillans, M.W.	2032	84	24.19	6- 67	2	1	0+1
Pinner, N.D.	32	0	–				
Piolet, S.A.	570	19	30.00	6- 17	1	1	–
Plunkett, L.E.	13469	435	30.96	6- 33	11	1	3
Pollock, A.W.	874	25	34.96	4- 43	–	–	–
Porter, J.A.	1673	62	26.98	4- 28	–	–	1
Porterfield, W.T.S.	138	2	69.00	1- 29	–	–	–
Poynton, T.	96	2	48.00	2- 96	–	–	–
Poysden, J.E.	429	6	71.50	3- 20	–	–	–

F-C	Runs	Wkts	Avge	Best	5wI	10wM	50wS
Pratt, D.T.P.	155	5	31.00	2- 51	–	–	–
Prince, A.G.	179	4	44.75	2- 11	–	–	–
Pringle, R.D.	674	22	30.63	5- 63	1	–	–
Procter, L.A.	1883	58	32.46	7- 71	2	–	–
Prowse, I.	121	2	60.50	1- 12	–	–	–
Pujara, C.A.	115	5	23.00	2- 4	–	–	–
Pyrah, R.M.	2527	55	45.94	5- 58	1	–	–
Quinn, M.R.	1556	53	29.35	4- 41	–	–	–
Rabada, K.	1344	60	22.40	9- 33	2	1	–
Raine, B.A.	2710	88	30.79	5- 43	2	–	1
Rankin, W.B.	7760	291	26.66	6- 55	8	–	1
Rashid, A.U.	13976	410	34.08	7-107	18	1	2
Ratnayake, D.E.M.	206	6	34.33	3- 72	–	–	–
Rayner, O.P.	7114	203	35.04	8- 46	7	1	–
Read, C.M.W.	90	0	–				
Redfern, D.J.	815	21	38.80	3- 33	–	–	–
Reece, L.M.	542	14	38.71	4- 28	–	–	–
Rhodes, W.M.H.	311	12	25.91	3- 42	–	–	–
Richardson, M.J.	13	0	–				
Riley, A.E.N.	4036	115	35.09	7-150	5	–	1
Rimmington, N.J.	2684	98	27.38	5- 27	3	–	–
Robinson, O.E.	1137	46	24.71	6- 33	1	–	–
Robson, A.J.	95	0	–				
Robson, S.D.	98	2	49.00	1- 4	–	–	–
Rogers, C.J.L.	133	1	133.00	1- 16	–	–	–
Roland-Jones, T.S.	6126	248	24.70	6- 50	12	2	1
Root, J.E.	1186	24	49.41	3- 33	–	–	–
Root, W.T.	6	0	–				
Rossington, A.M.	6	0	–				
Rouse, H.P.	425	6	70.83	3- 45	–	–	–
Rouse, T.D.	64	2	32.00	1- 3	–	–	–
Roy, J.J.	495	14	35.35	3- 9	–	–	–
Rudolph, J.A.	2637	59	44.69	5- 80	3	–	–
Rushworth, C.	6470	278	23.27	9- 52	16	2	3
Russell, C.J.	1566	38	41.21	4- 43	–	–	–
Rutherford, H.D.	32	0	–				
Ryder, J.D.	4143	149	27.80	6- 47	7	2	–
Sabin, L.M.	5	0	–				
Saeed Ajmal	15037	562	26.75	7- 19	38	7	1+1
Sakande, A.	279	9	31.00	3- 38	–	–	–
Salisbury, M.E.T.	995	19	52.36	4- 50	–	–	–
Salter, A.G.	2100	43	48.83	3- 5	–	–	–
Sammy, D.J.G.	6312	217	29.08	7- 66	10	–	–
Sanderson, B.W.	413	17	24.29	5- 50	1	–	–
Sandhu, G.S.	357	7	51.00	4- 49	–	–	–
Sangakkara, K.C.	150	1	150.00	1- 13	–	–	–
Santner, M.J.	1390	25	55.60	3- 51	–	–	–
Sayer, R.J.	352	4	88.00	2- 59	–	–	–
Scott, G.F.B.	121	2	60.50	2- 67	–	–	–
Senanayake, S.M.S.M.	7786	385	20.22	8- 70	32	6	0+3
Shah, O.A.	1505	26	57.88	3- 33	–	–	–
Shahid Afridi	7051	263	26.80	6-101	8	–	–
Shahzad, A.	7601	227	33.48	5- 46	4	–	–
Shantry, J.D.	6359	232	27.40	7- 60	11	2	2
Sheikh, A.	872	22	39.63	4- 97	–	–	–
Shreck, C.E.	16715	531	31.47	8- 31	23	2	4

F-C	Runs	Wkts	Avge	Best	5wI	10wM	50wS
Sibley, D.P.	64	1	64.00	1- 41	–	–	–
Siddle, P.M.	11867	426	27.85	8- 54	17	–	0+1
Sidebottom, R.J.	16963	706	24.02	7- 37	29	4	4
Slater, B.T.	36	0	–				
Smith, G.M.	6502	184	35.33	5- 42	4	–	–
Smith, G.P.	73	1	73.00	1- 64	–	–	–
Smith, R.A.J.	1095	28	39.10	3- 23	–	–	–
Smith, S.P.D.	3316	63	52.63	7- 64	1	–	–
Smith, T.C.	6508	226	28.79	6- 46	6	–	1
Smith, T.M.J.	3378	65	51.96	4- 35	–	–	–
Smith, W.R.	993	23	43.17	3- 34	–	–	–
Sohail Tanvir	6770	275	24.61	8- 54	18	3	0+1
Solanki, V.S.	4230	90	47.00	5- 40	4	1	–
Southee, T.G.	7399	269	27.50	8- 27	11	1	–
Starc, M.A.	5094	174	29.27	6- 51	7	–	–
Steel, C.T.	92	1	92.00	1- 39	–	–	–
Stevens, D.I.	8955	319	28.07	7- 21	12	1	2
Stevenson, R.A.	215	3	71.66	1- 15	–	–	–
Stirling, P.R.	593	15	39.53	2- 31	–	–	–
Stokes, B.A.	5485	180	30.47	7- 67	4	1	–
Stone, O.P.	1871	62	30.17	5- 44	2	–	–
Stoneman, M.D.	122	0	–				
Sykes, J.S.	1114	20	55.70	4-176	–	–	–
Tait, S.W.	5661	198	28.59	7- 29	7	1	0+1
Tavaré, W.A.	30	0	–				
Taylor, B.R.M.	225	4	56.25	2- 36	–	–	–
Taylor, J.M.R.	1659	39	42.53	4-125	–	–	–
Taylor, J.W.A.	176	0	–				
Taylor, L.R.P.L.	364	6	60.66	2- 4	–	–	–
Taylor, M.D.	1753	39	44.94	5- 75	2	–	–
Taylor, R.M.L.	3420	85	40.23	5- 55	3	–	–
Taylor, T.A.I.	1397	43	32.48	6- 61	2	–	–
ten Doeschate, R.N.	6596	195	33.82	6- 20	7	–	–
Thakor, S.J.	1463	29	50.44	3- 57	–	–	–
Thomas, A.C.	14412	547	26.34	7- 54	25	2	1
Thomas, I.A.A.	1390	43	32.32	4- 48	–	–	–
Thompson, H.L.	6	0	–				
Tomlinson, J.A.	11713	368	31.82	8- 46	12	1	2
Topley, R.J.W.	3223	125	25.78	6- 29	7	2	–
Tredwell, J.C.	14112	391	36.09	8- 66	12	3	1
Trego, P.D.	13091	367	35.67	7- 84	4	1	1
Tremlett, C.T.	13158	459	28.66	8- 96	13	–	–
Trescothick, M.E.	1551	36	43.08	4- 36	–	–	–
Trott, I.J.L.	3160	65	48.61	7- 39	1	–	–
Tye, A.J.	421	13	32.38	3- 47	–	–	–
Umar Akmal	286	5	57.20	2- 24	–	–	–
van der Gugten, T.	448	17	26.35	7- 68	2	1	–
van der Merwe, R.E.	2959	72	41.09	4- 59	–	–	–
Velani, K.S.	21	0	–				
Vince, J.M.	860	19	45.26	5- 41	1	–	–
Voges, A.C.	1761	52	33.86	4- 92	–	–	–
Wagg, G.G.	13083	385	33.98	6- 29	11	1	2
Wagner, N.	11225	414	27.11	7- 46	20	1	0+2
Wahab Riaz	10408	373	27.90	9- 59	15	5	0+2
Wainwright, D.J.	6879	179	38.43	6- 33	6	–	1
Wakely, A.G.	339	6	56.50	2- 62	–	–	–

261

F-C	Runs	Wkts	Avge	Best	5wI	10wM	50wS
Wallace, M.A.	3	0	–				
Waller, M.T.C.	493	10	49.30	3- 33	–	–	–
Warner, D.A.	433	6	72.16	2- 45	–	–	–
Watkinson, L.	137	2	68.50	1- 32	–	–	–
Watling, B.J.	8	0	–				
Watson, S.R.	6294	210	29.97	7- 69	7	1	–
Weighell, W.J.	179	1	179.00	1- 72	–	–	–
Weller, S.D.	247	11	22.45	3- 26	–	–	–
Wells, L.W.P.	1595	37	43.10	3- 35	–	–	–
Wells, T.J.	575	10	57.50	3- 68	–	–	–
Wessels, M.H.	115	3	38.33	1- 10	–	–	–
Westley, T.	2046	44	46.50	4- 55	–	–	–
Westphal, A.A.	251	8	31.37	3- 45	–	–	–
Westwood, I.J.	318	7	45.42	2- 39	–	–	–
Wheal, B.T.J.	393	8	49.12	4-101	–	–	–
Wheater, A.J.A.	86	1	86.00	1- 86	–	–	–
Wheeler, B.M.	2484	92	27.00	6- 60	3	–	–
White, G.G.	2108	47	44.85	4- 72	–	–	–
White, H.J.	116	2	58.00	2- 85	–	–	–
White, W.A.	6583	192	34.28	6- 25	7	–	–
Whiteley, R.A.	1626	29	56.06	2- 6	–	–	–
Whittingham, S.G.	109	1	109.00	1- 77	–	–	–
Willey, D.J.	4401	148	29.73	5- 29	5	1	–
Williams, B.P.R.	85	1	85.00	1- 66	–	–	–
Williams, D.R.	83	0	–				
Williamson, K.S.	3367	81	41.56	5- 75	1	–	–
Wilson, G.C.	89	0	–				
Winslade, J.R.	97	4	24.25	4- 20	–	–	–
Woakes, C.R.	9053	357	25.35	7- 20	15	3	2
Wood, C.P.	2699	96	28.11	5- 39	3	–	–
Wood, J.M.	68	2	34.00	2- 32	–	–	–
Wood, L.	1087	33	32.93	3- 27	–	–	–
Wood, M.A.	2700	99	27.27	5- 32	5	–	–
Wood, S.K.W.	92	3	30.66	3- 64	–	–	–
Wright, B.J.	174	2	87.00	1- 14	–	–	–
Wright, C.J.C.	10726	315	34.05	6- 22	9	–	1
Wright, L.J.	4862	120	40.51	5- 65	3	–	–
Wylie, B.A.	383	7	54.71	3- 14	–	–	–
Yardy, M.H.	2192	29	75.58	5- 83	1	–	–
Yasir Arafat	18593	773	24.05	9- 35	43	5	0+4
Zaib, S.A.	56	0	–				
Zain Shahzad	417	17	24.52	4- 33	–	–	–

LIMITED-OVERS CAREER RECORDS

Compiled by Philip Bailey

The following career records, to the end of the 2015 season, include all players currently registered with first-class counties. These records are restricted to performances in limited-overs matches of 'List A' status as defined by the Association of Cricket Statisticians and Historians now incorporated by ICC into their Classification of Cricket. The following matches qualify for List A status and are included in the figures that follow: Limited-Overs Internationals; Other International matches (e.g. Commonwealth Games, 'A' team internationals); Premier domestic limited-overs tournaments in Test status countries; Official tourist matches against the main first-class teams.

The following matches do NOT qualify for inclusion: World Cup warm-up games; Tourist matches against first-class teams outside the major domestic competitions (e.g. Universities, Minor Counties etc.); Festival, pre-season friendly games and Twenty20 Cup matches.

	M	Runs	Avge	HS	100	50	Wkts	Avge	Best	Econ
Abbott, K.J.	77	375	17.85	45*	–	–	94	29.98	4-21	5.13
Abell, T.B.	7	202	33.66	80	–	1	–	–	–	–
Adams, J.H.K.	99	3326	41.06	131	2	25	1	105.00	1-34	7.97
Adeel Malik	28	677	32.23	70	–	4	22	46.95	3-39	5.16
Ali, A.M.	8	155	19.37	84	–	1	0	–	–	5.16
Ali, M.M.	128	3634	30.28	158	9	16	81	38.96	3-28	5.39
Allenby, J.	103	2235	26.29	91*	–	11	82	33.17	5-43	4.92
Ambrose, T.R.	152	3229	30.46	135	3	16	–	–	–	151/29
Anderson, J.M.	247	366	9.15	28	–	–	343	28.15	5-23	4.83
Ansari, Z.S.	36	690	36.31	66*	–	3	35	29.14	4-42	5.86
Arshad, U.	7	32	16.00	25	–	–	4	61.25	3-80	6.93
Ashar Zaidi	78	2349	36.13	141	4	11	59	28.91	4-39	4.16
Azhar Mahmood	319	4555	22.00	101*	2	19	348	31.37	6-18	4.69
Azharullah, M.	48	69	6.27	9	–	–	72	26.68	5-38	5.47
Bailey, T.E.	7	12	–	5*	–	–	10	29.00	3-31	5.28
Bairstow, J.M.	70	1745	32.31	123	2	9	–	–	–	52/5
Balbirnie, A.	27	628	27.30	129	1	2	2	47.50	1-26	6.78
Ball, A.J.	26	163	13.58	28	–	–	22	35.50	3-36	5.68
Ball, J.T.	43	86	9.55	19*	–	–	50	29.28	4-25	5.61
Ballance, G.S.	82	3123	48.04	139	6	19	–	–	–	–
Bancroft, C.T.	18	339	19.94	66	–	3	–	–	–	–
Barker, K.H.D.	48	440	17.60	56	–	1	52	30.96	4-33	5.84
Barnard, E.G.	7	102	17.00	51	–	1	12	29.25	3-59	5.75
Barrow, A.W.R.	22	359	27.61	72	–	2	–	–	–	22/1
Batty, G.J.	237	2246	15.70	83*	–	5	218	32.28	5-35	4.58
Beer, W.A.T.	43	294	18.37	45*	–	–	37	40.10	3-27	5.17
Bell, I.R.	292	10184	40.25	158	11	73	33	34.48	5-41	5.29
Bell-Drummond, D.J.	21	624	34.66	83	–	6	0	–	–	7.50
Berg, G.K.	63	1072	25.52	75	–	5	40	38.22	4-24	5.54
Billings, S.W.	47	1380	41.81	143	3	9	–	–	–	34/6
Bird, J.M.	9	8	8.00	5*	–	–	10	33.10	3-39	4.43
Blake, A.J.	52	835	25.30	89	–	5	3	24.66	2-13	5.28
Bopara, R.S.	289	8717	40.17	201*	14	51	210	27.83	5-63	5.20
Borthwick, S.G.	71	786	19.65	87	–	4	59	34.25	5-38	5.90
Bragg, W.D.	32	749	27.74	88	–	5	1	54.00	1-11	7.36
Bravo, D.J.	221	3950	24.23	112*	2	13	264	27.73	6-43	5.21

L-O	M	Runs	Avge	HS	100	50	Wkts	Avge	Best	Econ
Bresnan, T.T.	246	2316	18.52	80	–	4	280	33.53	5-48	5.18
Briggs, D.R.	68	201	11.16	25	–	–	71	35.43	4-32	5.12
Broad, S.C.J.	138	559	11.89	45*	–	–	205	29.42	5-23	5.25
Brooks, J.A.	35	48	4.80	10	–	–	36	34.27	3-30	4.85
Broom, N.T.	111	3099	34.82	164	4	18	6	65.33	2-59	6.06
Brown, B.C.	47	513	20.52	60	–	3	–	–	–	43/9
Brown, K.R.	60	1867	39.72	129	2	10	0	–	–	17.00
Browne, N.L.J.	8	153	25.50	69	–	1	–	–	–	–
Buck, N.L.	36	80	8.88	21	–	–	43	36.55	4-39	6.18
Bull, K.A.	2	0	–	0	–	–	1	48.00	1-40	5.53
Burgess, M.G.K.	4	101	25.25	49	–	–	–	–	–	–
Burgoyne, P.I.	16	129	16.12	43	–	–	13	39.46	3-31	5.42
Burke, J.E.	9	90	12.85	26*	–	–	16	20.06	5-28	6.00
Burns, R.J.	22	751	35.76	95	–	5	–	–	–	–
Buttler, J.C.	123	3465	44.42	129	4	22	–	–	–	125/13
Cachopa, C.	48	1153	25.62	121	2	6	–	–	–	–
Carberry, M.A.	168	4650	32.97	150*	6	34	11	27.00	3-37	5.53
Carter, A.	20	35	5.83	12	–	–	26	27.00	4-45	6.41
Carver, K.	5	35	–	35*	–	–	2	54.00	2-40	4.90
Chappell, Z.J.	2	32	32.00	31	–	–	1	53.00	1-28	4.89
Chapple, G.	284	2062	17.77	81*	–	9	320	28.55	6-18	4.50
Chopra, V.	91	3506	42.75	115	7	24	0	–	–	6.00
Christian, D.T.	95	2271	33.39	117	2	9	92	33.09	6-48	5.46
Clark, G.	7	142	20.28	42	–	–	–	–	–	–
Clark, J.	24	336	25.84	72	–	1	13	45.92	2-27	6.21
Clarke, J.M.	5	242	80.66	131*	1	2	–	–	–	–
Clarke, R.	203	3679	25.02	98*	–	19	116	38.92	4-28	5.43
Claydon, M.E.	84	218	7.03	19	–	–	112	29.57	4-39	5.54
Coad, B.O.	7	3	–	2*	–	–	3	94.00	1-34	6.50
Cobb, J.J.	68	2239	37.94	137	6	11	24	49.62	3-34	5.86
Cockbain, I.A.	44	917	30.56	98*	–	7	–	–	–	–
Coleman, F.R.J.	40	745	21.91	70	–	5	–	–	–	–
Coles, M.T.	52	300	13.04	100	1	–	80	22.92	6-32	5.91
Collingwood, P.D.	411	10829	34.26	132	10	60	264	33.08	6-31	4.81
Compton, N.R.D.	114	3045	36.25	131	6	19	1	53.00	1- 0	5.21
Cook, A.N.	150	5204	37.71	137	9	31	0	–	–	3.33
Cooke, C.B.	60	1699	36.93	137*	2	10	–	–	–	22/2
Cork, G.T.G.	2	0	–	0	–	–	4	14.00	2-17	6.22
Cosgrove, M.J.	131	3849	31.04	121	4	29	18	59.33	2-21	6.32
Cosker, D.A.	248	823	11.12	50*	–	1	258	32.38	5-54	4.81
Cotton, B.D.	12	42	21.00	18*	–	–	15	31.46	3-11	5.27
Coughlin, P.	8	2	1.00	2*	–	–	2	109.50	1-34	4.76
Cowdrey, F.K.	22	541	31.82	75	–	4	10	42.80	3-32	5.21
Cox, O.B.	40	376	16.34	39	–	–	–	–	–	34/6
Crane, M.S.	6	18	9.00	16*	–	–	9	31.33	4-30	6.17
Critchley, M.J.J.	7	38	9.50	22*	–	–	6	40.66	4-48	5.54
Croft, S.J.	128	3200	34.04	107	1	25	57	37.08	4-24	5.41
Crook, S.P.	72	866	18.04	100	1	4	79	30.88	5-36	5.63
Curran, S.M.	10	98	24.50	42	–	–	15	30.00	4-32	5.37
Curran, T.K.	15	127	15.87	44	–	–	24	27.95	5-34	5.80

264

L-O	M	Runs	Avge	HS	100	50	Wkts	Avge	Best	Econ
Davey, J.H.	59	1065	24.76	91	–	5	74	24.41	6-28	5.52
Davies, A.L.	16	380	38.00	73*	–	3	–	–	–	16/3
Davies, S.M.	159	5063	37.50	127*	8	32	–	–	–	128/41
Dawson, L.A.	108	2180	30.27	113*	1	11	78	36.64	6-47	4.91
Denly, J.L.	119	3464	33.30	115	4	19	17	19.23	3-19	4.78
Dent, C.D.J.	43	943	27.73	151*	1	2	10	36.70	4-43	5.47
Dernbach, J.W.	125	198	7.33	31	–	–	192	28.00	6-35	6.00
Dexter, N.J.	95	1913	31.88	135*	2	8	38	51.97	3-17	5.60
Dickson, S.R.	5	52	13.00	47	–	–	–	–	–	–
D'Oliveira, B.L.	27	222	17.07	42	–	–	18	43.16	3-35	5.55
Donald, A.H.T.	4	49	24.50	37	–	–	–	–	–	–
Duckett, B.M.	21	479	29.93	69	–	3	–	–	–	22/3
Dunn, M.P.	1	0	–	0	–	–	2	16.00	2-32	5.33
Durston, W.J.	117	2963	35.27	134	5	14	52	38.19	3- 7	5.60
Eckersley, E.J.H.	30	680	26.15	108	1	3	–	–	–	18/1
Edwards, F.H.	78	131	10.07	21*	–	–	92	31.17	6-22	5.07
Edwards, G.A.	5	9	–	8*	–	–	2	100.50	1-29	7.44
Elstone, S.L.	38	671	22.36	75*	–	2	1	58.00	1-22	6.00
Ervine, S.M.	230	5267	30.44	167*	7	24	203	34.05	5-50	5.61
Evans, L.J.	27	462	22.00	50	–	1	0	–	–	8.20
Fell, T.C.	21	698	36.73	89	–	7	–	–	–	–
Finch, A.J.	114	4245	39.67	154	10	23	7	30.28	2-44	5.21
Finch, H.Z.	4	140	70.00	92*	–	1	0	–	–	2.00
Finn, S.T.	119	264	9.42	42*	–	–	169	28.31	5-33	5.09
Fisher, M.D.	13	62	31.00	34	–	–	11	39.18	3-32	5.39
Fletcher, L.J.	46	183	12.20	40*	–	–	45	37.42	4-44	5.48
Foakes, B.T.	18	308	19.25	56	–	2	–	–	–	13/2
Footitt, M.H.A.	35	28	4.66	11*	–	–	46	29.43	5-28	6.30
Foster, J.S.	210	3162	27.73	83*	–	15	–	–	–	233/59
Franklin, J.E.C.	268	5264	32.90	133*	4	30	211	34.87	5-42	4.93
Freckingham, O.H.	3	6	6.00	3*	–	–	3	72.00	2-38	8.64
Fuller, J.K.	37	399	22.16	45	–	–	58	25.17	6-35	5.57
Gabriel, S.T.	15	17	5.66	6*	–	–	20	24.10	4-34	4.31
Gale, A.W.	135	3468	30.42	125*	2	18	–	–	–	–
Gayle, C.H.	337	11698	38.22	215	25	63	222	32.03	5-46	4.55
Gibson, R.	5	19	6.33	9	–	–	5	31.60	1-17	5.44
Gidman, W.R.S.	46	615	25.62	76	–	2	42	30.85	4-36	4.85
Godleman, B.A.	38	930	29.06	109*	1	3	–	–	–	–
Gordon, R.O.	8	10	5.00	9*	–	–	10	38.10	3-25	6.68
Gregory, L.	36	405	20.25	105*	1	1	48	25.81	4-27	6.14
Griffiths, D.A.	26	30	15.00	12*	–	–	34	28.88	4-29	6.00
Griffiths, G.T.	5	7	–	5*	–	–	4	45.00	3-41	4.77
Groenewald, T.D.	83	598	18.68	57	–	2	87	32.78	4-22	5.43
Gubbins, N.R.T.	9	402	44.66	141	1	2	–	–	–	–
Gurney, H.F.	67	41	4.55	13*	–	–	71	36.25	5-24	5.60
Haggett, C.J.	10	57	8.14	36	–	–	8	46.87	2-54	6.69
Hain, S.R.	1	1	1.00	1	–	–	–	–	–	–
Hales, A.D.	110	3624	34.51	150*	9	18	0	–	–	15.00
Hammond, M.A.H.	3	0	0.00	0	–	–	5	19.40	2-18	5.10
Handscomb, P.S.P.	31	757	36.04	72	–	4	–	–	–	31/2

265

L-O	M	Runs	Avge	HS	100	50	Wkts	Avge	Best	Econ
Hannon-Dalby, O.J.	22	44	14.66	21*	–	–	35	26.68	5-27	5.96
Harinath, A.	6	105	26.25	52	–	1	0	–	–	5.33
Harris, J.A.R.	53	293	11.72	32	–	–	71	28.94	4-38	5.67
Harrison, J.	3	7	–	7*	–	–	2	75.00	2-51	7.14
Hastings, J.W.	81	871	19.35	69*	–	1	123	27.39	5-41	4.85
Hatchett, L.J.	16	9	4.50	5	–	–	19	33.15	3-44	5.64
Head, T.M.	20	550	30.55	108	1	3	2	88.50	2- 9	6.00
Helm, T.G.	3	0	–	0	–	–	4	16.50	3-27	3.88
Henry, M.J.	51	251	13.21	37*	–	–	83	25.63	6-45	5.47
Hepburn, A.	2	32	32.00	32	–	–	6	13.00	4-34	4.14
Higgins, R.F.	6	80	16.00	27	–	–	–	–	–	–
Hildreth, J.C.	176	4517	34.21	151	6	19	6	30.83	2-26	7.40
Hill, L.J.	15	283	20.21	86	–	1	–	–	–	6/1
Hodd, A.J.	63	858	23.18	91	–	2	–	–	–	62/12
Hogan, M.G.	49	115	14.37	27	–	–	82	24.46	5-44	4.82
Horton, P.J.	103	2542	31.00	111*	2	13	–	–	–	–
Hose, A.J.	8	168	21.00	46	–	–	–	–	–	–
Howell, B.A.C.	55	1304	38.35	122	1	7	36	37.25	3-37	5.00
Hudson-Prentice, F.J.	1	0	–	0	–	–	0	–	–	8.50
Hughes, A.L.	32	328	20.50	59*	–	1	26	38.53	3-31	5.30
Hughes, C.F.	69	1478	23.83	81	–	12	22	35.22	5-29	5.26
Hunn, M.D.	5	6	–	5*	–	–	5	38.20	2-31	5.78
Hurt, L.J.	1	15	15.00	15	–	–	2	29.50	2-59	7.37
Hutton, B.A.	8	66	22.00	33*	–	–	8	45.75	3-72	6.20
Ingram, C.A.	139	5426	45.21	130	12	34	13	30.92	2-13	5.22
Jackson, C.F.	4	34	–	34*	–	–	–	–	–	1/2
Jarvis, K.M.	47	130	8.66	33*	–	–	53	37.30	4-35	5.60
Javid, A.	29	507	33.80	43	–	–	12	63.33	3-48	5.93
Jennings, K.K.	21	574	44.15	71*	–	6	1	211.00	1- 9	6.39
Jones, R.A.	12	23	7.66	11*	–	–	4	117.25	1-25	6.94
Jordan, C.J.	57	341	11.75	38*	–	–	89	27.66	5-29	5.69
Joyce, E.C.	276	8905	38.38	146	14	52	6	51.50	2-10	7.02
Kapil, A.	20	315	26.25	59	–	1	5	58.80	1-18	7.57
Keogh, R.I.	19	323	20.18	61	–	3	1	257.00	1-49	5.46
Kerrigan, S.C.	33	28	3.11	10	–	–	23	52.47	3-21	5.28
Kervezee, A.N.	99	2494	29.34	121*	2	12	0	–	–	9.00
Kettleborough, J.M.	3	51	25.50	26	–	–	–	–	–	–
Key, R.W.T.	225	6469	32.18	144*	8	37	–	–	–	–
Kleinveldt, R.K.	134	1184	17.15	55	–	2	155	30.33	4-22	4.69
Klinger, M.	144	5958	49.23	140*	14	38	–	–	–	–
Knight, T.C.	9	16	5.33	10	–	–	9	35.66	3-36	5.35
Kohler-Cadmore, T.	15	318	22.71	71	–	1	–	–	–	–
Latham, T.W.M.	75	2033	33.88	130	2	11	–	–	–	50/3
Leach, J.	14	226	37.66	45*	–	–	15	37.46	4-30	5.74
Leach, M.J.	15	21	7.00	18	–	–	18	35.22	3-52	4.83
Leaning, J.A.	24	591	36.93	111*	1	4	7	20.14	5-22	5.42
Leask, M.A.	28	292	13.90	50	–	1	11	60.18	2-23	6.38
Lees, A.Z.	31	961	35.59	102	1	8	–	–	–	–
Levi, R.E.	98	3171	36.87	166	6	16	–	–	–	–
Liddle, C.J.	63	119	6.61	18	–	–	79	29.22	5-18	5.86

L-O	M	Runs	Avge	HS	100	50	Wkts	Avge	Best	Econ
Lilley, A.M.	10	20	6.66	10	–	–	15	21.40	4-30	5.17
Livingstone, L.S.	1	91	91.00	91	–	1	–	–	–	–
Lloyd, D.L.	14	89	11.12	32	–	–	9	33.00	4-10	5.10
Lumb, M.J.	202	5830	31.51	110	4	43	0	–	–	14.00
Lyth, A.	87	2388	32.27	109*	1	12	2	94.00	1- 6	6.26
McClenaghan, M.J.	80	190	12.66	34*	–	–	148	25.52	6-41	5.86
McCullum, B.B.	299	6966	30.28	170	8	35	–	–	–	301/17
McKay, C.J.	114	532	12.09	57	–	1	170	26.98	5-28	4.67
McLaren, R.	176	2582	31.48	88	–	11	222	27.27	5-38	5.09
MacLeod, C.S.	95	1752	21.62	175	3	5	20	40.50	3-37	5.53
Machan, M.W.	56	1808	36.89	126*	2	9	12	51.00	3-31	5.84
Madsen, W.L.	73	2222	40.40	138	3	14	9	15.22	3-27	4.41
Magoffin, S.J.	52	227	22.70	24*	–	–	65	31.40	4-58	4.71
Malan, D.J.	116	3796	39.95	156*	6	19	30	32.36	4-25	5.71
Marshall, H.J.H.	289	6916	27.66	122	6	46	4	73.75	2-21	6.23
Masters, D.D.	169	550	11.45	39	–	–	168	32.14	5-17	4.48
Meaker, S.C.	48	82	5.46	21*	–	–	48	38.47	4-47	6.23
Meschede, C.A.J.	36	300	16.66	40*	–	–	40	26.35	4- 5	5.59
Mickleburgh, J.C.	20	400	30.76	73	–	2	–	–	–	–
Middlebrook, J.D.	192	1737	20.19	57*	–	1	146	36.43	4-27	4.73
Miles, C.N.	22	35	7.00	12	–	–	29	31.24	4-29	5.90
Mills, T.S.	23	7	1.75	3*	–	–	22	35.77	3-23	5.97
Milne, A.F.	48	151	15.10	19*	–	–	71	28.81	5-45	5.25
Milnes, T.P.	3	22	11.00	16	–	–	3	59.00	2-73	7.69
Mitchell, D.K.H.	105	2572	33.40	107	2	15	58	35.41	4-19	5.57
Morgan, E.J.G.	261	7628	37.20	161	14	44	0	–	–	7.00
Morris, C.A.J.	15	37	12.33	16*	–	–	15	40.66	3-46	5.76
Morris, C.H.	55	683	25.29	90*	–	2	62	29.04	4-30	5.18
Muchall, G.J.	148	3477	34.08	101*	1	20	2	84.00	1-15	4.84
Mullaney, S.J.	79	1018	23.13	63*	–	5	70	29.61	4-29	4.90
Munsey, H.G.	6	75	25.00	40*	–	–	–	–	–	–
Murphy, D.	39	271	22.58	31*	–	–	–	–	–	23/11
Murtagh, T.J.	154	693	11.55	35*	–	–	198	29.46	4-14	5.19
Mustafizur Rahman	11	10	5.00	9	–	–	30	12.26	6-43	3.90
Mustard, P.	190	5138	31.13	143	7	32	–	–	–	200/47
Myburgh, J.G.	100	2371	28.22	112	1	14	25	60.80	2-22	5.06
Naik, J.K.H.	37	192	11.29	36*	–	–	30	42.06	3-21	5.33
Napier, G.R.	240	2939	18.60	79	–	14	287	26.04	7-32	5.28
Nash, C.D.	101	2837	31.17	124*	2	17	43	31.18	4-40	5.46
Neesham, J.D.S.	39	674	29.30	69	–	3	52	27.40	5-44	5.96
Newton, R.I.	25	616	28.00	88*	–	2	–	–	–	–
Nijjar, A.S.S.	3	21	21.00	21	–	–	1	107.00	1-39	5.09
Noema-Barnett, K.	63	1017	23.11	67	–	5	38	41.76	3-42	4.91
Northeast, S.A.	62	1677	32.25	132	2	9	–	–	–	–
Norwell, L.C.	7	7	7.00	6	–	–	11	26.09	6-52	5.97
O'Brien, I.E.	152	3528	30.41	142	3	15	113	33.77	4-13	5.35
O'Brien, N.J.	195	4670	30.52	121	3	29	–	–	–	150/34
Onions, G.	87	130	5.90	19	–	–	99	31.04	4-45	5.09
Overton, C.	21	216	14.40	49	–	–	22	36.00	3-37	5.02
Overton, J.	18	83	16.60	16*	–	–	24	29.37	4-42	6.24

267

L-O	M	Runs	Avge	HS	100	50	Wkts	Avge	Best	Econ
Palladino, A.P.	52	251	10.91	31	–	–	54	33.35	5-49	5.31
Parry, S.D.	72	260	15.29	31	–	–	93	27.29	5-17	4.92
Patel, J.S.	170	618	10.13	50	–	1	197	31.43	4-16	4.60
Patel, R.H.	10	0	0.00	0*	–	–	11	44.45	3-71	5.62
Patel, S.R.	208	5084	33.66	129*	4	28	192	30.50	6-13	5.27
Patterson, S.A.	68	184	16.72	25*	–	–	87	27.82	6-32	4.97
Payne, D.A.	55	76	10.85	18	–	–	98	22.42	7-29	5.65
Penrhyn Jones, D.	3	0	–	0*	–	–	2	55.00	1-22	10.31
Petersen, A.N.	178	5372	33.78	145*	7	32	8	46.00	2-48	5.52
Pettini, M.L.	173	4352	29.20	144	8	27	–	–	–	–
Pillans, M.W.	5	35	17.50	20*	–	–	7	24.14	3-37	4.97
Plunkett, L.E.	138	1299	21.65	72	–	3	166	31.59	4-15	5.45
Podmore, H.W.	6	1	–	1*	–	–	4	68.00	2-46	6.91
Porter, J.A.	4	5	–	5*	–	–	5	35.80	3-39	5.50
Porterfield, W.T.S.	193	5939	32.27	112*	9	34	–	–	–	–
Poynton, T.	28	173	11.53	40	–	–	–	–	–	17/5
Poysden, J.E.	13	20	6.66	10*	–	–	13	35.00	3-33	5.79
Pringle, R.D.	20	170	13.07	35	–	–	5	86.60	1-12	6.32
Procter, L.A.	22	252	28.00	97	–	2	12	37.58	3-29	6.26
Quinn, M.R.	16	105	15.00	36	–	–	22	36.59	3-19	5.69
Rabada, K.	22	60	6.66	22	–	–	30	33.50	6-16	5.33
Raine, B.A.	8	117	19.50	43	–	–	8	44.62	2-48	6.26
Rankin, W.B.	101	102	6.37	18*	–	–	120	28.53	4-34	4.92
Rashid, A.U.	108	1122	20.77	71	–	2	126	31.83	5-33	5.30
Rayner, O.P.	50	448	24.88	61	–	1	41	37.48	4-35	5.31
Read, C.M.W.	317	5297	29.42	135	2	21	–	–	–	300/73
Reece, L.M.	22	409	25.56	59	–	2	6	69.66	4-35	6.20
Rhodes, W.M.H.	16	185	16.81	46	–	–	10	28.80	2-22	5.41
Richardson, M.J.	4	117	39.00	56	–	1	–	–	–	2/0
Riley, A.E.N.	23	11	5.50	5*	–	–	19	40.57	2-32	5.58
Robinson, O.E.	7	53	17.66	30	–	–	3	75.00	2-61	6.25
Robson, A.J.	14	317	22.64	90	–	2	–	–	–	–
Robson, S.D.	14	354	29.50	88	–	2	–	–	–	–
Roderick, G.H.	33	652	29.63	104	1	4	–	–	–	33/4
Rogers, C.J.L.	167	5345	36.86	140	5	36	2	13.00	2-22	6.50
Roland-Jones, T.S.	43	270	15.88	31*	–	–	71	24.14	4-42	5.40
Root, J.E.	88	2849	39.02	121	7	13	24	49.50	2-10	5.50
Rossington, A.M.	19	426	30.42	82	–	3	–	–	–	12/2
Rouse, A.P.	3	15	5.00	7	–	–	–	–	–	3/2
Roy, J.J.	80	2379	33.50	141	7	11	0	–	–	12.00
Rudolph, J.A.	246	9747	48.97	169*	17	67	13	34.61	4-40	5.74
Rushworth, C.	50	96	8.72	38*	–	–	81	22.35	5-31	5.23
Russell, C.J.	8	2	–	1*	–	–	5	44.20	4-32	5.81
Rutherford, H.D.	47	1338	29.08	110	3	8	0	–	–	4.00
Ryder, J.D.	141	4024	33.25	115	7	22	46	35.52	4-39	5.75
Saeed Ajmal	226	537	6.97	33	–	–	346	25.09	5-18	4.37
Salt, P.D.	1	22	22.00	22	–	–	–	–	–	–
Salter, A.G.	17	90	18.00	36*	–	–	9	51.88	2-41	4.63
Sanderson, B.W.	11	14	14.00	12*	–	–	8	30.87	2-17	5.88
Sangakkara, K.C.	512	18630	43.02	169	36	116	–	–	–	510/123

L-O	M	Runs	Avge	HS	100	50	Wkts	Avge	Best	Econ
Santner, M.J.	24	606	26.34	86	–	3	29	30.55	3-31	4.93
Sayer, R.J.	6	32	6.40	22*	–	–	3	96.33	1-46	6.28
Scott, G.F.B.	1	4	4.00	4	–	–	0	–	–	9.33
Shahid Afridi	499	10869	25.04	124	8	58	509	33.73	7-12	4.62
Shahzad, A.	76	449	13.60	59*	–	1	112	26.96	5-51	5.37
Shantry, J.D.	61	164	11.71	31	–	–	82	28.85	4-29	5.77
Sheikh, A.	6	27	5.40	22	–	–	6	42.83	3-49	5.73
Shreck, C.E.	60	47	5.22	9*	–	–	73	31.01	5-19	5.16
Sibley, D.P.	3	43	43.00	37	–	–	–	–	–	–
Sidebottom, R.J.	186	552	11.04	32	–	–	198	30.97	6-40	4.47
Simpson, J.A.	57	757	24.41	82	–	4	–	–	–	41/7
Slater, B.T.	7	109	18.16	46	–	–	–	–	–	–
Smith, G.P.	40	959	27.40	135*	2	4	–	–	–	–
Smith, R.A.J.	9	19	6.33	9	–	–	7	36.42	3-48	6.53
Smith, T.C.	67	1505	34.20	117	2	10	77	28.48	4-48	5.28
Smith, T.M.J.	53	264	18.85	65	–	1	44	38.79	3-26	5.47
Smith, W.R.	102	2291	29.00	120*	2	18	12	29.75	2-19	5.59
Stevens, D.I.	278	6874	30.01	133	6	43	119	31.68	5-32	4.92
Stirling, P.R.	120	3530	31.80	177	8	13	49	36.46	4-11	4.74
Stokes, B.A.	99	2348	30.49	164	4	8	89	26.33	5-61	5.64
Stone, O.P.	17	90	22.50	24*	–	–	11	50.54	3-34	5.26
Stoneman, M.D.	52	1872	40.69	136*	5	10	–	–	–	–
Sykes, J.S.	18	41	6.83	15	–	–	15	38.40	3-34	5.42
Tavaré, W.A.	8	221	27.62	77	–	2	–	–	–	–
Taylor, B.R.M.	256	7648	33.84	145*	13	44	20	30.20	5-28	160/32
Taylor, J.M.R.	25	336	25.84	53	–	1	27	28.03	4-38	5.03
Taylor, J.W.A.	131	5100	52.04	146*	14	28	5	34.00	4-61	7.39
Taylor, L.R.P.L.	214	7486	43.52	132*	19	45	3	81.00	1-13	4.58
Taylor, M.D.	2	7	–	7*	–	–	4	22.25	2-43	6.43
Taylor, R.M.L.	46	595	19.19	48*	–	–	60	30.31	3-39	5.61
Taylor, T.A.I.	4	0	–	0	–	–	5	34.80	3-48	5.93
ten Doeschate, R.N.	185	5002	46.31	180	9	27	154	30.70	5-50	5.72
Thakor, S.J.	32	491	20.45	83*	–	4	28	30.03	4-49	5.83
Thomas, I.A.A.	4	1	1.00	1	–	–	3	55.33	2-64	6.38
Tomlinson, J.A.	36	53	5.30	14	–	–	39	29.48	4-47	5.23
Topley, R.J.W.	30	40	6.66	19	–	–	50	24.44	4-26	5.49
Tredwell, J.C.	246	1731	16.97	88	–	4	259	31.56	6-27	4.69
Trego, P.D.	161	3563	30.71	147	6	17	156	32.32	5-40	5.61
Trescothick, M.E.	372	12229	37.28	184	28	63	57	28.84	4-50	4.90
Trott, I.J.L.	250	8958	46.90	137	17	62	54	28.35	4-55	5.57
Tye, A.J.	8	114	28.50	28*	–	1	18	21.38	5-46	5.76
Umar Akmal	153	4048	34.01	104	4	26	2	41.50	1- 7	104/13
van der Gugten, T.	22	70	10.00	23	–	–	31	24.12	5-24	5.06
van der Merwe, R.E.	129	1701	24.30	93	–	6	174	25.99	5-26	4.74
Velani, K.S.	10	79	13.16	27	–	–	1	14.00	1-14	7.00
Vince, J.M.	89	2736	35.07	131	4	13	1	84.00	1-18	6.00
Voges, A.C.	171	5449	43.59	112*	5	41	33	46.00	3-25	5.18
Wagg, G.G.	116	1491	18.63	62*	–	2	127	33.79	4-35	5.90
Wagner, N.	71	405	11.91	42	–	–	113	26.61	5-34	5.24
Wahab Riaz	134	915	15.77	77	–	3	186	29.13	5-24	5.30

L-O	M	Runs	Avge	HS	100	50	Wkts	Avge	Best	Econ
Waite, M.J.	2	23	23.00	12	–	–	0	–	–	6.90
Wakely, A.G.	58	1429	29.77	102	1	9	5	21.40	2-14	4.86
Wallace, M.A.	201	2692	20.54	118*	2	7	–	–	–	181/45
Waller, M.T.C.	43	77	15.40	25*	–	–	33	37.45	3-39	5.53
Webb, J.P.	1	11	11.00	11	–	–	–	–	–	–
Wells, L.W.P.	16	107	9.72	23	–	–	6	28.00	3-19	5.11
Wells, T.J.	13	197	24.62	32*	–	–	5	48.20	2-45	7.77
Wessels, M.H.	143	3423	28.52	132	2	18	1	48.00	1- 0	5.87
Westley, T.	48	1447	36.17	111*	2	13	16	35.81	4-60	5.04
Westwood, I.J.	60	941	22.95	65	–	3	3	75.66	1-28	5.15
Wheater, A.J.A.	61	1014	24.73	135	2	3	–	–	–	22/7
White, G.G.	54	266	14.77	39*	–	–	54	28.55	5-35	5.22
White, W.A.	69	783	19.09	46*	–	–	66	37.21	6-29	6.47
Whiteley, R.A.	40	645	20.80	77	–	3	8	52.87	1-17	6.66
Willey, D.J.	67	1048	22.78	167	2	3	64	31.95	5-62	5.67
Williamson, K.S.	143	5433	46.43	145*	11	33	56	35.89	5-51	5.27
Wilson, G.C.	151	2830	22.82	113	1	17	–	–	–	117/24
Winslade, J.R.	1	0	–	0	–	–	1	61.00	1-61	9.38
Woakes, C.R.	109	1007	18.64	49*	–	–	116	36.64	6-45	5.66
Wood, C.P.	62	311	12.44	41	–	–	88	25.63	5-22	5.49
Wood, M.A.	25	54	9.00	15*	–	–	26	34.84	3-23	5.45
Wood, S.K.W.	9	63	10.50	32	–	–	5	32.60	2-24	5.43
Wright, C.J.C.	90	219	10.42	42	–	–	91	35.35	4-20	5.58
Wright, L.J.	183	3994	31.20	143*	9	12	111	38.11	4-12	5.34
Zaib, S.A.	3	27	13.50	16	–	–	0	–	–	10.00

FIRST-CLASS CRICKET RECORDS
To the end of the 2015 season
TEAM RECORDS
HIGHEST INNINGS TOTALS

1107	Victoria v New South Wales	Melbourne	1926-27
1059	Victoria v Tasmania	Melbourne	1922-23
952-6d	Sri Lanka v India	Colombo	1997-98
951-7d	Sind v Baluchistan	Karachi	1973-74
944-6d	Hyderabad v Andhra	Secunderabad	1993-94
918	New South Wales v South Australia	Sydney	1900-01
912-8d	Holkar v Mysore	Indore	1945-46
910-6d	Railways v Dera Ismail Khan	Lahore	1964-65
903-7d	England v Australia	The Oval	1938
900-6d	Queensland v Victoria	Brisbane	2005-06
887	Yorkshire v Warwickshire	Birmingham	1896
863	Lancashire v Surrey	The Oval	1990
860-6d	Tamil Nadu v Goa	Panjim	1988-89
850-7d	Somerset v Middlesex	Taunton	2007

Excluding penalty runs in India, there have been 34 innings totals of 800 runs or more in first-class cricket. Tamil Nadu's total of 860-6d was boosted to 912 by 52 penalty runs.

HIGHEST SECOND INNINGS TOTAL

770	New South Wales v South Australia	Adelaide	1920-21

HIGHEST FOURTH INNINGS TOTAL

654-5	England (set 696 to win) v South Africa	Durban	1938-39

HIGHEST MATCH AGGREGATE

2376-37	Maharashtra v Bombay	Poona	1948-49

RECORD MARGIN OF VICTORY

Innings and 851 runs: Railways v Dera Ismail Khan	Lahore	1964-65

MOST RUNS IN A DAY

721	Australians v Essex	Southend	1948

MOST HUNDREDS IN AN INNINGS

6	Holkar v Mysore	Indore	1945-46

LOWEST INNINGS TOTALS

12	†Oxford University v MCC and Ground	Oxford	1877
12	Northamptonshire v Gloucestershire	Gloucester	1907
13	Auckland v Canterbury	Auckland	1877-78
13	Nottinghamshire v Yorkshire	Nottingham	1901
14	Surrey v Essex	Chelmsford	1983
15	MCC v Surrey	Lord's	1839
15	†Victoria v MCC	Melbourne	1903-04
15	†Northamptonshire v Yorkshire	Northampton	1908
15	Hampshire v Warwickshire	Birmingham	1922

† *Batted one man short*

There have been 28 instances of a team being dismissed for under 20.

LOWEST MATCH AGGREGATE BY ONE TEAM

34 (16 and 18) Border v Natal	East London	1959-60

LOWEST COMPLETED MATCH AGGREGATE BY BOTH TEAMS

105	MCC v Australians	Lord's	1878

TIED MATCHES

Before 1949 a match was considered to be tied if the scores were level after the fourth innings, even if the side batting last had wickets in hand when play ended. Law 22 was amended in 1948 and since then a match has been tied only when the scores are level after the fourth innings has been completed. There have been 56 tied first-class matches, five of which would not have qualified under the current law. The most recent are:

Warwickshire (446-7d & forfeit) v Essex (66-0d & 380)	Birmingham	2003
Worcestershire (262 & 247) v Zimbabweans (334 & 175)	Worcester	2003
Habib Bank (245 & 178) v WAPDA (233 & 190)	Lahore	2011-12
Border (210 & 210) v Boland (219 & 201)	East London	2012-13

BATTING RECORDS
35,000 RUNS IN A CAREER

	Career	I	NO	HS	Runs	Avge	100
J.B.Hobbs	1905-34	1315	106	316*	**61237**	50.65	197
F.E.Woolley	1906-38	1532	85	305*	**58969**	40.75	145
E.H.Hendren	1907-38	1300	166	301*	**57611**	50.80	170
C.P.Mead	1905-36	1340	185	280*	**55061**	47.67	153
W.G.Grace	1865-1908	1493	105	344	**54896**	39.55	126
W.R.Hammond	1920-51	1005	104	336*	**50551**	56.10	167
H.Sutcliffe	1919-45	1088	123	313	**50138**	51.95	149
G.Boycott	1962-86	1014	162	261*	**48426**	56.83	151
T.W.Graveney	1948-71/72	1223	159	258	**47793**	44.91	122
G.A.Gooch	1973-2000	990	75	333	**44846**	49.01	128
T.W.Hayward	1893-1914	1138	96	315*	**43551**	41.79	104
D.L.Amiss	1960-87	1139	126	262*	**43423**	42.86	102
M.C.Cowdrey	1950-76	1130	134	307	**42719**	42.89	107
A.Sandham	1911-37/38	1000	79	325	**41284**	44.82	107
G.A.Hick	1983/84-2008	871	84	405*	**41112**	52.23	136
L.Hutton	1934-60	814	91	364	**40140**	55.51	129
M.J.K.Smith	1951-75	1091	139	204	**39832**	41.84	69
W.Rhodes	1898-1930	1528	237	267*	**39802**	30.83	58
J.H.Edrich	1956-78	979	104	310*	**39790**	45.47	103
R.E.S.Wyatt	1923-57	1141	157	232	**39405**	40.04	85
D.C.S.Compton	1936-64	839	88	300	**38942**	51.85	123
G.E.Tyldesley	1909-36	961	106	256*	**38874**	45.46	102
J.T.Tyldesley	1895-1923	994	62	295*	**37897**	40.60	86
K.W.R.Fletcher	1962-88	1167	170	228*	**37665**	37.77	63
C.G.Greenidge	1970-92	889	75	273*	**37354**	45.88	92
J.W.Hearne	1909-36	1025	116	285*	**37252**	40.98	96
L.E.G.Ames	1926-51	951	95	295	**37248**	43.51	102
D.Kenyon	1946-67	1159	59	259	**37002**	33.63	74
W.J.Edrich	1934-58	964	92	267*	**36965**	42.39	86
J.M.Parks	1949-76	1227	172	205*	**36673**	34.76	51
M.W.Gatting	1975-98	861	123	258	**36549**	49.52	94
D.Denton	1894-1920	1163	70	221	**36479**	33.37	69
G.H.Hirst	1891-1929	1215	151	341	**36323**	34.13	60
I.V.A.Richards	1971/72-93	796	63	322	**36212**	49.40	114
A.Jones	1957-83	1168	72	204*	**36049**	32.89	56
W.G.Quaife	1894-1928	1203	185	255*	**36012**	35.37	72
R.E.Marshall	1945/46-72	1053	59	228*	**35725**	35.94	68
M.R.Ramprakash	1987-2012	764	93	301*	**35659**	53.14	114
G.Gunn	1902-32	1061	82	220	**35208**	35.96	62

HIGHEST INDIVIDUAL INNINGS

501*	B.C.Lara	Warwickshire v Durham	Birmingham	1994
499	Hanif Mohammed	Karachi v Bahawalpur	Karachi	1958-59
452*	D.G.Bradman	New South Wales v Queensland	Sydney	1929-30
443*	B.B.Nimbalkar	Maharashtra v Kathiawar	Poona	1948-49
437	W.H.Ponsford	Victoria v Queensland	Melbourne	1927-28
429	W.H.Ponsford	Victoria v Tasmania	Melbourne	1922-23
428	Aftab Baloch	Sind v Baluchistan	Karachi	1973-74
424	A.C.MacLaren	Lancashire v Somerset	Taunton	1895
405*	G.A.Hick	Worcestershire v Somerset	Taunton	1988
400*	B.C.Lara	West Indies v England	St John's	2003-04
394	Naved Latif	Sargodha v Gujranwala	Gujranwala	2000-01
390	S.C.Cook	Lions v Warriors	East London	2009-10
385	B.Sutcliffe	Otago v Canterbury	Christchurch	1952-53
383	C.W.Gregory	New South Wales v Queensland	Brisbane	1906-07
380	M.L.Hayden	Australia v Zimbabwe	Perth	2003-04
377	S.V.Manjrekar	Bombay v Hyderabad	Bombay	1990-91
375	B.C.Lara	West Indies v England	St John's	1993-94
374	D.P.M.D.Jayawardena	Sri Lanka v South Africa	Colombo	2006
369	D.G.Bradman	South Australia v Tasmania	Adelaide	1935-36
366	N.H.Fairbrother	Lancashire v Surrey	The Oval	1990
366	M.V.Sridhar	Hyderabad v Andhra	Secunderabad	1993-94
365*	C.Hill	South Australia v NSW	Adelaide	1900-01
365*	G.St A.Sobers	West Indies v Pakistan	Kingston	1957-58
364	L.Hutton	England v Australia	The Oval	1938
359*	V.M.Merchant	Bombay v Maharashtra	Bombay	1943-44
359	R.B.Simpson	New South Wales v Queensland	Brisbane	1963-64
357*	R.Abel	Surrey v Somerset	The Oval	1899
357	D.G.Bradman	South Australia v Victoria	Melbourne	1935-36
356	B.A.Richards	South Australia v W Australia	Perth	1970-71
355*	G.R.Marsh	W Australia v S Australia	Perth	1989-90
355*	K.P.Pietersen	Surrey v Leicestershire	The Oval	2015
355	B.Sutcliffe	Otago v Auckland	Dunedin	1949-50
353	V.V.S.Laxman	Hyderabad v Karnataka	Bangalore	1999-00
352	W.H.Ponsford	Victoria v New South Wales	Melbourne	1926-27
352	C.A.Pujara	Saurashtra v Karnataka	Rajkot	2012-13
351	K.D.K.Vithanage	Tamil Union v SL Air	Katunayake	2014-15
350	Rashid Israr	Habib Bank v National Bank	Lahore	1976-77

There have been 202 triple hundreds in first-class cricket, W.V.Raman (313) and Arjan Kripal Singh (302*) for Tamil Nadu v Goa at Panjim in 1988-89 providing the only instance of two batsmen scoring 300 in the same innings.

MOST HUNDREDS IN SUCCESSIVE INNINGS

6	C.B.Fry	Sussex and Rest of England	1901
6	D.G.Bradman	South Australia and D.G.Bradman's XI	1938-39
6	M.J.Procter	Rhodesia	1970-71

TWO DOUBLE HUNDREDS IN A MATCH

244	202*	A.E.Fagg	Kent v Essex	Colchester	1938

TRIPLE HUNDRED AND HUNDRED IN A MATCH

333	123	G.A.Gooch	England v India	Lord's	1990
319	105	K.C.Sangakkara	Sri Lanka v Bangladesh	Chittagong	2013-14

DOUBLE HUNDRED AND HUNDRED IN A MATCH MOST TIMES

4	Zaheer Abbas	Gloucestershire	1976-81

TWO HUNDREDS IN A MATCH MOST TIMES

8	Zaheer Abbas	Gloucestershire and PIA	1976-82
8	R.T.Ponting	Tasmania, Australia and Australians	1992-2006
7	W.R.Hammond	Gloucestershire, England and MCC	1927-45
7	M.R.Ramprakash	Middlesex, Surrey	1990-2010

MOST HUNDREDS IN A SEASON

18	D.C.S.Compton	1947	16	J.B.Hobbs		1925

100 HUNDREDS IN A CAREER

	Total		100th Hundred	
	Hundreds	Inns	Season	Inns
J.B.Hobbs	197	1315	1923	821
E.H.Hendren	170	1300	1928-29	740
W.R.Hammond	167	1005	1935	679
C.P.Mead	153	1340	1927	892
G.Boycott	151	1014	1977	645
H.Sutcliffe	149	1088	1932	700
F.E.Woolley	145	1532	1929	1031
G.A.Hick	136	871	1998	574
L.Hutton	129	814	1951	619
G.A.Gooch	128	990	1992-93	820
W.G.Grace	126	1493	1895	1113
D.C.S.Compton	123	839	1952	552
T.W.Graveney	122	1223	1964	940
D.G.Bradman	117	338	1947-48	295
I.V.A.Richards	114	796	1988-89	658
M.R.Ramprakash	114	764	2008	676
Zaheer Abbas	108	768	1982-83	658
A.Sandham	107	1000	1935	871
M.C.Cowdrey	107	1130	1973	1035
T.W.Hayward	104	1138	1913	1076
G.M.Turner	103	792	1982	779
J.H.Edrich	103	979	1977	945
L.E.G.Ames	102	951	1950	915
G.E.Tyldesley	102	961	1934	919
D.L.Amiss	102	1139	1986	1081

MOST 400s: 2 – B.C.Lara, W.H.Ponsford

MOST 300s or more: 6 – D.G.Bradman; 4 – W.R.Hammond, W.H.Ponsford

MOST 200s or more: 37 – D.G.Bradman; 36 – W.R.Hammond; 22 – E.H.Hendren

MOST RUNS IN A MONTH

1294 (avge 92.42)	L.Hutton	Yorkshire	June 1949

MOST RUNS IN A SEASON

Runs			I	NO	HS	Avge	100	Season
3816	D.C.S.Compton	Middlesex	50	8	246	90.85	18	1947
3539	W.J.Edrich	Middlesex	52	8	267*	80.43	12	1947
3518	T.W.Hayward	Surrey	61	8	219	66.37	13	1906

The feat of scoring 3000 runs in a season has been achieved 28 times, the most recent instance being by W.E.Alley (3019) in 1961. The highest aggregate in a season since 1969 is 2755 by S.J.Cook in 1991.

1000 RUNS IN A SEASON MOST TIMES

28   W.G.Grace (Gloucestershire), F.E.Woolley (Kent)

HIGHEST BATTING AVERAGE IN A SEASON

(Qualification: 12 innings)

Avge			I	NO	HS	Runs	100	Season
115.66	D.G.Bradman	Australians	26	5	278	2429	13	1938
104.66	D.R.Martyn	Australians	14	5	176*	942	5	2001
103.54	M.R.Ramprakash	Surrey	24	2	301*	2278	8	2006
102.53	G.Boycott	Yorkshire	20	5	175*	1538	6	1979
102.00	W.A.Johnston	Australians	17	16	28*	102	–	1953
101.70	G.A.Gooch	Essex	30	3	333	2746	12	1990
101.30	M.R.Ramprakash	Surrey	25	5	266*	2026	10	2007
100.12	G.Boycott	Yorkshire	30	5	233	2503	13	1971

FASTEST HUNDRED AGAINST AUTHENTIC BOWLING

35 min	P.G.H.Fender	Surrey v Northamptonshire	Northampton	1920

FASTEST DOUBLE HUNDRED

113 min	R.J.Shastri	Bombay v Baroda	Bombay	1984-85

FASTEST TRIPLE HUNDRED

181 min	D.C.S.Compton	MCC v NE Transvaal	Benoni	1948-49

MOST SIXES IN AN INNINGS

23	C.Munro	Central Districts v Auckland	Napier	2014-15

MOST SIXES IN A MATCH

23	C.Munro	Central Districts v Auckland	Napier	2014-15

MOST SIXES IN A SEASON

80	I.T.Botham	Somerset and England		1985

MOST FOURS IN AN INNINGS

72	B.C.Lara	Warwickshire v Durham	Birmingham	1994

MOST RUNS OFF ONE OVER

36	G.St A.Sobers	Nottinghamshire v Glamorgan	Swansea	1968
36	R.J.Shastri	Bombay v Baroda	Bombay	1984-85

Both batsmen hit for six all six balls of overs bowled by M.A.Nash and Tilak Raj respectively.

MOST RUNS IN A DAY

390*	B.C.Lara	Warwickshire v Durham	Birmingham	1994

There have been 19 instances of a batsman scoring 300 or more runs in a day.

LONGEST INNINGS

1015 min	R.Nayyar (271)	Himachal Pradesh v Jammu & Kashmir Chamba		1999-00

HIGHEST PARTNERSHIPS FOR EACH WICKET

First Wicket

561	Waheed Mirza/Mansoor Akhtar	Karachi W v Quetta	Karachi	1976-77
555	P.Holmes/H.Sutcliffe	Yorkshire v Essex	Leyton	1932
554	J.T.Brown/J.Tunnicliffe	Yorkshire v Derbys	Chesterfield	1898

Second Wicket

580	Rafatullah Mohmand/Aamer Sajjad	WAPDA v SSGC	Sheikhupura	2009-10
576	S.T.Jayasuriya/R.S.Mahanama	Sri Lanka v India	Colombo	1997-98
480	E.Elgar/R.R.Rossouw	Eagles v Titans	Centurion	2009-10
475	Zahir Alam/L.S.Rajput	Assam v Tripura	Gauhati	1991-92
465*	J.A.Jameson/R.B.Kanhai	Warwickshire v Glos	Birmingham	1974

Third Wicket
624	K.C.Sangakkara/D.P.M.D.Jayawardena	Sri Lanka v South Africa	Colombo	2006
539	S.D.Jogiyani/R.A.Jadeja	Saurashtra v Gujarat	Surat	2012-13
523	M.A.Carberry/N.D.McKenzie	Hampshire v Yorkshire	Southampton	2011

Fourth Wicket
577	V.S.Hazare/Gul Mahomed	Baroda v Holkar	Baroda	1946-47
574*	C.L.Walcott/F.M.M.Worrell	Barbados v Trinidad	Port-of-Spain	1945-46
502*	F.M.M.Worrell/J.D.C.Goddard	Barbados v Trinidad	Bridgetown	1943-44
470	A.I.Kallicharran/G.W.Humpage	Warwickshire v Lancs	Southport	1982

Fifth Wicket
520*	C.A.Pujara/R.A.Jadeja	Saurashtra v Orissa	Rajkot	2008-09
494	Marchall Ayub/Mehrab Hossain Jr	Central Zone v East Zone	Bogra	2012-13
479	Misbah-ul-Haq/Usman Arshad	Sui NGP v Lahore Shalimar	Lahore	2009-10
464*	M.E.Waugh/S.R.Waugh	NSW v W Australia	Perth	1990-91
420	Mohd. Ashraful/Marshall Ayub	Dhaka v Chittagong	Chittagong	2006-07
410*	A.S.Chopra/S.Badrinath	India A v South Africa A	Delhi	2007-08
405	S.G.Barnes/D.G.Bradman	Australia v England	Sydney	1946-47
401	M.B.Loye/D.Ripley	Northants v Glamorgan	Northampton	1998

Sixth Wicket
487*	G.A.Headley/C.C.Passailaigue	Jamaica v Tennyson's	Kingston	1931-32
428	W.W.Armstrong/M.A.Noble	Australians v Sussex	Hove	1902
417	W.P.Saha/L.R.Shukla	Bengal v Assam	Kolkata	2010-11
411	R.M.Poore/E.G.Wynyard	Hampshire v Somerset	Taunton	1899

Seventh Wicket
460	Bhupinder Singh jr/P.Dharmani	Punjab v Delhi	Delhi	1994-95
371	M.R.Marsh/S.M.Whiteman	Australia A v India A	Brisbane	2014
366*	J.M.Bairstow/T.T.Bresnan	Yorkshire v Durham	Chester-le-Street	2015

Eighth Wicket
433	V.T.Trumper/A.Sims	Australians v C'bury	Christchurch	1913-14
392	A.Mishra/J.Yadav	Haryana v Karnataka	Hubli	2012-13
332	I.J.L.Trott/S.C.J.Broad	England v Pakistan	Lord's	2010

Ninth Wicket
283	J.Chapman/A.Warren	Derbys v Warwicks	Blackwell	1910
268	J.B.Commins/N.Boje	SA 'A' v Mashonaland	Harare	1994-95
261	W.L.Madsen/T.Poynton	Derbys v Northants	Northampton	2012
251	J.W.H.T.Douglas/S.N.Hare	Essex v Derbyshire	Leyton	1921

Tenth Wicket
307	A.F.Kippax/J.E.H.Hooker	NSW v Victoria	Melbourne	1928-29
249	C.T.Sarwate/S.N.Banerjee	Indians v Surrey	The Oval	1946
239	Aqil Arshad/Ali Raza	Lahore Whites v Hyderabad	Lahore	2004-05

BOWLING RECORDS
2000 WICKETS IN A CAREER

	Career	Runs	Wkts	Avge	100w
W.Rhodes	1898-1930	69993	**4187**	16.71	23
A.P.Freeman	1914-36	69577	**3776**	18.42	17
C.W.L.Parker	1903-35	63817	**3278**	19.46	16
J.T.Hearne	1888-1923	54352	**3061**	17.75	15
T.W.J.Goddard	1922-52	59116	**2979**	19.84	16
W.G.Grace	1865-1908	51545	**2876**	17.92	10
A.S.Kennedy	1907-36	61034	**2874**	21.23	15
D.Shackleton	1948-69	53303	**2857**	18.65	20
G.A.R.Lock	1946-70/71	54709	**2844**	19.23	14
F.J.Titmus	1949-82	63313	**2830**	22.37	16
M.W.Tate	1912-37	50571	**2784**	18.16	13+1
G.H.Hirst	1891-1929	51282	**2739**	18.72	15
C.Blythe	1899-1914	42136	**2506**	16.81	14
D.L.Underwood	1963-87	49993	**2465**	20.28	10

	Career	Runs	Wkts	Avge	100w
W.E.Astill	1906-39	57783	2431	23.76	9
J.C.White	1909-37	43759	2356	18.57	14
W.E.Hollies	1932-57	48656	2323	20.94	14
F.S.Trueman	1949-69	42154	2304	18.29	12
J.B.Statham	1950-68	36999	2260	16.37	13
R.T.D.Perks	1930-55	53771	2233	24.07	16
J.Briggs	1879-1900	35431	2221	15.95	12
D.J.Shepherd	1950-72	47302	2218	21.32	12
E.G.Dennett	1903-26	42571	2147	19.82	12
T.Richardson	1892-1905	38794	2104	18.43	10
T.E.Bailey	1945-67	48170	2082	23.13	9
R.Illingworth	1951-83	42023	2072	20.28	10
F.E.Woolley	1906-38	41066	2068	19.85	8
N.Gifford	1960-88	48731	2068	23.56	4
G.Geary	1912-38	41339	2063	20.03	11
D.V.P.Wright	1932-57	49307	2056	23.98	10
J.A.Newman	1906-30	51111	2032	25.15	9
A.Shaw	1864-97	24580	2026+1	12.12	9
S.Haigh	1895-1913	32091	2012	15.94	11

ALL TEN WICKETS IN AN INNINGS

This feat has been achieved 81 times in first-class matches (excluding 12-a-side fixtures).

Three Times: A.P.Freeman (1929, 1930, 1931)

Twice: V.E.Walker (1859, 1865); H.Verity (1931, 1932); J.C.Laker (1956)

Instances since 1945:

W.E.Hollies	Warwickshire v Notts	Birmingham	1946
J.M.Sims	East v West	Kingston on Thames	1948
J.K.R.Graveney	Gloucestershire v Derbyshire	Chesterfield	1949
T.E.Bailey	Essex v Lancashire	Clacton	1949
R.Berry	Lancashire v Worcestershire	Blackpool	1953
S.P.Gupte	President's XI v Combined XI	Bombay	1954-55
J.C.Laker	Surrey v Australians	The Oval	1956
K.Smales	Nottinghamshire v Glos	Stroud	1956
G.A.R.Lock	Surrey v Kent	Blackheath	1956
J.C.Laker	England v Australia	Manchester	1956
P.M.Chatterjee	Bengal v Assam	Jorhat	1956-57
J.D.Bannister	Warwicks v Combined Services	Birmingham (M & B)	1959
A.J.G.Pearson	Cambridge U v Leicestershire	Loughborough	1961
N.I.Thomson	Sussex v Warwickshire	Worthing	1964
P.J.Allan	Queensland v Victoria	Melbourne	1965-66
I.J.Brayshaw	Western Australia v Victoria	Perth	1967-68
Shahid Mahmood	Karachi Whites v Khairpur	Karachi	1969-70
E.E.Hemmings	International XI v W Indians	Kingston	1982-83
P.Sunderam	Rajasthan v Vidarbha	Jodhpur	1985-86
S.T.Jefferies	Western Province v Orange FS	Cape Town	1987-88
Imran Adil	Bahawalpur v Faisalabad	Faisalabad	1989-90
G.P.Wickremasinghe	Sinhalese v Kalutara	Colombo	1991-92
R.L.Johnson	Middlesex v Derbyshire	Derby	1994
Naeem Akhtar	Rawalpindi B v Peshawar	Peshawar	1995-96
A.Kumble	India v Pakistan	Delhi	1998-99
D.S.Mohanty	East Zone v South Zone	Agartala	2000-01
O.D.Gibson	Durham v Hampshire	Chester-le-Street	2007
M.W.Olivier	Warriors v Eagles	Bloemfontein	2007-08
Zulfiqar Babar	Multan v Islamabad	Multan	2009-10

MOST WICKETS IN A MATCH

19	J.C.Laker	England v Australia	Manchester	1956

MOST WICKETS IN A SEASON

Wkts		Season	Matches	Overs	Mdns	Runs	Avge
304	A.P.Freeman	1928	37	1976.1	423	5489	18.05
298	A.P.Freeman	1933	33	2039	651	4549	15.26

The feat of taking 250 wickets in a season has been achieved on 12 occasions, the last instance being by A.P.Freeman in 1933. 200 or more wickets in a season have been taken on 59 occasions, the last being by G.A.R.Lock (212 wickets, average 12.02) in 1957.

The highest aggregates of wickets taken in a season since the reduction of County Championship matches in 1969 are as follows:

Wkts		Season	Matches	Overs	Mdns	Runs	Avge
134	M.D.Marshall	1982	22	822	225	2108	15.73
131	L.R.Gibbs	1971	23	1024.1	295	2475	18.89
125	F.D.Stephenson	1988	22	819.1	196	2289	18.31
121	R.D.Jackman	1980	23	746.2	220	1864	15.40

Since 1969 there have been 50 instances of bowlers taking 100 wickets in a season.

MOST HAT-TRICKS IN A CAREER

7	D.V.P.Wright
6	T.W.J.Goddard, C.W.L.Parker
5	S.Haigh, V.W.C.Jupp, A.E.G.Rhodes, F.A.Tarrant

ALL-ROUND RECORDS
THE 'DOUBLE'

3000 runs and 100 wickets: J.H.Parks (1937)

2000 runs and 200 wickets: G.H.Hirst (1906)

2000 runs and 100 wickets: F.E.Woolley (4), J.W.Hearne (3), W.G.Grace (2), G.H.Hirst (2), W.Rhodes (2), T.E.Bailey, D.E.Davies, G.L.Jessop, V.W.C.Jupp, J.Langridge, F.A.Tarrant, C.L.Townsend, L.F.Townsend

1000 runs and 200 wickets: M.W.Tate (3), A.E.Trott (2), A.S.Kennedy

Most Doubles: 16 – W.Rhodes; 14 – G.H.Hirst; 10 – V.W.C.Jupp

Double in Debut Season: D.B.Close (1949) – aged 18, the youngest to achieve this feat.

The feat of scoring 1000 runs and taking 100 wickets in a season has been achieved on 305 occasions, R.J.Hadlee (1984) and F.D.Stephenson (1988) being the only players to complete the 'double' since the reduction of County Championship matches in 1969.

WICKET-KEEPING RECORDS
1000 DISMISSALS IN A CAREER

	Career	Dismissals	Ct	St
R.W.Taylor	1960-88	**1649**	1473	176
J.T.Murray	1952-75	**1527**	1270	257
H.Strudwick	1902-27	**1497**	1242	255
A.P.E.Knott	1964-85	**1344**	1211	133
R.C.Russell	1981-2004	**1320**	1192	128
F.H.Huish	1895-1914	**1310**	933	377
B.Taylor	1949-73	**1294**	1083	211
S.J.Rhodes	1981-2004	**1263**	1139	124
D.Hunter	1889-1909	**1253**	906	347
H.R.Butt	1890-1912	**1228**	953	275
J.H.Board	1891-1914/15	**1207**	852	355
H.Elliott	1920-47	**1206**	904	302
J.M.Parks	1949-76	**1181**	1088	93
R.Booth	1951-70	**1126**	948	178
L.E.G.Ames	1926-51	**1121**	703	418

	Career	Dismissals	Ct	St
D.L.Bairstow	1970-90	**1099**	961	138
G.Duckworth	1923-47	**1096**	753	343
H.W.Stephenson	1948-64	**1082**	748	334
J.G.Binks	1955-75	**1071**	895	176
T.G.Evans	1939-69	**1066**	816	250
A.Long	1960-80	**1046**	922	124
G.O.Dawkes	1937-61	**1043**	895	148
R.W.Tolchard	1965-83	**1037**	912	125
W.L.Cornford	1921-47	**1017**	675	342
C.M.W.Read	1997-2015	**1007**	957	50

MOST DISMISSALS IN AN INNINGS

9	(8ct, 1st)	Tahir Rashid	Habib Bank v PACO	Gujranwala	1992-93
9	(7ct, 2st)	W.R.James	Matabeleland v Mashonaland CD	Bulawayo	1995-96
8	(8ct)	A.T.W.Grout	Queensland v W Australia	Brisbane	1959-60
8	(8ct)	D.E.East	Essex v Somerset	Taunton	1985
8	(8ct)	S.A.Marsh	Kent v Middlesex	Lord's	1991
8	(6ct, 2st)	T.J.Zoehrer	Australians v Surrey	The Oval	1993
8	(7ct, 1st)	D.S.Berry	Victoria v South Australia	Melbourne	1996-97
8	(7ct, 1st)	Y.S.S.Mendis	Bloomfield v Kurunegala Youth	Colombo	2000-01
8	(7ct, 1st)	S.Nath	Assam v Tripura (on debut)	Gauhati	2001-02
8	(8ct)	J.N.Batty	Surrey v Kent	The Oval	2004
8	(8ct)	Golam Mabud	Sylhet v Dhaka	Dhaka	2005-06
8	(8ct)	D.C.de Boorder	Otago v Wellington	Wellington	2009-10
8	(8ct)	R.S.Second	Free State v North West	Bloemfontein	2011-12
8	(8ct)	T.L.Tsolekile	South Africa A v Sri Lanka A	Durban	2012

MOST DISMISSALS IN A MATCH

14	(11ct, 3st)	I.Khaleel	Hyderabad v Assam	Guwahati	2011-12
13	(11ct, 2st)	W.R.James	Matabeleland v Mashonaland CD	Bulawayo	1995-96
12	(8ct, 4st)	E.Pooley	Surrey v Sussex	The Oval	1868
12	(9ct, 3st)	D.Tallon	Queensland v NSW	Sydney	1938-39
12	(9ct, 3st)	H.B.Taber	NSW v South Australia	Adelaide	1968-69
12	(12ct)	P.D.McGlashan	Northern Districts v Central Districts	Whangarei	2009-10
12	(11ct, 1st)	T.L.Tsolekile	Lions v Dolphins	Johannesburg	2010-11
12	(12ct)	Kashif Mahmood	Lahore Shalimar v Abbottabad	Abbottabad	2010-11
12	(12ct)	R.S.Second	Free State v North West	Bloemfontein	2011-12

MOST DISMISSALS IN A SEASON

128	(79ct, 49st)	L.E.G.Ames			1929

FIELDING RECORDS
750 CATCHES IN A CAREER

1018	F.E.Woolley	1906-38	784	J.G.Langridge	1928-55
887	W.G.Grace	1865-1908	764	W.Rhodes	1898-1930
830	G.A.R.Lock	1946-70/71	758	C.A.Milton	1948-74
819	W.R.Hammond	1920-51	754	E.H.Hendren	1907-38
813	D.B.Close	1949-86			

MOST CATCHES IN AN INNINGS

7	M.J.Stewart	Surrey v Northamptonshire	Northampton	1957
7	A.S.Brown	Gloucestershire v Nottinghamshire	Nottingham	1966
7	R.Clarke	Warwickshire v Lancashire	Liverpool	2011

MOST CATCHES IN A MATCH

10	W.R.Hammond	Gloucestershire v Surrey	Cheltenham	1928
9	R.Clarke	Warwickshire v Lancashire	Liverpool	2011

MOST CATCHES IN A SEASON

78	W.R.Hammond	1928	77	M.J.Stewart	1957

ENGLAND LIMITED-OVERS INTERNATIONALS 2015

CARLTON MID ONE-DAY INTERNATIONAL TRI-SERIES

LIMITED-OVERS INTERNATIONALS

Sydney Cricket Ground, 16 January. Toss: England. **AUSTRALIA** won by three wickets. England 234 (47.5; E.J.G.Morgan 121, M.A.Starc 4-42, J.P.Faulkner 3-47). Australia 235-7 (39.5; D.A.Warner 127, C.R.Woakes 4-40). Award: M.A.Starc.

Woolloongabba, Brisbane, 20 January. Toss: India. **ENGLAND** won by nine wickets. India 153 (39.3; S.T.Finn 5-33, J.M.Anderson 4-18). England 156-1 (27.3; I.R.Bell 88*, J.W.A.Taylor 56*). Award: S.T.Finn.

Bellerive Oval, Hobart, 23 January. Toss: Australia. **AUSTRALIA** won by three wickets. England 303-8 (50; I.R.Bell 141, J.E.Root 69). Australia 304-7 (49.5; S.P.D.Smith 102*). Award: S.P.D.Smith.

W.A.C.A. Ground, Perth, 30 January. Toss: England. **ENGLAND** won by three wickets. India 200 (48.1; A.M.Rahane 73, S.T.Finn 3-36). England 201-7 (46.5; J.W.A.Taylor 82, J.C.Buttler 67, S.T.R.Binny 3-33). Award: J.W.A.Taylor.

FINAL, W.A.C.A. Ground, Perth, 1 February. Toss: England. **AUSTRALIA** won by 112 runs. Australia 278-8 (50; G.J.Maxwell 95, M.R.Marsh 60, J.P.Faulkner 50*, S.C.J.Broad 3-55). England 166 (39.1; G.J.Maxwell 4-46, M.G.Johnson 3-27). Award: G.J.Maxwell. Series award: M.A.Starc.

ICC CRICKET WORLD CUP

LIMITED-OVERS INTERNATIONALS

Melbourne Cricket Ground, 14 February. Toss: England. **AUSTRALIA** won by 111 runs. Australia 342-9 (50; A.J.Finch 135, G.J.Maxwell 66, G.J.Bailey 55, S.T.Finn 5-71). England 231 (41.5; J.W.A.Taylor 98*, M.R.Marsh 5-33). Award: A.J.Finch.
S.T.Finn took a hat-trick in the last three balls of Australia's innings.

Westpac Stadium, Wellington, 20 February. Toss: England. **NEW ZEALAND** won by eight wickets. England 123 (33.2; T.G.Southee 7-33). New Zealand 125-2 (12.2; B.B.McCullum 77). Award: T.G.Southee.
New Zealand won with 226 balls remaining – England's equal-heaviest defeat in terms of balls remaining.

Hagley Oval, Christchurch, 23 February. Toss: Scotland. **ENGLAND** won by 119 runs. England 303-8 (50; M.M.Ali 128, I.R.Bell 54, J.H.Davey 4-68). Scotland 184 (42.2; K.J.Coetzer 71, S.T.Finn 3-26). Award: M.M.Ali.

Westpac Stadium, Wellington, 1 March. Toss: England. **SRI LANKA** won by nine wickets. England 309-6 (50; J.E.Root 121). Sri Lanka 312-1 (47.2; H.D.R.L.Thirimanne 139*, K.C.Sangakkara 117*). Award: K.C.Sangakkara.

Adelaide Oval, 9 March. Toss: England. **BANGLADESH** won by 15 runs. Bangladesh 275-7 (50; Mahmudullah 103, Mushfiqur Rahim 89). England 260 (48.3; J.C.Buttler 65, I.R.Bell 63, Rubel Hossain 4-53). Award: Mahmudullah.

Sydney Cricket Ground, 13 March. Toss: England. **ENGLAND** won by nine wickets (D/L method). Afghanistan 111-7 (36.2/36.2). England 101-1 (18.1/25; I.R.Bell 52*). Award: C.J.Jordan (2-13).
Australia beat New Zealand by seven wickets in the final to win the tournament.

IRELAND v ENGLAND

LIMITED-OVERS INTERNATIONAL

The Village, Malahide, 8 May. Toss: England. **NO RESULT**. Ireland 56-4 (18). England debuts: Z.S.Ansari, J.J.Roy, J.M.Vince, D.J.Willey, M.A.Wood.

ENGLAND v NEW ZEALAND

ROYAL LONDON LIMITED-OVERS INTERNATIONALS

Edgbaston, Birmingham, 9 June. Toss: New Zealand. **ENGLAND** won by 210 runs. England 408-9 (50; J.C.Buttler 129, J.E.Root 104, A.U.Rashid 69, E.J.G.Morgan 50, T.A.Boult 4-55). New Zealand 198 (31.1; S.T.Finn 4-35, A.U.Rashid 4-55). Award: J.C.Buttler. England debut: S.W.Billings.
England's highest total in all LOIs; England's biggest winning margin (by runs).

The Oval, London, 12 June. Toss: New Zealand. **NEW ZEALAND** won by 13 runs (D/L method). New Zealand 398-5 (50; L.R.P.L.Taylor 119*, K.S.Williamson 93, M.J.Guptill 50). England 365-9 (46/46; E.J.G.Morgan 88, A.D.Hales 54, N.L.McCullum 3-86). Award: L.R.P.L.Taylor.

The Rose Bowl, Southampton, 14 June. Toss: England. **NEW ZEALAND** won by three wickets. England 302 (45.2; E.J.G.Morgan 71, B.A.Stokes 68, J.E.Root 54, T.G.Southee 3-44, B.M.Wheeler 3-63). New Zealand 306-7 (49; K.S.Williamson 118, L.R.P.L.Taylor 110, D.J.Willey 3-69). Award: K.S.Williamson.

Trent Bridge, Nottingham, 17 June. Toss: New Zealand. **ENGLAND** won by seven wickets. New Zealand 349-7 (50; K.S.Williamson 90, G.D.Elliott 55*, M.J.Guptill 53). England 350-3 (44; E.J.G.Morgan 113, J.E.Root 106*, A.D.Hales 67). Award: E.J.G.Morgan.

Riverside Ground, Chester-le-Street, 20 June. Toss: England. **ENGLAND** won by three wickets (D/L method). New Zealand 283-9 (50; M.J.Guptill 67, K.S.Williamson 50, B.A.Stokes 3-52). England 192-7 (25/26; J.M.Bairstow 83*, M.J.Santner 3-31). Award: J.M.Bairstow. Series award: K.S.Williamson.

NATWEST TWENTY20 INTERNATIONAL

Old Trafford, Manchester, 23 June. Toss: England. **ENGLAND** won by 56 runs. England 191-7 (20; J.E.Root 68). New Zealand 135 (16.2; K.S.Williamson 57, D.J.Willey 3-22, M.A.Wood 3-26). Award: J.E.Root. England debuts: S.W.Billings, D.J.Willey, M.A.Wood.

ENGLAND v AUSTRALIA

NATWEST TWENTY20 INTERNATIONAL

Sophia Gardens, Cardiff, 31 August. Toss: Australia. **ENGLAND** won by 5 runs. England 182-5 (20; E.J.G.Morgan 74, M.M.Ali 72*). Australia 177-8 (20; S.P.D.Smith 90). Award: M.M.Ali. England debut: R.J.W.Topley.

ROYAL LONDON LIMITED-OVERS INTERNATIONALS

The Rose Bowl, Southampton, 3 September. Toss: Australia. **AUSTRALIA** won by 59 runs. Australia 305-6 (50; M.S.Wade 71*, D.A.Warner 59, A.U.Rashid 4-59). England 246 (45.3; J.J.Roy 67). Award: M.S.Wade.

Lord's, London, 5 September. Toss: England. **AUSTRALIA** won by 64 runs. Australia 309-7 (50; S.P.D.Smith 70, M.R.Marsh 64, G.J.Bailey 54, B.A.Stokes 3-60). England 245 (42.3; E.J.G.Morgan 85, P.J.Cummins 4-56). Award: M.R.Marsh.

Old Trafford, Manchester, 8 September. Toss: England. **ENGLAND** won by 93 runs. England 300-8 (50; J.W.A.Taylor 101, J.J.Roy 63, E.J.G.Morgan 62). Australia 207 (44; A.J.Finch 53, M.M.Ali 3-32, L.E.Plunkett 3-49). Award: J.W.A.Taylor.

Headingley, Leeds, 11 September. Toss: Australia. **ENGLAND** won by three wickets. Australia 299-7 (50; G.J.Maxwell 85, G.J.Bailey 75, M.S.Wade 50*, D.J.Willey 3-51). England 304-7 (48.2; E.J.G.Morgan 92, P.J.Cummins 4-49). Award: E.J.G.Morgan.

Old Trafford, Manchester, 13 September. Toss: England. **AUSTRALIA** won by eight wickets. England 138 (33; M.R.Marsh 4-27, J.W.Hastings 3-21). Australia 140-2 (24.2; A.J.Finch 70*). Award: M.R.Marsh. Series award: M.R.Marsh. England debut: R.J.W.Topley.

PAKISTAN v ENGLAND

LIMITED-OVERS INTERNATIONALS

Sheikh Zayed Stadium, Abu Dhabi, 11 November. Toss: England. **PAKISTAN** won by six wickets. England 216 (49.4; E.J.G.Morgan 76, J.W.A.Taylor 60, Mohammad Irfan 3-35). Pakistan 217-4 (43.4; Mohammad Hafeez 102*, Babar Azam 62*, R.J.W.Topley 3-26). Award: Mohammad Hafeez.

Sheikh Zayed Stadium, Abu Dhabi, 13 November. Toss: England. **ENGLAND** won by 95 runs. England 283-5 (50; A.D.Hales 109, J.E.Root 63, J.J.Roy 54, Wahab Riaz 3-43). Pakistan 188 (45.5; Sarfraz Ahmed 64, C.R.Woakes 4-33, D.J.Willey 3-25). Award: A.D.Hales.

Sharjah Cricket Stadium, 17 November. Toss: Pakistan. **ENGLAND** won by six wickets. Pakistan 208 (49.5; C.R.Woakes 4-40). England 210-4 (41; J.W.A.Taylor 67*). Award: J.W.A.Taylor.

Dubai International Cricket Stadium, 20 November. Toss: England. **ENGLAND** won by 84 runs. England 355-5 (50; J.C.Buttler 116*, J.J.Roy 102, J.E.Root 71). Pakistan 271 (40.4; Shoaib Malik 52, Babar Azam 51, M.M.Ali 3-53, A.U.Rashid 3-78). Award: J.C.Buttler. Series award: J.C.Buttler.
J.C.Buttler took an England record 46 balls to reach his century, hitting an England record eight sixes in his innings. England's total of 355-5 is their highest outside England.

TWENTY20 INTERNATIONALS

Dubai International Cricket Stadium, 26 November. Toss: England. **ENGLAND** won by 14 runs. England 160-5 (20; S.W.Billings 53). Pakistan 146 (20; L.E.Plunkett 3-21, R.J.W.Topley 3-24). Award: S.W.Billings. England debut: J.M.Vince.

Dubai International Cricket Stadium, 27 November. Toss: England. **ENGLAND** won by 3 runs. England 172-8 (20; Shahid Afridi 3-15). Pakistan 169-8 (20; L.E.Plunkett 3-33). Award: L.E.Plunkett.

Sharjah Cricket Stadium, 30 November. Toss: England. **MATCH TIED (ENGLAND won one-over eliminator)**. England 154-8 (20). Pakistan 154-7 (20; Shoaib Malik 75, D.J.Willey 3-36). Award: Shoaib Malik.

ENGLAND'S RESULTS IN 2015

	P	W	L	T	NR
Limited Overs	26	12	13	–	1
Twenty20	5	4	–	1*	–
Overall	31	16	13	1*	1

* England awarded the victory after a one-over eliminator.

700 RUNS IN LIMITED-OVERS INTERNATIONALS IN 2015

	M	I	NO	HS	Runs	Avge	100	50	S/Rate
E.J.G.Morgan	25	23	1	121	967	43.95	2	7	93.79
J.E.Root	20	18	1	121	723	42.52	3	4	91.98

20 WICKETS IN LIMITED-OVERS INTERNATIONALS IN 2015

	Pl	O	M	R	W	Avge	Best	4wI	Econ
S.T.Finn	18	149	10	858	31	27.67	5-33	3	5.75
M.M.Ali	19	162.4	9	768	23	33.39	3-32	–	4.72
C.R.Woakes	17	137.1	5	778	21	37.04	4-33	3	5.67

LIMITED-OVERS INTERNATIONALS CAREER RECORDS

These records, complete to 7 April 2016, include all players registered for county cricket for the 2015 season at the time of going to press, plus those who have appeared in LOI matches for ICC full member countries since 1 December 2014.

ENGLAND – BATTING AND FIELDING

	M	I	NO	HS	Runs	Avge	100	50	Ct/St
M.M.Ali	36	35	4	128	856	27.61	2	3	11
T.R.Ambrose	5	5	1	6	10	2.50	–	–	3
J.M.Anderson	194	79	43	28	273	7.58	–	–	53
Z.S.Ansari	1	–	–	–	–	–	–	–	–
J.M.Bairstow	12	10	2	83*	260	32.50	–	1	10/1
G.S.Ballance	16	15	1	79	279	21.21	–	2	8
G.J.Batty	10	8	2	17	30	5.00	–	–	4
I.R.Bell	161	157	14	141	5416	37.87	4	35	54
S.W.Billings	5	4	–	41	90	22.50	–	–	1
R.S.Bopara	120	109	21	101*	2695	30.62	1	14	35
S.G.Borthwick	2	2	–	15	18	9.00	–	–	–
T.T.Bresnan	85	64	20	80	871	19.79	–	1	20
D.R.Briggs	1	–	–	–	–	–	–	–	–
S.C.J.Broad	121	68	25	45*	529	12.30	–	–	27
J.C.Buttler	70	61	10	129	1798	35.25	4	7	87/9
M.A.Carberry	6	6	–	63	114	19.00	–	1	2
G.Chapple	1	1	–	14	14	14.00	–	–	–
R.Clarke	20	13	–	39	144	11.07	–	–	11
P.D.Collingwood	197	181	37	120*	5092	35.36	5	26	108
A.N.Cook	92	92	4	137	3204	36.40	5	19	36
S.M.Davies	8	8	–	87	244	30.50	–	1	8
J.L.Denly	9	9	–	67	268	29.77	–	2	5
J.W.Dernbach	24	8	1	5	19	2.71	–	–	5
S.T.Finn	65	28	12	35	131	8.18	–	–	13
J.S.Foster	11	6	3	13	41	13.66	–	–	13/7
H.F.Gurney	10	6	4	6*	15	7.50	–	–	1
A.D.Hales	29	28	–	112	962	34.35	2	6	6
C.J.Jordan	27	20	6	38*	154	11.00	–	–	18
E.C.Joyce †	17	17	–	107	471	27.70	1	3	6
R.W.T.Key	5	5	–	19	54	10.80	–	–	1
M.J.Lumb	3	3	–	106	165	55.00	1	–	1
S.C.Meaker	2	2	–	1	2	1.00	–	–	–
E.J.G.Morgan †	137	128	20	124*	4012	37.14	7	24	53
P.Mustard	10	10	–	83	233	23.30	–	1	9/2
G.Onions	4	1	1	1	1	1.00	–	–	–
S.D.Parry	2	–	–	–	–	–	–	–	–
S.R.Patel	36	22	7	70*	482	32.13	–	1	7
L.E.Plunkett	34	30	11	56	414	21.78	–	1	10
W.B.Rankin †	7	2	1	4	5	2.50	–	–	–
A.U.Rashid	25	17	5	69	294	24.50	–	1	8
C.M.W.Read	36	24	7	30*	300	17.64	–	–	41/2
J.E.Root	68	64	6	125	2572	44.34	8	12	32
J.J.Roy	20	19	–	102	558	29.36	1	3	5
A.Shahzad	11	8	2	9	39	6.50	–	–	4
R.J.Sidebottom	25	18	8	24	133	13.30	–	–	6
B.A.Stokes	39	34	2	70	685	21.40	–	4	18
J.W.A.Taylor	27	26	5	101	887	42.23	1	7	7
R.J.W.Topley	10	5	4	6	7	7.00	–	–	2
J.C.Tredwell	45	25	11	30	163	11.64	–	–	14

283

	M	I	NO	HS	Runs	Avge	100	50	Ct/St
M.E.Trescothick	123	122	6	137	4335	37.37	12	21	49
I.J.L.Trott	68	65	10	137	2819	51.25	4	22	14
J.M.Vince	1	–	–	–	–	–	–	–	1
D.J.Willey	13	7	3	13*	58	14.50	–	–	5
C.R.Woakes	43	34	8	42*	486	18.69	–	–	21
M.A.Wood	7	3	2	13	26	26.00	–	–	1
L.J.Wright	50	39	4	52	707	20.20	–	2	18

ENGLAND – BOWLING

	O	M	R	W	Avge	Best	4wI	R/Over
M.M.Ali	292.4	5	1437	38	37.81	3-32	–	4.91
J.M.Anderson	1597.2	125	7861	269	29.22	5-23	13	4.92
G.J.Batty	73.2	1	366	5	73.20	2-40	–	4.99
I.R.Bell	14.4	0	88	6	14.66	3- 9	–	6.00
R.S.Bopara	310	11	1523	40	38.07	4-38	1	4.91
S.G.Borthwick	9	0	72	0	–	–	–	8.00
T.T.Bresnan	703.3	35	3813	109	34.98	5-48	4	5.42
D.R.Briggs	10	0	39	2	19.50	2-39	–	3.90
S.C.J.Broad	1018.1	56	5364	178	30.13	5-23	10	5.26
M.A.Carberry	1	0	12	0	–	–	–	12.00
G.Chapple	4	0	14	0	–	–	–	3.50
R.Clarke	78.1	3	415	11	37.72	2-28	–	5.30
P.D.Collingwood	864.2	14	4294	111	38.68	6-31	4	4.96
J.W.Dernbach	205.4	6	1308	31	42.19	4-45	1	6.35
S.T.Finn	557.4	35	2839	98	28.96	5-33	6	5.09
H.F.Gurney	75.5	4	432	11	39.27	4-55	1	5.69
C.J.Jordan	222	4	1338	40	33.45	5-29	1	6.02
S.C.Meaker	19	1	110	2	55.00	1-45	–	5.78
G.Onions	34	1	185	4	46.25	2-58	–	5.44
S.D.Parry	19	2	92	4	23.00	3-32	–	4.84
S.R.Patel	197.5	4	1091	24	45.45	5-41	1	5.51
L.E.Plunkett	267.1	7	1578	45	35.06	3-24	–	5.90
W.B.Rankin	53.1	3	241	10	24.10	4-46	1	4.53
A.U.Rashid	203.2	2	1199	27	44.40	4-55	2	5.89
J.E.Root	141	2	814	12	67.83	2-15	–	5.77
A.Shahzad	98	5	490	17	28.82	3-41	–	5.00
R.J.Sidebottom	212.5	12	1039	29	35.82	3-19	–	4.88
B.A.Stokes	213.2	2	1314	36	36.50	5-61	2	6.15
R.J.W.Topley	77.1	6	410	16	25.62	4-50	1	5.31
J.C.Tredwell	350.4	18	1666	60	27.76	4-44	3	4.75
M.E.Trescothick	38.4	0	219	4	54.75	2- 7	–	5.66
I.J.L.Trott	30.3	0	166	2	83.00	2-31	–	5.44
D.J.Willey	96	7	539	19	28.36	3-25	–	5.61
C.R.Woakes	338.3	12	1959	56	34.98	6-45	6	5.78
M.A.Wood	59	1	344	5	68.80	1-25	–	5.83
L.J.Wright	173	2	884	15	58.93	2-34	–	5.11

† *E.C.Joyce has also made 39 appearances for Ireland; E.J.G.Morgan has also made 23 appearances for Ireland; and W.B.Rankin has also made 37 appearances for Ireland (see below).*

LOI

AUSTRALIA – BATTING AND FIELDING

	M	I	NO	HS	Runs	Avge	100	50	Ct/St
A.C.Agar	2	1	–	5	5	5.00	–	–	2
G.J.Bailey	71	68	8	156	2498	41.63	3	18	34
S.M.Boland	6	1	–	2	2	2.00	–	–	3
J.A.Burns	6	6	–	69	146	24.33	–	1	2
D.T.Christian	19	18	5	39	273	21.00	–	–	10
M.J.Clarke	245	223	44	130	7981	44.58	8	58	106
M.J.Cosgrove	3	3	–	74	112	37.33	–	1	–
N.M.Coulter-Nile	13	8	4	16	60	15.00	–	–	3
P.J.Cummins	18	7	4	11*	34	11.33	–	–	5
X.J.Doherty	60	23	16	15*	101	14.42	–	–	19
J.P.Faulkner	50	38	16	116	873	39.68	1	4	14
A.J.Finch	57	55	1	148	2078	38.48	7	10	29
B.J.Haddin	126	115	16	110	3122	31.53	2	16	170/11
J.W.Hastings	20	16	9	48*	180	25.71	–	–	5
J.R.Hazlewood	17	3	3	5*	5	–	–	–	–
M.C.Henriques	6	6	1	12	36	7.20	–	–	1
M.G.Johnson	153	91	32	73*	951	16.11	–	2	35
U.T.Khawaja	5	5	1	50	108	27.00	–	1	2
N.M.Lyon	10	4	3	8*	12	12.00	–	–	1
C.J.McKay	59	31	10	30	190	9.04	–	–	7
M.R.Marsh	30	28	6	102*	870	39.54	1	6	13
S.E.Marsh	50	49	2	151	1857	39.51	3	12	11
G.J.Maxwell	62	57	7	102	1710	34.10	1	13	35
J.S.Paris	2	–	–	–	–	–	–	–	1
J.L.Pattinson	15	8	4	13	42	10.50	–	–	3
K.W.Richardson	12	4	2	19	30	15.00	–	–	1
G.S.Sandhu	2	–	–	–	–	–	–	–	–
S.P.D.Smith	72	59	7	149	2082	40.03	5	9	42
M.A.Starc	46	19	11	52*	163	20.37	–	1	12
M.P.Stoinis	1	1	–	4	4	4.00	–	–	–
A.C.Voges	31	28	9	112*	870	45.78	1	4	7
M.S.Wade	61	64	6	75	1173	24.43	–	7	79/7
D.A.Warner	71	69	2	178	2537	37.86	5	14	27
S.R.Watson	190	169	27	185*	5757	40.54	9	33	64
C.L.White	88	74	15	105	2037	34.52	2	11	37
A.Zampa	2	1	–	2	2	2.00	–	–	–

AUSTRALIA – BOWLING

	O	M	R	W	Avge	Best	4wI	R/Over
A.C.Agar	11	0	57	2	28.50	1-12	–	5.18
S.M.Boland	58	0	379	5	75.80	2-59	–	6.53
D.T.Christian	121.1	4	595	20	29.75	5-31	1	4.91
M.J.Clarke	430.5	7	2146	57	37.64	5-35	2	4.98
M.J.Cosgrove	5	0	13	1	13.00	1-1	–	2.60
N.M.Coulter-Nile	108.4	3	583	22	26.50	4-48	1	5.36
P.J.Cummins	146.1	5	832	33	25.21	4-49	2	5.69
X.J.Doherty	465.2	17	2224	55	40.43	4-28	3	4.77
J.P.Faulkner	385.4	9	2171	67	32.40	4-48	2	5.62
A.J.Finch	9.1	0	48	2	24.00	1-2	–	5.23
J.W.Hastings	172.5	5	825	24	34.37	4-58	1	4.77
J.R.Hazlewood	141.1	11	660	27	24.44	5-31	2	4.67
M.C.Henriques	34	1	157	5	31.40	3-32	–	4.61
M.G.Johnson	1248.1	74	6038	239	25.26	6-31	12	4.83
N.M.Lyon	91	7	464	12	38.66	4-44	1	5.09
C.J.McKay	494.1	38	2364	97	24.37	5-28	6	4.78
M.R.Marsh	155	2	874	29	30.13	5-33	2	5.63
G.J.Maxwell	303.4	6	1689	42	40.21	4-46	2	5.56

	O	M	R	W	Avge	Best	4wI	R/Over
J.S.Paris	16	0	93	1	93.00	1-40	–	5.81
J.L.Pattinson	121.1	6	681	16	42.56	4-51	1	5.62
K.W.Richardson	101	9	540	14	38.57	5-68	1	5.34
G.S.Sandhu	20	0	107	3	35.66	2-49	–	5.35
S.P.D.Smith	174.2	1	931	27	34.48	3-16	–	5.34
M.A.Starc	364.2	20	1769	90	19.65	6-28	11	4.85
M.P.Stoinis	4	0	17	0	–	–	–	4.25
A.C.Voges	50.1	1	276	6	46.00	1- 3	–	5.50
D.A.Warner	1	0	8	0	–	–	–	8.00
S.R.Watson	1077.4	35	5342	168	31.79	4-36	3	4.95
C.L.White	55.1	2	351	12	29.25	3- 5	–	6.36
A.Zampma	20	0	102	3	34.00	2-57	–	5.10

SOUTH AFRICA – BATTING AND FIELDING

	M	I	NO	HS	Runs	Avge	100	50	Ct/St
K.J.Abbott	24	10	4	23	70	11.66	–	–	7
H.M.Amla	131	128	9	159	7358	52.13	22	29	67
F.Behardien	41	34	9	70	767	30.68	–	4	16
Q.de Kock	57	57	3	138*	2319	42.94	10	5	80/3
M.de Lange	4	–	–	–	–	–	–	–	–
A.B.de Villiers	200	192	34	162*	8621	54.56	24	48	164/5
F.du Plessis	87	84	10	133*	2944	39.78	5	20	46
J.P.Duminy	150	135	31	150*	4028	38.73	4	21	64
D.Elgar	6	5	1	42	98	24.50	–	–	3
Imran Tahir	54	18	10	23*	82	10.25	–	–	13
C.A.Ingram	31	29	3	124	843	32.42	3	3	12
R.K.Kleinveldt	10	7	–	43	105	15.00	–	–	4
R.McLaren	54	41	15	71*	485	18.65	–	1	13
D.A.Miller	82	73	21	138*	1819	34.98	2	8	37
M.Morkel	106	40	15	25	214	8.56	–	–	30
C.H.Morris	11	6	1	62	96	19.20	–	1	1
W.D.Parnell	46	25	9	56	373	23.31	–	1	5
A.N.Petersen	21	19	1	80	504	28.00	–	4	5
A.M.Phangiso	16	10	2	20	66	8.25	–	–	3
V.D.Philander	30	19	7	30*	151	12.58	–	–	6
K.Rabada	14	7	3	19*	50	12.50	–	–	3
R.R.Rossouw	29	28	2	132	860	33.07	2	4	22
J.A.Rudolph	45	39	6	81	1174	35.57	–	7	11
D.W.Steyn	112	46	10	35	292	8.11	–	–	26
R.E.van der Merwe	13	7	3	12	39	9.75	–	–	3
M.N.van Wyk	17	17	1	82	425	26.56	–	4	10/1
D.Wiese	6	6	1	41*	102	20.40	–	–	–

SOUTH AFRICA – BOWLING

	O	M	R	W	Avge	Best	4wI	R/Over
K.J.Abbott	179.1	9	887	27	32.85	4-21	1	4.95
F.Behardien	119.4	2	675	14	48.21	3-19	–	5.64
M.de Lange	34.5	1	198	10	19.80	4-46	1	5.68
A.B.de Villiers	32	0	202	7	28.85	2-15	–	6.31
F.du Plessis	32	0	189	2	94.50	1- 8	–	5.90
J.P.Duminy	458.3	8	2407	55	43.76	3-29	–	5.24
D.Elgar	16	1	67	2	33.50	1-11	–	4.18
Imran Tahir	476.3	21	2219	92	24.11	5-45	6	4.65
C.A.Ingram	1	01	17	0	–	–	–	17.00
R.K.Kleinveldt	85.3	6	448	12	37.33	4-22	1	5.23
R.McLaren	400.3	13	2102	77	27.29	4-19	5	5.24

SOUTH AFRICA – BOWLING (continued)

	O	*M*	*R*	*W*	*Avge*	*Best*	*4wI*	*R/Over*
M.Morkel	889	43	4385	180	24.36	5-21	9	4.93
C.H.Morris	80.3	1	512	13	39.38	3-74	–	6.36
W.D.Parnell	351.1	16	1957	65	30.10	5-48	4	5.57
A.N.Petersen	1	01	17	0	–	–	–	17.00
A.M.Phangiso	144.5	5	661	16	41.31	3-43	–	4.56
V.D.Philander	213.1	20	986	41	24.04	4-12	2	4.62
K.Rabada	125	7	604	30	20.13	6-16	3	4.83
R.R.Rossouw	7.3	0	44	1	44.00	1-17	–	5.86
J.A.Rudolph	4	0	26	0	–	–	–	6.50
D.W.Steyn	933.5	68	4539	175	25.93	6-39	7	4.86
R.E.van der Merwe	117.3	2	561	17	33.00	3-27	–	4.77
D.Wiese	49	0	316	9	35.11	3-50	–	6.44

WEST INDIES – BATTING AND FIELDING

	M	*I*	*NO*	*HS*	*Runs*	*Avge*	*100*	*50*	*Ct/St*
S.J.Benn	34	22	6	31	138	8.62	–	–	5
J.Blackwood	2	2	–	9	11	5.50	–	–	1
C.R.Brathwaite	7	7	–	18	71	10.14	–	–	2
D.J.Bravo	164	141	24	112*	2968	25.36	2	10	73
D.M.Bravo	84	81	10	124	2283	32.15	2	16	27
J.L.Carter	13	12	1	50*	212	19.27	–	1	5
J.Charles	35	35	–	130	1015	29.00	2	4	19/1
S.S.Cottrell	2	2	2	2*	3	–	–	–	1
N.Deonarine	31	29	3	65*	682	26.23	–	4	9
F.H.Edwards	50	22	14	13	73	9.12	–	–	4
A.D.S.Fletcher	18	18	–	54	265	14.72	–	2	5/3
C.H.Gayle	266	261	17	215	9166	37.56	22	46	113
J.O.Holder	35	23	7	57	372	23.25	–	2	9
L.R.Johnson	6	6	–	51	98	16.33	–	1	2
N.O.Miller	46	26	12	51	264	18.85	–	1	17
J.N.Mohammed	2	2	–	4	6	3.00	–	–	–
S.P.Narine	55	37	9	36	291	10.39	–	–	12
D.Ramdin	129	100	22	169	1924	24.66	2	7	171/6
R.Rampaul	92	40	11	86*	362	12.48	–	1	14
K.A.J.Roach	67	42	26	34	216	13.50	–	–	16
A.D.Russell	51	43	9	92*	985	28.97	–	4	11
D.J.G.Sammy	126	105	30	89	1871	24.94	–	9	67
M.N.Samuels	177	167	26	133*	4806	34.08	9	26	47
L.M.P.Simmons	68	65	3	122	1958	31.58	2	16	28
D.R.Smith	105	89	5	97	1560	18.57	–	8	31
J.E.Taylor	81	38	8	43*	255	8.50	–	–	19

WEST INDIES – BOWLING

	O	*M*	*R*	*W*	*Avge*	*Best*	*4wI*	*R/Over*
S.J.Benn	282.5	14	1332	34	39.17	4-18	3	4.70
J.Blackwood	3	0	16	0	–	–	–	5.33
C.R.Brathwaite	40	1	226	3	75.33	2-35	–	5.65
D.J.Bravo	1085.1	38	5874	199	29.51	6-43	7	5.41
J.L.Carter	7.1	0	45	3	15.00	2-14	–	6.27
J.Charles	0.5	0	12	0	–	–	–	14.40
S.S.Cottrell	13	0	107	2	53.50	2-39	–	8.23
N.Deonarine	83.3	2	475	6	79.16	2-18	–	5.68
F.H.Edwards	356.2	23	1812	60	30.20	6-22	2	5.08
C.H.Gayle	1203.4	38	5739	163	35.20	5-46	4	4.76
J.O.Holder	271.2	21	1542	48	32.12	4-13	3	5.68
N.O.Miller	324.1	16	1509	41	36.80	4-43	2	4.65

WEST INDIES – BOWLING (continued)

	O	M	R	W	Avge	Best	4wI	R/Over
J.N.Mohammed	6	0	25	0	–	–	–	4.16
S.P.Narine	492.1	32	2006	77	26.05	5-27	5	4.07
R.Rampaul	672.1	33	3434	117	29.35	5-49	10	5.10
K.A.J.Roach	558.1	40	2782	99	28.10	6-27	5	4.98
A.D.Russell	353.4	13	2066	64	32.28	4-35	5	5.84
D.J.G.Sammy	826	41	3851	81	47.54	4-26	1	4.66
M.N.Samuels	816.5	22	3932	85	46.25	3-25	–	4.81
L.M.P.Simmons	26	0	172	1	172.00	1- 3	–	6.61
D.R.Smith	454.2	18	2285	61	37.45	5-45	4	5.02
J.E.Taylor	667.3	34	3390	124	27.33	5-48	4	5.07

NEW ZEALAND – BATTING AND FIELDING

	M	I	NO	HS	Runs	Avge	100	50	Ct/St
C.J.Anderson	40	36	5	131*	1016	32.77	1	4	8
T.A.Boult	32	12	8	21*	58	14.50	–	–	5
D.A.J.Bracewell	13	7	1	30	59	9.83	–	–	2
N.T.Broom	22	22	3	71	333	17.52	–	1	1
D.G.Brownlie	10	9	1	47	203	25.37	–	–	4
A.P.Devcich	10	9	–	58	177	19.66	–	1	3
G.D.Elliott	83	69	11	115	1976	34.06	2	11	17
J.E.C.Franklin	110	80	27	98*	1270	23.96	–	4	26
M.J.Guptill	129	126	14	237*	4844	43.25	10	30	66
M.J.Henry	25	9	4	48*	86	17.20	–	–	8
T.W.M.Latham	38	37	6	110*	917	29.58	1	4	21/1
M.J.McClenaghan	48	14	10	34*	108	27.00	–	–	4
B.B.McCullum	260	228	28	166	6083	30.41	5	32	262/15
N.L.McCullum	84	62	11	65	1070	20.98	–	4	41
H.J.H.Marshall	66	62	9	101*	1454	27.43	1	12	18
A.W.Mathieson	1	1	1	0*	0	–	–	–	–
K.D.Mills	170	101	34	54	1047	15.62	–	2	42
A.F.Milne	33	12	6	36	130	21.66	–	–	16
C.Munro	12	9	–	85	244	27.11	–	2	1
J.D.S.Neesham	19	16	5	42*	238	21.63	–	1	7
H.M.Nicholls	10	9	2	82	219	31.28	–	2	6
J.S.Patel	39	13	7	34	88	14.66	–	–	12
L.Ronchi	70	54	8	170*	1159	25.19	1	3	88/8
H.D.Rutherford	16	29	1	171	755	26.96	1	1	11
J.D.Ryder	48	42	1	107	1362	33.21	3	6	15
M.J.Santner	14	11	5	48	294	49.00	–	–	5
I.S.Sodhi	10	3	–	5	5	1.66	–	–	2
T.G.Southee	99	54	19	32	384	10.97	–	–	23
L.R.P.L.Taylor	171	157	27	131*	5707	43.90	15	32	110
D.L.Vettori	291	183	55	83	2201	17.19	–	4	86
B.M.Wheeler	6	4	3	39*	58	–	–	–	1
K.S.Williamson	93	87	9	145*	3666	47.00	7	25	38
G.H.Worker	2	2	1	21	41	41.00	–	–	–

NEW ZEALAND – BOWLING

	O	M	R	W	Avge	Best	4wI	R/Over
C.J.Anderson	222.3	10	1349	55	24.52	5-63	3	6.06
T.A.Boult	281.2	25	1355	59	22.96	5-27	5	4.81
D.A.J.Bracewell	111.2	13	549	17	32.29	3-31	–	4.93
A.P.Devcich	41	1	221	4	55.25	2-33	–	5.39
G.D.Elliott	217	8	1179	39	30.23	4-31	1	5.43
J.E.C.Franklin	641.2	34	3354	81	41.40	5-42	1	5.22
M.J.Guptill	17.1	0	92	2	46.00	2- 7	–	5.35

	O	M	R	W	Avge	Best	4wI	R/Over
M.J.Henry	208.3	12	1131	51	22.17	5-30	6	5.42
M.J.McClenaghan	389.2	11	2313	82	28.20	5-58	7	5.94
N.L.McCullum	589.2	6	2956	63	46.92	3-24	–	5.01
A.W.Mathieson	4	0	40	1	40.00	1-40	–	10.00
K.D.Mills	1371.4	127	6485	240	27.02	5-25	9	4.72
A.F.Milne	243.5	5	1259	31	40.61	3-49	–	5.16
C.Munro	9	0	43	0	–	–	–	4.77
J.D.S.Neesham	107.2	1	687	20	34.35	4-42	2	6.40
J.S.Patel	300.4	9	1513	42	36.02	3-11	–	5.03
J.D.Ryder	67.5	0	412	12	34.33	3-29	–	6.07
M.J.Santner	81.2	1	519	15	34.60	3-31	–	6.38
I.S.Sodhi	78	2	417	9	46.33	3-38	–	5.34
T.G.Southee	807.4	52	4318	135	31.98	7-33	6	5.34
L.R.P.L.Taylor	7	0	35	0	–	–	–	5.00
D.L.Vettori	2303.2	98	9495	297	31.96	5- 7	9	4.12
B.M.Wheeler	51.3	3	315	8	39.37	3-63	–	6.11
K.S.Williamson	180.3	1	1013	27	37.51	4-22	1	5.61
G.H.Worker	1	0	5	0	–	–	–	5.00

INDIA – BATTING AND FIELDING

	M	I	NO	HS	Runs	Avge	100	50	Ct/St
R.Ashwin	102	58	18	65	658	16.45	–	1	30
S.T.R.Binny	14	11	3	77	230	28.75	–	1	3
J.J.Bumrah	1	–	–	–	–	–	–	–	–
R.Dhawan	3	2	1	9	12	12.00	–	–	–
S.Dhawan	74	73	3	137	3078	43.97	9	17	34
M.S.Dhoni	272	238	66	183*	8744	50.83	8	60	254/86
Gurkeerat Singh	3	3	1	8	13	6.50	–	–	1
Harbhajan Singh	234	126	35	49	1213	13.32	–	–	71
R.A.Jadeja	126	87	30	87	1849	32.43	–	10	43
K.M.Jadhav	4	4	1	105*	146	48.66	1	–	2
V.Kohli	171	163	23	183	7212	51.51	25	36	83
D.S.Kulkarni	8	1	1	2*	2	–	–	–	2
B.Kumar	57	30	8	31	207	9.40	–	–	17
A.Mishra	31	9	3	9	28	4.66	–	–	4
Mohammed Shami	47	21	11	25	109	10.90	–	–	16
M.K.Pandey	4	3	1	104*	181	90.50	1	1	–
A.R.Patel	22	15	6	17*	91	10.11	–	–	12
A.M.Rahane	67	65	2	111	2093	33.22	2	15	37
S.K.Raina	223	192	35	116*	5568	35.46	5	36	100
A.T.Rayudu	31	28	7	124*	952	45.33	2	5	10
I.Sharma	80	28	13	13	72	4.80	–	–	19
M.M.Sharma	26	9	5	11	31	7.75	–	–	6
R.G.Sharma	148	142	23	264	5008	42.08	10	28	51
B.B.Sran	3	–	–	–	–	–	–	–	1
M.K.Tiwary	12	12	1	104*	287	26.09	1	1	4
J.D.Unadkat	7	–	–	–	–	–	–	–	–
R.V.Uthappa	46	42	6	86	934	25.94	–	6	19/2
M.Vijay	17	16	–	72	339	21.18	–	1	9
U.T.Yadav	57	19	12	17	52	7.42	–	–	15

INDIA – BOWLING

	O	M	R	W	Avge	Best	4wI	R/Over
R.Ashwin	928.3	34	4507	142	31.73	4-25	1	4.85
S.T.R.Binny	81.4	4	439	20	21.95	6- 4	1	5.37
J.J.Bumrah	10	0	40	2	20.00	2-40	–	4.00

INDIA – BOWLING (continued)

	O	M	R	W	Avge	Best	4wI	R/Over
R.Dhawan	25	0	160	1	160.00	1-74	–	6.40
M.S.Dhoni	6	0	31	1	31.00	1-14	–	5.16
Gurkeerat Singh	10	0	68	0	–	–	–	6.80
Harbhajan Singh	2059.5	83	8872	265	33.47	5-31	5	4.30
R.A.Jadeja	1042.2	44	5080	147	34.55	5-36	6	4.87
V.Kohli	101.5	1	636	4	159.00	1-15	–	6.24
D.S.Kulkarni	67.2	2	359	13	27.61	4-34	1	5.33
B.Kumar	469.5	44	2298	60	38.30	4- 8	2	4.89
A.Mishra	274.4	17	1296	49	26.44	6-48	3	4.71
Mohammed Shami	390.5	26	2166	87	24.89	4-35	5	5.54
A.R.Patel	170.2	7	807	28	28.82	3-39	–	4.73
S.K.Raina	347.2	4	1769	36	49.13	3-34	–	5.09
A.T.Rayudu	18	1	111	3	37.00	1- 5	–	6.16
I.Sharma	622.1	29	3563	115	30.98	4-34	6	5.72
M.M.Sharma	186.5	12	1020	31	32.90	4-22	1	5.45
R.G.Sharma	98.5	2	515	8	64.37	2-27	–	5.21
B.B.Sran	26.2	1	170	3	56.66	3-56	–	6.45
M.K.Tiwary	22	1	150	5	30.00	4-61	1	6.81
J.D.Unadkat	52	5	209	8	26.12	4-41	1	4.01
R.V.Uthappa	0.2	0	0	0	–	–	–	0.00
M.Vijay	6	0	37	1	37.00	1-19	–	6.16
U.T.Yadav	444.5	19	2666	79	33.74	4-31	3	5.99

PAKISTAN – BATTING AND FIELDING

	M	I	NO	HS	Runs	Avge	100	50	Ct/St
Aamer Yamin	3	2	1	62	63	63.00	–	1	–
Ahmed Shehzad	75	75	1	124	2510	33.91	6	13	26
Anwar Ali	22	16	5	43*	321	29.18	–	–	4
Asad Shafiq	58	56	4	84	1318	25.34	–	9	13
Azhar Ali	33	33	3	102	1249	41.63	2	7	4
Azhar Mahmood	143	110	26	67	1521	18.10	–	3	37
Babar Azam	9	9	1	83	375	46.87	–	5	6
Bilal Asif	3	3	–	38	40	13.33	–	–	2
Bilawal Bhatti	10	7	1	39	89	14.83	–	–	2
Ehsan Adil	6	4	1	15	27	9.00	–	–	–
Fawad Alam	38	36	12	114*	966	40.25	1	6	10
Hammad Azam	11	7	2	36	80	16.00	–	–	4
Haris Sohail	22	21	3	89*	774	43.00	–	7	9
Iftikhar Ahmed	2	2	–	5	8	4.00	–	–	1
Imad Wasim	6	3	–	61	77	25.66	–	1	2
Junaid Khan	52	23	11	25	60	5.00	–	–	5
Misbah-ul-Haq	162	149	31	96*	5122	43.40	–	42	66
Mohammad Amir	17	14	4	73*	168	16.80	–	1	6
Mohammad Hafeez	175	175	10	140*	5356	32.46	11	28	63
Mohammad Irfan	59	33	21	12	48	4.00	–	–	10
Mohammad Rizwan	15	13	3	75*	348	34.80	–	3	10
Mohammad Sami	87	46	19	46	314	11.62	–	–	19
Nasir Jamshed	48	48	3	112	1418	31.51	3	8	13
Rahat Ali	14	7	4	6*	8	2.66	–	–	1
Saad Nasim	3	3	1	77*	99	49.50	–	1	–
Saeed Ajmal	113	70	24	33	324	7.04	–	–	25
Sami Aslam	1	1	–	45	45	45.00	–	–	–
Sarfraz Ahmed	58	43	7	101*	1077	29.91	1	3	53/17
Shahid Afridi	393	364	27	124	8027	23.81	6	39	127
Shoaib Malik	232	209	31	143	6129	34.43	8	35	81
Sohaib Maqsood	26	25	2	89*	735	31.95	–	5	9

	M	I	NO	HS	Runs	Avge	100	50	Ct/St
Sohail Tanvir	62	40	11	59	399	13.75	–	1	15
Umar Akmal	111	100	16	102*	2913	34.67	2	20	77/13
Umar Gul	126	64	17	39	451	9.59	–	–	15
Wahab Riaz	69	51	13	54*	546	14.36	–	2	20
Yasir Arafat	11	8	3	27	74	14.80	–	–	2
Yasir Shah	15	7	2	32*	76	15.20	–	–	4
Younus Khan	265	255	23	144	7249	31.24	7	48	135
Zafar Gohar	1	1	–	15	15	15.00	–	–	–
Zulfiqar Babar	5	5	3	14*	35	17.50	–	–	–

PAKISTAN – BOWLING

	O	M	R	W	Avge	Best	4wI	R/Over
Aamer Yamin	17	1	89	1	89.00	1-38	–	5.23
Ahmed Shehzad	19.1	0	140	2	70.00	1-22	–	7.30
Anwar Ali	154.3	1	944	18	52.44	3-66	–	6.11
Azhar Mahmood	1040.2	58	4813	123	39.13	6-18	5	4.62
Asad Shafiq	2	0	18	0	–	–	–	9.00
Azhar Ali	39	0	213	4	53.25	2-26	–	5.46
Bilal Asif	22	1	96	5	19.20	5-25	1	4.36
Bilawal Bhatti	68.1	4	439	6	73.16	3-37	–	6.44
Ehsan Adil	37.3	0	223	4	55.75	1-31	–	5.94
Fawad Alam	66.2	0	377	5	75.40	1- 8	–	5.68
Hammad Azam	33	0	169	2	84.50	1-21	–	5.12
Haris Sohail	76	0	444	9	49.33	3-45	–	5.84
Iftikhar Ahmed	10	0	49	1	49.00	1-31	–	4.90
Imad Wasim	43.1	1	205	7	29.28	3-36	–	4.74
Junaid Khan	407.2	24	2147	78	27.52	4-12	3	5.27
Misbah-ul-Haq	4	0	30	0	–	–	–	7.50
Mohammad Amir	148.4	9	667	30	22.23	4-28	1	4.48
Mohammad Hafeez	1096.2	43	4499	129	34.87	4-41	1	4.10
Mohammad Irfan	513.1	30	2523	81	31.14	4-30	2	4.91
Mohammad Sami	714	42	3567	121	29.47	5-10	4	4.99
Rahat Ali	113.1	1	658	18	36.55	3-40	–	5.81
Saad Nasim	6	0	46	0	–	–	–	7.66
Saeed Ajmal	1000	50	4182	184	22.72	5-24	8	4.18
Shahid Afridi	2933.1	75	13572	393	34.53	7-12	13	4.62
Shoaib Malik	1210.5	36	5591	151	37.02	4-19	1	4.61
Sohaib Maqsood	9	0	42	1	42.00	1-16	–	4.66
Sohail Tanvir	491.3	24	2566	71	36.14	5-48	4	5.22
Umar Gul	979.4	67	5068	173	29.29	6-42	6	5.17
Wahab Riaz	532.1	19	2954	94	31.42	5-46	5	5.55
Yasir Arafat	69	2	373	4	93.25	1-28	–	5.40
Yasir Shah	126	1	656	18	36.44	6-26	2	5.20
Younus Khan	47.2	1	288	3	96.00	1- 3	–	6.08
Zafar Gohar	10	0	54	2	27.00	2-54	–	5.40
Zulfiqar Babar	49	1	246	4	61.50	2-52	–	5.02

SRI LANKA – BATTING AND FIELDING

	M	I	NO	HS	Runs	Avge	100	50	Ct/St
P.V.D.Chameera	9	5	3	13*	36	18.00	–	–	2
L.D.Chandimal	107	96	18	111	2427	31.11	2	15	43/3
T.M.Dilshan	327	300	41	161*	10216	39.44	22	47	119/1
R.M.S.Eranga	17	10	7	12*	34	11.33	–	–	5
A.N.P.R.Fernando	7	4	3	3*	3	–	–	–	1
P.L.S.Gamage	5	2	2	0*	0	–	–	–	1
M.D.Gunathilaka	6	5	–	65	117	23.40	–	1	1

	M	I	NO	HS	Runs	Avge	100	50	Ct/St
H.M.R.K.B.Herath	71	30	15	17*	140	9.33	–	–	14
D.S.N.F.G.Jayasuriya	3	2	1	11*	11	11.00	–	–	–
D.P.M.D.Jayawardena	443	413	38	144	12381	33.01	17	75	212
S.H.T.Kandamby	39	36	6	93*	870	29.00	–	5	7
C.K.Kapugedera	97	79	7	95	1551	21.54	–	8	30
F.D.M.Karunaratne	13	11	1	60	153	15.30	–	1	3
K.M.D.N.Kulasekara	173	116	35	73	1273	15.71	–	4	43
R.A.S.Lakmal	42	18	11	8	29	4.14	–	–	9
S.L.Malinga	191	96	29	56	475	7.08	–	1	28
A.D.Mathews	169	140	38	139*	4067	39.87	1	28	39
B.A.W.Mendis	87	42	19	21*	188	8.17	–	–	15
B.M.A.J.Mendis	54	40	10	72	604	20.13	–	1	13
S.S.Pathirana	3	3	–	33	66	22.00	–	–	1
M.D.K.Perera	5	4	–	30	44	11.00	–	–	–
M.D.K.J.Perera	51	49	3	116	1259	27.36	2	7	20
N.L.T.C.Perera	110	81	13	80*	1178	17.32	–	5	49
K.T.G.D.Prasad	24	12	6	31*	129	21.50	–	–	1
S.Prasanna	25	22	2	42	193	9.65	–	–	3
S.M.A.Priyanjan	23	20	2	74	420	23.33	–	2	7
K.C.Sangakkara	397	373	40	169	13975	41.96	25	90	396/96
S.M.S.M.Senanayake	49	33	11	42	290	13.18	–	–	19
T.A.M.Siriwardana	13	10	1	66	262	29.11	–	2	4
W.U.Tharanga	180	172	9	174*	5407	33.17	13	28	33
H.D.R.L.Thirimanne	107	87	12	139*	2586	34.48	4	16	34
J.D.F.Vandersay	3	1	1	7*	7	–	–	–	–

SRI LANKA – BOWLING

	O	M	R	W	Avge	Best	4wI	R/Over
P.V.D.Chameera	50.1	0	349	10	34.90	3-51	–	6.95
T.M.Dilshan	967.1	22	4706	106	44.39	4- 4	3	4.86
R.M.S.Eranga	112.2	4	652	20	32.60	3-46	–	5.80
A.N.P.R.Fernando	57.2	2	337	7	48.14	2-55	–	5.87
P.L.S.Gamage	37	2	224	2	112.00	1-59	–	6.05
H.M.R.K.B.Herath	540.2	18	2362	74	31.91	4-20	1	4.37
D.S.N.F.G.Jayasuriya	5	0	26	1	26.00	1-15	–	5.20
D.P.M.D.Jayawardena	98.5	1	563	8	70.37	2-56	–	5.69
S.H.T.Kandamby	29	1	173	2	86.50	2-37	–	5.96
C.K.Kapugedera	44	0	225	2	112.50	1-24	–	5.11
F.D.M.Karunaratne	1.4	0	11	0	–	–	–	6.60
K.M.D.N.Kulasekara	1301.4	103	6339	186	34.08	5-22	4	4.86
R.A.S.Lakmal	318	18	1777	59	30.11	4-30	1	5.58
S.L.Malinga	1534.3	88	8082	291	27.77	6-38	16	5.26
A.D.Mathews	772.1	48	3581	102	35.10	6-20	2	4.63
B.A.W.Mendis	692.2	34	3324	152	21.86	6-13	10	4.80
B.M.A.J.Mendis	222.5	2	1134	28	40.50	3-15	–	5.08
S.S.Pathirana	29	1	200	3	66.66	2-70	–	6.89
M.D.K.Perera	16	0	81	2	40.50	1-17	–	5.06
N.L.T.C.Perera	677.5	23	3889	123	31.61	6-44	6	5.73
K.T.G.D.Prasad	169.1	4	976	32	30.50	3-17	–	5.76
S.Prasanna	208.1	6	1106	22	50.27	3-32	–	5.31
S.M.A.Priyanjan	44.1	1	233	5	46.60	2-11	–	5.27
S.M.S.M.Senanayake	393	11	1874	53	35.35	4-13	1	4.76
T.A.M.Siriwardana	44.1	1	244	8	30.50	2-27	–	5.52
H.D.R.L.Thirimanne	17.2	0	94	3	31.33	2-36	–	5.42
J.D.F.Vandersay	13	1	104	2	52.00	2-55	–	8.00

A.N.P.R.Fernando is also known as N.Pradeep.

LOI **ZIMBABWE – BATTING AND FIELDING**

	M	I	NO	HS	Runs	Avge	100	50	Ct/St
R.W.Chakabva	34	31	1	45	454	15.13	–	–	20/3
B.B.Chari	4	4	–	39	76	19.00	–	–	2/1
T.L.Chatara	27	18	10	23	99	12.37	–	–	3
C.J.Chibhabha	93	93	2	99	2225	24.45	–	16	31
E.Chigumbura	196	182	24	117	4128	26.12	2	19	69
T.S.Chisoro	8	6	3	12	37	12.33	–	–	5
C.K.Coventry	39	35	1	194*	831	24.44	1	3	19/1
A.G.Cremer	61	43	12	58	519	16.74	–	1	21
C.R.Ervine	47	44	6	130*	1400	36.84	2	8	23
S.M.Ervine	42	34	7	100	698	25.85	1	2	5
K.M.Jarvis	24	15	5	13	52	5.20	–	–	6
L.M.Jongwe	22	19	3	46	236	14.75	–	–	10
R.Kaia	1	–	–	–	–	–	–	–	–
T.P.Kamungozi	14	11	6	12*	27	5.40	–	–	6
N.Madziva	11	11	2	25	57	6.33	–	–	3
T.Maruma	16	15	–	32	140	9.33	–	–	8
H.Masakadza	165	164	4	178*	4649	29.05	4	30	65
W.P.Masakadza	10	5	–	10	14	2.80	–	–	4
S.F.Mire	10	10	–	52	198	19.80	–	2	2
P.J.Moor	7	7	–	52	180	25.71	–	2	1
C.B.Mpofu	68	35	19	6	40	2.50	–	–	10
T.Mupariwa	39	31	10	33	184	8.76	–	–	9
C.T.Mutombodzi	11	10	1	27	112	12.44	–	–	4
R.Mutumbami	28	26	2	74	531	22.12	–	3	21/5
T.Muzarabani	6	5	2	3	6	2.00	–	–	–
J.C.Nyumbu	19	14	4	18	46	4.60	–	–	7
T.Panyangara	64	48	13	33	227	6.48	–	–	9
V.Sibanda	124	123	4	116	2898	24.35	2	20	42
Sikandar Raza	55	52	5	141	1431	30.44	3	4	23
B.R.M.Taylor	167	166	15	145*	5258	34.82	8	32	98/20
D.T.Tiripano	7	5	2	13*	24	8.00	–	–	–
P.Utseya	164	132	48	68*	1406	16.73	–	4	50
B.V.Vitori	19	10	3	20*	63	9.00	–	–	2
M.N.Waller	56	52	3	99*	896	18.28	–	4	16
S.C.Williams	95	93	13	102	2675	33.43	1	24	33

ZIMBABWE – BOWLING

	O	M	R	W	Avge	Best	4wI	R/Over
T.L.Chatara	244	19	1269	37	34.29	3-35	–	5.20
C.J.Chibhabha	254	10	1515	33	45.90	4-25	1	5.96
E.Chigumbura	688.1	23	4003	95	42.13	4-28	1	5.81
T.S.Chisoro	61	4	247	11	22.45	3-16	–	4.04
A.G.Cremer	488.2	19	2318	74	31.32	6-46	4	4.74
S.M.Ervine	274.5	10	1561	41	38.07	3-29	–	5.67
K.M.Jarvis	202.5	9	1221	27	45.22	3-36	–	6.01
L.M.Jongwe	143.5	11	759	25	30.36	5- 6	1	5.27
T.P.Kamungozi	106	1	548	12	45.66	2-36	–	5.16
N.Madziva	81.4	2	494	20	24.70	4-49	1	6.04
T.Maruma	37.3	1	230	4	57.50	2-50	–	6.13
H.Masakadza	297.5	5	1571	38	41.34	3-39	–	5.27
W.P.Masakadza	88.1	7	376	15	25.06	4-21	1	4.26
S.F.Mire	35.3	0	230	5	46.00	3-49	–	6.47
C.B.Mpofu	544	37	2930	72	40.69	6-52	3	5.38
T.Mupariwa	330.3	23	1647	57	28.89	4-39	3	4.98
C.T.Mutombodzi	51.5	0	278	6	46.33	2-33	–	5.36
T.Muzarabani	44.5	2	231	7	33.00	2-32	–	5.15
J.C.Nyumbu	140.4	3	738	17	43.41	3-42	–	5.24

ZIMBABWE – BOWLING (continued)

	O	M	R	W	Avge	Best	4wI	R/Over
T.Panyangara	532.5	41	2987	64	46.67	3-28	–	5.60
V.Sibanda	44.3	1	265	3	88.33	1-12	–	5.95
Sikandar Raza	176	6	895	22	40.68	3-40	–	5.08
B.R.M.Taylor	66	0	406	9	45.11	3-54	–	6.15
D.T.Tiripano	56.5	5	324	12	27.00	5-63	1	5.70
P.Utseya	1428.3	65	6239	133	46.90	5-36	3	4.36
B.V.Vitori	161.2	4	946	26	36.38	5-20	2	5.86
M.N.Waller	73	0	390	6	65.00	1- 9	–	5.34
S.C.Williams	433.1	14	2159	37	58.35	3-23	–	4.98

BANGLADESH – BATTING AND FIELDING

	M	I	NO	HS	Runs	Avge	100	50	Ct/St
Abul Hasan	6	2	–	3	4	2.00	–	–	1
Al-Amin Hossain	14	7	5	2*	4	2.00	–	–	1
Anamul Haque	30	27	–	120	950	35.18	3	3	10
Arafat Sunny	16	11	7	15	48	12.00	–	–	5
Imrul Kayes	58	58	1	101	1548	27.15	1	12	19
Jubair Hossain	3	1	–	5	5	5.00	–	–	1
Liton Das	9	9	1	36	124	15.50	–	–	8
Mahmudullah	125	108	29	128*	2629	33.27	2	14	38
Mashrafe Mortaza	158	118	21	51*	1428	14.72	–	1	49
Mominul Haque	26	24	1	60	543	23.60	–	3	4
Mushfiqur Rahim	158	145	21	117	3920	31.61	4	22	126/38
Mustafizur Rahman	9	5	3	9	15	7.50	–	–	2
Nasir Hossain	56	45	7	100	1231	32.39	1	6	33
Rubel Hossain	67	34	18	17	89	5.56	–	–	11
Sabbir Rahman	23	19	4	57	482	32.13	–	2	13
Shakib Al Hasan	157	149	24	134*	4398	35.18	6	30	39
Soumya Sarkar	16	16	2	127*	692	49.42	1	4	11
Taijul Islam	2	–	–	–	–	–	–	–	–
Tamim Iqbal	153	152	3	154	4713	31.63	6	32	35
Taskin Ahmed	14	6	3	2	3	1.00	–	–	3

BANGLADESH – BOWLING

	O	M	R	W	Avge	Best	4wI	R/Over
Abul Hasan	32	1	219	0	–	–	–	6.84
Al-Amin Hossain	100.3	7	523	21	24.90	4-51	2	5.20
Arafat Sunny	138.2	8	600	24	25.00	4-27	2	4.33
Jubair Hossain	19	0	114	4	28.50	2-41	–	6.00
Mahmudullah	597	14	3031	70	43.30	3- 4	–	5.07
Mashrafe Mortaza	1310.2	104	6169	203	30.38	6-26	6	4.70
Mominul Haque	36	1	175	7	25.00	2-13	–	4.86
Mustafizur Rahman	75.2	4	321	26	12.34	6-43	3	4.26
Nasir Hossain	158.2	3	727	19	38.26	3-26	–	4.59
Rubel Hossain	508.2	20	2846	87	32.71	6-26	6	5.59
Sabbir Rahman	26.1	0	173	2	86.50	1-12	–	6.61
Shakib Al Hasan	1335.1	75	5746	206	27.89	5-47	7	4.30
Soumya Sarkar	7	0	32	0	–	–	–	4.57
Taijul Islam	17	2	69	4	17.25	4-11	1	4.05
Tamim Iqbal	1	0	13	0	–	–	–	13.00
Taskin Ahmed	102	4	564	21	26.85	5-28	1	5.52

ASSOCIATES – BATTING AND FIELDING

	M	I	NO	HS	Runs	Avge	100	50	Ct/St
A.Balbirnie (Ireland)	22	21	1	97	451	22.55	–	2	2
P.K.D.Chase (Ireland)	1	–	–	–	–	–	–	–	–
F.R.J.Coleman (Scotland)	16	14	–	70	211	15.07	–	1	8
J.H.Davey (Scotland)	25	23	5	64	452	25.11	–	2	8
E.C.Joyce (Ireland)	39	38	4	116*	1273	37.44	2	8	14
A.N.Kervezee (Netherlands)	39	36	3	92	924	28.00	–	4	18
M.A.Leask (Scotland)	10	9	1	50	179	22.37	–	1	3
C.S.MacLeod (Scotland)	34	32	3	175	742	25.58	2	2	13
M.W.Machan (Scotland)	23	22	–	114	734	33.36	1	3	4
E.J.G.Morgan (Ireland)	23	23	2	115	744	35.42	1	5	9
D.Murphy (Scotland)	8	7	2	20*	58	11.60	–	–	8/3
T.J.Murtagh (Ireland)	14	8	4	23*	81	20.25	–	–	3
K.J.O'Brien (Ireland)	94	85	11	142	2340	31.62	2	11	43
N.J.O'Brien (Ireland)	74	73	8	80*	1954	30.06	–	15	49/7
W.T.S.Porterfield (Ireland)	84	83	3	112*	2460	30.75	7	11	42
W.B.Rankin (Ireland)	37	16	11	7*	35	7.00	–	–	6
S.W.Poynter (ireland)	3	2	–	8	15	7.50	–	–	6
P.R.Stirling (Ireland)	62	61	1	177	2033	33.88	5	9	25
R.M.L.Taylor (Scotland)	15	14	5	46*	154	14.00	–	–	6
R.N.ten Doeschate (Netherlands)	33	32	9	119	1541	67.00	5	9	13
T.van der Gugten (Netherlands)	4	2	–	2	4	2.00	–	–	–
B.T.J.Wheal (Scotland)	1	1	1	2*	2	–	–	–	–
G.C.Wilson (Ireland)	63	61	7	113	1428	26.44	1	10	48/10

ASSOCIATES – BOWLING

	O	M	R	W	Avge	Best	4wI	R/Over
A.Balbirnie	10	0	68	2	34.00	1-26	–	6.80
J.H.Davey	169.5	14	899	43	20.90	6-28	3	5.29
A.N.Kervezee	4	0	34	0	–	–	–	8.50
M.A.Leask	33.5	0	226	2	113.00	1-26	–	6.67
C.S.MacLeod	65	2	342	8	42.75	2-26	–	5.26
M.W.Machan	67	2	384	9	42.66	3-31	–	5.73
T.J.Murtagh	111	9	509	17	29.94	4-32	1	4.58
K.J.O'Brien	463.5	22	2417	77	31.38	4-13	2	5.21
W.B.Rankin	283.2	19	1391	43	32.34	3-32	–	4.90
P.R.Stirling	288.4	7	1303	30	43.43	4-11	1	4.51
R.M.L.Taylor	118.5	5	617	20	30.85	3-39	–	5.19
R.N.ten Doeschate	263.2	18	1327	55	24.12	4-31	3	5.03
T.van der Gugten	21	3	85	8	10.62	5-24	1	4.04
B.T.J.Wheal	8.1	0	44	1	44.00	1-44	–	5.38

LIMITED-OVERS INTERNATIONALS RESULTS

1970-71 to 7 April 2016

This chart excludes all matches involving multinational teams.

	Opponents	Matches	E	A	SA	WI	NZ	I	P	SL	Z	B	Ass	Tied	NR
England	Australia	136	51	80	–	–	–	–	–	–	–	–	–	2	3
	South Africa	56	24	–	28	–	–	–	–	–	–	–	–	1	3
	West Indies	88	42	–	–	42	–	–	–	–	–	–	–	–	4
	New Zealand	83	36	–	–	–	41	–	–	–	–	–	–	2	4
	India	93	38	–	–	–	–	50	–	–	–	–	–	2	3
	Pakistan	76	45	–	–	–	–	–	29	–	–	–	–	–	2
	Sri Lanka	64	30	–	–	–	–	–	–	34	–	–	–	–	–
	Zimbabwe	30	21	–	–	–	–	–	–	–	8	–	–	–	1
	Bangladesh	16	13	–	–	–	–	–	–	–	–	3	–	–	–
	Associates	22	19	–	–	–	–	–	–	–	–	–	1	–	2
Australia	South Africa	88	–	46	39	–	–	–	–	–	–	–	–	3	–
	West Indies	135	–	70	–	59	–	–	–	–	–	–	–	3	3
	New Zealand	130	–	87	–	–	37	–	–	–	–	–	–	–	6
	India	123	–	72	–	–	–	41	–	–	–	–	–	–	10
	Pakistan	93	–	58	–	–	–	–	31	–	–	–	–	1	3
	Sri Lanka	91	–	56	–	–	–	–	–	31	–	–	–	–	4
	Zimbabwe	30	–	27	–	–	–	–	–	–	2	–	–	–	1
	Bangladesh	19	–	18	–	–	–	–	–	–	–	1	–	–	–
	Associates	22	–	21	–	–	–	–	–	–	–	–	0	–	1
S Africa	West Indies	58	–	–	43	13	–	–	–	–	–	–	–	1	1
	New Zealand	65	–	–	38	–	22	–	–	–	–	–	–	–	5
	India	70	–	–	42	–	–	25	–	–	–	–	–	–	3
	Pakistan	72	–	–	47	–	–	–	24	–	–	–	–	–	1
	Sri Lanka	60	–	–	29	–	–	–	–	29	–	–	–	1	1
	Zimbabwe	38	–	–	35	–	–	–	–	–	2	–	–	–	1
	Bangladesh	17	–	–	14	–	–	–	–	–	–	3	–	–	–
	Associates	22	–	–	22	–	–	–	–	–	–	–	0	–	–
W Indies	New Zealand	61	–	–	–	30	24	–	–	–	–	–	–	–	7
	India	116	–	–	–	60	–	53	–	–	–	–	–	1	2
	Pakistan	127	–	–	–	69	–	–	55	–	–	–	–	3	–
	Sri Lanka	54	–	–	–	27	–	–	–	24	–	–	–	–	3
	Zimbabwe	45	–	–	–	35	–	–	–	–	9	–	–	–	1
	Bangladesh	28	–	–	–	19	–	–	–	–	–	7	–	–	2
	Associates	22	–	–	–	19	–	–	–	–	–	–	2	–	1
N Zealand	India	93	–	–	–	–	41	46	–	–	–	–	–	1	5
	Pakistan	98	–	–	–	–	42	–	53	–	–	–	–	1	2
	Sri Lanka	95	–	–	–	–	45	–	–	41	–	–	–	1	8
	Zimbabwe	38	–	–	–	–	27	–	–	–	9	–	–	1	1
	Bangladesh	25	–	–	–	–	17	–	–	–	–	8	–	–	–
	Associates	13	–	–	–	–	13	–	–	–	–	–	0	–	–
India	Pakistan	127	–	–	–	–	–	51	72	–	–	–	–	–	4
	Sri Lanka	149	–	–	–	–	–	83	–	54	–	–	–	1	11
	Zimbabwe	60	–	–	–	–	–	48	–	–	10	–	–	2	–
	Bangladesh	32	–	–	–	–	–	26	–	–	–	5	–	–	1
	Associates	27	–	–	–	–	–	25	–	–	–	–	2	–	–
Pakistan	Sri Lanka	147	–	–	–	–	–	–	84	58	–	–	–	1	4
	Zimbabwe	54	–	–	–	–	–	–	47	–	4	–	–	1	2
	Bangladesh	35	–	–	–	–	–	–	31	–	–	4	–	–	–
	Associates	28	–	–	–	–	–	–	26	–	–	–	1	–	1
Sri Lanka	Zimbabwe	47	–	–	–	–	–	–	–	39	7	–	–	–	1
	Bangladesh	38	–	–	–	–	–	–	–	33	–	4	–	–	1
	Associates	20	–	–	–	–	–	–	–	19	–	–	1	–	–
Zimbabwe	Bangladesh	67	–	–	–	–	–	–	–	–	28	39	–	–	–
	Associates	62	–	–	–	–	–	–	–	–	43	–	16	1	2
Bangladesh	Associates	35	–	–	–	–	–	–	–	–	–	24	11	–	–
Associates	Associates	180	–	–	–	–	–	–	–	–	–	–	172	1	7
		3720	319	535	337	373	309	448	452	362	122	98	206	31	128

MERIT TABLE OF ALL L-O INTERNATIONALS

	Matches	Won	Lost	Tied	No Result	% Won (exc NR)
Australia	867	535	292	9	31	63.99
South Africa	546	337	188	6	15	63.46
Pakistan	857	452	379	8	18	55.66
India	890	448	396	7	39	52.64
West Indies	734	373	329	8	24	52.53
England	664	319	316	7	22	49.68
Sri Lanka	765	362	366	4	33	49.45
New Zealand	701	309	348	6	38	46.60
Bangladesh	312	98	210	–	4	31.81
Zimbabwe	471	122	334	5	10	28.57
Associate Members (v Full*)	273	34	231	1	7	12.78

* Results of games between two Associate Members and those involving multi-national sides are excluded from this list; Associate Members have participated in 453 LOIs, 180 LOIs being between Associate Members.

TEAM RECORDS

HIGHEST TOTALS

† Batting Second

443-9	(50 overs)	Sri Lanka v Netherlands	Amstelveen	2006
439-2	(50 overs)	South Africa v West Indies	Johannesburg	2014-15
438-9†	(49.5 overs)	South Africa v Australia	Johannesburg	2005-06
438-4	(50 overs)	South Africa v India	Mumbai	2015-16
434-4	(50 overs)	Australia v South Africa	Johannesburg	2005-06
418-5	(50 overs)	South Africa v Zimbabwe	Potchefstroom	2006-07
418-5	(50 overs)	India v West Indies	Indore	2011-12
417-6	(50 overs)	Australia v Afghanistan	Perth	2014-15
414-7	(50 overs)	India v Sri Lanka	Rajkot	2009-10
413-5	(50 overs)	India v Bermuda	Port of Spain	2006-07
411-8†	(50 overs)	Sri Lanka v India	Rajkot	2009-10
411-4	(50 overs)	South Africa v Ireland	Canberra	2014-15
408-5	(50 overs)	South Africa v West Indies	Sydney	2014-15
404-5	(50 overs)	India v Sri Lanka	Kolkata	2014-15
402-2	(50 overs)	New Zealand v Ireland	Aberdeen	2008
401-3	(50 overs)	India v South Africa	Gwalior	2009-10
399-6	(50 overs)	South Africa v Zimbabwe	Benoni	2010-11
399-9	(50 overs)	England v South Africa	Bloemfontein	2015-16
398-5	(50 overs)	Sri Lanka v Kenya	Kandy	1995-96
398-5	(50 overs)	New Zealand v England	The Oval	2015
397-5	(44 overs)	New Zealand v Zimbabwe	Bulawayo	2005
393-6	(50 overs)	New Zealand v West Indies	Wellington	2014-15
392-6	(50 overs)	South Africa v Pakistan	Pretoria	2006-07
392-4	(50 overs)	India v New Zealand	Christchurch	2008-09
391-4	(50 overs)	England v Bangladesh	Nottingham	2005
387-5	(50 overs)	India v England	Rajkot	2008-09
385-7	(50 overs)	Pakistan v Bangladesh	Dambulla	2010
383-6	(50 overs)	India v Australia	Bangalore	2013-14
377-6	(50 overs)	Australia v South Africa	Basseterre	2006-07
376-2	(50 overs)	India v New Zealand	Hyderabad, India	1999-00
375-3	(50 overs)	Pakistan v Zimbabwe	Lahore	2015
374-4	(50 overs)	India v Hong Kong	Karachi	2008
373-6	(50 overs)	India v Sri Lanka	Taunton	1999
373-8	(50 overs)	New Zealand v Zimbabwe	Napier	2011-12
372-6	(50 overs)	New Zealand v Zimbabwe	Whangarei	2011-12
372-2	(50 overs)	West Indies v Zimbabwe	Canberra	2014-15
371-9	(50 overs)	Pakistan v Sri Lanka	Nairobi	1996-97
370-4	(50 overs)	India v Bangladesh	Dhaka	2010-11
369-5	(50 overs)	New Zealand v Pakistan	Napier	2014-15

368-5	(50 overs)	Australia v Sri Lanka	Sydney	2005-06
368-4	(50 overs)	Sri Lanka v Pakistan	Hambantota	2015
365-2	(50 overs)	South Africa v India	Ahmedabad	2009-10
365-9†	(46 overs)	England v New Zealand	The Oval	2015
364-7	(50 overs)	Pakistan v New Zealand	Sharjah	2014-15
363-7	(55 overs)	England v Pakistan	Nottingham	1992
363-3	(50 overs)	South Africa v Zimbabwe	Bulawayo	2001-02
363-5	(50 overs)	New Zealand v Canada	Gros Islet	2006-07
363-5	(50 overs)	India v Sri Lanka	Colombo (RPS)	2008-09
363-4	(50 overs)	West Indies v New Zealand	Hamilton	2013-14
363-5	(50 overs)	India v Sri Lanka	Cuttack	2014-15
363-9	(50 overs)	Sri Lanka v Scotland	Hobart	2014-15
362-1†	(43.3 overs)	India v Australia	Jaipur	2013-14
362-3	(50 overs)	Australia v Scotland	Edinburgh	2013
361-5	(42 overs)	South Africa v West Indies	Centurion	2014-15
361-8	(50 overs)	Australia v Bangladesh	Dhaka	2010-11
360-4	(50 overs)	West Indies v Sri Lanka	Karachi	1987-88
360-5	(50 overs)	New Zealand v Sri Lanka	Dunedin	2014-15

The highest score for Zimbabwe is 351-7 (v Kenya, Mombasa, 2008-09), and for Bangladesh 329-6 (v Pakistan, Dhaka, 2014-15).

HIGHEST TOTALS BATTING SECOND

WINNING:	438-9	(49.5 overs)	South Africa v Australia	Johannesburg	2005-06
LOSING:	411-8	(50.0 overs)	Sri Lanka v India	Rajkot	2009-10

HIGHEST MATCH AGGREGATES

872-13	(99.5 overs)	South Africa v Australia	Johannesburg	2005-06
825-15	(100 overs)	India v Sri Lanka	Rajkot	2009-10

LARGEST RUNS MARGINS OF VICTORY

290 runs	New Zealand beat Ireland	Aberdeen	2008
275 runs	Australia beat Afghanistan	Perth	2014-15
272 runs	South Africa beat Zimbabwe	Benoni	2010-11
258 runs	South Africa beat Sri Lanka	Paarl	2011-12
257 runs	India beat Bermuda	Port of Spain	2006-07
257 runs	South Africa beat West Indies	Sydney	2014-15
256 runs	Australia beat Namibia	Potschefstroom	2002-03
256 runs	India beat Hong Kong	Karachi	2008
245 runs	Sri Lanka beat India	Sharjah	2000-01
243 runs	Sri Lanka beat Bermuda	Port of Spain	2006-07
234 runs	Sri Lanka beat Pakistan	Lahore	2008-09
233 runs	Pakistan beat Bangladesh	Dhaka	1999-00
232 runs	Australia beat Sri Lanka	Adelaide	1984-85
231 runs	South Africa beat Netherlands	Mohali	2010-11
229 runs	Australia beat Netherlands	Basseterre	2006-07
224 runs	Australia beat Pakistan	Nairobi	2002
221 runs	South Africa beat Netherlands	Basseterre	2006-07
217 runs	Pakistan beat Sri Lanka	Sharjah	2001-02
215 runs	Australia beat New Zealand	St George's	2006-07
215 runs	West Indies beat Netherlands	Delhi	2010-11
214 runs	South Africa beat India	Mumbai	2015-16
212 runs	South Africa beat Zimbabwe	Centurion	2009-10
210 runs	New Zealand beat USA	The Oval	2004
210 runs	Sri Lanka beat Canada	Hambantota	2010-11
210 runs	England beat New Zealand	Birmingham	2015
209 runs	South Africa beat West Indies	Cape Town	2003-04
208 runs	South Africa beat Kenya	Cape Town	2001-02
208 runs	Australia beat India	Sydney	2003-04
208 runs	West Indies beat Canada	Kingston	2009-10
206 runs	New Zealand beat Australia	Adelaide	1985-86
206 runs	Sri Lanka beat Netherlands	Colombo (RPS)	2002-03

298

206 runs	South Africa beat Bangladesh	Dhaka	2010-11
205 runs	Pakistan beat Kenya	Hambantota	2010-11
203 runs	Australia beat Scotland	Basseterre	2006-07
203 runs	West Indies beat New Zealand	Hamilton	2013-14
202 runs	England beat India	Lord's	1975
202 runs	South Africa beat Kenya	Nairobi	1996-97
202 runs	Zimbabwe beat Kenya	Dhaka	1998-99
202 runs	New Zealand beat Zimbabwe	Napier	2011-12
201 runs	South Africa beat Ireland	Canberra	2014-15
200 runs	India beat Bangladesh	Dhaka	2002-03
200 runs	New Zealand beat India	Dambulla	2010
200 runs	Australia beat Scotland	Edinburgh	2013

LOWEST TOTALS (Excluding reduced innings)

35	(18.0 overs)	Zimbabwe v Sri Lanka	Harare	2003-04
36	(18.4 overs)	Canada v Sri Lanka	Paarl	2002-03
38	(15.4 overs)	Zimbabwe v Sri Lanka	Colombo (SSC)	2001-02
43	(19.5 overs)	Pakistan v West Indies	Cape Town	1992-93
43	(20.1 overs)	Sri Lanka v South Africa	Paarl	2011-12
44	(24.5 overs)	Zimbabwe v Bangladesh	Chittagong	2009-10
45	(40.3 overs)	Canada v England	Manchester	1979
45	(14.0 overs)	Namibia v Australia	Potschefstroom	2002-03
54	(26.3 overs)	India v Sri Lanka	Sharjah	2000-01
54	(23.2 overs)	West Indies v South Africa	Cape Town	2003-04
55	(28.3 overs)	Sri Lanka v West Indies	Sharjah	1986-87
58	(18.5 overs)	Bangladesh v West Indies	Dhaka	2010-11
58	(17.4 overs)	Bangladesh v India	Dhaka	2014
58	(16.1 overs)	Afghanistan v Zimbabwe	Sharjah	2015-16
61	(22.0 overs)	West Indies v Bangladesh	Chittagong	2011-12
63	(25.5 overs)	India v Australia	Sydney	1980-81
63	(18.3 overs)	Afghanistan v Scotland	Abu Dhabi	2014-15
64	(35.5 overs)	New Zealand v Pakistan	Sharjah	1985-86
65	(24.0 overs)	USA v Australia	Southampton	2004
65	(24.3 overs)	Zimbabwe v India	Harare	2005
67	(31.0 overs)	Zimbabwe v Sri Lanka	Harare	2008-09
67	(24.4 overs)	Canada v Netherlands	King City	2013
67	(24.0 overs)	Sri Lanka v England	Manchester	2014
68	(31.3 overs)	Scotland v West Indies	Leicester	1999
69	(28.0 overs)	South Africa v Australia	Sydney	1993-94
69	(22.5 overs)	Zimbabwe v Kenya	Harare	2005-06
69	(23.5 overs)	Kenya v New Zealand	Chennai	2010-11
70	(25.2 overs)	Australia v England	Birmingham	1977
70	(26.3 overs)	Australia v New Zealand	Adelaide	1985-86
70	(23.5 overs)	West Indies v Australia	Perth	2012-13
70	(24.4 overs)	Bangladesh v West Indies	St George's	2014

The lowest for England is 86 (v A, Manchester, 2001).

LOWEST MATCH AGGREGATES

73-11	(23.2 overs)	Canada (36) v Sri Lanka (37-1)	Paarl	2002-03
75-11	(27.2 overs)	Zimbabwe (35) v Sri Lanka (40-1)	Harare	2003-04
78-11	(20.0 overs)	Zimbabwe (38) v Sri Lanka (40-1)	Colombo (SSC)	2001-02

BATTING RECORDS

5000 RUNS IN A CAREER

		LOI	I	NO	HS	Runs	Avge	100	50
S.R.Tendulkar	I	463	452	41	200*	18426	44.83	49	96
K.C.Sangakkara	SL/Asia/ICC	404	380	41	169	14234	41.98	25	93
R.T.Ponting	A/ICC	375	365	39	164	13704	42.03	30	82
S.T.Jayasuriya	SL/Asia	445	433	18	189	13430	32.36	28	68
D.P.M.D.Jayawardena	SL/Asia	448	418	39	144	12650	33.37	19	77

		LOI	I	NO	HS	Runs	Avge	100	50
Inzamam-ul-Haq	P/Asia	378	350	53	137*	11739	39.52	10	83
J.H.Kallis	SA/Afr/ICC	328	314	53	139	11579	44.36	17	86
S.C.Ganguly	I/Asia	311	300	23	183	11363	41.02	22	72
R.S.Dravid	I/Asia/ICC	344	318	40	153	10889	39.16	12	83
B.C.Lara	WI/ICC	299	289	32	169	10405	40.48	19	63
T.M.Dilshan	SL	327	300	41	161*	10269	39.44	22	47
Mohammad Yousuf	P/Asia	288	272	40	141*	9720	41.71	15	64
A.C.Gilchrist	A/ICC	287	279	11	172	9619	35.89	16	55
M.Azharuddin	I	334	308	54	153*	9378	36.92	7	58
P.A.de Silva	SL	308	296	30	145	9284	34.90	11	64
C.H.Gayle	WI/ICC	269	264	17	215	9221	37.33	22	47
M.S.Dhoni	I/Asia	275	241	67	183*	8918	51.25	9	60
Saeed Anwar	P	247	244	19	194	8824	39.21	20	43
S.Chanderpaul	WI	268	251	40	150	8778	41.60	11	59
D.L.Haynes	WI	238	237	28	152*	8648	41.37	17	57
A.B.de Villiers	SA/Afr	200	192	34	162*	8621	54.56	24	48
M.S.Atapattu	SL	268	259	32	132*	8529	37.57	11	59
M.E.Waugh	A	244	236	20	173	8500	39.35	18	50
Yuvraj Singh	I/Asia	293	268	39	139	8329	36.37	13	51
V.Sehwag	I/Asia/ICC	251	245	9	219	8273	35.05	15	38
H.H.Gibbs	SA	248	240	16	175	8094	36.13	21	37
Shahid Afridi	P/Asia/ICC	398	369	27	124	8064	23.57	6	39
S.P.Fleming	NZ/ICC	280	269	21	134*	8037	32.40	8	49
M.J.Clarke	A	245	223	44	130	7981	44.58	8	58
S.R.Waugh	A	325	288	58	120*	7569	32.90	3	45
A.Ranatunga	SL	269	255	47	131*	7456	35.84	4	49
Javed Miandad	P	233	218	41	119*	7381	41.70	8	50
Younus Khan	P	265	255	23	144	7249	31.24	7	48
V.Kohli	I	171	163	23	183	7212	51.51	25	36
Salim Malik	P	283	256	38	102	7170	32.88	5	47
N.J.Astle	NZ	223	217	14	145*	7090	34.92	16	41
G.C.Smith	SA/Afr	197	194	10	141	6989	37.98	10	47
M.G.Bevan	A	232	196	67	108*	6912	53.58	6	46
G.Kirsten	SA	185	185	19	188*	6798	40.95	13	45
A.Flower	Z	213	208	16	145	6786	35.34	4	55
I.V.A.Richards	WI	187	167	24	189*	6721	47.00	11	45
G.W.Flower	Z	221	214	18	142*	6571	33.52	6	40
Ijaz Ahmed	P	250	232	29	139*	6564	32.33	10	37
A.R.Border	A	273	252	39	127*	6524	30.62	3	39
R.B.Richardson	WI	224	217	30	122	6248	33.41	5	44
H.M.Amla	SA	131	128	9	159	6204	52.13	22	29
M.L.Hayden	A/ICC	161	155	15	181*	6133	43.80	10	36
Shoaib Malik	P	232	209	31	143	6129	34.43	8	35
B.B.McCullum	NZ	260	228	28	166	6083	30.41	5	32
D.M.Jones	A	164	161	25	145	6068	44.61	7	46
D.C.Boon	A	181	177	16	122	5964	37.04	5	37
J.N.Rhodes	SA	245	220	51	121	5935	35.11	2	33
Ramiz Raja	P	198	197	15	119*	5841	32.09	9	31
R.R.Sarwan	WI	181	169	33	120*	5804	42.67	5	38
C.L.Hooper	WI	227	206	43	113*	5761	35.34	7	29
S.R.Watson	A	190	169	27	185*	5757	40.54	9	33
L.R.P.L.Taylor	NZ	171	157	27	131*	5707	43.90	15	32
S.K.Raina	I	223	192	35	116*	5568	35.46	5	36
W.J.Cronje	SA	188	175	31	112	5565	38.64	2	39
M.E.K.Hussey	A	185	157	44	109*	5442	48.15	3	39
I.R.Bell	E	161	157	14	141	5416	37.87	4	35
W.U.Tharanga	SL/Asia	180	172	9	174*	5407	33.17	13	28
A.Jadeja	I	196	179	36	119	5359	37.47	6	30
Mohammad Hafeez	P	175	175	10	140*	5356	32.46	11	28
D.R.Martyn	A	208	182	51	144*	5346	40.80	5	37
B.R.M.Taylor	Z	167	166	15	145*	5258	34.82	8	32

		LOI	I	NO	HS	Runs	Avge	100	50
G.Gambhir	I	147	143	11	150*	**5238**	39.68	11	34
A.D.R.Campbell	Z	188	184	14	131*	**5185**	30.50	7	30
R.S.Mahanama	SL	213	198	23	119*	**5162**	29.49	4	35
C.G.Greenidge	WI	128	127	13	133*	**5134**	45.03	11	31
Misbah-ul-Haq	P	162	149	31	96*	**5122**	43.40	–	42
P.D.Collingwood	E	197	181	37	120*	**5092**	35.36	5	26
A.Symonds	A	198	161	33	156	**5088**	39.75	6	30
Abdul Razzaq	P/Asia	265	228	57	112	**5080**	29.70	3	23
R.G.Sharma	I	148	142	21	264	**5008**	42.08	10	28

The most for Bangladesh is 3977 in 135 innings by Shakib Al Hasan.

HIGHEST INDIVIDUAL INNINGS

264	R.G.Sharma	India v Sri Lanka	Kolkata	2014-15
237*	M.J.Guptill	New Zealand v West Indies	Wellington	2014-15
219	V.Sehwag	India v West Indies	Indore	2011-12
215	C.H.Gayle	West Indies v Zimbabwe	Canberra	2014-15
209	R.G.Sharma	India v Australia	Bangalore	2013-14
200*	S.R.Tendulkar	India v South Africa	Gwalior	2009-10
194*	C.K.Coventry	Zimbabwe v Bangladesh	Bulawayo	2009
194	Saeed Anwar	Pakistan v India	Madras	1996-97
189*	I.V.A.Richards	West Indies v England	Manchester	1984
189*	M.J.Guptill	New Zealand v England	Southampton	2013
189	S.T.Jayasuriya	Sri Lanka v India	Sharjah	2000-01
188*	G.Kirsten	South Africa v UAE	Rawalpindi	1995-96
186*	S.R.Tendulkar	India v New Zealand	Hyderabad	1999-00
185*	S.R.Watson	Australia v Bangladesh	Dhaka	2010-11
183*	M.S.Dhoni	India v Sri Lanka	Jaipur	2005-06
183	S.C.Ganguly	India v Sri Lanka	Taunton	1999
183	V.Kohli	India v Pakistan	Dhaka	2011-12
181*	M.L.Hayden	Australia v New Zealand	Hamilton	2006-07
181	I.V.A.Richards	West Indies v Sri Lanka	Karachi	1987-88
178*	H.Masakadza	Zimbabwe v Kenya	Harare	2009-10
178	D.A.Warner	Australia v Afghanistan	Perth	2014-15
177	P.R.Stirling	Ireland v Canada	Toronto	2010
175*	Kapil Dev	India v Zimbabwe	Tunbridge Wells	1983
175	H.H.Gibbs	South Africa v Australia	Johannesburg	2005-06
175	S.R.Tendulkar	India v Australia	Hyderabad, India	2009-10
175	V.Sehwag	India v Bangladesh	Dhaka	2010-11
175	C.S.MacLeod	Scotland v Canada	Christchurch	2013-14
174*	W.U.Tharanga	Sri Lanka v India	Kingston	2013
173	M.E.Waugh	Australia v West Indies	Melbourne	2000-01
172*	C.B.Wishart	Zimbabwe v Namibia	Harare	2002-03
172	A.C.Gilchrist	Australia v Zimbabwe	Hobart	2003-04
172	L.Vincent	New Zealand v Zimbabwe	Bulawayo	2005
171*	G.M.Turner	New Zealand v East Africa	Birmingham	1975
171*	R.G.Sharma	India v Australia	Perth	2015-16
170*	L.Ronchi	New Zealand v Sri Lanka	Dunedin	2014-15
169*	D.J.Callaghan	South Africa v New Zealand	Pretoria	1994-95
169	B.C.Lara	West Indies v Sri Lanka	Sharjah	1995-96
169	K.C.Sangakkara	Sri Lanka v South Africa	Colombo (RPS)	2013
169	D.Ramdin	West Indies v Bangladesh	Basseterre	2014
167*	R.A.Smith	England v Australia	Birmingham	1993
166	B.B.McCullum	New Zealand v Ireland	Aberdeen	2008
164	R.T.Ponting	Australia v South Africa	Johannesburg	2005-06
163*	S.R.Tendulkar	India v New Zealand	Christchurch	2008-09
163	D.A.Warner	Australia v Sri Lanka	Brisbane	2011-12
162*	A.B.de Villiers	South Africa v West Indies	Sydney	2014-15
161*	S.R.Watson	Australia v England	Melbourne	2010-11
161*	T.M.Dilshan	Sri Lanka v Bangladesh	Melbourne	2014-15
161	A.C.Hudson	South Africa v Netherlands	Rawalpindi	1995-96
161	J.A.H.Marshall	New Zealand v Ireland	Aberdeen	2008

160*	T.M.Dilshan	Sri Lanka v India	Hobart	2011-12
160	Imran Nazir	Pakistan v Zimbabwe	Kingston	2006-07
160	T.M.Dilshan	Sri Lanka v India	Rajkot	2009-10

The highest for Bangladesh is 154 by Tamim Iqbal (v Zimbabwe, Bulawayo, 2009).

HUNDRED ON DEBUT

D.L.Amiss	103	England v Australia	Manchester	1972
D.L.Haynes	148	West Indies v Australia	St John's	1977-78
A.Flower	115*	Zimbabwe v Sri Lanka	New Plymouth	1991-92
Salim Elahi	102*	Pakistan v Sri Lanka	Gujranwala	1995-96
M.J.Guptill	122*	New Zealand v West Indies	Auckland	2008-09
C.A.Ingram	124	South Africa v Zimbabwe	Bloemfontein	2010-11
R.J.Nicol	108*	New Zealand v Zimbabwe	Harare	2011-12
P.J.Hughes	112	Australia v Sri Lanka	Melbourne	2012-13
M.J.Lumb	106	England v West Indies	North Sound	2013-14
M.S.Chapman	124*	Hong Kong v UAE	Dubai	2015-16

Shahid Afridi scored 102 for P v SL, Nairobi, 1996-97, in his second match having not batted in his first.

Fastest 100	31 balls	A.B.de Villiers (149)	SA v WI	Johannesburg	2014-15
Fastest 50	16 balls	A.B.de Villiers (149)	SA v WI	Johannesburg	2014-15

15 HUNDREDS

		Inns	100	E	A	SA	WI	NZ	I	P	SL	Z	B	Ass
S.R.Tendulkar	I	452	49	2	9	5	4	5	–	5	8	5	1	5
R.T.Ponting	A	365	30*	5	–	2	2	6	6	1	4	1	1	1
S.T.Jayasuriya	SL	433	28	4	2	–	1	5	7	3	–	1	4	1
V.Kohli	I	163	25	2	5	1	3	2	–	2	6	1	3	–
K.C.Sangakkara	SL	380	25	4	2	2	–	2	6	2	–	–	5	2
A.B.de Villiers	SA	192	24	2	1	–	5	1	6	3	2	3	–	1
H.M.Amla	SA	128	22	2	1	–	4	2	2	2	3	3	1	2
C.H.Gayle	WI	264	22	2	–	3	–	2	4	3	2	1	1	3
T.M.Dilshan	SL	300	22	2	1	2	–	3	4	2	–	2	4	2
S.C.Ganguly	I	300	22	1	1	3	3	–	–	3	4	3	1	4
H.H.Gibbs	SA	240	21	2	3	–	5	2	2	2	1	2	1	1
Saeed Anwar	P	244	20	–	1	2	4	–	4	–	7	2	–	–
B.C.Lara	WI	289	19	1	3	3	–	2	–	5	2	1	1	1
D.P.M.D.Jayawardena	SL	418	19*	5	–	1	3	4	2	–	–	–	1	2
M.E.Waugh	A	236	18	1	–	2	3	3	3	1	1	3	1	–
D.L.Haynes	WI	237	17	2	6	–	–	2	2	4	1	–	–	–
J.H.Kallis	SA	314	17	1	1	–	4	3	2	1	3	1	–	1
N.J.Astle	NZ	217	16	2	1	1	1	–	5	2	–	3	1	–
A.C.Gilchrist	A	279	16*	2	–	2	–	2	1	1	6	1	–	1
L.R.P.L.Taylor	NZ	157	15	3	1	–	1	–	2	3	1	2	2	–
V.Sehwag	I	245	15	1	–	1	–	2	–	3	4	1	2	1
Mohammad Yousuf	P	273	15	–	1	2	6	–	2	–	–	2	1	–

* = Includes hundred scored against multi-national side. The most for England is 12 by M.E.Trescothick (in 122 innings), for Zimbabwe 8 by B.R.M.Taylor (167), and for Bangladesh 6 by Shakib Al Hasan (157) and Tamim Iqbal (153) .

HIGHEST PARTNERSHIP FOR EACH WICKET

1st	286	W.U.Tharanga/S.T.Jayasuriya	Sri Lanka v England	Leeds	2006
2nd	372	C.H.Gayle/M.N.Samuels	West Indies v Zimbabwe	Canberra	2014-15
3rd	258	D.M.Bravo/D.Ramdin	West Indies v Bangladesh	Basseterre	2014
4th	275*	M.Azharuddin/A.Jadeja	India v Zimbabwe	Cuttack	1997-98
5th	256*	D.A.Miller/J.P.Duminy	South Africa v Zimbabwe	Hamilton	2014-15
6th	267*	G.D.Elliott/L.Ronchi	New Zealand v Sri Lanka	Dunedin	2014-15
7th	177	J.C.Buttler/A.U.Rashid	England v New Zealand	Birmingham	2015
8th	138*	J.M.Kemp/A.J.Hall	South Africa v India	Cape Town	2006-07
9th	132	A.D.Mathews/S.L.Malinga	Sri Lanka v Australia	Melbourne	2010-11
10th	106*	I.V.A.Richards/M.A.Holding	West Indies v England	Manchester	1984

BOWLING RECORDS

200 WICKETS IN A CAREER

		LOI	Balls	R	W	Avge	Best	5w	R/Over
M.Muralitharan	SL/Asia/ICC	350	18811	12326	534	23.08	7-30	10	3.93
Wasim Akram	P	356	18186	11812	502	23.52	5-15	6	3.89
Waqar Younis	P	262	12698	9919	416	23.84	7-36	13	4.68
W.P.J.U.C.Vaas	SL/Asia	322	15775	11014	400	27.53	8-19	4	4.18
Shahid Afridi	P/Asia/ICC	398	17620	13632	395	34.51	7-12	9	4.62
S.M.Pollock	SA/Afr/ICC	303	15712	9631	393	24.50	6-35	5	3.67
G.D.McGrath	A/ICC	250	12970	8391	381	22.02	7-15	7	3.88
B.Lee	A	221	11185	8877	380	23.36	5-22	9	4.76
A.Kumble	I/Asia	271	14496	10412	337	30.89	6-12	2	4.30
S.T.Jayasuriya	SL	445	14874	11871	323	36.75	6-29	4	4.78
J.Srinath	I	229	11935	8847	315	28.08	5-23	3	4.44
D.L.Vettori	NZ/ICC	295	14060	9674	305	31.71	5- 7	2	4.12
S.K.Warne	A/ICC	194	10642	7541	293	25.73	5-33	1	4.25
S.L.Malinga	SL	191	9207	8082	291	27.77	6-38	7	5.26
Saqlain Mushtaq	P	169	8770	6275	288	21.78	5-20	6	4.29
A.B.Agarkar	I	191	9484	8021	288	27.85	6-42	2	5.07
Z.Khan	I/Asia	200	10097	8301	282	29.43	5-42	1	4.93
J.H.Kallis	SA/Afr/ICC	328	10750	8680	273	31.79	5-30	2	4.84
A.A.Donald	SA	164	8561	5926	272	21.78	6-23	2	4.15
J.M.Anderson	E	194	9584	7861	269	29.22	5-23	2	4.92
Abdul Razzaq	P/Asia	265	10941	8564	269	31.83	6-35	3	4.69
Harbhajan Singh	I/Asia	236	12479	8973	269	33.35	5-31	3	4.31
M.Ntini	SA/ICC	173	8687	6559	266	24.65	6-22	4	4.53
Kapil Dev	I	225	11202	6945	253	27.45	5-43	1	3.72
Shoaib Akhtar	P/Asia/ICC	163	7764	6169	247	24.97	6-16	4	4.76
K.D.Mills	NZ	170	8230	6485	240	27.02	5-25	1	4.72
M.G.Johnson	A	153	7489	6038	239	25.26	6-31	3	4.83
H.H.Streak	Z/Afr	189	9468	7129	239	29.82	5-32	1	4.51
D.Gough	E/ICC	159	8470	6209	235	26.42	5-44	2	4.39
C.A.Walsh	WI	205	10822	6918	227	30.47	5- 1	1	3.83
C.E.L.Ambrose	WI	176	9353	5429	225	24.12	5-17	4	3.48
Abdur Razzak	B	153	7965	6065	207	29.29	5-29	4	4.56
Shakib Al Hasan	B	157	8011	5746	206	27.89	5-47	1	4.30
Mashrafe Mortaza	B/Asia	160	7957	6277	204	30.76	6-26	1	4.73
C.J.McDermott	A	138	7460	5018	203	24.71	5-44	1	4.03
C.Z.Harris	NZ	250	10667	7613	203	37.50	5-42	1	4.28
C.L.Cairns	NZ/ICC	215	8168	6594	201	32.80	5-42	1	4.84

SIX WICKETS IN AN INNINGS

8-19	W.P.J.U.C.Vaas	Sri Lanka v Zimbabwe	Colombo (SSC)	2001-02
7-12	Shahid Afridi	Pakistan v West Indies	Providence	2013
7-15	G.D.McGrath	Australia v Namibia	Potschefstroom	2002-03
7-20	A.J.Bichel	Australia v England	Port Elizabeth	2002-03
7-30	M.Muralitharan	Sri Lanka v India	Sharjah	2000-01
7-33	T.G.Southee	New Zealand v England	Wellington	2014-15
7-36	Waqar Younis	Pakistan v England	Leeds	2001
7-37	Aqib Javed	Pakistan v India	Sharjah	1991-92
7-51	W.W.Davis	West Indies v Australia	Leeds	1983
6- 4	S.T.R.Binny	India v Bangladesh	Dhaka	2014
6-12	A.Kumble	India v West Indies	Calcutta	1993-94
6-13	B.A.W.Mendis	Sri Lanka v India	Karachi	2008
6-14	G.J.Gilmour	Australia v England	Leeds	1975
6-14	Imran Khan	Pakistan v India	Sharjah	1984-85
6-14	M.F.Maharoof	Sri Lanka v West Indies	Mumbai	2006-07
6-15	C.E.H.Croft	West Indies v England	Kingstown	1980-81
6-16	Shoaib Akhtar	Pakistan v New Zealand	Karachi	2001-02
6-16	K.Rabada	South Africa v Bangladesh	Dhaka	2015
6-18	Azhar Mahmood	Pakistan v West Indies	Sharjah	1999-00
6-19	H.K.Olonga	Zimbabwe v England	Cape Town	1999-00
6-19	S.E.Bond	New Zealand v Zimbabwe	Harare	2005

6-20	B.C.Strang	Zimbabwe v Bangladesh	Nairobi	1997-98
6-20	A.D.Mathews	Sri Lanka v India	Colombo (RPS)	2009-10
6-22	F.H.Edwards	West Indies v Zimbabwe	Harare	2003-04
6-22	M.Ntini	South Africa v Australia	Cape Town	2005-06
6-23	A.A.Donald	South Africa v Kenya	Nairobi	1996-97
6-23	A.Nehra	India v England	Durban	2002-03
6-23	S.E.Bond	New Zealand v Australia	Port Elizabeth	2002-03
6-25	S.B.Styris	New Zealand v West Indies	Port of Spain	2002
6-25	W.P.J.U.C.Vaas	Sri Lanka v Bangladesh	Pietermaritzburg	2002-03
6-26	Waqar Younis	Pakistan v Sri Lanka	Sharjah	1989-90
6-26	Mashrafe Mortaza	Bangladesh v Kenya	Nairobi	2006
6-26	Rubel Hossain	Bangladesh v New Zealand	Dhaka	2013-14
6-26	Yasir Shah	Pakistan v Zimbabwe	Harare	2015-16
6-27	Naved-ul-Hasan	Pakistan v India	Jamshedpur	2004-05
6-27	C.R.D.Fernando	Sri Lanka v England	Colombo (RPS)	2007-08
6-27	M.Kartik	India v Australia	Mumbai	2007-08
6-27	K.A.J.Roach	West Indies v Netherlands	Delhi	2010-11
6-28	H.K.Olonga	Zimbabwe v Kenya	Bulawayo	2002-03
6-28	J.H.Davey	Scotland v Afghanistan	Abu Dhabi	2014-15
6-28	M.A.Starc	Australia v New Zealand	Auckland	2014-15
6-29	B.P.Patterson	West Indies v India	Nagpur	1987-88
6-29	S.T.Jayasuriya	Sri Lanka v England	Moratuwa	1992-93
6-29	B.A.W.Mendis	Sri Lanka v Zimbabwe	Harare	2008-09
6-30	Waqar Younis	Pakistan v New Zealand	Auckland	1993-94
6-31	P.D.Collingwood	England v Bangladesh	Nottingham	2005
6-31	M.G.Johnson	Australia v Sri Lanka	Pallekele	2011
6-35	S.M.Pollock	South Africa v West Indies	East London	1998-99
6-35	Abdul Razzaq	Pakistan v Bangladesh	Dhaka	2001-02
6-38	Shahid Afridi	Pakistan v Australia	Dubai	2009
6-38	S.L.Malinga	Sri Lanka v Kenya	Colombo (RPS)	2010-11
6-39	K.H.MacLeay	Australia v India	Nottingham	1983
6-39	D.W.Steyn	South Africa v Pakistan	Port Elizabeth	2013-14
6-41	I.V.A.Richards	West Indies v India	Delhi	1989-90
6-42	A.B.Agarkar	India v Australia	Melbourne	2003-04
6-42	Umar Gul	Pakistan v England	The Oval	2010
6-43	D.J.Bravo	West Indies v Zimbabwe	St George's	2012-13
6-43	M.A.Starc	Australia v India	Melbourne	2014-15
6-43	Mustafizur Rahman	Bangladesh v India	Dhaka	2015
6-44	Waqar Younis	Pakistan v New Zealand	Sharjah	1996-97
6-44	N.L.T.C.Perera	Sri Lanka v Pakistan	Pallekele	2012
6-45	C.R.Woakes	England v Australia	Brisbane	2010-11
6-46	A.G.Cremer	Zimbabwe v Kenya	Harare	2009-10
6-47	C.R.Woakes	England v Sri Lanka	Pallekele	2014-15
6-48	A.Mishra	India v Zimbabwe	Bulawayo	2013
6-49	L.Klusener	South Africa v Sri Lanka	Lahore	1997-98
6-50	A.H.Gray	West Indies v Australia	Port of Spain	1990-91
6-52	C.B.Mpofu	Zimbabwe v Kenya	Nairobi (Gym)	2008-09
6-55	S.Sreesanth	India v England	Indore	2005-06
6-59	Waqar Younis	Pakistan v Australia	Nottingham	2001
6-59	A.Nehra	India v Sri Lanka	Colombo (RPS)	2005

HAT-TRICKS

Jalaluddin	Pakistan v Australia	Hyderabad	1982-83
B.A.Reid	Australia v New Zealand	Sydney	1985-86
C.Sharma	India v New Zealand	Nagpur	1987-88
Wasim Akram	Pakistan v West Indies	Sharjah	1989-90
Wasim Akram	Pakistan v Australia	Sharjah	1989-90
Kapil Dev	India v Sri Lanka	Calcutta	1990-91
Aqib Javed	Pakistan v India	Sharjah	1991-92
D.K.Morrison	New Zealand v India	Napier	1993-94
Waqar Younis	Pakistan v New Zealand	East London	1994-95
Saqlain Mushtaq	Pakistan v Zimbabwe	Peshawar	1996-97
E.A.Brandes	Zimbabwe v England	Harare	1996-97
A.M.Stuart	Australia v New Zealand	Melbourne	1996-97

Saqlain Mushtaq	Pakistan v Zimbabwe	The Oval	1999
W.P.J.U.C.Vaas	Sri Lanka v Zimbabwe	Colombo (SSC)	2001-02
Mohammad Sami	Pakistan v West Indies	Sharjah	2001-02
W.P.J.U.C.Vaas[1]	Sri Lanka v Bangladesh	Pietermaritzburg	2002-03
B.Lee	Australia v Kenya	Durban	2002-03
J.M.Anderson	England v Pakistan	The Oval	2003
S.J.Harmison	England v India	Nottingham	2004
C.K.Langeveldt	South Africa v West Indies	Bridgetown	2004-05
Shahadat Hossain	Bangladesh v Zimbabwe	Harare	2006
J.E.Taylor	West Indies v Australia	Mumbai	2006-07
S.E.Bond	New Zealand v Australia	Hobart	2006-07
S.L.Malinga[2]	Sri Lanka v South Africa	Providence	2006-07
A.Flintoff	England v West Indies	St Lucia	2008-09
M.F.Maharoof	Sri Lanka v India	Dambulla	2010
Abdur Razzak	Bangladesh v Zimbabwe	Dhaka	2010-11
K.A.J.Roach	West Indies v Netherlands	Delhi	2010-11
S.L.Malinga	Sri Lanka v Kenya	Colombo (RPS)	2010-11
S.L.Malinga	Sri Lanka v Australia	Colombo (RPS)	2011
D.T.Christian	Australia v Sri Lanka	Melbourne	2011-12
N.L.T.C.Perera	Sri Lanka v Pakistan	Colombo (RPS)	2012
C.J.McKay	Australia v England	Cardiff	2013
Rubel Hossain	Bangladesh v New Zealand	Dhaka	2013-14
P.Utseya	Zimbabwe v South Africa	Harare	2014
Taijul Islam	Bangladesh v Zimbabwe	Dhaka	2014-15
S.T.Finn	England v Australia	Melbourne	2014-15
J.P.Duminy	South Africa v Sri Lanka	Sydney	2014-15
K.Rabada	South Africa v Bangladesh	Mirpur	2015

[1] The first three balls of the match. Took four wickets in opening over (W W W 4 wide W 0).
[2] Four wickets in four balls.

WICKET-KEEPING RECORDS

100 DISMISSALS IN A CAREER

Total			LOI	Ct	St
482†‡	K.C.Sangakkara	Sri Lanka/Asia/ICC	360	384	98
472‡	A.C.Gilchrist	Australia/ICC	287	417	55
424	M.V.Boucher	South Africa/Africa	295	402	22
346	M.S.Dhoni	India/Asia	275	257	89
287‡	Moin Khan	Pakistan	219	214	73
242†‡	B.B.McCullum	New Zealand	185	227	15
233	I.A.Healy	Australia	168	194	39
220‡	Rashid Latif	Pakistan	166	182	38
206‡	R.S.Kaluwitharana	Sri Lanka	187	131	75
204‡	P.J.L.Dujon	West Indies	169	183	21
189	R.D.Jacobs	West Indies	147	160	29
187	Kamran Akmal	Pakistan	154	156	31
181	B.J.Haddin	Australia	126	170	11
177	D.Ramdin	West Indies	129	171	6
165	D.J.Richardson	South Africa	122	148	17
165†‡	A.Flower	Zimbabwe	213	133	32
163†‡	A.J.Stewart	England	170	148	15
162	Mushfiqur Rahim	Bangladesh	158	124	38
154‡	N.R.Mongia	India	140	110	44
145	T.Taibu	Zimbabwe/Africa	150	112	33
136†‡	A.C.Parore	New Zealand	179	111	25
126	Khaled Masud	Bangladesh	126	91	35
124	R.W.Marsh	Australia	92	120	4
103	Salim Yousuf	Pakistan	86	81	22

† Excluding catches taken in the field. ‡ Excluding matches when not wicket-keeper.

SIX DISMISSALS IN AN INNINGS

6	(6ct)	A.C.Gilchrist	Australia v South Africa	Cape Town	1999-00
6	(6ct)	A.J.Stewart	England v Zimbabwe	Manchester	2000
6	(5ct/1st)	R.D.Jacobs	West Indies v Sri Lanka	Colombo (RPS)	2001-02
6	(5ct/1st)	A.C.Gilchrist	Australia v England	Sydney	2002-03
6	(6ct)	A.C.Gilchrist	Australia v Namibia	Potchefstroom	2002-03
6	(6ct)	A.C.Gilchrist	Australia v Sri Lanka	Colombo (RPS)	2003-04
6	(6ct)	M.V.Boucher	South Africa v Pakistan	Cape Town	2006-07
6	(5ct/1st)	M.S.Dhoni	India v England	Leeds	2007
6	(6ct)	A.C.Gilchrist	Australia v India	Baroda	2007-08
6	(5ct/1st)	A.C.Gilchrist	Australia v India	Sydney	2007-08
6	(6ct)	M.J.Prior	England v South Africa	Nottingham	2008
6	(6ct)	J.C.Buttler	England v South Africa	The Oval	2013
6	(6ct)	M.H.Cross	Scotland v Canada	Christchurch	2013-14
6	(5ct/1st)	Q.de Kock	South Africa v New Zealand	Mt Maunganui	2014-15
6	(6ct)	Sarfraz Ahmed	Pakistan v South Africa	Auckland	2014-15

FIELDING RECORDS

100 CATCHES IN A CAREER

Total			LOI	Total			LOI
218	D.P.M.D.Jayawardena	Sri Lanka/Asia	448	113	Inzamam-ul-Haq	Pakistan/Asia	378
160	R.T.Ponting	Australia/ICC	375	111	S.R.Waugh	Australia	325
156	M.Azharuddin	India	334	110	L.R.P.L.Taylor	New Zealand	171
140	S.R.Tendulkar	India	463	109	R.S.Mahanama	Sri Lanka	213
133	S.P.Fleming	New Zealand/ICC	280	108	P.D.Collingwood	England	197
131	J.H.Kallis	South Africa/Africa/ICC	328	108	M.E.Waugh	Australia	244
130	Younus Khan	Pakistan	265	108	H.H.Gibbs	South Africa	248
130	M.Muralitharan	Sri Lanka/Asia	350	108	S.M.Pollock	South Africa/Africa/ICC	303
127	A.R.Border	Australia	273	106	M.J.Clarke	Australia	245
127	Shahid Afridi	Pakistan/Asia/ICC	398	105	M.E.K.Hussey	Australia	185
124	R.S.Dravid	India/Asia/ICC	344	105	G.C.Smith	South Africa/Africa	197
123	S.T.Jayasuriya	Sri Lanka/Asia	445	105	J.N.Rhodes	South Africa	245
120	C.L.Hooper	West Indies	227	100	I.V.A.Richards	West Indies	187
120	B.C.Lara	West Indies/ICC	299	100	S.K.Raina	India	223
114	C.H.Gayle	West Indies/ICC	269	100	S.C.Ganguly	India/Asia	311
114	T.M.Dilshan	Sri Lanka	327				

The most for Zimbabwe is 86 by G.W.Flower (221), and for Bangladesh 49 by Mashrafe Mortaza (158).

FIVE CATCHES IN AN INNINGS

5	J.N.Rhodes	South Africa v West Indies	Bombay (BS)	1993-94

APPEARANCE RECORDS

250 MATCHES

463	S.R.Tendulkar	India	311	S.C.Ganguly	India/Asia
448	D.P.M.D.Jayawardena	Sri Lanka/Asia	308	P.A.de Silva	Sri Lanka
445	S.T.Jayasuriya	Sri Lanka/Asia	303	S.M.Pollock	South Africa/Africa/ICC
404	K.C.Sangakkara	Sri Lanka/Asia/ICC	299	B.C.Lara	West Indies/ICC
398	Shahid Afridi	Pakistan/Asia/ICC	295	M.V.Boucher	South Africa/Africa
378	Inzamam-ul-Haq	Pakistan/Asia	295	D.L.Vettori	New Zealand/ICC
375	R.T.Ponting	Australia/ICC	293	Yuvraj Singh	India/Asia
356	Wasim Akram	Pakistan	288	Mohammad Yousuf	Pakistan/Asia
350	M.Muralitharan	Sri Lanka/Asia/ICC	287	A.C.Gilchrist	Australia/ICC
344	R.S.Dravid	India/Asia/ICC	283	Salim Malik	Pakistan
334	M.Azharuddin	India	280	S.P.Fleming	New Zealand/ICC
328	J.H.Kallis	South Africa/Africa/ICC	275	M.S.Dhoni	India/Asia
327	T.M.Dilshan	Sri Lanka	273	A.R.Border	Australia
325	S.R.Waugh	Australia	271	A.Kumble	India/Asia
322	W.P.J.U.C.Vaas	Sri Lanka/Asia	269	C.H.Gayle	West Indies/ICC

269	A.Ranatunga	Sri Lanka	260	B.B.McCullum	New Zealand	
268	M.S.Atapattu	Sri Lanka	251	V.Sehwag	India/Asia/ICC	
268	S.Chanderpaul	West Indies	250	C.Z.Harris	New Zealand	
265	Abdul Razzaq	Pakistan/Asia	250	Ijaz Ahmed	Pakistan	
265	Younus Khan	Pakistan	250	G.D.McGrath	Australia/ICC	
262	Waqar Younis	Pakistan				

The most for England is 197 by P.D.Collingwood, for Zimbabwe 221 by G.W.Flower, and for Bangladesh 175 by Mohammad Ashraful.

The most consecutive appearances is 185 by S.R.Tendulkar for India (Apr 1990-Apr 1998).

100 MATCHES AS CAPTAIN

LOI			W	L	T	NR	% Won (exc NR)
230	R.T.Ponting	Australia/ICC	165	51	2	12	75.68
218	S.P.Fleming	New Zealand	98	106	1	13	47.80
193	A.Ranatunga	Sri Lanka	89	95	1	8	48.10
191	M.S.Dhoni	India	104	72	4	11	57.77
178	A.R.Border	Australia	107	67	1	3	61.14
174	M.Azharuddin	India	90	76	2	6	53.57
150	G.C.Smith	South Africa/Africa	92	51	1	6	63.88
147	S.C.Ganguly	India/Asia	76	66	–	5	53.52
139	Imran Khan	Pakistan	75	59	1	4	55.55
138	W.J.Cronje	South Africa	99	35	1	3	73.33
129	D.P.M.D.Jayawardena	Sri Lanka	71	49	1	8	58.67
125	B.C.Lara	West Indies	59	59	–	7	50.42
118	S.T.Jayasuriya	Sri Lanka	66	47	2	3	57.39
109	Wasim Akram	Pakistan	66	41	2	–	60.55
106	S.R.Waugh	Australia	67	35	3	1	63.80
105	I.V.A.Richards	West Indies	67	36	–	2	65.04

The most for England is 69 by A.N.Cook, for Zimbabwe 86 by A.D.R.Campbell, and for Bangladesh 69 by Habibul Bashar.

100 LOI UMPIRING APPEARANCES

209	R.E.Koertzen	South Africa	09.12.1992	to	09.06.2010
200	B.F.Bowden	New Zealand	23.03.1995	to	06.02.2016
181	S.A.Bucknor	West Indies	18.03.1989	to	29.03.2009
178	Alim Dar	Pakistan	16.02.2000	to	11.11.2015
174	D.J.Harper	Australia	14.01.1994	to	19.03.2011
174	S.J.A.Taufel	Australia	13.01.1999	to	02.09.2012
172	D.R.Shepherd	England	09.06.1983	to	12.07.2005
146	R.B.Tiffin	Zimbabwe	25.10.1992	to	18.10.2015
139	D.B.Hair	Australia	14.12.1991	to	24.08.2008
137	S.J.Davis	Australia	12.12.1992	to	17.06.2015
122	E.A.R.de Silva	Sri Lanka	22.08.1999	to	13.06.2012
112	B.R.Doctrove	West Indies	04.04.1998	to	20.01.2012
111	I.J.Gould	England	20.06.2006	to	08.02.2016
107	D.L.Orchard	South Africa	02.12.1994	to	07.12.2003
100	R.S.Dunne	New Zealand	06.02.1989	to	26.02.2002
100	N.J.Llong	England	17.06.2006	to	31.01.2016

INTERNATIONAL TWENTY20 RECORDS

MATCH RESULTS
2004-05 to 14 March 2016

Opponents		Matches	E	A	SA	WI	NZ	I	P	SL	Z	B	Ass	Tied	NR
England	Australia	13	5	7	–	–	–	–	–	–	–	–	–	–	1
	South Africa	11	3	–	7	–	–	–	–	–	–	–	–	–	1
	West Indies	12	4	–	–	8	–	–	–	–	–	–	–	–	–
	New Zealand	13	8	–	–	–	4	–	–	–	–	–	–	–	1
	India	8	5	–	–	–	–	3	–	–	–	–	–	–	–
	Pakistan	13	9	–	–	–	–	–	3	–	–	–	–	1	–
	Sri Lanka	6	2	–	–	–	–	–	–	4	–	–	–	–	–
	Zimbabwe	1	1	–	–	–	–	–	–	–	0	–	–	–	–
	Bangladesh	0	0	–	–	–	–	–	–	–	–	0	–	–	–
	Associates	4	1	–	–	–	–	–	–	–	–	–	2	–	1
Australia	South Africa	17	–	11	6	–	–	–	–	–	–	–	–	–	–
	West Indies	11	–	5	–	6	–	–	–	–	–	–	–	–	–
	New Zealand	5	–	4	–	–	0	–	–	–	–	–	–	–	1
	India	12	–	4	–	–	–	8	–	–	–	–	–	–	–
	Pakistan	13	–	5	–	–	–	–	7	–	–	–	–	–	1
	Sri Lanka	8	–	2	–	–	–	–	–	6	–	–	–	–	–
	Zimbabwe	1	–	0	–	–	–	–	–	–	1	–	–	–	–
	Bangladesh	3	–	3	–	–	–	–	–	–	–	0	–	–	–
	Associates	1	–	1	–	–	–	–	–	–	–	–	0	–	–
S Africa	West Indies	9	–	–	6	3	–	–	–	–	–	–	–	–	–
	New Zealand	14	–	–	10	–	4	–	–	–	–	–	–	–	–
	India	10	–	–	4	–	–	6	–	–	–	–	–	–	–
	Pakistan	11	–	–	6	–	–	–	5	–	–	–	–	–	–
	Sri Lanka	5	–	–	3	–	–	–	–	2	–	–	–	–	–
	Zimbabwe	3	–	–	3	–	–	–	–	–	0	–	–	–	–
	Bangladesh	4	–	–	4	–	–	–	–	–	–	0	–	–	–
	Associates	3	–	–	3	–	–	–	–	–	–	–	0	–	–
W Indies	New Zealand	10	–	–	–	3	4	–	–	–	–	–	–	–	3
	India	4	–	–	–	2	–	2	–	–	–	–	–	–	–
	Pakistan	4	–	–	–	2	–	–	2	–	–	–	–	–	–
	Sri Lanka	8	–	–	–	2	–	–	–	6	–	–	–	–	–
	Zimbabwe	3	–	–	–	2	–	–	–	–	1	–	–	–	–
	Bangladesh	6	–	–	–	3	–	–	–	–	–	2	–	–	1
	Associates	4	–	–	–	2	–	–	–	–	–	–	1	–	1
N Zealand	India	4	–	–	–	–	4	0	–	–	–	–	–	–	–
	Pakistan	14	–	–	–	–	6	–	8	–	–	–	–	–	–
	Sri Lanka	15	–	–	–	–	7	–	–	6	–	–	–	1	1
	Zimbabwe	6	–	–	–	–	6	–	–	–	0	–	–	–	–
	Bangladesh	3	–	–	–	–	3	–	–	–	–	0	–	–	–
	Associates	4	–	–	–	–	4	–	–	–	–	–	0	–	–
India	Pakistan	7	–	–	–	–	–	5	1	–	–	–	–	1	–
	Sri Lanka	10	–	–	–	–	–	6	–	4	–	–	–	–	–
	Zimbabwe	4	–	–	–	–	–	3	–	–	1	–	–	–	–
	Bangladesh	4	–	–	–	–	–	4	–	–	–	0	–	–	–
	Associates	5	–	–	–	–	–	4	–	–	–	–	0	–	1
Pakistan	Sri Lanka	15	–	–	–	–	–	–	10	5	–	–	–	–	–
	Zimbabwe	9	–	–	–	–	–	–	9	–	0	–	–	–	–
	Bangladesh	9	–	–	–	–	–	–	7	–	–	2	–	–	–
	Associates	7	–	–	–	–	–	–	7	–	–	–	0	–	–
Sri Lanka	Zimbabwe	3	–	–	–	–	–	–	–	3	0	–	–	–	–
	Bangladesh	5	–	–	–	–	–	–	–	4	–	1	–	–	–
	Associates	5	–	–	–	–	–	–	–	5	–	–	0	–	–
Zimbabwe	Bangladesh	9	–	–	–	–	–	–	–	–	4	5	–	–	–
	Associates	12	–	–	–	–	–	–	–	–	5	–	6	1	–
Bangladesh	Associates	15	–	–	–	–	–	–	–	–	–	10	4	–	1
Associates	Associates	119	–	–	–	–	–	–	–	–	–	–	116	–	3
		534	38	42	52	33	42	41	59	45	12	20	129	9	12

308

	Matches	Won	Lost	Tied	NR	Win %
Afghanistan	44	28	16	0	0	63.63
India	68	41	25	1	1	61.19
South Africa	87	52	34	0	1	60.46
Pakistan	102	59	40	3	0	57.84
Netherlands	42	23	17	0	2	57.50
Sri Lanka	80	45	33	1	1	56.96
Ireland	53	24	23	0	6	51.06
Australia	84	42	39	2	1	50.60
Papua New Guinea	6	3	3	0	0	50.00
England	81	38	38	1	4	49.35
New Zealand	88	42	39	5	2	48.83
West Indies	71	33	33	3	2	47.82
Scotland	40	15	22	0	3	40.54
Hong Kong	20	8	12	0	0	40.00
Bangladesh	58	20	36	0	2	35.71
Kenya	29	10	19	0	0	34.48
United Arab Emirates	18	6	12	0	0	33.33
Oman	13	4	8	0	1	33.33
Nepal	11	3	8	0	0	27.27
Zimbabwe	51	12	38	1	0	23.52
Canada	19	4	14	1	0	21.05
Bermuda	3	0	3	0	0	0.00

INTERNATIONAL TWENTY20 RECORDS
(To 14 March 2016)

TEAM RECORDS
HIGHEST INNINGS TOTALS † Batting Second

260-6	Sri Lanka v Kenya	Johannesburg	2007-08
248-6	Australia v England	Southampton	2013
241-6	South Africa v England	Centurion	2009-10
236-6†	West Indies v South Africa	Johannesburg	2014-15
231-7	South Africa v West Indies	Johannesburg	2014-15
225-7	Ireland v Afghanistan	Abu Dhabi	2013-14
221-5	Australia v England	Sydney	2006-07
219-4	South Africa v India	Johannesburg	2011-12
218-4	India v England	Durban	2007-08
215-5	Sri Lanka v India	Nagpur	2009-10
215-3	Sri Lanka v West Indies	Pallekele	2015-16
215-6	Afghanistan v Zimbabwe	Sharjah	2015-16
214-5	Australia v New Zealand	Auckland	2004-05
214-6	New Zealand v Australia	Christchurch	2009-10
214-4†	Australia v New Zealand	Christchurch	2009-10
214-7	England v New Zealand	Auckland	2012-13
213-4	Australia v England	Hobart	2013-14
211-5	South Africa v Scotland	The Oval	2009
211-4†	India v Sri Lanka	Mohali	2009-10
211-3	Sri Lanka v Pakistan	Dubai	2013-14
210-5	Afghanistan v Scotland	Edinburgh	2015
209-3	Australia v South Africa	Brisbane	2005-06
209-2	West Indies v New Zealand	Lauderhill	2012
209-6†	England v Australia	Southampton	2013
208-8	West Indies v England	The Oval	2007
208-2†	South Africa v West Indies	Johannesburg	2007-08
206-7	Sri Lanka v India	Mohali	2009-10
205-6	West Indies v South Africa	Johannesburg	2007-08
205-4	West Indies v Australia	Colombo (RPS)	2012-13
205-5	Australia v South Africa	Johannesburg	2015-16

The highest total for Zimbabwe is 200-2 (v New Zealand, Hamilton, 2011-12) and for Bangladesh is 190-5 (v Ireland, Belfast, 2012).

LOWEST COMPLETED INNINGS TOTALS † Batting Second

39 (10.3)	Netherlands v Sri Lanka	Chittagong	2013-14
53 (14.3)	Nepal v Ireland	Belfast	2015
56† (18.4)	Kenya v Afghanistan	Sharjah	2013-14
60† (15.3)	New Zealand v Sri Lanka	Chittagong	2013-14
67 (17.2)	Kenya v Ireland	Belfast	2008
68† (16.4)	Ireland v West Indies	Providence	2009-10
69† (17.0)	Hong Kong v Nepal	Chittagong	2013-14
69† (17.4)	Nepal v Netherlands	Amstelveen	2015
70	Bermuda v Canada	Belfast	2008
71 (19.0)	Kenya v Ireland	Dubai	2011-12
72 (17.1)	Afghanistan v Bangladesh	Dhaka	2013-14
72	Nepal v Hong Kong	Colombo (PSS)	2014-15
73 (16.5)	Kenya v New Zealand	Durban	2007-08
73† (16.4)	UAE v Netherlands	Dubai	2015-16
74 (17.3)	India v Australia	Melbourne	2007-08
74† (19.1)	Pakistan v Australia	Dubai	2012
75† (19.2)	Canada v Zimbabwe	King City (NW)	2008-09
78 (17.3)	Bangladesh v New Zealand	Hamilton	2009-10
78† (18.5)	Kenya v Scotland	Aberdeen	2013
79† (14.3)	Australia v England	Southampton	2005
79-7†	West Indies v Zimbabwe	Port of Spain	2009-10
80† (16.0)	Afghanistan v South Africa	Bridgetown	2009-10
80† (15.5)	New Zealand v Pakistan	Christchurch	2010-11
80† (17.2)	Afghanistan v England	Colombo (RPS)	2012-13
80† (14.4)	England v India	Colombo (RPS)	2012-13

The lowest total for South Africa is 100 (v Pakistan, Centurion, 2012-13), for Sri Lanka 82 (v India, Visakhapatnam, 2015-16), and for Zimbabwe 84 (v New Zealand, Providence, 2009-10).

BATTING RECORDS
1000 RUNS IN A CAREER

Runs			M	I	NO	HS	Avge	50	R/100B
2140	B.B.McCullum	NZ	71	70	10	123	35.66	15	136.2
1751	T.M.Dilshan	SL	74	73	11	104*	28.24	13	120.5
1666	M.J.Guptill	NZ	57	55	7	101*	34.70	10	129.6
1611	Umar Akmal	P	75	72	13	94	27.30	8	122.9
1595	D.A.Warner	A	57	57	3	90*	29.53	12	140.7
1571	J.P.Duminy	SA	68	62	19	96*	36.53	8	121.7
1545	Mohammad Hafeez	P	75	73	3	86	22.07	8	113.9
1493	D.P.M.D.Jayawardena	SL	55	55	8	100	31.76	10	133.1
1406	C.H.Gayle	WI	45	43	3	117	35.15	14	142.5
1382	K.C.Sangakkara	SL	56	53	9	78	31.40	8	119.5
1372	Shoaib Malik	P	74	70	16	75	25.40	5	110.7
1368	V.Kohli	I	38	35	9	90*	52.61	13	133.0
1366	S.R.Watson	A	54	52	4	124*	28.45	11	145.0
1363	H.Masakadza	Z	47	47	2	93*	30.28	10	120.4
1333	E.J.G.Morgan	E	56	55	11	85*	30.29	7	133.1
1315	Shahid Afridi	P	94	86	12	54*	17.77	4	148.9
1287	Mohammad Shahzad	Af	44	44	2	118*	30.64	10	136.0
1258	A.B.de Villiers	SA	67	64	9	79*	22.87	7	128.8
1204	R.G.Sharma	I	55	48	11	106	32.54	11	128.6
1176	K.P.Pietersen	E	37	36	5	79	37.93	7	141.5
1165	L.R.P.L.Taylor	NZ	68	60	12	63	24.27	5	120.6
1162	S.K.Raina	I	57	48	11	101	31.40	4	133.2
1154	A.D.Hales	E	39	39	5	116*	33.94	8	135.1
1092	Tamim Iqbal	B	49	49	5	103*	24.81	5	115.3
1082	Yuvraj Singh	I	51	44	9	77*	30.91	8	139.4

HIGHEST INDIVIDUAL INNINGS

Score	Balls				
156	63	A.J.Finch	A v E	Southampton	2013
124*	71	S.R.Watson	A v I	Sydney	2015-16
123	58	B.B.McCullum	NZ v B	Pallekele	2012-13
122	60	Babar Hayat	HK v Oman	Fatullah	2015-16
119	56	F.du Plessis	SA v WI	Johannesburg	2014-15
118*	67	Mohammad Shahzad	Af v Z	Sharjah	2015-16
117*	51	R.E.Levi	SA v NZ	Hamilton	2011-12
117	57	C.H.Gayle	WI v SA	Johannesburg	2007-08
116*	56	B.B.McCullum	NZ v A	Christchurch	2009-10
116*	64	A.D.Hales	E v SL	Chittagong	2013-14
114*	70	M.van Wyk	SA v WI	Durban	2014-15
111*	62	Ahmed Shehzad	P v B	Dhaka	2013-14
106	66	R.G.Sharma	I v SA	Dharmasala	2015-16
104*	57	T.M.Dilshan	SL v A	Pallekele	2011
103*	63	Tamim Iqbal	B v Oman	Dharmasala	2015-16
101*	69	M.J.Guptill	NZ v SA	East London	2012-13
101	60	S.K.Raina	I v SA	Gros Islet	2009-10
100	64	D.P.M.D.Jayawardena	SL v Z	Providence	2009-10
100	58	R.D.Berrington	Sc v B	The Hague	2012

The highest score for Zimbabwe is 93* by H.Masakadza (v B, Khulna, 2015-16).

HIGHEST PARTNERSHIP FOR EACH WICKET

1st	171*	M.J.Guptill/K.S.Williamson	NZ v P	Hamilton	2015-16
2nd	166	D.P.M.D.Jayawardena/K.C.Sangakkara	SL v WI	Bridgetown	2009-10
3rd	152	A.D.Hales/E.J.G.Morgan	E v SL	Chittagong	2013-14
4th	161	D.A.Warner/G.J.Maxwell	A v SA	Johannesburg	2015-16
5th	119*	Shoaib Malik/Misbah-ul-Haq	P v A	Johannesburg	2007-08
6th	101*	C.L.White/M.E.K.Hussey	A v SL	Bridgetown	2009-10
7th	91	P.D.Collingwood/M.H.Yardy	E v WI	The Oval	2007
8th	80	P.L.Mommsen/S.M.Sharif	Sc v Ne	Edinburgh	2015
9th	63	Sohail Tanvir/Saeed Ajmal	P v SL	Dubai	2013-14
10th	31*	Wahab Riaz/Shoaib Akhtar	P v NZ	Auckland	2010-11

BOWLING RECORDS
45 WICKETS IN A CAREER

Wkts			Matches	Overs	Mdns	Runs	Avge	Best	R/Over
93	Shahid Afridi	P	94	341.2	4	2243	24.11	4-11	6.57
85	Umar Gul	P	60	200.3	2	1443	16.97	5- 6	7.19
85	Saeed Ajmal	P	64	238.2	2	1516	17.83	4-19	6.36
78	S.L.Malinga	SL	62	217.5	–	1582	20.28	5-31	7.26
66	B.A.W.Mendis	SL	39	147.3	5	952	14.42	6- 8	6.45
65	S.C.J.Broad	E	56	195.3	2	1491	22.93	4-24	7.62
61	Shakib Al Hasan	B	50	179.5	1	1200	19.67	4-15	6.67
57	D.W.Steyn	SA	44	144.1	2	941	16.50	4- 9	6.52
55	K.M.D.N.Kulasekara	SL	48	170.1	6	1220	22.18	4-32	7.16
55	N.L.McCullum	NZ	61	182.1	–	1257	22.85	4-16	6.90
51	G.P.Swann	E	39	135.0	4	859	16.84	3-13	6.36
48	G.H.Dockrell	Ire	39	116.4	1	730	15.20	4-20	6.25
47	Sohail Tanvir	P	50	175.3	3	1268	26.97	3-12	7.22
46	R.Ashwin	I	38	145.0	2	992	21.56	4- 8	6.84
46	Mohammad Hafeez	P	60	166.2	1	1106	24.04	4-10	6.64
46	T.G.Southee	NZ	38	137.0	2	1182	25.69	5-18	8.62
45	K.J.O'Brien	Ire	51	114.3	–	750	16.66	3- 8	6.55
45	M.Morkel	SA	39	138.4	9	1022	22.71	4-17	7.37

BEST FIGURES IN AN INNINGS

6- 8	B.A.W.Mendis	SL v Z	Hambantota	2012-13
6-16	B.A.W.Mendis	SL v A	Pallekele	2011
5- 3	H.M.R.K.B.Herath	SL v NZ	Chittagong	2013-14
5- 6	Umar Gul	P v NZ	The Oval	2009
5- 6	Umar Gul	P v SA	Centurion	2012-13
5-13	Elias Sunny	B v Ire	Belfast	2012
5-13	Samiullah Shenwari	Af v K	Sharjah	2013-14
5-18	T.G.Southee	NZ v P	Auckland	2010-11
5-19	R.McLaren	SA v WI	North Sound	2009-10
5-19	Ahsan Malik	Neth v SA	Chittagong	2013-14
5-20	N.Odhiambo	K v Sc	Nairobi (Gym)	2009-10
5-23	D.Wiese	SA v WI	Durban	2014-15
5-24	A.C.Evans	Sc v Neth	Edinburgh	2015
5-26	D.J.G.Sammy	WI v Z	Port of Spain	2009-10
5-27	M.R.J.Watt	Sc v Neth	Dubai	2015-16
5-31	S.L.Malinga	SL v E	Pallekele	2012-13
4- 2	S.O.Tikolo	K v Sc	Dubai	2013-14
4- 6	S.J.Benn	WI v Z	Port of Spain	2009-10
4- 7	M.R.Gillespie	NZ v K	Durban	2007-08
4- 7	Mudassar Bakhari	Neth v UAE	Dubai	2015-16
4- 8	Umar Gul	P v A	Dubai	2009
4- 9	D.W.Steyn	SA v WI	Port Elizabeth	2007-08
4-10	Mohammad Hafeez	P v Z	Harare	2011
4-10	R.S.Bopara	E v WI	The Oval	2011

HAT-TRICKS

B.Lee	Australia v Bangladesh	Melbourne	2007-08
J.D.P.Oram	New Zealand v Sri Lanka	Colombo (RPS)	2009
T.G.Southee	New Zealand v Pakistan	Auckland	2010-11
N.L.T.C.Perera	Sri Lanka v India	Ranchi	2015-16

WICKET-KEEPING RECORDS
25 DISMISSALS IN A CAREER

Dis			Matches	Ct	St
60	Kamran Akmal	Pakistan	54	28	32
52	M.S.Dhoni	India	63	35	17
48	D.Ramdin	West Indies	52	30	18
45	K.C.Sangakkara	Sri Lanka	56	25	20
44	Mushfiqur Rahim	Bangladesh	53	22	22
39	Mohammad Shahzad	Afghanistan	44	20	19
32†	B.B.McCullum	New Zealand	71	24	8
29	Q.de Kock	South Africa	25	22	7
28†	A.B.de Villiers	South Africa	67	21	7
25	N.J.O'Brien	Ireland	30	15	10
25	W.Barresi	Netherlands	32	25	–

† *Excluding catches taken in the field.*
The most for England is 20 (17 ct, 3 st) by C.Kieswetter.

MOST DISMISSALS IN AN INNINGS

5 (3 ct, 2 st)	Mohammad Shahzad	Afghanistan v Oman	Abu Dhabi	2015-16
4 (4 ct)	A.C.Gilchrist	Australia v Zimbabwe	Cape Town	2007-08
4 (4 ct)	M.J.Prior	England v South Africa	Cape Town	2007-08
4 (4 ct)	A.C.Gilchrist	Australia v New Zealand	Perth	2007-08
4 (4 st)	Kamran Akmal	Pakistan v Netherlands	Lord's	2009
4 (3 ct, 1 st)	N.J.O'Brien	Ireland v Sri Lanka	Lord's	2009
4 (4 ct)	M.S.Dhoni	India v Afghanistan	Gros Islet	2009-10

4 (2 ct, 2 st)	A.B.de Villiers	South Africa v West Indies	North Sound	2009-10
4 (3 ct, 1 st)	G.C.Wilson	Ireland v Kenya	Dubai	2011-12
4 (4 ct)	A.B.de Villiers	South Africa v Zimbabwe	Hambantota	2012-13
4 (4 ct)	M.S.Dhoni	India v Pakistan	Colombo (RPS)	2012-13
4 (2 ct, 2 st)	Q.de Kock	South Africa v Pakistan	Dubai	2013-14
4 (4 ct)	W.Barresi	Netherlands v Kenya	Dubai	2013-14
4 (4 st)	D.Ramdin	West Indies v Pakistan	Dhaka	2013-14
4 (1 ct, 3 st)	R.Mutumbami	Zimbabwe v Scotland	Nagpur	2015-16

FIELDING RECORDS
25 CATCHES IN A CAREER

Total			Matches	Total			Matches
41	L.R.P.L.Taylor	New Zealand	68	29	Shahid Afridi	Pakistan	94
38	A.B.de Villiers	South Africa	67	28	D.J.G.Sammy	West Indies	60
34	Umar Akmal	Pakistan	75	28	Shoaib Malik	Pakistan	74
32	J.P.Duminy	South Africa	68	27	P.W.Borren	Netherlands	40
30	D.J.Bravo	West Indies	55	27	S.K.Raina	India	57
30	D.A.Warner	Australia	57	26	D.A.Miller	South Africa	42
29	M.J.Guptill	New Zealand	57	26	T.M.Dilshan	Sri Lanka	74

The most for England is 23 by E.J.G.Morgan.

MOST CATCHES IN AN INNINGS

4	D.J.G.Sammy	West Indies v Ireland	Providence	2009-10
4	P.W.Borren	Netherlands v Bangladesh	The Hague	2012
4	C.J.Anderson	New Zealand v South Africa	Port Elizabeth	2012-13
4	L.D.Chandimal	Sri Lanka v Bangladesh	Chittagong	2013-14
4	A.M.Rahane	India v England	Birmingham	2014
4	Babar Hayat	Hong Kong v Afghanistan	Dhaka	2015-16

APPEARANCE RECORDS
60 APPEARANCES

94	Shahid Afridi	Pakistan	67	A.B.de Villiers	South Africa
75	Mohammad Hafeez	Pakistan	64	Saeed Ajmal	Pakistan
75	Umar Akmal	Pakistan	63	M.S.Dhoni	India
74	T.M.Dilshan	Sri Lanka	62	S.L.Malinga	Sri Lanka
74	Shoaib Malik	Pakistan	62	A.D.Matthews	Sri Lanka
71	B.B.McCullum	New Zealand	61	N.L.McCullum	New Zealand
68	J.P.Duminy	South Africa	60	D.J.G.Sammy	West Indies
68	L.R.P.L.Taylor	New Zealand	60	Umar Gul	Pakistan

The most for England is 56 for S.C.J.Broad and E.J.G.Morgan.

25 MATCHES AS CAPTAIN

			W	L	T	NR	%age wins
62	M.S.Dhoni	India	36	24	1	1	59.01
48	W.T.S.Porterfield	Ireland	24	20	–	4	54.54
41	D.J.G.Sammy	West Indies	22	16	1	2	56.41
39	Shahid Afridi	Pakistan	18	20	1	–	46.15
34	P.W.Borren	Netherlands	20	13	–	1	60.60
30	P.D.Collingwood	England	17	11	–	2	60.71
29	Mohammad Hafeez	Pakistan	17	11	1	–	58.62
28	G.J.Bailey	Australia	14	13	1	–	50.00
28	B.B.McCullum	New Zealand	13	14	–	1	48.14
28	D.L.Vettori	New Zealand	13	13	2	–	46.42
27	G.C.Smith	South Africa	18	9	–	–	66.66
27	F.du Plessis	South Africa	16	11	–	–	59.25
27	S.C.J.Broad	England	11	15	–	1	42.30

INDIAN PREMIER LEAGUE 2015

The eighth IPL tournament was held in India between 8 April and 24 May.

Team	P	W	L	T	NR	Pts	Net RR
1 Chennai Super Kings (3)	14	9	5	–	–	18	+0.70
2 Mumbai Indians (4)	14	8	6	–	–	16	–0.04
3 Royal Challengers Bangalore (7)	14	7	5	–	2	16	+1.03
4 Rajasthan Royals (5)	14	7	5	–	2	16	+0.06
5 Kolkata Knight Riders (2)	14	7	6	–	1	15	+0.25
6 Sunrisers Hyderabad (6)	14	7	7	–	–	14	–0.23
7 Delhi Daredevils (8)	14	5	8	–	1	11	–0.04
8 Kings XI Punjab (1)	14	3	11	–	–	6	–1.43

1st Qualifying Match: At Wankhede Stadium, Mumbai, 19 May (floodlit). Toss: Mumbai Indians. **MUMBAI INDIANS** won by 25 runs. Mumbai Indians 187-6 (20; L.M.P.Simmons 65, D.J.Bravo 3-40). Chennai Super Kings 162 (19; S.L.Malinga 3-23). Award: K.A.Pollard (Mumbai Indians, 41 in 17b).

Elimination Final: At Maharashtra C.A.Stadium, Pune, 20 May (floodlit). Toss: Royal Challengers Bangalore. **ROYAL CHALLENGERS BANGALORE** won by 71 runs. Royal Challengers Bangalore 180-4 (20; A.B.de Villiers 66, Mandeep Singh 54*). Rajasthan Royals 109 (19). Award: A.B.de Villiers.

2nd Qualifying Match: At JSCA International Stadium, Ranchi, 22 May (floodlit). Toss: Chennai Super Kings. **CHENNAI SUPER KINGS** won by three wickets. Royal Challengers Bangalore 139-8 (20; A.Nehra 3-28). Chennai Super Kings 140-7 (19.5; M.E.K.Hussey 56). Award: A.Nehra.

FINAL: At Eden Gardens, Kolkata, 24 May (floodlit). Toss: Chennai Super Kings. **MUMBAI INDIANS** won by 41 runs. Mumbai Indians 202-5 (20; L.M.P.Simmons 68, R.G.Sharma 50). Chennai Super Kings 161-8 (20; D.R.Smith 57, M.J.McClenaghan 3-25). Award: R.G.Sharma. Series award: A.D.Russell (Kolkata Knight Riders).

IPL winners:	2008	Rajasthan Royals	2009	Deccan Chargers
	2010	Chennai Super Kings	2011	Chennai Super Kings
	2012	Kolkata Knight Riders	2013	Mumbai Indians
	2014	Kolkata Knight Riders		

TEAM RECORDS
HIGHEST TOTALS

263-5 (20)	Bangalore v Pune	Bangalore	2013
246-5 (20)	Chennai v Rajasthan	Chennai	2010

LOWEST TOTALS

58 (15.1)	Rajasthan v Bangalore	Cape Town	2009
67 (15.2)	Kolkata v Mumbai	Mumbai	2008

LARGEST MARGINS OF VICTORY

140 runs	Kolkata (222-3) v Bangalore (82)	Bangalore	2008
10 wickets	Mumbai (154-7) v Deccan (155-0)	Mumbai	2008
10 wickets	Rajasthan (92) v Bangalore (93-0)	Bangalore	2010
10 wickets	Mumbai (133-5) v Rajasthan (134-0)	Mumbai	2011
10 wickets	Rajasthan (162-6) v Mumbai (163-0)	Jaipur	2012
10 wickets	Punjab (138) v Chennai (139-0)	Mohali	2013
10 wickets	Delhi (95) v Bangalore (99-0)	Delhi	2015

Delhi beat Punjab by ten wickets in a reduced game in 2009.

BATTING RECORDS
700 RUNS IN A SEASON

Runs			Year	M	I	NO	HS	Ave	100	50	6s	4s	R/100B
733	C.H.Gayle	Bangalore	2012	15	14	2	128*	61.08	1	7	59	46	160.7
733	M.E.K.Hussey	Chennai	2013	17	17	3	95	52.35	–	6	17	81	129.5
708	C.H.Gayle	Bangalore	2013	16	16	4	175*	59.00	1	4	51	57	156.2

HIGHEST SCORES

Score	Balls				
175*	66	C.H.Gayle	Bangalore v Pune	Bangalore	2013
158*	73	B.B.McCullum	Kolkata v Bangalore	Bangalore	2008
133*	73	A.B.de Villiers	Bangalore v Mumbai	Mumbai	2015
128*	62	C.H.Gayle	Bangalore v Delhi	Delhi	2012
127	56	M.Vijay	Chennai v Rajasthan	Chennai	2010

FASTEST HUNDRED

30 balls	C.H.Gayle (175*)	Bangalore v Pune	Bangalore	2013

MOST SIXES IN AN INNINGS

17	C.H.Gayle	Bangalore v Pune	Bangalore	2013

HIGHEST STRIKE RATE IN A SEASON (Qualification: 100 runs or more)

R/100B	Score	Balls			
204.34	188	92	B.B.McCullum	Kolkata	2008

HIGHEST STRIKE RATE IN AN INNINGS (Qualification: 25 runs, 350+ strike rate)

R/100B	Score	Balls			
400.0	28	7	J.A.Morkel	Chennai v Bangalore	Chennai	2012
387.5	31	8	A.B.de Villiers	Bangalore v Pune	Bangalore	2013
385.7	27*	7	B.Akhil	Bangalore v Deccan	Hyderabad	2008
372.7	41	11	A.B.de Villiers	Bangalore v Mumbai	Bangalore	2015
350.0	35	10	C.H.Gayle	Bangalore v Hyderabad	Hyderabad	2015

BOWLING RECORDS
25 WICKETS IN A SEASON

Wkts			Year	P	O	M	Runs	Avge	Best	4w	R/Over
32	D.J.Bravo	Chennai	2013	18	62.3	–	497	15.53	4-42	1	7.95
28	S.L.Malinga	Mumbai	2011	16	63.0	2	375	13.39	5-13	1	5.95
28	J.P.Faulkner	Rajasthan	2013	16	63.1	2	427	15.25	5-16	2	6.75
26	D.J.Braveo	Chennai	2015	17	52.2	–	426	16.38	3-22	–	8.14

BEST BOWLING FIGURES IN AN INNINGS

6-14	Sohail Tanvir	Rajasthan v Chennai	Jaipur	2008
5- 5	A.Kumble	Bangalore v Rajasthan	Cape Town	2009
5-12	I.Sharma	Deccan v Kochi	Kochi	2011
5-13	S.L.Malinga	Mumbai v Delhi	Delhi	2011

MOST ECONOMICAL BOWLING ANALYSIS

O	M	R	W				
4	1	6	0	F.H.Edwards	Deccan v Kolkata	Cape Town	2009
4	1	6	1	A.Nehra	Delhi v Punjab	Bloemfontein	2009

MOST EXPENSIVE BOWLING ANALYSIS

O	M	R	W				
4	0	66	0	I.Sharma	Hyderabad v Chennai	Hyderabad	2013
4	0	65	0	U.T.Yadav	Delhi v Bangalore	Delhi	2013
4	0	65	1	Sandeep Sharma	Punjab v Hyderabad	Hyderabad	2014
4	0	63	2	V.R.Aaron	Delhi v Chennai	Chennai	2012
4	0	63	0	A.B.Dinda	Pune v Mumbai	Mumbai	2013
4	0	62	0	M.G.Neser	Punjab v Bangalore	Mohali	2013
4	0	60	2	R.McLaren	Kolkata v Mumbai	Mumbai	2013

ENGLAND WOMEN INTERNATIONALS

The following players have played for England since 1 September 2014. Details correct to 17 March 2016, England's first game in the ICC Women's World T20.

BEAUMONT, Tamsin ('**Tammy**') Tilley, b Dover, Kent 11 Mar 1991. RHB, WK. Kent 2007 to date. Diamonds 2007-12. Sapphires 2008. Emeralds 2011-13. **Tests**: 2 (2013 to 2014); HS 12 v I (Wormsley) 2014. **LOI**: 23 (2009-10 to 2014); HS 44 v I (Taunton) 2012. **IT20**: 36 (2009-10 to 2015-16); HS 29* v NZ (Bridgetown) 2013-14.

BRUNT, **Katherine** Helen, b Barnsley, Yorks 2 Jul 1985. RHB, RMF. Yorkshire 2004 to date. Sapphires 2006-08. Diamonds 2011-12. **Tests**: 10 (2004 to 2015); HS 52 v A (Worcester) 2005; BB 6-69 v A (Worcester) 2009. **LOI**: 84 (2004-05 to 2015-16); HS 31 v A (Worcester) 2015; BB 5-18 v A (Wormsley) 2011. **IT20**: 50 (2005 to 2015); HS 35 v WI (Arundel) 2012; BB 3-6 v NZ (Lord's) 2009.

CROSS, Kathryn ('**Kate**') Laura, b Manchester, Lancs 3 Oct 1991. RHB, RMF. Lancashire 2005 to date. Sapphires 2007-08. Emeralds 2012. **Tests**: 3 (2013-14 to 2015); HS 4* v A (Canterbury) 2015; BB 3-29 v I (Wormsley) 2014. **LOI**: 12 (2013-14 to 2015-16); HS 4* v I (Scarborough) 2014; BB 5-24 v NZ (Lincoln) 2014-15. **IT20**: 4 (2013-14 to 2014-15); HS – ; BB 2-27 v NZ (Whangarei) 2014-15.

EDWARDS, **Charlotte** Marie, b Huntingdon, Cambs 17 Dec 1979. RHB, LB. East Anglia 1994-99. Kent 2000 to date. N Districts 2000-01 to 2002-03. Diamonds 2006-12. Sapphires 2013. W Australia 2014-15. MBE 2009. CBE 2014. *Wisden* 2013. **Tests**: 23 (1996 to 2015, 10 as captain); HS 117 v NZ (Scarborough) 2004; BB 2-28 v A (Harrogate) 1998. **LOI**: 191 (1997 to 2015-16, 117 as captain); HS 173* v Ire (Pune) 1997-98; BB 4-30 v SL (Colombo, PSS) 2010-11. **IT20**: 90 (2004 to 2014-15, 88 as captain); HS 92* v A (Hobart) 2013-14; BB 3-21 v SL (Colombo, NCC) 2010-11.

ELWISS, **Georgia** Amanda, b Wolverhampton, Staffs 31 May 1991. RHB, RMF. Staffordshire 2004-10. Sapphires 2006-12. Diamonds 2008. Australia CT 2009-10 to 2010-11. Emeralds 2011. Sussex 2011 to date. Rubies 2013. **Tests**: 1 (2015); HS 46 and BB – (v A (Canterbury) 2015. **LOI**: 14 (2011-12 to 2015-16); HS 61 v SA (Johannesburg) 2015-16; BB 3-17 v I (Wormsley) 2012. **IT20**: 11 (2011-12 to 2015-16); HS 18 v SA (Paarl) 2015-16; BB 2-30 v NZ (Invercargill) 2011-12.

FARRANT, Natasha ('**Tash**') Eleni (Sevenoaks S), b Athens, Greece 29 May 1996. LHB, LM. Kent 2012 to date. Sapphires 2013. **LOI**: 1 (2013-14); HS 1* and BB 1-14 v WI (Port of Spain) 2013-14. **IT20**: 8 (2013 to 2015-16); HS 1* and BB 2-15 v P (Loughborough) 2013.

GREENWAY, **Lydia** Sophie, b Farnborough, Kent 6 Aug 1985. LHB, OB. Kent 2000 to date. Diamonds 2008. Sapphires 2013. **Tests**: 14 (2002-03 to 2015); HS 70 v SA (Shenley) 2003. **LOI**: 126 (2003 to 2015-16); 125* v SA (Potchefstroom) 2011-12. **IT20**: 80 (2004 to 2015); HS 80* v A (Southampton) 2013.

GRUNDY, **Rebecca** Louise, b Solihull, Warwicks 12 Jul 1990. LHB, SLA. Warwickshire 2007 to date. Rubies 2013. **LOI**: 7 (2014-15 to 2105-16); HS 1* v NZ (Mt Maunganui) 2014-15 – twice; BB 3-36 v NZ (Lincoln) 2014-15 – twice. **IT20**: 10 (2013-14 to 2015-16); HS 2* v A (Hove) 2015; BB 2-13 v SL (Sylhet) 2013-14.

GUNN, **Jennifer** ('**Jenny**') Louise, b Nottingham 9 May 1986. RHB, RMF. Nottinghamshire 2001 to date. Emeralds 2006-08. S Australia 2006-07 to 2007-08. Diamonds 2007. W Australia 2008-09. Yorkshire 2011. Rubies 2012-13. MBE 2014. **Tests**: 11 (2004 to 2014); HS 62* and BB 5-19 v I (Wormsley) 2014. **LOI**: 129 (2003-04 to 2015-16); HS 73 v NZ (Taunton) 2007; BB 5-22 v P (Louth) 2013. **IT20**: 87 (2004 to 2015-16, 3 as captain); HS 69 v SL (Colombo, NCC) 2010-11; BB 5-18 v NZ (Bridgetown) 2013-14.

HAZELL, Danielle ('Danni'), b Durham 13 May 1988. RHB, OB. Durham 2002-04. Sapphires 2006-13. Emeralds 2007. Yorkshire 2008 to date. Diamonds 2011-12. **Tests**: 3 (2010-11 to 2013-14); HS 15 v A (Perth) 2013-14; BB 2-32 v A (Sydney) 2010-11. **LOI**: 41 (2009-10 to 2015-16); HS 24* v Ire (Kibworth) 2010; BB 3-22 v SL (Colombo, NCC) 2010-11. **IT20**: 66 (2009-10 to 2015-16); HS 18* v WI (Arundel) 2012; BB 4-12 v WI (Hove) 2012.

JONES, Amy Ellen, b Solihull, Warwicks 13 Jun 1993. RHB, WK. Warwickshire 2008 to date. Diamonds 2011. Emeralds 2012. Rubies 2013. **LOI**: 9 (2012-13 to 2015-16); HS 41 v SL (Mumbai, BS) 2012-13. **IT20**: 12 (2013 to 2015-16); HS 14 v A (Melbourne) 2013-14 and 14 v SA (Johannesburg) 2015-16.

KNIGHT, Heather Clare, b Rochdale, Lancs 26 Dec 1990. RHB, OB. Devon 2008-09. Emeralds 2008-13. Berkshire 2010 to date. Sapphires 2011-12. Tasmania 2014-15 to date. **Tests**: 5 (2010-11 to 2015); HS 157 v A (Wormsley) 2013; BB 1-7 v I (Wormsley) 2014. **LOI**: 55 (2009-10 to 2015-16); HS 79 v NZ (Mt Maunganui) 2014-15; BB 4-47 v NZ (Mt Maunganui) 2014-15 – separate matches. **IT20**: 29 (2010-11 to 2015-16); HS 30 v NZ (Whangarei) 2014-15; BB 3-10 v NZ (Whangarei) 2014-15 – separate matches.

MARSH, Laura Alexandra, b Pembury, Kent 5 Dec 1986. RHB, RMF/OB. Sussex 2003-10. Rubies 2006-07. Emeralds 2008. Sapphires 2011. Kent 2011 to date. New South Wales 2015-16. Otago 2015-16. **Tests**: 7 (2006 to 2015); HS 55 v A (Wormsley) 2013; BB 3-44 v I (Leicester) 2006. **LOI**: 72 (2006 to 2015); HS 67 v Ire (Kibworth) 2010; BB 5-15 v P (Sydney) 2008-09. **IT20**: 58 (2007 to 2014-15); HS 54 v P (Galle) 2012-13; BB 3-17 v WI (Basseterre) 2010.

SCIVER, Natalie Ruth, b Tokyo, Japan 20 Aug 1992. RHB, RM. Surrey 2010 to date. Rubies 2011. Emeralds 2012-13. **Tests**: 3 (2013-14 to 2015); HS 49 and BB 1-30 v A (Perth) 2013-14. **LOI**: 20 (2013 to 2015); HS 66 v A (Taunton) 2015; BB 3-19 v WI (Port of Spain) 2013-14. **IT20**: 29 (2013 to 2015-16); HS 47 and BB 4-15 v A (Cardiff) 2015.

SHRUBSOLE, Anya, b Bath, Somerset 7 Dec 1991. RHB, RMF. Somerset 2004 to date. Rubies 2006-12. Emeralds 2006-13. **Tests**: 4 (2013 to 2015); HS 14 v I (Wormsley) 2014; BB 4-51 v A (Perth) 2013-14. **LOI**: 34 (2008 to 2015-16); HS 29 v NZ (Mt Maunganui) 2014-15; BB 5-17 v SA (Cuttack) 2012-13. **IT20**: 42 (2008 to 2015-16); HS 10* v SA (Paarl) 2015-16; BB 5-11 v NZ (Wellington) 2011-12.

TAYLOR, Sarah Jane, b Whitechapel, London 20 May 1989. RHB, WK. Sussex 2004 to date. Rubies 2006-12. Emeralds 2008-13. Wellington 2010-11 to 2011-12. S Australia 2014-15 to date. **Tests**: 8 (2006 to 2015); HS 40 v I (Wormsley) 2014. **LOI**: 101 (2006 to 2015-16); HS 129 v SA (Lord's) 2008. **IT20**: 76 (2006 to 2015); HS 77 v A (Chelmsford) 2013.

WINFIELD, Lauren, b York 16 Aug 1990. RHB, WK. Yorkshire 2007 to date. Diamonds 2011. Sapphires 2012. Rubies 2013. **Tests**: 2 (2014 to 2015); HS 35 v I (Wormsley) 2014. **LOI**: 14 (2013 to 2015-16); HS 31 v WI (Port of Spain) 2013-14. **IT20**: 15 (2013 to 2015); HS 74 v SA (Birmingham) 2014.

WYATT, Danielle ('Danni') Nicole, b Stoke-on-Trent, Staffs 22 Apr 1991. RHB, OB. Staffordshire 2005-12. Emeralds 2006-08. Sapphires 2011-12. Victoria 2011-12. Nottinghamshire 2013 to date. **LOI**: 36 (2009-10 to 2015-16); HS 40 v WI (Mumbai) 2012-13 and 40 v SA (Centurion) 2015-16; BB 3-7 v SA (Cuttack) 2012-13. **IT20**: 62 (2009-10 to 2015-16); HS 41 v P (Loughborough) 2012; BB 4-11 v SA (Basseterre) 2010.

WOMEN'S LIMITED-OVERS RECORDS

1973 to 7 April 2016
RESULTS SUMMARY

	Matches	Won	Lost	Tied	NR	% Won (exc NR)
Australia	288	222	59	1	6	78.72
England	300	171	117	2	10	58.96
India	225	117	103	1	4	52.94
West Indies	141	70	66	1	4	51.09
New Zealand	296	146	142	2	6	50.34
South Africa	131	62	61	1	7	50.00
Sri Lanka	129	51	73	–	5	41.12
Trinidad & Tobago	6	2	4	–	–	33.33
Pakistan	124	38	84	–	2	31.14
Ireland	130	38	87	–	5	30.40
Bangladesh	18	4	13	–	1	23.52
Jamaica	5	1	4	–	–	20.00
Netherlands	101	19	81	–	1	19.00
Denmark	33	6	27	–	–	18.18
International XI	18	3	14	–	1	17.64
Young England	6	1	5	–	–	16.66
Scotland	8	1	7	–	–	12.50
Japan	5	–	5	–	–	0.00

TEAM RECORDS
HIGHEST INNINGS TOTALS

455-5 (50 overs)	New Zealand v Pakistan	Christchurch	1996-97
412-3 (50 overs)	Australia v Denmark	Mumbai	1997-98
397-4 (50 overs)	Australia v Pakistan	Melbourne	1996-97
376-2 (50 overs)	England v Pakistan	Vijayawada	1997-98

LARGEST RUNS MARGIN OF VICTORY

408 runs	New Zealand beat Pakistan	Christchurch	1996-97
374 runs	Australia beat Pakistan	Melbourne	1996-97

LOWEST INNINGS TOTALS

22 (23.4 overs)	Netherlands v West Indies	Deventer	2008
23 (24.1 overs)	Pakistan v Australia	Melbourne	1996-97
24 (21.3 overs)	Scotland v England	Reading	2001

BATTING RECORDS
2000 RUNS IN A CAREER

Runs		Career	M	I	NO	HS	Avge	100	50
5992	C.M.Edwards (E)	1997-2016	191	180	23	173*	38.16	9	46
5301	M.Raj (I)	1999-2016	164	149	42	114*	49.54	5	40
4844	B.J.Clark (A)	1991-2005	118	114	12	229*	47.49	5	30
4814	K.L.Rolton (A)	1995-2009	141	132	32	154*	48.14	8	33
4101	S.C.Taylor (E)	1998-2011	126	120	18	156*	40.20	8	23
4064	D.A.Hockley (NZ)	1982-2000	118	115	18	117	41.89	4	34
3468	S.R.Taylor (WI)	2008-2016	90	89	13	171	45.63	5	23
3261	S.J.Taylor (E)	2006-2016	101	94	12	129	39.76	5	16
2957	S.W.Bates (NZ)	2006-2016	84	81	8	168	40.50	7	16
2951	A.J.Blackwell (A)	2003-2016	122	108	23	114	34.71	3	21
2919	H.M.Tiffen (NZ)	1999-2009	117	111	16	100	30.72	1	18

Runs		Career	M	I	NO	HS	Avge	100	50
2856	A.Chopra (I)	1995-2012	127	112	21	100	31.38	1	18
2844	E.C.Drumm (NZ)	1992-2006	101	94	13	116	35.11	2	19
2728	L.C.Sthalekar (A)	2001-2013	125	111	22	104*	30.65	2	16
2630	L.M.Keightley (A)	1995-2005	82	78	12	156*	39.84	4	21
2554	L.S.Greenway (E)	2003-2016	126	111	26	125*	30.04	1	12
2438	S.J.McGlashan (NZ)	2002-2016	134	125	16	97*	22.36	–	14
2201	R.J.Rolls (NZ)	1997-2007	104	91	3	114	25.01	2	12
2150	D.J.S.Dottin (WI)	2008-2016	90	85	9	95	28.28	–	16
2124	M.M.Lanning (A)	2011-2016	45	45	3	135*	50.57	8	9
2121	J.A.Brittin (E)	1979-1998	63	59	9	138*	42.42	5	8
2091	J.Sharma (I)	2002-2008	77	75	7	138*	30.75	2	14
2047	S.Nitschke (A)	2004-2011	80	69	9	113*	34.11	1	14
2035	A.E.Satterthwaite (NZ)	2007-2016	80	76	6	109	29.07	2	11
2002	N.J.Browne (NZ)	2002-2014	125	102	28	63	27.05	–	10

HIGHEST INDIVIDUAL INNINGS

229*	B.J.Clark	Australia v Denmark	Mumbai	1997-98
173*	C.M.Edwards	England v Ireland	Pune	1997-98
171	S.R.Taylor	West Indies v Sri Lanka	Mumbai	2012-13
168	S.W.Bates	New Zealand v Pakistan	Sydney	2008-09
157	R.H.Priest	New Zealand v Sri Lanka	Lincoln	2015-16
156*	L.M.Keightley	Australia v Pakistan	Melbourne	1996-97
156*	S.C.Taylor	England v India	Lord's	2006
154*	K.L.Rolton	Australia v Sri Lanka	Christchurch	2000-01
153*	J.Logtenberg	South Africa v Netherlands	Deventer	2007
151	K.L.Rolton	Australia v Ireland	Dublin	2005

HIGHEST PARTNERSHIP FOR EACH WICKET

1st	268	S.J.Taylor/C.M.G.Atkins	England v South Africa	Lord's	2008
2nd	262	H.M.Tiffen/S.W.Bates	New Zealand v Pakistan	Sydney	2008-09
3rd	244	K.L.Rolton/L.C.Sthalekar	Australia v Ireland	Dublin	2005
4th	224*	J.Logtenberg/M.du Preez	South Africa v Netherlands	Deventer	2007
5th	188*	S.C.Taylor/J.Cassar	England v Sri Lanka	Lincoln	2000-01
6th	139*	S.J.McGlashan/N.J.Browne	New Zealand v South Africa	Bowral	2008-09
7th	104*	S.J.Tsukigawa/N.J.Browne	New Zealand v England	Chennai	2006-07
8th	85*	S.L.Clarke/N.J.Shaw	England v Scotland	Reading	2001
9th	73	L.R.F.Askew/I.T.Guha	England v New Zealand	Chennai	2006-07
10th	58	A.Sharma/G.Sultana	India v England	Taunton	2012

BOWLING RECORDS
100 WICKETS IN A CAREER

		LOI	Balls	R	W	Avge	Best	4w	R/Over
C.L.Fitzpatrick (A)	1993-2007	109	6017	3023	180	16.79	5-14	11	3.01
J.Goswami (I)	2002-2016	148	7189	3812	175	21.78	6-31	6	3.18
L.C.Sthalekar (A)	2001-2013	125	5964	3646	146	24.97	5-35	2	3.66
N.David (I)	1995-2008	97	4892	2305	141	16.34	5-20	6	2.82
A.Mohammed (WI)	2003-2016	93	4293	2335	130	17.96	7-14	11	3.26
J.L.Gunn (E)	2004-2016	129	5288	3337	120	27.80	5-22	5	3.78
S.R.Taylor (WI)	2008-2016	90	3918	2035	108	18.84	4-17	5	3.11
H.A.S.D.Siriwardene (SL)	2003-2016	93	4218	2639	106	24.89	4-11	6	3.75
C.E.Taylor (E)	1988-2005	105	5140	2443	102	23.95	4-13	2	2.85
E.A.Perry (A)	2007-2016	73	3472	2504	102	24.54	5-19	3	4.32
I.T.Guha (E)	2001-2011	83	3767	2345	101	23.21	5-14	4	3.73
N.Al Khadeer (I)	2002-2012	78	4036	2402	100	24.02	5-14	5	3.57

SIX OR MORE WICKETS IN AN INNINGS

7- 4	Sajjida Shah	Pakistan v Japan	Amsterdam	2003
7- 8	J.M.Chamberlain	England v Denmark	Haarlem	1991
7-14	A.Mohammed	West Indies v Pakistan	Dhaka	2011-12
7-24	S.Nitschke	Australia v England	Kidderminster	2005
6-10	J.Lord	New Zealand v India	Auckland	1981-82
6-10	M.Maben	India v Sri Lanka	Kandy	2003-04
6-10	S.Ismail	South Africa v Netherlands	Savar	2011-12
6-20	G.L.Page	New Zealand v Trinidad & T	St Albans	1973
6-20	D.B.Sharma	India v Sri Lanka	Ranchi	2015-16
6-31	J.Goswami	India v New Zealand	Southgate	2011
6-32	B.H.McNeill	New Zealand v England	Lincoln, NZ	2007-08

WICKET-KEEPING AND FIELDING RECORDS
100 DISMISSALS IN A CAREER

Total			LOI	Ct	St
133	R.J.Rolls	New Zealand	104	89	44
115	T.Chetty	South Africa	76	82	33
114	J.Smit	England	109	69	45
113	S.J.Taylor	England	101	73	40

SIX DISMISSALS IN AN INNINGS

6 (4ct, 2st)	S.L.Illingworth	New Zealand v Australia	Beckenham	1993
6 (1ct, 5st)	V.Kalpana	India v Denmark	Slough	1993
6 (2ct, 4st)	Batool Fatima	Pakistan v West Indies	Karachi	2003-04
6 (4ct, 2st)	Batool Fatima	Pakistan v Sri Lanka	Colombo (PSS)	2011

50 CATCHES IN THE FIELD IN A CAREER

Total			LOI	Career
52	L.S.Greenway	England	126	2003-2016
52	C.M.Edwards	England	191	1997-2016
51	J.Goswami	India	148	2002-2016

FOUR CATCHES IN THE FIELD IN AN INNINGS

4	Z.J.Goss	Australia v New Zealand	Adelaide	1995-96
4	J.L.Gunn	England v New Zealand	Lincoln	2014-15

APPEARANCE RECORDS
125 APPEARANCES

191	C.M.Edwards	England	1997-2016
164	M.Raj	India	1999-2016
148	J.Goswami	India	2002-2016
141	K.L.Rolton	Australia	1995-2009
134	S.J.McGlashan	New Zealand	2002-2016
129	J.L.Gunn	England	2004-2016
127	A.Chopra	India	1995-2012
126	L.S.Greenway	England	2003-2016
126	S.C.Taylor	England	1998-2011
125	N.J.Browne	New Zealand	2002-2014
125	L.C.Sthalekar	Australia	2001-2013

MOST CONSECUTIVE APPEARANCES

109	M.Raj	India	17.04.2004 to 07.02.2013

100 MATCHES AS CAPTAIN

			Won	Lost	No Result	
117	C.M.Edwards	England	72	38	7	2005-2016
101	B.J.Clark	Australia	83	17	1	1994-2005

WOMEN'S INTERNATIONAL TWENTY20 RECORDS

2004 to 12 March 2016

MATCH RESULTS SUMMARY

	Matches	Won	Lost	Tied	NR	Win %
England	94	66	25	2	1	70.96
Australia	88	53	33	2	–	60.22
West Indies	87	48	33	4	2	56.47
New Zealand	83	46	34	2	1	56.09
India	62	32	30	–	–	51.61
South Africa	65	27	37	–	1	42.18
Pakistan	65	27	35	2	1	42.18
Sri Lanka	60	16	41	–	3	28.07
Ireland	37	8	29	–	–	21.62
Bangladesh	26	5	21	–	–	19.23
Netherlands	11	–	10	–	1	0.00

WOMEN'S INTERNATIONAL TWENTY20 RECORDS
(To 12 March 2016)

TEAM RECORDS
HIGHEST INNINGS TOTALS

205-1	South Africa v Netherlands	Potchefstroom	2010-11
191-4	West Indies v Netherlands	Potchefstroom	2010-11
191-4	Australia v Ireland	Sylhet	2013-14
188-3	New Zealand v Sri Lanka	Christchurch	2015-16
186-7	New Zealand v South Africa	Taunton	2007
186-1	Australia v Ireland	Dublin	2015
185-2	Australia v Pakistan	Sylhet	2013-14
184-4	West Indies v Ireland	Dublin	2008
180-5	England v South Africa	Taunton	2007
180-5	New Zealand v West Indies	Gros Islet	2010

HIGHEST INNINGS TOTAL BATTING SECOND

165-2	England (set 164) v Australia	The Oval	2009

LOWEST COMPLETED INNINGS TOTALS † Batting Second

57† (19.4)	Sri Lanka v Bangladesh	Guangzhou	2012-13
58-9†	Bangladesh v England	Sylhet	2013-14
60† (16.5)	Pakistan v England	Taunton	2009
60 (19.4)	New Zealand v England	Whangarei	2014-15

BATTING RECORDS
1100 RUNS IN A CAREER

Runs			M	I	NO	HS	Avge	50	R/100B
2403	C.M.Edwards	E	90	88	13	92*	32.04	10	106.3
2005	S.J.Taylor	E	76	74	11	77	31.82	15	110.7
1962	S.R.Taylor	WI	68	67	12	90	35.67	17	101.9†
1944	S.W.Bates	NZ	78	76	3	94*	26.63	12	106.7
1655	M.M.Lanning	A	61	60	6	126	30.64	7	117.8
1624	D.J.S.Dottin	WI	82	81	16	112*	24.98	10	123.1†
1410	M.Raj	I	55	53	14	67	36.15	8	95.4†
1195	A.J.Blackwell	A	85	73	15	61	20.60	1	94.3
1187	L.S.Greenway	E	80	69	22	80*	25.25	2	96.5
1172	Bismah Maroof	P	62	57	15	65*	27.90	4	85.1

† No information on balls faced for games at Roseau on 22 and 23 February 2012.

HIGHEST INDIVIDUAL INNINGS

Score	Balls				
126	65	M.M.Lanning	A v Ire	Sylhet	2013-14
116*	71	S.A.Fritz	SA v Neth	Potchefstroom	2010-11
112*	45	D.J.S.Dottin	WI v SA	Basseterre	2010
96*	53	K.L.Rolton	A v E	Taunton	2005
94*	61	S.W.Bates	NZ v P	Sylhet	2013-14
92*	59	C.M.Edwards	E v A	Hobart	2013-14

HIGHEST PARTNERSHIP FOR EACH WICKET

1st	170	S.A.Fritz/T.Chetty	SA v Neth	Potchefstroom	2010-11
2nd	118*	S.W.Bates/A.L.Watkins	NZ v A	Taunton	2009
3rd	124	T.D.Smartt/S.A.C.A.King	WI v Neth	Potchefstroom	2010-11
4th	147*	K.L.Rolton/K.A.Blackwell	A v E	Taunton	2005
5th	118	S.F.Daley/D.J.S.Dottin	WI v SA	Basseterre	2010
6th	68	K.L.Rolton/A.J.Blackwell	A v SA	Taunton	2009
7th	51	S.R.Taylor/M.R.Aguilleira	WI v SL	Cayon	2010
8th	39	L.E.Kaushalya/K.A.D.A.Kanchana	SL v I	Ranchi	2015-16
9th	33*	D.Hazell/H.L.Colvin	E v WI	Bridgetown	2013-14
10th	23*	L.N.McCarthy/E.J.Tice	Ire v SL	Dublin	2013

BOWLING RECORDS
55 WICKETS IN A CAREER

Wkts			Matches	Overs	Mdns	Runs	Avge	Best	R/Over
97	A.Mohammed	WI	80	273.3	5	1432	14.76	5-10	5.23
73	E.A.Perry	A	75	243.2	4	1396	19.12	4-12	5.73
72	S.F.Daley	WI	68	227.1	8	1113	15.45	5-15	4.89
68	D.Hazell	E	66	250.2	6	1307	19.22	4-12	5.22
63	H.L.Colvin	E	50	186.5	4	971	15.41	4- 9	5.19
61	A.Shrubsole	E	42	140.4	4	777	12.73	5-11	5.52
60	L.C.Sthalekar	A	54	199.2	1	1161	19.35	4-18	5.82
59	S.R.Taylor	WI	68	180.1	4	957	16.22	3-10	5.31
58	J.L.Gunn	E	87	173.5	–	1114	19.20	5-18	6.40
56	Sana Mir	P	63	217.2	7	1090	19.46	4-13	5.01
56	L.A.Marsh	E	58	216.3	4	1139	20.33	3-17	5.26
55	S.Ismail	SA	54	187.4	6	1065	19.36	3- 5	5.67

FIVE OR MORE WICKETS IN AN INNINGS

6-17	A.E.Satterthwaite	NZ v E	Taunton	2007
5-10	A.Mohammed	WI v SA	Cape Town	2009-10
5-11	A.Shrubsole	E v NZ	Wellington	2011-12
5-11	J.Goswami	I v A	Visakhapatnam	2011-12
5-12	A.Mohammed	WI v NZ	Bridgetown	2013-14
5-15	S.F.Daley	WI v SL	Colombo (RPS)	2012-13
5-16	P.Roy	I v P	Taunton	2009
5-16	S.L.Quintyne	WI v E	Bridgetown	2013-14
5-18	J.L.Gunn	E v NZ	Bridgetown	2013-14
5-22	J.L.Hunter	A v WI	Colombo (RPS)	2012-13

HAT-TRICKS

Asmavia Iqbal	Pakistan v England	Loughborough	2012
Ekta Bisht	Sri Lanka v India	Colombo (NCC)	2012-13
M.Kapp	South Africa v Bangladesh	Potchefstroom	2013-14

N.R.Sciver	England v New Zealand	Bridgetown	2013-14		
Sana Mir	Pakistan v Sri Lanka	Sharjah	2014-15		

WICKET-KEEPING RECORDS
30 DISMISSALS IN A CAREER

Dis			Matches	Ct	St
65	S.J.Taylor	England	76	20	45
59	R.H.Priest	New Zealand	59	31	28
53	T.Chetty	South Africa	62	32	21
50	Batool Fatima	Pakistan	45	11	39
46	M.R.Aguilleira	West Indies	73	23	23
40	J.M.Fields	Australia	37	25	15
34	A.J.Healy	Australia	62	14	20
31	S.Naik	India	31	10	21

FIVE DISMISSALS IN AN INNINGS

5 (1ct, 4st) Kycia A.Knight	West Indies v Sri Lanka	Colombo (RPS)	2012-13	
5 (1ct, 4st) Batool Fatima	Pakistan v Ireland	Dublin	2013	
5 (1ct, 4st) Batool Fatima	Pakistan v Ireland	Dublin	2013	

FIELDING RECORDS
25 CATCHES IN A CAREER

Total			Matches	Total			Matches
51	J.L.Gunn	England	87	30	S.A.C.A.King	West Indies	70
50	L.S.Greenway	England	80	29	A.J.Blackwell	Australia	85
33	J.E.Cameron	Australia	64	28	S.J.McGlashan	New Zealand	71
33	S.W.Bates	New Zealand	78				

FOUR CATCHES IN AN INNINGS

4	L.S.Greenway	England v New Zealand	Chelmsford	2010

APPEARANCE RECORDS
70 APPEARANCES

90	C.M.Edwards	England	76	S.J.Taylor	England
87	J.L.Gunn	England	75	E.A.Perry	Australia
85	A.J.Blackwell	Australia	73	M.R.Aguilleira	West Indies
82	D.J.S.Dottin	West Indies	72	S.A.Campbelle	West Indies
80	L.S.Greenway	England	71	S.J.McGlashan	New Zealand
80	A.Mohammed	West Indies	70	S.A.C.A.King	West Indies
78	S.W.Bates	New Zealand			

30 MATCHES AS CAPTAIN

			W	L	T	NR	%age wins
88	C.M.Edwards	England	64	22	1	1	73.56
70	M.R.Aguilleira	West Indies	38	28	2	2	55.88
61	Sana Mir	Pakistan	24	34	2	1	40.00
46	M.du Preez	South Africa	23	22	–	1	51.11
41	S.W.Bates	New Zealand	21	19	1	–	51.21
34	H.A.S.D.Siriwardene	Sri Lanka	9	23	–	2	28.15

MCCA FIXTURES 2016

Sun 24 April   **KNOCK-OUT TROPHY**

Falkland	Berkshire v Dorset (1)
North Devon	Devon v Cornwall (1)
Nantwich	Cheshire v Staffordshire (2)
Shrewsbury	Shropshire v Herefordshire (2)
March	Cambridgeshire v Norfolk (3)
Grantham	Lincolnshire v Northumberland (3)
Ampthill	Bedfordshire v Suffolk (4)
Harpenden	Hertfordshire v Buckinghamshire (4)

Sun 1 May   **KNOCK-OUT TROPHY**

Truro	Cornwall v Berkshire (1)
Wormsley	Oxfordshire v Devon (1)
Colwall	Herefordshire v Cheshire (2)
Abergavenny	Wales MC v Shropshire (2)
Furness	Cumberland v Cambridgeshire (3)
Manor Park	Norfolk v Lincolnshire (3)
Gerrards Cross	Buckinghamshire v Bedfordshire (4)
Warminster	Wiltshire v Hertfordshire (4)

Sun 8 May   **KNOCK-OUT TROPHY**

Wargrave	Berkshire v Oxfordshire (1)
North Perrott	Dorset v Cornwall (1)
Chester, Boughton H	Cheshire v Wales MC (2)
Himley	Staffordshire v Herefordshire (2)
Bracebridge Heath	Lincolnshire v Cumberland (3)
Benwell Hill	Northumberland v Norfolk (3)
Dunstable	Bedfordshire v Wiltshire (4)
Warminster	Wiltshire v Suffolk (4)

Sun 15 May   **KNOCK-OUT TROPHY**

Exmouth	Devon v Berkshire (1)
Bicester & N Ox	Oxfordshire v Dorset (1)
Oswestry	Shropshire v Cheshire (2)
Newport	Wales MC v Staffordshire (2)
March	Cambridgeshire v Lincolnshire (3)
Penrith	Cumberland v Northumberland (3)
Harpenden	Hertfordshire v Bedfordshire (4)
Warminster	Wiltshire v Suffolk (4)

Sun 22 May   **KNOCK-OUT TROPHY**

Werrington	Cornwall v Oxfordshire (1)
Bashley	Dorset v Devon (1)
Eastnor	Herefordshire v Wales MC (2)
Leek	Staffordshire v Shropshire (2)
Fakenham	Norfolk v Cumberland (3)
Jesmond	Northumberland v Cambridgeshire (3)
Chesham	Buckinghamshire v Wiltshire (4)
Bury St Edmunds	Suffolk v Hertfordshire (4)

Sun 29 – Tue 31 May   **MCCA CHAMPIONSHIP**

Wisbech	Cambridgeshire v Norfolk

Sun 5 – Tue 7 June   **MCCA CHAMPIONSHIP**

Burnham	Buckinghamshire v Northumberland
Tattenhall	Cheshire v Wiltshire
St Austell	Cornwall v Oxfordshire

Carlisle	Cumberland v Suffolk
Colwall	Herefordshire v Berkshire
Bishop's Stortford	Hertfordshire v Staffordshire
Sleaford	Lincolnshire v Bedfordshire
Whitchurch	Shropshire v Dorset
Pontarddulais	Wales MC v Devon

Sun 12 June — **KNOCK-OUT TROPHY – Quarter-finals**

Match 1	Winner Gp 2 v Runner-up Gp 3
Match 2	Winner Gp 1 v Runner-up Gp 4
Match 3	Winner Gp 4 v Runner-up Gp 1
Match 4	Winner Gp 3 v Runner-up Gp 2

Sun 19 – Tue 21 June — **MCCA CHAMPIONSHIP**

Luton Town & Ind	Bedfordshire v Buckinghamshire
Henley	Berkshire v Wales MC
Saffron Walden	Cambridgeshire v Hertfordshire
Bournemouth	Dorset v Cheshire
Eastnor	Herefordshire v Devon
Aston Rowant	Oxfordshire v Shropshire
Longton	Staffordshire v Cumberland
Bury St Edmunds	Suffolk v Northumberland
Corsham	Wiltshire v Cornwall

Sun 3 – Tue 5 July — **MCCA CHAMPIONSHIP**

Falkland	Berkshire v Cheshire
High Wycombe	Buckinghamshire v Cumberland
Sandford	Devon v Wiltshire
North Perrott	Dorset v Herefordshire
Hertford	Hertfordshire v Lincolnshire
Burnopfield	Northumberland v Bedfordshire
Bridgnorth	Shropshire v Cornwall
West Brom Dartmth	Staffordshire v Norfolk
Copdock	Suffolk v Cambridgeshire
Usk	Wales MC v Oxfordshire

Sun 10 July — **KNOCK-OUT TROPHY – Semi-finals**

| tbc | Winner Match 3 v Winner Match 4 |
| tbc | Winner Match 2 v Winner Match 1 |

Sun 17 – Tue 19 July — **MCCA CHAMPIONSHIP**

Bedford School	Bedfordshire v Staffordshire
Alderley Edge	Cheshire v Devon
Truro	Cornwall v Dorset
Netherfield	Cumberland v Cambridgeshire
Cleethorpes	Lincolnshire v Suffolk
Manor Park	Norfolk v Buckinghamshire
Jesmond	Northumberland v Hertfordshire
Gt & Little Tew	Oxfordshire v Herefordshire
Shifnal	Shropshire v Berkshire
South Wilts	Wiltshire v Wales MC

Sun 24 – Tue 26 July — **MCCA CHAMPIONSHIP**

| Manor Park | Norfolk v Lincolnshire |

Sun 31 July – Tue 2 August — **MCCA CHAMPIONSHIP**

Clare College	Cambridgeshire v Bedfordshire
Nantwich	Cheshire v Shropshire
Grampound Road	Cornwall v Berkshire
Exeter	Devon v Oxfordshire
Bournemouth	Dorset v Wales MC

Brockhampton	Herefordshire v Wiltshire
Long Marston	Hertfordshire v Buckinghamshire
Grantham	Lincolnshire v Cumberland
Manor Park	Norfolk v Northumberland
Ipswich School	Suffolk v Staffordshire
Sun 14 – Tue 16 August	**MCCA CHAMPIONSHIP**
Flitwick	Bedfordshire v Hertfordshire
Finchampstead	Berkshire v Dorset
Tring Park	Buckinghamshire v Suffolk
Sedbergh School	Cumberland v Norfolk
Sidmouth	Devon v Cornwall
Jesmond	Northumberland v Cambridgeshire
Banbury	Oxfordshire v Cheshire
Knypersley	Staffordshire v Lincolnshire
Abergavenny	Wales MC v Herefordshire
Devizes	Wiltshire v Shropshire
Wed 24 August	**KNOCK-OUT TROPHY**
Wormsley	FINAL
Sun 28 – Wed 31 August	**MCCA CHAMPIONSHIP**
Wormsley	FINAL

MCCA KNOCK-OUT TROPHY GROUPS

Group 1	*Group 2*	*Group 3*	*Group 4*
Berkshire	Cheshire	Cambridgeshire	Bedfordshire
Cornwall	Herefordshire	Cumberland	Buckinghamshire
Devon	Shropshire	Lincolnshire	Hertfordshire
Dorset	Staffordshire	Norfolk	Suffolk
Oxfordshire	Wales MC	Northumberland	Wiltshire

SECOND XI CHAMPIONSHIP FIXTURES 2016

THREE-DAY MATCHES

APRIL		
Mon 18	Radlett	Middlesex v Essex
	Northampton	Northants v Leics
	EFSG	Warwicks v Notts
Tue 19	Beckenham	Kent v MCC YC
Mon 25	Swarkestone	Derbyshire v Leics
	Southampton	Hampshire v Somerset
	Manchester	Lancashire v Warwicks
	Radlett	Middlesex v MCC YC
MAY		
Mon 2	Northern CC	Lancashire v Derbyshire
	Taunton Vale	Somerset v Sussex
Tue 3	Guildford	Surrey v Glamorgan
Wed 4	Desborough T	Leics v Worcs
Mon 9	Bristol CC	Glos v Essex
	H Wycombe	MCC YC v Surrey
	Notts SC	Notts v Derbyshire
Tue 10	Mumbles	Glamorgan v Middlesex
	Desborough T	Northants v Lancashire
Mon 16	Southampton	Hampshire v MCC YC
	Liverpool	Lancashire v Notts
Tue 17	EFSG	Warwicks v Durham
Mon 23	Taunton	Somerset v Middlesex
Tue 24	B Stortford	Essex v Glamorgan
	Kidderminster	Worcs v Northants
Wed 25	Polo Farm	Kent v Glos
Mon 30	Richmond	Middlesex v Surrey
JUNE		
Wed 1	Eastbourne	Sussex v MCC YC
Mon 6	Hinckley	Leics v Notts
Tue 7	Billericay	Essex v Kent
	EFSG	Warwicks v Yorkshire
	Stourbridge	Worcs v Durham
Mon 13	Uxbridge	Middlesex v Hampshire
	York	Yorkshire v Leics
Tue 14	Darlington	Durham v Derbyshire
	Newport	Glamorgan v Somerset
	tbc	Glos v Sussex
	Worksop Coll	Notts v Northants
Mon 20	Southampton	Hampshire v Glos
Tue 21	Brandon	Durham v Lancashire
	Panteg	Glamorgan v MCC YC
	Polo Farm	Kent v Somerset
	Northampton	Northants v Derbyshire
	Scarborough	Yorkshire v Worcs
Mon 27	Neath	Glamorgan v Hampshire
	Cheam	Surrey v Essex
Tue 28	Desborough T	Leics v Warwicks
	Weetwood	MCC Univs v Lancashire
	Taunton Vale	Somerset v Glos
	Blackstone	Sussex v Kent
JULY		
Mon 4	Todmorden	Lancashire v Yorkshire
	Radlett	Middlesex v Glos
	EFSG	Warwicks v MCC Univs
Tue 5	Derby	Derbyshire v Worcs
	Canterbury	Kent v Glamorgan
	Notts SC	Notts v Durham
Mon 11	Denby	Derbyshire v Warwicks
	Southampton	Hampshire v Surrey
	Urmston	Lancashire v Leics
	Kidderminster	MCC Univs v Worcs
	Preston Nom	Sussex v Middlesex
Mon 18	New Malden	Surrey v Kent
Tue 19	Chester-le-St	Durham v Northants
	Desborough T	Leics v MCC Univs
	Trent College	Notts v Yorkshire
	Blackstone	Sussex v Essex
Wed 20	H Wycombe	MCC YC v Somerset
Mon 25	Desborough T	Leics v Durham
	Notts SC	Notts v MCC Univs
Tue 26	Belper Mead	Derbyshire v Yorkshire
	Newclose IoW	Hampshire v Kent
	H Wycombe	MCC YC v Essex
	Rugby School	Northants v Warwicks
	Bath	Somerset v Surrey
	RGS Worcester	Worcs v Lancashire
Wed 27	Abergavenny	Glamorgan v Sussex
AUGUST		
Mon 1	Shenley	MCC YC v Glos
Tue 2	Coggeshall	Essex v Hampshire
	Weetwood	MCC Univs v Derbyshire
	Mkt Harboro	Northants v Yorkshire
	RGS Worcester	Worcs v Notts
Wed 3	New Malden	Surrey v Sussex
Mon 8	Halstead	Essex v Somerset
	Desborough T	MCC Univs v Northants
Tue 9	Bath	Glos v Glamorgan
	Beckenham	Kent v Middlesex
	York	Yorkshire v Durham
Mon 15	Horsham	Sussex v Hampshire
	Barnt Green	Warwicks v Worcs
	Stamford Brg	Yorkshire v MCC Univs
Tue 16	Bath	Glos v Surrey
Mon 22	S N'berland	Durham v MCC Univs
SEPTEMBER		
Tue 6	tbc	FINAL (Four days)

SECOND XI TROPHY FIXTURES 2016

ONE-DAY

APRIL		
Tue 5	Richmondshire	Durham v Worcs
Thu 28	Radlett	Middlesex v MCC YC
MAY		
Tue 3	Barnsley	Yorkshire v Unicorns
Wed 4	Cov/N Wrwk	Warwicks v Unicorns
Thu 5	Neston	Lancashire v Derbyshire
Mon 9	Northampton	Northants v Lancashire
Thu 12	Horsham	Sussex v Hampshire
Thu 19	Southampton	Hampshire v MCC YC
Mon 23	Burnopfield	Unicorns v Durham
Wed 25	Repton School	Derbyshire v Warwicks
Tue 31	Taunton Vale	Somerset v Glamorgan
JUNE		
Wed 1	Notts SC	Notts v Warwicks
Thu 2	Sunbury	Middlesex v Surrey
	Taunton Vale	Somerset v Glos
Mon 6	Horsham	Sussex v Surrey
	Knowle & Dor	Warwicks v Yorkshire
Thu 9	Loughborough	Leics v Notts
	Gt & Little Tew	Unicorns v Northants
Fri 10	Loughborough	Leics v Unicorns
Wed 15	Challow & C	Unicorns v Worcs
Thu 16	Pudsey Cong	Yorkshire v Leics
Mon 20	Brandon	Durham v Lancashire
	Panteg	Glamorgan v MCC YC
	Polo Farm	Kent v Somerset
	Northampton	Northants v Derbyshire
Wed 22	Billericay	Essex v Middlesex
Mon 27	East Grinstead	Sussex v Kent
Thu 30	Worksop Coll	Notts v Derbyshire
	New Malden	Surrey v Essex
JULY		
Mon 4	Derby	Derbyshire v Worcs

	Canterbury	Kent v Glamorgan
	Kibworth	Leics v Northants
	Caythorpe	Notts v Durham
Thu 7	Southampton	Hampshire v Surrey
	Westhoughton	Lancashire v Yorkshire
	Radlett	Middlesex v Glos
Thu 14	Preston Nom	Sussex v Middlesex
Mon 18	Chester-le-St	Durham v Northants
	Blackstone	Sussex v Essex
Tue 19	H Wycombe	MCC YC v Somerset
Wed 20	Newport	Glamorgan v Hampshire
Fri 22	tbc	Glos v Surrey
Mon 25	Alvaston & B	Derbyshire v Yorkshire
	Southampton	Hampshire v Kent
	H Wycombe	MCC YC v Essex
	Bath	Somerset v Surrey
	RGS Worcester	Worcs v Lancashire
Tue 26	St Fagans	Glamorgan v Sussex
AUGUST		
Mon 1	Worcester	Worcs v Notts
Thu 4	Shenley	MCC YC v Glos
Fri 5	Coggleshall	Essex v Hampshire
	tbc	Glos v Kent
Mon 8	Bath	Glos v Glamorgan
	Cov/N Wrwk	Warwicks v Leics
	York	Yorkshire v Durham
Wed 10	RGS Worcester	Worcs v Warwicks
Thu 11	Halstead	Essex v Somerset
	Bowdon	Lancashire v Leics
Fri 12	Beckenham	Kent v Middlesex
	Finedon Dol	Northants v Notts
Fri 19	tbc	Semi-finals
Thu 25	tbc	FINAL

SECOND XI TWENTY20 CUP FIXTURES 2016

APRIL		
Thu 14	Shenley	MCC YC v Glamorgan
Mon 18	Beckenham	Kent v MCC YC
Thu 21	Radlett	Middlesex v Essex
Thu 28	Southampton	Hampshire v Somerset
	Sale	Lancashire v Warwicks
Fri 29	Derby	Derbyshire v Leics
MAY		
Tue 3	Kibworth	Leics v Worcs
	Finedon Dol	Northants v Warwicks
	Taunton Vale	Somerset v Sussex
Thu 5	Birmingham	Warwicks v Notts

Fri 6	Purley	Surrey v Glamorgan
Mon 9	Port Talbot	Glamorgan v Middlesex
Tue 10	Kibworth	Leics v Durham
Thu 12	Bristol CC	Glos v Essex
	H Wycombe	MCC YC v Surrey
Fri 13	Derby	Derbyshire v Notts
	Taunton Vale	Somerset v Essex
Mon 16	Cardiff	Glamorgan v Glos
	Uxbridge	Middlesex v Kent
	Stowe School	Northants v Yorkshire
	Purley	Surrey v Sussex
	Birmingham	Warwicks v Durham

328

WOMEN'S FIXTURES 2016

PRINCIPAL FIXTURES 2016

CC1	Specsavers County Championship Division 1
CC2	Specsavers County Championship Division 2
F	Floodlit
FCF	First-Class Friendly
LOI	Royal London Limited-Overs International

50L	Royal London One-Day Cup
T20	NatWest T20 Blast
[T20]	Other Twenty20 match
IT20	NatWest Twenty20 International
TM	Investec Test Match
MCCU	MCC University
Uni	University match

Sun 20 – Wed 23 March
FCF	Abu Dhabi	MCC v Yorkshire

Thu 31 March – Sat 2 April
Uni	Cambridge	Cambridge MCCU v Essex
Uni	Bristol	Glos v Durham MCCU
Uni	Oxford	Oxford MCCU v Worcs
Uni	The Oval	Surrey v Loughboro MCCU
Uni	Birmingham	Warwicks v Leeds/Brad MCCU

Mon 4 – Wed 6 April
Uni	Southampton	Hampshire v Cardiff MCCU

Tue 5 – Thu 7 April
Uni	Cambridge	Cambridge MCCU v Notts
Uni	Chester-le-St	Durham v Durham MCCU
Uni	Canterbury	Kent v Loughboro MCCU
Uni	Oxford	Oxford MCCU v Northants
Uni	Hove	Sussex v Leeds/Brad MCCU

Sun 10 – Wed 13 April
CC1	Chester-le-St	Durham v Somerset
CC1	Southampton	Hampshire v Warwicks
CC1	Nottingham	Notts v Surrey
CC2	Chelmsford	Essex v Glos
CC2	Northampton	Northants v Sussex
CC2	Worcester	Worcs v Kent

Mon 11 – Wed 13 April
Uni	Cambridge	Cambridge MCCU v Lancashire
Uni	Derby	Derbyshire v Durham MCCU
Uni	Cardiff	Glamorgan v Cardiff MCCU
Uni	Leicester	Leics v Loughboro MCCU
Uni	Oxford	Oxford MCCU v Middlesex
Uni	Leeds	Yorkshire v Leeds/Brad MCCU

Sun 17 – Wed 20 April
CC1	Manchester	Lancashire v Notts
CC1	Lord's	Middlesex v Warwicks
CC1	Leeds	Yorkshire v Hampshire
CC2	Cardiff	Glamorgan v Leics
CC2	Bristol	Glos v Derbyshire
CC2	Hove	Sussex v Essex

Sun 17 – Tue 19 April
Uni	Taunton V	Somerset v Cardiff MCCU

Sun 24 – Wed 27 April
CC1	Chester-le-St	Durham v Middlesex
CC1	The Oval	Surrey v Somerset
CC1	Birmingham	Warwicks v Yorkshire
CC2	Derby	Derbyshire v Glamorgan
CC2	Chelmsford	Essex v Northants
CC2	Bristol	Glos v Worcs
CC2	Leicester	Leics v Kent

Sun 1 – Wed 4 May
CC1	Southampton	Hampshire v Middlesex
CC1	Nottingham	Notts v Yorkshire
CC1	The Oval	Surrey v Durham
CC1	Taunton	Somerset v Lancashire
CC2	Canterbury	Kent v Glamorgan
CC2	Northampton	Northants v Derbyshire
CC2	Hove	Sussex v Leics
CC2	Worcester	Worcs v Essex

Sun 8 – Wed 11 May
CC1	Manchester	Lancashire v Hampshire
CC1	Lord's	Middlesex v Notts
CC1	Birmingham	Warwicks v Somerset
CC1	Leeds	Yorkshire v Surrey
CC2	Derby	Derbyshire v Sussex
CC2	Cardiff	Glamorgan v Worcs
CC2	Canterbury	Kent v Glos
CC2	Leicester	Leics v Northants

Sun 8 – Tue 10 May
FCF	Chelmsford	Essex v Sri Lankans

Fri 13 – Sun 15 May
FCF	Leicester	Leics v Sri Lankans

Sun 15 – Wed 18 May
CC1	Chester-le-St	Durham v Lancashire
CC1	Nottingham	Notts v Warwicks
CC1	Taunton	Somerset v Yorkshire
CC1	The Oval	Surrey v Middlesex
CC2	Chelmsford	Essex v Derbyshire
CC2	Bristol	Glos v Glamorgan
CC2	Northampton	Northants v Kent
CC2	Worcester	Worcs v Sussex

Thu 19 – Mon 23 May

TM1	Leeds	ENGLAND v SRI LANKA

Fri 20 May

T20 F	Chelmsford	Essex v Surrey
T20 F	Bristol	Glos v Sussex
T20 F	Canterbury	Kent v Somerset
T20 F	Leicester	Leics v Northants
T20 F	Nottingham	Notts v Warwicks
T20	Worcester	Worcs v Durham

Sat 21 May

T20	Manchester	Lancashire v Derbyshire

Sun 22 – Wed 25 May

CC1	Southampton	Hampshire v Notts
CC1	Manchester	Lancashire v Surrey
CC1	Lord's	Middlesex v Somerset
CC1	Birmingham	Warwicks v Durham
CC2	Derby	Derbyshire v Kent
CC2	Bristol	Glos v Northants
CC2	Leicester	Leics v Worcs
CC2	Cardiff	Glamorgan v Essex

Thu 26 May

T20 F	The Oval	Surrey v Glamorgan

Fri 27 – Tue 31 May

TM2	Chester-le-St	ENGLAND v SRI LANKA

Fri 27 May

T20 F	Manchester	Lancashire v Durham
T20	Uxbridge	Middlesex v Hampshire
T20 F	Northampton	Northants v Derbyshire
T20 F	Birmingham	Warwicks v Worcs
T20 F	Leeds	Yorkshire v Leics

Sat 28 – Tue 31 May

CC1	Nottingham	Notts v Durham
CC1	Taunton	Somerset v Surrey
CC2	Northampton	Northants v Essex
CC2	Hove	Sussex v Derbyshire

Sun 29 May – Wed 1 June

CC1	Northwood	Middlesex v Hampshire
CC1	Leeds	Yorkshire v Lancashire
CC2	Canterbury	Kent v Leics
CC2	Worcester	Worcs v Glos

Wed 1 June

T20 F	Chester-le-St	Durham v Notts
T20 F	Cardiff	Glamorgan v Essex
T20 F	Hove	Sussex v Somerset

Thu 2 June

T20 F	Southampton	Hampshire v Kent
T20	Northwood	Middlesex v Glos
T20	Worcester	Worcs v Yorkshire

Fri 3 June

T20 F	Derby	Derbyshire v Leics
T20 F	Cardiff	Glamorgan v Hampshire
T20	Beckenham	Kent v Glos
T20 F	Manchester	Lancashire v Yorkshire
T20 F	Northampton	Northants v Worcs
T20	Taunton	Somerset v Essex
T20 F	Hove	Sussex v Surrey
T20 F	Birmingham	Warwicks v Durham

Sat 4 June

T20	Leicester	Leics v Durham
T20	Nottingham	Notts v Lancashire

Sun 5 June

50L	Southampton	Hampshire v Essex
50L	Beckenham	Kent v Surrey
50L	Manchester	Lancashire v Warwicks
50L	Leicester	Leics v Durham
50L	Taunton	Somerset v Glos
50L	Worcester	Worcs v Derbyshire

Mon 6 June

50L F	Cardiff	Glamorgan v Glos
50L F	Nottingham	Notts v Northants
50L F	Hove	Sussex v Essex

Tue 7 June

50L	Derby	Derbyshire v Durham
50L	Radlett	Middlesex v Hampshire
50L F	Leeds	Yorkshire v Worcs
50L F	Birmingham	Warwicks v Leics

Wed 8 June

50L F	Cardiff	Glamorgan v Sussex
50L F	Bristol	Glos v Middlesex
50L F	Northampton	Northants v Lancs
50L F	Nottingham	Notts v Warwicks
50L F	The Oval	Surrey v Somerset
T20 F	Canterbury	Kent v Hampshire

Thu 9 – Mon 13 June

TM3	Lord's	ENGLAND v SRI LANKA

Thu 9 June

T20 F	The Oval	Surrey v Hampshire

Fri 10 June

T20 F	Chelmsford	Essex v Middlesex
T20 F	Bristol	Glos v Glamorgan
T20 F	Manchester	Lancashire v Leics
T20 F	Nottingham	Notts v Derbyshire
T20	Taunton	Somerset v Surrey
T20 F	Hove	Sussex v Kent
T20 F	Birmingham	Warwicks v Yorkshire
T20	Worcester	Worcs v Northants

Sun 12 June

50L	Chesterfield	Derbyshire v Yorkshire

50L	Chester-le-St	Durham v Worcs
50L	Chelmsford	Essex v Somerset
50L	Canterbury	Kent v Glamorgan
50L	Blackpool	Lancashire v Notts
50L	Northampton	Northants v Leics
50L	Hove	Sussex v Middlesex

Tue 14 June
50L	Cardiff	Glamorgan v Middlesex
50L F	Bristol	Glos v Hampshire
50L	Canterbury	Kent v Somerset
50L	Guildford	Surrey v Sussex
50L	Scarborough	Yorkshire v Northants

Wed 15 June
50L	Chester-le-St	Durham v Notts
50L	Chelmsford	Essex v Kent
50L F	Southampton	Hampshire v Surrey
50L F	Manchester	Lancashire v Yorkshire
50L	Taunton	Somerset v Glamorgan
50L F	Birmingham	Warwicks v Derbyshire
50L	Worcester	Worcs v Leics

Thu 16 June
T20 F	Chelmsford	Essex v Glos
T20 F	Manchester	Lancashire v Northants
T20 F	Lord's	Middlesex v Surrey

Fri 17 June
T20 F	Derby	Derbyshire v Warwicks
T20 F	Cardiff	Glamorgan v Kent
T20 F	Bristol	Glos v Somerset
T20 F	Southampton	Hampshire v Sussex
T20 F	Leicester	Leics v Worcs
T20 F	Northampton	Northants v Durham
T20 F	The Oval	Surrey v Middlesex
T20 F	Leeds	Yorkshire v Notts

Sat 18 June
T20	Worcester	Worcs v Notts

Sun 19 – Wed 22 June
CC1	The Oval	Surrey v Notts
CC2	Chelmsford	Essex v Leics
CC2	Cardiff	Glamorgan v Kent

Sun 19 June
T20	Taunton	Somerset v Hampshire
T20	Birmingham	Warwicks v Lancashire
T20	Leeds	Yorkshire v Derbyshire

Mon 20 – Thu 23 June
CC1	Chester-le-St	Durham v Yorkshire
CC1	Manchester	Lancashire v Warwicks
CC2	Derby	Derbyshire v Worcs

Tue 21 June
LOI F	Nottingham	England v Sri Lanka

Wed 22 – Sat 25 June
CC2	Arundel	Sussex v Northants

Thu 23 June
T20	Lord's	Middlesex v Somerset

Fri 24 June
LOI F	Birmingham	England v Sri Lanka
T20 F	Derby	Derbyshire v Notts
T20 F	Chester-le-St	Durham v Yorkshire
T20 F	Chelmsford	Essex v Hampshire
T20 F	Cardiff	Glamorgan v Surrey
T20 F	Canterbury	Kent v Middlesex
T20 F	Manchester	Lancashire v Worcs
T20 F	Leicester	Leics v Warwicks

Sat 25 June
T20	Southampton	Hampshire v Glos
T20	The Oval	Surrey v Essex

Sun 26 – Wed 29 June
CC1	Southampton	Hampshire v Somerset
CC1	Lord's	Middlesex v Lancashire
CC1	Birmingham	Warwicks v Notts
CC2	Canterbury	Kent v Derbyshire
FCF	Chester-le-St	Durham v Sri Lanka A
FCF	Leeds	Yorkshire v Pakistan A

Sun 26 June
LOI	Bristol	England v Sri Lanka
T20	Northampton	Northants v Leics
T20	Arundel	Sussex v Glos

Mon 27 – Thu 30 June
CC2	Leicester	Leics v Glos

Wed 29 June
LOI F	The Oval	England v Sri Lanka

Thu 30 June
T20 F	Chester-le-St	Durham v Worcs
T20 F	Canterbury	Kent v Sussex

Fri 1 July
T20 F	Chelmsford	Essex v Kent
T20 F	Nottingham	Notts v Durham
T20	Taunton	Somerset v Glos
T20 F	Hove	Sussex v Middlesex
T20 F	Birmingham	Warwicks v Northants
T20	Worcester	Worcs v Derbyshire
T20 F	Leeds	Yorkshire v Lancashire
	Lord's	Oxford U v Cambridge U

Sat 2 – Tue 5 July
CC1	Guildford	Surrey v Warwicks
CC2	Hove	Sussex v Glamorgan

Sat 2 July
LOI	Cardiff	England v Sri Lanka

Sun 3 – Wed 6 July
CC1 Chester-le-St Durham v Hampshire
CC1 Nottingham Notts v Lancashire
CC1 Scarborough Yorkshire v Middlesex
CC2 Chelmsford Essex v Kent
CC2 Worcester Worcs v Leics
FCF Leicester Pakistan A v Sri Lanka A

Sun 3 – Tue 5 July
FCF Taunton Somerset v Pakistanis

Sun 3 July
T20 Chesterfield Derbyshire v Northants

Mon 4 – Thu 7 July
CC2 Chesterfield Derbyshire v Northants
FCF Oxford Oxford U v Cambridge U

Tue 5 July
IT20 ^{F} Southampton England v Sri Lanka

Wed 6 July
T20 ^{F} Bristol Glos v Surrey

Thu 7 July
T20 ^{F} Cardiff Glamorgan v Sussex
T20 Taunton Somerset v Kent

Fri 8 – Sun 10 July
FCF Hove Sussex v Pakistanis

Fri 8 July
T20 ^{F} Bristol Glos v Kent
T20 ^{F} Southampton Hampshire v Essex
T20 ^{F} Leicester Leics v Derbyshire
T20 Richmond Middlesex v Glamorgan
T20 ^{F} Northampton Northants v Notts
T20 ^{F} The Oval Surrey v Somerset
T20 Worcester Worcs v Lancashire
T20 ^{F} Leeds Yorkshire v Warwicks

Sat 9 July
T20 Nottingham Notts v Worcs

Sun 10 – Wed 13 July
CC1 Taunton Somerset v Middlesex
CC1 Birmingham Warwicks v Hampshire
CC2 Northampton Northants v Worcs

Sun 10 – Wed 13 July
FCF Worcester Pakistan A v Sri Lanka A

Sun 10 July
T20 Chesterfield Derbyshire v Yorkshire
T20 Chester-le-St Durham v Leics
T20 Cardiff Glamorgan v Glos

Mon 11 – Thu 14 July
CC1 The Oval Surrey v Yorkshire

Tue 12 July
T20 ^{F} Leicester Leics v Notts

Wed 13 – Sat 16 July
CC2 Cheltenham Glos v Essex

Wed 13 July
T20 ^{F} Derby Derbyshire v Lancashire

Thu 14 – Mon 18 July
TM1 Lord's **ENGLAND v PAKISTAN**

Thu 14 July
T20 ^{F} Southampton Hampshire v Glamorgan

Fri 15 July
 Newport Glamorgan v Pakistan A
T20 ^{F} Chester-le-St Durham v Northants
T20 Tunbridge W Kent v Surrey
T20 ^{F} Leicester Leics v Lancashire
T20 Nottingham Notts v Yorkshire
T20 Taunton Somerset v Middlesex
T20 ^{F} Hove Sussex v Hampshire
T20
^{F} Worcester Worcs v Warwicks
 Derby Derbyshire v Sri Lanka A

Sat 16 – Tue 19 July
CC1 Southport Lancashire v Durham

Sun 17 – Wed 20 July
CC1 Southampton Hampshire v Surrey
CC1 Nottingham Notts v Somerset
CC2 Colwyn Bay Glamorgan v Derbyshire
CC Tunbridge W Kent v Sussex

Sun 17 July
T20 Cheltenham Glos v Essex
T20 Birmingham Warwicks v Leics

Mon 18 July
 Cheltenham Pakistan A v Sri Lanka A

Tue 19 July
 Cheltenham England Lions v Pakistan A
T20 ^{F} Northampton Northants v Warwicks

Wed 20 – Sat 23 July
CC2 Cheltenham Glos v Leics

Wed 20 July
T20 ^{F} Leeds Yorkshire v Durham

Thu 21 July
 Northampton England Lions v Sri Lanka A
T20 ^{F} Chelmsford Essex v Sussex
T20 ^{F} Lord's Middlesex v Surrey

Fri 22 – Tue 26 July
TM2 Manchester **ENGLAND v PAKISTAN**

Fri 22 July

F	Northampton	Pakistan A v Sri Lanka A
T20 F	Derby	Derbyshire v Worcs
T20 F	Chester-le-St	Durham v Lancashire
T20 F	Cardiff	Glamorgan v Somerset
T20 F	Southampton	Hampshire v Middlesex
T20 F	Canterbury	Kent v Essex
T20 F	The Oval	Surrey v Sussex
T20 F	Birmingham	Warwicks v Notts
T20 F	Leeds	Yorkshire v Northants

Sun 24 July

	Canterbury	England Lions v Pakistan A
50L	Chelmsford	Essex v Surrey
50L	Cheltenham	Glos v Sussex
50L	Leicester	Leics v Yorkshire
50L	Lord's	Middlesex v Kent
50L	Northampton	Northants v Durham
50L	Welbeck Col	Notts v Derbyshire
50L	Taunton	Somerset v Glamorgan
50L	Birmingham	Warwicks v Worcs

Mon 25 July

	Canterbury	England Lions v Sri Lanka A

Tue 26 July

50L F	Chelmsford	Essex v Glamorgan
50L F	Southampton	Hampshire v Kent
50L	Leicester	Leics v Lancashire
50L	Taunton	Somerset v Middlesex
50L	Birmingham	Warwicks v Northants

Wed 27 July

50L F	Derby	Derbyshire v Lancashire
50L	S N'berland	Durham v Notts
50L F	The Oval	Surrey v Glos
50L F	Hove	Sussex v Hampshire
50L	Worcester	Worcs v Northants
50L	Scarborough	Yorks v Notts

Thu 28 July

T20 F	Lord's	Middlesex v Essex
T20 F	Hove	Sussex v Glamorgan

Fri 29 – Sat 30 July

	Worcester	Worcs v Pakistan

Fri 29 July

T20 F	Chester-le-St	Durham v Derbyshire
T20 F	Chelmsford	Essex v Glamorgan
T20 F	Bristol	Glos v Middlesex
T20 F	Southampton	Hampshire v Somerset
T20 F	Manchester	Lancashire v Warwicks
T20 F	Northampton	Northants v Yorkshire
T20 F	Nottingham	Notts v Leics
T20 F	The Oval	Surrey v Kent

Sat 30 July

50L	Taunton	Somerset v Sussex

Sun 31 July

50L	Chester-le-St	Durham v Yorkshire
50L	Swansea	Glamorgan v Hampshire
50L	Canterbury	Kent v Glos
50L	Leicester	Leics v Notts
50L	Lord's	Middlesex v Essex
50L	Northampton	Northants v Derbyshire
50L	Worcester	Worcs v Lancashire

Mon 1 August

50L F	Derby	Derbyshire v Leics
50L F	Manchester	Lancashire v Durham
50L F	Nottingham	Notts v Worcs
50L F	The Oval	Surrey v Glamorgan
50L F	Leeds	Yorkshire v Warwicks

Tue 2 August

50L F	Bristol	Glos v Essex
50L F	Southampton	Hampshire v Somerset
50L F	Lord's	Middlesex v Surrey
50L F	Hove	Sussex v Kent

Wed 3 – Sun 7 August

TM3	Birmingham	ENGLAND v PAKISTAN

Wed 3 – Sat 6 August

CC2	Swansea	Glamorgan v Northants
CC2	Canterbury	Kent v Worcs

Thu 4 – Sun 7 August

CC1	Southampton	Hampshire v Lancashire
CC1	Lord's	Middlesex v Surrey
CC1	Taunton	Somerset v Durham
CC1	Leeds	Yorkshire v Warwicks
CC2	Colchester	Essex v Sussex
CC2	Leicester	Leics v Derbyshire

Mon 8 August

T20 F	tbc	Quarter-final 1

Tue 9 August

T20 F	tbc	Quarter-final 2

Wed 10 August

T20 F	tbc	Quarter-final 3

Thu 11 – Mon 15 August

TM4	The Oval	ENGLAND v PAKISTAN

Thu 11 August

T20 F	tbc	Quarter-final 4

Sat 13 – Tue 16 August

CC1	Manchester	Lancashire v Yorkshire
CC1	Lord's	Middlesex v Durham
CC1	Nottingham	Notts v Hampshire
CC1	Birmingham	Warwicks v Surrey

CC2	Derby	Derbyshire v Essex
CC2	Northampton	Northants v Leics
CC2	Hove	Sussex v Glos
CC2	Worcester	Worcs v Glamorgan

Wed 17 August

50L^F	tbc	Quarter-finals 1 & 2

Thu 18 August

50L^F	tbc	Quarter-finals 3 & 4

Sat 20 August

T20^F	Edgbaston	Semi-finals and FINAL

Tue 23 – Fri 26 August

CC1	Chester-le-St	Durham v Warwicks
CC1	Taunton	Somerset v Hampshire
CC1	The Oval	Surrey v Lancashire
CC1	Scarborough	Yorkshire v Notts
CC2	Cardiff	Glamorgan v Sussex
CC2	Bristol	Glos v Kent
CC2	Leicester	Leics v Essex
CC2	Worcester	Worcs v Northants

Wed 24 August

LOI^F	Southampton	England v Pakistan

Sat 27 August

LOI	Lord's	England v Pakistan

Sun 28 August

50L	tbc	Semi-final 1

Mon 29 August

50L^F	tbc	Semi-final 2

Tue 30 August

LOI^F	Nottingham	England v Pakistan

Wed 31 August – 3 September

CC1	Chester-le-St	Durham v Notts
CC1	Southampton	Hampshire v Yorkshire
CC1	Manchester	Lancashire v Somerset
CC1	Birmingham	Warwicks v Middlesex
CC2	Derby	Derbyshire v Glos

CC2	Chelmsford	Essex v Worcs
CC2	Northampton	Northants v Glamorgan
CC2	Hove	Sussex v Kent

Thu 1 September

LOI^F	Leeds	England v Pakistan

Sun 4 September

LOI	Cardiff	England v Pakistan

Tue 6 – Fri 9 September

CC1	Nottingham	Notts v Middlesex
CC1	Taunton	Somerset v Warwicks
CC1	The Oval	Surrey v Hampshire
CC1	Leeds	Yorkshire v Durham
CC2	Cardiff	Glamorgan v Glos
CC2	Beckenham	Kent v Northants
CC2	Leicester	Leics v Sussex

Wed 7 September

IT20^F	Manchester	England v Pakistan

Mon 12 – Thu 15 September

CC1	Chester-le-St	Durham v Surrey
CC1	Manchester	Lancashire v Middlesex
CC1	Leeds	Yorkshire v Somerset
CC2	Derby	Derbyshire v Leics
CC2	Chelmsford	Essex v Glamorgan
CC2	Northampton	Northants v Glos
CC2	Hove	Sussex v Worcs

Sat 17 September

50L	Lord's	FINAL

Tue 20 – Fri 23 September

CC1	Southampton	Hampshire v Durham
CC1	Lord's	Middlesex v Yorkshire
CC1	Taunton	Somerset v Notts
CC1	Birmingham	Warwicks v Lancashire
CC2	Bristol	Glos v Sussex
CC2	Canterbury	Kent v Essex
CC2	Leicester	Leics v Glamorgan
CC2	Worcester	Worcs v Derbyshire

First published in 2016
by HEADLINE PUBLISHING GROUP

Front cover photograph Ben Stokes (England and Durham)
© Getty Images

Back cover photograph Moeen Ali (England and Worcestershire)
© Action Images

1

Cataloguing in Publication Data is available from the British Library

ISBN 978 1 4722 3254 0

Typeset in Times by
Letterpart Limited, Caterham on the Hill, Surrey

Printed and bound in Great Britain by
Clays Ltd St Ives plc

HEADLINE PUBLISHING GROUP
An Hachette UK Company
Carmelite House
50 Victoria Embankment
London EC4Y 0DZ

www.headline.co.uk
www.hachette.co.uk